Citizenship and the State in the Middle East

APPROACHES AND APPLICATIONS

Edited by

NILS A. BUTENSCHON,

URI DAVIS, and

MANUEL HASSASSIAN

SYRACUSE UNIVERSITY PRESS

Library of Congress Cataloging-in-Publication Data

Citizenship and the state in the Middle East : approaches and applications / edited by
Nils A. Butenschon, Uri Davis, and Manuel Hassassian. — 1st ed.
    p.   cm. — (Contemporary issues in the Middle East)
Papers presented at an international conference held Nov. 1996 in Oslo and organized
by the University of Oslo, Dept. of Political Science.
Includes bibliographical references and index.
ISBN 0-8156-2829-3 (pbk. : alk. paper)
1. Citizenship—Middle East—Congresses.   2. Political participation—Middle
East—Congresses.   3. Civil society—Middle East—Congresses.   4. Political culture—Middle
East—Congresses.   5. Middle East—Politics and government—Congresses.   I. Butenschøn,
Nils A. (Nils August), 1949–   II. Davis, Uri.   III. Hassassian, Manuel S. (Manuel Sarkis),
1954–   IV. Universitetet i Oslo. Institutt for statsvitenskap.   V. Series.
JQ1758.A92 C58 2000
323.6′0956—dc21   00-021079

Manufactured in the United States of America

Contents

Illustrations

Figures

Tables

Preface

AS A FIELD OF STUDY, citizenship has gained much attention over the last few years, not the least in Europe, where the viability of existing nation-states has been questioned in view of the challenge emerging from the sub-national level (in ethnic and religious mobilization, for example) as well from processes of regional integration and globalization. Where do these processes leave the individual citizen—his or her rights and obligations vis-à-vis the state as well as his or her role in shaping the political future? Can the traditional ideas of democratic citizenship survive these challenges?

The challenges faced by contemporary Middle Eastern states are no less acute than in Europe, but the nature of these challenges may be different. There is a growing literature on the nature of the state in the Middle East, but the question of citizenship in this context has not been systematically addressed in the same way.

Citizenship refers to a legal relationship between the individual and the state. It can be viewed from a number of angles, but is inseparably related to the nature of political authority of the state. It further designates the legal and institutional foundations of individual rights as well as obligations toward state authorities. Citizenship is a certificate of membership in a political community and thus represents political identities and loyalties. It regulates the access of the individual to the civil, political, social, and material resources of the state and can be seen as a core concept in the analysis of political and social relations in any state.

This volume, *Citizenship and the State in the Middle East: Approaches and Applications,* and its sister volume, *Gender and Citizenship in the Middle East,* edited by Suad Joseph, represent a pioneering attempt to approach the Middle East from a citizenship perspective. It is the first systematic undertaking of its kind, bringing together contributions by experts from many fields of study with the purpose of effecting a deeper insight into the complex nature of Middle Eastern states and politics.

Both volumes include theoretical chapters as well as case studies. The present volume has two main sections. The first part introduces the citizenship approach from the perspective of both social sciences and international human rights law. The applicability of the approach in a Middle Eastern context is discussed both in general terms and with reference to individual countries. This part also includes a chapter each on Lebanon and Kuwait. The second part focuses specifically on Israel and Palestine. The sister volume investigates the gendering of citizenship in Middle Eastern politics. After the editor's theoretical introduction, the volume divides the Middle East into four regional areas to offer fifteen country case studies. Taken together we believe the reader is offered the first comprehensive overview of the subject.

It was essential for a four-member editorial committee residing in three different continents and traveling internationally, one of whom (Manuel Hassassian) lives under Israeli occupation, to agree a division of labor and support each other when circumstances beyond their control intervened with the work.

Suad Joseph introduced the project to the publisher. She assumed sole responsibility for the editorial work of the volume *Gender and Citizenship in the Middle East*. As the international conference had few papers on gender and citizenship, she solicited entirely new contributions for this volume. None of the chapters in this volume (except for an earlier version of the introduction) was presented at the conference. Nils Butenschon, Uri Davis, and Manuel Hassassian were responsible for the editorial work for *Citizenship and the State in the Middle East*.

Butenschon and Davis did the better part of the editorial work for the present volume in consultation with Hassassian. Butenschon assumed the main responsibility for the organization of the international conference and the funding for the project, negotiated the contract with the publisher, and coordinated the editorial work and international correspondence with contributors. Davis brought to the project the international networking and driving force that made the project possible, assumed responsibility for coordination of correspondence and administration in geographical Palestine, and organized several of the editorial committee meetings. Hassassian provided the anchor for the project at Bethlehem University, coordinated among Palestinian contributors, and hosted two editorial committee meeting and two delegations from the University of Oslo.

The problem of transliteration is well-known to authors of works on the Middle East in non-Semitic languages. There are no standard solutions. The problem is particularly evident with edited books like this one. In this case, we resolved to allow each of our contributors his or her preferred style of transliteration.

The publication of these two volumes completes the sustained five-year individual and collective efforts of the four editors. In 1992, Tim Niblock and Uri Davis, both still at the Department of Politics, University of Exeter (UK), and Nils Butenschon and Rania Maktabi at the Department of Political Science, University of Oslo, started to discuss the possibility of cooperation based on a shared academic interest in questions of citizenship and democratization in the Middle East.

The project took off when Niblock and Davis received funding from the Economic and Social and Research Council (ESRC) of the United Kingdom in 1993 for their research proposal "Creating the Basis for Democracy in the Middle East: Conceptions of Citizenship in the Levant" (award ref. no. R0023446201). Shortly after the award of the ESRC grant, Niblock and Davis moved to the Centre for Middle Eastern and Islamic Studies (CMEIS), University of Durham, where the bulk of the research project was administered and carried out (1993–95).

On a parallel track in Oslo, Butenschon and Maktabi received funding from the Norwegian Research Council for their project "The Politics of Citizenship in the Middle East." In the academic year 1993–94, Butenschon joined Niblock and Davis at CMEIS for his sabbatical year, at which time the conceptual and administrative guidelines were established for an international conference in Oslo called "Citizenship and the State in the Middle East." Also in 1994, Butenschon and Manuel Hassassian of the Faculty of Arts, Bethlehem University, established a working relationship, and Hassassian was invited to join the convening committee of this international conference.

On an independent track, Suad Joseph had applied to and was funded by the American Council of Learned Societies/Social Science Research Council, in 1994, to carry out field work on how children in a village in Lebanon learn their concepts of citizenship, nationality, and rights. She also guest-edited a special issue of *Middle East Reports* on gender and citizenship in the Middle East, which appeared in 1996 (vol. 26, no. 1). In 1996 she proposed to Omar Traboulsi of Oxfam, U.K., to fund two conferences, one on citizenship in Lebanon and one on gender and citizenship in Lebanon. Both conferences were funded and were held in 1997. The first was co-organized with Walid Moubarak and Antoine Messarra and co-funded by the Fredrik Ebert Foundation. The second was co-organized with Najla Hamadeh and Jean Said Makdisi and co-funded by the Ford Foundation, Cairo. Both conference proceedings are to appear in Arabic in 1999.

The conference on Citizenship and the State in the Middle East was organized as a separate project within the framework of the University of Oslo's Programme of Cooperation with Palestine universities. The Palestinian Council of Higher Education (now part of the Palestinian Ministry of Higher Education) directed and coordinated the program on the Palestinian side. Through 1994 and 1995, the Programme of Cooperation was developed by the two sides in the form of thirteen project proposals and was presented to the Norwegian Agency for Development and Cooperation (Norad) for funding. In 1996, four projects were accepted for funding, among them the international conference "Citizenship and the State in the Middle East." (In1997, the administration of the funding was taken over by the National Programme for University Cooperation in Norway, NUFU.) Nils Butenschon was program coordinator on the Norwegian side, Manuel Hassassian on the Palestinian side. Uri Davis represented Durham University as the third convening partner.

The Department of Political Science, University of Oslo, organized the conference, with encouragement and support from the Faculty of Social Sciences and the university leadership. On 22–24 November 1996, more than one hundred participants from five continents met in Oslo. The conference was video-taped and excerpts shown on Channel 2 of the Norwegian Broadcasting Corporation on two consecutive weekends in May 1997. The project was also awarded the University of Oslo 1997 prize for distinguished educational achievement.

Subsequent to the conference, Suad Joseph (who presented a paper on gender and citizenship in the Middle East) agreed to join the members of the convening committee to form the editorial committee for the two volumes, and the editorial committee was co-opted by the new international journal *Citizenship Studies* as Middle East regional committee. The editorial committee held its first meeting in Oslo right after the conference and benefited greatly from the advice of Bryan Turner, founding editor of *Citizenship Studies* and director of the Citizenship Center at Deakin University at the time. Meeting in Oslo, Bethlehem, Jerusalem, Sakhnin, and Syracuse, the editorial committee used the conference papers as the groundwork for the two-volume project.

The members of the editorial committee extend their special thanks to the funding institutions that have made this research and publication project possible: the Economic and Social Research Council (ESCR) of the UK, the Norwegian Research Council, and the Norwegian Agency for Development and Cooperation (Norad). We also want to thank our own institutions, which have contributed extra finance, infrastructure, and moral support—particularly the Universities of Bethlehem, Durham, and Oslo, and their relevant academic and administrative departments, but also the Department of Politics, University of Exeter; University of California at Davis; *Citizenship Studies,* Cambridge University; MIFTAH (Consultancy Office), Kefar Shemayahu, Arab Institute for Vocational Completion, Sakhnin. Special thanks to the Royal Norwegian Ministry for Foreign Affairs, which assisted us whenever necessary.

Special thanks also to the late Anton Sarsour, executive vice president, Bethlehem University; Evelyn Ebsworth, vice-chancellor, University of Durham; Ronald Gallagher, vice-chancellor, Bethlehem University; and Lucy Smith, rector, University of Oslo, for their personal involvement and active support. In this connection, we particularly appreciate visits of Ronald Gallagher to Oslo and Lucy Smith to Bethlehem in support of the project.

On a more personal note, there are a great number of additional people we would like to thank warmly for their support, commitment, extra work hours, comments, and advice—notably, all those who presented papers and made contributions at the international conference.

Particular thanks are also due to all those at the University of Oslo who contributed practical help in setting up and conducting the conference: Tone Lund (administrative head, Department of Political Science) and her entire staff; Willy Egset (research assistant and conference coordinator); and the rest of Butenschon's project group of ten graduate students, who contributed both academically and with practical assistance. Also, the assistance provided by Olve Sorensen and later by Mette Topnes at the Department of International Relations in all matters related to funding institutions (applications, transfer of money, reports, etc.—a huge amount of paperwork!) was indispensable.

We are also grateful to those who contributed to the completion of this first volume. Among them, Hana' Jahshan, administrative officer at Bethleham University, must be mentioned. With gentle firmness she took care of most practical arrangements in Bethlehem's cooperation with Oslo and Durham and whenever the editorial committee met in Bethlehem. Atle Hommersand, a member of the student project group in Oslo, deserves a special thanks for his assistance to Nils Butenschon in copyediting the manuscript for this volume. His patience and availability were particularly helpful in the last stage of the work, as Butenschon took over the demanding job as director of the Norwegian Institute of Human Rights, University of Oslo, in 1998. Also, Christopher Saunders, who works as a language consultant for Norwegian academic institutions, made invaluable contributions in the final proofreading stage.

Last, but not least, we extend our thanks to Syracuse University Press. We are indebted to Director Robert Mandel, who took personal interest in the project and facilitated the concluding editorial committee meeting in Syracuse. Acquisitions editor Mary Selden Evans directed the final preparation of the manuscript with authority and a generous approach toward the authors.

All this said, the final product presented here is inescapably our own responsibility.

Contributors

Nils Butenschon is director of the Norwegian Institute of Human Rights at the University of Oslo, on internal leave since 1998 from the Department of Political Science, where he is associate professor of international relations specializing in Middle East politics. He was deputy head of the department and director of International and Post-Graduate Studies 1996–98. In 1993–94 he was visiting professor at the Centre for Middle Eastern and Islamic Studies, University of Durham. His latest publication in English is "The Oslo Agreement: From the White House to Jabal Abu Ghneim," in *After Oslo: New Realities, Old Problems,* edited by G. Giacaman and D. J. Lønning (1998).

Uri Davis is Honorary Research Fellow at the Centre for Middle Eastern and Islamic Studies, University of Durham, and at the Institute of Arab and Islamic Studies, University of Exeter. Dr. Davis has been at the forefront of the defense of human rights, notably Palestinian rights, since 1965 and pioneered critical research on Zionism and Israel since the mid-1970s. He has published extensively in these fields, including *Israel: An Apartheid State* (1990) and *Citizenship and the State: Comparative Study of Citizenship Legislation in Israel, Jordan, Palestine, Syria, and Lebanon* (1997). Dr. Davis is Observer-Member, Palestine National Council and chairman, AL-BEIT: Association for the Defence of Human Rights in Israel.

Asbjørn Eide is senior fellow at the Norwegian Institute of Human Rights. He was among the Institute's founders in 1987 and its director until 1998. He is member of the United Nations Sub-Commission for Prevention of Discrimination and Protection of Minorities and chairman of the sub-commission's Working Group on Minorities.

Manuel S. Hassassian is professor of international politics and relations and is currently executive vice president of Bethlehem University. His areas of specialization are comparative politics, with emphasis on Middle East politics and the Armenian National Movement, and political theory. His latest publications include *Palestine: Factionalism in the National Movement 1919–1939* (1990) and *The Historical Evolution of the Armenian Question and the Conflict over Nagorno Karabagh* (1990). Dr. Hassassian is a member of the editorial board of the *Arab Political Science Journal* and the *Palestine-Israel Journal*. He is also a core member of International Consultative Group of the Center for Strategic and International Studies (Washington D.C.) and of Search for Common Ground (Washington D.C.).

Sara Helman is lecturer at the Department of Behavioral Sciences, Ben Gurion University. Her research interests are in the sociology of citizenship, social movements, and political identities. She has published in *Citizenship Studies* and other international journals and is currently working on social identities and the military, and on the politics of ethnicity and religion in Israel.

Raymond Hinnebusch is professor of international relations and Middle East politics at the University of St. Andrews, Scotland. He is the author of many works on Egypt and Syria, including *Egyptian Politics under Sadat* (1985) and *Authoritarian Power and State Formation in Ba'thist Syria* (1990).

Anis Kassim is a lawyer who currently practices law in Jordan and Palestine. He is member of the board of the Palestinian Independent Commission for Citizens' Rights and editor-in-chief of the *Palestine Yearbook of International Law*.

Rebecca Kook is assistant professor at the Department of Politics and Government at Ben Gurion University, Israel. Dr. Kook's research interests focus on theories of nationalism and citizenship, and she has written on issues related to national identity in both Israel and the United States.

Anh Nga Longva is associate professor in social anthropology at the University of Bergen, Norway. Her publications are based on fieldwork in the Gulf and include *Walls Built on Sand: Migration, Exclusion and Society in Kuwait* (1997) and *Democracy Between Tribalism, Islam and the Welfare State: Perspectives from Kuwait and Bahrain* (forthcoming).

Rania Maktabi is a political scientist currently working on her Ph.D. thesis at the Fafo Institute for Applied Social Science in Oslo, where she has worked as a research fellow for several years. The thesis is entitled "Membership and Participation in Divided Societies: The Politics of Citizenship in Jordan, Kuwait and Lebanon."

Beverley Milton-Edwards is a reader at the School of Politics and assistant director of the Centre for the Study of Ethnic Conflict at Queen's University of Belfast. She is the author of *Islamic Politics in Palestine* (1996) and *Contemporary Politics in the Middle East* (1999).

Christopher Parker is a Ph.D. candidate at the Center for Third World Studies–Middle East Studies Center of the University of Ghent, Belgium. He is the author of *Resignation or Revolt? Socio-Political Development and the Challenges of Peace in Palestine* (1999).

Zeev Rosenhek is lecturer at the Department of Sociology and Anthropology, Hebrew University, Jerusalem. He conducts research in the areas of the political economy of the welfare state, state-society relations, stratification and ethnicity, and labor migration.

Michael Shalev is chair of the Department of Sociology and Anthropology at Hebrew University. He has been a notable contributor to the critical wave in Israeli social science since the 1980s and is currently interested in the politics of economic liberalization in Israel and advanced capitalist economies. He is the author of *Labour and the Political Economy in Israel* (1992).

Mary Ann Tétreault is professor of political science at Iowa State University. She has written extensively on Middle Eastern energy policy and gender politics, and is the author of *Stories of Democracy: Politics and Society in Contemporary Kuwait* (1999).

Bryan Turner has held professorial positions at a number of universities and is currently professor of Sociology at the University of Cambridge. He is the founding editor of the journal *Citizenship Studies* and the author of many standard works of relevance for the present book, including *Weber and Islam* (1974), *Marx and the End of Orientalism* (1978), *Capitalism and Class in the Middle East* (1984), *Citizenship and Capitalism* (1986), and *Orientalism, Postmodernism and Globalism* (1994). He is currently editing a twelve-volume study of early Orientalism for Routledge.

PART ONE

APPROACHES

1

State, Power, and Citizenship in the Middle East

A Theoretical Introduction

NILS A. BUTENSCHON

The Citizenship Perspective

WHEN ALTERNATIVE MODELS for a good society are discussed in the relevant academic literature, a most fundamental question is seldom asked: Who are *the people?* How do we define *the society* whose interests we cherish? If we want democracy, who is the demos that constitutes the basis for democratic institutions? As Margaret Canovan (1996) points out, such questions are "easily overlooked by theorists who approach questions of justice in abstract and universal terms while tacitly taking for granted the territorial and legal limits of the state within which they happen to be writing" (28).[1]

Implicitly, of course, we make more or less precise judgments about the nature of our own society or any society under discussion. But in failing to present thorough arguments and make such judgments explicit, we may overlook extremely important questions of relevance for the discussion of a good (or just, etc.) society. For example, if we take the demographic and geographic boundaries of the society for granted—and accordingly the sociocultural or ideological meaning associated with them—we effectively close the room for alternative definitions and interpretations.[2]

---

1. For an excellent elaboration of this argument, see Canovan (1996), especially chapters 3 and 4.

2. This exclusion of alternatives may of course be the effect of lack of precision or inability

Consequently, the discourse on democracy and good governance is typically dominated by questions pertaining to the role of the state in the economy, models of political participation, the rule of law, the role of traditional values in politics, and so on. These are important questions in their own right, but can be meaningfully discussed only when there is *already* an established agreement on who legitimately constitute "the society." What kind of criteria are applied when the distinction is drawn between those who are included and those who are not in the political community under discussion?

This is where the citizenship perspective comes into the picture. It is not a unified theoretical position—as demonstrated by the range of contributions to this book. What distinguishes this approach is its level of analysis, which can be defined as the contractual relationship (in the broadest possible meaning of *contractual*) between the state and the inhabitants under its jurisdiction. Under what conditions are such relationships created, how are rights and obligations codified and perceived by the parties, what are the modalities for changing the terms, and what instruments of retribution are available to the parties in case of conflict? The question "who are the people" is of particular relevance when an established political order breaks down, when a country or a region undergoes dramatic political upheavals or faces fundamental challenges to the existing order. What is the purpose of organizing political communities with sovereignty over territorial entities, whose interests should be represented, how should a state deal with demographic differences and social conflict? In the real world, such questions arise only *after* the state itself has been established—as a result of military conquest, colonial design, or a larger territorial reorganization agreed upon by external powers. Many of the more important parameters of a new order have then already been imposed: the territorial boundaries of the new states, their demographic composition, and their position in a new security system. Both Europe and the Middle East have been subject to such painful experiences throughout this century. Consequently, point zero in the process of building states is not a situation where you have a *unified* people ready to build a state as it sees fit. More often, you have an unstable situation with a number of groups and elites who compete for territorial control and institutional power. The outcome of these struggles (with or without external intervention) will determine who will constitute the political center and who will be more or less excluded from influence in the emerging political system.

---

to think in alternative perspectives, but it may also be a conscious strategy of excluding threatening worldviews.

The citizenship approach is a cross-disciplinary approach. From a legal point of view, the contractual relationships between the state and its inhabitants are manifested in a variety of legal statuses allocated to different segments of the population (according to age, sex, family affiliation, ethnic identity, duration of residence in the country, etc.), as codified in the legal system of particular countries. On another level, states have obligations toward every individual under their jurisdiction under international human rights law, as explained in detail by Asbjørn Eide in chapter 5 of this book.

Social scientists (sociologists, political scientists, social anthropologists) seek to interpret and explain these different contractual relations in the context of wider social, cultural, or political structures that characterize state-society relations. As a political scientist, I am particularly concerned with the significance of citizenship with regard to the distribution of power and the nature of political institutions in a country, and with how the founding principles of states are expressed more widely in certain patterns of citizenship policies.

The power of citizenship is probably best known by those who are denied it: the right to carry a passport and be protected by a state; the right to abode; the right to membership in a political community with access to decision-making institutions and public welfare. Citizenship is a scarce public good that is distributed by the state, a source of collective identity and an instrument of political control. As Michael Walzer (1983 [1994]) puts it, membership is "the primary good that we distribute to one another" (31). It is the right to have rights.

But the nature and scope of rights and obligations that go into the concept of citizenship vary greatly from country to country. These variations may easily become hidden behind the veil of formal sovereignty and the concept of nationality that is applicable to all internationally recognized states. I suggest that variations in the conditions of citizenship from one country to another can be taken to reflect differences in key principles of power distribution. The significance of a citizenship approach is that it allows us to unveil important aspects of the architecture of power-relations between rulers and ruled, and to analyze the logic of these relations.

The theoretical reasoning that justifies this approach is that citizenship is a major institutional control mechanism that regulates the distribution of rights and obligations in a society, including access to decision-making arenas and state-controlled economic resources. Thus, state authorities and their rivals tend to be involved in legal and political struggles involving the modus operandi of citizenship in individual countries.

Whether or not the state leadership is able to control or even dictate the outcome of these processes depends on the nature of the regime and its governance capacity. In most Middle Eastern countries, citizenship matters are regarded as important for state security and thus are firmly held in the hands of centralized authorities.

Citizenship is not something that exists only in the form of legal regulations, institutional mechanisms, and ideological or cultural constructs. As a prime criterion of membership, it belongs to the core dynamics of any politically organized society and should also be understood in that context. Consequently, what I broadly call "the politics of citizenship" in a given country is taken here to be an analytical gateway to insight into the dynamics of regime formation in that country and its *raison d'etat*, its *state-idea*. Furthermore, for reasons that are explained in more detail below, this approach to the nature of political power is of particular relevance if our empirical focus happens to be the Middle East, a region where the purpose of state power seems to be an unresolved question as much today as at any time before.

The politics of citizenship, as an analytical category, covers more than citizenship *policies*—i.e., the legal and practical-political ways in which state authorities handle questions of citizenship. It covers any arena of social interaction where citizenship comes into the picture as an instrument of power distribution. Indeed, most modern discourses on citizenship harbor a normative-holistic approach whereby citizenship is seen as a mechanism of societal integration, equal participation, and economic justice. In this way, citizenship has become a very broad concept with the danger of being emptied of a specific meaning.

A useful point of departure for any discussion on contemporary concepts of citizenship is T. H. Marshall's classic article "Citizenship and Social Class," originally published in 1950. Marshall identifies three stages in the formation of modern citizenship in Europe, each characterized by a specific functional sphere or arena for politics of citizenship.

The first of the three stages in the development of a complete citizenship defines the scope of individual freedom and security (such as the rights to property, personal liberty, and justice) institutionalized in a system for the rule of law. This forms what Marshall calls *civil citizenship*. This stage emerged in the wake of the French Revolution as a liberal conception of the state consolidated in Europe.

Political citizenship is the second stage and refers to participation in the political arena (such as the right to vote and be elected to positions in political institutions), which was introduced on an increasingly broader scale in the nineteenth century.

The final stage in Marshall's ideal model is *social citizenship*, which encompasses rights to social security and welfare, both closely linked to mechanisms of economic redistribution. This dimension of citizenship was on the political center stage of European countries in the twentieth century.[3]

More recently, the concept of citizenship has been stretched in new directions to cover postindustrial discourses on state-society relations. *Cultural citizenship, global citizenship,* and even *ecological citizenship* have been introduced by different scholars with references to what they see as important challenges of the contemporary world, including globalization and the alleged crisis of the nation-state (van Steenbergen 1994, 3). Bryan Turner (1986) pursues this line of thought to its logical conclusion when he states that "citizenship is not simply about class and capitalism, but it also involves debates about the social rights of women, children, the elderly and even animals" (11). Turner's point is, as he also explains in chapter 2 of this book, that citizenship as a membership institution cannot easily extend protection and care to "nonmembers" within the community, which presents contemporary citizenship theory with important challenges from a perspective of universal human rights. Turner's question is how citizenship theory might be developed to propose just and reasonable solutions to the dilemma of inclusion and exclusion inherent in the conception of citizenship.

Thus, the potential applicability of a citizenship-based approach to various social categories seems to be almost unlimited. But when we turn to the fundamental challenges of political stability and democracy in the Middle East, I think we need a back-to-basics approach with a focus on how political communities are constituted in the first place. For that purpose, an important contribution to the conceptualization of citizenship is the distinction, introduced by Uri Davis in chapter 3 in this volume, between *jinsiyya* citizenship and *muwatana* citizenship. The former concept ("passport citizenship" in Davis's terminology) designates the individual's right of abode in the state where he or she is a citizen. The latter concept ("democratic citizenship") designates, in addition to the individual's right of abode, also his or her equal access to the civil, political, social, and economic resources of the state of his or her citizenship. The distinction between the two concepts is, symbolically, the distinction between illegitimate and legitimate male offspring of a household, with only the latter entitled to equal inheritance rights. The disinction is particularly useful for conceptualizing the legislation and the application of first- and second-class citizenship in Middle

---

3. This way of organizing political development conceptually is characteristic of many studies of modernization and nation building written mostly in the 1960s and 1970s. See, for example, Bendix (1977) and Rokkan (1975). For a more detailed discussion of Marshall, see Barbalet (1988).

Eastern states (illegal under international law) as well as the mechanisms employed to veil such legislation and practice from the scrutiny of world community.

We have to remember that the historic experience that influenced Marshall, Reinhard Bendix (1964 [1977]), Stein Rokkan (1975), and many subsequent Western-based contributors to modern theories of citizenship was first and foremost the gradual formation and integration of the nation-state, as we have come to know the contemporary democratic welfare state in Western Europe. The overriding pattern in the formation of these states was the extension of citizenship rights, step by step, to include new sections of the population and new spheres of the political and economic system, all the time within the framework of given territories. By and large, most of the advanced industrial countries had reached a level of nation building, as defined by Marshall's final stage, by the 1960s or 1970s. Now people started to ask, Where do we go from here? Why stop at social citizenship, Marshall's final stage? Why stop at the borders of nation-states? Why not include the entire world community, future generations, animals, and nature as such?[4]

Questions like these can be asked only if you accept the logic of Marshall's incremental approach, whereby each new sequence of social integration builds on the former. Social citizenship is inconceivable without an established political citizenship (and an industrial economy), and political citizenship presupposes civil citizenship. Progressive ideas of extending citizenship rights beyond the Marshallian model are based on the assumption that civil, political, and social rights are historically secured beyond doubt, at least in principle, and can be taken for granted as stepping stones for further advancements. This assumption is, however, not applicable without important qualifications in the context of Middle Eastern political history (or if applied to many other regions of the world, parts of Europe included). This point is emphasized by Raymond Hinnebusch in the concluding paragraph of his contribution to this volume: "In the Middle East, the 'premature' granting of socioeconomic rights—before industrial takeoff—means that current democratization there is likely to be accompanied by the *opposite* of the Western experience—not the *expansion,* but the *reversal* of such rights." What is so special, then, with the Middle East from a political development point of view?

---

4. Such questions were asked from a communitarian perspective. Neoliberalists, on the other hand, questioned the role of the state as the regulator of welfare and power distribution, and had considerable success in the 1980s in their campaign for the retreat of the state in favor of the market as the basic regulatory mechanism in society.

Political Development and Patterns of Authority
in the Middle East

The formation of contemporary political communities in the Middle East cannot be neatly organized into historical sequences whereby one stage follows the other in a seemingly logical manner. On the contrary, the region—particularly the Arab Middle East—was not given the chance (or did not seize the opportunity, according to some) to develop a modernizing strategy based on indigenous conceptions of human dignity, legitimate authority, solidarity, and other fundamental aspects of social and political organization. The political history of the late-nineteenth-century and early-twentieth-century Middle East was dominated by the struggle for control over the shrinking, and later collapsing, Ottoman Empire. As a consequence, a number of local and regional wars were waged throughout the twentieth century with origins in well-established patterns of imperial and colonial rule in the Middle East. External great powers have always been present in one way or the other, directly or indirectly, particularly in times of war and postwar situations. As a result, it is almost impossible to draw clear distinctions between structures and processes of *national* as opposed to *international* relations of the Middle East.[5] Indeed, state formation in the Middle East cannot be studied solely as a process endogenous to the region itself, as most students of Western European state building take for granted.

The modern political history of the Middle East has left the region with painful experiences and deep uncertainties about the purpose and principles of organizing political communities and states. This theme has attracted considerable and growing academic interest over the last ten to fifteen years. A number of observations seem to justify a special focus on the region, particularly the Arab Middle East (see, for example, Luciani 1990, Khoury and Kostiner 1991, Owen 1992, Ayubi 1995). One is the paradoxical persistence of the ruling elites and regimes that came to power in the Arab countries after the political upheavals in the region in the 1950s and 1960s. In spite of continued widespread political turmoil, including violent outbursts of popular discontent, and in spite of civil, local, and regional wars and external interference, the established Arab political order has, with few qualifications,[6] not been radically changed since the early 1970s. It is as if

5. This is a characteristic feature of what S. B. Cohen (1973) calls a geostrategic "shatterbelt," where the combined effects of global powers struggling for control of the region, on the one hand, and local groups in conflict, on the other, create endemic regional instability and unpredictability.

6. Such qualifications include the unification of North and South Yemen and the change of

the political structures of Arab states have been frozen for some twenty-five years; by and large the established regimes have responded to internal and external opposition and challenges by tightening their grips on power and strengthening every line of defense. Ask yourself how many rulers from the early 1970s still hold on to power today. A striking element in this picture is how most of the "revolutionary" Arab republics (particularly Iraq, Syria, Libya, and Algeria) have failed to meet expectations of facilitating broad public participation in the political and economic development of their countries. The promises of Nasserism, Ba'athism, and their off-shoots have not only not been fulfilled, but betrayed by small groups of rulers primarily concerned with the protection of their own power base (L. Anderson 1991).

This stagnation in politicostructural dynamics in the Arab world differs sharply from the expectations and predictions that characterized many well-known studies written under the impression of the post–World War II pan-Arab mobilization and radical transformation in the region. Such studies include Daniel Lerner's *The Passing of Traditional Society* (1958), Manfred Halpern's *The Politics of Social Change in the Middle East and North Africa* (1963), Hisham Sharabi's *Nationalism and Revolution in the Arab World* (1966), and Michael C. Hudson's *Arab Politics: The Search for Legitimacy* (1977). These works and others had varying ideas about where the Arab political systems were heading, but most authors believed that traditional and autocratic patterns of government would give way inevitably to more "modern," "rational," or "progressive" regimes. What we have experienced, however, is that radical Arab republics have degenerated into personal dictatorships or bureaucratic authoritarianism, that the dynastic monarchies have adapted surprisingly well to the modern world without introducing basic democratic reforms, and that the most forceful and popular political opposition to the existing order comes from mobilized religious groups, not from a "progressive" and "rational" opposition with a secularized Western political model (liberal or socialist) in mind.

Of the classical works mentioned above, Michael C. Hudson's *Arab Politics* deserves special attention here. Hudson presents a comprehensive account of political dynamics in the Arab world in the 1960s and early 1970s within the context of classical theories of political science. The rich analysis of the book makes it worthwhile reading still today, even though the agenda of the Arab political and intellectual discourse has changed.

Hudson puts special emphasis on "governance capacity" in his attempt to explain mechanisms of political change and stability, but omits any reference to the institution of citizenship in this connection. This omission is, in my

---

regime in Sudan to an Islamist government. These changes have had limited impact on the rest of the region, however.

opinion, a major weakness in his analysis because citizenship can be considered the organizing principle of state-society relations in modern states. This volume is an attempt to demonstrate that point.

In itself, the phenomenon of citizenship does not presuppose equality, democracy, or a vibrant society of citizens (civil society).[7] The basic quality of citizenship is that of a contractual relationship: it regulates the legal status of the individual inhabitants of a state (by implication including noncitizens) and sets the rules for participation in political institutions and access to public resources. In this sense, citizenship *constitutes* political communities within the territorial boundaries of states; in short, citizenship is the organizing principle of modern states. It draws lines between members and nonmembers, between those who are included and those excluded from specific rights and obligations regulated by the authorities. The patterns of these dividing lines reflect the internal sociolegal boundaries of the state as a membership organization. Thus, citizenship laws and regulations constitute a major mechanism that manifests *legal classes* in a society.

The authority to define or the ability to control the content of a state's citizenship policy—laws, regulations, and their practical application of inclusion and exclusion—means a pronounced influence on the basic parameters of that state, including the distribution of rights and obligations between groups and consequently whether or not the nature of a particular citizenship is democratic. This kind of influence is of particular significance if the legitimacy of the existing regime (or the state itself) is challenged by groups with the capacity to mobilize serious opposition, which is so often the case in the Middle East.

Citizenship and the "Territorial Trap"

In the period after the Cold War, we have witnessed a global trend of crumbling state authority and governance capacity, as well as a corresponding growth in the number of internal conflicts. This trend has often been interpreted—wrongly in my opinion—as a historic sign that the modern state as we came to know it in the twentieth century is about to lose its relevance as a coherent unit of political decision making. According to this view, new challenges on both the global level (*globalization*) and the subnational level (*regionalization*) make the sovereign nation-state a less relevant entity for solving political problems and meeting personal or collective aspirations.

---

7. For historic reasons, however, *citizenship* carries connotations to the state of being "free," with reference to city dwellers in Europe who freed themselves from feudal relations of servitude (Fraser and Gordon 1994, 95).

What such popular analyses ignore, however, is that most cases of internal struggles are conflicts over the central institutions of state power with the aim of taking over (or holding on to) the symbols of sovereignty and the control of resources and instruments of power that accompany them. Qualitatively new ways of organizing political communities, which could replace the sovereign nation-state, are not emerging. The discussions on a possible European citizenship within the European Union does not evade this territorial trap. This is basically a question of extending the territorial applicability of existing citizenship rights, not of dissociating citizenship rights from state and territory. Pure and unlimited state sovereignty is difficult to imagine and define in practical terms and has never been a reality, not under the conditions of the Cold War and not in the present situation. What we have seen in a number of conflict-ridden regions lately should be understood as struggles for the reordering of state boundaries and control of monopoly powers. New bases for political loyalties are thus in the process of being formed now that the old structure of global bipolarity is gone—and with it the old patterns of discipline and loyalties it imposed on regional states.

In short, responses to changes in global relations of power the last decade of the twentieth century indicate basic weaknesses in the post–World War II and postcolonial state system, but not a crisis of the modern state as a model of political organization. On the contrary, the various internal conflicts—focused as they are on traditional symbols and institutions of national sovereignty—confirm the significance of the state as the unrivaled framework for collective political organization.

As already indicated, citizenship should basically be considered a principle of power distribution that significantly forms the boundaries of a political system. These boundaries are lines of defense and channels of influence to the core institutions of the state. All political regimes must establish such boundaries in order to function as a decision-making unit. These boundaries, in effect, are materialized in the form of political institutions and legal mechanisms. What principles of inclusion and exclusion are applied in the formation of such institutions and mechanisms? Where in the political system do we find the arenas that are decisive for forming principles of inclusion and exclusion? And how are these principles reflected in state policies and institutional arrangements?

Citizenship and Regime Formation in the Middle East

As a contractual relationship between the state and its inhabitants, citizenship is only one among a complex set of formal and informal structures that characterize a state-society. The modern idea of citizenship, however, is that citizenship supersedes all other patterns of authority, and that this principle is a prerequisite for an all-inclusive and democratic citizenship. Modernization in this sense is the process of gradual integration of the inhabitants of the state whereby traditional and primordial authority patterns and contractual relations are replaced by legally codified universal rights and obligations. Everyone is equal before the law, and none is outside the law. The state commands monopolistic control over coercive means within its jurisdiction. No other authority structure in society—be it based on the family, religious leadership, or tribal organization—can legitimately demand loyalty from one of its members in a way that contradicts his or her obligations toward the state.

We know that in the real world this ideal model of transition from traditional to modern society—for example, Ferdinand Tönnies's gesellschaft or Max Weber's legal-rational authority—is not represented, not in Europe and even much less in the Middle East.[8] As regards the Arab Middle East, Michael Hudson (1977) discerns four dimensions of traditional authority: *patriarchal, consultative, Islamic,* and *feudal* (82–84). Each of these dimensions is deeply rooted in Arab history and is legacies of sultanic and Islamic imperial rule. When Hudson finds that there is a "crisis of authority" in the Arab world, it is for two main reasons:[9] first, the traditional structures of authority contradict the logic of the state-centered modern conception of authority, and second, there are tensions between the traditional dimensions of authority. With reference to the first point, Hudson explains in Weberian terms that

[t]he traditional bases of authority have been weakened but have not disappeared, while rational-legal types of authority have arisen but are not strong. The coexistence of contradictory types of authority is a drain on overall system legitimacy. Arabs are still socialized into accepting traditional rationales for obedience based on kinship, religion, dynastic depotism, and feudalism. Yet at the same time, they are influenced by Western ideologies which justify authority on altogether different grounds like "the will of the people." But in the absence of effective structures of political participation, how is the will of the

8. This transition has been famously conceptualized in the form of dichotomies by some of the pioneers of social sciences, such as Emil Durkheim (*organic* vs. *mechanical* solidarity), Ferdinand Tönnies (*Gemeinshaft* vs. *Gesellschaft*), and Max Weber (*traditional* and *charismatic* authority vs. *legal-rational*). For a recent study of these and more contemporary positions on modernity and nationalism, see Paul James (1996).

9. Hudson wrote his book in the mid-1970s and must be read with that in mind. But I still think his account of the legitimacy problem in Arab politics is the best and most comprehensive from a political science point of view.

people to be ascertained? All sorts of politicians and groups can and do claim to be authentic representatives of the popular will. But there is usually no accepted, legitimized procedure for ascertaining which among them is the most authentic embodiment of this will. Accordingly, force is frequently the arbiter of the locus of authority. (82–83)

As for the second reason, the tension between traditional dimensions of authority, Hudson sees "tensions and contradictions: on the one hand [the promotion of] absolutism and blind obedience—a shepherd-flock relationship[,] but on the other hand, . . . demands for egalitarianism and participation." Summing up, Hudson contends, "In the absence of a coherent foundation for authoritative rule, there is a disproportionate reliance on personality and individual leadership to legitimize rule" (82–83).

An analysis of traditional authority structures and the persistence of such structures also informs Ilya Harik's (1990) typology of Arab political systems. He distinguishes four main types of regimes, three of which are based on the traditional patterns of authority referred to by Hudson. These three types can be distributed along a dimension with different combinations of religious and secular authority, from the strongest combination (*imam-sheikh systems,* where a religious leader is also the leader of the ruling dynasty)[10] via *alliance systems* (where the religious leadership commands the legal system and sanctions the dynastic rule of the state)[11] to systems based primarily on secular authority *(sheikh systems).*[12] Along with these systems come what Harik calls *bureaucratic-military oligarchies,* characterized by a strong central power and personal authoritarian rule. Such systems are to be found most typically in North Africa (Egypt, Libya, Algeria, Tunisia) with precedents in the Ottoman era. Located far away from the imperial center, these territories were often ruled by military oligarchies on behalf of the sultan with a large degree of autonomy. The best-known example is the rule of Muhammed Ali in Egypt in the early nineteenth century. A more contemporary model is Mustafa Kemal (Atatürk) and his authoritarian reformism (Kemalism) of the new Turkish state in the late 1920s and 1930s. Kemal was heavily influenced by European nationalism and republicanism, and set out to build a strong, modern, centralized, and secular Turkish state. Kemal's rule was also the first instance in the Middle East of a regime based on the idea of popular sovereignty and not a dynastic or religious conception of state authority. It is characteristic that the founding fathers of mod-

10. Oman would be a contemporary example.
11. Saudi Arabia is a strong candidate here.
12. Kuwait falls clearly into this category.

ern Tunisia, Algeria, and Egypt (Habib Bourgiba, Houari Boumedienne, and Gamal Abdel Nasser, respectively) all had Atatürk as an important source of inspiration for their own revolutionary aspirations (Richards and Waterbury 1990, 302).

Kemal's program for the transformation of the core Ottoman territory into a modern Turkish nation-state—which included such radical steps as a total separation of state and mosque, the introduction of the Latin alphabet, and a general deorientalization of public and private cultural attributes within the confines of the new Turkish republic—was not easy to copy in Egypt or any other Arab country. Although the North African societies were not unambiguously Arab, Islamic civilization could not be eradicated altogether from the public sphere of the state, inseparable as it was and is from Arab political identity and history. Following the Suez Crisis in 1956, Gamal Abdel Nasser emerged not only as the savior of the *Egyptians*, but as the new leader of "the Arab nation." Nasserism became the program of transforming the Arab world from a backward region artificially partitioned into state territories and ruled by Western-dominated feudal lords. Nasser was expected to lead the Arabs toward a unified political commonwealth that could stand up against any power that would try to dominate the Arabs again. So, in a sense, Nasserism was a revolt against or a redefinition of certain dimensions of traditional Arab authority (notably the concentration of authority in a class of notables and the importance of kinship groups in Arab politics) by invoking a progressive interpretation of other dimensions—such as the consultative tradition, whereby the leader's authority derives from communal acceptance and participation in decision making, and the patriarchal tradition, which refers to the habitual deference accorded to the father in the Arab family (Hudson 1977, 83–84). As has been demonstrated over the last decades of the twentieth century, Nasserism failed to unify Arab political identity and accordingly also to unify the Arab peoples politically.[13] The dilemmas and paradoxes of Arab identity are no less relevant today. On the political level, they are probably most visible in the conflict between religious and secular conceptions of political authority; on the academic level, we see them reflected in numerous conferences on the Middle East, where "unity, diversity, identity" seem to be among the most popular themes.

Can what we here call a citizenship approach be of any help to clarify these dilemmas and paradoxes? The authors of this volume may differ

---

13. Malcolm Kerr's *The Arab Cold War* (1971) is a classical study of the failed attempt to unify permanently Egypt and Syria (and later to include Iraq) in the form of the United Arab Republic.

widely in general academic or political outlook, but we agree that approaching Middle East politics from a citizenship perspective offers an important analytical strategy that has so far not been systematically pursued. The approach is both *specific* in its empirical focus (the contractual relationship between the rulers and the ruled) and *universal* in its theoretical assumptions (the question of citizenship in one country is comparable to but empirically different from the question of citizenship in any other country). Thus, the dilemmas and paradoxes experienced in the context of the established order of Arab states are unique only as far as the historical and cultural references are concerned, but they are not necessarily unique as challenges in the process of creating political authority and building states. The same reasoning is valid in the case of Israel and the "nonstate" of Palestine,[14] which is why a number of chapters in this book discuss the Israeli-Palestinian dimension.

As already indicated, state and nation building involves basically the establishment of political institutions with monopolized authority in the entire state territory and the integration of the population into that polity. The structure of citizenship relations is a key factor in these processes, not only from the perspective of individual rights, but also from the perspective of the state's capacity to create political loyalties and manage communal conflicts. As Bendix (1977) and Rokkan (1975) have demonstrated, successful nation building can be understood *as* the gradual extension of citizenship rights both in scope and inclusiveness.

Political Organization of State Territories: A Typology

In order to locate the question of citizenship more precisely in the processes of state and nation building, I suggest below a typology of normative principles for constituting political communities within state territories. The purpose of the typology is to help us answer questions such as: Who are considered legitimate members of the collectivity that is to be organized within the jurisdiction of the state? How does the state relate to fragmented identities and group conflicts, to individuals or groups who reject the legitimacy of state authority, and to individuals or groups who are not considered legitimate members of the state (or national) community?

Again, in the real world we find as many answers to these and related questions as there are states, but for the sake of the theoretical argument I

14. This expression was used, for the first time as far as I know, by Professor Ibrahim Abu-Lughod of Birzeit University, Palestine, in a keynote address to the Oslo Conference, which is the basis for this book.

TABLE 1.1
Principles of Distribution of Rights

Distribution of Rights	Discriminatory	Non-discriminatory
Group-based	Hegemonic systems	Consociational Democracy
Individually based		Majoritarian Democracy

think it is possible to discern three qualitatively different normative conceptions (or models) of contractual relations between the state and the population under its jurisdiction, forming one of the two dimensions of the typology. Let us designate these conceptions *singularism, pluralism,* and *universalism.* What distinguishes them from each other is, first, whether the organizational principle of state institutions is based on *collective* or *individual* membership. To what extent is the status of the individual subject under the state's jurisdiction dependent on his or her group affiliation? The second question focuses on whether the state allocates rights on a discriminatory basis—i.e., whether or not the state applies *a systematic principle of differentiation* between individuals or groups in its allocation of rights and duties.

These distinctions can be summarized as shown in table 1.1.

The other dimension of the proposed typology of political regimes is the nature of the *territorial principle* applied in organization the state. Is there congruence between the politicogeographical organization of the state and its sociocultural demographic structure? How can a fragmented sociocultural structure be represented in territorial terms? Or should it be represented territorially? In this context, we can distinguish between the *unitary state, the fragmented state,* and *separate states* (see table 1.2, below).

Singularism

Singularism refers to the idea that the state community is constituted by a single and specific collective identity, and that the state is the embodiment of that identity. This principle can be found as the basis of authority and political organization in a number of Middle Eastern states. In the case of Saudi Arabia, a tribal principle of paternalistic kinship norms, consultative practices, Islamic law, and neofeudal royal patronage is applied to secure political hegemony by the constituent family, the Saudis (Hudson 1977, 105). Israel is an example where the principle of jus sanguinis (citizenship by law of blood) forms the overriding mechanism in the process of Jewish state building in Palestine. This mechanism—as operationalized in a set of laws, regulations, and implementing agencies—contributes effectively to

TABLE 1.2

Political Organization of State Territories

A Typology

Constitutional Principles	Territorial Principles		
	The Unitary State	The Fragmented State	Separate Territories
Singularism	Hegemonic systems	Imposed self-rule	Ethnic "Homelands"
Pluralism	Consociational systems	Cantonization	Separate states
Universalism	Majoritarian systems	Federation/Con-federation	Separate states

Jewish control over territory and political institutions by excluding non-Jews from access to and effective participation in centers of power. In Turkey, the linguistic-ethnic conception of Turkishness is the normative foundation of national integration to the extent that non-Turkish identities (notably the Kurdish identity) are not accepted as legitimate; in Iran, the Islamic *umma* (community of believers) constitutes the raison d'être of political authority and organization, and the idea of its redemption legitimizes political control by the Shi'ite religious leadership on all levels of government.

The reason why I group these otherwise extremely different regimes together as "hegemonic" is that they are all based on a singularistic state-idea that is both *organic* and *programmatic*. It is organic in the sense that the constituent community is considered an indivisible whole whose existence and interests have a superior moral value. It is programmatic in the sense that the state is considered to have a historical mission in the realization of the constituent community's fundamental aspirations. Thus, the state is not neutral in the way it relates to group identities and intergroup conflicts in the population, but is more or less partisan in its promotion of the status and interests of the titular community.

To what extent this role of the state creates manifest conflict or not depends of course on the historical context of each individual case. But particularly in situations where the privileged position of the titular community is rejected or seriously challenged by other groups, citizenship regulations present themselves to the authorities as a most effective measure for control of access to state territories, public resources, and political institutions.

Furthermore, by according different citizenship status to different groups and thus creating more or less identifiable legal classes in society, the singularistic state may easily create rivalries and conflicts between nontitular communities and thus prevent a unified front of opposition (the classic strategy of divide and rule). To the extent that such strategies are applied, we will see a system of *hierarchical citizenship,* creating a demographic structure of first- and second-class citizens (and more levels if needed). Finally, a characteristic feature of singularistic states is that they tend to be centralized with relatively large public resources allocated to a rigorous control system (including an omnipresent security police) mandated to detect any opposition to the core principles of state authority.

In terms of regime categorization of the states mentioned above, Saudi Arabia would classify as a *dynastic* state, Turkey and Israel as *ethnocracies,* and contemporary Iran as a *theocracy.* Let us have a closer look at ethnocracies and how they relate to plural and universalist principles of state organization.

Singularism in a Comparative Perspective: The Case of Ethnocracies

Singularism as a state-building principle is by no means unique to the states of the Middle East or to the contemporary world. As Rogers Brubaker (1996) shows, the European states that emerged from the disintegration of the Ottoman, Habsburg, and Romanov empires in the interwar period (1918–45) in Europe were founded on the basis of what I call organic and programmatic state-ideas (*nationalizing states* in Brubaker's term). According to him, this pattern seemed to repeat itself in the 1990s in countries that were formerly part of the Soviet Union, Yugoslavia, and Czechoslovakia, a development that could be seen as a challenge to assumptions and predictions in the established literature on nation building.[15]

More specifically, Brubaker's definition of a nationalizing state fits the category of ethnocratic singularism. In an earlier work (Butenschon 1993), I suggest that an ethnocracy should be understood as a separate regime formation with specific modes of power distribution and corresponding political dynamics (13). In short, I define an ethnocracy as *a state that allocates citizenship according to specific ethnic criteria (as normally spelled out in a nationality law).* This definition is a generalization of observed patterns first and foremost in the Middle East. Brubaker's definition of a nationalizing state is in effect very similar, but takes its empirical references mostly from Eastern Europe. A nationalizing state is a state

15. According to Brubaker (1996, 82–83), the political patterns of ethnic nationalism in former communist Europe challenge some of the paradigmatic assumptions in theoretic literature on nation building from the 1960s and 1970s, particularly the idea that ethnicity is an impediment to nation building.

understood to be the state *of* and *for* a particular ethnocultural "core nation" whose language, culture, demographic position, economic welfare, and political hegemony must be protected and promoted by the state. The key elements here are (1) the sense of "ownership" of the state by a particular ethnocultural nation that is conceived as distinct from the citizenry or permanent resident population as a whole, and (2) the "remedial" or "compensatory" project of using state power to promote the core nation's specific (and heretofore inadequately served) interests. (Brubaker 1996, 103)[16]

I indicated earlier that, in the Middle Eastern context, both Israel and Turkey qualify as ethnocracies. There is a very important difference between these two cases, however, that has important consequences on the level of the two states' ethnic policies. Whereas Israel is founded on the idea that all Jews of the world in principle belong in "the Land of the Jews" (Eretz Israel) and that the historic mission of modern Jewish nationalism (Zionism) is to territorialize the (bulk of) world Jewry ("ingathering the exiles"), modern Turkish nationalism (Kemalism) seeks to integrate and homogenize the entire population of Turkey on the basis of a modernized conception of Turkishness. Whereas Israel does not intend to integrate or assimilate the indigenous non-Jewish population of Palestine into the core national collective, Kemalist nation building precludes any ethnonational differentiation within the borders of Turkey. Any significant organized non-Turkish communal life is considered a threat to the integrity of the state and must not be tolerated. Accordingly, everyone who accepts identification with Turkish national culture (or, rather, who does not openly defy this culture, as understood by the authorities) is recognized as full and equal members of the nation. Those who do not accept this conception of national loyalty have no legitimate rights to participate in the life of the nation. The message to the Kurdish population of Turkey is clear: either accept that you are an inseparable part of the Turkish nation and be welcome as equals or face the consequences (such as forced assimilation, political repression, forced relocation).

From an Israeli-Zionist point of view, the Palestinians (either those who live in the State of Israel, in the Israeli-occupied territories, or in other countries as refugees) are not candidates for membership in the core nation of the state. On the contrary, the mere existence of the Palestinian people is a major strategic impediment to the realization of classical Zionist ambitions. Consequently, the Zionist solution to nation building is to exclude

---

16. If I am correct in my contention that *ethnocracy* and *nationalizing state* reflect more or less identical regime patterns, it indicates that the underlying theoretical assumptions are fruitful and could be pursued as the basis for more systematic comparative research.

the non-Jewish population from the constituent demos. This forms the logical background of a segregational policy that erects defensive walls of legal, institutional, and physical kinds to prevent Palestinians access to land, institutions, or other rights that could threaten Jewish hegemony in historic Palestine. The other side of the coin is, of course, that Zionist ethnocracy has provoked a Palestinian counterforce that seeks to correct the imbalance, and an inherently unstable relationship has been created between Israeli Jews and Palestinian Arabs. Singularism is in the long run extremely costly for both privileged and underprivileged, a proposition that was tragically substantiated during the Intifada, the Palestinian uprising between 1987 and 1993. Predictably, a need will be felt in such situations to find lasting solutions accepted as reasonable by the most important groups on both sides. In the course of that process, however, painful decisions will have to be made that will determine who should be included and who should be excluded from membership (citizenship) in the future political entity (or entities) of the territory and the modalities of these memberships.

In the context of the Israeli-Palestinian peace process, such questions belong to the final status negotiations, which, at the time of writing, are still to be commenced. A most important aspect of these talks will be to determine the status of the Palestinian refugees. Who and how many are they, and what is the nature of their legitimate rights, if any, to return to their country of origin? The continued existence of a Palestinian refugee population of several million represents not only a political and humanitarian problem, but also a potential reservoir of Palestinian population growth in Palestine, a fact that is of paramount importance in the context of ethnocratic politics and that more than anything explains the consistent Israeli rejection of the repatriation of Palestinian refugees to their homeland. The Israeli Law of Return—which guarantees any Jew and his or her immediate family automatic rights to immigration, settlement, and citizenship in Israel—should also be understood with a view to its strategic significance. It is a law that not only symbolically confirms Israel's purpose as a state for all Jews, but also opens up the gates of Israel for a potentially enormous reservoir of Jewish population growth in Israel. But this factor is not due to appear on the negotiating table in the upcoming final status negotiations.

In short, a large number of alternative demographic boundaries could be drawn in the Israeli-Palestinian context and would constitute either a more or less homogenous or heterogeneous demos as the basis for building one (or more) future state(s) in the territory of pre-1948 Palestine. These alternatives are illustrated in figure 1.1.

The point I want to make by this discussion is that a close examination of what Richard Hartshorne (1950) once called the *state-idea*, the founding

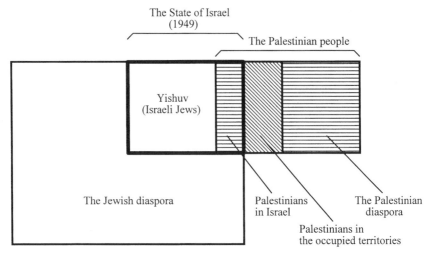

Fig. 1.1 **Alternative Demographic Boundaries in the Israeli-Palestinian Context**

principles of state organization, is essential if we want to understand the logic and patterns of political dynamics in a particular country. Singularism is one such founding principle, but as we have seen, this principle can be given very different expressions and formulations with considerable consequences in terms of citizenship policies. The second part of this book investigates different aspects of citizenship policies in the Israeli-Palestinian context.[17]

Pluralism

Pluralism refers, in our context, to a conception of the national community as composed of separate subgroups without programmatic predominance accorded to any of these groups. This conception forms the normative core of political systems of *power sharing*, which differs fundamentally from singularistic systems. Power sharing is rejected explicitly and in principle by singularism. The role of the state in plural systems is not to promote a specific communal identity, but to facilitate politics of compromise that give the different groups a fair say in the political decision-making processes.

Politics within such constitutional frameworks tend to focus on inter-group bargaining for the best possible deal within the confines of agreed principles of power sharing (as stated in a constitution or other formal or informal agreements with a comparable status). The government itself is

---

17. For a thorough discussion of aspects of ethnic division in contemporary Israel, see also a special issue of *Ethnic and Racial Studies* 21, no. 3 (May 1998), edited by Martin Blumer.

composed of leading representatives from the most salient groups (with positions normally allocated on the basis of relative numerical strength) in order to guarantee governmental neutrality toward intergroup conflict and bargaining. This, in effect, implies that all major governmental decisions that impinge upon intergroup relations have to be passed on the basis of consensus. Thus, the government in such cases is typically weak; it does not represent a strong and centralized institution with independent powers to impose specific solutions to conflicts between the groups represented in the power-sharing setup.[18] Internal peace is based on mutual respect, a general loyalty toward established procedures and rules of conduct, as well as a shared interest in protecting the political architecture of the system.

In the theoretical literature, such principles of government are usually referred to as *consociationalism,* as introduced by Arend Lijphart (1969 and 1977).[19] Lijphart wanted to demonstrate that intergroup conflict and political instability is not necessarily a characteristic feature of plural (socioculturally fragmented) societies, as was often contended in Anglo-American social science of the 1950s and 1960s. Lijphart's own empirical reference was the smaller continental European democracies (Holland, Belgium, Austria, and Switzerland). None of these countries is homogeneous, but every one is relatively democratic and stable. The critical factor that explains this stability is, according to Lijphart, that the elites of the most important segments have been able to agree upon a power-sharing formula based on the specific historical experiences and structural characteristics of the country. Finding such a formula is a question of creative "political engineering."

Lijphart's political engineering is applicable only in cases where the constituent groups are able to agree on a definition of demos—i.e., the demographic structure of the population that is to be organized in a state-society. This definition identifies the "collective individuals" who will be partners in power sharing. Thus, the individual member of the society is accorded his or her legal status by virtue of belonging to a specific group; citizenship becomes in effect an *indirect* relationship between a citizen and the state because group affiliation determines the nature of that individual's relationship to the state.

How do we distinguish singularism from pluralism? As can be seen from this discussion, there is one basic similarity between singularism and plural-

---

18. If, however, these groups are challenged by another group that for some reason is not party to the power-sharing institutions, they may of course agree to join forces to fight the rebels (or, more unlikely, to invite the rebels to share power with them).

19. His model of consociational democracy is most fully worked out in *Democracy in Plural Societies* (1977). For a discussion of the consociational model, see Butenschon (1985).

ism: both regard certain sociocultural collective identities as *irreducible* and as constituting fundamental premises for state and nation building. The underlying consociational presumption is that attempts by a central government either to eradicate or to merge firmly established subnational identities for purposes of creating "unity" (referred to as "standardization of national culture" in literature on nation building) most probably will be faced by severe opposition from groups who feel their integrity or even existence threatened. Better then to let such particular identities merge into a common overriding identity in a later stage of system development when everyone feels ready for it. Such unification should not, contend pluralists, be regarded as predetermined by modernization or as a precondition for successful nation building.

But consociationalism has been criticized for blurring the distinctions between hegemonic group relations (singularistic systems) and more equal group relations (democratic pluralism). One should not take for granted that every case of group conflict in a country is best solved by a system of power sharing based on existing identities. Lijphart's own suggestions for a system of power sharing in South Africa in the early 1980s (Lijphart 1985), for example, were strongly criticized by proponents of black majority rule. His suggestions were seen as a way of preserving elements of white ethnocracy (known as apartheid) and of preventing a thorough democratization of South Africa. Also, Lijphart's presentation of Israel as a "semiconsociational democracy" (1977, 129) is indeed questionable in terms of definitions and distinctions.[20] Here, he restricts himself to an analysis of the *Jewish* society in Israel because the Palestinian population falls outside what is generally considered in Israel to be the national community. The basic questions again arise: How is demos constituted? Who are legitimate partners in the state-building endeavor? What characterizes a situation of "equality" between groups? When do we consider a specific relation between two or more groups to be "hegemonic"?

In a Middle Eastern context, Lebanon is the best-known example of a political system based on power sharing, in important ways closely resembling Lijphart's model. Still today, however, people cannot quite agree whether consociationalism in Lebanon has been a success story, a failure, or both. The fact that the Lebanese power-sharing system survived the Lebanese civil war (1975–90)—however modified by the Taif Agreement that ended the war—can be interpreted as both a weakness and a strength of the

---

20. *Semiconsociationalism* refers specifically to the relative institutional autonomy of the Jewish Orthodox community in Israel and the customary rule of including minority religious parties in governmental coalitions.

prewar system. The outbreak of the civil war might be seen as produced by weaknesses in the consociational system in that it demonstrated the inability of the system to solve intergroup conflict (i.e., the inability of a consensus-based government to impose solutions to conflicts between the constituent groups).

Rania Maktabi presents a critical discussion of the Lebanese consociational system in her contribution to this volume (see chapter 7). She clearly disagrees with Arend Lijphart's statement (made shortly after the outbreak of the civil war) that "consociationalism in Lebanon must be judged to have performed satisfactorily for more than thirty years" (1977, 149). Analyzing the Lebanese system and its roots in the post–World War I formation of the state, particularly with a fresh and close look at the 1932 census, Maktabi finds it questionable to consider Lebanon a pluralist system and says that it has features consistent with ethnocracy (a hegemonic system). I find her observations interesting because they illustrate both the theoretical problems of identifying basic characteristics of political systems and the fruitfulness of applying a citizenship approach.

The important point here is that the two kinds of regime are based on a common organizational principle: in both cases, the status of individual persons in relation to the state and their chances of being fully integrated as members of the political community follow a fundamental group-based logic, normatively justified with reference to the state-idea. In both cases, the political system reflects more or less balanced contractual relations between the state and constituent groups, even though the state (the government and state institutions) is accorded, in principle, a very different role in these contractual relations (partisanism versus neutralism).

We can point to at least two main reasons why it may be difficult to distinguish clearly between a partisan and a neutral state (or between a hegemonic and a plural regime) in specific empirical cases like Lebanon. First, a hegemonic regime tends not to be consistently hegemonic in every way it relates to different groups in society. From a rational choice perspective (which explains actions consistently on the basis of self-interest), the regime normally tends to compromise, create alliances to secure a broad power base, contain conflicts, and so on. In short, the regime seeks to maintain hegemony on behalf of the titular group (of which the state is the embodiment) at the *lowest possible costs*. If at all possible within the realm of acceptable concessions, a rational political leadership will modify discriminatory practices in ways that can produce loyalty and support (or at least reduce the level of opposition) from lower-class citizens. Second, plural regimes may not always be as plural as the definition would indicate. The specific balance of power between constituent groups—on which plural regimes is based and as expressed in a formal or informal constitutional agreement—may not in the real world reflect either equality between the groups or neutrality of the state. So, to the extent that one group in fact dominates important institutions of the power-sharing system (for example, by having decisive control over coercive or legal mechanisms), we have a regime with more or less hegemonic features.

Universalism

In the previous sections, we discussed two of the three principles presented in table 1.2. The third principle, *universalism*, refers to the normative presumption that group-specific identities within a political community are irrelevant when it comes to each individual member's status and rights vis-à-vis the state. The political community (the demos, that is) constitutes the universe within which every adult and sane person is considered equal. Rights and obligations are anchored in the individual qua citizen, with no qualifications whatsoever because of his or her group affiliation (cf. table 1.1). This is clearly an expression of the classical model of democratic citizenship and is reflected in the Universal Declaration of Human Rights adapted by the United Nations in 1948.

From a singularistic perspective, the singular ethnocultural group constitutes a "universe" in its own right, irrespective of its share of the state population, and the political system is considered "democratic" to the extent that the members of this universe are secured basic equality in political rights. Universalism, in contrast, defines political communities in *territorial* terms. Anyone within the jurisdiction of a particular state enjoys—in principle— equal rights before the law. This implies that in cases where the population of the state territory is 100 percent homogeneous in an ethnocultural sense, *singularism* would not be a meaningful term; the hegemonic group and the "universe" would empirically refer to the same demographic entity. The basic difference, then, between the two principles lies in the way in which the demos is constituted—as an ethnoculturally or a territorially defined political community. The South African transition from apartheid to democracy as confirmed by the general elections in 1994 can illustrate the point. What took place with the adoption of the new interim Constitution and electoral system was a major redefinition of South Africa as a political community. Democratic citizenship (i.e., the boundaries of the demos) was extended to include the entire territorial population of South Africa on the basis of a universalist conception of citizenship, irrespective of the singularistic race distinctions of the apartheid era. The new system was, however, not of a pure majoritarian kind. The interim Constitution should be seen as an

outcome of negotiations and a compromise between the old regime, dominated by the National Party, and the would-be leadership of a new South
Africa, dominated by the African National Congress (ANC). It was based
on the principle that no group should be dominated by any other group,
which is a basic element in any system of pluralism and power sharing. The
white minority was ready to give up their political ascendancy (which they
at this stage saw would be impossible to defend in the long run) in return
for guarantees, in the interim Constitution, of governmental veto power
and commitments from the ANC of limited interventions in the economic
power bases of the white community. With the enactment of the "final"
Constitution of 4 December 1996, most of these guarantees and commitments have been removed. As Siri Gloppen (1997) concludes in her study
of the constitutional process in South Africa, "Explicit power-sharing arrangements are out, at least with regard to the jewel in the crown, that of
executive power. The system of the 'final' constitution is basically majoritarian, but one in which the opposition has considerably more impact than
in a standard majoritarian democracy" (240). For our purposes, the political
system of the transitional stage in South Africa demonstrates how a pluralist
system can be adapted as a compromise solution in situations of deep-seated
group conflict or theoretically can be conceived as an intermediate stage in
a political development from ethnocratic singularism toward democratic
universalism.

Conclusion

This introduction does not reflect in any systematic way or do justice to
the richness in theoretical reasoning and empirical analysis contained in the
chapters throughout this book. It has been informed and indeed inspired by
these contributions as the editorial work has progressed. But what has been
presented here is basically my own approach to citizenship as a field of study
from a political science point of view. In spite of this obvious limitation, my
ambition has been to demonstrate the academic relevance of a broad citizenship approach for the purpose of penetrating fundamental problems of
modern political development in general and in particular in the Middle
East. And, above all, I hope that the reader has been given the necessary
impetus to explore further the theme of citizenship and the state in the
Middle East as developed in this book and its sister volume.

2

Islam, Civil Society, and Citizenship

Reflections on the Sociology of Citizenship and Islamic Studies

BRYAN S. TURNER

THE TYPICAL UNDERLYING QUESTION behind much sociological research on citizenship is: What are the principal features of a society that explain the historical absence or contemporary underdevelopment of democratic citizenship? Investigations usually then proceed to examine some missing structural feature that will account for this historical aberration—for example, the peculiar configuration of municipal organizations or some ideological feature of the juridical system. This approach can produce interesting and fruitful results, but it is often combined with an optimistic assumption that, once installed, democracies tend to be enduring, robust political arrangements that are not easily undermined or eradicated. In short, the democratic conditions of modern citizenship are seen to be accumulative, sequential, self-generating, and immune to catastrophic erosion.

These assumptions about absences (in terms of missing structures, faulty legal systems, and underdeveloped ideologies) are typical of classical Orientalism, which sought to explain the apparent failures of Islamic societies in terms of the militaristic history of Islam, patrimonial empires, the absent bourgeoisie, and the peculiarities of the history of the Islamic city. This orientalist account presents world history in terms of the West versus the rest (Turner 1978). The comparative history of democratic citizenship often compares the failure of Islam to produce democracy against the benchmark of Western success. However, if we treat citizenship as the modern product of the political revolutions that started in 1790, then we might place the

28

alleged "failure" of Islam to produce a viable form of civil society within a much shorter time frame. There may well be problems for "late starts" in terms of the evolution of civil society. These orientalist accounts of civil society in any case are characteristically silent about the role of organized slavery and the domestic status of women in their analysis of the cradle of democracy in classical Greece and Rome (Finley 1983).

Often the failure of democracy and civil society in Islamic cultures is explained in cultural terms. Again borrowing from Max Weber, it is argued that the inner-wordly asceticism of the Christian West is an important lever in the historical growth of Western patterns of modernity, which in turn supports civil society. If this argument is specifically developed as an interpretation of the political role of Puritanism, then the seventeenth-century Puritans were hardly noted for their liberal tolerance of diversity and difference. They did not support individualism in the sense of cultivating diversity of political perspectives. Like the Taliban of modern Afghanistan, the English Puritans wanted "Godly Rule," not liberal individualism.I also assume that the Abrahamic faiths have more in common than their superficial differences; hence, differences in democracy are probably not easily explained by religion alone.

These Western assumptions about the inevitability of the liberal democratic revolution have in recent years become increasingly triumphalist, assertive, and confident. With the collapse of organized communism and the implosion of the Soviet Empire, liberal theorists in the West have tended to assume that, whereas centralized communist regimes are inclined to internal crisis and demolition, there is a historical logic driving societies toward an expansion of democracy. Ceteris paribus, rational men, who are not morally corrupted, will choose democracy over dictatorship and egalitarian citizenship over slavery. In a modern environment, according to Richard Rorty (1993), they will choose liberal capitalism over all other systems, and if they are especially wise, they will plump for *American* liberal capitalism. As a consequence within this triumphalist vision of modernity, democratic citizenship is seen to be the rule rather than the exception. The most comprehensive statement of this view of democracy as the Universal History of mankind has been presented by Francis Fukuyama (1992) in *The End of History and the Last Man*. In his survey of world history, starting with the French and American Revolutions, Fukuyama (1992, 49–50) notes that the number of democracies have increased from three in 1790 to sixty-one in 1990.

Within this Whig interpretation of postcommunist history, the Cold War has ended with the destruction of communism, and there are no significant international hurdles for the continuing expansion of liberal democracy.

During the postwar period, therefore, the two principal global ideologies were communism and liberal capitalism. With the demise of communism, liberal democracy is seen by many commentators to enjoy a virtual monopoly over political belief. The "end of ideology," which was proclaimed by political scientists such as Daniel Bell (1960) in the 1960s, came true in the 1990s with the end of Cold War politics.

Within this triumphalist liberal context, the global status of Islam and Islamic politics has come to assume some urgency. Will fundamentalist Islam come to replace communism as the principal threat to Western, secular triumphalism? Will Islam become a successful capitalist system with suitably liberal and democratic institutions? This view of fundamentalist Islam as resistant to the processes of secularization and liberalism has been in particular championed by the late Ernest Gellner (1983a), for whom the world of Islam is the only exception to the universal impact of liberal secularism and, with the demise of communism and the eruption of the Iranian Revolution, the only significant challenge to the ideological hegemony of the capitalist West. Indeed, for Gellner, militant Islam has replaced both nationalism and Marxism as the principal challenge to Western leadership because Islam, whether in Iran or Algeria or Afghanistan, has emerged as the carrier and expression of Third World aspirations for and frustrations against Western consumerism and Western political arrogance.

My objection to many of these triumphalist assumptions is not primarily that they are sociologically invalid. It is more that they are unduly optimistic and historically premature. The underlying assumption of my approach to democratic citizenship is rather remote from this triumphalist version of the rebirth of the ideal of civil society (Gellner 1994a, 1) because I argue that democratic citizenship is precarious and vulnerable. It is difficult to create and easy to destroy. It may be useful at the outset to provide a list of the presuppositions that guide this argument.

I am pessimistic, but hopefully more realistic than the Whig version of the history of democratic citizenship because my argument is that citizenship is the exception not the rule; it is politically fragile and socially precarious, and it is not historically cumulative. The achievement of "deep citizenship" (Clarke 1996) is sociologically uncertain and contingent. Citizenship, if we accept the arguments of T. H. Marshall (1950) with respect to the English case, took three centuries to create from the constitutional settlement of 1688 to the formation of the welfare state in 1948. Marshallian citizenship was constructed around three fundamental rights—legal, political, and social citizenship—and was institutionalized in terms of the jury system, parliament, and welfare. However, Marshall failed to analyze economic forms of citizenship (such as workers' control, employees' share ownership, and industrial democracy), and hence many critics have suggested that economic rationalism and Thatcherite consumerism have undermined, or at least brought about an erosion of, citizenship in modern Britain. The essential point of this argument is that citizenship as a scale of rights is not necessarily cumulative. Many contemporary British sociologists thus believe that citizenship needs rethinking as a consequence of Thatcherite economic restructuring (Bulmer and Rees 1996, Roche 1992).

Contemporary theories of democracy, active citizenship, and civil society have to confront the submerged, tragic history of postwar Europe and especially postcommunist Europe, which has been characterized by ethnic conflict, interregional hostility, religious conflicts, denial of indigenous rights, and genocide. Without underestimating the economic miracle of postwar reconstruction and the absence of conventional warfare, one has to take seriously in any adequate theory of citizenship the problem of accounting for Bosnia, Northern Ireland, the Basque nationalist struggles, and the denial of Muslim aspirations for recognition within a European context. Within a broader geopolitical context, any robust theory of civil rights would need to address questions of active citizenship and participatory civil society in Afghanistan and Chechny. It would need to examine the issue of civil liberty with respect to the indigenous peoples of the Arctic Circle. The failure of the West to provide support for Kurdish rights on a systematic and consistent basis is also an indictment of Western international relations policy. While European social scientists have been celebrating the triumph of democracy following the symbolically significant fall of the Berlin Wall, one conclusion of Yugoslavia is that peace in Eastern Europe and in the Soviet Empire more generally was a function of the presence of the Russian army and of the integration brought about by the Communist Party. Although communism stifled political dissent in Eastern Europe, it also suppressed ethnic conflict and civil war.

Although critical of many aspects of Western modernization and sympathetic to many aspects of postmodern theory, I adopt a possibly unpopular and controversial view—that citizenship is a function of modernization and that failures of citizenship are failures of successful patterns of modernization. This position does not and should not mean equating modernization with Westernization. Citizenship is literally the triumph of gesellschaft over gemeinschaft, or in more elaborate terminology from the sociology of Weber, it is the replacement of closed/personal social relationships by open/impersonal social relationships, or the historical supremacy of markets over villages (Weber 1968). Markets most clearly illustrate the growth of social relations that are between strangers and that are open and associational. In the language of Ferdinand Tönnies (1957), citizenship requires a society organized around associations rather than communities. The concepts of citizenship and civil society are historically and etymologically tied to the rise of bourgeois society and bourgeois civility, and they express ideologically and culturally the rise of urban civilizations and urbane cultures. They are, one might say, antagonistic to the rural, pagan, traditional world. One can argue that Islamic fundamentalism as a global social movement attempts to combine, in Weber's terms, a set of open social relations based on communal, not associational, values and practices; the Household of Faith is, in this sense, a globalized village.

Although this chapter does not support epistemological relativism as a necessary principle, the concepts *civil society* and *citizenship* are specifically modern concepts. The term *citizenship* denotes a city dweller who enjoys certain rights of immunity and corresponding privileges. As an urban status, citizenship is tied to the legal history of the burgh and the borough. It is also connected with the historical formation of the nation-state, within which nationalism provided the civil religion (the social cement) that bound together the disparate elements of civil society. Modern citizenship in the West is a product of the American and French Revolutions with their notions of equality and individualism, and of the industrial revolution, which brought in a new division of labor. Although the term *citizen* can be found in the writings of, for example, Samuel von Pufendorf (1632–94), I argue (Turner and Hamilton 1994) that *citizenship* be restricted to nineteenth-century notions of political membership. We may also come to the conclusion that is more or less explicit in Weber's theory of citizenship in *The City* (1981): the ensemble of bourgeois concepts that surround democratic theory are specific to the West. Such a position finds support in the debate about "the Islamization of Science," where writers such as A. H. AbuSulayman argue that the term *democracy,* with its secular notions of political relations, cannot be easily translated into Arabic (Stenberg 1996). *Democracy* may be translated as *ash-shura* or "consultation," which is compatible with divine revelation.

Similarly, *civil society* is an expression of Western political discourse in which writers such as Hegel and Marx attempted to think about the linkages between the individual and the state. However, it was Adam Ferguson in *An Essay on the History of Civil Society* in 1773 who analyzed the importance of the shift from aristocratic to mercantile society and the decline of the warrior in favor of an economic ethic. The rise of the theory of civil society was a product of the social crisis of the seventeenth century, which was created by massive economic changes under the impact of imperial expansion (Seligman 1992). There are, of course, many variations in this theory, but at the analytical core of each is a separation of spheres, in particular

TABLE 2.1

A Historical Model of Citizenship

Period	*Person*	*Rights*
City-state	Denizen	Legal rights
Nation-state	Citizens	Political rights
Welfare-state	Social citizens	Social rights
Global capitalism	Humans	Human rights

the division between the political (the state) and the socioeconomic (the market). From my point of view, the emphasis given in Weber's sociology to the autonomy of society in the city-state is important. In addition, it was Alexis de Tocqueville's reflections on American democracy in terms of the role of voluntary associations that has produced the core debate about "associative democracy" in contemporary political theory (Cohen and Rogers 1995). Within this paradigm, a robust democracy requires (1) an expanding middle class with a commitment to liberal tolerance; (2) a viable media and public relations system that will support open debate; (3) a universal notion of citizenship that will contain the particularistic force of personal and communal ties; and (4) a large space of voluntary associations that will bind individuals to society and create effective patterns of social integration.

These reflections on the growth of citizenship suggest a model of Western evolution. Citizenship evolves out of the notion of a denizen of an urban space, which, however, is replaced by a stronger notion of citizenship in the autonomous city-state of medieval society. This conception is the basis of Weber's model of city politics. Within Marshall's model, this notion of political citizenship is expanded through the welfare state into social citizenship. Finally, the globalization of contemporary society indicates a growing importance of general human rights regardless of nationality (see table 2.1).

We cannot, however, take the cosy or comforting view that modernization is painless or uniformly enlightened. Because the spread of urban citizenship required the extension of the nation-state as its political shell, it also involved the exclusion and on many occasions the destruction of local, traditional, and tribal cultures. The marginalization and exclusion of the "Celtic fringe" in the United Kingdom is historically a classic example of the growing dominance of the Westminster model of citizenship founded on an assumption of ethnic and religious homogeneity (Hechter 1975). Citizenship is necessarily a contradictory force. It creates an internal space of social rights and solidarity, and thus an external, exclusionary force of nonmembership.

This inclusionary/exclusionary dynamic is one explanation of continuing ethnic violence in Central Africa, where the modern boundaries of nationalistic states do not correspond with ancient boundaries between such ethnic communities as the Tutsi and Hutu. One mechanism for the genocidal conflict has been the fact that the Banyarwanda have been stripped of citizenship by Zaire.

Such an argument forces one as a matter of logic to accept the Weberian conclusion that primary groups (tribes, clans, and families), or what the Egyptian sociologist Saad Eddin Ibrahim (1992) calls "primordial associations," are inimical to the successful function of nation-state citizenship because they inhibit or contradict the full force of *gesellschaftlich* processes. I consider below the view that it is primary loyalties in many Islamic societies that corrode the foundation of urban citizenship. Such a position requires me to embrace what one might call the classical liberal view that the growth of civil society requires, above all, the existence of independent voluntary associations and institutions that link the anomic individual to the abstract state. On the basis of this model, modernization theorists characteristically criticized traditional societies for their failure to expunge "primordial associations" in favor of genuine, universalistic, neutral forms of urban association and secular sociality. My argument, however, (a) rejects any simplistic West/East contrast in favor of a picture of world history so brilliantly developed by Marshall G. S. Hodgson (1993) in which the hub of global civilizations is placed on the interface between three lettered traditions from the Axial Age in the Indo-Mediterranean region—namely, the Sanskrit, the Irano-Semitic, and the Hellenic, and (b) notes that one of the enduring problems of Western citizenship has been precisely the strength of primordial associations—for example, the Mafia, which is a classic illustration of a communal welfare agency operating outside the law in favor of individuals who have claims upon this "familial" organization.

If citizenship is the politicocultural expression of the successful growth of the nation-state through the nineteenth and twentieth centuries, then it is an incomplete or unfinished version of universalistic rights, which are embraced, for example, in United Nations legislation on *human* rights. Globalization politically involves the growing importance of human rights over nation-state citizenship rights. Human rights and citizenship rights often collide in the modern state, where those who suffer from state legislation will appeal to a "higher" court. The global process of indigenous rights presents the paradox of particular or local claims being expressed against state citizenship structures.

Such a view of rights draws me to take a position on universalism versus the indigenization of knowledge and on the assertion of local juridical systems against universal legal codes. For the majority of sociologists, relativism provides an easy way out of this dilemma. Indeed, Weber's sociology is often seen to be the principal expression of sociological relativism, and it was for this reason that Weberian sociology of law became the target of criticisms from philosophers such as Leo Strauss (1950), who defended natural law notions against Weber's perspectivism.

My solution is to defend universalism in systems such as natural law with an ontological argument about human frailty and social precariousness (Turner 1993b). Because all human beings qua humans are subject to universal biological limitations (which I call "frailty"), there is a social need for protection against existential and social precariousness—protection that is provided by human rights. This argument is a variation on the Hobbesian theme that "the life of man [is] . . . nasty, brutish, and short." The test case of the depth of citizenship and the adequacy of human rights is the capacity of a state or political community to protect the physically weak—the elderly, the sick, children, and mothers—and to show compassion toward minorities, which might be expressed as a capacity to tolerate difference. On this ontological argument about frailty, a measure of political maturity will be the institutionalization of an ethic of care and compassion for those who are members as well as those who are not. My position at this level is derived from feminist theories of care. But here is the problem of citizenship (at least conventional, nationalist, or state citizenship): it cannot easily extend protection and care to nonmembers, and these so-called nonmembers are not only "other people" but also social categories such as children, the unborn, the mentally ill, or the profoundly disabled. In fact, sensitivity to disability as a stigmatizing label may be the best indicator of the capacity of civil society to protect individuals who are in the cultural boundary of personality and membership. In this respect, Japanese cultural negativity toward persons with physical and mental disabilities indicates the strong pressures toward the exclusion of "outsiders" in Japanese civil society.

For some critics, this attempt to combine a universalistic doctrine of rights with a feminist theory of care and compassion might appear contradictory. Feminism and postmodernism have been sensitive to difference and care, often regarding categories such as citizenship as necessarily patriarchal. My universalistic position, however, is not based on some idea of knowledge or rationality as the basis of universalism, but on the idea that frailty and sympathy are the empirical and normative foundations of the political community. It also assumes that citizenship is an incomplete expression of rights. By combining these two aspects, my argument leads to a criticism of local or indigenous customs that sustain female subordination or oppression, even where women themselves appear to defend their customary sub-

ordination or marginalization. This position is particularly relevant to many
customary practices in Muslim societies, such as the adoption of the head
scarves for women or the Taliban fundamentalists' imposition of a curfew on
women in public spaces in Afghanistan. These seclusions of women to the
domestic sphere and their exclusion from civil society are not compatible
with the extension of public citizenship to women; they perpetuate the historic regulation of women, which in traditional Afghanistan often meant the
status of a "house slave." The seclusion of women from public space is not
an essential tradition of Islam as a religion and is incompatible with the
status of women in the Qu'ran. I can also defend this view via Hodgson
(1974) in terms of the progressive and liberating force of Islam as a global
religion, which presents a universal spiritual challenge.

Finally, although citizenship is much discussed in recent sociology, it is
rarely explained. Essentially I take the position that citizenship is typically
the unintended consequence of social struggles and political violence—the
Weberian sociology of fate. I develop what we might call a conflict model of
democratic citizenship. Warfare, occupation, and civil wars can often produce unintentionally the modernizing force necessary to erode gender hierarchies, status divisions, and the presence of primordial associations within
the public domain. In *Citizenship and Capitalism* (1986), I tried to show
how migration, social struggles, and warfare can often lay the foundations
for advances in citizenship. This model was developed in response to the
static version of the sociology of citizenship in the work of sociologists like
Marshall.

A Definition of Citizenship

Two contradictory principles organize human societies. They are structured around issues of scarcity, which results in exclusionary arrangements
such as gender divisions, racial orders, social classes, and status groups, but
they also promote social solidarity. In sociology, these contradictory principles are characteristically referred to as the allocative and integrative functions. In a secular society, especially where social inequality is intensified by
economic rationalism, citizenship functions as a foundation of social solidarity, namely as a civil religion. One can explore the scope of citizenship
studies through an examination of identity, civic virtue, and community.

◆   ◆   ◆

Citizenship involves the institutionalization of political and social rights
within the juridical framework of the nation-state; it often produces important tensions, therefore, between social and human rights because social

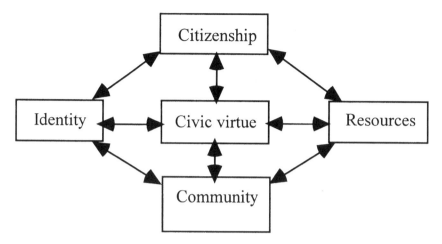

Fig. 2.1 **A Sociological Model of Citizenship**

rights are national, whereas human rights are global. Marshall developed a theory of postwar societies through an analysis of the relationships between social class, welfare, and citizenship, but he was unable to incorporate ethnic and religious differences into his study of modern citizenship. His theory is also weak in dealing with economic citizenship and with the rights of women and children, and he failed to analyze the impact of international contexts and globalization on citizenship (Andrews 1991, Beiner 1995, Bulmer and Rees 1996, Roche 1992, Turner and Hamilton 1994).

One may define citizenship as an ensemble of rights and obligations that give individuals a formal legal identity; these legal rights and obligations have been put together historically as sets of social institutions such as the jury system, parliaments, and welfare states. Citizenship has traditionally been a fundamental topic of philosophy and politics, but from a sociological point of view, we are interested in those institutions in society that embody or give expression to the formal rights and obligations of individuals as members of a political community. Figure 2.1 provides a summary of the key components of citizenship in modern societies.

This sociological approach attempts to comprehend the institutions of citizenship and social identity, the nature of inequality, and access to socio-economic resources. Sociologists have been concerned to understand how the institutions of citizenship protect individuals and groups from the negative outcomes and unintended vagaries of the market in a capitalist society. This focus on the redistributive potential of citizenship institutions (the allocative function) has provided the basis for sociological approaches to questions about justice and equality. Thus, citizenship controls the access of individuals and groups to scarce resources in society. Once these legal rights and obligations are institutionalized as formal status positions, they give people formal entitlements to scarce resources in society. *Resources* are primarily economic resources such as social security, health care entitlements, subsidized housing, retirement packages, or taxation concessions, but they also include access to culturally desirable "goods" such as, within a traditional liberal framework, rights to speak one's own language in the public arena or rights relating to religious freedoms. These resources therefore include not only the traditional economic resources of housing, health, income, and employment, but also cultural resources such as education, knowledge, religion, and language.

It is conceptually useful to think of three types of resources—economic, cultural, and political—alongside which there are three forms of rights: economic rights, which are related to basic needs for food and shelter; cultural rights, which include both access to welfare and access to education; and finally, political rights, which cover the conventional area of liberal concern such as individual freedoms and rights to expression through political means such as parliaments. These rights may be collectively referred to as *social* rights as distinct from *human* rights because they typically presuppose membership of a nation-state.

The first thing to emphasize about citizenship is that it controls access to the scarce resources of society, and hence this allocative function is the basis of a profound conflict in modern societies over citizenship membership criterion. To use the terminology of Max Weber's political sociology (Parkin 1979), social closure is an elementary form of group solidarity, producing an inevitable alienation and stigmatization of "outsiders." This "fear of diversity," which underlines social closure, is in many respects the social driving force behind political theory as such (Saxonhouse 1992). The boundaries of the state produce an enduring crisis of belonging for marginal communities in an ethnically plural society, and in this negative sense, citizenship is about the policing of borders (Connolly 1995).

Any benchmark of citizenship would have to include some notion of egalitarian openness to difference and otherness as an essential ingredient of liberal democracy. Who gets citizenship clearly indicates the prevailing formal criteria of inclusion/exclusion within a political community, and how these resources—following citizenship membership—are allocated and administered largely determines the economic fate of individuals and families. In any assessment of modern citizenship, we need to examine carefully how the status of women, children, and minority groups is managed in terms of this inclusionary/exclusionary dynamic. The first benefit of citizenship is social membership.

Another aspect of citizenship is that it confers, in addition to a legal status, a particular cultural identity on individuals and groups. The notion of the "politics of identity" indicates an important change in the nature of contemporary politics. Whereas much of the struggle over citizenship in the early stages of industrialization was about class membership and class struggle in the labor market, citizenship struggles in late-twentieth-century society were often about claims to cultural identity and cultural history. These struggles were about sexual identity, gay rights, gender equality, and aboriginality. Most debates about citizenship in contemporary political theory are about the question of contested collective identity in a context of radical pluralization (Mouffe 1992b). Citizenship and civic virtues are once more seen to be an essential ingredient of a civilized and pluralistic democracy. This concern for the political threat to civic culture in a market society has been associated with a reappraisal of Mill's liberalism (Bobbio 1987, 1989), the importance of pluralism (Hirst 1989), and the role of voluntary associations in democracy (Cohen and Rogers 1995). The cultural dimension of citizenship is now an essential component of citizenship studies, especially in a context where there is political ambiguity around the analysis of cultural fragmentation and simulation brought about by postmodernization.

The final component of this sociological model of citizenship is the idea of a political community as the basis of citizenship; this political community is typically the nation-state. When individuals become citizens, they not only enter into a set of institutions that confer upon them rights and obligations, acquire an identity, and are socialized into civic virtues, but they also become members of a political community with a particular territory and history. In order to have citizenship, they have to be, at least in most modern societies, bona fide members of a political community. Generally speaking, it is rather unusual for people to acquire citizenship if they are not simultaneously members of a political community—that is, a nation-state. One should notice here an important difference between human rights and citizenship. In general, citizenship is a set of rights and obligations that attach to members of formally recognized nation-states within the system of nations; hence, it corresponds to legal membership of a nation-state. Citizenship identities and citizenship cultures are national identities and national cultures.

In classical sociological theory, there are a number of models of civil society. In the Durkheimian version, civil society emerges with the secularization of religion and provides through a network of professional groups, guild structures, and occupational associations a regulatory mechanism or moral control over hedonistic individual behavior in a competitive capitalist environment. Civil society is essentially a solidaristic and ethical structure that connects the anomic individual to the state (Durkheim 1992). In the tradition of de Tocqueville, voluntary associations (churches, community groups, and neighborhood associations) protect individual differences and cultural variation against the potential tyranny of a mass democracy and the ideology of equality of opportunity. In the Hegelian-Marxist tradition of civil society theory, which found its fullest expression in Antonio Gramsci, civil society was considered the terrain of freedom of action and moral responsibility that lies between the coercive arm of the state and the deterministic necessities of the economic base. It was over this moral terrain that the intellectual vanguard of the party should seek leadership through an ideological hegemony against the traditional cultural leadership of the Roman Catholic Church and its priesthood.

These theories share in common the notions that (1) civil society is an intermediary institution between atomistic individuals and the state in capitalism; (2) civil society has a positive moral character and is essential for the civilized existence of individuals against the power of the state and the anarchy of the marketplace; (3) civil society is changing rapidly with the growth of the marketplace through capitalism and the bureaucratization of state power; and (4) civil society is an arena over which the intellectuals struggle to secure hegemonic leadership of the working class and the masses.

Although the traditional literature on civil society takes a positive interpretation of voluntary associations and other intermediary groups, the role of those associations is in fact far more problematic than this summary statement would suggest. Secondary associations can also have a negative impact on democratic processes precisely because they articulate sectional, specific, and particular interests. For example, lobby groups can often represent the attitude of so-called NIMBYism ("not in my back yard"). This general problem of sectional interest is often referred to, following its discussion by James Madison in *The Federalist,* no. 10, as the "Mischief of Faction" in which a "minority faction" can determine the condition of the majority (Cohen and Rogers 1995). An associative democracy can work only if there is considerable decentralization and devolution of powers and responsibilities, but, given the threat of the mischief of faction, regulative devices and mechanisms are also needed to guarantee, for example, minimal and egalitarian standards of public services. In short, there must be a framework of state regulation if the free play of associations is to have any benefit for civil society.

In contemporary Arabic literature on the theory of civil society, there are a number of contested positions. Sami Zubaida (1992) has provided a useful summary of two such dominant orientations to the notion of civil society in Islam. First, there is the thesis that an evolution of civil society took place in the Arab world before the Second World War in terms of a growth of voluntary associations (occupational groupings, trade associations, trade unions, and so forth); these associations were attacked by the radical populist states during the 1950s and 1960s. A renaissance of Arab voluntary organizations, community development associations, and nongovernmental organizations occurred in the 1970s and 1980s as a result of the "retreat" of the state and the introduction of economic liberalization, which is associated with an expansion of the educated middle classes and the growing authority of professional syndicates and associations. Zubaida argues that this process of liberalization is threatened by Islamic fundamentalism. The second thesis is represented by those who argue that, against the bureaucratic tendencies of Nasserism, there was an informal network of Islamic groups, which constituted a civil society; this view presents a communal/ Islamic understanding of everyday society outside the state. These Islamic associations are related to pilgrimage, the teaching of the Qu'ran, and sociomedical services.

Zubaida disputes both views, arguing—correctly, as I see it—that economic liberalization will in fact require effective state intervention and that in Egypt the liberalization of the economy is dependent on the state. The state limits the growth of autonomous voluntary associations in Ibrahim's sense (1992), but permits the continuity of the informal Islamic networks favored by Bishri. The result is an "authoritarian communalism" that favors the control of the masses at the local level by a new Islamic grassroots leadership. The exclusive and authoritarian nature of this movement is illustrated by its attacks on Copts in the towns and villages of Upper Egypt; there is also considerable hostility to women's rights. Zubaida concludes, therefore, that strong legal reforms are an essential element of any rejuvenated civil society in Egypt to protect it against "primordial institutions."

Social citizenship expands with the general process of modernization (i.e., the growth of secularism, the erosion of particularism as an organizing principle of society, the extension of citizenship institutions to all sectors of society, the urbanization of the population, and thus the expansion of formal education for all). As Benedict Anderson (1991) has argued, the growth of nationalism and the creation of an imaginary community of the nation are a function of the revolution of print. It is the newspaper industry that "quietly and continuously (produces) that remarkable confidence of community in anonymity which is the hallmark of modern nations" (36). In a peculiar way, these theories of nationalism bring us back to the extensively criticized views of Daniel Lerner (1958) in *The Passing of Traditional Society,* for whom modernization involves substituting a neutral communication system based on print for a personal communication system based on word of mouth. In the terms of Marshall McLuhan's *Understanding Media* (1964), it replaces a hot medium with a cool one.

We can indeed see the emergence of *cultural citizenship* by means of an educational revolution that extends democratic rights into the arena of mass higher education, involving the emergence of expectations about universal literacy and participation in the national culture. Perhaps only Karl Mannheim (1992) has adequately understood the importance of this "pedagogical revolution" for the growth of contemporary democracies. Although I generally support such an interpretation of cultural citizenship, we do not need to accept the evolutionary assumptions of conventional modernization theory. What produces an expansion of citizenship, in Marshall's terms, from legal to political to social rights? On this causal issue, Marshall was largely silent. In *Citizenship and Capitalism* (Turner 1986), I argued that citizenship expands where hierarchical and particularistic dimensions of social stratification are destroyed by violent or traumatic historical events and social movements. The thesis was that mass migration (such as the movement of European populations to North America), modern warfare (the impact Second World War on social attitudes in the United Kingdom), and social movements (worker-class struggles for industrial rights in nineteenth-century Europe) had the unintended consequences of increasing demands for social rights—that is, for citizenship. A similar argument about the impact of comradeship in arms on Greek society has been made by Michael Mann (1986), who claims that the military tactics (such as the formation of the phalanx) of the heavily armed hoplites generated an interdependency between these soldiers. This social structure reduced the importance of kin organization in favor of a collective political commitment—that is, an embryonic democracy. This whole position might be derived from Marx's theory of revolution and in particular from his views on the fixedness of societies that are dominated by the Asiatic mode of production. The unintended consequence of British colonialism in India was to bring about modernization, which undercut the traditional system of castes, oriental bureaucracy, and land ownership. In his articles in the *New York Daily Tribune,* Marx claimed that the introduction of the railway system, newspapers, military organization, and private property in land had revolutionized the stagnant mode of production in India and brought about the first modern revolution in Indian society (Marx and Engels 1972). Indeed, India had

TABLE 2.2

Typology of Citizenship

Below	*Above*	
Active Revolutionary France	Mixed active/passive Constitutional monarchy Britain	Public
Mixed active/passive Liberalism USA	Passive Plebiscitary Germany	Private

entered "history" for the first time. This view of India and of social change generally was a materialist adaptation of Hegel's idealist philosophy of history.

Conflict Model of Citizenship

There are different types of citizenships, which embrace different levels of active involvement in the public domain (Turner 1990). The typology given in table 2.2 illustrates the notions of active and passive citizenship in European history.

Active citizenship is more than a formal or legal definition of political membership. It involves a civic culture within which there is a strong sense of moral obligation and commitment to society. Active citizenship is a positive involvement in the affairs of the public arena in the defense of democracy. The modern theory of civic culture involves a *rational-activist model* of the citizen, who is motivated to protect and sustain the democratic ethic of civil society. A successful democracy requires citizens to be active and involved in politics and "that their participation be informed, analytic and rational" (Almond 1989, 64). Active citizenship as an ideal somewhat romantically reconstructs the history of democracy with its appeal to the norms of Roman society and the rhetoric of republican virtues. There is a nostalgic reference to the moral values of Cicero and the importance of the public domain in the civil society of Rome. However, it is clearly important for a democracy that its citizens be properly informed and that they should participate in elections and public office on the basis of adequate knowledge and information. It is for this reason that democratic politics requires an effective, mass education system and a media industry that conveys a flow of relevant information. The current enthusiasm for "electronic democracy" is a reflection of anxiety about the monopolistic control of the global media industry, the erosion of news by the public relations industry, and the decline of the public sphere.

This distinction between active and passive involves a model of European history and was developed originally as a critique of Michael Mann's article on citizenship as a ruling-class strategy (Mann 1993). Mann has argued that there are a variety of forms of citizenship with different historical backgrounds. However, these forms of citizenship share a common component—namely, that they were responses by the dominant class to the emergent and increasingly radical working class during the early stages of industrialization, when the "dangerous classes" represented a potential challenge to the ruling class. Citizenship functions, according to Mann, as a mechanism for the incorporation of the radical working class within the nation-state. By contrast, it can be argued that active citizenship, which is not handed down from above but grasped from below by radical social movements, may be revolutionary; for example, in the French and American Revolutions, there developed a form of citizenship that was grasped from below by popular struggle and by popular social movements.

The second dimension of the typology refers to the moral status of the public arena. Greek classical politics developed in a culture where the private space of domestic social relations was defined as a deprivation (*privatus*). The argument here is that a positive view of the moral quality of public life facilitates the enhancement of citizenship. In the French Revolution, there was also a clear sense of the public arena as a place where citizens could act as political agents and secure new social rights. The model of citizenship that I have developed in this chapter attempts to make a distinction between active or revolutionary citizenship and passive citizenship. Active citizenship is the product of social struggles within which there is a clear and decisive notion of the value of the public over the private. Such a pattern of radical citizenship contrasts significantly with passive citizenship, which is cultivated by the state in terms of a limited nimber of entitlements for citizens. The classical illustration of passive citizenship is the English case in the aftermath of the revolutionary wars of the seventeenth century. The so-called Glorious Settlement of the late seventeenth century brought to an end the revolutionary struggles against the aristocracy and ushered in a long history of gradualism in English politics. The use of the plebiscite is simply a mechanism for selecting leaders and does not assume active engagement in politics apart from casting a vote. Having conducted an election and appointed a government, a leader can rule arbitrarily once in power because the leader does not consult with political supporters. In Weber's political sociology, a plebiscite is simply a way of installing a type of leadership that is not necessarily answerable to its electorate *after* an election. The French Revolution created an active sense of citizenship in a European revolutionary tradition, but by contrast Germany had a passive notion of citizenship. In Weber's analysis of German politics, he advocated the importance of what he called plebiscitory democracy—that is, a democracy based on strong leadership and passive forms of citizenship. Weber was of course skeptical about democracy as a form of politics; he suggested that the only choice is between leadership democracy with a mass-party bureaucracy or leaderless and aimless democracy. In any case, in Germany, Lutheranism created a weak sense of the public arena because it assumed that good citizens were people who accepted moral values appropriate to ethical actions in the private domain of the home. It also created a sense of the public arena as a dangerous and evil domain. The state exists because human beings are fallen creatures. By contrast, consider individualistic liberalism and the revolutionary struggle to create the United States as an independent nation. It created a constitution with a strong sense of democracy from below, where congregationalism and Protestant asceticism favored trust in self-government and participatory citizenship. However, this sense of republican virtue has been converted into private "habits of the heart" (Bellah et al. 1985), and U.S. democracy is weakened by the emphasis on the private in liberalism, which, in granting individual rights (freedom of speech and freedom of association), has a weak sense of the public domain. England emerged as a top-down democracy in which, because of the monarchical settlement of the late seventeenth century, there is a patriarchal idea of the Parliament and the monarchy, where the citizen is a subject of the queen. Nevertheless, there is a sense of the public arena being morally acceptable because in English culture Lutheranism was never particularly strong and Anglicanism provided a model of public events that was not privatized.

The third dimension of the typology is the distinction between universalism versus particularism. Is the form of citizenship based on a particulartistic definition of membership around race or ethnicity, or is ethnic membership replaced by universalist notions of membership? The central paradox of modern citizenship is the relationship between solidarity and scarcity. Citizenship is a form of civil religion that binds separate and anomic individuals together into a single community; in short, against the conflictual impulse of a class society, citizenship creates a foundation of modern solidarity, but it does so as an insurance scheme that distributes welfare to its citizens. Where this solidaristic function is based on a nationalist civil religion, citizenship can also be a powerful exclusionary mechanism. Because the nation-state is indeed a nationalistic polity, citizenship may typically assume a racist dimension by grounding the definition of membership in a blood relationship.

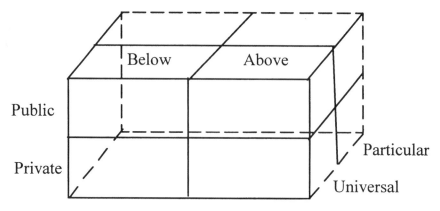

Fig. 2.2 **Three-Dimensional Typology of Citizenship**

Membership of the polity is then determined by an exclusive and particularistic dimension of race. In many Western formations of citizenship, there is an unstable blend of liberal principles of equality and nationalist principles of exclusivity, but there are also illustrations of volatile racism—for example, in the case of national socialism and the Nazi state.

We can now apply this three-dimensional model (active/passive, public/private, universal/particular) to Arabic societies. (See figure 2.2.)

(a) Nasserism represents a top-down passive form of citizenship, which, because it embraced—at least officially—a secular, pan-Arabic and nationalist ideology, avoided the difficulties of an extreme particularistic or exclusionary definition of the polity; Ba'athism perhaps represents a stronger version of particularism. The growing importance of the Muslim Brotherhood in Egypt and elsewhere threatens the nascent civil society with "primordial institutions." Indeed, the word *brotherhood* itself indicates the presence, in Weber's terms, of closed/communal ties within the open/associational world of state arrangements.

(b) The Iranian Revolution was clearly a bottom-up struggle against the Pahlavi regime, which, driven by the political philosophy and sociology of Ali Shariati, embraced a populist form of Islamic radicalism that was open and inclusionary. The ulema, the mosque, and the traditional markets were sites for social struggle and constituted a civil society outside the state (Kamali 1995). The revolution itself was eventually dominated by clerics, displaced peasantry, and alienated workers. As Shi'ism came to dominate official discourse, the radical legacy of Ali Shariati was eventually submerged.

(c) The radical Islamic opposition in Afghanistan is also clearly a bottom-up revolution against imperialism (especially Soviet colonization). However, the bitter intergroup struggles have articulated traditional patterns of seg-

mentation into *qawm*, where local commanders cannot offer any real national leadership and where their power rests on a patronage network linked into the flow of international goods (arms, money, drugs, and other commodities). The exclusionary Islamic ideology of the Taliban, with its puritanical hatred of foreigners and regulation of women, is one result of this traditional political struggle.

(d) In other societies in the Middle East, similar patterns of neofundamentalist ideology and influence can be noticed. Islamic groups from the neofundamentalist wing of Islamic politics have infiltrated the professions, the military, and the Islamic banking institutions, and the result is a fundamentalization of society at the grass roots. New Islamic spaces are created in local schools, lending libraries, cooperatives. These developments follow the Tariq al-Bishri model of civil society. These Islamic spaces are "liberated zones" free from Western influences (alcohol, video, films, cafes, and so on). In these spaces, women are forced back into the veil, and there is a moralization of society (Roy 1994a). Neofundamentalist groups also replace and take over the traditional control of the Sufi orders over the peasantry and the urban masses. The result is a passive form of citizenship, which is combined with particularist definitions of the insider/outsider relationship.

(e) The Palestinian struggles both inside and outside Israel present a case of active citizenship struggles over rights, a relatively secular ideology of egalitarian membership, and an understanding of the importance of participatory associations. The Palestinian community has yet to build the educational and civil structures to sustain this promising basis, and it is now confronted with an Israeli government that is fundamentally ambivalent about the peace process.

(f) The Zionist movement itself, following the Borochov model, is an active struggle for citizenship, based on the colonization and occupation of a hostile social and geographical terrain. Its struggle with the British and then the Arabs had the egalitarian and participatory consequences that I predict in the conflict model, but the secular and emancipatory elements of its socialist doctrines were constrained and undermined by the paradox that the Israeli claim to the land is ultimately based in religious mythology and lore. Thus, the impact of conservative and orthodox Jewish elements has produced a highly particularistic and indeed racist definition of political membership.

Conclusion

Citizenship emerged with the city-state and created an idea of the denizen, whereas nation-states created a primitive notion of citizenship based on political rights. This latter form was followed by the welfare state, where we have social citizenship based upon social rights. In this historical model, the question is: What might come next? One answer may be found in global capitalism, where there is an emerging notion of human rights. As the world economy becomes more and more globalized, more workers will travel between economies in search of employment; there will be increasing conflict in the labor market over access to global resources. The sovereignty of the nation-state is eroded by global market trends so that more and more of the national economy is owned by international corporations, and it may be that traditional forms of citizenship cannot express or do not correspond to the idea of an increasingly global market.

◆   ◆   ◆

This model of the history of citizenship can have either an optimistic or a pessimistic conclusion. The optimistic one is that through the United Nations and through agreements about human rights, we can manage the problem of interstate violence, terrorism, and conflict. The pessimistic one is that in fact we do not have cumulative citizenship; what we have is a breakdown of citizenship. Nation-states no longer adequately provide citizenship for their members, and instead we have a growing war of megacities and megaeconomies against each other. Human rights will not be protected because the so-called new world order operates in the interests of a small number of powerful economies through the mechanism of the World Bank, the International Monetary Fund, and the General Agreement on Tariffs and Trade (Muzaffar 1993). The pessimistic view of the future is that societies such as China will break down into megacities warring with each other, that the international links in the economy will undermine traditional notions of citizenship, and that the political future will be a much more insecure and uncertain environment. Regardless of these historical changes, the idea of citizenship is a central aspect of the modern struggle for democracy and an essential concept for the analysis of international conflict over scarce resources within a world economy.

3

Conceptions of Citizenship in the Middle East

State, Nation, and People

URI DAVIS

A NARRATIVE—any narrative, including academic narrative—is both part of the overarching context of constituted human reality and correlatively a representation of the power relationships and intentions of individuals, organizations, and political parties acting in this context. In other words, as a representation, narrative reflects an existing power system, including the activity necessary to maintain it, as well as the intended political efforts to change and reform it.

Economic, social, and political action is thought and imagined, inter alia, in conceptual narrative, and the importance of the narrative is that it simultaneously and correlatively conceptualizes both existing social and political

This chapter is based on work carried out in the framework of the UK Economic and Social Research Council (ESRC)–funded research program at the Department of Politics, University of Exeter, and the Centre for Middle Eastern and Islamic Studies (CMEIS), University of Durham (award reference no. R00023446201), on citizenship and the state in the Middle East (1993–1995) of which Professor Tim Niblock and I were award holders. The substance of this essay is included in Uri Davis, "The Question of Citizenship," *Citizenship and the State: A Comparative Study of Citizenship Legislation in Israel, Jordan, Palestine, Syria, and Lebanon* (Reading: Ithaca, 1997).

The essay was first presented as Guest Lecture at the Lunchtime Seminar, Department of Political Science, University of Oslo, 21 November 1996. I am grateful to the staff and students who attended the lecture for their critical comments

49

reality and the power relations obtaining therein as well as the intentions and the value orientations of the narrator.

In this essay, the emphasis on clarity and accurate (politically correct) conceptual definitions is not motivated by my phenomenological or semantic interests, but rather by my typically political and pragmatic commitments. The purpose of this study is to make a contribution toward the constitution of an academic and political narrative on the subject of citizenship that does not implode into a conceptual and moral self-contradiction. Needless to say, the development of such a narrative is of particular significance for individuals, organizations, and political parties in the Middle East and elsewhere who are committed to act for a reform of the existing power relations in the region with the view to their replacement with democratic regimes predicated on the principles of separation of religion from the state, equality of rights, and reciprocity.

As noted above, economic, social, and political action is thought and imagined, inter alia, in conceptual narrative. In order to project an alternative political future predicated on democratic power relations, it is necessary to formulate an academic and political narrative that is able to represent such a reform as a worthwhile objective in consistent terms. Thus, it is incumbent upon individuals, organizations, and political parties who are committed to such a reform to construct a narrative that will reflect their intentions as clearly as possible.

Words, as we all well know, can illuminate as well as veil. The purpose of this work is to illuminate and make a contribution to the construction of a clearer academic narrative on the subject of citizenship. As an academic and a documentalist, I wish to conclude this introduction with the observation that it is only in the relationship between text and context that we can hope to find enlightenment.

Before progressing further into case studies, it is necessary to attend to some of the basic terms and dichotomies underpinning this essay, specifically *citizenship, secularism, state* and *society, nation* and *people, sovereignty* and *independence, freedom* and *oppression.*

Citizenship

Citizenship is defined in this work as a certificate regulating the relationship between the individual and the state, and specifically for the purpose of this study between the individual and the modern state, whose midwives were the American and the French Revolutions of 1776 and 1789 respectively. The right to citizenship is a right won by the people from the state through struggle (sometimes revolution), often at huge sacrifice, against the sustained resistance of the state.

As indicated in the introduction to this chapter, the conceptual point of departure for this work is the classification of citizenship as datum, as a certificate. In Western liberal democratic states, citizenship represents a recognized basic claim of the individual vis-à-vis the state of which he is a citizen, a right to equal access to the resources of the state—the civil resources of the state (e.g., the courts of law), the power-political resources (e.g., vote and election), the social services resources (e.g., welfare, education), and the material resources (e.g., land, water).

Those who are familiar with the literature would note that the above classification diverges somewhat from T. H. Marshall's (1950) classical dissertation on citizenship, where he proposed to divide citizenship into three parts or three elements: civil, political, and social.

Here, an explicit material element is added. The certificate of citizenship is valid only if issued by the recognized authorities of an internationally recognized state. But the certificate of citizenship is not a passport. Thus, people may be citizens of a given state but not have passports because, for instance, they do not travel outside the territory of the said state. Passports may expire; citizenship certificates do not. In this essay, the meaning of the term *passport* is confined to the narrow designation of a document issued by the recognized authorities of a recognized state to its citizens, and only to its citizens, for the purpose of travel outside the internationally recognized borders of the said state. In other words, and by the definition given above, only citizens travel on passports.

Furthermore, for the purpose of this study, the term *travel document* is limited also to the designation of travel documents issued by recognized states. Other forms of travel documents (e.g., United Nations [UN] papers) are ignored in this study.

The importance of stipulating a consistent definition of what constitutes a passport is further highlighted by the review of the situation in the field, notably Palestine. Hundreds of thousands of the inhabitants in the occupied West Bank carry travel documents named "two-year Jordanian passports," but their holders are stateless and not citizens of the state that issued the document. The newly established Palestinian Authority has now also issued travel documents called "passport/travel documents,"[1] but the holders of these documents are also stateless. Issued by the Palestinian Authority under

---

1. The PLO is reported to have insisted (against Israeli refusal) on naming these documents "*passports*." The compromise reached in the Agreement on Gaza Strip and Jericho Area, Annex II "Protocol Concerning Civil Affairs, Clause 27 (f), "Population Registry and Documentation," reads as follows: "Exit abroad through the passages or through Israeli points of exit by residents of the Gaza and the Jericho Area shall only be possible by means of an agreed passport/travel document." This title shall be written on the cover in letters of equal size.

the terms of the Israel-PLO agreements known as the Oslo Agreements, these documents are not passports as defined here, nor are they travel documents equivalent to Jordanian travel documents or Israeli travel documents because they are not issued by a state.

The critical difference between a passport and a travel document is that whereas citizens (who have the right of abode) have the corollary right to a passport and can claim their right from the state, noncitizens (who do not have the right of abode) have no right to a travel document and may apply for the document from the state and are given a travel document only at the pleasure of the sovereign.

In my research for this essay, it became clear to me that the UN terminology as codified in the Universal Declaration of Human Rights is insufficient to account for the reality of the relationship between citizenship and the state (in the Middle East and elsewhere) as it has developed since 1948. The declaration addresses the question of citizenship by stipulating that "Everyone has the right to a nationality and No one shall be arbitrarily deprived of his nationality nor denied the right to change his nationality" (Article 15[1–2]). Since then, the distinction between *nationality* and *citizenship* has become established. It is just as possible for two individuals or two constituencies to be of the same nationality yet unequal citizens of the same state, as it is for them to be of different nationalities and unequal citizens of the same state. Thus, as of the commencement of the British Nationality Act in 1981, the common nationality of all citizens of the independent Commonwealth countries and of citizens of the United Kingdom (UK) and colonies is legally conceptualized as *Commonwealth citizenship.* But British nationality (Commonwealth citizenship) does not confer the right of abode in the UK and may be represented by, for example, British Dependent Territory Citizenship (BDTC) and British Overseas Citizen (BOC) passports.[2] British citizenship, on the other hand, confers the right of abode in the UK and is represented by a "British citizenship passport." Additional terms are needed to distinguish between different classes of citizenship, and the English language cannot provide these terms.

On the other hand, Arabic political and legal language makes a number of relevant terminological distinctions, which are useful in this context. At least four Arabic terms could be used as synonyms to the English *citizenship*: *ra'wiyya* (archaic), *taba'iyya, jinsiyya,* and *muwatana*—all are translated as "citizenship/nationality."[3] I found the linguistic distinction in Arabic be-

---

2. As well as British Nationals (Overseas) [BN(O)] and British Protected Persons (BPP) passports.

3. *Ra'wiyya* is derived from the root *r'w*, of which (among other terms) the nouns *ra'in*

tween *jinsiyya* and *muwatana* to be most illuminating. It provided an important conceptual tool directly relevant to the subject of this study.

In this work, the "guts of citizenship," to borrow Fransman's (1989, 139) phrase, is designated as *jinsiyya* ("passport citizenship"), representing the right of abode. Rights of equal access to the civil, political, social, and economic resources of the state are designated by the term *muwatana* ("democratic citizenship").[4] The distinction is useful because, as the case studies indicate, all countries of the Levant (as well as, in fact, many countries throughout the world, including the United Kingdom) have evaded United Nations censure for violation of the 1973 UN International Convention on the Elimination of All Forms of Racial Suppression and Punishment of the Crime of Apartheid (specifically Article 2c) by resorting to a legal and administrative distinction between "passport" citizenship *(jinsiyya)* and "democratic" citizenship *(muwatana)*.[5]

(shepherd) and *ra'iya* (flock) are also formed. *Taba'iyya* from the root *tb'* (forming inter alia *tabi'* [belonging, subordinate, dependent]). *Jinsiyya*—from the root *jns* (forming *jins* [species and also sex]). *Muwatana*—from the root *wtn*, forming *wataniyya* (patriotism) and *watan* (homeland).

It is in order to note here other important Arabic terminological distinctions whose semantic fields are relevant to our narrative on citizenship. The following definitions and translations from the Arabic will be consistently employed: *sh'ab* (pl., *shu'ub*), people; *umma*, nation; *qawmiyya*, nationalism (the national sentiment); *tajannus*, naturalization; *iqama*, residence. The distinction dovetails with the established classification of citizenship legislation in the member states of the League of Arab States as *Qanun al-Jinsiyya* (Citizenship Law).

4. There obtains an asymmetrical legal relationship between *jinsiyya* and *muwatana*. Democratic citizenship rights always include passport citizenship rights. The converse does not necessarily apply.

The successful crafting of the conceptual framework for this study was achieved through collaborative and reciprocal efforts and developed by Tim Niblock and me in a series of working sessions in Exeter and Durham. The classification of citizenship as a datum, as a certificate, was an Uri Davis contribution; the distinction between *jinsiyya* and *muwatana* was a Tim Niblock contribution; and the normative definition of *muwatana* as democratic citizenship was again Uri Davis's.

5. In this work, the term *racial discrimination* (or *racism*) is applied as defined in UN Conventions and Covenants, namely, "[A]ny distinction, exclusion, restriction or preference based on race, colour, descent, or national or ethnic origin which has the purpose or the effect of nullifying or impairing the cognition, enjoyment or exercise, on an equal footing, of human rights and fundamental freedoms in the political, economic, social, cultural or any other field of public life" (International Convention on the Elimination of All Forms of Racial Discrimination, 1966, Part I, Article 1, quoted in Brownlie 1992, 149–50). And the "crime of apartheid" includes "similar policies and practices of racial segregation and discrimination as practiced in South Africa, [and] shall apply to the following inhuman acts committed for the purpose of establishing and maintaining domination by one racial group of persons over any other racial group of persons and systematically oppressing them: . . . . (c) Any legislative measures and

By instituting a two-tier citizenship, one *jinsiyya* and the other *muwatana,* it was possible for legislators of at least two states in the region (Jordan and Israel) to create large constituencies, namely large Palestinian constituencies, which can only be characterized by the surreal Orwellian designation "pretend citizens" or "part citizens." They are citizens (they have valid full-term passports), but they have no rights or only partial rights.

In the case of Jordan, the people concerned are Palestinians whose ordinary residence was the West Bank. For four decades (since the annexation of the West Bank to the Hashemite Kingdom of Jordan in 1950), they were citizens of Jordan. In 1988, they were made stateless by a royal decree disengaging the West Bank from Transjordan and were issued two-year passports—namely, travel documents (laissez-passer).

As of 1995, however, they were issued five-year passports, indistinguishable from the passports carried by Jordanian citizens. Yet these passports do not represent access to resources of the Hashemite Kingdom of Jordan or the right of abode in the state whose passports they carry. The right of abode and the rights of citizenship in Jordan are now recognized only for passport holders who also carry yellow Jordanian identity cards. West Bank residents carry green Jordanian identity cards. They have no citizens' rights in Jordan.

In the case of Israel, the remnants of the Palestinian people who survived the mass expulsions of 1948 and remained in the territories that fell under Israeli sovereignty became Israeli citizens.[6] They were allowed equal access to civil and political rights, including participation on equal footing in the electoral political process, but are denied equal access to the social and material resources of the state. For example, the Palestinian citizens of Israel have right of abode there, but more than 92 percent of the territory of the State of Israel is reserved by law only to persons recognized by the state to be "Jews" (see the discussion of Israeli citizenship "by return" below).

To elaborate the case, in Israel a legal distinction obtains between the Jewish citizens of the state who have *muwatana* ("democratic citizen-

---

other measures calculated to prevent a racial group or groups from participation in the political, social, economic and cultural life of the country and the deliberate creation of conditions preventing the full development of such a group or groups, in particular by denying to members of a racial group or groups basic human rights and freedoms, including the right to form recognized trade unions, the right to education, the right to leave and return to their country, the right to a nationality, the right to freedom of movement and residence, the right to freedom of opinion and expression, and the right to freedom of peaceful assembly and association" (International Convention on the Suppression and Punishment of the Crime of Apartheid, 1973, Article 2(c), quoted in Brownlie 1992, 163–64).

    6. Not all, though. It is established that some 20 percent were classified as "present absentees." Their citizenship status was finally regularized in 1980.

ship")—representing the right of equal access to the civil, political, social, and economic resources of the state, including *jinsiyya,* the right of abode— and the non-Jewish (Palestinian) citizens of the state who have the same *jinsiyya* ("passport citizenship") rights as the Jewish citizens, but not the same *muwatana* citizenship rights. Thus, the Palestinian citizens of Israel have equal access to the courts of law (civil rights) and equal access to the political process of voting and elections (political rights) but not to the welfare and educational resources of the state (social rights) or to its land and water resources (economic rights). The distinction thus reveals two separate classes of Israeli citizenship, segregating between nearly one million Palestinian citizens of Israel versus more than four million Jewish citizens.

The choice between obfuscation and illumination is a fundamental normative strategic choice for all students working in the various disciplines of the humanities. The foremost obstacle to illumination is reification. The fact that one human being is classified as a citizen of a given state and another human being is also classified as a citizen does not (in itself) make them "equal" legal persons. A British citizen and a British Dependent Territories citizen share the same British nationality: they are both Commonwealth citizens (prior to 1983 also known as "British subjects"), but they do not have equality of rights in Britain. The fact that one piece of paper is entitled "passport" and another piece of paper is also entitled "passport" does not (in itself) make them "equal" legal documents. A Palestinian citizen of Israel travels on the same passport as a Jewish citizen of Israel, but they do not have equality of rights in Israel.

Note on Secularism

In this text, the term *secularism* and its derivatives designate adherence to the principle of separation of the state from the church. Reference to *the church* in this text should be read (unless otherwise required) as reference to the church, the mosque, and the synagogue.

State and Society

The state is not a universal attribute of human society. The history of human stateless (primitive) societies is chronologically longer than the history of state (civilized) societies. The distinguishing feature of the state is its foundation in occupation and conquest.[7] The paradigm of state formation is

7. For example, William I, surnamed the Conqueror, styled Willielmus Rex Anglorum, "b at Falaise, 1025; illegitimate son of Robert II, Duke of Normandy. Duke of Normandy in 1035; King of England *by conquest* 14 October 1066, crowned in Westminster Abbey 25 De-

territorial conquest—not voluntary membership. New states are formed by conquest, or by a process of disintegration of the conqueror administration and the takeover of the state by a native political party or an external invader, or by breakup into component states or new states. The official histories of all states trace their origin to an act of conquest or resistance to conquests; namely, the origin of the state is in human action. States are instruments created by men and women. As such, therefore, the state is secular by definition.

The phenomenology of the state in general is a relatively simple matter. All states rest on three interrelated foundations: law (police, court, and jail administration of justice), conscription, and taxation (Diamond 1974, 255–80). The origin of state authority is state monopoly of violence, which is also its defining characteristic. As such, the state is by definition not a voluntary association (see further discussion on freedom and oppression, below). The integrated formulation of the order of the state is the rule of law. On the other hand, society in general is not a human creation. We do not know man except as man in society. The origin of human society is not in human action. Society in general is not an instrument created by men and women. Society is given to us as created. The origins of society in general, like the origins of the universe, are a mystery.

The phenomenology of society in general is not a simple matter at all. As students of the field are acutely aware, all distinctions in this context must be regarded as analytical, aiming to introduce consistent terms of classification and coherent narratives into normative contexts that are inevitably always politically and ideologically loaded. For the purpose of this work, the origin of the various articulations of societal authority, notably the nation, are identified as being fundamentally voluntary. In other words, it is submitted here that the defining characteristic of any given society (in contradistinction to the state) is the voluntary origin of its societal authority.

The Nation

This work follows the body of scholarship that attends to national identity as a fact of consciousness (see, for instance, B. Anderson 1991, Gellner 1983b, Hobsbawm 1990). Under the category *nation,* three analytically separate and historically interrelated primary affiliations can be classified. These three affiliations constitute in various specific combinations the identity of any given nation.

---

cember 1066" ("Royal Lineage" 1959, 49, emphasis added). I am indebted to Tony Benn, member of parliament, for the reference.

Kinship designates all such social affiliations as define the qualifications for membership in the nation (the boundary or identity of the nation) in terms of and by reference to a shared historical and/or mythological origin of a common ancestor. *Tribal homeland* designates all such social affiliations as define the qualifications for membership in the nation in terms of and by reference to a shared historical and/or mythological origin of a common fatherland or motherland. *Confession* designates all such social affiliations as define the qualifications for membership in the nation in terms of and by reference to a shared historical and/or mythological origin of a common deity or religious tradition.

Language is advisedly not listed among the defining elements of the nation (national identity) as a fact of consciousness because it is patently the case that different nationalities may share "the same" language (consider, for instance, the English and Scottish nationalities in the UK).

In the context of this study, a *nation* is defined as an imagined community, a collectivity bound by a shared fact of consciousness, whose constitutive characteristics consist of interrelated references to a shared historical and/or mythological common father (or mother) and/or common fatherland (or motherland) and/or common deity (or religious tradition).

It is a recurring submission in this work that failure clearly to separate kinship, tribal homeland, and confession (or, generally speaking, nationality) in law from the state inevitably results in the same kind of damage to human rights as failure to clearly separate church, mosque, or the synagogue in law from the state. In the latter case, the wedding of church and the state in law invariably results in the prostitution of both the church and the state in the form of fundamentalism. In the former case, failure to separate nationality from the state in law invariably results in the prostitution of both the people and the state in various forms of racial discrimination, culminating in sectarianism, apartheid, and genocide (Orr 1981, Butenschon 1993).

The tributaries of kinship, tribal homeland, and confessional—affiliations that converge to constitute the changing flow of national identity—have distinct and very different meanings when considered as a fact of consciousness under the voluntary category of self-government and autonomy, on the one hand, and when considered as an ideological construct harnessed as a legitimizing principle for state and as the compulsory monopoly of violence underpinning the authority of the state as a fact of law, on the other.

In both cases, the term *national identity* is spelled the same, but the meaning of the term, its signification, and its denotation in each case represents two qualitatively distinct phenomena. The first is cultural and designates an affiliation that is fundamentally voluntary, whereas the second is political and designates an ideological construct or an ideological process recruited by the state to rationalize policies of state government and the involuntary implementation of these policies under the sanction of the law.

Out of the discussion so far there emerges an emphatic need to designate separate terms for the two phenomena of "nationality": (1) nationality as recognized by the members of the national community, considered from the point of view *voluntary* association of self-government and autonomy, and predicated on varying "cocktails" of kinship, tribal homeland, and confession (national identity); (2) nationality as recognized by the state, considered from the point of view of *compulsory* stipulation of the legal language and predicated, in the case of the democratic state, on the separation of ethnic narrative from the legal narrative of the state. There exists an appropriate term available to designate the latter phenomenon of nationality, which is conceptualized not as a fact of consciousness (national identity) but as a fact of law. This term is *people*. Assuming equal citizenship, there can be only one people, although in recognition of its political history, the state may be bi- or multilingual.

The benefit of establishing a firm and clear analytical distinction between the social construct of the nation—an imagined community bound together on a voluntary basis by a shared fact of consciousness—on the one hand, and the political construct of the people as a legal community bound together on an involuntary basis by a force of law of the state in whose sovereign territory they are ordinarily resident, on the second hand, becomes evident in the discussion below on national self-determination.

Here, suffice it to point out that this conceptual distinction makes available for an incumbent or alternative government of any given state, notably the binational or multinational state, an adequate and politically correct legal conceptual instrument to address its multinational constituency of citizens, the collective body of citizens, in nontribal terms. That instrument is the term *bi-* or *multilingual people*. The advantages of this term are that, applied in this way, it can be readily integrated into international official and legal language, and that it does not draw and does not need to draw from religious or ethnic narratives in order to define official or legal issues.

It was proposed above that nationality as a fact of consciousness and a fundamentally voluntary identity be defined (and indeed is commonly defined) in tribal terms. Language was advisedly not listed among the defining features of national identity because it is patently the case that different nationalities as defined above may share "the same" language. Not so the people. It is a requirement of the state, definitely of the modern state, institutionalized through the system of compulsory state schooling and education, that all the people ordinarily resident in its sovereign territory partake in the official language of the state or in one of its official languages. The people, the community bound together on an involuntary basis by the force of law of the state (as distinct from the nation bound together by a national identity that may traverse the political boundaries of any given state) is a collectivity defined in terms of their official language or more than one of their official languages—all of this assuming equal citizenship.

Such distinctions are evident in the citizenship laws of most member states of the United Nations Organization. In most states, naturalization requires acquisition of some knowledge of the official language or one of the official languages. The majority of member states of the United Nations Organization are bi- and multilingual states. Assuming equal citizenship, all states have one people and most states are bi- or multilingual. Most states have not one official language, but a plurality of official languages. In most cases, the number of different nationalities in a state is higher than the number of official languages. For example, take the case of Britain: one British people, two officially recognized languages (English and Welsh), and a rainbow of nationalities (e.g., Pakistani, Indian, Jamaican, Irish, Scottish, English, and Welsh). In postapartheid South Africa, there is one South African people, eleven official languages (Afrikaans, English, Ndebele, Pedi, Shutu, Siswati, Tsonga, Tswana, Venda, Xhosa, and Zulu), and, likewise, an even greater number of nationalities, officially referred to as ethnic groups. Norway: one Norwegian people, three official languages (Bokmal, Nynorsk, and Sami) and similarly a rainbow of nations (Africans, Pakistani, Filipinos, Danes, Swedes, Sami, Nordmenn, etc.).

It follows from the terminological definitions developed hitherto that, based on the principle of separation of nationality from the state and assuming equal citizenship, the state—definitely the modern democratic state, where the certificate of citizenship represents equal access to the civil, social, political, and material resources of the state—is compatible with only one people, a single body of equal citizens. It is also compatible with bi- or multilingualism, but only with the proviso that the national affiliation of the citizen remains strictly in his or her private domain and, like his or her sexual preferences or religious preferences, does not become a matter of law.

It is only in political systems that do not maintain equal citizenship that the narrative of single peoplehood does not obtain and that the idea of single peoplehood is fractured. In these circumstances, an interim solution must be developed for the period of transition and common struggle from apartheid of two or more unequal citizenships to the democracy of single citizenship.[8] The argument for the principle of separation of nationality

8. I have attempted to develop elsewhere such an interim solution, predicated on the renewal of the usage of the linguistic term *Hebrew* to identify the people whose historical origin

from the state, the decoupling of nationality from the state, represents an argument against the idea of the nation-state and for the alternative norm of the nonnational state.

I strongly believe that on the basis of the conceptual and legal framework developed above national pluralism and multicultural diversity can flourish on the surface of the modern world, where all territories are subject to the sovereignty of one state or another. It is my view that on the basis of the conceptual and legal framework developed above a plurality of cultural self-determination (cultural autonomy and self-government) can be maintained on an equal footing among all nationalities without collapsing into apartheid, ethnic cleansing, and genocide, and strengthen the single peoplehood of equal citizens rather than otherwise.

The People

The idea of the democratic state—a government of the people, by the people, for the people based on the principle of separation of religion from the state—was a new idea born with the American Revolution of 1776 and the French Revolution of 1789, and culminating in the Universal Declaration of Human Rights in 1948 and the Geneva Conventions and their additional protocols of 1949. The adjective *democratic* is predicated on two terms, the *demos* (the people) and *kratos* (rule), and the conjunction *democratic state* in this study assumes the underlying liberal principle of separation of religion from the state. (See "Note on Secularism," above). Critical to our concern, however, remains the question "Who are the people?"

Since Woodrow Wilson's Fourteen Points outlining the framework for the post–World War I peace settlement, the concept of national self-determination became the legitimizing principle of the modern international order regulated by the League of Nations and subsequently (after World War II) by the United Nations. In terms of the conventions of modern international relations narrative, the terms *people* and *nation* are almost synonymous. The classification of any given collectivity as a people (or a nation) is read as entailing a political statement regarding the right of the collectivities concerned to "national self-determination," which, in turn, is conventionally read to mean recognition of their "right" to independence— namely, statehood. This political philosophy is typically reflected, for instance, in the United Nations Declaration on the Granting of Independence

---

is in the Zionist immigration to and settlement in Palestine and who are currently officially classified in the State of Israel as *Jewish* (*New Socialism: A Quarterly for New Socialist Thought* (Hebrew edition) 1 [1996]: 29–40).

to Colonial Countries and Peoples (1960), where recognition of a collectivity as a people or a nation entails the right to "the exercise of their sovereignty" and the defense of "the integrity of their national territory" (Brownlie 1992, 28–30).

It is patently clear, however, that this conceptual political framework has failed to meet the requirements of bi- or multinational situations (the majority of the cases the world over), where the "national territory" is the patrimony of not one single nation but of a plurality of nations and where the "exercise of sovereignty" by one nation has frequently collapsed into ethnic cleansing and genocide. It is in this political context that the clear distinction between people and nation, between citizenship and nationality, can make significant contribution to the complex legal and political interrelationship between questions of self-determination, autonomy, citizenship, and democracy, and provide new thinking and a new understanding of citizenship in general and in the Middle East in particular.[9]

The idea of the independent and sovereign nation-state has been historically an ideological formula for massive human disaster. It seems that the only ideology that can be wedded to the state as the principle of legitimation that does not necessarily entail racism (e.g., apartheid) or ethnic cleansing (genocide) is the modern ideology of universal human rights. A study aiming to contribute to the making of a new and alternative conceptual framework for a political narrative based on the principles of separation of religion from the state, equality of rights, and reciprocity should therefore address the question of who are the people (the demos) on behalf of whose interest the democratic state is regarded as a necessary instrument and who, by the token of being classified as the legally relevant people, are entitled as citizens to equal access to the civil, political, social, and material resources of the state.

It has already been suggested that this conceptual alternative be predicated on the principle of separation of the nation from the state and that consistent democratic political narrative would be hugely advanced if the term *people* be reserved to designate the collective body of citizens of any given state. Thus, the British people (the collective body of British citizens) belong to at least three nations (English, Scottish, and Welsh), and it is the British people who are the demos of a future, democratic, multinational Britain, where the right of national self-determination (cultural autonomy,

9. In developing these distinctions I am indebted to Fouzi al-Asmar and the late Naim Khadar and the discussion sesions held in Bradford and Brussels leading to the publication of *Towards a Socialist Republic of Palestine* (London and Kefar Shemaryahu: Ithaca Press and Miftah (Key) Publishers, 1978) and to my past association with Akiva Orr.

self-government) would be guaranteed to the (at least) three nations of Britain in a written constitution. I agree with Tony Benn that the root weakness of the democratic tradition in Britain is the absence of a written constitution. Benn (Benn and Hood, 1993) correctly points out that without a written constitution, "British democracy is fragile and under great threat. The monarch retains, in law, substantial powers, such that a coup under the Crown would be quite legal" (73). Assuming a normative paradigm where statelessness is abolished and where all individuals who were made refugees after the publication of the Universal Declaration of the Human Rights in 1948 are offered the choice of dual citizenship, both the citizenship of their country of origin and the citizenship of their host state, we can then accept that the proper people of the democratic state can be only the body of citizens ordinarily resident in the territory occupied by the state, subject to its legislation, and liable to its taxation. It is this body of people, the demos of the democratic state, its citizens, who (as taxpayers) have a claim to equal access to the civil, political, social, and material resources of the state.

The legal origin of citizenship in the Middle East is rooted in the Ottoman Citizenship Law of 19 January 1869 and the Treaty of Peace, signed at Lausanne, 24 July 1923, between the British Empire, France, Italy, Japan, Greece, Rumania, and the Serb-Croat-Slovene State on the one part and Turkey on the second part, formalizing the defeat of the Ottoman Empire and the surrender by Turkey of any rights and titles whatsoever over former Ottoman territories situated outside the frontiers of modern Turkey as laid down in the said Treaty of Peace.

Section II of the treaty ("Nationality"), Article 30, stipulates as follows:

> Turkish subjects habitually resident in territory which in accordance with the provisions of the present Treaty is detached from Turkey will become *ipso facto* in the conditions laid down by the local law, nationals of the State to which such territory is transferred. (*League of Nations Treaty Series*, vol. 28, nos. 1–4 [1924], 29)

Historically two principles were evoked as the foundation of modern citizenship: citizenship by law of blood (jus sanguinis) and citizenship by law of the soil (territory)—namely, place of birth (jus soli). Modern citizenship in the Middle East is predicated, as it ought to be, on jus soli. And the answer to the question "Who are the people?" of each state in the Levant at the time when it came into being in the wake of the Lausanne Treaty of Peace must surely be all the inhabitants of the territory that, having been detached from Turkey, came under the sovereignty of another state. It is the departure from this normative and legal foundation that has resulted in the worse abuses of ethnic cleansing in the region, notably the dispossession and expulsion of the Palestinian people from territories that came under Israeli sovereignty.

Sovereignty and Independence

Sovereignty is not independence, and independence is not sovereignty. Not every independent member state of the United Nations organization is also a sovereign state. In the UN, there are member states, such as Andorra, which are independent but not sovereign. Andorra is a state recognized by the UN, with full vote at the UN General Assembly, as well as embassies and missions with other states represented in the UN—but it is not a sovereign state. The sovereignty of Andorra is vested with the Count de Foix, whose duties are vested today with the president of the French Republic in personal capacity and with the bishop of Urgell in Spain. Andorra has a constitution, a parliament, and a police force, but not an army. Andorra is an independent state—not a sovereign state. For the purpose of this presentation, a state is defined as an *independent state* if and when it obtains recognition by the UN and a seat with the UN General Assembly, and as a *sovereign state* if and when it commands recognized armed forces patrolling its international borders. In terms of this distinction, the State of the Vatican is a sovereign state (it has a recognized army, the Swiss Guards), whereas Andorra is not. We ought not regard the question of sovereignty frivolously because sovereignty, represented first and foremost in the command of recognized armed forces patrolling the international borders of the state, vests the sovereign with ultimate control of the land, water, and airspace demarcated by the said international borders.

The distinction between independence and sovereignty would bear repeating: in this work, a state is defined as independent if it is a recognized voting member of the United Nations General Assembly and as sovereign if it is in command of recognized armed forces patrolling its international borders. I follow Thomas Hobbes (1968) in identifying the locus of sovereignty in the state as such, not in the people (as identified by John Locke, Jean-Jacques Rousseau). The people, as defined in this study, are not sovereign; the people are free. The state is a construct in the hands of the people and, like all instruments and human constructs, can if necessary be dismantled by the people. Taking as a point of departure twentieth-century literature on the subject of sovereignty, I follow Alan James (1986).

Like James, I am now convinced that the attempts to conceptualize sovereignty primarily in terms of power, let alone illimitable power, are less than productive. Thus, for instance, Preston King defines sovereignty as "[T]he power or authority which comprises the attributes of an ultimate arbitral agent—whether persons or a body of persons—entitled to make decisions or settle disputes within a political hierarchy with some degree of finality" (Miller 1983, 492–93). King further refines the definition, noting that the ability to make such decisions implies independence from external powers and ultimate authority or dominance over internal groups. He identifies four primary attributes of sovereignty: (1) location, in that it is the highest power in any politicolegal hierarchy; (2) sequence, in that it is the ultimate power of decision within such a hierarchy; (3) effect, in that it is general, influencing the overall flow of action within the said hierarchy; and (4) autonomy, in that the sovereign is independent in its relations with other agents, internal or external, domestic or foreign.

The definition seems to be clearly lacking. A cursory review of the domain of international relations would reveal that according to this definition, no member state of the United Nations is sovereign—namely, independent in their relationships with other states.

David Held (1989) identifies five "gaps" or disjunctions in the relations between the political theory of the sovereign state and the nature of twentieth-century world. These gaps he lists as (1) "world economy," (2) "hegemonic powers and power blocs," (3) "international organizations," (4) "international law," and (5) "the end of domestic policy." He maintains that the operation of states in an ever more complex international system limits their autonomy and infringes on their sovereignty, at least such sovereignty as is classically conceived as an illimitable and indivisible form of political power. He concludes that "if sovereignty as a concept is to retain its analytical and normative forces—as the rightful capacity to take final decisions and make and enact the law within a given community—it has to be conceived as divided among a number of agencies and limited by the way the very nature of this plurality and the rules and procedures which protect it" (238). Here, as well, much confusion is entailed by the misplaced conception of sovereignty in terms of power, let alone illimitable power. In the process, one essential feature of sovereignty, its unitary attribute, is lost in Held's exposition. To my understanding, sovereignty can be recognized as sovereignty because it is indivisible and unitary. Sovereignty conceived as divided is not sovereignty, but something else.

More than thirty years earlier, Stanley Benn (1955, 122), following a parallel line of thinking and having identified six senses in which the term *sovereignty* might be meaningfully employed, concluded that "in the light of this analysis it would appear to be a mistake to treat 'sovereignty' as denoting a genus of which the species can be distinguished by suitable adjectives, and there would seem to be a strong case for giving up so Protean a word" (quoted in A. James 1986, 6).

Alan James (1986) takes the discussion out of what he terms this terminological "quagmire" by seeking to anchor the definition of sovereignty in state practice in the twentieth century, especially in its middle and later parts, pursuing the question of how, nowadays, sovereign states give meaning to the word *sovereignty* when they refer to that which makes them eligible for international life: "States may not be verbally explicit about the nature of their sovereignty, meaning that which entitles them to seek admission to the international hurly-burly. But their actions make the meaning which they attach to the term 'sovereignty' entirely plain" (1986, 22). In his review of the process of transformation of former colonial dependencies into sovereign statehood, James concludes, utilizing actual state practice and following Manning (1962), that the sovereignty on which state international activity is based is "constitutional independence," or constitutional separateness ("insularity" in Manning's terms)—namely, that a state is regarded as sovereign in the international domain if its constitution is not part of a larger constitutional arrangement.

The clarity of James's insight is very appealing, as indeed is his subsequent explication of the three main features of sovereignty: it is legal, unitary, and absolute. Unlike Held's proposition, James's definition retains the elegance of the classical theory of sovereignty in that it anchors sovereignty squarely to the state and insists on its unitary condition. His definition, however, collapses in the face of the reality of the transformation of the European Community (EC) into the European Union (EU). James published his work in 1986, six years before the conclusion of the Maastricht Treaty in February 1992 or, more precisely, before the date of the coming into force of the Maastricht Treaty in November 1993, following which the constitutions of the member states of the EU have indeed become a part of a larger constitutional arrangement.

I propose that a state be defined and recognized as sovereign (as distinct from independent) if and when it has security forces officially classified and internationally recognized as an army (as distinct from a police force) to patrol its international borders. I believe this definition to be superior to James's definition. Thus, in terms of my definition, the constituent member states of the EU remain sovereign because inside the framework of the EU, each member state continues to maintain a separate and recognized army patrolling its internationally recognized borders. It is only if and when the armies of the constituent members of the EU are legally reclassified as police forces that the sovereignty of EU member states will be lost and the EU will have been transformed into a federal state like the United States.

The definition also sheds new light on the classification of apartheid South Africa's Bantustans. In apartheid South Africa, Bantustans were divided into two classes: (1) *independent homelands* (Transkei, Ciskei, and Buphuthatswana; and (2) *homelands* (Venda, Qwa Qwa, Kangwane, Gazankulu, and Qwazulu). Independent homelands had their own police and armed forces (Transkei Defense Forces [TDF], Ciskei Defense Forces [CDF], and Buphuthatswana Defense Forces [BDF]). Homelands did not have their own security forces. In the homelands, both polices forces and armed forces were South African.

It seems in order to note here that in the framework of the Oslo peace process, Israel and the Labor Zionist leadership of Shimon Peres conceptualized for the Palestinians a hybrid South African apartheid homeland, a middle creature between an apartheid homeland and an independent homeland—namely, a Palestinian political entity with police forces but no Palestinian armed forces, or an independent State of Palestine, not a sovereign State of Palestine. Both under Peres and Labor Zionism and under Netanyahu and Likud, ultimate control of land, water, and airspace delineated by internationally recognized borders patrolled by army, navy, and air force—in other words, sovereignty—are to be firmly denied to the projected Palestinian entity and are to remain firmly in Israeli hands.

In sum, it follows from my argument that whereas all sovereign states are by definition independent, not all independent states are necessarily sovereign. It is also in order to point out that the distinction between sovereignty and independence may allow, under certain circumstances, for new Bantustans to be introduced to the international community in the guise of "independent states" in Palestine and elsewhere.

The distinction I have developed helps explain Israel's insistence on ultimate control, in the framework of the Oslo I and Oslo II Agreements negotiated with the Palestine Liberation Organization (PLO), over the international crossings along the British Mandate boundaries between Palestine and the Hashemite Kingdom of Jordan and Egypt, as well as over the Gaza seaport and airport—let alone its insistence on legally defining the Palestinian security forces as police forces—not as an army. My distinction also explains the insistence of all such official and semiofficial Israeli think tanks as have recommended the option of a State of Palestine alongside the State of Israel that the proposed State of Palestine be demilitarized—a state with no army.

I submit that the Israeli insistence on the demilitarization of any prospective State of Palestine has little to do with security considerations and has everything to do with outright Israeli rejection of Palestinian sovereignty on any part of geographical Palestine.

Since the signing of the Camp David Accords between Israel and Egypt in 1979 there has been complete agreement between the Israeli Labor Party and the Likud Party on this question. It is an error to interpret the readiness of the Zionist Labor Party to consider the option of a minuscule State of Palestine alongside the State of Israel as readiness to roll back Israeli sovereignty from any part of the territory of British Mandate Palestine. Both Labor and Likkud are committed to the maintenance of Israeli sovereignty over the entire territory of British Mandate Palestine, and both envision a Palestinian "autonomy" ("Bantustan") under Israeli sovereignty. The only difference between the parties is that the Labor Party argues that, given the persistence of the Palestinian Arab people, the long-term interests of Israeli diplomacy and Zionist policy may benefit from an international recognition of Palestine as an independent state, a member state in the United Nations organization, whereas the Likud Party argues vehemently against recognition of a State of Palestine in any form whatsoever. From a Zionist point of view, the Israeli Labor Party position is probably the better position.

Freedom and Oppression

Membership (or otherwise) in societal (including religious) associations is fundamentally voluntary. It is, in final analysis, a matter of individual choice. Membership in societal associations can be transformed through state intervention (e.g., legislation), whereupon it ceases to be a matter of individual choice and is augmented into a question of law, enforced in final analysis by resort to the state monopoly of violence (police, army, taxation). When this happens, oppression begins, and freedom is compromised.

Thus, the objection of parents to the marriage of their children outside the community is not "like" the incorporation of the confessional religious code into the law books of the state, which applies state machinery of law enforcement to disallow mixed marriages. The former is fundamentally voluntary; the latter is antidemocratic and a blatant violation of the Universal Declaration of Human Rights.[10]

---

10. The parallel Orthodox Jewish religious argument is represented by the anti-Zionist Neturei Karta (Guardians of the [Holy] City). They regard Zionism to be the worst expression of Jewish apostasy. They argue forcefully that the legitimate ingathering of the Jewish diaspora in the Land of Israel can come about only as a result of divine intervention in human history— namely, in the End of Days and as part of Messianic redemption. Any attempt by Jews to

In the final analysis, it is and always was possible to break away from the kinship affiliation into which one was born (e.g., through mixed marriage), from one tribal homeland to another diaspora (e.g., through rejection of a mythological common territory of origin or emigration), from any given confessional affiliation (e.g., through conversion), from customary dress (e.g., through adoption of Western attire). The price may be high and the pain harsh, but the break does not entail jail, taxation, or conscription. On the other hand, where the state highjacks into its legal system such communal attributes as, for instance, a tribal kinship code (resulting in apartheid) or a tribal homeland territorial code (resulting in chauvinism) or all or parts of the communal religious code (resulting in clericalism), then freedom of choice ends and oppression begins.

Whereas affiliation to any given religious association (e.g., mosque, church, synagogue), national association (e.g., ethnic school), or civil association (e.g., trade union) is fundamentally voluntary, paying taxes to the state is not. Submission to the order of custom or a societal organization is distinctly and qualitatively different from submission to the rule of law. The former is, in the final analysis, voluntary, the latter compulsory. One breaks the law on pain of jail, conscription, or taxation. It is in this sense that the law is compulsory in a way that national and societal affiliations are not. The state is an organization that has at its disposal the capacity to impose the compulsory sanction of jail, conscription, and taxation. National (kin, tribal homeland, or confessional) organizations, unless hijacked and usurped or prostituted by the state, do not have at their disposal these instruments of sanction, and it is precisely in this sense that they are voluntary forms of organization in a way that tax-paying residence in the state is not.

This distinction is paradigmatic to this study: *voluntary association* means voluntary national and societal affiliation, and *involuntary affiliation* is subjection to authority of the sovereign state under the penalty of jail, conscription, or taxation.

In the Middle East (as elsewhere), the imperative of secular democratic citizenship (e.g., equality before the law) conflicts with two well-established and entrenched interrelated political traditions, the first claiming the su-

---

intervene through secular political action in what is properly and strictly the domain of the holy, the domain of God, is the gravest sin a Jew could commit. They regard political Zionism on religious grounds as the enemy of the Jews; they do not recognize the legitimate existence of the State of Israel as a Jewish state; and they deny the claim of the State of Israel to represent all Jewish diaspora communities morally or legally or in any other way.

For the secular equivalent of the anti-Zionist Orthodox Jewish position, see *RETURN Magazine*, nos. 1–5, BM 8999, London WC1N 3XX.

premacy of one chosen confession over the state (fundamentalism) and the second proclaiming the supremacy of one chosen nation (sectarianism). They aim to replace the voluntary foundation of religious, national, and societal associations with involuntary state sanction. The former aims to make adherence to religious law compulsory by means of the law enforcement instruments of the state; the latter seeks adherence to the imagined boundaries of the nation. It is in this sense and in this way that both fundamentalism and sectarianism represent gross violations of the universal secular value of political freedom and are correctly identified as tyrannical.

Modernity can be phenomenologically characterized as the process of secularization of the state in the name of the principle of separation of religion from the state. The progressive separation of the state from the church was accompanied by the emergence of universal democratic values as the principle of legitimization of the state.

Over the past two hundred years, since the American and the French Revolutions, the process of secularization and democratization of the state and the consolidation of the hegemonious position of liberal values in the West has been greatly advanced on a global scale, particularly after the Second World War and the establishment of the UN in 1945. The imperative of secular citizenship in modern democratic states can be characterized as the process of replacement of kin, tribal homeland, and confession as values of legitimation of the state with liberal values—notably, the values of the Universal Declaration of Human Rights.

Although the conceptual awareness that the necessary condition for the combat of fundamentalism is the categorical and uncompromising insistence on the principle of separation of religion from the state is well established in modern Western political traditions, the conceptual and political requirements for the combat of sectarianism are not sufficiently developed.

It is a repeated contention of this work that it is not possible to bring the process of the democratization of the modern state in general and in the Middle East in particular to completion without the separation of nationality from the state and respect for the universal right to citizenship.

4

Gender, Citizenship, and State in the Middle East

MARY ANN TÉTREAULT

Sovereignty and Citizenship

ALL THE BOUNDED AREAS on modern world maps are called *nation-states,* but their qualities as political communities vary enormously. Most, in fact, are far from fulfilling the requirements of *nations*—named populations sharing a territory, a mythic past, a popular culture, and a common political economy (Smith 1991, 14; also Connor 1994). Some also are questionable as *states*—compulsory political organizations governing a specific territory within which they claim a monopoly of the legitimate use of force (M. Weber 1978, 54; Jackson 1990). The lack of analytic and substantive clarity in the meaning of *nation-state* as either a conceptual category or a political form affects the theory and practice of citizenship—membership of a nation-state that inscribes an ensemble of public rights and responsibilities incumbent on persons by virtue of that membership.

The nation-state (state) is defined by a set of conflicts over legitimacy (C. Weber 1995, 3). Those conflicts that center on relations within states determine the parameters of citizenship and also of *internal* or *positive sovereignty,* the authority and obligations of the state vis-à-vis civil society. Those that center on relations among states determine the parameters of *external* or *negative sovereignty.* External sovereignty refers to the principle of political equivalence of nation-states that makes each one's internal affairs forbidden territory to the others (Jackson 1990, 27; also Rosenberg 1990). These terms are analogous to Isaiah Berlin's (1969) definitions of positive and

70

negative liberty, but the two kinds of sovereignty are more closely interdependent than the two concepts of liberty.

External sovereignty became a political norm in Europe during the era of royal absolutism and began to be codified in treaties following the wars of religion in the seventeenth century. At first it applied to great powers only, and it did not preclude imperial ventures of various types well into the twentieth century (Doyle 1986, Jackson 1990). External sovereignty was founded on the notion of an "exchange between god and a monarch" (C. Weber 1995, 123). This "truth" allowed a state to represent itself and to recognize others (Greenfeld 1992). It is in this sense that John Ruggie's (1986) comparison of sovereignty to private property is meant. The "owner" of the state was the sovereign, the king—*l'état, c'est moi.* Gradually, this idea of the state as a possession of its ruler gave way to conceptions of the sovereign nation-state—that is, a state that belongs to its citizens (B. Anderson 1991, 20–22).

The meaning of *citizen,* a concept with linguistic and normative roots in the city-states of the ancient world, is linked to contemporary understandings of the nature of the political community to which the citizen belongs. What is meant by *citizen* varies over time, across political divisions, and according to a person's status. A citizen of fifth-century Athens had different rights and obligations than a citizen of fifth-century Sparta, and, in both places, the rights and obligations of male and female citizens were different. Even today, when "there is virtually no spot on the globe not included in a bounded, continuous stretch of space . . . disjunct . . . categorical . . . and exhaustive" (Geertz 1994, 9), the human beings dwelling on these pieces of geography are differently organized, protected, and obligated depending on where they live and who they are.

Cynthia Weber (1995) argues that sovereignty today is legitimated by "a transference of authority . . . between a domestic community and its government apparatus" (7). Legitimation rests on acceptance by a domestic community of a social contract describing "the popular mode whereby a citizenry represents itself and submits itself to the authority of the state so long as the state performs as the reflection of the will of its citizenry" (C. Weber 1995, 8). Unlike the absolutist state, which recognized only one citizen,[1] most states today include as citizens the majority of their adult

---

1. Under absolutism, the monarch was the only citizen. Writing about the modern development of politics in northern Europe, Patricia Springborg (1986) puts it this way: "In these latter systems (excluding northern Italian city states and the free cities of the Hansa League) participation in free and equal institutions is only a recent part of history, and absolutism, where the only public person was the king, was once the dominant mode" (200).

inhabitants. Their consent to be governed is the basis of internal sovereignty, produced by the contingent actions of citizens and state engaged in negotiating and fulfilling a social contract.

Consequently, sovereignty in the modern world is less like private property and more like a condominium defined by contestations. One such contestation centers on the nature of the community; another defines how the state and members of this community are mutually specified and obligated. In contrast to the image of a one-time surrender of political autonomy to a ruler, such as the one depicted by Thomas Hobbes in *Leviathan,* the boundaries of the domestic community and the provisions of the social contract operating between any state and its citizens are generally understood as corresponding to "moving averages" that are constantly reformulated and recalculated.

The field of contestations between states and societies that shape positive sovereignty is linked to the field of contestations among states themselves that shape negative sovereignty. These fields produce a different set of moving averages that mark the boundaries of legitimate external intervention. Robert Jackson (1990) argues that external sovereignty has become such a dominating idea since 1945 that legitimate intervention by other states, even in the affairs of a state that is severely abusive of its domestic population, is normatively precluded most of the time. Perhaps as a result, a third set of contestations defining sovereignty has been mounted by transnational actors and movements, many organized to protest human rights violations by states.

The mutual invention of sovereignty and citizenship is ongoing. One reason for this is the fluidity of the field describing state-inhabitant relations. Within most states and across all states, the status of various members of domestic communities differs widely. We can think of this range of statuses as grouped around two "ideal types" of state-inhabitant relations (Sadri 1992). One type creates *citizens,* free persons who are autonomous and equal partners in civil and political life. Each citizen is unique. This "plurality" (Arendt 1967) allows all of them together to construct their state as a corporate expression of the values, interests, and desires of an entire community, a definition that goes back to Aristotle (1981; also Finley 1963 and C. James 1986). The other type creates *subjects,* persons subjected to a ruler's will. Subjects are not autonomous partners engaging in civil life. They are part of the landscape of the ruler's estate. Like the deer in his forest or the fish in his rivers, they are not consulted when a ruler divides his property among his children or sells it to pay his debts.[2] Perhaps no state

---

2. The movement of the Plantagenet estates between France and England is one example

today can boast of citizens who are entirely free, equal, and fully incorpo-rated into political life; however, nearly every state harbors subjects of var-ious sorts, among them persons who are nominally citizens.

Citizens and Subjects

Citizenship and the nation-state as mutually contingent phenomena are fundamental characteristics of modernity. Anthony Giddens (1991) defines modernity as the

> institutions and modes of behavior established first of all in post-feudal Europe, but which in the twentieth century increasingly have become world-historical in their impact. "Modernity" can be understood as roughly equiva-lent to "the industrialized world." . . . A second dimension is capitalism. . . . Each of these can be distinguished analytically from the institutions of surveil-lance, the basis of the massive increase in organisational power associated with the emergence of modern social life. . . . This dimension can in turn be sepa-rated from control of the means of violence. . . . Modernity produces certain distinct social forms, of which the most prominent is the nation-state. (14–15)

Today's citizens and nation-states are creatures of modernity, but subjects belong to "the dynastic realm," a political order associated with a hierarchi-cal and heteronomous premodern past. "Kingship organizes everything around a high centre. Its legitimacy derives from divinity, not from popula-tions, who, after all, are subjects, not citizens. . . . [I]n the older imagining, . . . states were defined by centres, borders were porous and indistinct, and sovereignties faded imperceptibly into one another" (B. Anderson 1991, 19). Dynastic cycles governed by such concepts as the Mandate of Heaven and life cycles during which parents produce children to take their places in a cosmically regulated pattern of recapitulation without change—without "progress"—are divinely ordained pathways of life (Marr 1981).

Different understandings of the person in the world operate in the dynas-tic realm and in modernity. In Benedict Anderson's conception of the "older imagining," the world is monadic and timeless. Although each per-son—every thing—in it is singular, each also is iconic and essential, one self-contained facet of a complex crystalline structure—eternity—containing all of them at the same time. Destiny, one's location in the crystal, determines each life. As in Verdi's 1861 opera, *La forza del destino*, destiny may be

of property changing hands for dynastic reasons, the sale by Napoléon of Louisiana to Thomas Jefferson another.

interpreted by clerical intermediaries, but it cannot be altered. This image of the world is captured in a Christian prayer, the Gloria: "As it was in the beginning, is now, and ever shall be, world without end." Muslims say "It was written" to convey a similar sense of destiny over which human will has no power to prevail.

The modern world in Anderson's (1991) conception is pluralistic; it exists in "homogeneous empty time . . . measured by clock and calendar" (24). In this world, persons and things exist in their particularity. Cosmology is separate from history, which is shaped by human agency and is materially rather than spiritually manifested. In the modern world, we speak of "individuals," but this status is synonymous with atomization and interchangeability rather than with singularity.[3] The individual, unlike the "soul," is neither unique nor immortal: to paraphrase Andy Warhol, everyone gets to be famous, but only for fifteen minutes.

Ernest Gellner (1983b) offers a less cosmic but still recognizably hierarchical and heteronomous image of premodern social orders that he terms "agro-literate" society. Unlike Anderson, who sees the modern citizen almost as a spontaneous product of the spread of literacy and "print capitalism" (a profit-seeking, industrialized publishing industry), Gellner points to the modern nation-state as the chief creator of its own equal and functionally interchangeable citizens. They are produced by "exo-socialization, education proper"—mass education provided via a state-supported national system as compared to the individualized training of agro-literate persons by parents, priests, and tutors (37). In this view, the modern citizen is a commodity purposely designed for multiple uses by the modern state (38). In turn, modern citizens create the modern state by generating and consuming the economic and political resources that maintain its legitimacy and sovereignty.

Educated citizens of modern states are assumed to be autonomous, interchangeable, and, not incidentally, politically equal. However, some inhabitants of these political communities are none of these things. Gellner (1983b) defines them as "entropy-resistant" (65). They are marked in some obvious and unerasable way that allows their fellows to reject and discrimi-

---

3. The apparently odd coupling of singularity with sameness and of uniformity with individuality is reproduced through costumes. Writing about the variability in women's clothing during the romantic period, Anne Hollander (1994) observes that " 'woman' became a sort of single primitive force, encountered by individual men in the form of dramatically varied samples which were nonetheless believed to be only superficially different, sisters under the differently colored skin. . . . [T]he faces might as well be all the same, just as if the same doll were dressed in many different ways. [At the same time, men's clothing was becoming more uniform with the result that] the individual character of each man is made more important" (98).

nate against them, and sometimes they suffer discrimination as an intended outcome of state policy. For example, some members of the community may be defined legally as having different entitlements to the resources of exosocialization or equal access as adults to participation in the political, economic, and social life of the community.

Concrete illustrations of such rejection and discrimination can be found throughout history. In the United States of the eighteenth and nineteenth centuries, for example, slaves were counted as three-fifths of a citizen for the purpose of political representation but had no social, economic, or political rights, including the right to vote for "their" representatives. Women were counted as full citizens for the purpose of representation but had no political rights and only highly limited social and economic rights. In the twentieth century, Israeli Arabs are denied citizenship rights equal to those of Israeli Jews and even some rights that are available to Jews who are citizens of other countries (Tekiner 1994, Peled and Shafir 1996). Jewish Israeli women have inferior rights and obligations as compared to Jewish Israeli men (Jorgensen 1994, Sharoni 1995). Each of these inequalities represents a dynastic element in a modern political body.

Tradition refers to the remnants of the dynastic realm in the modern world. When we speak of tradition and traditional life, we convey images of timelessness and subjection that imply the existence of people whose positions in life are determined by essential qualities independent of their individuality. Indeed, we do not even see individuality, in the sense of intersubjectivity, as a characteristic of such people. Whereas only the religious may attribute essential qualities to divine will, most of us employ terms such as *nature* or *culture* that amount to much the same thing. Hidden behind this vocabulary are the assumptions of the older imagining: the interconnected concepts of legitimate subjection and the inherent inability of subjects to "progress" or "develop"—to be or become like ourselves.

In almost every political community, the persons most associated with tradition in this sense are women, and, as a result, the concept of citizenship is profoundly gendered (e.g., Mosse 1985, Pateman 1988, Yuval-Davis and Anthias 1989, Peterson 1994). In societies incorporating slave populations, this same distinction is made and is sometimes emphasized by parallel analyses of the essentially defective or incomplete natures of women and slaves. For example, Aristotle differentiated between male and female citizens as well as between slaves and free men with respect to their moral capacity. Both women and slaves were judged as inherently incapable of rationality and the ability to exercise authority (also Ortner 1974, Garlan 1988). Their inherent moral inferiority was reflected in social norms that defined the bodies of subordinates as the instruments of the dominant.

Now property is part of a household . . . [and] in any special skill the availability of the proper tools will be essential for the performance of any task. . . . Any piece of property is an assemblage of such tools; a slave is a sort of living piece of property . . . in spite of being a man, he is a piece of property, i.e., a tool. . . . [T]he rule of free over slave, male over female, man over boy, all are different, because while parts of the soul are present in each case, the distribution is different. Thus the deliberative faculty of the soul is not present at all in a slave; in a female it is present but ineffective; in a child present but undeveloped. (Aristotle 1981, 1253b23, 1254a1–9, 1259b32)

Moral inferiority excludes such persons from an entitlement to participate as equals in political life. Natural subjects never can be citizens.

Citizenship, Nationality, and Gender

Citizenship should be distinguished from *nationality,* a politically mediated classification conferred by states according to bureaucratic rules. The development of the concept of nationality is associated with nineteenth-century nationalist ideologies and mass movements, and with attempts by states to impose controls on selected populations. Nationalist ideologies and movements identify a political community with a territory and with a common history, language, religion, culture, and customary ties to that territory (e.g., Connor 1994, Kellas 1991, Moynihan 1993, Smith 1991). Often associated with separatist movements in decaying nineteenth-century empires, nationalism is identified by Rousseau as the mainspring of the "general will" of a state (cited in Waltz 1959, 174). Nationalism drove the French Revolution and the imperialism of Napoleon. A number of scholars, among them Anthony Smith (1991) and James Kellas (1991), argue that nationalist identification characterized some populations at much earlier periods.

Nationalism is a powerful ideology with intense religious overtones (Manzo 1996, Smith 1991). It replaces "God the father . . . [by] lay[ing] claim to the fruits of divinity identified in the Old Testament," allowing nationalist leaders "legimately [to] demand the sacrifice of human life as a means of collective immortality" (Manzo 1996, 17; also Elshtain 1991). Nationalists associate legitimacy with primordial identities and relationships, and consequently are neither egalitarian nor modern in the sense of reflecting values such as equality or freedom of choice. Nationalism naturalizes the hierarchical principles characteristic of the dynastic realm as legitimate in modern states. Nationalist ideologies direct the inclusion or exclusion of particular persons or groups from citizenship when their adherents control the state and challenge the sovereignty of existing states when they do not (Hobsbawm 1990).

Nationality as a formal political identity developed toward the end of the nineteenth century. Not coincidentally, this also was a period featuring extensive voluntary and involuntary migration across political boundaries. Nationality as a claim that a person belongs to a particular state was developed to identify those who did not belong—that is, refugees, formerly colonized persons, and other "illegal aliens" (Manzo 1996). Nationality also affirmed a state's authority over former residents living abroad whose behavior and treatment were thought to reflect on the reputations of their country of origin (Guy 1992). Bureaucracies in receiving and sending states were charged with classifying members of the population as "citizens" or "aliens." However, merely calling someone a citizen and issuing a passport do not replace premodern social hierarchies with the egalitarian societies envisioned in modern liberal political theory, particularly for citizens who are women. This brings me to a second reason why there is such fluidity in the concept of citizenship.

Citizenship's gendered quality embeds a dualism in how it is understood. This dualism operates both as a paradigm that models ideal—gendered—relationships between states and citizens (e.g., Combs-Schilling 1989, Hunt 1992) and as a vulnerable point or fault line attracting conflict over the respective levels, modes, and expressions of autonomy appropriate to citizens and states generally. For example, the model of citizenship implied by liberal political theory is brotherhood. Whether one traces the development of this concept philosophically (e.g., Aristotle 1985, Pateman 1988) or psychoanalytically (e.g., Freud 1930, 1958; Brown 1985; Hunt 1992), the brotherhood envisioned by liberal theorists from John Locke to John Rawls is exactly that, brotherhood. It rejects half of the dynastic concept of patriarchal rule, the rule of the fathers, but does not question the other half, the subjection of women to men and particularly of wives to husbands (Pateman 1988, Okin 1989). Even otherwise impeccable liberals such as John Stuart Mill (1929), who wrote with his wife, Harriet Taylor, an impassioned attack on female subjection (see also Rose 1983), drew the line at permitting married women to exercise the same degree of autonomy as their spouses (Okin 1979, 226–27). Well into the twentieth century and virtually everywhere in the world, wives were the subjects of their husbands and thus could not be autonomous citizens (e.g., Mill 1929; Okin 1989; Boswell 1990; Tétreault 1994c, 1997a).

The normative and positive absence of women from theories of citizenship was and is echoed in social practices and laws that discriminate between women and men with respect to both citizenship and nationality (Mayer 1995a, 1995b; Guy 1992; Peters and Wolper 1995). For example, a Kuwaiti woman married to a national of another state loses some of her rights as a citizen of her natal state. This denial of rights extends to her children, who are identified by the Kuwaiti state as aliens of the same nationality as their fathers rather than as dual nationals or as persons with a right to choose between their parents' nationalities at the age of majority (Tétreault and al-Mughni 1995).

Gender and the Construction of Citizenship in the Middle East

Gender inequality persists in theories and practices of citizenship all over the world. In most cases, it is excused as a practice with a long legal and social tradition or one sanctioned by religious customs and values (Mayer 1995a and 1995b) or both. An academic explanation for its persistence in Middle Eastern states is that it is the result of a long stagnation in the development of Islamic law. As a direct result of "clos[ing] . . . the door of *ijtihad* (interpretation)," Muslim law regulating personal status—such things as marriage, inheritance, custody, and some civil rights—was frozen:

> Islamic law is conservative in procedure: In the tenth century . . . the consensus of the majority of legal scholars determined that the elaboration of law was complete. Independent interpretation was deemed to be no longer necessary. . . . Henceforth, the role of jurists was to follow or imitate *(taqlid)* the established authoritative doctrines of the law schools. . . . [T]he dynamic relationship between *ijtihad* and *ijma* [consensus] was severed. *Ijma* became the infallible consensus of scholars. (Esposito 1982, 10–11)

Islamic law also is conservative in substance, the result of incorporating dynastic practices that were common during the time when legal development halted. As John Esposito (1982) notes, "traditional" Islamic law on personal status was corrupted by the tenth-century assimilation of non-Qu'ranic social practices such as female seclusion and veiling (11). Germaine Tillion (1983) emphasizes that even in circumstances where Qu'ranic injunctions are explicit, such as in the establishment of inheritance rights for women, local communities describing themselves as Islamic commonly violate religious norms in favor of patriarchal values.

Among the ironies of the end of the era of *ijtihad,* the principle that had made Islamic law so dynamic and innovative, was the setback it imposed on the egalitarian spirit of the Muslim religion. The basic material sources of Islamic law, the Qu'ran and the Sunnah (the normative behavior of the Prophet), are noteworthy for their detailed specification of rights for women far in advance of contemporary social practice. Some scholars see this as a Quranic "intent" to be egalitarian and progressive with respect to gender

(Esposito 1982, Mernissi 1987). Muslim feminists and Muslim fundamentalists both point to Islam as a religion that protects women's rights (e.g., Mernissi 1987, Roy 1994a), but how they see Islam in this regard depends on whether they emphasize the spirit or the letter of the law. Feminists concentrate on Islam's egalitarianism and the parts of Qu'ran and the Sunnah that establish positive rights for women. Fundamentalists stress those parts of the Muslim tradition that highlight gender differences—women's allegedly greater physical weakness and emotionalism—to support theories of gender complementarity. Thus, requiring that women receive a share of an inheritance is interpreted by feminists as a recognition of women's equality, whereas the specification of the woman's share as only half that of a man is interpreted by fundamentalists as signifying women's inferiority.

A second support for gender inequality in the Middle East is the tradition of communal jurisprudence within the same state in matters of personal status, such as marriage and divorce. Such group distinctions are said to be "traditional" and are attributed to the Ottoman millet system, but in practice they are found in states such as Kuwait that were not part of the Ottoman Empire and in Jewish Israel, which rejects Muslim traditions. However such group distinctions are interpreted, they deny equal protection under the law. Deniz Kandiyoti (1992) argues that confessionally based legal distinctions are accommodations by modernizing Middle Eastern states to the demands of traditionalist and anti-Western elements among their populations, a strategy embedded in the discourse of "authenticity" that also is used to describe conflicts between governing regimes and their challengers throughout the region. Kandiyoti associates this pattern of accommodation with low levels of state legitimacy and deficiencies in civil society. Fatima Mernissi (1995) sees them in a similar light: "Since the abolition of slavery, only women and minorities are left as a test for the state to modernize itself. . . . This is why most of the debate on democracy in the Muslim world circles endlessly around the explosive issue of women's liberation" (44).

Theories of citizenship in the Middle East also are shaped by reactions to imperialism. Leila Ahmed (1992) shows how the depiction by British writers of Egyptian women as abused subjects of Egyptian men was used to provide moral justification for British imperialism in Egypt. That this depiction was cynical rather than principled is evident in her sketch of one of the chief "defenders" of the rights of Egyptian women, the British consul general Lord Cromer (Evelyn Baring), who was a charter member of an organization established to oppose the extension of social and political rights to British women (Ahmed 1992, 151–55).

The fairly widespread obsession of representatives of Western imperial powers regarding the sexuality of subject populations (Ahmed 1992, Mabro 1991, Alloula 1986) dictated the utility of gender politics as an instrument of rule and of resistance to that rule, but how it was used depended on local traditions and the particular circumstances of national liberation movements. In Confucian Vietnam, for example, analyses of traditional gender relations were used to disguise normative and structural arguments against French colonial rule. Conservative Vietnamese nationalists continued to emphasize "the family as the foundation of society and female subordination as the foundation of the family"; at the same time, radical nationalists invited their fellows "to see women as one of many oppressed groups in their society and revolution as a way to liberate them all" (Tétreault 1994a, 112). The dominance of the radicals in Vietnam's revolution, in part due to the time and effort it took to expel the French (and later the Americans) and consequently the need to mobilize women as full participants in the struggle for national liberation, explains the domination of radical ideology and political practice during the revolution and after.

In contrast, in former European dependencies in the Middle East, the imperialists' deployment of gender as a fulcrum for applying leverage to weaken local regimes tended to be internalized as an attack on nation and religion. For example, during the Iranian Revolution, "female sexuality offer[ed] a fertile ground over which to insist upon the distinctiveness and purity of the Iranian Islamic culture in order to launch a counter-attack [against what was depicted as a corrupt, Westernized regime]" (Farhi 1994, 260). Even in Algeria, which, like Vietnam, was forced to struggle at great cost and for many years against a colonial power that employed gender to divide and exploit the local population, the participation of women in the liberation war did not change male consciousness with regard to the nature of women or their proper place in Algerian society because male dominance and female subordination were so deeply embedded as integral national identity (e.g., Fanon 1967; see also Lazreg 1994, Lemsine 1993, Shaaban 1988).

Links between nationalist revolutionary movements and the extension of equal citizenship to women are fragile everywhere in the world, not only in the Middle East (Tétreault 1994b). This stems from the relative autonomy of sex-gender systems from the states in which they operate (Busch and Mumme 1994, 348; also Rubin 1975).[4] How any society constructs gender

---

4. Gayle Rubin (1975) defines a sex-gender system as the construction of two genders by exaggerating the differences between women and men and by suppressing the similarities between them. This system produces a gendered division of labor in the family, the economy, and the state. The purpose of a sex-gender system is to control female sexuality, but the contingent

is related to how it constructs its state and economy, but historically specific examples of any one of these three interacting fields (sex-gender system, state, economy) are neither independent of nor completely determined by the others. This is why undergoing a revolution is no guarantee that every last crumb of an old regime will be swept away (Tocqueville 1955). Virtually every society, no matter how nominally "modern," includes traditional arrangements that have survived from the past and are expressed not only in sex-gender systems, the primary repositories for tradition, but also in states and economies.

In Middle East scholarship, such survivals often are thought to be unique. Interpreted as Middle Eastern "exceptionalism," they are variously conceived as products of Islam (Huntington 1994, Lewis 1993), tribalism (al-Naqeeb 1990, Sharabi 1988), overly strong societies (Migdal 1988), and poorly legitimated states (Hudson 1977). I argue that the Middle East is not exceptional; what appears to some as uniquely problematic is more likely to be the result of a conflation of the particular survivals under consideration with the strategies of particular rulers and regimes (a similar point is made in Bromley 1994). These connections are perhaps most clearly visible in "traditional" regimes. Whether, like Morocco's, they claim ancient roots or, like Kuwait's, they spring from more recent exercises in state building, their legitimation is linked explicitly and simultaneously to female subordination and the divine dispensation claimed by dynastic regimes generally. As long as their rulers can maintain powerful hegemonic ideologies embedded in religious and social tenets and practices, they anticipate also being able to maintain stable social orders with themselves at the head.

> The construction and maintenance of a body of ideological communications is . . . a social process and cannot be explained merely as the formal working out of an internal cultural logic. The development of an overall hegemonic pattern or "design for living" is not so much the victory of a collective cognitive logic or aesthetic impulse as the development of redundancy—the continuous repetition, in diverse instrumental domains, of the same basic propositions regarding the nature of constructed reality. (Wolf 1982, 388)

Elaine Combs-Schilling (1989) has examined this phenomenon in Morocco. She argues that religious rituals such as the celebration of the Prophet's birthday and the annual ram sacrifice performed during the

---

development of political and economic systems with sex-gender systems results in a degree of interdependence that makes it difficult to effect lasting structural change at any level without changing all.

month of the Haj were remodeled by Moroccan rulers beginning in the fourteenth century to shore up their eroding dynastic authority. Popular rituals of first marriage were explicitly incorporated in order to bring the regime-mediated patriarchal and patrimonial design for living into every household. Each ritual, public and private, includes parallel kinesthetic and visual patterns strengthening perceptions that the experience it exalts is both connected to the other rituals and "ineffable, part of the very structure of being":

> During the 'Alawi era, local marriage ceremonies renewed the monarchy. . . . In local rites, the sharifi monarch gave young men—and by extension young women—their coming of age. The groom was metaphorically transformed into the ruler at the beginning of the ceremonies and remained the ruler until the bride's blood was spilled. Through the transformation, the ruler's role as archetypal man, reproductive exemplar, was affirmed. (Combs-Schilling 1989, 189)

Haya al-Mughni and I (1995) have examined a parallel strategy adopted by the Kuwaiti ruling family in the late 1970s. The Kuwaiti regime sought to buttress a political position weakened, ironically, by economic success. The Kuwaiti state commanded significant oil rents and had initiated a system of redistributing oil income in such a way that the autonomy of Kuwaiti citizens was significantly enhanced (Tétreault 1995). The result was an explosion in the number and diversity of economically and socially mobile Kuwaitis. Rapid social change was added to long-standing political pressures from members of the traditional merchant class against the ruling family's twentieth-century venture into autocratic rule (Tétreault 1991). Popular perceptions foreclosed a simple appeal to tradition as sufficient to legitimate the regime as it had become; too many Kuwaitis perceived their tradition as protodemocratic (Tétreault forthcoming). To them, the ruling family had achieved its political status only with the consent of other leading families and was bound by this tradition to be responsive to Kuwaiti citizens. Defying this assumption, in 1975, the amir, Sabah al-Salim, shut down the Kuwaiti Parliament and suspended a host of civil liberties presumably protected by the Kuwaiti Constitution. At a stroke, all Kuwaiti citizens became subjects.

A new amir, Jabir al-Ahmad, acceded to the rulership in 1977 following his uncle's death. Finding himself the target of criticism for failing to remove the subject status of Kuwaiti citizens, he inaugurated a campaign of national unity under the slogan *"al-usra al-waheda,"* the one/united family. Schoolchildren were encouraged to refer to the amir as "Baba Jabir," Father

Jabir, and a new national anthem and a pledge of allegiance were adopted. Popular criticism continued however, and in 1978 another tack was taken when the amir made a speech declaring his support for national renewal in the form of an "Islamization of the state" (Tétreault and al-Mughni 1995, 72). The explicit incorporation of religious sanctions, along with reinforcing rituals—secular as well as religious—to support Kuwait's patrimonial and patriarchal regime, repeats in multiple domains the basic proposition that the Al Sabah have the right to rule Kuwait as they choose. The key symbolic role played by gender in popular Islam, along with support by the ruling family for fundamentalist Islamists,[5] cements the continued subordination of women into the foundation of the regime's stability (al-Mughni 1993, Tétreault and al-Mughni 1995, al-Mughni forthcoming, Tétreault forthcoming).

Links between gender subordination and religion also are used to legitimate postrevolutionary regimes. One example is Iran, whose revolutionary Islamism started out far removed from the "back to the ninth century" canard many in the West employed to describe it (Roy 1994a, 58). During the 1978–79 revolution, a "retraditionalization" of women's dress formed part of a cultural attack on a broad spectrum of "Westernizing" policies initiated by Shah Mohammad Reza Pahlevi (Farhi 1994). At the same time, female Iranian revolutionaries were integral members of the Islamist movement and central to the vision of postrevolutionary Iranian society held by many of the proponents of political Islam (Roy 1994a, 58–59). Religious revolutionary ideologues were forced to devise images and rituals that simultaneously foreclosed independent female agency while they exalted women's participation as revolutionary activists.

> 'Ali Shariati . . . found a perfect solution [to the problem of defining authentic Muslim womanhood] in the fusion of the true Muslim woman and the revolutionary and anti-imperialist woman. . . . Shariati's ideal woman, Fatemeh (Mohammad's daughter), is simple and pure. She is totally dedicated to Islam and the legacy of her father but she is also a true companion to her husband and a dedicated mother to her children. Most importantly, however, she is a militant, challenging political injustice and respecting just authority. (Farhi 1994, 260)

Mobilized into the revolution and transformed into its most enduring symbol, Iranian women marching in their chadors may have missed the significance of the choice of Fatemeh as their model. They expected autonomy

---

5. Olivier Roy (1994a) emphasizes the difference in gender politics between fundamentalist and neofundamentalist Islamists, who urge female seclusion and subordination, and political Islamists, who incorporate women as activists in their movements.

and equal rights to result from their successful struggles. But as women in postrevolutionary societies around the world have all too often discovered (e.g., Park 1994, Ranchod-Nilsson 1994), the symbolic value of women, their reproductive power, and the competition they represent to socially and economically marginal men (Mernissi 1992, Tétreault forthcoming) make them the instrument of choice for political manipulation by male elites seeking to dominate postrevolutionary regimes. Iranian women who had the temerity to demand liberation openly following the ouster of the Shah were criticized as contaminated by imperialist values, and those who discarded their veils found themselves disciplined by street gangs in which former revolutionaries were heavily represented (Moghissi 1994, 133). Meanwhile, the new government rushed to suspend Iran's 1975 Family Protection Law, which had enhanced women's status by banning polygamy and giving women the right to divorce their husbands and to seek custody of their children (Mirhosseini 1995).

One of Ayatollah Ruhollah Khomeini's first political acts following his return to Iran was a 7 March 1979 speech demanding the reveiling of women. Iranian women responded the next day—International Women's Day—by marching in the streets, calling strikes, and presenting the government with an eight-page manifesto in defense of their rights. The order to reveil was promptly rescinded, but this apparent victory was short-lived. Iran had no autonomous women's organizations to sustain an opposition feminist movement. Perhaps as problematic was the decision by Iranian leftists to join Islamists in denouncing the women's protests as having been instigated by "loyalists and *agents provocateurs*" (Moghissi 1994, 143). With no male allies and no protected space from which to organize to defend their interests,[6] Iranian feminists were politically isolated within a short time. Haideh Moghissi (1994) argues that the success of the by no means united Islamist leaders in neutralizing the only group that had openly challenged them gave them the confidence to go on to attack and defeat others who were threatening their domination of postrevolutionary Iran. Once again, the subjection of women can be seen as part of a comprehensive strategy to curtail citizen autonomy for the population as a whole.

Secular postrevolutionary regimes are no less likely than their Islamist counterparts to glorify traditional gender roles and behaviors as a way to maintain their hold on power. Isam al-Khafaji (1995) analyzes the orchestration of violence against women in Iraq following the first Gulf War as a strategy to deflect political opposition, discredit liberalism among Iraqi

---

6. The term *protected space* refers to a domain substantially free by law and custom from intrusion by the state or by powerful social groups.

youth, reaffirm the power of men over women in Iraqi society, and—not incidentally—raise the birthrate. The chief tool to accomplish these goals was Resolution 111 of the Revolutionary Command Council, passed on 28 February 1990. The resolution "empowered Iraqi male citizens to murder their wives, sisters, mothers, aunts, nieces and even their female cousins, if any of these was found to have adulterous relations" (al-Khafaji 1995, 17). Despite or perhaps even because of the efforts of Iraqi women to support and sustain their families throughout eight years of war, Iraq's provincial Ba'athist leaders tried to reconcile the need for women's participation with an ideology emphasizing manhood and the centrality of military experience to the Iraqi national identity.

> In such an atmosphere, it was only natural to look upon those who could perform [civilian] duties as an inferior species. Women, intellectuals and non-Iraqis working in Iraq belonged to this category. They were always reminded that, thanks to the heroes defending their honor, they were able to live their ordinary lives. The repeated reference of the official discourse to the concept "honor" served to reiterate the subordinate role of women in Iraqi society. . . . In defending the honor of Iraqi women, the male fighters were at the same time defending their honor, because dishonoring women sexually was a powerful means of attacking social cohesion. (al-Khafaji 1995, 18)

Iraq's state-directed rape of Iraqi women (for examples see Makiya 1993, Brooks 1994), along with the state's sanction of private sexual violence against female citizens, also relies on tradition and what, in another context, historian David Newbury has termed "the yearnings of youth mixed with the strategies of statesmen" (quoted in Tétreault 1997b, 428). That this mixture also supports the subjection of male populations is rarely visible to those eager to assert their manhood by abusing women, which is also a function of the persistence of what Sana al-Khayyat (1990) terms the "traditional oppression" of women in modern Iraq.

Implications

Since 1945, external sovereignty has taken precedence over internal sovereignty as a principle guiding international relations. This shift has had a number of consequences on relations among states and between states and citizens. In the community of nation-states, external sovereignty boosts the status of weak states in international bodies and provides grounds for challenging intervention by foreigners. Internally, the delegitimation of external intervention removes an important check on state governments in their domestic relations. Thus, internationally, the weak state has gained in stature, but in consequence citizens as well as subject populations and groups are more vulnerable to domestic repression both by agents of the state and by dominant elements in civil society.

Modernization counters some of the loss in power suffered by subject populations. The erosion of traditional relations of production has weakened traditional patterns of social control and political allegiance, forcing governments to respond if they wish to remain in power. States seek to develop their economies both to improve their competitive positions vis-à-vis other states and to satisfy popular demands at home for economic and social welfare. National economic development and integration require that populations be transformed into "labor," a process that includes developing and channeling nationalist ideologies that focus citizen loyalties on the state and away from competing identities and social structures such as family and religion that also claim citizen loyalty and support. To increase the stake of citizens in the welfare of the state, governments extend citizenship rights to nationals, thereby building a constituency for the regime as well as laying the basis to claim expanded obligations in the form of positive support for the state (Greenfeld 1992, Salamé 1994b).

State and economy are linked to a sex-gender system that produces the ideological justification for a gendered division of economic and political power. These mutually constituting systems compose an overall design in which the same basic propositions are repeated in diverse instrumental domains. These systems are destabilized when a different design intrudes, one based on propositions that challenge the hegemony of the status quo. Gender relations are a point of potential vulnerability because of their centrality to all three systems. Especially as economies become more open as a result of modernization, those occupying positions of authority in hierarchical political and familial systems may feel compelled to join forces to ensure their mutual survival, resulting in alliances between governments and family patriarchs to confine status changes to the modernizing economy. One strategy is to cripple women's capacity to compete against men for the most desirable jobs or to defend themselves against subjection to the men in their families and governments through the exercise of political and legal rights.

Patriarchs and politicians appeal to tradition, particularly religion, to buttress their efforts to keep women in their place (Mayer 1995b). This tactic is seldom criticized in international forums. However, some citizen observers are quick to condemn their own states and international bodies for failing to intervene to defend human rights abroad. In response to gender discrimination and other human rights abuses, transnational social movements have mobilized to focus attention on and channel collective action against these behaviors and policies. The economic dependence of developing countries on transnational institutions whose political agendas support women's rights amplifies the efforts of these movements. These trends highlight the consequences of state collapse, including declines in state legitimacy, and demonstrate a reordering of loyalties and efforts toward more direct involvement by individuals and nonstate corporate actors in international and transnational politics.

Gender is one of the axes around which this reordering is taking place as proponents of change implement a new ethic of intervention and thus a different understanding of sovereignty and international relations. The range and number of nongovernmental organizations represented at international conferences, such as the September 1995 United Nations Fourth World Conference on Women held in Beijing, show the rising importance of gender in the development of structures and strategies contesting the dominance of states over decisions affecting citizens and their rights. The ideologies of such groups based in the Middle East span the ideological spectrum from feminism to fundamentalism (Crossette 1996, 3). This diversity argues for the state to adopt the role of arbiter rather than partisan, to embrace positive sovereignty and participatory politics to preserve its own authority as well as to protect its citizens and ameliorate conflict. The demands of movement activists will continue to be made either way, propelling both the theory and the practice of citizenship toward fundamental change in the Middle East and elsewhere.

5

Citizenship and International Human Rights Law

Status, Evolution, and Challenges

ASBJØRN EIDE

Allocation of Citizenship—
A Matter for International Law?

EACH STATE DETERMINES under its own laws who its nationals are, but the state is far from free to set whatever rules it wants. Increasingly stringent standards are set by international law. The dominant view for a long time was that the allocation of nationality was purely a matter for domestic jurisdiction and legislation. This is now changing. Although the state can still set its own laws in those areas, principles and rules have recently emerged in international law containing requirements for domestic legislation regarding the allocation of nationality and citizenship to individuals. The main cause of change is the dynamic development of international human rights law, which is redefining the basic character of international law. The process of change is still in its early stages, however, and considerable controversies remain concerning the scope of regulation in international law. Important legislative efforts have been made in recent years,[1] and the International Law Commission of the United Nations is presently preparing a set of articles on nationality in relation to state succession, where human rights considera-

1. The most recent international document is the European Convention on Nationality, adopted by the Council of Europe and opened for signature in 1997.

tions are taken into account.[2] This chapter explores the evolution and its implications.[3]

The Two Faces of International Law

For purposes of analysis, contemporary international law can be seen partly as *interstate law* and partly as the *common law of states*. As interstate law, it regulates relations between states; as the common law of states, it contains principles and rules to be applied inside all societies. International human rights law now covers part of the field traditionally covered in national constitutions.[4] The most important component of the common law of states is the law of universal human rights. This law does not regulate matters between states but contains universal requirements for the domestic legal order of every state.

International law as it was understood for about 150 years, from about 1800 to 1945, was almost exclusively an interstate law.[5] It developed as a consequence of the emergence and proliferation of nation-states. Its logic was based on the notion of state sovereignty; whatever international rules there were reflected the self-interest of sovereign states to coexist peacefully. It regulated issues of relevance for interstate relations and served as a basis for solving disputes between states. It was usually defined as the law that governed relations between states. Only states were subjects of international law in the sense that only they had rights and duties under that law.

International law was quite distinct from domestic law. States recognized each other's sovereignty, which was understood to give them full freedom to determine their own domestic legislation, but the states developed rules—partly through practice and partly through formal agreements called

2. See Vaclav Mikulka, Special Rapporteur, International Law Commission, *Third Report on Nationality in Relation to the Succession of States*, UN Doc. A/CN.4/480, 27 February 1997.

3. Significant contributions to the study of the human rights impact on nationality or citizenship can be found in Chan (1991), Donner (1994), Schram and Ziemele (1999), and Ziemele (1998).

4. International human rights laws cover and expand what in the past and often also in the present are contained in national constitutions as "bills of rights" or "guarantees for the individual." An increasing number of national constitutions give priority to international human rights law over national law.

5. What follows in the text is a highly condensed description of dominant conceptions during the period referred to, glossing over the considerable developments taking place during that period, which would require a much more nuanced analysis if space had allowed. For the development of nineteenth-century conceptions of international law, see, in particular, David Kennedy (1996), and for the period between World War I and World War II, see Nathanial Berman (1993).

treaties—to determine the extent and limits of jurisdiction held by sovereign states over territory and persons. When domestic law or its implementation caused harm to other states, the latter were not necessarily bound to respect the domestic law of the other state. A major function of international law was to resolve disputes that might arise in such cases.

Until the emergence of the League of Nations after World War I, there existed no central authority to legislate, administrate, or even adjudicate traditional law. A modest beginning was made with the league and in particular with the Permanent Court of International Justice (PCIJ), but these were only minor modifications of an otherwise thoroughly decentralized legal system. It has been described as a horizontal law because its impact depended on the willingness of reciprocal self-limitation by states.

Although much of the traditional interstate law remains operative today, it has been significantly expanded in scope and has undergone substantial institutional development. Two major phenomena have reflected and contributed to these changes: the enormous growth in intergovernmental organizations, which have become necessary to regulate the expanding areas of cooperation between states, and the introduction of human rights into international law.

International human rights law is not interstate law regulating matters of disputes between states, but constitutes the core element of the emerging common law of states. It establishes a set of universal requirements for the legal and administrative order of every state. Matters previously within the domestic jurisdiction of each state have now become subjects of international concern and regulation. International supervisory bodies have emerged to push for compliance with universal norms.

The process of change in the basic logic of international law started with the adoption of the United Nations Charter in 1945 and was given direction by the adoption of the Universal Declaration of Human Rights in 1948. Human rights law now stands as the most dynamic part of international law, fundamentally different from traditional branches of international law. In few areas can this difference be observed so clearly as in citizenship issues and the treatment of noncitizens.

International human rights law is built on the Universal Declaration of Human Rights (UDHR). A great number of conventions and declarations have been adopted at the global and regional level to give substance and detail to the UDHR. It is a law in the making, and its full implications have not yet been realized. One of the most important features of the UDHR is its insistence on popular sovereignty, or democracy. Article 21(3) reads: "The will of the people shall be the basis of the authority of government; this will shall be expressed in periodic and genuine elections which shall be by universal and equal suffrage and shall be held by secret vote or by equivalent free voting procedures." This raises the questions: Who forms "the people," and when is the suffrage universal? These questions are fundamental to the operation of democracy, which is deeply affected by the citizenship legislation, which in turn is one of the reasons why human rights law and citizenship regulation interact.

Nationality Versus Citizenship: A First Semantic Excursion

Semantics and substance sometimes get confused. The two words *national* and *citizen* are often used as synonyms, but they are at other times used as separate concepts with different meanings. It is not always clear what is intended. This ambiguity affects discourse on the subject. In the English-language doctrine of international law, the word *citizen* is rarely encountered; there is—at least until recently—an almost exclusive reference to *nationality.* To complicate matters further, these terms have different meanings in legal and in social sciences.

The focus in this chapter is on legal usage. Unless otherwise stated, the words *national* and *nationality* refer to a legal relationship between a person and a state. The nature of that legal relationship is examined further below. The word *national* as used in international law does not indicate the ethnic origin of the person. A Palestinian Arab can therefore be an Israeli national; a Sami can be a Norwegian national.[6]

In another widespread usage, mainly in nonlegal contexts, *nationality* is used to denote an ethnonational identity. The Tamil Tigers in Sri Lanka claim that the Tamils there constitute "a nation without a state"; Kurds similarly claim that they form a "nation without a state," and their members would then define themselves to be of Tamil or Kurdish "nationality."

In some societies, the ethnic approach to nationality was given legal consequences. The former Soviet Union and former Yugoslavia were designated "multinational states," with a meaning quite different from the Western notion of *multinational*—for example, in the term *multinational corporations.* The USSR and former Yugoslavia were called multinational because of the existence inside their territory of several *titular nationalities,* ethnonational groups that were assigned to particular union republics. The titular nationality of Georgia were the Georgians, in Armenia the Armenians, and so on. The designation was also used at the lower level of territorial subdivision: in

6. For example, the European Convention on Nationality, Article 2, Definitions, reads: "For the purpose of this Convention: 'nationality' means the legal bond between a person and a State and does not indicate the person's ethnic origin."

Georgia, there were autonomous areas for the Ossetians, the Abkhazians, the Adjarians, and so on in many other places.

For the purposes of international relations, as long as the USSR existed, they were all nationals of the Soviet Union, whatever titular nationality they belonged to. So it was also for the Yugoslavs, but for internal usage there existed a second-level citizenship that was not linked to ethnicity.[7] For the purposes of international law, the ethnonational link is generally irrelevant: a national of a country is a person who is held to be a subject in or member of a sovereign state.

Having made clear the distinction between legal and social science or anthropological usages of the word *national,* we should now turn to the next source of confusion: the ambiguity in legal usage of the words *national* and *citizen.* The analysis of the relationship between those words can best be done after an explanation of the evolution of international law, on the one hand, and of human rights instruments, on the other.

Pre-1945 International Law and Disputes over Nationality

The evolution of what is generally called international law has gone through several stages.[8] In very general terms, three stages can be identified: the first or "classic" stage is the period from the sixteenth century to the Napoleonic wars; the second stage starts with the end of the Napoleonic wars and ends with World War II; and the third stage—in which we still live—starts with the adoption of the United Nations Charter.

The first of these stages was the period of intellectual exploration and systematization during the transition from the medieval notions of a universal law to the emergence and consolidation of what is loosely called nationstates. During this period, a combination was made of logic from natural law and reflections about the requirements of the emerging society of sovereign states.[9]

The second stage, starting at the end of the Napoleonic wars and finding its clearest articulation during the second part of the nineteenth century and the first part of the twentieth century, was characterized by two things: a rejection of natural law reasoning in favor of positivism and a reliance on the prevalence of sovereign, independent states bound by no other rules than

---

7. For a description, see UNHCR (1997).

8. More precisely, the stages refer to the way in which international law has been understood and presented by the doctrine, which to various degrees has been affected by state practice and in turn has influenced state practice.

9. The great authors of the time were Gentili, Vitoria, Suarez, Grotius, Pufendorff, and Vattel.

those to which they had given their consent, be it by participation in the creation of custom or by formal agreements. In this essay, I refer to this second stage in the evolution of international law as *traditional international law*.[10]

In regard to questions of nationality, the position in traditional international law can best be exemplified by a statement in the advisory opinion given in 1923 by the Permanent Court of International Justice concerning the Tunis and Morocco Nationality Decrees:

> The question whether a certain matter is or is not solely within the jurisdiction of a State is an essentially relative question; it depends upon the development of intentional relations. Thus, in the present state of international law, questions of nationality are, in opinion of this Court, in principle within this reserved domain. (PCIJ 1923, ser. B, no. 4)

In this statement, two points are made: one, that questions of nationality were, in 1923, in principle solely within the domestic jurisdiction of states, and two, that the answer to the question whether something is solely within the domestic jurisdiction of a state can change when international relations change. And indeed they have changed substantially since 1923. Since then, human rights law has become a part of international law, and international relations and many international institutions have been established to monitor and promote human rights performance. As a consequence, allocation of citizenship is no longer solely within the domestic jurisdiction of states.

A brief examination of approaches to nationality and its significance for traditional international law can illustrate the differences to the present time.

Determination of the nationality of a given person was significant at that point in two respects: a state could impose duties on its nationals to a much larger extent than it could do on nonnationals, and the state could protect its own nationals abroad if it so wanted. The right of protection was not a right of the individual but of the state concerned, which could use it at its discretion.

The question of nationality was important as an aspect of the law of intervention. During the nineteenth and early twentieth centuries, Western states faced weaker states or other political units—particularly in Latin America, the former Ottoman Empire, and later the Balkans, Turkey, and also parts of Asia. A major issue was the scope and limits of intervention.

---

10. The second stage could be subdivided into the period up to the peace conferences in 1899–1909, at which time the history of multilateral agreements seriously started; then the period from the beginning of the twentieth century until the time of the League of Nations, followed by the period of extreme nationalism until World War II.

Western states asserted a right to protect their nationals abroad by insisting on the application to such persons of what they called minimum standards of civilization. Seen from its positive aspects, this asserted right can be considered a precursor of international protection of human rights because the focus was on the protection of the life, liberty, dignity, and property of their nationals abroad.

Very often in practice, however, the protection by Western states of their nationals abroad was related to financial activities (Nussbaum 1954 215–18). Private, Western investors and creditors operating in Latin America, the Balkans, or the Middle East sometimes discovered that the foreign state that had borrowed or guaranteed bonded loans was unable or unwilling to live up to its obligations. In such cases, Western creditors called on their own government to protect their property. The inequality in power relations resulted sometimes in direct international financial control being imposed on the country concerned (for example, Tunisia 1869, Egypt 1876, Turkey 1880) or in direct, military intervention (such as that of Napoleon III in Mexico in 1861).

Latin American countries led the opposition to these interventions and promoted the so-called Calvo doctrine, according to which a foreign creditor would not be entitled to a higher protection than that of domestic creditors who had to submit to the domestic rules and regulations applicable to such a situation.

A legal question that sometimes arose was whether the person protected by a given Western state was indeed a national of that country. Although there was general agreement that every state was entitled to legislate in nationality matters and thereby to determine the allocation of nationality, international law had to determine whether that allocation had to be respected by other states and by the international community through its organizations. In order to settle this question, international arbitrations and tribunals had to grapple with the question of the criteria by which other states had to accept the nationality legislation of the country that sought to protect the person concerned. This is where international law developed the notion of the need of a genuine link between the state and the person claimed to be its national.

This issue appeared in the Nottebohm case, which arose from a pre-1945 dispute dealt with by the International Court of Justice in 1955. Although I can discuss the case only briefly here, it is extensively covered in existing doctrine (Brownlie 1990, 397; Donner 1994, 59). The state of Liechtenstein brought a case against Guatemala to the International Court of Justice for restitution of property wrongfully seized by the government of Guatemala between 1942 and 1946 from a person who was claimed to be a national of Liechtenstein. The question before the court was whether Guatemala had to treat Mr. Nottebohm as a Liechtenstein national. Mr. Nottebohm was born in Germany and lived there until he migrated to Guatemala, at twenty-four years of age, in 1905. He was arrested by Guatemalan authorities in 1943. His property had been seized the year before because Guatemala was nominally at war with Germany and considered him an enemy national.

In 1939, before a state of war existed between the two countries, Mr. Nottebohm had been granted the nationality of Liechtenstein and renounced his German nationality. The issue in the case was whether Guatemala was obliged to respect the Liechtenstein act in bestowing on him its nationality. The International Court of Justice (1955) decided by eleven to three that Nottebohm's Liechtenstein nationality had been granted under such circumstances that Liechenstein was not entitled to extend its protection to him. The court found that the factual connection between Liechtenstein (where Nottebohm had never lived) and Nottebohm was not sufficiently close. The court then presented its own view of what constitutes nationality: "Nationality is a legal bond having as its basis a social fact of attachment, a genuine connection of existence, interests and sentiments, together with the existence of reciprocal rights and duties" (23). This view has since been referred to as the requirement of a genuine link. It can also be formulated in a different way: a state cannot at its own discretion and at random extend its own nationality to persons of foreign nationality living in other states, even if the beneficiary accepts it.

Another set of questions with which pre–World War II international law had to grapple involved disputes over nationality in cases of state succession. When the state exercising sovereign power over a populated territory was replaced by another state, there arose the question of the nationality of persons domiciled in the transferred territory. Traditional law perceived this mainly as a question of the allocation of subjects between the two states involved. International law was concerned with the relation of the states involved, not with the human beings affected.

The general approach was that when the territory was the subject of a change of sovereignty, the inhabitants of the territory were presumed automatically to become the "nationals" of the new sovereign. Gradually, however, it was accepted that if such persons refused to accept the new nationality, they could keep their previous one, but this would often require that they leave the transferred territory.

The normal effect of the annexation of territory by the British Crown, whatever may be the source or cause of the annexation, for instance, a treaty of

cession, or subjugation by war, is that the nationals of the State whose territory is annexed, if resident thereon, become British subjects; in practice, however, it is becoming increasingly common to give such nationals an option,
either by the treaty of cession or by an Act of Parliament, to leave the territory
and retain their nationality. (Lord McNair, quoted by Brownlie 1990, 662, n.
35)

As further illustrations, some of the peace settlements after World War I can
be mentioned. The Minorities Treaty regarding Poland signed at Versailles
provided in Article 4 that

Poland admits and declares to be Polish nationals ipso facto and without the
requirements of any formality persons of German, Austrian, Hungarian or
Russian nationality who were born in the said territory of parents habitually
resident there, even if at the date of the coming into force of the present
Treaty they are not themselves habitually resident there. Nevertheless, within
two years after coming into force of the present Treaty, these persons may
make a declaration before the competent Polish authorities in the country in
which they are resident stating that they abandon Polish nationality, and they
will then cease to be considered as Polish nationals. In this connection a declaration by a husband will cover his wife and a declaration by parents will cover
their children under 18 years of age. (Brownlie 1990, 662, n. 35)

Article 6 states:

All persons born in Polish territory who are not born nationals of another
State shall ipso facto become Polish nationals. (Brownlie 1990, 662, n. 35)

As pointed out by Brownlie (1990), other peace treaties after World War
I—including those of St Germain, Trianon, and Paris—had similar provisions (662).

The Origin of Human Rights Law
and its Significance for Citizenship

Because human rights in the post–World War II period gradually have
been made universal, the content of the term *nationality* has also changed
from the attribution of subjects between states to a substantive concept. Its
content is better expressed by the term *citizenship* than by *nationality*, notwithstanding the fact that the latter term remains the most commonly used
in international law. Before I discuss the impact of human rights on international law after World War II, it may be useful to explore the conceptualiza-

tion of citizenship in the formative period of human rights at the national level, or more precisely "the rights of man."

The close link between the development of the concept of human rights and of citizenship is captured in the title of the French Declaration of 1789—"Declaration of the Rights of Man and the Citizen." In that year, the main actors in the French Revolution were still cosmopolitan in outlook. They did not initially make much of a difference between the rights of man in general and the rights of the citizen in particular. Most of the rights were to be enjoyed by every man (it was still a male-oriented approach), whereas some other rights—mainly those related to political participation— were to be enjoyed by citizens only.

This is not the place to review at length the emergence and evolution of the concept and function of citizenship in the Western tradition, but some attention should be given to the fact that the modern concept of citizenship was born with the French Revolution and coincided to a large extent with the institution of citizenship in Britain and the United States. To the east in Europe the situation was quite different, starting with Germany.

There were, of course, earlier roots. Concepts of citizenship were known in Greek and Roman times, but disappeared during the medieval period until the beginning of the modern period. Its modern revival took place as a part of a transition from feudalism and was initially literally a question of citizenship, where *citizen* is derived from *city*. The initial citizens were the members of the networks of corporations within the emerging cities. The burghers (those living inside the city wall) had to some extent disengaged themselves from the feudal order dominating the rural communities surrounding them, where the systems of status and inequalities still remained intact. In England, the term *citizen* originally referred to a member of a borough or local municipal corporation, whereas the word *subject* was used to emphasize the individual's subordinate position relative to the monarch or state. The distinction between *subject* and *citizen* is important here: the citizen had rights as well as a corresponding set of duties, whereas the subject simply was the target of the duties and demands imposed by superiors, ultimately the king.

The French Revolution was the watershed in conceptualizing citizenship. Rogers Brubaker (1994) has pointed out that there were four aspects of the French Revolution that together contributed to the content and function that citizenship has in our time. One was the bourgeois aspect of the revolution, the consolidation and extension of the freedoms required for the functioning of the bourgeoisie, the burghers who no longer were content to remain inside the city walls but whose economic and professional activities required the elimination of the many blockages of feudalism. *Citoyeneté* or citizenship was first and foremost about freedoms and equality before the law and about the right to private property—the key challenges of the burghers against the vestiges of the feudal society, aristocratic privileges and royal arbitrariness. This corresponds to the first stage in the achievement of civil rights and property rights in Britain, where the "Glorious Revolution" in 1688–89 was an early high point and in which the theory of social contract as spelled out by John Locke played such an essential role.

The second aspect contributing to citizenship was the French Revolution as a democratic revolution through its insistence on political rights. Urban citizenship, in the sense of membership in the decision-making bodies within the cities, was already known but had been on the decline due to the efforts by the centralizing, territorially oriented French monarch to eliminate the privileges of the cities. Brubaker (1994) shows that through the democratic aspect of revolution, political rights were sought to be institutionalized as citizenship rights, transposing them from the plane of the city-state to that of the nation-state and transforming them from a privilege to a general right. He does admit that it was not a full-fledged democratic revolution because women were excluded from politics, and the male citizens were divided into *citoyens actifs* (who were given political rights) and *citoyens passifs* (who were not). A similar dichotomy had emerged in Britain. John Locke, it will be remembered, although an early advocate of "peoples' sovereignty," had also envisaged that only holders of property should form part of the collective "sovereign" and thus have political rights, and he appears to have been concerned with only male property owners.

In spite of its limitations, the French Revolution was decisive for the development of the modern institution of national citizenship by linking civil rights to political rights. It is another matter that it still took a long struggle in France during the nineteenth century to effectively ensure political rights for all adult men, and for women it was not obtained until the first part of the twentieth century.

A widely used reference is to T. H. Marshall's seminal lectures, "Citizenship and Social Class" (1950), in which he presented his view of the historical development in the West of those attributes vital to effective citizenship. His focus was on the internal, integrating aspects of the evolution of citizenship. He distinguished three stages in this evolution, tracing the formative period in the life of each of these types of rights to a different century.

Civil rights had been the great achievement of the eighteenth century, laying the foundation of the notion of equality of all members of society before the law; political rights were the principal achievement of the nineteenth century by allowing for increasingly broader participation in the exercise of sovereign power; social rights were the contribution of the twentieth century, making it possible for all members of society to enjoy satisfactory conditions of life. This chronology gave a fairly correct description of the British development, but does not quite correspond to the evolution in other countries, such as Germany or those farther to the east of Europe.[11]

What nevertheless makes T. H. Marshall particularly interesting and of particular relevance to this paper is that the three components he described—civil, political, and social—formed the main building blocks for the comprehensive system of rights contained in the UDHR of 1948. Civil, political, economic, social, and cultural rights have been made into a package of international human rights, and the different rights are interdependent and therefore indivisible.[12] This is a point repeatedly made by the United Nations, in particular at the World Conference on Human Rights held in Vienna under United Nations auspices in 1993.

Implicit in the description by Marshall is that the three elements have formed part of a long process of social integration. One of the main functions of the contemporary system of human rights is to include, to equalize, to protect. The relationship between human rights and citizenship still has to be examined, however.

The Citizen and the Alien

The consolidation of the notion of citizenship as a *national* bond between the government and the inhabitants also has a reverse side: to exclude, to draw lines between those who are inside and those who are outside. The older notion of citizenship had functioned as a criterion of social exclusion, by dividing the privileged participants from those who were mere subjects of duties. It had served also to distinguish the city-dwellers from the rural population. To illustrate its emergence and significance, a further discussion of the French developments is useful.

The third aspect of the French Revolution discussed by Brubaker (1994) is the national revolution, which T. H. Marshall did not address because it was not relevant to his theme. But its legacy has had great impact on the everyday life of millions throughout the world. Brubaker argues that this aspect was neither intended nor foreseen by those who started the revolution in 1789, but emerged only during the most radical stage of the revolution, in the years 1793–94. It was a move away from the cosmopolitan spirit prevailing during the early years, when "like-minded foreigners" such

11. The continued relevance of T. S. Marshall's analysis of citizenship is discussed in Bulmer and Rees (1996).

12. See Eide (1998).

as Thomas Paine were made citizens of France in recognition of the fact that they shared the same spirit of freedom and equality as the French revolutionary. During those early years, the French Revolution was portrayed as the beginning of a European-wide revolution, in collaboration with the newly independent United States, for freedom and equality for all.

Due in part to its missionary zeal to undermine the conservative and aristocratic old regimes of Europe, France soon became embroiled in armed conflict first with the monarchies of Austria and Prussia, and soon with most of the European powers. Inside France this resulted, by 1793–94, in the outburst of a xenophobic nationalism produced partly from the wars with external enemies and partly from factional struggles inside France. A climate of extreme suspicion and fear engulfed France—suspicion of any alien but also of internal factions that might knowingly or unknowingly be in the service of external enemies. As a consequence, the French Convention adopted a series of measures specifically against foreigners, establishing a system of registration and surveillance, ordering expulsions, and excluding foreigners from all political functions. The transition from an exceptionally cosmopolitan atmosphere to raving xenophobia took a period of only four or five years.

It was in this context that the distinction between the French and the non-French was made much clearer and rigid than it ever had been before. Whereas the bourgeois and the political revolutions had highlighted the integrative function and the inclusiveness of the citizenship concept by insisting on freedom and equality, the national revolution emphasized its excluding function, by requiring clear demarcation between those who were French citizens and those who were not. Thus, according to Brubaker (1992), "the revolution created a legal and a moral frontier between members of different nation-states. Abolishing legal and moral boundaries and divisions inside the nation-state (France), it crystallized legal and moral boundaries and division between nation-states. Thus, it engendered both the modern nation-state and modern nationalism" (48).[13]

There was, according to Brubaker, a fourth aspect of the French Revolution that also influenced the citizenship conception and its function: the bureaucratic revolution. The French Revolution abolished the vestiges of

13. On this point, I would prefer to replace the word *nation-state* with *state-nation*. I would also prefer to say that the French Revolution engendered one form of nationalism, which I would call *civic nationalism*, to be contrasted with *ethnonationalism*. France became a state-nation in the sense that it took the existing boundaries of the state as its basis and sought to include everyone within it as part of the nation, irrespective of ethnic or religious background. The nationalism was civic in the sense that it at least in principle was sought to be built on the implementation of human rights as the substantive content of citizenship.

the seigneurial system—the complex sets of privileges, the many different sets of jurisdictions—and thereby created an immediate link between the state and the citizen, "freed from the various separate, local, urban, and provincial powers in order to create the civil unity of the state," as Karl Marx expressed it (quoted in Brubaker 1992, 98). This made possible direct taxation, required military service from every citizen, and a statewide common regulation of foreigners.

The French Revolution generated the upsurge of a national patriotism that led to the emergence of a modern mass army and that was skillfully exploited by Napoléon in his conquest of large parts of Europe. That, in turn, contributed to the development of another form of nationalism—the ethnonationalist wave, which started during the early years of the nineteenth century and engulfed much of Central and Eastern Europe in the latter part of that century, culminating with World War I and the interlude of the two interwar decades before World War II was unleashed. This ethnonationalism served both to unite and to split. It served to unite areas that had a relatively common culture and ethnicity, but that had evolved as separate feudal power holders or city-states (Germany, Italy)[14] or had been split between different occupants (Poland). It served to split empires with a multiethnic composition (the Ottoman and the Habsburg empires, which were split during a long, drawn out process during the nineteenth century and the first part of the twentieth century, culminating during World War I.) The multiethnic tsarist empire was also rent by ethnonationalist sentiments, but kept them under control until the Russian Revolution, at which time it shed the Baltic area and Bessarabia. The rest was, in the words of Ernest Gellner, "placed under an entirely new management" (1994, 30) with the name Soviet Union, which reoccupied the Baltic states and Bessarabia (now Moldavia) but finally dissolved at the end of 1991.

Ethnonationalism in Central and Eastern Europe can be seen as late aftereffects of the French Revolution and the Napoleonic wars. Full-fledged ethnonationalist ideology has three components. First, nations are to be defined in ethnic terms, referring to a common past history, tradition, and preferably a common language. Second, a nation should have its own state, so the society composing a state should as far as possible be congruent with the nation. Third, the loyalty of members of nations to their nation should override all other loyalties.

Ethnonationalism engenders its own approach to citizenship, creating serious obstacles to the implementation of human rights and in particular to

---

14. Germany was gradually united into one country in mid–nineteenth century under Prussian leadership (Bismarck). The unification of Italy took place at about the same time.

the allocation of citizenship on an impartial basis. It emphasizes state bor-
derlines on grounds of ethnicity: ethnonationalists would prefer that only
members of the same ethnic group should have a place within the territory.
At its worst, this preference gives rise to ethnic cleansing, in open or more
disguised forms. Because massive ethnic cleansing is strongly condemned in
our time, alternative modes of "cleansing" are utilized that create special
difficulties for members of ethnic groups to obtain citizenship. Ethnonationalist preferences also express themselves in selectivity in subsequent allocation of citizenship, which is given by preference to persons of the same
ethnic group, even to the extent that some of them are offered a direct and
immediate right to citizenship (Germany, Israel), whereas others at best
have to go through long and difficult processes of naturalization and in
some places do not obtain citizenship even if they have lived within the
territory for generations.

Ethnonationalists are less concerned with the substantive content of citizenship than with its function as criteria for exclusion. In some cases, they
also make use of a differentiation in the content of citizenship, reserving the
broadest rights to those persons belonging to the hegemonic ethnic groups
but presenting a more narrow set of rights to the others. Israel is one of the
clearest cases in point, but certainly not the only one. This practice flies in
the face of the principle of equality and nondiscrimination, which is at the
very foundation of modern human rights.

With regard to the addition of new citizens after the state has been established, civic nationalism normally applies the principle of jus soli: acquisition
of citizenship by everyone born on the territory.[15] Those states that fall in the
ethnonationalist camp tend to use the principle of jus sanguinis, where the
right to citizenship generally is limited to the children of those who already
are citizens. Moderate forms of ethnonationalism have flexible combinations
of jus sanguinis and jus soli: they make it a nearly absolute right for persons
who are born in the country to obtain citizenship on request when they
reach maturity, provided they in the meantime have had a period of uninterrupted residence (in the case of Norway, the required length of residence is
seven years). Most of these forms also allow for the naturalization of other
persons after a period of residence. A few jus sanguinis countries, such as
Germany and Switzerland, do not extend an automatic right to citizenship
to anyone solely on the basis of long residence. There are in those countries
persons of the second and even third generation after immigration who are
unable to obtain citizenship.

---

15. Some limitations are nearly everywhere applied, however.

Semantics Revisited: Explaining the Possible
Difference between *National* and *Citizen*

Having observed that traditional international law was concerned mainly with which country a person "belonged to" in cases of dispute with other states, we can better understand the limited scope of the concept behind the term *national* during that time. Before an act of the U.S. Congress made them citizens, for example, American Indians were sometimes referred to as *noncitizen nationals.* They were nationals for the purpose of international law, but they were not U.S. citizens: they lived in reservations with extended self-government. They were not taxed under U.S. law; they did not have the normal rights of U.S. citizens, nor did they have the same duties. The category of noncitizen nationals is still used in U.S. law.

There are also other states that in their legislation have divided their subjects into those who have a higher or privileged status, designated *citizens,* and those who are nationals but not citizens. This has happened mainly in the legislation of (former) colonial metropoles or other states that have had dependencies, protectorates, or other non-self-governing entities under their control. Thus, in the case of the United Kingdom, the inhabitants of dependencies, whatever their internal status under the British Nationality Act of 1981, are considered to have the status of British nationals for purposes of international law. In the past, Italian law also knew a distinction between citizens and colonial subjects, the latter being regarded as nationals in the international sphere.[16]

The special situations described above appear to have arisen in situations of colonial relations or dependencies, where the inhabitants were not allocated full political rights in the core territory of the sovereign country. They could not vote in the British or U.S. national election, they could not hold public office there, and in some cases they did not even have the right of abode there, but they were treated as nationals for the purposes of classical international law—i.e., to make it clear that they "belonged" to the British or the Americans as the case might be and that the right of diplomatic protection would be applied to them.

In these rather special cases, nationality is distinguished from citizenship, but these situations are gradually disappearing because they occur mainly in relation to nonself-governing territories (NSGTs). It has been one of the most consistent—and successful—activities of the United Nations to bring to an end in almost all cases the status of NSGT, which is incompatible with

16. See further Brownlie (1990, 396).

the principle of self-determination. Most of the territories defined by the United Nations as NSGTs have during the process of decolonization either become independent states or have merged in full rights with a sovereign states. The category of noncitizen nationals is by now a marginal phenomena and is therefore not further examined here.

With the introduction of modern human rights law, the emphasis is different: Which individuals should, according to international law, have full rights within the country in which he or she lives? This issue is better covered by the concept of citizenship than by nationality. When the word "nationality" is used in international human rights law, it can be assumed that the word *national* is synonymous with *citizen* unless there is clear evidence to the contrary.

International Human Rights Law and Reduction in the Legal Significance of Citizenship

The introduction of human rights law has reduced the difference, under international law, between the rights of citizens and noncitizens. In general terms, states are obliged to ensure the enjoyment of human rights for everyone within their territories and subject to their jurisdiction. The UDHR states that the rights contained within it shall be enjoyed by everyone, without discrimination; thus, they shall be enjoyed also by noncitizens. The question still remains: In regard to specific persons, which government has the responsibility to ensure the enjoyment of human rights? In very general terms, it can be argued that every state holds the trust, under international law, to secure human rights for those who live on its territory. The United Nations Covenant on Civil and Political Rights (CCPR), Article 2(1) reads as follows:

> Each State Party to the present Covenant undertakes to respect and to ensure to all individuals within its territory and subject to its jurisdiction the rights recognized in the present Covenant, without distinction of any kind, such as race, colour, sex, language, religion, political or other opinion, national or social origin, property, birth or other status.

The state shall ensure the rights contained in the covenant for all individuals (not only citizens) within the territory of the state, and there shall be no distinction made in the enjoyment of these rights. There are some important exceptions, but the main rule should be clear: citizens and noncitizens should enjoy most of the civil rights contained in that covenant without distinctions being made.

The European Convention for the Protection of Human Rights and Fundamental Freedoms has the same scope: Article 1 states that the state parties shall secure to everyone within their jurisdiction the rights and freedoms defined in the convention.

The Convention on the Rights of the Child is even more explicit in its Article 2(1):

> States Parties shall respect and ensure the rights set forth in the present Convention to each child within their jurisdiction without discrimination of any kind, irrespective of the child's or his or her parent's or legal guardian's race, colour, sex, language, religion, political or other opinion, national, ethnic or social origin, property, disability, birth or other status.

The International Covenant on Economic, Social, and Cultural Rights, Article 2(2), requires the state parties to guarantee that the rights contained in the covenant will be exercised without discrimination on grounds listed there, such as national or social origin. Article 2(3), however, contains an exception: *developing* countries can determine to what extent they would guarantee for nonnationals the economic rights contained in the covenant. Antithetically, no such distinction can be made by industrialized countries. Other factors, such as legal residence, work permit, and other elements may be relevant, but not citizenship as such.

Citizenship Still Matters

Although the UDHR established that human rights were to be enjoyed by everyone, at least two of its articles contain restricting language—Article 21 on political rights and Article 13 on the right to freedom of movement.

Article 21, paragraph 1, of the UDHR and Article 25(c) of the International Covenant on Civil and Political Rights deal with the right to take part in the government of *one's country,* directly or through freely chosen representatives. Equally important is the right of everyone to equal access to public service in one's own country.

The enjoyment of human rights is precarious when the person does not have the citizenship of her or his country of residence. Political rights are among the most precious of all human rights because their enjoyment makes it possible to influence laws and policies of the country and therefore also to be able to protect one's own interests and value. When large numbers of individuals belonging to minorities are denied citizenship, it is difficult to ensure reasonable protection for them. Such a denial can also seriously weaken the functioning of democracy, which is supposed to ensure peaceful settlement of conflicts through effective participation by all groups.

Article 13 of the UDHR and Article 12 of the CCPR deal with freedom of movement. Everyone, citizen or not, is entitled to move freely and reside within the borders of the state and to leave any country, including his own, but the right to enter a country is limited to "his own country." This latter stipulation would at first sight be understood to limit the right of entry as a human right to citizens only, but it cannot be understood in so rigid a way. The Human Rights Committee, which is the official body supervising the implementation of the covenant, has noted that in some circumstances a noncitizen may enjoy protection under Article 12 of the covenant. For example, considerations of nondiscrimination, prohibition of inhuman treatment, and respect for family ties will have to be taken into account.

It can probably also be argued that principles of legality and due process would have to be fulfilled. Noncitizens who seek return can be denied the right to reenter only within the same limits as they can be expelled, as set out in CCPR Article 13; consequently, the denial of a right to return would have to be based on preexisting law, and the person should have the right to submit reasons against the denial of reentrance, to have the case reviewed, and to be represented before the competent authority designed for this purpose. These requirements are set out in greater detail in Protocol 7 to the European Convention for the Protection of Human Rights and Fundamental Freedoms and would seem to be a reasonable interpretation of the general right to an effective remedy.

Ambiguities in international human rights law exist also with regard to protection of minorities: Are such rights limited to citizens only, or are they also given to resident noncitizens? In national practice, they are often limited to citizens, but this is hardly in conformity with international human rights law. Article 27 of the International Covenant on Civil and Political Rights dealing with rights of persons belonging to minorities does not have restrictive language that can be interpreted to limit its application to citizens. Consequently, the general rule in Article 2 of this covenant must apply, under which the rights have to be secured to everyone in the territory and subject to the jurisdiction of the state. The United Nations Human Rights Committee has therefore made it clear that Article 27 confers rights on all persons belonging to minorities that "exist" in a state party and that these rights therefore apply also to noncitizens.

In sum, what is clear is that political rights *can* be limited to citizens only, though every state is free to be more generous than that. The right to return is more precarious for resident noncitizens than for citizens. Whereas citizens normally cannot be expelled from her or his country, noncitizens are at greater risk, but there is no absolute freedom of states to expel noncitizens, and persons who have obtained some form of permanent or lasting residence can be expelled only under rather stringent conditions.

A Human Right to Citizenship?

Having noted that most human rights shall be ensured to everyone within the jurisdiction of the state but that some important rights are limited to citizens, we must examine the next question: Is there a human right to obtain citizenship?

The first international instrument directly addressing this question was the UDHR itself. Its Article 15 reads: "Everyone has the right to a nationality. No one shall be arbitrarily deprived of his nationality, nor denied the right to change his nationality." It should be noted that this article has not been followed up with any correspondingly comprehensive provision in legally binding conventions. Nevertheless, Article 15 is of great importance in indicating the evolution of the human rights approach to nationality.[17]

Before we take a closer look at Article 15, mention should be made of various recent international instruments with a bearing on nationality.

The Convention on the Elimination of All Forms of Discrimination against Women, adopted in 1979, deals in Article 9 with the question of nationality. The states parties undertake to grant men and women equal rights to acquire, change, or retain their nationality. They shall ensure in particular that neither marriage to an alien nor change of nationality by a husband during marriage shall automatically change the nationality of a wife, render her stateless, or force upon her the nationality of the husband.

Article 1 of the Convention on the Nationality of Married Women states that:

> Each Contracting State agrees that neither the celebration nor the dissolution of a marriage between one of its nationals and an alien, nor the change of nationality by the husband during marriage, shall automatically affect the nationality of the wife.

Article 7 of the Convention on the Rights of the Child of 1989 has now become an almost universal instrument, with 191 states parties to it; only two have not yet ratified. Article 7 provides that

---

17. Schram and Ziemele (1999), passim, provides a detailed analysis of Article 15 and its follow-up.

1. The child shall be registered immediately after birth and shall have the right from birth to a name, *the right to acquire a nationality* and, as far as possible, the right to know and be cared for by his or her parents.

2. States Parties shall ensure the implementation of these rights in accordance with their national instruments in this field, *in particular where the child would otherwise be stateless.* [emphasis mine]

At the regional level, the Inter-American Convention on Human Rights of 1978 deals in Article 20 with the right to a nationality:

1. Every person has the right to a nationality.

2. Every person has the right to the nationality of the state in whose territory he was born if he does not have the right to any other nationality.

3. No one shall be arbitrarily deprived of his nationality or of the right to change it.

Regarding *Amendments to the Naturalization Provisions of the Constitution of Costa Rica,* the Inter-American Court of Human Rights in its Advisory Opinion of 1984 concluded that the right to a nationality is an inherent human right recognized in international law.[18]

The Council of Europe adopted in 1997 the European Convention on Nationality, which contains the most updated expression of legal opinion on the right to nationality at the regional level.

Interpretation of Article 15 of the Universal Declaration of Human Rights

Article 15, as the main international provision dealing with the right to nationality from a human rights perspective, must be interpreted in light of the international instruments adopted at global and regional level. It must also be understood in the light of the broad package of rights in the UDHR. As pointed out in the preceding section, it had established that "everyone" is entitled to enjoy the rights contained in the declaration with two major exceptions—political rights (Article 21) and the right to return (Article 13). Article 15 seeks to remedy these exceptions by making it a right in itself to have a nationality and thus to enjoy the complete package of rights, including those of Articles 13 and 21 of the UDHR and of the corresponding provisions in subsequent human rights instruments.

In the interpretation of Article 15, there are at least four issues to be

18. For further discussion of the approach to nationality in human rights law by the Inter-American Court on Human Rights see Chan (1991, 5–6).

discussed: *(a)* the meaning of *nationality* in this context; *(b)* the duty bearer against whom the right to a nationality can be addressed, *(c)* the prohibition of arbitrary deprivation of nationality, and *(d)* the right to change a nationality.

The Meaning of Nationality in Article 15

The ambiguity of the term *nationality* and its relation to *citizenship* has been discussed. When it appears in a human rights text, it is clearly intended to refer to rights rather than to whose subject the person is, and it goes beyond the question of diplomatic protection in international relations. Although admittedly there was some ambiguity in the positions of those who drafted the text, the only reasonable meaning of the word *nationality* in this human rights provision is a right to citizenship.

Which State Is the Duty Bearer?

Although everyone has the right to citizenship, Article 15 does not say citizenship in *which* country or which state is obliged to provide the person with its citizenship. The presumption must be, however, that the duty bearer is the state in which the person lives, unless special factors justify a denial of that right to particular persons. Quite clearly, the normal interest of the individual to a right to nationality is to have the citizenship of the country where that person has chosen to make her or his home.

If a state seeks to implement the UDHR, including Article 15, in good faith but deprives a person of citizenship or denies a request for it by a resident, that state has to show legitimate cause for its exclusion of that person. An exploration of such legitimate causes is therefore in order here.

In practical terms, the question arises in regard to persons who *(a)* already have the citizenship of the state concerned but are in risk of losing it, *(b)* live in a territory that has come under new sovereignty and thus need a new citizenship, *(c)* are stateless, or *(d)* have moved from their countries of citizenship to another country. These issues will be discussed in turn.

The Right to Retain Acquired Citizenship

A citizenship once acquired cannot be arbitrarily withdrawn (UDHR, Article 15, European Convention on Nationality Article 4[c]). Before the era of human rights, citizenship or nationality was sometimes arbitrarily withdrawn, sometimes even on the grounds of race or ethnicity. One of the worst examples is Nazi Germany's German Reich Citizenship Law of 1935, one of the so-called Nuremberg Laws, by which German citizenship was limited to "persons of German or cognate blood." This step was one of the first in the process leading to the Holocaust, affecting Jews, Romanis, and others who did not have "German or cognate blood." It was ethnonationalism at its extreme. Such collective deprivation on ethnic grounds would today be a gross violation of human rights.

Because nationality cannot be arbitrarily withdrawn, there is a need to clarify the conditions under which it can legitimately be withdrawn. Withdrawal can be applied only to individuals and under conditions previously set out in national law. Such law cannot permit withdrawal unless reasonable conditions are met. The most recent formulation of such conditions is found in the European Convention on Nationality, Article 7, which must be considered to reflect the current level of understanding of the human rights requirement of nationality legislation.

Under the European Convention on Nationality, Article 7, withdrawal is permissible only under the following conditions: when nationality has been acquired through fraudulent conduct; when the person voluntarily acquires another nationality; when the person voluntarily takes service in foreign military force; when the person has settled in another country, and there is no genuine link to the previous country; and when the person has shown a conduct that is seriously prejudicial to the vital interests of the state.

The state can, of course, withdraw the citizenship at the request of the person concerned. This follows from the right of everyone to change their citizenship (UDHR, Article 15), which means that the person acquires another citizenship. States are normally not entitled, however, to accept a renunciation of its nationality by a person who would thereby become stateless (European Convention on Nationality, Article 8[1]), which follows also from the general obligation to cooperate in the elimination of statelessness.

Right to Retain Original Citizenship
in Cases of State Succession

A question that has some similarity to withdrawal arises in cases of what in legal terms is called *state succession*—i.e., when a territory is the subject of change of sovereignty. Four situations of state succession can be identified: *(a)* unification of states; *(b)* transfer of part of the territory to another state, *(c)* dissolution of a state and the emergence of several newly independent states, and *(d)* separation of part of the territory to become an independent state. The problems of citizenship arise for the residents of the territory who already were citizens of the previous state.

The first type of does not give rise to doubt: the old citizenship is replaced by citizenship of the unified country. In the other situations, evidence from practice has been that nationality (citizenship) follows the territory. Although residents should have an automatic option of citizenship of the state where his or her territory of residence is included (an issue further discussed below), it is doubtful whether the person concerned also has an option of retaining the original citizenship even if the territory of residence is now under a different state's sovereignty.

Such questions arose frequently in the process of decolonization, where at least some of the inhabitants of the colonies wanted to retain the nationality of the colonial metropole, be it the United Kingdom, France, or another country.

The general presumption has been that nationality follows the territory, which means that the domicile of the person determines the future citizenship, but there have been and continue to be important exceptions where persons are given a right to opt for their previous nationality. Complex situations arose during the process of decolonization. In some cases, a distinction was made between "the indigenous"—those who belonged to the ethnic groups habitually living in the state that now became independent— and those who ethnically originated from the colonial metropolitan country or from other parts of the colonial possessions of the metropole. The latter were given the option to retain their previous nationality, whereas the "indigenous" were denied that option and had to accept the citizenship of the new state.[19]

Because the colonial system is now practically eliminated and had particularities that are not compatible with modern human rights law, it will not be further examined here. The rule of thumb is that the person has the right to become a citizen of the country in which she or he resided at the time of change, but may sometimes have the option to retain the old citizenship. The conditions under which the person can be denied the citizenship of the country of residence are discussed below. The option to retain the old citizenship can be more restrictive and has in practice depended on factors such as the territorial origin or the place of birth of the person concerned. International law has little guidance to give in these matters.

The third type of situation—the total dissolution of a state and the emergence of several newly independent states—is different. Because the country has gone, the old citizenship no longer exists and cannot therefore be re-

---

19. For details on these practices, see Donner (1994). Variations can be observed between the French and Dutch practice of granting independence through treaties (Donner 1994, 274–76) and the British practice that leaves it to the legislation of the newly independent states and U.K. legislation.

tained. Citizenship has to be determined anew for all. As a general rule of thumb, residents will be given the citizenship of the new state in which they live and cannot normally demand to become a citizen of one of the other states emerging out of the dissolution. Such other states are, of course, free to offer their citizenship but are not obliged to do so unless special reasons therefore exist.

Right to Obtain the Citizenship of the State of Residence in Cases of State Succession

Summarizing the practice observed in previous times, Brownlie (1990) concludes that "the evidence is overwhelmingly in support of the view that the population follows the change of sovereignty in matters of nationality" (661–62). He cites as evidence the practice after World War I, including the Versailles and associated treaties, which contained a number of provisions, more or less uniform in content, relating to changes of sovereignty that exhibited all the variations of state succession. He recognizes, however, that there is as yet no rule of international law under which the nationals of the predecessor state automatically acquire the nationality of the successor state because international law cannot have such a direct effect, nor does the practice of states show that this inevitably is the result of the change of sovereignty. "As a rule, however, States have conferred their nationality on the former nationals of the predecessor State, and in this regard one may say that there is, in the absence of statutory provisions of municipal law, a *presumption* [emphasis mine] of international law that municipal law has this effect" (Brownlie 1990, 662). As a consequence of Article 7(2) of the Convention on the Rights of the Child, at least one point can be made with great certitude: a child born on a state's territory has to be given the citizenship of that country if it otherwise would be stateless. Thus, insofar as children otherwise stateless are concerned, the principle of jus soli has now become universal law. 191 states have ratified the convention; the United States, which is the main state that has not ratified it, applies in any case the jus soli principle.

This apart, the best guidance to advanced legal opinion on these matters is to be found in the European Convention on Nationality, Articles 18 and 19. Preferably, the matter should be settled by treaty between the states concerned (Article 19), but ultimately the decision is with the separate states.

The principles to be followed in making such decisions shall, according to Article 18, take into account human rights, including the principle that everyone has a right to a nationality and that statelessness shall be avoided. The burden of avoiding statelessness by extending citizenship will fall mainly on the country of residence, and as mentioned above, this practice will at least be followed with regard to children born on that territory.

In addition, the following factors shall be taken into account:

(a) the genuine and effective link of the person to the state, *(b)* the habitual residence of the person concerned at the time of state succession, *(c)* the will of the person concerned, and *(d)* the territorial origin of the person concerned. The fourth factor does not mean the ethnic origin of the person, but the territorial. It would have to be determined by the established place of residence at the time of state succession, at least if that person has lived in that territory from birth.

A convergence of several of the factors would determine the matter. Thus, a person's wanting to have the citizenship of the country of residence and living there from birth would strongly point in the direction of a right to that citizenship. Doubts can arise only when the person has only recently arrived in that part of the territory or has retained strong links with the other state.

In sum, the evolution of human rights–inspired international law at present gives reason to conclude as follows. In cases of state succession, citizens of the former state who live habitually (as distinct from temporarily) on the territory under new sovereignty are entitled to obtain the citizenship of the state that has obtained sovereignty over the territory. Such persons shall always have the option to accept the offer of citizenship of the other country concerned but are not obliged to take it, and the other country is not generally obliged to offer it except when the factors mentioned in Article 18 converge to make that the most reasonable solution. Both states are obliged to ensure that statelessness does not occur, and the burden of proof will fall on the state of domicile to show that it has legitimate cause to deny citizenship to any person habitually resident there.

Current Drafting by the International Law Commission

The International Law Commission is the body set up under the Charter of the United Nations to study the progressive development of international law and its codifications. Due to the urgency of nationality questions, the International Law Commission has since 1993 sought to develop a nonbinding instrument regarding the impact of state succession on the nationality of natural and legal persons. In 1994, the commission appointed Mr. Vaclav Mikulka as special rapporteur for the topic, who presented in 1995 his first report (A/CN.4/467) and in 1996 the second report (A/CN. 4/474). A working group of the commission was set up to give guidance to its work.

The working group concluded that the result of the work on the subject should take the form of a nonbinding instrument consisting of articles with commentaries based on the following principles: *(a)* the right of every individual who had the nationality of the predecessor state on the date of the succession of states to the nationality of at least one of the states concerned; *(b)* the corollary obligation of states concerned to prevent that person who, on the date of the succession of states, had the nationality of the predecessor state and had his or her habitual residence on the respective territories of the states concerned from becoming stateless as a result of such succession; *(c)* the obligation to enact promptly national legislation concerning nationality and other connected issues arising in relation with state succession, and to ensure that individuals concerned would be apprised, within a reasonable time period, of the effect of such legislation on their nationality and the consequences of a possible exercise of an option on their status; *(d)* the obligation of states concerned, without prejudice to their policy in the matter of multiple nationality, to give consideration to the will of individuals whenever they are equally qualified, either in whole or in part, to acquire the nationality of two or several such states; *(e)* the obligation not to discriminate; *(f)* the prohibition of arbitrary decisions concerning the acquisition and withdrawal of nationality and the exercise of the right of option; *(g)* the obligation that relevant applications be issued promptly and that decisions be issued in writing and open to administrative or judicial review; *(h)* the obligation to take all necessary measures to ensure the protection of the basic human rights and freedoms of persons having their habitual residence on the territory or otherwise under the jurisdiction of such states during the interim period between the date of the succession of states and the date when their nationality would be determined; *(i)* the obligation that a reasonable time limit be granted to comply with a requirement to transfer one's residence out of the territory of a state concerned following the voluntary renunciation of that state's nationality, whenever such requirement is contained in the legislation of that state; *(j)* the obligation to adopt all reasonable measures to enable a family to remain together or to be reunited, whenever the application of a state's internal law or of treaty provisions would infringe on the unity of such family; *(k)* the obligation of states concerned to consult and negotiate in order to determine whether the state succession had any negative consequences with respect to the nationality of individuals and other related aspects of their status, and, if so, to seek a solution of these problems through negotiations; *(l)* the rights and obligations of states other than the states concerned when confronted with cases of statelessness resulting from noncompliance by the latter with the provisions of the future instrument.[20]

In 1997, the commission adopted on first reading a set of twenty-seven articles with commentaries, which were submitted to the Sixth Committee (Legal) of the General Assembly for comments.

The draft articles on nationality in relation to state succession are divided into two parts. Part I contains general provisions applicable in all cases of succession of states, and Part II consists of provisions relating to specific categories of succession of states.

The draft set of articles is based on the fundamental principle that every individual has the right to the nationality of at least one of the states involved in the succession if he or she had the nationality of the predecessor state on the date of the succession of states (Article 1). States thus have the obligation to take all appropriate measures to prevent such persons from becoming stateless as a result of the succession (Article 3). A general presumption exists that persons acquire the nationality of the successor state on the date of such succession if they had the nationality of the predecessor state and reside in the territory affected by the succession, but there are exceptions (Article 4). Special emphasis is given to the will of individuals whenever they are qualified to acquire the nationality of more than one state involved in the succession. In such cases, they are to be granted a right of option (Article 10).

Other issues addressed in Part I concern the enactment of legislation on nationality and connected questions (Article 5); the effective date of attribution of nationality following the succession (Article 6); and the nationality to be attributed to nationals of the predecessor states residing in a state that is not involved in the succession (Article 7).

In giving effect to the provisions of Part I in specific situations, states are to take into account the provisions of Part II (Article 19), which contains more detailed rules on the attribution of nationality in the following four specified cases of succession of States. They are: transfer of part of the territory (section 1); unification of states (section 2); dissolution of a state (section 3); and separation of part or parts of the territory (section 4).

The draft also contains a provision stating explicitly that, without prejudice to the right to a nationality, the provision applies to the affects of a succession of states occurring in conformity with international law and, in

---

20. The deliberations of the International Law Commission are found in the Official Records of the General Assembly, 48th sess., supp. no. 10 (A/48/10); 49th sess., supp. no. 10 (A/49/10); and 50th sess., supp. no. 10 (A/50/10).

particular, with the principles of international law embodied in the Charter of the United Nations (Article 27).

Right to Obtain Citizenship of the State of Residence in Cases of State Restoration

It is sometimes argued that situations of state restoration should be treated differently from cases of state succession (Ziemele 1998). State restoration occurs when a previously independent state for some time has been incorporated into a larger entity but subsequently has regained its independence. The prime examples from recent times are the three Baltic states that were incorporated into the Soviet Union in 1940 and regained their independence in 1991.

The justification used to claim that situations of state restoration do not have to follow the rules applying to state succession is that restored states can reinstate the legislation on nationality as it stood before their incorporation and thereby determine the allocation of nationality at restored independence based on that previous law. This argument can be used only when the incorporation is a result of illegal use of force. If several states have merged through a lawful process based on consent and application of the relevant constitutional principles of each state, and if after a prolonged period of time they restore their separate statehood, the situation would have to be treated in the same way as state succession when a larger entity dissolves, as discussed above. Under human rights law, everyone has the right to freedom of movement and residence within a state (UDHR, Article 13; CCPR, Article 12). Thus, everyone can move to any part of the larger state and settle down there. Should the larger state subsequently be dissolved, everyone who is habitually resident in any of the restored states must be given the citizenship of that restored state if they so want. Exceptions would be applicable only if the merger has been of short duration.

The main problem arises when incorporation of previously independent states has resulted from illegal threat or use of force, which arguably happened to the Baltic states in 1940. These situations should be kept separate from cases of wartime occupation of territory where incorporation has not taken place. The occupying power is not entitled to transfer parts of its own civilian population to the occupied territory (Geneva Convention Relative to the Protection of Civilian Persons in Time of War, Article 49 i.f.). At the end of occupation, such illegal settlers from the enemy state would normally not be entitled to demand citizenship in the state established when the occupation is brought to an end.

The question of citizenship in restored states after a longtime incorporation of doubtful legality is different. If looked at from a human rights perspective, it matters little for the persons living in a country what the origin of the incorporation was if they have settled there in good faith assuming that it was their own country. If the incorporation has lasted for a prolonged period of time, migrations within the larger entity may have taken place on a large scale. When the settlements have continued over two or more generations before restoration takes place, the question of citizenship cannot be treated in the same way as it would at the end of an occupation, even if the incorporation initially was achieved through the use of force. It is, on the other hand, not obvious that those who settled after the incorporation or their descendents have an automatic right to citizenship in the restored country, even if they had citizenship of the larger state entity before restoration of independence.

Due to their established domicile, however, such people cannot be treated as regular aliens. As a minimum, the same rules should apply as in case of succession for resident nonnationals who were nationals of the larger entity or the predecessor state. If they do not immediately acquire citizenship, they shall have the right to remain in the restored state and enjoy equality of treatment with nationals of the restored state with regard to social and economic rights, including access to work, but with one exception: until they obtain citizenship, they can be excluded from such public service as involves the exercise of sovereign power (European Convention on Nationality, Article 20).

In the case of the Baltics, the incorporation lasted for half a century. Large numbers of inhabitants are second- or third-generation descendants of persons who arrived from other parts of the Soviet Union during the period of incorporation. Two of the three Baltic states, Latvia and Estonia, reactivated the citizenship law in existence prior to the incorporation and excluded from automatic citizenship those who had arrived during the period of incorporation and their descendants, some of whom lived there in the third generation and very many in the second generation. They have recognized, however, that those who had been domiciled in these states in general have a right to remain and cannot therefore be expelled. A gradual but rather slow process of naturalization is at present taking place, and they have recognized that children born after the restored independence who would otherwise be stateless should be given citizenship.

Language policies can become a problem in such cases. In normal cases of succession, it would be unjustified to require knowledge of the official language of the newly sovereign state as a condition of citizenship if that language was previously not a requirement in the territory where the person is domiciled. In the cases of regular naturalization of immigrants, it may be justified to demand that the immigrant seeking naturalization have a good command of the official language. For persons who have already lawfully resided in the territory as citizens of the larger state where two or more official languages existed and who were not required to master more than one, it would not be reasonable to demand such a command of an official language.

New Arrivals: Human Rights Requirements to Naturalization?

The discussion above has dealt with persons who had already established a residence on the territory at the time of state succession or state restoration. The remaining question is whether new arrivals or their descendants have any rights related to citizenship in their country of arrival. We are not here concerned with children born on the territory to parents who are already citizens. In all societies, they automatically become citizens. The concern here is with the fate of noncitizen arrivals or their children.

Many states practice the principle of jus soli, which means that children born on the territory as a general rule get the citizenship of that country even if their parents were not citizens. Others restrict themselves to jus sanguinis, meaning that only children born of parents who already are citizens automatically *(ex lege)* obtain citizenship.

As a consequence of the evolution of human rights law, even those who otherwise apply the jus sanguinis principle have to apply the principle of jus soli to children born on their territory who would otherwise be stateless. Most immigrants, however, have preexisting citizenship in their country of departure, and their children cannot therefore demand citizenship on the basis of statelessness.

For persons who do not become citizens *ex lege,* states can bestow citizenship through naturalization. Does international law contain requirements or restrictions regarding naturalization?

The first point to be made is that a state cannot impose its citizenship on new arrivals or their descendants if they do not want it. But the opposite question is more important and more controversial: Is the host country obliged, at any stage, to naturalize those who have become permanent residents in the country? This is indeed an area where states have so far considered themselves entirely free to make their own rules, a practice which, however, is now also changing. An illustration of the evolving legal approaches is found in the European Convention on Nationality, Article 6 (acquisition of nationality), where in section 3 it is provided that states in their internal law shall provide for the possibility of naturalization of persons lawfully and habitually resident on its territory, and in such legislation the time of residence required before an application can be lodged should not exceed ten years.

The question whether the state can make distinctions between applicants for naturalization is also controversial. This domestic prerogative has traditionally been jealously guarded, and international law remains weak on the point, but it is changing also in this matter. Groups of neighboring or like-minded countries sometimes make special arrangements, on a basis of reciprocity, for immigrants coming from one of the other states in the group. This practice is considered to be in conformity with international law.

But can states otherwise make a distinction, for example, on grounds of ethnicity or culture? Such a distinction could be held to be a violation of the International Covenant on the Elimination of All Forms of Racial Discrimination adopted by the U.N. General Assembly, particularly its Article 5(d)(iii). Under that article, the state parties shall guarantee the right of nationality to everyone, without distinction as to race, color, or national or ethnic origin. The implication seems to be that preference cannot be given to particular ethnic groups among those who seek naturalization. In practice, several countries continue to give such preference. It must be admitted that international law is still weak and vague on this issue.

Here, also, the European Convention on Nationality gives guidance: its Article 5, on nondiscrimination, states that the rules of a state party shall not contain distinctions or include any practices that amount to discrimination on the grounds of sex, religion, race, color, or national or ethnic origin. Furthermore, states shall be guided by the same principle of nondiscrimination between its nationals (citizens), whether they are nationals by birth or have acquired its nationality subsequently.

Citizenship and the Elimination of Statelessness

Since the end of World War II, the international community has been deeply concerned with the elimination of statelessness. The International Convention on the Reduction of Statelessness was adopted in 1961, and the United Nations High Commissioner for Refugees (UNHCR) was appointed as the agency to which claims for assistance can be addressed. The UNHCR has in recent years been confronted with an increasing number of problems of statelessness arising from situations of state succession or state restoration. It is therefore of the greatest urgency to develop clear guidance to the allocation of citizenship in such situations.[21]

A major gain was made with the Convention on the Rights of the Child

---

21. Some of the problems faced by the UNHCR in recent years are discussed in Batchelor (1995a and 1995b).

and its Article 7, referred to above. Because it is ratified by 191 countries, it is practically universal. A child born of stateless parents shall normally be given the citizenship of the country in which he or she is born. As an adult, the person can of course later renounce that citizenship if she or he has another and preferred option of citizenship. Although a faithful implementation of Article 7 would reduce the scope of statelessness, it does not solve the problem of children born in a country to parents who have a different nationality, which for political or other reasons they do not want to have.

Conclusion

International human rights law has affected not only the allocation of citizenship, but also the relevance of the distinction between citizens and noncitizens.

The modern concept of citizenship implies a quest for integration at the national level without distinction based on race, color, religion, gender, national or other origin. Generations ago it left behind the original meaning of *citizen* as the elite members of an urban core (the city) and has come to embrace all who are nationals. It is also an aspect of the process toward democratization, seeking to ensure that all groups in society can participate and thereby contribute to peaceful management of tensions and conflicts.

The modern concept of citizen is still an aspiration rather than a reality in many parts of the world. It requires a willingness to integrate rather than exclude in whole or in part, and it requires integration without assimilation.

In legal terms, each state can itself determine by law its rules concerning allocation, acquisition, and deprivation of citizenship, but international standards have to be taken into account. The net requirement is that everyone permanently residing in a given country should be entitled to the citizenship of that country unless the person falls into a category of permissible exceptions. The task is therefore to determine which are the permissible exceptions.

As has been shown in this chapter, the presumption is that everyone residing in a given territory when the state first becomes independent with its present borders or those who live in territories subsequently added to the state should have the option to become citizen of that country through state succession. In cases of state succession, individuals will often have an option to choose the citizenship of either the predecessor state or the successor state. The stronger claim is toward the state where the person resides, unless the person has a stronger link to the predecessor state and has a justified preference for that state.

In cases of state restoration, the solution should depend on the length of incorporation and the nature of the original incorporation. The longer the incorporation has lasted, the greater the similarity with state succession, and thus the solutions just mentioned can also be used. Incorporation that took place due to illegal use of force can weaken the presumption that persons who have settled during the period of incorporation should automatically be eligible to obtain their citizenship *ex lege*. When such persons have become permanent residents, however, they should at least have preferential access to naturalization.

Under any circumstance, a solution should be found that prevents persons from becoming stateless as consequence of succession or restoration. Children of stateless persons should be given the citizenship of the country in which they are born.

Immigrants, including refugees, who arrive after independence or restoration of it do not have an immediate right to citizenship but have to make use of the national rules and regulations of naturalization. Here also, however, international law is increasingly making its demands felt: there should be no discrimination in the nationality legislation, including that part that deals with naturalization. The length of residence before an application for naturalization can be made should not be too long; the European convention sets a limit of ten years.

A word of caution should be said at the end: although international human rights law contains significant rules applicable to the allocation, change, and withdrawal of citizenship, it is necessary also to recognize that the human rights part of international law suffers from serious weaknesses. Many states successfully resist international regulation of matters that the states still consider to be within their internal jurisdiction.

Human rights law is in a process of evolution. Universality of human rights has to be achieved through constant efforts; it is not something that has been effectively established merely by the United Nations General Assembly's adoption of the Universal Declaration of Human Rights in 1948. Partly as a consequence of increasing interdependence, partly also because of the quickly expanding international civil society consisting of thousands of international NGOs, the impact of international human rights law is becoming progressively stronger. The increasing interdependence has led also to the establishment and functioning of international institutions and agencies that make use of human rights law in their discourse with the authorities of the countries where they have a mandate. This interdependence is particularly felt in Europe: the Council of Europe, the High Commissioner on National Minorities, the Commissioner for Human Rights and Democratic Development of the Council of the Baltic Sea Countries, and the European Union are all making their demands for compliance. The Council of Europe, through its new Convention on Nationality of 1997, is starting to address these issues with greater determination.

In the Americas, the inter-American system of human rights protection has taken the nationality regulation seriously as a matter of human rights. For the rest of the world, the protection of the right to a nationality rests with the United Nations, which in these matters is rather weak, mainly because of the slow acceptance in many places of human rights in general. The preparation by the International Law Commission of articles on nationality in relation to the succession of states shows that human rights considerations are becoming increasingly prominent in nationality matters.

The regulation of citizenship in international law is therefore very much a law in the making, but the direction is clear. Human rights considerations are superseding self-serving preferences of dominant ethnic or religious elites in the individual states.

6

Liberalization Without Democratization in "Post-Populist" Authoritarian States

Evidence from Syria and Egypt

RAYMOND A. HINNEBUSCH

In all societies two classes of people appear—a class that rules and a class that is ruled.

—Gaetano Mosca, *The Ruling Class*

The specific form in which unpaid surplus labour is pumped out of the direct producers determines the relationship between rulers and ruled . . . the corresponding form of state.

—Karl Marx, *Kapital,* vol. 3

IS THE PRACTICAL EMPOWERMENT of theoretical citizenship, with enforceable rights and meaningful political participation, a natural by-product of modernization? A resurrected version of modernization theory imagines that economic growth, the spread of literacy, and mass communications erode primordial isolation and generate a multitude of differentiated interests; beyond a certain threshold, this more mobilized, complex society, it is claimed, cannot be governed by purely authoritarian means. Once *political liberalization*—greater political pluralism, rule of law, and less state control over society—begins, it becomes ever more difficult, in this view, for regimes to obstruct the generalization of political rights to the whole population. This extension of *democratization* implies a combination of contestation—specifically, competitive elections—with mass inclusion in the political process. Against this universalism stand the arguments for Middle Eastern exceptionalism, which hold that a distinctive political culture has short-circuited the correlation between socioeconomic development and the declining viability of authoritarian rule. The facts are more complicated than either of these views. On the one hand, political liberalization has swept across the Middle East. However, democratization is little in evidence there.

Is political liberalization simply a first step on the road to democratization? Although the global spread of democracy has put modernization theory back in fashion, there are opposing political traditions in which *liberalization without democratization,* far from being an anomaly, is the norm. In Mosca's (1935) elitist approach, effective participation is everywhere limited to a "political class," the active organized minority on which the top elite depends to dominate the unorganized majority. Liberal forms are no deterrent to continued elite rule and indeed can more effectively appease the so-called political class without conceding accountability to the broader citizenry. If the citizenry becomes more politically mobilized with modernization, therefore less easily governable by force, its interests also become more differentiated, whereas elites develop more sophisticated political technologies of control; although the ruling class may be briefly opened to plebeian strata through revolution or co-optation, it tends to be self-perpetuating. Marxism and its descendants argue that liberal forms are perfectly compatible with the dominance of power by the bourgeoisie; although popular struggle can extract a widening of democratic rights, liberal forms cannot assume much authentic democratic content as long as private wealth translates into public power and the economy is outside the sphere of public accountability. In these traditions, the retardation of democratization has less to do with a cultural lag than with the universal realities of elitism and of political economy. As Turner (chapter 2 in this volume) remarks, citizenship is everywhere the exception, not the rule. In the light of this, what is the significance of current political "reform" in the Middle East?

This essay argues that:

1. Modernization does indeed increase the *propensity and capacity of the populace to participate,* putting mounting pressures on authoritarian regimes, and political culture does not immunize Middle Easterners to this universal tendency. However, if the objective conditions are not right, this attitudinal change is not enough to make for democratization.

2. Political economy—specifically, a *balance between the state and social forces*—determines whether objective conditions are right. As Huntington (1968) suggests, the state must possess the legitimacy and institutions to incorporate rising social forces without praetorian breakdown. On the other hand, as Barrington Moore (1966), insists, "no bourgeoisie, no democracy" (418): the bourgeoisie is the main social force potentially strong and demo-

cratic enough to check state power and extract political reform, and bourgeois civil society is the crucible of citizenship. Further, whereas political liberalization depends on a state-bourgeois power-sharing alliance, democratization depends on a "democratic coalition" of the bourgeoisie and the masses to extract democratization from the state. The prospects for such alliances are decisively shaped by the configurations of capitalist development. In much of the Middle East, this chiefly means the way the requisites of capital accumulation have forced *authoritarian-populist* states into *postpopulist* strategies. Such a scenario may actually require some political liberalization, but it also entails a rollback of socioeconomic rights, which deters a bourgeois-mass alliance on behalf of democratization.

3. Elites have designed postpopulist strategies and structures to cope with the contradiction between the increased participatory demands unleashed by modernization and the requisites of capital accumulation. Specifically, limited political liberalization provides the conditions for a state-bourgeois alliance while obstructing the emergence of a bourgeoisie-mass democratic coalition. Political liberalization may widen space for civil society and thereby enhance associational habits among a newly emerging political class, but, in empowering them far more than the mass citizenry, it initially leads to a *less equal* distribution of real influence rather than to democratization. Thus, there is no necessary positive relation between political liberalization and democratization.

Political Culture, Modernization, and Islam

According to the cultural exceptionalism argument, the main explanation for the apparent immunity of the Middle East to democratization is an inherited incompatible political culture. This essay argues that culture is less an independent variable than a dependent one—reshaped, despite certain lags, by changes in objective circumstances: political reform depends on whether objective conditions *undermine or reinforce* the nondemocratic aspects of the inherited culture.

In the cultural exceptionalism argument, a history of military conquest states, bureaucratic empires, tribal structures, and patriarchal families transmits a dominance-submission and primordial culture that deters the activism and universalistic attitudes needed for civil society. Political ties are said to be predominately personal and primordial; the typical units of action are small groups and client networks seeking immediate and particular benefits, rather than classes or associational groups motivated by issues and seeking to influence law and policy or extract democratic political rights (Roy 1994b, 270–81; Springborg 1975).

In reality, the persistence of this cultural behavior varies greatly. On the one hand, as modernization theory holds, where economic development and social mobilization have advanced, culture has altered. Education, literacy, urbanization, and mass communications have endowed the Middle East population with far greater potentially empowering resources than those offered in the premodern era. That the culture of passivity and clientalism is undermined by social mobilization is evidenced by the greater political activism of those milieu—campus, factory, and urban street—most exposed to it and by the greater decline of traditional legitimacy in those states—generally the republics as opposed to the tribal monarchies—where the population is most mobilized.

Where "traditional" behavior persists, it is less an unchanging cultural artifact than a contingent product of objective conditions—namely, an *adaptation to authoritarian rule*—and of the few participatory opportunities made available by elite strategies. On the one hand, where the state controls the economy and bureaucratic structures deter political pluralization, clientalism is replicated as a rational strategy of competition for scarce resources, and the expansion of politicization is manifest not in pluralistic politics, but in the democratization of clientage networks—that is, their extension from a small upper class to the middle and even to deprived strata, often through corporatist structures.

On the other hand, where the strategies of authoritarian elites have widened opportunities for participation, citizens have rapidly taken advantage of them to engage in politics with many of the marks of "modernity" (Hinnebusch 1983). Thus, in Syria under the pre-1970 Ba'th, a populist political strategy made a difference for participation propensities. The Ba'th Party and its popular auxiliaries deliberately recruited formerly nonparticipant plebeian strata, notably youth and the peasantry, in the 1960s and 1970s, and by the 1980s the party was overwhelmingly a party of the lower middle and lower classes. That this participation was not purely nominal is suggested by evidence that recruits' attitudes and motivations were shaped by rational class interest. For example, attitudes toward income distribution varied according to class: employers and rich peasants preferred more freedom for the private sector and defended the right of inheritance, whereas workers opposed these platforms. Ideology was a salient factor in political recruitment and was associated with greater efficacy and activism. Moreover, greater exposure to modernization *did* increase political consciousness: the educated lower middle strata were more ideological, whereas uneducated rurals were more likely to have lower ideology, efficacy, and participation levels. The decline of this activism has followed a postpopulist shift in elite strategies, not a resurgence of traditional culture.

Similarly, in Egypt, Sadat's postpopulist authoritarian regime, seeking to appease and win over the bourgeoisie, allowed the formation of opposition parties, which would give the old leaders of the liberal Wafd Party, repressed under Nasser, an opportunity to resurrect their party. Recruitment to the "New Wafd," far from being random, was a function of class interest: the vast majority of recruits were of upper- or upper-middle-class status and drawn to the party by its ideology of liberalization and by a determination to help dismantle the remnants of the Nasserist regime. That the Wafd's entry into politics has not propelled democratization is best explained by its lack of ideological appeal to the mass public—its failure to lead a democratic coalition—not by traditional culture.

Indeed, the association of liberal ideology with the Wafd's upper-status recruits and of populism with the Ba'th's lower-status activists is exactly what is expected of "modern" rational political participation. *This evidence suggests that modernization theory carries considerable validity at the level of political culture: modernization does increase the propensity to participate in modern ways.* The fact is that when even modest participation channels are opened, increases in rational activism result, which suggests that the democratization of political structures is the key to political cultural change rather than that such change is a requisite of democratization.

For the cultural exceptionalists, Islam and particularly political Islam, supposedly the world's only remaining ideological alternative to Western liberalism, is what makes the region so distinctively resistant to democratization. Islam's insistence on the fusion of religion and politics—a "sovereignty of God" that obviates the need for debate or consent—and its preference for unity over pluralism and community over individual or minority rights are said to be antidemocratic. Because Islam is the main ideology of mass opposition, the rise of the masses may result in theocracy rather than democracy.

Whatever the validity of these claims, Islam arguably has contrary democratic-friendly tendencies. Islamic movements have pushed for and facilitated the contraction in the scope of state power, which is essential to a more autonomous civil society. Islam is *more compatible* with other aspects of democratic culture—majoritarianism and mass participation—than some other cultures, notably the inegalitarian Hindu and Confucian civilizations, where some democratization has advanced. Moreover, some Islamic movements have accepted the inevitability of pluralist competition and the need to promote the Islamization of politics through consent.

Democratization must be made compatible with capitalist development, so Islamic attitudes toward capitalism are crucial, and these attitudes are ambivalent, not opposed. Reflecting the worldview of their largely petit bourgeois constituencies, Islamic movements are hostile to aristocratic concentrations of wealth, but they approve private property, especially small property, and embrace the market, on condition it is regulated in the interests of equality and mass welfare. Islamic movements therefore tend to waver between attacks on the inegalitarian consequences of capitalism and defense of property and the market; they typically seek the "middle way" of a capitalism regulated by Islam, but can easily split between populist and procapitalist variants.

Rather than expressing an unchanging culture or dogma, Islamic political movements thus vary significantly according to objective circumstances. Variation stems partly from their character as a reaction to the policies of the regime in power. In the populist stage, when small private property is threatened by the state, Islam takes conservative forms; in the postpopulist stage, if Islamic notables succeed on the liberalized market and accumulate wealth, the movement may maintain its procapitalist tilt, but the threat to the artisan and small business community from the penetration of Western monopolies and commodities pulls the other way. Modernization, reflected in increased recruitment of educated youth into Islamic movements, has also shaped the course of Islamic revival: on the one hand, a more "modernized" activist and pluralist version of Islam, as in Turkey, but, on the other hand, to the extent youth are excluded from employment and political participation, a greater militancy and an effort to mobilize the victims of economic liberalization under a populist banner, as in Algeria.

The real challenge of political Islam is the fact that political reform, representing the main mass opposition to incumbent regimes, cannot proceed far without a détente or pact by which Islamists accept and are accepted into the established system. Mainstream Islamist movements, in fact, seek integration into the political order, not its overthrow (Kramer 1994, 204). Whether regimes attempt to integrate or exclude them is likely to depend on whether they accept postpopulist strategies—specifically economic liberalization—or attempt to mobilize the victims of that liberalization. In short, Islamic ideology, per se, is neither uniform or uniformly incompatible with pluralist models of development; rather, political economy and elite strategies determine whether Islamic and pluralist politics are compatible.

Political Economy: From Populism to Bourgeois Reincorporation

The political economy of development in the Middle East has been the main obstacle to democratization. First, late development made for weak or dependent bourgeoisies, which, barely differentiated from the landed notability, had little interest in a democratic coalition. Delayed dependent development and the struggle against imperialism gave rise to authoritarian-populist states seeking autonomous national development. The product of revolts by the rising salaried middle class against traditional elites, these regimes established autonomy of the dominant classes through redistributive strategies, including nationalization and land reform; creation of public-sector economies; and the mobilization of middle-cum-lower-class coalitions incorporated through single-party and corporatist structures. These strategies—inclusionary in that they mobilized formerly passive mass strata—paradoxically also enhanced regime autonomy and enabled the state to repress the rudiments of pluralist politics. Their strategy of state-led import substitute industrialization marginalized the private sector in favor of state investment and made much of the public dependent on the state for employment, hence in no position to demand political rights. But these regimes eschewed a Stalinist-type extraction of resources from the masses; on the contrary, their populism fostered consumption rather than accumulation: mass support was build on a tacit "social contract" in which the public accorded support or acquiescence in return for nationalist accomplishments, economic security, and populist welfare—made manifest in subsidized food, state employment, land distribution, and free education. Some of these states, notably Nasser's Egypt, achieved considerable nationalist legitimacy, even Gramscian ideological hegemony, until this was shattered by the 1967 defeat by Israel. Post-1967 legitimacy deficits were, however, compensated for in the seventies by the availability of oil "rent," which sustained state dominance of the economy and gave it patronage resources to appease restive constituencies (Ayubi 1995, 196–223; Richards and Waterbury 1990, 184–237, 302–17). In leveling an already weak bourgeoisie, these authoritarian-populist regimes neutralized societal checks on state power and, by incorporating the masses, obstructed a democratic coalition.

Populist states have entered a postpopulist era, however, in which the requisites of capitalist development have become a major determinant of policy. Statist strategies were exhausted as public sectors—burdened by militarism, patronage, and populist consumption—failed to become engines of capital accumulation. Nevertheless, a state bourgeoisie was generated in the heart of the state, with accumulated capital for which it sought investment outlets, while the private sector was kept alive by state subcontracting and middleman activities. Statist economic crises were met by economic liberalization policies meant to revive the private sector as the main or at least a complementary engine of capital accumulation and to facilitate a switch from import substitute to export strategies. The success of these strategies has depended on the construction of a new state-bourgeois alliance and on the rollback of reliance on the mass citizenry as the regime's main support base. That success is also associated with vulnerability to the demands of international economic institutions and with increasing dependency on international investment and aid. The scenario is thus favorable to political liberalization but not to democratization.

On the one hand, the exhaustion of statism forces increased reliance on private investment and requires regimes to overcome the historic alienation of the capitalist class. Investors cannot readily be brought to trust regimes that once expropriated private property unless they are convinced that ruling elites seek a real partnership with them. Moreover, capital will not risk investment (other than in short-term speculative ventures) unless it enjoys effective, if not privileged, access to decision makers and unless increasing rule of law curbs the arbitrariness of the state. The durability of economic liberalization and the predictability of the investment climate depend on the bourgeoisie acquiring a share of power by which it can counter corrupt elites from above and populist demands from below. As taxation of the private sector becomes an ever more important source of state revenue, business has to be convinced to pay taxes, especially income tax, by according it representation in the policy process. For all these reasons, postpopulist strategies require some political liberalization.

Once it starts, such liberalization may foster the conditions for its own durability. The growth of the bourgeoisie—partly autonomous, partly state dependent—creates a force that has both some power to check the state and a stake in the status quo. Liberalization advances the deepening of a certain civil society, largely among business and professional associations. In this more complex market society, economic policymaking can no longer be confined to bureaucratic politics, and the state must increasingly govern through bargains with the bourgeoisie rather than by decrees that run roughshod over its interests (Ehteshami and Murphy 1996).

On the other hand, the compatibility of capitalist development and democratization is far more problematic. Although democracy is indeed associated with *developed* capitalist economies, the requisite of capitalism in *developing* economies that are entering supposedly "postpopulist" scenarios is arguably an obstacle to it (Pool 1993). Early capitalist development requires primitive capital accumulation favoring investors at the expense of labor and—in the Middle East—rolling back the populist social contract. To be sure, in the early *infitah* (opening up) stage, there is frequently an influx of loans and rent combined with an import boom, increasing the wealth and conspicuous consumption of the "*infitah* bourgeoisie" but not initially damaging the lower strata. This phase typically ends in debt, making the state vulnerable to structural adjustment imposed by the International Monetary Fund (IMF). Populist rollback is also required to create the necessary investment climate, and—as import substitute industrialization gives way to export strategies—to increase export competitiveness through lowered costs. Austerity measures cut welfare subsidies, public-sector spending, and state employment. Privatization, redundancies, and removal of labor protections follow. Although new private investment can make up for some job losses, high population growth and welfare cuts mean that the proportion of the marginalized population is likely to grow, not decline, at least in the early stages of the new capitalism. Economic liberalization could, in the long term, stimulate small industries, but the most immediate result is likely to be increased foreign competition, an end to subsidies, and a wave of small business bankruptcies. In fact, the postpopulist phase has meant increasing inequality throughout the Middle East (Farsoun and Zacharia 1995, Ehteshami and Murphy 1996).

Populist rollback has been accompanied by popular revolt—or "food riots"—in many Middle East countries (Seddon 1994). It has been argued that the public can be brought to accept economic austerity in return for political rights (Richards 1995). Attempts have, indeed, been made in the Middle East to manage economic discontent through political concessions, but these attempts have normally made for a very controlled and limited political liberalization very vulnerable to reversal and, for several reasons, have not led into sustained democratization.

First, the middle class, the "natural constituency" for democracy elsewhere, is ambivalent toward it in the Middle East. The bourgeoisie, considering democracy to potentially empower mass resistance to economic liberalization, is unenthusiastic about it. The large stratum of the middle class that is salaried and state dependent is normally threatened by economic liberalization; it is less likely to be won over to it though democratization than to use the latter to make common cause with the masses against the former. Whereas the small business class, under economic pressure, often turns to the Islamic opposition, the Westernized professional and intellectual upper middle strata fear that democratization means Islamic electoral victories threatening to liberal personal rights.

Nor would mass resistance to economic liberalization necessarily be assuaged by democratization. On the contrary, populist regimes have so accustomed the people to social and labor rights that they likely use political rights to make demands that, if they increased the welfare role of the state, could raise taxes, consumption, and debt, and therefore deter investors. If the masses accept austerity, there is a risk it would be conditional on the upper classes bearing their fair share of the burden, a demand likely to lead to capital flight. Ironically, whether the masses can be accommodated to populist rollback may depend on Islamic movements, the opposition force enjoying the greatest mass legitimacy: Can their alternative welfare provision buffer the costs of economic liberalization, and will they choose to accommodate the masses to capitalism rather than mobilize them against it?

In setting bourgeois and mass interests at odds, the postpopulist political economy is a major obstacle to the democratic coalition needed to extract democracy from the state. Indeed, managing economic liberalization may actually require a "harder" form of authoritarian state.[1]

Variations in Political Reform: State-Bourgeoisie Alliance and Islamic Incorporation

Although postpopulist political economy facilitates political liberalization while deterring democratization, variations in political change among countries depend on *the configuration of social coalitions*. A comparative study of Syria and Egypt suggests that (1) variations in political liberalization can be predicted by the extent that a postpopulist alliance of state and bourgeoisie is solidified through economic liberalization; and (2) prospects for democratization vary according to the ability of regimes or the bourgeoisie or both to reach an accommodation with political Islam.

Syria

In Syria, the postpopulist process remains incomplete, economic liberalization modest, and political liberalization rudimentary. Although the beginnings of an *infitah* alliance of the state with the commercial bourgeoisie dates to the early 1970s, the regime has been able to maintain its hegemony

---

1. It is true that economic liberalization and authoritarianism are no longer as associated in some Third World regions as they are in the Middle East, especially where some industrialization has succeeded as in the NICs. I would, however, argue that Third World democratization is fragile and that the distinction between such limited democracies and the Middle East's liberalized authoritarian regimes is a matter of degree rather than a qualitative distinction. Some comparative studies suggest that liberalization cannot proceed very far into thorough democratization if economic liberalization policies are to hold. Haggard and Kaufman (1992) found that "democracies" succeed at economic reform when they are based on a narrow coalition insulated from popular demands, but they fail when popular groups are organized. In many developing regions, such as Latin America, populist rollback required for the "capital-deepening" stage of industrialization (O'Donnell 1973)—which may be ahead for the Middle East—was accomplished by "hard" bureaucratic-authoritarian regimes, and only after they had done the job and intimidated the masses by draconian repression did the middle class push for widened political liberalization. Democratization depended on mass depoliticization or remained conditional: the mass public was accorded political rights as long as it did not use them to obstruct economic liberalization (O'Donnell and Schmitter 1986).

over society by balancing between the private and state sectors, and between its old peasant constituency and a new bourgeois one. The alliance was gradually deepened by a second wave of liberalization in the 1990s when a new investment law sparked a private investment boom. However, state-private joint ventures remain limited, and international capital is not part of the liberalizing alliance in Syria—in good part because Syrian eligibility for it depends on reaching accommodation with Israel.

At the core of the state-bourgeoisie alliance stands a "military-mercantile complex" of Alawi officers and Damascene merchants, a complex deepened in the nineties by partnerships between the children of the Ba'thi elite and the Sunni bourgeoisie. But the bourgeoisie, in good part dependent on regime contracts and protection and engaged in corrupt practices with it, presents no common demand for greater power sharing and seemingly has no more interest in democratization than has the regime. The state-business alliance, moreover, remains fragile. It is retarded by the sectarian divide and the consequent dearth of intermarriages between the Alawi political elite and the largely Sunni bourgeoisie. The Alawi elite has accepted the bourgeoisie as a junior partner, but the latter want a full partnership and deeply resent the payoffs to Alawi barons needed to do business. Neither side yet wholly trusts the other.

On the other hand, the state-dependent middle class and the rural, labor, and minority elements of the regime constituency retain a stake in statist-populist policies that the regime has contracted but not abandoned. Privatization of the public sector is not on the agenda. Populist policies were severely contracted by economic crisis and austerity in the eighties, but the regime has not attacked many measures, such as the labor and agrarian relations laws, which benefit its lower-class constituency at the expense of investors. The regime has enough access to rent—oil exports, Arab aid—to permit it to service its constituency and to shield it from total dependence on the investment and taxation of the private sector. Its international economic dependency, being diversified, has given it the ability to resist IMF liberalization prescriptions (Hinnebusch 1993a, Perthes 1994).

Political Islam in Syria has the potential to advance political liberalization but not democratization. In the past, it expressed both the resentment of pious Sunnis against the dominance of sectarian minorities in the Ba'th regime and the resistance of the damaged bourgeoisie and souk petite bourgeoisie to Ba'thist socialism. It was thus incompatible with the Ba'th's populist stage, and in the 1980s the regime deployed massive repression to turn back an Islamic rebellion. The ideology of Syrian political Islam seems quite compatible with postpopulist economic liberalization, however: for example, its 1980s manifesto called for free trade, privatization, and an end to populist market regulation. As such, prospects for political liberalization in Syria are enhanced by the extent to which economic liberalization, in making for an economically less intrusive state and in easing the sectarian gap, generates a détente between the Ba'th regime and the Islamic bourgeoisie. On the other hand, Syrian Islam is unlikely to put together a democratic coalition able to extract democratization; Syrian Islam does not appeal to the victims of economic liberalization and is a largely urban phenomenon, lacking the ability to mobilize the villages, whose continued incorporation into regime political structures makes them, in any case, relatively unavailable (Hinnebusch 1996).

Egypt

In the Egyptian case, economic liberalization has gone a great deal further in dismantling state controls over the economy and in generating a state-bourgeoisie alliance. The Sadat era produced the new *infitah* bourgeoisie, the *infitah* boom, and rising debt, which made Egypt vulnerable to IMF conditionality for debt rescheduling. This scenario produced much further integration into the world market in the 1990s—advanced by such policies as a floating convertible currency, trade liberalization, and the raising of interest rates and energy prices to "world levels." The public sector persists, but is being gradually privatized, and the private, foreign, and joint sectors are much larger than in Syria. The bourgeoisie is larger and more diversified, and has extensive transnational connections: a symbol of this growth is the emergence of the powerful American-Egyptian Chamber of Commerce. The amalgamation of the originally middle-class military elite and families of old and new wealth is complete, and with the alienation of the bourgeoisie having largely been overcome, the regime can much more readily afford to share power with it than in Syria (Hinnebusch 1993b).

Initially, U.S. and Arab aid allowed the regime to avoid much attack on populism, and it quickly retreated in the face of the first popular backlash, the 1977 food riots. But the reduction of subsidies has since proceeded relentlessly if incrementally, shifting resources from mass welfare to the service of elite interests; thus, slashes in welfare spending have been paralleled by purchases of expensive U.S. arms. Populist regulations such as price controls have been much more thoroughly eliminated than in Syria and the labor law is being targeted. The first big test of populist rollback is the reversal of Nasser's Agrarian Relations Law—in the name of private property rights—which threatens to make thousands of tenants landless and has already stimulated protest and repression. As the health of the economy has come to depend on foreign aid and private investment, the regime has had to put the structural adjustment demands of international economic institutions and the expectations of investors before any efforts to placate the mass public. Little remains of the regime's former populist alliance as it has increasingly reneged on the social contract (Hinnebusch 1993b, 1993c; Owen 1994).

The prospect of democratization through regime détente with political Islam is more complicated in Egypt than Syria because political Islam is more variegated in Egypt. The Muslim Brotherhood, conservative and anti-socialist under Nasser, was initially co-opted by Sadat's de-Nasserization. Its leaders are wealthy notables who consider private ownership natural and are silent on economic issues. Although they oppose Westernization at the ideological level, many of them, as well as the Islamic investment houses and banks, have made huge profits on the same international economic connections and through many of the same speculative black-market activities as the Westernized *infitah* bourgeoisie. They have increasingly accepted political pluralism and sought to be admitted to the political contest.

In such a case where political Islam accepts contestation and economic liberalization, not only is its political incorporation compatible with a widening of pluralism, but if Islamic movements accommodate the mass following to the market and promote private welfare networks to substitute for state populism, they may even advance the chances of democratization. Unlike the fragmented secular opposition, the Islamic opposition could check the power of the state and its bourgeois allies while ensuring mass interests were not wholly disregarded; the state could, in turn, balance and dilute Islamic demands. If an Islamic bourgeoisie mobilizes its mass base to extract political rights, Islam could even provide the missing formula for a democratic coalition.

Of course, where radical Islam mobilizes discontent among the victims of economic liberalization in a challenge to the postpopulist order, its admission to the political game is not readily compatible with capitalist development. In the Sadat and Mubarak eras, a radical wing of the Islamic movement became a vehicle for opposition to postpopulist policies, chiefly formed by the lower middle class and especially partly educated youthful urban migrants lacking stable employment. This wing of Egyptian political Islam took on a more populist color—namely, the attacks by the Gamiyyat al-Islamiyya on the corruption and inequality brought on by the *infitah*, on the contraction of welfare services for the poor while the *infitah* bourgeoisie flaunted its new wealth, and on the spread of Westernized lifestyles among the rich (Hinnebusch 1985, 198–208).

Thus, regime strategies toward Islamic movements depend in great part on the movements' compatibility with postpopulist development. When radical populist Islam dominates, limited political liberalization incorporating mainly the secular bourgeoisie may make political sense: it strengthens the regime vis-à-vis the Islamists, and it encourages the bourgeoisie and secular middle class, alarmed at the Islamic challenge, to defer demands for wider democratization. On the other hand, even if political Islam is not fully compatible with regime strategies, inclusion may nevertheless moderate Islamic demands just as the admission of radical parties into politics in the West was accompanied by their moderation. Indeed, the Mubarak regime, faced with an Islamic opposition with both conservative and radical wings, initially seemed to be following a successful strategy of differentiating among them, co-opting the moderates and thereby marginalizing the radicals. However, it is now pursuing a more exclusionary strategy—hence ruling out democratization in practice.

Why—if the Egyptian and even more the Algerian cases are any indicator—do experiments at inclusion of Islamic movements in the postpopulist Middle East seem so problematic? One main obstacle is that inclusion depends on the incumbent regime possessing considerable legitimacy, but postpopulist authoritarian regimes lack the traditional or nationalist legitimacy that the state in the West enjoyed in the era of democratization. They never had traditional legitimacy, but they also lose their nationalist legitimacy insofar as their integration into the world capitalist system results in Western economic dependence, cultural penetration, deference to Western power in foreign affairs, and an undesired accommodation with a triumphant Israel. What makes the Islamic nature of the opposition movements so dangerous for postpopulist regimes is, therefore, less their nonsecular character than the fact that regimes suffering nationalist delegitimation are handicapped in any contest with a social force possessing more convincing indigenous symbols of legitimation than their own.[2]

In summary, Middle Eastern Islam is not an insurmountable obstacle to democratization: it fosters political activism that, if channeled through the established order, could enhance pluralization, legitimize an indigenous capitalism, and even lead into democratization. The main obstacle is the absence of Huntington's (1968) condition for democratization: regimes having the political legitimacy to incorporate mass social forces safely without praetorian breakdown.

2. The importance of nationalist legitimation for democratization is well illustrated by the case of Jordan. Although political liberalization was initiated to defuse food riots in 1989, it was consolidated during the second Gulf War when King Hussein won nationalist legitimacy for his stand against Western intervention. When his realignment with the United States and peace with Israel eroded this legitimacy, and opposition began to contest these policies, the liberalization experiment was curbed, and the regime opted to depend on external support rather than domestic legitimation (Kramer 1994, 218–22; Andoni 1996b).

Elite Strategy in Practice:
Limited Liberalization for the "Haves"

If political economy determines one structural condition of political liberalization and democratization—the social forces needed to extract such reforms from the state—then elite strategies reflect and affect the other one, namely, attempts to generate the legitimacy and political structures to incorporate these forces without praetorian breakdown. Modernization theory predicts that, to avoid destabilization, the state must adapt to the more pluralized, mobilized society that development creates through structural differentiation and pluralization. But the pluralist threshold at which this adaptation is necessary is very indeterminate, and there are potentially many incremental stages in the political reform process. For elites, a strategy of *separating* political liberalization from democratization minimizes the risks of change.

Political liberalization merely requires the relaxation of state controls over society and the according of greater autonomy to executive and elite-run governing institutions such as the legislature and judiciary. Democratization requires much more: the creation of an autonomous, mass-incorporating political infrastructure, which confers on the public some power to hold elites accountable. In the Middle East, elites seek the reverse: the regime autonomy thought needed to manage the contradiction between rising political activism stimulated by social mobilization and the requisites of capitalist development. As such, the process proceeds under strict control from above, measured out, as President Mubarak put it, in "doses" proportionate to Egypt's ability to absorb them (Makram-Ebeid 1989, 423). As in the case of Syria's President Assad, disorder results when political structures are too advanced for a country's economic level (FBIS 1990, BBC 1992).

Political liberalization can actually enhance the autonomy of the top elite: if military or bureaucratic interests or the ruling party resist economic liberalization, an opening to the bourgeoisie allows the elite to co-opt and channel their countervailing influence on behalf of postpopulist strategies; diversifying their coalitions better enables elites to balance above these competing interests and to steer a course that suits them. Limited political pluralism also satisfies some of the autonomy demands of a more differentiated society that is less readily directed from above by an overburdened state. Elites may even permit enough opening to win the support of wider groups and to recharge legitimacy long enough to impose economic austerity or spread the blame for it—but only as long as they can use corporatist structures, controlled elections, and so on to keep the process from ending in democratization. And, if rolling back populism requires repressive power against mass resistance, the executive always holds such power in reserve, keeping firm control of the military and police (Ehteshami and Murphy 1996).

Despite the limited nature of political reform, it is by no means unimportant. Limited political liberalization means opening new access to those more mobilized classes that are expected to support and benefit from economic liberalization, while seeking to balance or even demobilize those victimized by or opposed to it. But there may be significant variations in the outcomes of political liberalization—in who wins power sharing and who is excluded. This distinction is arguably more important among Arab states than any superficial variations in levels of democratic practice. A comparison of Syria, where the political liberalization process is rudimentary, and Egypt, where it is well advanced, not only illustrates the range of variation in outcomes and the forces determining this range, but also demonstrates that a greater extent of political liberalization by no means corresponds to a more equitable distribution of power among social forces.

Syria

In Syria, political liberalization has been carefully designed to strengthen, not change, the regime (Kienle 1994). On-and-off bursts of very limited liberalization have been associated with the need of the ruling elite to co-opt or appease the bourgeoisie and middle class. In 1970, Assad, in a struggle with his radical-socialist rivals in the Ba'th Party, appealed to the urban educated and commercial classes for support with a relaxation of political and economic controls. After a setback in the 1980s, when Islamic rebellion invited near-totalitarian repression, political decompression in the early 1990s was associated with the need to revitalize the private sector and, to a lesser degree, to satisfy pent up middle-class expectations unleashed by democratization in Eastern Europe.

Political liberalization has, however, remained much more limited in Syria than in most other Arab countries, for several reasons. On the one hand, it could unleash the pent up resentments of older elements of the bourgeoisie who have never forgiven the Ba'th for its socialist reforms, or it might enable political Islam to play the sectarian card. On the other hand, pressures for political liberalization have been readily contained: the bourgeoisie seems prepared to defer demands for more power in return for business freedom and security, and the middle class and intelligentsia are fragmented and isolated from the masses. The regime evidently has enough legitimacy to widen its social coalition through strictly limited political liberalization, but not enough to go further.

A substantial political decompression has certainly taken place by comparison to the draconian rule of the 1980s. The relaxation of state control over society and the economy is manifest in greater personal freedom to travel, get rich, and consume. But checks on state encroachment are rudimentary: there is no judicial or press independence comparable to Egypt, and professional syndicates have not been allowed even the autonomy the Egyptians won under Sadat. Party pluralization hardly exists. A few tiny middle-class parties subservient to the regime are tolerated. Assad downgraded the role of the mass political party, the Ba'th, but it remains the most effective political institution in Syria, and, incorporating the state-dependent middle class and the village, it cannot readily be transformed into a party of business, like the postpopulist Egyptian ruling party, the National Democratic Party (NDP). Nor are there any liberal parties with the stature of the Egyptian Wafd waiting in the wings for further liberalization.

On the other hand, ambitious businessmen have been co-opted into Parliament as independents. The Chamber of Commerce, speaking for the bourgeoisie, has acquired growing corporatist-like access to cabinet decision making. This access has transformed Syrian corporatism from a populist version in which the worker and peasant unions enjoyed privileged access to the more conventional arrangement in which the regime balances between popular and bourgeois interest groups. However, access for mass interest groups remains relatively more effective than in Egypt: the trade unions have blocked public-sector privatization, and the peasant union has preempted any rollback in agrarian reform. In the Syrian case, therefore, the mass public actually seems to retain greater clout to defend its interests precisely because a lower level of political liberalization has not permitted the growth of business interest groups or opened channels of influence comparable to that enjoyed by the Egyptian bourgeoisie. To the extent significant elements of the mass public remain so incorporated into the regime, they are unavailable to oppositionist movements, liberal or Islamic, thus obstructing a democratic coalition against the state. The regime is more autonomous of the bourgeoisie, but because its relations with the bourgeoisie are less secure, it can less easily afford to offend its populist constituency than can the regime in Egypt.

Egypt

The Egyptian case, where Sadat pioneered limited liberalization in the 1970s, is a much more advanced experiment (Hinnebusch 1985, 1990). Unlike Assad, Sadat aimed to virtually transform the social base of Nasser's regime. Early survival depended on winning bourgeois support against his

Nasserist opponents, and his determination to reverse many Nasserist policies required shifting the regime from its reliance on the military, bureaucracy, and Nasser's mass constituency to a greater dependence on the Egyptian landed and business classes internally and on the United States externally. The state remained essentially authoritarian, with enormous power concentrated in the presidential monarchy. But, under Sadat and Mubarak, its role in the economy and society contracted, allowing a revival of the private sector and a restoration of personal freedoms—curbed under Nasser—for those with the resources to enjoy them. The regime came gradually to share power with the business, landed, and professional strata, which made up its main constituency. This power sharing was channeled through Parliament, interest groups, the judiciary, and the press, but the mass public was largely excluded from it.

The courts and rule of law now protect the rights of some Egyptians much more effectively than they did under Nasser. The judiciary achieved a substantial measure of autonomy as the regime steered clear of the purges of judges that intimidated it under Nasser. Restrictions on the right to travel were abolished, and private property rights are now considered inviolable. Political rights are far less secure, but they were broadened by comparison to the Nasser era, when the political police were much feared; private criticism of the regime is now unguarded. The courts canceled several fraudulent elections and biased election laws, and allowed the formation of new parties the regime had rejected.

But the uneven empowerment of social classes by political liberalization was evident even in the enforcement of rights and the role of the judiciary. Courts played a role in rolling back Nasserist reforms, ruling the 1960s nationalizations had been unconstitutional and their victims entitled to compensation, and proving themselves zealous in protecting the legal rights of high officials charged with abuse of public property, but they had no comparable record in defending the small property of slum dwellers who had been displaced to build highways and hotels for the "haves." Also, the exercise of political rights varied greatly according to one's social status. On occasion, middle-class figures used the courts to challenge government policies, notably in the famous Pyramid Plateau controversy. For students or workers, however, strikes, public demonstrations, and the possession of antigovernment tracts made them liable to arrest and imprisonment. When courts dismissed charges against political offenders, the regime took to referring political cases to military or exceptional courts. There is now widespread abuse of the human rights of suspected Islamic subversives.

The most striking manifestation of what could be called partial pluralization for the "haves" in post-Nasserist Egypt was the enlivening of the interest-group game, which had been deadened under Nasser's tight corporatism. Controls over syndicates by Nasser's official party, the Arab Socialist Union (ASU), were dismantled, and regime intervention in syndicate elections became far less overt. As regime controls were relaxed, many existing interest groups became vehicles for the expression of bourgeois interests. For example, the Engineer's Syndicate became an advocate for construction interests seeking to commit the government to invest scarce resources in a network of highways and flyovers chiefly of benefit to well-off motorists at a time when public transport was being squeezed. The Chamber of Commerce successfully lobbied against periodic efforts by the Ministry of Supply to fix profit margins and by the Ministry of Finance to raise customs duties. The Egyptian Businessmen's Association, a product of *infitah,* won semi-institutionalized access to parliamentary committees and is even consulted over cabinet-level initiatives. On the other hand, in the 1980s and 1990s, once Islamists captured a number of professional syndicates and seemed poised to turn them into autonomous forces able to challenge the regime, the regime attacked their autonomy. Political liberalization granted from above to Westernized capitalist forces was acceptable, but the takeover of corporatist structures from below by indigenous forces was not.

At the same time, the trade unions, which under Nasser had pride of place in the corporatist system, were brought under tighter control. Under Sadat, as trade unions protested the effects of economic liberalization with strikes, public marches, and disturbances, government intervention in syndicate elections increased, hostile union leaders were purged, and more moderate union leaders were co-opted through the ruling party or appointment as ministers of labor. Public-sector workers, the best organized, were soon deterred from active resistance by the realization that a reserve army of the unemployed coveted their jobs in an era of job insecurity. To be sure, in the 1980s, as public-sector jobs were threatened by privatization and by proposals to reduce labor rights under the Nasserite labor law, trade unions became assertive in defense of the public sector and struck alliances with opposition parties and public-sector managers to derail privatization proposals. But by the 1990s, under relentless IMF pressure, privatization was moving ahead, and trade union resistance was crumbling. As the market economy spreads, unions still do not enjoy the right to strike and, unlike bourgeois interest groups, are kept firmly under corporatist control.

Under political liberalization, Parliament was given greater autonomy from the executive, and opposition parties were permitted to win a small minority of parliamentary seats. The result was that Parliament became another key arena in which the regime's bourgeois constituency could articulate its interests, albeit within the broader lines of presidential policy, whereas other interests were effectively excluded. Under Nasser, 50 percent of parliamentary seats were, in principle at least, reserved for workers and peasants in order to dilute the traditional dominance of the rural notability; by 1987, a majority were rural notables, and 80 of 450 deputies identified themselves as business executives: as more real power over economic regulation and budgetary matters flowed downward to Parliament, business executives found it worthwhile to join the ruling party and to work to put the right people on parliamentary committees.

These committees became breeding grounds for an endless stream of initiatives that sought to reverse statist or populist regulation of the private sector. Parliament regularly turned back government proposals for more equitable distribution of the tax burden—for example, taxing lucrative orchards. From the education committee sprang proposals for a private university, and from the planning and budget committee, opposition to periodic increases in workers salaries. The agricultural committee, representing landlords, carried on a relentless campaign against the Nasser-era agrarian relations law, which restricted rents and gave tenants quasi-property rights. In 1975, Parliament raised rents and diluted tenant security after a debate in which speaker after speaker detailed landlord grievances against peasants, while not one peasant voice—in a parliament 50 percent of which is theoretically workers and peasants—was raised against them. In 1995, the committee went further and proposed a "reform" that would phase out all tenancy contracts; although this law had the potential to inflict great hardship on thousands of tenants who had for more than four decades enjoyed a modicum of security, peasants were virtually voiceless in the debate over the bill, with only a handful of deputies from the tiny Nasserite and National Progressive Unionist parties (NPUP) speaking and voting against it. Dominated by the regime's National Democratic Party, Parliament cannot be a vehicle for the demands of those outside the favored regime-bourgeoisie alliance.

Political parties are the main modern instruments of mass political mobilization. On the face of it, the pluralization of the party system could have made it an instrument of mass incorporation—turning political liberalization into democratization. Party pluralism in Egypt turns out, however, to be largely a manifestation of strictly limited liberalization. Sadat initially permitted opposition parties to provide a safety valve for the discontent of those—notably on the left—who could not be incorporated into the ruling party and might otherwise have resorted to violence against his de-Nasserization of Egypt. Party pluralization also served as a divide-and-rule strategy. Sadat encouraged Islamists to enter the political arena to challenge the power of the left; by the 1990s, fear of Islamists had pushed the left-wing

National Progressive Unionist Party into a virtual alliance with the regime, and politically active secular intellectuals increasingly accepted Mubarak's claims that democracy had to be limited if the Islamists were not to sweep all before them.

The rules and practices of the party system were clearly stacked: the parties law excluded parties based on the main cleavages (class) or the most burning issues (religion). Unfair electoral laws, significant electoral irregularities, patronage resources and electronic media monopoly at the command of the state, strict containment of the opposition's freedom to campaign, and police intimidation of opposition activists—all restricted the opposition parties' ability to mobilize the mass public and ensured that the government party achieved an overwhelming majority in every election. When opposition parties have taken themselves seriously and started to make breakthroughs in the mobilization of resistance to government policies, they have faced repression, as in Sadat's famous 1981 crackdown.

In so hobbling the secular opposition parties, the regime has obstructed their ability to bring segments of the public into the political arena under democratic leadership. The Islamic movement, the one political force already enjoying authentic mass roots and with the potential to mobilize majorities, has also been sharply restricted. Islamic parties were not permitted to form, although their use of the opposition labor and liberal parties as vehicles was tolerated in the 1980s; by the 1990s, the regime was effectively cracking down even on the moderate Muslim Brotherhood. It was the decline of the opposition parties' ability to mobilize public opinion against regime economic policies in the 1990s that gave the regime the confidence to implement IMF-imposed structural reforms.

The Egyptian case shows, therefore, that the likely outcome of political liberalization in a postpopulist regime is discriminatory or lopsided empowerment, not democratization. *A limited pluralization that opens access points to those with resources while providing no effective means for the mobilization of those with no resources, the have-nots—indeed, discouraging such countervailing power—only accentuates class bias in the policy process.*

Conclusion: Citizenship in the Crucible of Political Economy

There is no reason to be optimistic about democratization in the Middle East, but it is *political economy*—the requisites of capitalist development—more than *political culture* that is the main constraint on it. Political Islam, per se, is no insurmountable barrier to pluralization. Nor is there convincing evidence that a distinctive political culture retards the propensity and capacity for political participation, which modernization theory rightly argues is a universal concomitant of socioeconomic development. If given the channels and freedoms, Middle Easterners will exercise their political rights in a rational way. As modernization expands the base of potential participation, regimes find it harder to govern in the purely authoritarian ways, which simply repress participation demands. This *does not* mean they must democratize, but it does require that they find ways to channel and contain these demands.

As Mosca (1935) points out, the citizens never rule; only a politically active stratum of them does. But elite strategies are decisive in determining *who* gets access to—recruitment into and influence over—the ruling stratum, while citizenship rights represent elite concessions giving ordinary people certain minimal claims on scarce resources (Turner, chapter 2 in this volume). Authoritarian regimes contract and expand participation opportunities and citizenship rights in a *selective* way designed to appease and co-opt potential constituents while weakening rivals or elements of the population they seek to control. The Egyptian and Syrian cases have indicated that nondemocratic strategies remain viable, but differences in them do differentially empower different strata. This is no merely capricious development attributable to culture. Rather, the choice of constituents and enemies, of inclusion and exclusion, depends on a regime's stage and strategy of economic development.

In the *populist stage,* regimes sought to replace weak or dependent capitalist classes with statist engines of development benefiting the new middle class and, to a degree, the mass public. Populist authoritarianism initially widened opportunities for the middle and lower classes while narrowing it for the upper classes. Thus, in the establishment of Ba'th rule in Syria, a regime attacking an old ruling class needed to mobilize mass support and to establish a single-party and corporatist state structure that, for a while, satisfied some participatory aspirations of the previously excluded. In defining citizenship to mean certain minimal entitlements on scarce resources, populist regimes reversed some of the inegalitarian consequences of the distribution of property and the market. But these rights, being largely granted from above—Turner's "passive citizenship"—rather than extracted via struggle from below, were only too readily reversed when the failure of statism required regimes to create the conditions of private capital accumulation. *Postpopulist* political liberalization, fully mature in Egypt, empowers unevenly, turning the populist strategy on its head: it increases the influence and access of the bourgeoisie while containing or even excluding that of the mass public. If citizenship mediates between the state and the anarchy of the market (Turner, chapter 2 in this volume), its selective acquisition means that the haves will enjoy enforcable rights (notably property rights), but those most in need, the have-nots, will bear the burdens of the return to the market, which requires the rollback of labor rights.

That the political economy of development is the key to moving from liberalization to democratization should be evident from even a cursory location of the Middle East in comparative perspective. Crude modernization theory may imagine the global replication of the Western (British) model in which liberal structures (parliament and elections) are democratized once development empowers the masses and makes their claim for inclusion irresistible. However, evolutionary democratic incorporation in the West was accompanied not just by mass politicization but also by an economic expansion large enough that demands for economic redistribution could be accommodated without civil war or massive capital disinvestment. In later developers, capital accumulation has normally been associated with authoritarian rule for the haves. And even where economic growth has permitted a move toward democratization, as in the Latin American and East Asian new industrialized countries (NICS), it is still very much conditional on the masses refraining from using political rights to demand economic redistribution, while the military waits in the wings. In the Middle East, the "premature" granting of socioeconomic rights—before industrial takeoff—means current democratization there is likely to be accompanied by the opposite of the Western experience—not the *expansion*, but the *reversal* of such rights. As such, there is no need for cultural explanations of the Middle East's democracy deficit: in scenarios where the demands of citizenship are likely to outrun those of primitive capital accumulation, the former is likely to be sharply constrained until, and if, the latter is accomplished.

7

State Formation and Citizenship in Lebanon

The Politics of Membership and Exclusion in a Sectarian State

RANIA MAKTABI

Qu'est ce qu'une famille òu l'on trouve moitié d'étrangers?
—George Samné, 1921[1]

THE PEOPLE OF LEBANON have not been counted since 1932. Nearly eight decades have passed, and nobody actually knows for certain the precise number of people in the country or the size of the eighteen acknowledged confessional sects. For a country where the political system is founded on political representation according to the relative size of these sects, carrying out population censuses involves the continuous renegotiation of the political organization formula according to the demographic fluctuations within each sect. The Lebanese regime, however, has since 1932 evaded officially updating a count of its citizens and thereby determining the demographic strength of each community. Instead, the regime has relied on the cross-confessional National Pact, which was agreed on at the eve of independence in 1943 and which stipulates that political representation was to reflect the relative sizes of the sects as rendered in the 1932 census.

---

1. Quoted in Zamir (1982, 41). Samné's article was entitled "La question du Liban ou la quadrature de la cercle," published in *Correspondance d'Orient* (Paris), 8 May 1921.

Perhaps most clearly, the sensitivity accorded to the demographic structure in the country is illustrated in the politics of citizenship that reflects the authorization process where legal regulations as well as political considerations determine membership in the Lebanese state. I maintain that, since the creation of modern Lebanon in 1920, the regime has applied citizenship policies in order to monitor the Lebanese citizenry and to form its Constitution in a way that would buttress its rule. Citizenship policies were applied to reinforce the size of the Christian citizen population through the naturalization of Christian immigrants and refugees. At the same time, the regime undermined the size of the Muslim citizen population by excluding stateless persons from membership in the state and by denying Lebanese citizenship to long-term immigrants of Muslim background.

It was not until 1994, following the fifteen-year-long civil war, that a citizenship decree was issued allowing up to 120,000 persons to become Lebanese citizens (*Al-Hayat*, 22 July 1994).[2] A significant number of the naturalized had been either stateless or long-term residents in the country, and their inclusion as citizens of the state had been on the political agenda several times since the mid-1960s without being accomplished. The citizenship decree heralded a new approach toward naturalization of noncitizens, breaking with the citizenship policies established after independence. The decree was characterized as an important step toward national unification by some groups, whereas others voiced strong criticism against the inclusion of "foreigners" as members of the Lebanese citizenry.[3]

How do we explain the regime's reluctance in counting its population? Why were large groups of inhabitants excluded from the citizenry? What was the role of the politics of citizenship in Lebanon before the civil war broke out in 1975?

The relationship between the *regime* (i.e., the organization of political power) and the *politics of citizenship* (i.e., structures and processes of membership in the state) is at the center of this article. I seek to identify some of the political motives that lie behind the politics of citizenship in Lebanon before the civil war in 1975. The Lebanese state is analyzed as a membership organization where both formal-legal regulations and political objectives control admission.

Using an analysis of the politics of citizenship, I argue that Lijphart's (1977) classification of the Lebanese regime as a consociational democracy

---

2. The names of persons who were naturalized by decree were issued in the official newspaper *(Al-jarida al-rasmiyya)* on 30 June 1994.

3. Some estimates and figures regarding the Lebanese population are rendered later in the chapter.

disregards critical factors in the Lebanese political system that contribute to a better understanding of the outbreak of the civil war in 1975. Rather than a consociational democracy, the Lebanese regime was closer to an *ethnocracy,* where political organization was based on democratic institutions, but also on policies that restricted access to these institutions according to ethnic affiliation (Butenschon 1993). The politics of citizenship played a central role in sustaining the political aspirations of one ethnic group in an ethnically divided society and can be seen as a set of policies that restricted access to democratic institutions.

From a Consociationalist to an Ethnocratic Understanding of the Lebanese Regime

Lijphart (1977) indicates that "consociationalism in Lebanon must be judged to have performed satisfactorily for more than thirty years" (149). His theory of consociational democracy focuses on the degree of elite accommodation and its effect on stable democratic governance in plural societies. He points out that political elites are able to transcend and solve conflicts that arise between and among different sects, despite the existence of social, economic, and political cleavages in deeply divided societies. Through accommodation, elites are able to reach agreements that stabilize the political system and ensure democratic governance. According to him, the unwritten National Pact of 1943 agreed on between the Maronite president and the Sunni prime minister "marked the beginning of consociational democracy in Lebanon" (1969, 217).

Despite the National Pact's being an agenda for consensus at the time of agreement, I argue that, rather than laying the basis for democratic governance, it cemented and reinforced structural mechanisms of exclusion that were established after the formation of the Lebanese state in 1920. These exclusive structures monitored membership in the state according to ethnic affiliation in ways that could not lay the basis for democratic governance, leading eventually to the outbreak of the civil war in 1975. Rather than laying the basis for an intercommunal modus operandi for the Lebanese regime in 1943, the pact was an endorsement of the status quo because it legitimized further a particular view regarding the distribution of power in Lebanon that had crystallized more than a decade earlier.

Among the central mechanisms of exclusion embodied by the National Pact we find the 1932 census, which served as a guideline for political organization in Lebanon; representation in the government, Parliament, and the bureaucracy was to reflect the relative size of the sects as rendered in that census. A closer look at the census reveals interesting details that reflect a particular view regarding who were considered legitimate or illegitimate members of the Lebanese state, *and reflects* the view expressed by the pre–civil war regime.

A New Reading of the 1932 Census

As a document, the 1932 census has played a central role in the organization of political power in Lebanon.[4] It showed that the Christian Maronites constituted 29 percent, the Sunni Muslims 22.5 percent, and the Shi'ite Muslims 20 percent of the citizen population at that time (Sluglett and Farouk-Sluglett 1993, 144). Using these percentages, Lijphart (1977) indicates that "the main sects are the Maronite Christians (about 30 percent of the population in the mid 1950s), the Sunni Muslims (20 percent), Shi'ite Muslims (18 percent), and Greek Orthodox (11 percent)" (147).

A translation of the 1932 census table as presented is rendered in table 7.1, along with the original version of the census results (table 7.2). A closer look at the original version of the census brings to light surprising details that give rise to several questions.

(1) Why does the census pay such a significant attention to the Lebanese emigrant population? (2) Why is the number of emigrants and information about tax payment rendered in such detail? (3) Why does the date 30 August 1924 play such an important role in the census? (4) How is the category *foreigners* defined? Why are foreigners not specified according to religious affiliation as the categories *emigrants* and *residents* are? (5) Why did the regime abide by the results of this census for more than four decades? Some answers to these questions can be discerned by analyzing the politics of membership and citizenship in Lebanon.

The State as a Membership Organization

Walzer (1994) indicates that "the distribution of membership[,] . . . in any ongoing society, is a matter of political decision" (40). States (through the governing regime) thus apply certain political standards and have absolute authority to include or exclude persons as members of state.

In Western democracies, the concept of citizenship is most often related to the set of rights and obligations that a citizen is entitled to within a given state. The approach presented here focuses on citizenship as membership in a given territorial state. Aspects of membership highlight the legal classifica-

---

4. I am indebted to Mr. Hussein Quteish, who first put me on the track of looking closer at the 1932 census in an undated article in *Kull Shay'*.

TABLE 7.1

The Results of the 1932 Census

Summary Results of the Census of Inhabitants of the Lebanese Republic which Occurred in 1932 According to the Regulation of the Higher Census Committee

Residents				Emigrants			
				Before 30 August, 1924		After 30 August, 1924	
				pays taxes	does not pay	pays taxes	does not pay
Residents	793,396	Sunni	178,100	2,653	9,840	1,089	3,623
Emigrants	254,987	Shiite	155,035	2,977	4,543	1,770	2,220
Foreigners	61,297	Druze	53,334	2,067	3,205	1,183	2,295
	1,109,680	Maronite	227,800	31,697	58,457	11,434	21,809
		Greek Catholic	46,709	7,190	16,544	1,855	4,038
		Greek Orthodox	77,312	12,547	31,521	3,922	9,041
		Protestant	6,869	607	1,575	174	575
		Armenian Orthodox	6,102	1	60	191	1,718
		Armenian Catholic	5,890	9	50	20	375
		Syriac Orthodox	2,723	6	34	3	54
		Syriac Catholic	2,803	9	196	6	101
		Jews	3,588	6	214	7	188
		Chaldean Orthodox	190	0	0	0	0
		Chaldean Catholic	548	0	6	0	19
		Miscellaneous	6,393	212	758	59	234
			793,396	59,981	127,003	21,713	46,290
	Thereof			Males	Females	Males	Females
				44,749	15,232	72,447	54,556
	Before August 1924	186,984		Pays fees and does not pay before 30 August, 1924			
				16,578	5,135	26,246	20,044
	After August 1924	68,003		Pays fees and does not pay after 30 August, 1924			
		254,987					

1 October 1932

President of the Higher Census Committee
Director of Interior Affairs
Sign: Subhi Abun-Nasr

Source: *al-jarida al-rasmiyya* no. 2718, 10 October 1932

tion of inhabitants within states as *citizens* and *noncitizens*, differentiating thereby between inhabitants who are regarded by the governing regime as the state's legitimate subjects and those who are not.

One reason for the prerogative that states exercise in forming membership policies is that admitting or excluding potential appliers has significant consequences on political organization within the state. Although inhabitants of a given state are residents, only citizens—i.e., residents who have citizenship—are eligible for the protection of the state if they abide by the informal or formal contract that defines authority in the state. In democracies, citizenship policies are thus membership policies that regulate admission to political participation in a state; they are applied to differentiate

TABLE 7.2

The Results of the 1932 Census (in Arabic)

الجريدة الرسمية

العدد ٨٧١ تاريخ ٥/ ١٠/١٩٣٤

صفحة ٥

خلاصة نتيجة الاحصاء

لسكان الجمهورية اللبنانية

الذي جرى في سنة ١٩٣٢ وفقاً لقرار لجنة الاحصاء العليا

لا يدفع	بدفم رسوم	لا يدفع	يدفم رسوم	مقيمون		
بعد ٣٠ اب سنة ١٩٢٤		قبل ٣٠ اب سنة ١٩٢٤				
٣٦٢٣	١٠٨٦	٩٨٤٠	٢٦٥٣	١٧٨١٠٠ سني	مقيمون ٧٩٣٣٩٦
٢٢٢٠	١٧٧٠	٤٥١٣	٢٩٧٧	١٥٥٠٣٥ شيعي	مهاجرون ٢٥٤٩٨٧
٢٢٩٥	١١٨٣	٣٣٠٥	٢٠٦٧	٥٣٣٣٤ درزي	اجانب ٦١٢٩٧
٢١٨٠٩	١١٤٣٤	٥٨١٥٧	٣١٦٩٧	٢٢٧٨٠٠ ماروني	١١٠٩٦٨٠
٤٠٣٨	١٨٥٥	١٦٥٤٤	٧١٩٠	٤٦٧٠٩ روم كاثوليك	
٩٠٤١	٣٦٢٢	٣١٥٢١	١٢٥٤٧	٧٧٣١٢ روم ارثوذكس	
٥٧٥	١٧٤	١٥٧٥	٦٠٧	٦٨٦٩ بروتستانت	
١٧١٨	١٩١	٦٠	١	٢٦١٠٢ ارمن ارثوذكس	
٣٧٥	٢٠	٥٠	٩	٥٨٩٠ ارمن كاثوليك	
٥٤	٣	٣٤	٦	٢٧٢٣ سريان ارثوذكس	
١٠١	٦	١١٦	٩	٢٨٠٣ سريان كاثوليك	
١٨٨	٧	٢١٤	٦	٣٥٨٨ موسوي	
٠	٠	٠	٠	١٩٠ كلدان ارثوذكس	
١٩	٠	٦	٠	٥٤٨ كلدان كاثوليك	
٢٣٤	٥٩	٢٥٨	٢١٢	٦٣٩٣ متفرقه	
٤٦٢٩٠	٢٦٧١٣	١٢٧٠٠٣	٥٩٩٨١	٧٩٣٣٩٦	

انات	ذكور	انات	ذكور	يكون
٥٤٥٥٦	٧٢٤٤٧	١٥٢٣٢	٤٤٧٤٩	
	قبل ٣٠ اب سنة ١٩٢٤ يدفع رسوم ولا يدفع			١٨٦٩٨١ قبل اب سنة ١٩٢٤
٢٠٠٤٤	٢٦٦٢٦	٥١٣٥	١٦٥٧٨	
	بعد ٣٠ اب سنة ١٩٢٤ يدفع رسوم ولا يدفع			٦٨٠٠٣ بعد اب سنة ١٩٢٤
				٢٥٤٩٨٧

في ١ تشرين الاول سنة ١٩٣٢

رئيس لجنة الاحصاء العليا

مدير الداخلية

الامضاء : صبحي ابو النصر

between those who are eligible for legitimate rule formation and those who are not. Citizens are able to voice legitimate demands, form rules, and enforce the application of these rules to all members within society, including noncitizens.

Membership in a state is channeled through one authoritative agent, the state's governing regime, and has all-encompassing effects on a person. Citizenship accords the citizen with access to a range of resources at the state's disposal, depending on the level of modernization as reflected in political, social, and economic institutions: civil resources (legal protection and access to the courts of law); social resources (welfare, education, and health services); political resources (voting, political representation); and economic resources (use of the state's land and water, work permits, jobs in the state administration, legal inheritance, right to purchase property). The right of permanent abode in the territories of the state is also an important ingredient of citizenship rights (Abdallah 1986, Brubaker 1992, Davis 1997, Marshall 1965).

Membership in Sectarian States

In sectarian states, the main ideological and political cleavages run along ethnic lines (linguistic, religious, or racial). Lebanon and other deeply divided societies—such as former Yugoslavia, Israel, Lithuania, Latvia, Estonia, Northern Ireland, and South Africa—represent challenging cases regarding the organization of political power and the accommodation of various group interests. These states face continuous disputes among groups that reflect the ethnic cleavages in society, disputes usually regarding the principles and mechanisms of governance. As "*the* organization in society that effectively establishes . . . rules of behavior" (Migdal 1988, xx, emphasis in original), the state is often at the center of continuous struggle between the various ethnic groups in achieving control over the natural and institutional resources of the state.

Nationalism and ideals regarding democratic governance politicize the question of membership in sectarian states. Although ethnic communities have been provided with national aspirations of self-governance, the ideal of one man one vote transformed the demographic strength of each community into a political determinant: the greater the numeric strength of an ethnic community, the more powerful its political influence and thereby its ability to implement its own political aspirations vis-à-vis the other ethnic groups. In sectarian states, according to Butenschon (1993), one ethnic group among many usually manages to secure the most important instruments of state power and to subordinate all considerations concerning the distribution of power to the basic intention of perpetuating its rule (5).

In Lebanon and several other sectarian states, we can discern, as Butenschon (1993) indicates, "a parallel development of two conflictual modes of political organisation; on the one hand a fabric of democratic institutions and on the other policies designed to restrict the access to these institutions according to ethnic affiliation" (4–5). He identifies regimes that primarily or in a fundamental way are based on the latter mode of political organization as *ethnocracies*. An ethnocracy is defined as

> a political regime which, in contrast to democracy, is instituted on the basis of *qualified rights to citizenship* and with *ethnic affiliation* (defined in terms of race, descent, religion, or language) as the distinguishing principle. The raison d'être of the ethnocracy is to secure that the most important instruments of state power are controlled by a specific ethnic collectivity. . . . Ethnocracies are characterized by their *control system*—the legal, institutional, and physical instruments of power deemed necessary to secure ethnic dominance. . . . Ethnocracy . . . denotes regimes that express the identity and aspirations of one ethnic group in an ethnically divided society. It is a form of government based on the rule of one ethnic group over other groups. The constitutional and institutional character of an ethnocratic regime can be seen as the *outcome* of or a *stage* in a conflict where ethnic collectivities struggle for control over space, natural resources, and political institutions. (1993, 5–6, emphasis in original)

Butenschon's approach to the study of sectarian states as ethnocracies proves fruitful in discerning the parallel development of democratic institutionsand the policies that reveal the ethnocratic character of the Lebanese regime.

Although there developed, on the one hand, a set of democratic institutions such as a representative parliament and governmental rule, the political system had preset proportional representative quotas for the different sects. The National Pact legitimized the institution of fixed quotas based on the relative size of the sects as rendered in the 1932 census. These quotas were not altered in light of demographic changes, thus maintaining the built-in majority status of Christian political representation in general and Maronite dominance in particular. The preset representation quotas functioned as a policy that guarded the prerogatives of the Maronite sect. Until the outbreak of the civil war, representatives of the Maronite sect secured key political positions in the government, the army, and the Deuxieme Bureau (internal security), as well as sensitive positions in the state administration, such as in the Directory General of Personal Affairs (DGPA) and the Directory General of Public Security (DGPS). As a collectivity, Christians outnumbered Muslims by a ratio of six to five in the Cabinet and the Parliament until 1984, resulting in a net Christian political dominance. Phares

(1995) indicates that one of the main objectives of the Christian political establishment immediately after the creation of modern Lebanon in 1920

> was to guarantee full control of governmental institutions. Profiting from the Muslim boycott of the administration, prominant Christian families sent their members to occupy different echelons of the ministries. Since this period, Lebanon's governmental apparatus was mostly controlled by the Christian element. Christian domination of the bureaucracy was also seen by the political establishment as a way to give additional support to the Lebanese identity of the state.[5] (80)

The Christians are today still regarded as being overrepresented in the government and in the bureaucracy relative to the current estimated size of the religious communities (Drysdale and Blake 1985, 199–200; Perthes 1992, 419).

Although governance in Lebanon was based on a presumably democratic principle, Cabinet members' right to veto decisions they deemed unfavorable developed into an instrument for maintaining the status quo in favor of the Christian-dominated regime. Demands for new population censuses that would assess demographic changes and pave the way for political rearrangements were repeatedly vetoed by Christian representatives.

Another indication of the dual development of both democratic institutions and mechanisms that restrain participation is illustrated through the politics of citizenship. Although the Lebanese regime professed democratic governance in the form of parliamentary rule and free elections, the politics of citizenship emerged as an effective instrument in restricting political participation and representation according to ethnic affiliation. In reaction to the political participation of members of opponent groups, the regime barred the inclusion of citizens who might jeopardize the dominant position of Christian groups. Through the politics of citizenship, I argue that persons who belonged to Christian sects—Armenians, Chaldeans, Christian Palestinians, and Syriacs—were favored as members of the Lebanese state and were thereby included as citizens, whereas persons who belonged to Muslim sects—the populations of Wadi Khaled and the Seven Villages, the Kurds, the stateless, immigrants and refugees of Muslim background—were disfavored as members of the state and were thereby excluded from the citizenry.

In order to maintain its prerogatives, the Lebanese regime relied on a

---

5. At the time, Muslim political leaders saw the creation of the Lebanese state as opposed to their national aspirations where unification with Syria was sought.

control system whereby legal measures were applied to prevent the inclusion of new members in the Lebanese citizenry. Official identity cards and citizenship certificates played a central role in regulating the legal, social, economic, and security status of large segments of the inhabitant population. Administrative institutions such as the DGPA and the DGPS,[6] as well as administrative measures such as population censuses, the Personal Status Registry, and other personal registries,[7] turned into effective control instruments at the hands of the ruling regime in documenting, sealing, and manipulating entry into the Lebanese citizenry.

Estimates and Figures of the Lebanese Population

We have to rely on semiofficial samples and plausible estimations in order to assess the population of Lebanon because no official census has been carried out since 1932. The Ministry of Information issued figures in 1985 indicating that the total Lebanese population was 5,659,215. This figure, however, includes long-term Lebanese emigrants and their descendants, who permanently live outside the country. In addition, large numbers of Lebanese left the country during the civil war (1975–89), many of them acquiring citizenship in their countries of residence. A United Nations (UN) estimate rendered the size of the population in 1995 at approximately 3 million (United Nations 1994) while the World Bank estimated the size of the population at approximately 4 million (World Bank 1994–95). It is unclear whether the Palestinian population is included in those figures. According to UN figures, there were at the time 334,659 registered Palestinians in Lebanon (*UNRWA* 1994, 7).[8]

When asked about estimations regarding the number of Lebanese, Bishara Mirhij,[9] former minister of interior and one of the three persons who signed the citizenship decree in 1994, replied:

Nobody knows. Lebanon is an extremely mobile society. The matter is complicated by the war; newborns after 1975 are not officially registered. Persons who have been dead for decades are still registered as living and have not been crossed off. There is a whole generation that only possesses *ikhraj qayd*. We

6. In Arabic, the DGPA is *Al-mudiriyya al-'amma lil-ahwal al-shakhsiyya*. The directory is popularly called '*An-nufus*'. The DGPS is *Al-mudiriyya al-'amma lil-amn al'am*.

7. In Arabic, *Sijilat al-ahwal al-madaniyya, sijilat al-quyud, aqlam al-nufus*.

8. See Salam (1994, 18–20) for an updated discussion of the size of the Palestinian community in Lebanon. He estimates the Palestinian population to number between 280,000 and 320,000.

9. Mirhij was reelected as member of parliament in the elections of 1996.

have the problem of ID forgeries, as well as corruption among the local officials. The issue of counting our population is difficult and sensitive.[10] (interview with author, 5 February 1996)

Political analysts indicate that the issuing of numbers and figures in Lebanon is treated as state secrets (Dagher 1993). According to Hussein Quteish, journalist and former political advisor to the Speaker of Parliament
(1989–92), the DGPA probably has good estimates; however, it "does not
issue figures nor does it announce them; it even hides them. If it is pressed
it gives false figures, or it informs that it does not have the exact numbers"
(*Kull Shay'*, undated article provided by Mr. Quteish). The difficulties related to producing population estimates are part and parcel of the political
sensitivity that encompasses citizenship policies in sectarian states.

The Palestinian community impinges on the analysis of the noncitizen
population resident in Lebanon and the general discourse concerning citizenship policies. Palestinian refugees form the largest single group of noncitizen inhabitants in Lebanon, probably equaling up to 10 percent of the
total population. The presence of the Palestinian community is used by
Lebanese citizens as a reason for not including yet another group that might
further complicate the intricate Lebanese political system. However, the
politics of citizenship as practiced by the Lebanese regime since the 1920s
indicates that selective citizenship policies were applied before the Palestinian refugees came to Lebanon. The Palestinians certainly exacerbated the
demographic imbalance in favor of Muslim groups, but the Palestinians did
not *create* this imbalance, which existed already in 1920, nearly three decades before their arrival in 1948. Furthermore, it is indicative of the citizenship policies of the ethnocratic regime in Lebanon that large segments of
the Christian Palestinian population, who generally belonged to higher-class
echelons than their Muslim compatriots, received Lebanese citizenship in
the 1950s and 1960s.[11]

10. Authorization cards issued by a local official *(mukhtar)* who has the authority to certify
persons who reside in his district. *Ikhraj qayd* were introduced following the outbreak of the civil
war in 1975 when all issuing of official ID cards stopped. *Ikhraj qayd* are still issued as the only
authoritative personal ID cards, and have to be renewed every six months. In 1993, the Ministry of Interior announced that new ID cards would be introduced in the foreseeable future, but
no measures have yet been taken in that matter (see *Al-Nahar,* 6 July 1994).

11. According to 1987 UNRWA estimates, thirty thousand Palestinians have become
Lebanese citizens (Salam 1994, 19). Rosemary Sayigh (1994) indicates that "Christians among
[middle-class urban Palestinians] were at first easily granted Lebanese nationality. . . . Middle-
class Muslims could also obtain nationality by paying lawyers and proving Lebanese ancestry"
(23). She further states that "[e]ase of naturalization for middle-class Palestinians ended in the
mid-1960s. Every application had to be passed by every memeber of the Cabinet, giving Ka-
ta'eb ministers the power to veto" (33).

Citizenship Legislation in Lebanon

Disputes regarding the identity of the state are closely related to the still unresolved conflicts concerning the *definition of the citizenry*. Who, if not its own population, is to decide what Lebanon is? We are left with this basic question: Who is Lebanese? Or, in legal and social scientific words: What are the rules and principles that determine the construction and formation of the Lebanese citizenry?

The existent citizenship legislation in Lebanon can be seen as legal guidelines for defining the citizenry in any given state. The foundation of Lebanese citizenship is rooted in the Lausanne Treaty of 24 July 1923. Following the defeat of the Ottoman Empire, this treaty regulated the legal status of former Ottoman subjects.[12] In Lebanon, the treaty was put in effect on 30 August 1924 through Resolution 2825 *(qarar)* issued by the French high commissioner. Article 1 stipulates that "[a]ny person who was a Turkish subject [*taba'a*] and resided in the territories of Greater Lebanon on August 30, 1924, is confirmed as a Lebanese subject and is regarded from now on as having lost the Turkish citizenship."[13] A follow-up resolution established Lebanese citizenship through Resolution 15 on 19 January 1925, whereby children of Lebanese fathers, foreign women married to Lebanese, persons born on the territories of Greater Lebanon, and foreigners resident for five uninterrupted years in Lebanon were entitled to Lebanese citizenship.[14] The current citizenship law in Lebanon is constituted of several pieces of legislation, the most important of which are Resolutions 2825 and 15 (Isam Ni'man,[15] interview with author 10 February 1996).[16]

Legal documents, however, can be interpreted and applied in different modes. What is apparent is that existing citizenship regulations have tended

12. The Lausanne Treaty was signed by Turkey on one side and Great Britain, France, Italy, Japan, and Yugoslavia on the other. The treaty indicated in Articles 30–36 that all former Ottoman subjects residing in the regions detached from Turkey are to enjoy the citizenship of the state to which regional sovereignty has been transferred (Abdallah 1986, 35).

13. Full text of Regulation 2825 is found in Karam (1993, 212–13).

14. See Karam (1993, 209–11) and Abdallah (1986, 224–27) for the full text of the Resolution 15.

15. Ni'man is a lawyer and former member of parliament (1992–96) who has worked with the question of citizenship. In 1984 and again in 1988, he forwarded a bill for a new citizenship law in Lebanon (See *Al-'Amal*, 12 December 1984).

16. The formation of a citizenship law has been on the political agenda since 1975. The call for an updated law was stipulated in Article 6 of the Taif Agreement of 1989. Several governmental committees have been appointed in order to prepare for a new citizenship law. A proposal for a new citizenship law was finally presented by Minister of Interior Michel Al-Murr in 1999 (*Al-Anwar*, 8 June 1999).

to be interpreted in a way that satisfies specific ideas concerning who is seen as preferred members of the state. By conceiving Lebanon as a Christian home in a predominantly Muslim area, the Lebanese regime has preferred to include members of Christian rather than Muslim background in order to secure a Christian majority as basis for its rule. On the one hand, Christian emigrants and their offspring have been seen as potential citizens in a state, defined by the regime, to be a Christian refuge. On the other hand, stateless persons and other noncitizen residents, predominantly of Muslim background, who live on Lebanese territories have been defined as not belonging to the Lebanese nation, but rather to the Muslim Arab nation.

The Creation of Greater Lebanon in 1920

The creation of modern Lebanon was to a large degree the product of Maronite national aspirations with French Mandate policy as midwife.[17] At the turn of the twentieth century, the political ambitions of the Maronite community consisted of three separate demands: an independent state, extended borders, and French protection (Zamir 1985, 4). Following the disintegration of the Ottoman Empire in 1918, France assumed the right to rule the autonomous Province of Mount Lebanon *(sanjak)* on behalf of the League of Nations at the San Remo Conference on 28 April 1920. Under the French Mandate, the Maronites opted for the enlargement of the province, arguing that it was not economically viable as an independent state. They repeatedly called for the inclusion of four regions regarded as integral parts of their envisaged homeland: Tripoli and the district of 'Akkar in the north, the Beqa' Valley in the east, the district of Jabal 'Amel in the south, and the coastal towns of Tyre, Sidon in the south, and Beirut.

Despite French reluctance regarding the inclusion of predominantly Muslim areas, Greater Lebanon was established on 1 September 1920 to the satisfaction of Maronite leaders. The conviction of the Maronites regarding extended borders "was so powerful that they totally ignored the implication of such a demand; namely the inclusion of a large Muslim population within the larger entity" (Zamir 1985, 37). Whereas the Maronites had constituted a majority in the *sanjak,* in Greater Lebanon they became a minority. The population of the *sanjak* in 1911 totaled 414,800, approximately 80 percent of whom were Christians, with the Maronites comprising 58 percent of that group. In the areas annexed to the *sanjak,* the Christians

17. Lebanon thus became a French Mandate, although French governance was not formally approved by the League of Nations until July 1922, and the approval was not effective before September 1923 (Mansfield 1973, 57).

comprised 35 percent of the population after 1920, with the Maronites a mere 14 percent (Dagher 1993; Zamir 1985, 98–99).

The demographic constitution of the new Lebanese entity reflected not only the altered proportional strength between the different confessional communities. More critical were the political aspirations expressed by the population in the annexed territories. Many inhabitants, most notably the Sunni community, resented their enforced detachment from Syria and regarded Greater Lebanon as an artificial entity. They repeatedly insisted on being reunited with Syria, which they envisaged as their Arab homeland.[18]

Upon the fulfillment of the Maronite national aspirations with the establishment of Greater Lebanon, a new era began in which administrative instruments and control mechanisms supported the political objective of upholding the Maronite state-idea of Lebanon:[19] a predominantly Christian state with strong ties to the West. How were the Maronites to achieve a politically dominant position in Greater Lebanon when they constituted less than one-third of the resident population in 1920?

The Politics of Citizenship: Squaring the Demographic Circle

Already in May 1921, George Samné, a Lebanese immigrant in France, expressed his views on the insolvable problem the Maronites faced in Greater Lebanon. They had either to detach the annexed areas in order to retain a Christian majority and thereby identity or to retain the enlarged borders, which would necessitate a different approach toward Syria and the Muslim population. "By striving to realize these two goals simultaneously the Lebanese Christians were attempting to attain the impossible—in Samné's words 'the squaring of a circle.'" (Zamir 1982, 40).[20]

Another prominent Maronite political figure, Emile Eddé,[21] foresaw the

18. The Sunnis had supported Faisal's apppointment as king of Syria in 1919 and were eager to see the formation of Lebanon united with Syria before Faisal was expelled by the French in July 1920.

19. The *state-idea* refers to conceptions regarding the identity of the state and to normative foundations expressing what the purpose of the state should be and who is to constitute its members (see Butenschon 1993, 15–18).

20. Together with Shukri Ghanem, George Samné organized a group of Syrian and Lebanese Christian immigrants in France, the Comité Central Syrien, which supported French control over the Levant. Samné was editor of *Correspondance Syrien,* where he published a series of articles during 1921 and 1922 pointing at the differences between the autonomous Province of Mount Lebanon prior to 1920 and the enlarged Greater Lebanon after 1920 (Zamir 1982, 40–41).

21. Eddé was a member of the first and third Lebanese deputation to the Paris Conference

political dilemma that a large Muslim population in Greater Lebanon would entail. Already in 1926, he suggested that French Mandate officials relinquish the town of Tripoli and the region of South Lebanon to Syria in order to decrease the size of the Muslim population. In a memorandum presented to French authorities in 1932,[22] he argued that territorial reduction of Greater Lebanon is essential in order to "permit [Lebanon] in having a more consistent Christian majority" (quoted in Zamir 1985, 232). Eddé suggested that Tripoli be transformed into a free city under direct French control, in which Christian inhabitants would obtain Lebanese citizenship, whereas Muslim inhabitants would obtain Syrian citizenship. He explained:

> In this way, Lebanon would number 55,000 Muslims less, which would constitute an agreeable result. . . . There is also room to make the whole region of South Lebanon, which is composed of a very large Muslim Shiite majority, an autonomous entity. Thanks to this second amputation, Lebanon will be quit of nearly 140,000 Shiite and Sunni Muslims, and remain with a Christian majority equaling approximately 80 percent of its entire population.[23] (quoted in ibid., 232–33)

Territorial reduction did not materialize as a means of decreasing the Muslim majority in the Lebanese state. However, other means, peculiarly in line with Eddé's views regarding the use of citizenship as a political instrument, were deployed in the aftermath of the census in order to reduce the political impact of the Muslim majority in Greater Lebanon. In an effort to defend and maintain the Christian character of the state, the Maronite regime applied citizenship policies that sought to weaken the demographic basis and political representation of opponent groups and to strengthen the demo-

---

in 1919–20, which demanded the creation of Greater Lebanon. He served as prime minister in 1929–30 and was president in 1936–41 (Zamir 1978, 232).

22. According to Zamir (1978), the memorandum itself is not dated, but a note attached to it is dated 29 August 1932 and identifies the writer as "M. Eddé, député Libanais" (232). The date corresponds to two weeks before the census ended on 14 September 1932 and only one month before the results of the census were officially presented on 5 October 1932. Eddé most probably knew the preliminary results of the census and reacted swiftly by proposing a radical solution to the population figures that showed that the number of Christian and Muslim Lebanese residents were more or less equal.

23. Eddé knew, however, that his ideas of relinquishing parts of the territories of Greater Lebanon would be seen as acts of treason by the Maronite community, whose leaders regarded Greater Lebanon as the result of their nationalist aspirations of an independent homeland. According to Zamir (1978), Eddé later dropped these ideas either due to personal conviction that it was possible to cooperate with the Muslims in the regime, or due to a perception that the territorial reduction of Lebanon was not attainable (234).

graphic and political basis of Christian groups. By excluding significant numbers of Muslim inhabitants from the Lebanese citizenry, the regime buttressed its rule along ethnocratic principles.

The main instrument in attaining the political goal of maintaining a Christian majority was the politics of citizenship, which evolved into a mechanism of control. The politics of citizenship included several elements: (1) politicizing the role of the 1921 and 1932 census by changing their character from administrative measures into legal registries, which served the political objectives of the ethnocratic regime; (2) the regime's consistent use of the "emigrant card"—i.e., the inclusion of registered emigrants before 1924 and their offspring as part of the Lebanese citizenry, counterbalancing the Muslim majority of residents on Lebanese territories; (3) inconsistent interpretations of existing citizenship legislation; (4) inaccurate personal registries; (5) the presence of the state in the courts of law in appeals for citizenship; (6) the Maronite president's absolute authority in approving or disapproving all applications for citizenship; (7) administrative personal registries as control instruments.

These elements amounted to effective control instruments at the hands of the regime in its endeavor to square the Lebanese circle between 1920 and 1975. The remaining part of this essay discusses the main factors that laid the basis for the politics of citizenship in Lebanon and that shaped membership policies along ethnic lines, buttressing the ethnocratic character of the regime.

The 1921 Census

On 9 March 1921, the French Mandate issued Resolution 763 for the purpose of counting the residents in Lebanon (Abdallah 1986, 29). In the local press, the high commissioner stated that the census was necessary for purely administrative purposes, including the forthcoming elections to be held in 1922. The census and the elections were strongly opposed by the Muslims, who refrained from registering as Lebanese subjects because registration could be interpreted as a recognition of the Lebanese state.[24] The French high commissioner, however, carried out the census and later issued Regulation 1307, dated 10 March 1922, which declared that until a regulation concerning Lebanese citizenship was to be issued, all subjects registered

24. Sunni notables met with Gouraud, the French high commissioner, to object against the census. Gouraud agreed to define them as "citizens of Beirut" (Zamir 1985, 130). McDowall (1996) indicates, "Throughout the 1920s and the 1930s, many [inhabitants in Lebanon] made their reluctance as citizens of the Lebanese state clear" (11).

in the 1921 census would be recognized as Lebanese (Abdallah 1986, 29–30).

Citizenship regulations (Resolution 2825, Resolution 15, and Decree 398) stipulated that a person seeking to obtain Lebanese citizenship had to prove that he or she was residing on Lebanese territory on 30 August 1924. In this respect, registration in the 1921 census became an important certification proving residency on Lebanese territories on 30 August 1924 as required by the citizenship regulations. Despite it being announced as an administrative measure when it was carried out, the 1921 census became an official authoritative source that played an important role in 1932 when the second census ever taken in Lebanon was carried out.

The 1921 census illustrated the first indications of problems connected with carrying out a population census under colonial rule. In addition to politically motivated persons who opposed the creation of Greater Lebanon and refrained from being counted, others either evaded enumeration for fear of being forced to enlist in the mandate army or were unconcerned and ignorant of the political repercussions of the census.[25]

The 1932 Census

A new reading of the 1932 census (see table 7.1) is essential in understanding how demographic distribution, confessional affiliation, and political representation are related because the system of political representation in Lebanon has been based on the relative size of the confessional groups as rendered in that census.[26]

With Decree 8837, dated 15 January 1932, the population census was announced, and the rules for the enumeration process were lined up. Many of the instructions rendered were later to serve as part of the Lebanese citizenship legislation. At a time when the national identification of the population was not yet settled, the census aimed at counting "all Lebanese and foreigners that reside on Lebanese territories" (Article 19). The idea of a national identity was still foreign to most sects, with the exception of the Maronites, who viewed Lebanon as the fulfillment of their political aspirations. The young state had barely taken its first steps regarding the forma-

25. Longrigg (1958), a longtime British official in the Middle East during the Mandate period indicates: "The [1921] census produced was highly imperfect, for the reasons (those of concealment, misunderstanding, falsification, conjectures, and motives peculiar to the communities) which in such countries always prevent accurate personal registration" (126).

26. The census ended on 14 September 1932. Decree 1 was issued, indicating the distribution of seats among the confessional sects. The results of the census were published in the official newspaper (*Al-jarida al-rasmiyya*) on 5 October 1932.

tion of its political structure following the establishment of the Constitution in 1926. The census was therefore an important building block in the state-formation process of the Lebanese state because it defined the electorate.

We can observe the ethnocratic rudiments of the politics of citizenship in the 1932 census by discerning the impact of some articles as rendered in the decree. First, Article 13 mentions specifically that "refugees from Turkish territories such as Armenians, Syriacs, Chaldeans and Greeks of Turkish origin, shall be counted as Lebanese provided they were found on Lebanese territories on August 30, 1924 according to Regulation 2825." Common to these groups is their Christian background. Whereas Christian groups are specified, refugee groups with Muslim affiliation, such as the Kurds, and nomad bedouin groups who lived in areas bordering to Syria are not specified as having the right to be counted as Lebanese. Article 12 stipulates that only bedouins who reside on Lebanese territories more than six months are to be counted as Lebanese, an instruction that resulted in the exclusion of bedouins partly because they could not prove the length of their residence on Lebanese territories. Citizenship regulations were later to be interpreted in such a way that refugees of Christian background did not have to prove their residence on 30 August 1924, whereas other previously Ottoman subjects of Muslim background had to provide documents proving residence on that precise date.

Second, the enumeration and definition of the status *foreigners* is not clearly specified in the census instructions. It is, however, clear that a foreigner need not be a citizen in another state. Article 13 indicates that in order to count inhabitants as Lebanese they are to present identity cards *(tathakir nufus)* to the census committee or to *prove residence* on Lebanese territories on 30 August 1924. The article further points out that those who came to Lebanese territories after that date, did not acquire Lebanese citizenship, and are unable to prove their residence on Lebanese territory on the given date are to be counted as foreigners and are to be registered without citizenship (i.e., stateless). In fact, it is unclear whether the census committee registered those that did not have citizenship as foreigners, or whether this legal status was held for persons who were actually citizens of other states. As a result, persons unable to prove residence on 30 August 1924 (by showing ID cards from the 1921 census or other official documentation) were registered as foreigners, despite their not being citizens of other states. This understanding is further affirmed by Article 18, which indicates that "each Lebanese is obliged to obtain an identity card [*tathkarat hawiyya*], while foreigners can choose [to produce or disclose an ID card] in that matter." The question is whether presenting ID cards on a voluntary basis was instrumental in excluding inhabitants who did not have any ID cards or citizenship whatsoever, thus legally designating them foreigners. A group of residents known as "the concealed" *(al-maktumin)*—i.e., nonregistered stateless persons—was created following the 1932 census. Common for this group was (and is) their residence in the northern and southern parts of the country, areas with a predominantly Muslim population.

Third, the 1932 census included the Lebanese emigrant population that was predominantly Christian. The inclusion of the emigrant population is a central point in understanding the state-idea of the Christian-dominated regime in Lebanon. This point explains also partly why the updating of the population census after 1932 has been repeatedly vetoed. Christian members of the government have insisted on including the emigrant population as part of the Lebanese citizenry, whereas Moslem members have opposed the inclusion of the emigrants and objected against granting emigrants the right to be represented politically. The issue of including the emigrant population and their offspring is still unresolved.

The inclusion of emigrants and the exclusion of residents by registering them as foreigners in 1932 can be seen as political measures that exemplify how the politics of citizenship function as a mechanism of control. These measures emphasize the ethnocratic character of the Lebanese regime. As a result, the demographic proportion of Christians was increased along with their political influence, but the demographic proportion of Muslim residents decreased along with their political representation, thereby buttressing the powers of the Christian-dominated regime. The next section deals with the emigrant card as part of ethnocratic governance.

The Emigrant Card

The Lebanese have a long history as a nation of emigrants. At the end of the nineteenth and the beginning of the twentieth centuries, thousands of Lebanese, mostly Christians, migrated to the West. Emigration was caused by several factors: it became easier to obtain travel permits following the fall of the Ottoman Empire, close religious links with the West, education, and trade. Zamir (1985) indicates that an estimated one hundred thousand Lebanese, about a quarter of the Mount Lebanon's population, emigrated between 1900 and 1914, a demographic drain that was presented as an argument for the extension of Mount Lebanon's territorial boundaries. Christians claimed that more territory would reduce emigration and enable those Lebanese who had already emigrated to return (15). Emigration rates, however, did not decrease among Christians despite the creation of Greater Lebanon.

Apparently, Maronite political and religious leaders, anticipating the increased demographic strength of the Muslim communities in Greater Lebanon because of Christian emigration, saw the inclusion of emigrants, the great majority being Christians, in the 1921 and 1932 censuses as a means of increasing the demographic strength of Christians and thereby their political influence. The inclusion of emigrants occurred only after strong disagreement with the French Mandate authorities, however. In a letter dated 26 February 1921, Anton Jumayyel wrote to his friend Yousef al-Sawda, head of the Administrative Council and a noted Maronite political figure at the time,[27] saying:

> The French High Commissioner is against the idea of entering emigrants in the census, the Muslims support him. . . . No doubt you know the expected aim. Without the emigrants, we become a minority, and the coming elections will see another majority eager to vote for unity with Syria. The French High Commissioner does not dare to announce his policy because he knows we will rebel. He intends to remove the emigrants, which will secure a Muslim majority, Shi'ite and Druze, in the new assembly. We are worried.[28] (cited in Dagher 1993)

Despite French disagreement, the Maronite leaders succeeded in entering the number of emigrants in the census and including them in the political calculations in the formation of the assembly in 1921.[29] The census gave the following results: resident citizens, 609,068; emigrants, 130,784; total number of Lebanese, 710,562. Emigrants thus equaled 18.4 percent of the population (Dagher 1993).

In 1932, emigrants were again included, this time forming an even more substantial part of the population (see table 7.1). The census indicated that residents numbered 793,396, emigrants 254,987, and foreigners 61,297. Interestingly, emigrants were defined as belonging to the "inhabitants of the Lebanese Republic" as rendered in the title of the table. The total number of inhabitants, as defined by the regime, amounted to 1,109,680; 1,048,383 were regarded as citizens. Of these "inhabitants," 23 percent were in reality emigrants—i.e., not resident on Lebanese territories. The percentage of the

27. The Administrative Council (Al-majlis al-idari) was the local government of Mount Lebanon during the Ottoman period and continued to function under the French Mandate.

28. The letter is rendered in Lohéac (1978).

29. Zamir (1985) and Phares (1995) indicate that Lebanese Christian emigrants were strong proponents for the creation of Greater Lebanon. Despite their small number, the emigrants had close contact with French authorities and exercised strong influence on French policy in Lebanon.

emigrant population in relation to the resident Lebanese population had increased to 24 percent of the Lebanese citizenry, up from the 18.4 percent of the 1921 census.

Almost one-fourth of the Lebanese citizenry resided outside the Lebanese territory, as indicated by the results of the 1932 census; 73 percent of these emigrants had left before 1924, but they increased the size of the Christian population significantly. Emigration figures are even more telling when the sizes of the Christian and Muslim emigrants are compared. Whereas 35 percent of the total Christian citizenry were emigrants, Muslim emigrants constituted only 9 percent of the Muslim citizenry.[30] What becomes evident is that the number of resident Christians exceeded the number of resident Muslims by 14,065 persons, a number reached by including the approximately 40,000 Armenian refugees who settled in Lebanon after 1920 (Zamir 1985, 100) and by administratively labeling approximately 60,000 persons of predominantly Muslim background as foreigners. Moreover, when we exclude the emigrant population in order to assess the constitution of the resident Lebanese population we find that the resident Christian Lebanese majority over the resident non-Christian Lebanese population is marginal, around 500 persons (396,946 Christians and 396,450 non-Christians).

The census illustrates that the representation of predominantly Christian emigrant Lebanese was given great concern, whereas the large groups of residents on Lebanese territories were not given administrative attention and were labeled as foreigners. Table 7.1 shows how the category *emigrants* is specified in detail in Decree 8837, but the category *foreigners,* counting more than 60,000 residents on Lebanese territories at the time, was not only vaguely defined in Articles 13 and 18, but totally neglected in the summary. The category *foreigner* is not listed as part of the resident population, nor are foreigners broken into religious categories, a specification that would have indicated the group's Muslim affiliation. This negligence supports the assumption that the census committee was more preoccupied by the political representation of predominantly Christian nonresident emigrants than by the predominantly Muslim inhabitants actually residing on

---

30. In the 1932 census, Christian emigrants numbered 216,259, whereas Christian residents numbered 400,534. Christian emigrants thus constituted 35 percent of all Christian citizens and 21 percent of the total Lebanese citizenry. Muslim emigrants numbered 37,465, whereas Muslim residents numbered 386,469. Muslim emigrants constituted thus 9 percent of total Muslim citizens, and 3.5 percent of the total Lebanese citizenry. These figures exclude the group defined as "miscellaneous," which numbered 6,393 residents and 1,263 emigrants.

Lebanese territories. The strict requirements applied in proving residency on the required date succeeded in excluding from the Lebanese citizenry a substantial number of residents who were not able to prove their residence on the required date, 30 August 1924.

The decisive date 30 August 1924, critical in ascertaining Lebanese citizenship, is central in the 1932 census. The link between emigrant status and the date officially required for obtaining Lebanese citizenship is also revealing. By specifying the exact date in the census, the authoritative importance of that date for obtaining Lebanese citizenship is underlined. The people most affected were inhabitants who either were not able to produce documents or other official certificates that might enable them to obtain citizenship or were not aware of the political implications resulting from not arranging their legal status in their place of residence.

It is more puzzling to understand why the distribution of tax-paying and non-tax-paying emigrants is emphasized in the decree. Apparently, by this emphasis the regime wanted to indicate that many emigrant citizens were still contributing financially to their homeland and thereby had the right to be represented. The well-known slogan from the American Revolution that equates tax paying with representation is applicable here. However, tax-paying emigrants amounted to approximately one-third of all emigrants, leaving 68 percent emigrants who did not pay taxes, but who nevertheless were represented politically in their homeland.

The first parliamentary assembly following the 1932 census was formed on 1 January 1934. It included fourteen Christian and eleven Muslim representatives (Decree 1), institutionalizing Christian supremacy in the government, the Parliament, and the state administration.

Inconsistent Interpretations of Existing Citizenship Legislation

The errors and deficiencies of the enumeration and enrollment in personal registries, as indicated above, gave rise to demands by persons that they be enrolled in the registries, which would enable them to obtain Lebanese citizenship. In this process, the application of existing citizenship legislation proved to be an intricate matter. Abdallah (1986) indicates that whereas some courts interpreted citizenship regulations strictly, others exercised milder requirements when processing citizenship cases (45–46). Among the most widely debated and inconsistently interpreted elements of the citizenship legislation is Regulation 2825, which stipulated that persons who resided on Lebanese territories on 30 August 1924 are confirmed as

Lebanese citizens (Karam 1993, 50–52; Abdallah 1986, 43–52). Controversy emerged on one main issue: How were noncitizens claiming to be Lebanese to *prove residence* on the required date?

Some judges interpreted *presence* mildly, taking into account the *probability of residence* on Lebanese territories; others were stricter, demanding documentation certifying such presence. According to Abdallah (1986), even judges within the same court had different interpretations of Regulation 2825. In one case, the court of appeal of Beqa' regarded a couple of refugees who came to Zahle in 1923 as Lebanese citizens on account of their probable continued presence on Lebanese territories on 30 August 1924. In another case, the court of appeal of Beirut did not accept official documents indicating enrollment in the refugee registries of Sidon on 9 March 1925, maintaining it to be insufficient proof of residence on the required date 30 August 1924, despite documentation that the appellant resided in the refugee camp of Jubeil between 1922 and 1925 (Abdallah 1986, 45–46).

The discourse regarding the interpretation of *presence* on Lebanese territories as required in Regulation 2825 ended partly when the regime issued Decree 398 on 26 November 1949, specifying more accurately that persons seeking to obtain Lebanese citizenship had to *document* residence by providing certification of historical character. The most restrictive interpretations regarding proof of residence on Lebanese territories were thus applied. A person seeking to obtain Lebanese citizenship had to present "all documents that prove his Lebanese origin such as registration in old personal records of him or one of his ancestors, official documents issued by the administration or the district, notifying him or his family in kinship books and family history, or the like" (Karam 1993, 227).[31] The Lebanese regime is not unique in issuing and requiring official documentation in order to verify the legal status of its inhabitants. What is remarkable are the strict preconditions set by the regime in documenting domicile on Lebanese territories during a period when the young state was under colonial rule and endured significant internal political upheavals, among them the very definition of the citizenry.

Apparently, the ethnocratic regime, eager to form and maintain the Lebanese state as a predominantly Christian state, applied citizenship legislation in ways that buttressed its own interests. It was not in the interest of the regime to increase the size of opponent groups by including them as members of the Lebanese state, a step that would reduce the comparative size and thereby the political leverage of the dominant Maronite sect within

31. Full Arabic text of Decree 398 is rendered in Karam (1993, 227–28)

the sectarian state. Strict requirements were therefore applied in order to limit the inclusion as members of the state any non-Christian people who claimed to be Lebanese.

Inaccurate Personal Registries

An unknown number of persons and families were not registered by the census committees in 1932, either because of willful evasion on their part or because of administrative shortcomings and errors on the part of the committees (Abdallah 1986, 36–37). In addition, many persons were born after the last census without being officially enrolled in personal registries *(aqlam al-quyud, sijilat an-nufus)* because of administrative shortcomings by local religious leaders. These deficiencies regarding personal registries resulted in an increasing number of Lebanese residents who did not officially exist in the state's personal registries. Although there is no direct mention of the confessional affiliation of persons applying for citizenship, common for all the undocumented persons is residence in areas predominantly inhabited by Muslims that were added to Mount Lebanon in 1920.

Nonregistration resulted in inaccuracies in the personal registries. What is more important, the authorities showed no interest in straightening up these inaccuracies, choosing instead to maintain the legally insecure status of the persons involved. Persons who where either not registered or stateless continued to be regarded as "foreigners" by the authorities. Administratively, their cases were handled by the DGPS, which regulated the presence of noncitizens.

Isam Ni'man indicates six main groups who, following the deficiencies of the 1932 census, inaccurate personal registration, as well as territorial amputations of Lebanese territories in 1922, constituted the bulk of persons demanding Lebanese citizenship after independence in 1943. In addition, he adds two groups of citizens of other states who, because of their long-term residence in the country also were applicants for Lebanese citizenship (*Ad-Diar,* 10 December 1992, 16 May 1993):

1. *Persons whose official legal status is concealed (maktumin):* These persons' names were deleted administratively from local personal registries following the 1932 census. Local committees deleted the names of members in families that had ten or more children, "not believing it to be possible" to have such big hatches, according to Isam Ni'man (interview with author, 10 February 1996). This group also includes children born of Lebanese parents in exile, who were either denied registration or not able to register at councils.

2. *Persons whose births were not registered (mahrumin)*. Many spouses registered their marriage at the local Muslim sheikhs who in turn did not inform the authorities. Children born to these officially unregistered marriages became "legally unregistered offspring." Their names were not listed in official personal registries, preventing them from obtaining citizenship. In other cases, male children were not enrolled in personal registries because parents feared forced conscription in the mandate army.

3. *The population of the Seven Villages (al-qura al-sab')*.[32] Following the Paulet-Newcombe Agreement,[33] concluded between the French and British Mandate powers on 3 February 1922, these villages in South Lebanon were detached from Greater Lebanon and annexed to Northern Palestine.[34] The agreement was, however, not promulgated until the Jerusalem Agreement on 2 February 1926, enabling the inhabitants to claim Lebanese citizenship on the basis of their residence on Lebanese territories on 30 August 1924 (Abdallah 1984, 30). The population of these villages was registered in the 1921 census, and their records are found in the personal registries of the District of Tyre (Alawiyya 1984, 7). Following the creation of the State of Israel in 1948, the inhabitants of these villages came to Lebanon as refugees and were soon registered as "Palestine refugees." An indication of their Lebanese roots is their Shi'ite background, which separates them from the predominantly Sunni Muslim and Christian Palestinians. Many former inhabitants of the Seven Villages have tried to obtain Lebanese citizenship, indicating Lebanese ancestry, and their enrollment in personal registries that still exist in the South Lebanese town of Tyre.

4. *The population of Wadi Khaled*.[35] Former nomads of bedouin background who—for different reasons, including their nomadic style of life and attempts at evading centralized governance and taxation—failed to acquire and present evidence that they resided for at least six months on Lebanese territories as required by Decree 8837. Their legal status and citizenship was, until 1993, officially categorized as *qayd ad-dars* (under consideration).

32. In reality, the Seven Villages are thought to include twenty-five villages. Among the biggest are Salha, Qadas, al-Malikiyya, al-Khalisa, Hounin, Abl al-Qamh, Tarabeikha, and Yousha' (Abdallah 1986, 30; Alawiyya 1984, 5).

33. Full text of the Paulet-Newcombe Agreement is rendered in Karam (1993, 186–206).

34. According to the Lebanese, these villages were eventually restored through the Rhodes Armistice Accords of 1949, a document that Lebanese authorities believe lays the basis of Lebanese sovereignty over these villages (Sayigh 1994, 18). In a footnote, Sayigh refers to F. Hof, *Galilee Divided: The Israel-Lebanese Frontier 1916–1948* (Boulder: Westview Press), 56–59.

35. *Wadi* means "valley" in English. The Valley includes sixteen villages in the northern region of 'Akkar bordering to Syria. 'Akkar was one of the four regions included in the formation of Greater Lebanon in 1920.

This group is estimated to include seven thousand persons (*Al-Nahar*, 2 July 1994; Abdallah 1986, 37).

5. *Foreigners.* This group is made up of citizens of foreign states who have married Lebanese women and whose contact with their original countries has ceased.

6. *Refugees.* These persons are non-Lebanese (excluding Palestinians) who have emigrated from their countries of birth and resided in Lebanon. They belong to both Muslim and Christian sects and have diverging ethnic affiliation, such as Arab, Kurd, Syriac, Chaldean, and Assyrian.

The number of stateless and noncitizen persons within these groups increased, and citizenship cases became more complicated as time passed. Among the reasons behind increased numbers of noncitizens and stateless persons, we find demographic increase and patriarchal citizenship laws whereby children inherited the legal status of their fathers.

Presence of the State in Court Appeals

With the passing of time after the 1932 census, the number of stateless persons—refugees as well as long-term noncitizen residents—increased rapidly, thereby enlarging the size of the noncitizen population in Lebanon. Abdallah (1986) indicates a parallel inflation in the number of legal appeals whereby persons demanding Lebanese citizenship presented their cases in court. Apparently, these cases also intensified the legal disputes and incongruencies in the interpretation of citizenship legislation. He notes, "[Disputes] became aggravated reaching a serious level which was reflected by court decisions, the writings of interpreters, and the generalizations of the Ministry of Justice. . . . Disagreement did not end before the issuing of Law 67/68 dated 4–12 1967, concerning the representation of the state in courts" (178).

Legally, Law 67/68 changed the character of lawsuits regarding citizenship. Instead of being handled as appeals of requests, they were now considered appeals of dispute, which necessitated the presence of a specific opposing part, namely the state, "due to the effect of these cases on public order [*al-nitham al-'am*]" (Abdallah 1986, 183–84). Article 1 of Law 67/68 states, "Only courts of first instance and none others shall handle the appeals of those whose legal identity is concealed subject to the provisions of the Lausanne Treaty and *Regulation 2825* issued on August 30, 1924"[36] Article 2 states, "The above-mentioned appeals are not handled without the presence of the state as a principle part" (quoted in Abdallah 1986, 228).

---

36. In Arabic, "courts of the first instance" is *al-mahakim al-ibtida'iyya*. "Concealed" (*maktumin*) refers to persons whose official legal status is concealed.

Politically, the law had a dramatic effect. It practically closed the door of naturalization, enabling the regime, through its strengthened hold on the legal institutions of the state, to stop lawsuits in which persons previously had succeeded in proving their right to citizenship in court by evidencing the requirements set by citizenship legislation.[37] The presence of the state (through the Judicial Board[38] at the Ministry of Justice) in all legal disputes regarding citizenship prevented in practice the handling of citizenship appeals. The ethnocratic regime thus strengthened its authoritative position and capability in maintaining its exclusive citizenship policies. In the aftermath of Law 67/68, stateless persons and persons whose official identity was "concealed" *(maktumin)* received an identification certificate indicating that the bearer's citizenship was "under consideration" *(jinsiyyat qayd ad-dars)* (Abdallah 1986, 20).

Although the legal status of stateless residents on Lebanese territories was not solved, statelessness had become a matter of dispute between subjects demanding citizenship and a regime reluctant to admit Muslim members to the citizenry. By the late 1960s, more than thirty years after the 1932 census, the regime was facing demands that threatened the basis of its state-idea: a predominantly Christian state where the identity and aspirations of the Maronite sect would be expressed. In addition to demographic changes in favor of the Muslim segments of the population, an increase in the number of Muslim citizens as members of the state further endangered the existence of the Christian-dominated regime, in a country where political representation was supposed to correspond with the relative size of the sects. In face of voiced demands by segments of the population to be included as members of the state, the regime sharpened its ethnocratic rule by applying more severe measures to the politics of citizenship. With the issuing of Law 67/68, the ethnocratic character of the regime was strengthened, further bolstering its control over membership in the state.

Absolute Authority of the President

In Lebanon, naturalization of persons applying for citizenship occurs following the issuing of a decree signed by the president, the prime minister,

---

37. Antoine Messara, a professor in political science and participant in a nongovernmental seminar dealing with the issue of stateless people and refugees in May 1993 indicates that the problem with the existing citizenship legislation is not its content but the fact that its implementation was prevented in court: "hatha al-qanun la yushakkil 'a'iqan wa huwa lam yutabbaq 'amaliyyan bisabab da'wat al-qada' ila tajmid tatbiqihi" (*Al-Nahar,* 21 July 1993).

38. In Arabic, *hay'at al-qadaya.*

and the minister of the interior after all the required documents have been presented to the bureaucracy. The executive power is not obliged to grant citizenship, even if the requirements set by citizenship legislation are met. Citizenship is seen as a bestowed privilege; it is not a right to which a person is entitled (Karam 1993, 93; Abdallah 1986, 89).

The introduction of Law 67/68 froze the procedures of citizenship applications. Politically, this legal step considerably increased the power of the Maronite president. The president had always had the prerogative of approving applications for naturalization, but following the introduction of Law 67/68, his role became even more consolidated as sole authoritarian body to consent to the applications of citizenship. The law further underlined the authority of the executive power. From then on, a tradition was instituted whereby citizenship was bestowed by decree on selected applicants at the end of each president's term (Habib Ifram,[39] interview with author, February 1996).

Administrative Personal Registries as Control Instruments

In the absence of population censuses that render vital statistical information on the constitution of the population, other administrative measures and institutions came to play a central role in the ethnocratic regime's endeavor to survey the ethnic constitution of the Lebanese population. Among the most important state institutions we find two directories placed under the Ministry of Interior: the DGPA, which surveys Lebanese citizens, and the DGPS, which surveys the noncitizen population. Both directories register births, marriages, deaths, and—central to our analysis—the confessional affiliation of each person resident on Lebanese territories. In addition, there are personal registries *(qalam quyud, aqlam an-nufus)* in all the country's districts, in which only Lebanese citizens, at least those who have been reported, are registered.[40] An indication of the tight connection between administrative and political elements is the close link between statistics and personal status as demonstrated by the original name of the DGPA. During

39. Ifram is leader of the Lebanese Committee for Naturalization *(lajnat at-tajnis).*

40. It is important to underline the word *reported* as we are dealing with a society where personal and family affairs are dealt with by the religious communities. At the time studied (1920s and 1930s), there did not exist established routines for demographic annotation. Births and deaths were, and still are, monitored by the religious communities, making the religious leaders responsible for informing the state administration. In some cases, these religious leaders did not carry out their administrative responsibilities, resulting in the creation of the problem of "concealed" persons.

the 1940s, it was called the Department of Statistics and Personal Affairs.[41] The powers accorded to the DGPA are illustrated by the issuing of Decree 1822, dated 6 September 1944, which entrusted to it the following authority:

> The director of personal registries is able to delete illegal enrolment [in the personal registries] after investigation and getting the permission of the Minister of Interior. The civil courts continue to handle the belonging [*tabi' iyya*] of the person whose enrolment [in the personal registries] has been administratively deleted [*al-mashtub qaydahu idariyyan*].[42]

Interestingly, this decree added a paragraph to Article 21 of Decree 8837 (which announced the 1932 census), fourteen years after the census was carried out. The names of persons living in the Seven Villages, detached from Lebanon and included in Palestine between 1922 and 1926, and the names of members of families with a great number of children were deleted (*Al-Hayat*, 5 May 1993; *Ad-Diar*, 10 December 1992 and 16 May 1993). The deleting of names from the registry more than a decade after the carrying out of the census illustrates a regime eager to exclude from the citizenry even more members defined as "undesired" than those already excluded.

According to lawyer Joseph Karam (1993), "the similarity between appeals for personal registration [*da' wa nufus*] and appeals for citizenship [*da' wa jinsiyya*] made the courts differentiate between them, having in mind the importance such appeals have on the legal and social level." He indicates that whereas "appeals for personal registration rely on its own laws, which are the registration of personal affairs laws, appeals for citizenship rely on citizenship laws, which are distinct from the laws of personal affairs" (160–61). Despite the legal distinction between the two kinds of appeals, I argue that appeals by persons who wanted to be enrolled in personal registries and appeals for citizenship are inseparable. Put in a political setting, appeals for enrollment in personal registries are linked with appeals for citizenship because citizenship legislation requires proof of enrollment in official historical registries as well as a stamp of approval from the DGPA and the DGPS (Alawiyya 1984, 24–25; Abdallah 1986, 94). The legal distinction set by the authorities between the two kinds of appeal should rather

---

41. The department is referred to in Decree 398, see Karam (1993, 227).

42. Decree 1822 was added in 1944 to Decree 8837, which was issued in 1932, i.e. twelve years earlier. In Lebanon, the president, the prime minister, and the minister of the interior can issue a decree jointly. Through a decree, an existing law can be changed by adding or deleting a paragraph. That is what happened to Decree 8837, which was corrected through Decree 1882. See full text of Decree 8837 in Karam 1993, 219–26. Decree 1822 is rendered on page 225.

be understood as another measure of control applied in order to restrict membership regulations into the Lebanese citizenry.

The role of the DGPS as a mechanism of control is also apparent in administrative procedures that manifest the exclusive traits of the regime by keeping the legal identity of substantial groups of persons undefined. In 1960, the directory counted all foreign subjects residing in the country and grouped them in three categories: (1) those whose citizenship of origin was certified; (2) those who argued that their custodians (parents or guardians) had mismanaged their registration at birth; and (3) those who denied having any citizenship whatsoever. As a result of the need to document uncertified subjects, the DGPS equipped the latter two groups with ID cards indicating that the person's citizenship was "unspecified" (*ghayr mu'ayyana*). Following the issuing of Law 67/68 in 1967, these cards were withdrawn and replaced by ID cards that indicated that the citizenship of the bearer was "under consideration" (*qayd ad-dars*). (Abdallah 1986, 20, 83–86; *Al-Nahar*, 2 July 1994).

State-Formation and Citizenship

The state-formation process of the Lebanese state evolved with the territorial birth of Greater Lebanon in 1920, whereby the political, administrative, and legal institutions of the state developed. The definition of the citizenry, the subjects whom the state and its regime are meant to represent, constitutes a fundamental element of state formation. Whereas the territorial delineation of state borders was the result of negotiations among colonial powers, membership policies in the territorial entity created were mainly at the hands of indigenous forces. In Lebanon, the regime was able to exploit the parallel development of the state apparatus and the definition of the citizenry, shaping the latter in accordance with its state-idea. The Maronite-dominated regime conceived the new territorial entity of Greater Lebanon as a predominantly Christian homeland, inhabited by citizens with Christian background. The process of forming the desired citizenry involved the official documentation of inhabitants legitimized as members or delegitimized as nonmembers of the state. In this process, enrollment in personal registries, documentation of residence, and the introduction of identity cards were applied by the authorities as elements in the politics of citizenship.

Not only was the state apparatus being formed during the 1920s, but the basis and formation of citizenship legislation, as well as the registration of the inhabitants in Lebanon, occurred during a historical period that saw the downfall of one colonial power (the Ottoman) and the institution of another (the French). These changes gave rise to political and social upheavals that, under foreign rule, caused deficiencies that were not settled at the time. What is disputable is the manner in which enrollment, personal registries, and citizenship demands were handled by the ruling regime after independence. The deficiencies of the 1932 census were not only maintained, but severely aggravated by the introduction of restrictive regulations, strict interpretations of existing citizenship legislation, and the authoritative power gathered at the hands of the Christian-dominated regime in selecting members of the state. Faced with unfavorable demographic changes, the regime intensified the use of the politics of citizenship as a control mechanism in order to maintain its rule.

Citizenship as a Demographic Control Instrument

In the aftermath of the creation of Greater Lebanon in 1920 until the outbreak of the civil war in 1975, the Maronite-dominated regime promoted its own state-idea of Lebanon as the homeland of predominantly Christian inhabitants in an Arab world predominantly inhabited by Muslims. Faced with the dilemma of becoming a numeric minority, the Maronites defined the demographic foundation of Christian rule as a critical factor for buttressing their political dominance.

According to Zamir (1985), the Maronites were eager to enlarge the territorial basis of Mount Lebanon (in which they had constituted a numerical majority), but were either blind to or did not assess the political and repercussions of the demographic inclusion of Muslim inhabitants (219). He indicates that "the small size of the Christian majority led the French authorities and the Lebanese Christians themselves to seek ways of reversing the demographic trend" by reducing the rate of Christian emigration, restricting exit permits, and encouraging Christians to resettle in the country (100). Through the politics of citizenship, whereby predominantly Christian groups were included as members of the state, but predominantly Muslim groups were excluded, the regime "sought ways" (as Zamir puts it) to reverse the demographic trend in order to favor Christian numerical supremacy.

The sensitivity of statistical information in a sectarian state paved the way for the instrumentality of administrative registries at the hands of the regime when applying and effecting its citizenship policies. As a result of the lack of regular official population censuses, the administration of personal registries and the departments dealing with the registration of the population acquired a political character. In light of changes defined as unfavorable to the regime's interests—i.e., the increased size and thereby potential political power of the Muslim citizen population—the regime tightened its grip further on the politics of citizenship.

In contexts where demographic strength is reflected in political influence, as the case is in sectarian states, I maintain that membership in ethnic communities loses its voluntary character and becomes heavily politicized. In Lebanon, the registration archives indicating the ethnic membership of the population were transformed into effective control mechanisms at the hands of the regime. Davis (1997) indicates that "the Lebanese legislator, reflecting the political confessionalism besetting modern Lebanon since its independence, seems to be haunted by an obsession with the question of confessional loyalty, and carries the obsession into the Lebanese citizenship legislation" (154). The "obsession with confessional loyalty" can be understood as an expression of the fundamental importance of personal registration in a multisectarian state, whereby the regime seeks to control the sectarian composition of the citizenry.

Conclusion

A revision of the importance attributed to the National Pact agreed upon in 1943 is necessary in light of the unsolved dilemmas regarding the identity of the Lebanese state. Among these dilemmas is the definition of the citizenry, which was not settled when independence was gained. The pact implicitly included structural unequal access to membership and citizenship in the Lebanese state because it adopted the biased results of the 1932 census as a basic guideline for political organization.

Lijphart's (1977) classification of Lebanon as a consociational democracy incorporates at face value the envisaged conceptions regarding democratic power sharing as defined by the dominant sects in 1943. He does not, however, sufficiently problematize the particular principles on which power sharing was built. More specifically, he disregards the inherent dilemmas in an agreement that institutionalized proportional representation, taking the questionable and biased results of the 1932 census as a basis for proportionality. The incumbent exclusive mechanisms embodied in the census and its application as an instrument of control at the hands of the governing regime are thereby implicitly included in Lijphart's analysis of the Lebanese polity as a consociational democracy. Lijphart thus disregards central aspects of exclusion from political participation as revealed by the politics of citizenship practiced in Lebanon. He explains the outbreak of the civil war mainly as the result of "the inflexible institutionalization of consociational principles" (149). Focusing on aspects that restricted membership in the Lebanese polity, however, allows us to analyze more closely this "inflexibility" as exercised by the Lebanese regime prior to the civil war.

As an ethnocracy, the Lebanese regime preferred to rely on control mechanisms—among them the politics of citizenship, which monitored membership in the Lebanese state along ethnic lines—in order to maintain the prerogatives of the Christian-dominated government. Under ethnocratic rule, there developed a peculiar group of stateless persons of predominantly Muslim background who were not welcomed as members of the state. Another expression of ethnocratic governance was the prevention of Muslim segments from acquiring political representation that corresponded to their relative size within the population. Governance in Lebanon was stable, yes, but it was not democratic, as Lijphart states.

The controversies following the citizenship decree in 1994 indicate that the Lebanese state is still enduring a post-Ottoman disorder, whereby central political questions have yet to be settled—among them, "Who is to constitute the Lebanese demos?" The citizenship decree in 1994, however, did not reconcile the diverse views regarding the state-idea of the Lebanese state because the Christian elite, particularly the Maronites, hold on to their claim of including long-term emigrants and their offspring as part of the Lebanese citizenry. Moreover, the issuing of a new citizenship law as stipulated in the Taif Agreement has been postponed. Apparently, the regime opted for a decree because it represented the least complex option to the solution to the problematic status of its stateless and long-term noncitizen inhabitants. On the one hand, the decree singled out the Palestinian community as the main noncitizen group in the country. On the other hand, it avoided dealing with the legal and political aspects of large numbers of potential emigrants of Lebanese origin who would be able to acquire citizenship as a result of a new citizenship law. It is feared that the political inclusion and potential representation of an unknown but substantially large group of potential citizens might further exacerbate the confessional political power imbalance in the country.

Questions regarding numbers and figures and their fundamental impact on political organization in Lebanon are still unanswered. In 1933, the Maronite patriarch Huwayik maintained that "the issue of minorities and majorities and their attitude toward us do not concern us; Lebanon is a Christian nation" (quoted in Phares 1995, 82). In face of the demographic changes that have occurred during the past decades, the issue of minorities and majorities is apt to be resolved politically. The prospects for these negotiations are more fruitful—although not necessarily less violent—when the identity of the state is not defined by the ruling regime a priori as it was on the creation of the Lebanese state in 1920.

8

Citizenship in the Gulf States

Conceptualization and Practice

ANH NGA LONGVA

THE STUDY OF CITIZENSHIP has undergone substantial change since the publication in 1950 of T. H. Marshall's pioneering work *Citizenship and Social Class*. It has become increasingly common to view citizenship not merely as a legal status entailing a set of formal rights and responsibilities, but also as a vehicle for nationalism and a focus for defining national identity. Citizenship is indeed the key concept without which the idea of the nation-state cannot be translated into practice. Like the nation-state, it was evolved in Europe and has been exported to the rest of the world in the wake of modern state building. But whereas *state* and *nation* have frequently been problematized by students of the non-Western world, the conceptualization and practice of citizenship have been, until recently, the object of limited analytical scrutiny. The assumption seems to be that we are dealing with a universal institution that is understood and practiced in the same manner in all societies and under all circumstances.

On the basis of empirical data from the Gulf region, more particularly Kuwait, this chapter argues that citizenship, although strictly speaking a legal device to organize the relations between individuals and state, is thought of in cultural and not universal terms, at least at this relatively early stage of state building in the region. From the point of view of the ordinary man and woman, citizenship is not an abstract institution that comes with a string of political rights and responsibilities attached to it; rather, it is a relationship between two social categories, *individual* and *state*, complexly mediated by ideas of authority, legitimacy, and allegiance. As is the case with all ideas, these categories are cultural constructs subject to social circumstances and historical variations.

Of particular importance here is how the *state* is defined and what is considered the legitimate overarching political entity to which the individual owes his or her allegiance. I show that in Kuwait the state is conceived of by some as being the political embodiment of a specific "imagined community," located on a specific territory and with a specific common history; for others, the important aspect of the state is its leadership, in this case the Al (or Ahl) Sabah ruling family. Whether the state is defined in one way or the other has profound implications for the manner in which the Kuwaiti individual understands the notion of citizenship and the rights and responsibilities it entails.

Two facts color both conceptualizations:

First, the modern state of Kuwait was established more or less at the same time as the national oil industry took off. Right from the beginning, the people have been dealing with a "do-gooder" state that offered to the citizens an encompassing, cradle-to-grave welfare system built upon a rentier economy and the labor of foreign migrant workers. To the majority of Kuwaitis, the state-citizen relationship is therefore not a confrontational relationship but one that comes closer to a kinship or, at least, a patron-client relationship. The state is at best generous, at worst passive and inefficient, but it is seldom viewed as violent and repressive.

Second, in the eyes of most Kuwaitis, the state of Kuwait—regardless of how it is defined—is an integral part of two supranational entities, the Arab community and the Muslim community. Although the connection between Kuwaiti citizenship and Arab identity is rejected, for obvious reasons, by the Shi'a minority of Persian origin, the linkage between Kuwaiti citizenship and Muslim identity is a pervasive assumption and an object of wide agreement.

The practice of citizenship in any society reflects the way the members of this society conceive of the political actors (*state* and *citizen*) and the ties binding them. Such conceptualizations are for the most part implicit and frequently overshadowed by conventional rhetoric that may bear only slight resemblance to reality. It takes exceptional events to bring them to the surface. The 1990 invasion of Kuwait by Iraq was such an event: it not only uncovered the difference between the European and the Kuwaiti conceptualizations of citizenship, it also laid bare the complexities and variations that characterize the way the different groups in Kuwaiti society understand the concept.

A Do-gooder State

Citizenship (as the French *citoyenneté*) derives from the root word *city*. As a concept, it arose in the context of the town and reflects the historical relationship between an individual and his city. In fact, the word citizen in English originally referred to a freeman of a city; later it came to mean civilian. Only relatively recently has the word come to mean "native of or naturalized by a state." Citizenship is thus at heart an urban phenomenon.

The first thing that strikes the student of citizenship in the non-Western world is that, when translated into many non-European languages, the term often loses its original urban connotation. There are two words in Arabic used to denote citizenship. Neither is directly connected to the ideas of city and nation, but at least one is related to other important native categories. These varying linguistic constructions are a first indication of possible differences in the way the notions of citizenship and nationality are understood and practiced in the West and the non-Western world.

Kuwait is a case in point. The settlement of Kuwait was created on the northwestern shore of the Gulf in the early 1700s by the Bani Utub, a group of families from the Anaiza tribe who fled central Arabia toward the end of the seventeenth century following a series of severe droughts (Abu-Hakima 1982). Pearl diving, sea trade with the rest of the Gulf and with the Indian Ocean, and caravan trade with the hinterland were the sources of the settlement's livelihood up to the end of World War II. As a small community of migrants living in an arid environment and entirely dependent on trade, the Kuwaitis have exhibited throughout their history an astonishing political stability unique in the context of Arabia. Ever since approximately 1752, the Utub families have chosen a male from the House of Sabah to take care of trade, the most important and prestigious activity. The merchants, whose work generated the revenues on which the town depended for its existence, were—and still are—the indisputable aristocracy of Kuwait, and they administered the affairs of Kuwait.[1] The Al Sabah *shaikh*,

---

1. The merchants may no longer have much political clout since the advent of oil, which put all the power in the hands of the Al Sabah. But they are still the richest class in Kuwait, and by holding on to their endogamous pattern of marriage, they have succeeded in preserving their social prestige almost intact. Today, the merchants are overwhelmingly Western-educated and have a strikingly Western lifestyle, many of them spending part of the year in Europe or the United States. In parliamentary politics, the majority adhere to secular liberal groupings (there are no official political parties in Kuwait) especially the Tajamu'a al dusturi (the Constitutional Gathering) and the Minbar al demoqrati (Democratic Forum). The words *dustur* (constitution) and *demoqratiyya* (democracy) recur like a leitmotiv in the merchant-political discourse,

"appointed" by his peers to administer the town, was initially at most primus inter pares; he was never the merchants' overlord. It has been claimed both by scholars and by the Kuwaitis themselves that this original division of tasks, which has sometimes been described as a political "pact" (Salamé 1994a), accounts for the fact that, alone among the Gulf states, Kuwait had a tradition of checks and balances between the ruler and the mercantile elite long before the notion of democracy was introduced in the region. It also accounts for Kuwait being so far the only Gulf state where the idea of parliamentary politics has endured in spite of many ups and downs.

Throughout the eighteenth and nineteenth centuries, the Kuwaitis skillfully maneuvered to retain their independence from the powers in the region, in particular the Ottomans, to whom eastern Arabia nominally belonged. But by the end of the nineteenth century, events made it increasingly clear that, in order for this small emirate to survive as an autonomous entity, it would have to align itself more closely either with Britain (which had gained a permanent naval presence in the lower Gulf through its treaties with the Trucial States and Bahrain) or with the Ottomans in Iraq for protection.[2] In 1899, Kuwait entered into a secret treaty with Great Britain whereby the latter promised to assist it in case of external aggression; in return, the *shaikh* of Kuwait pledged not to cede, sell, or lease any of his territory to any power without Britain's consent (Crystal 1995).

Oil was discovered in 1938, but World War II delayed its exploitation until 1946. Today, Kuwait has one of the largest oil reserves in the Middle East. Since independence in 1961, the country has undergone vast transformations. Politically, the advent of oil put an end to the balance of power between the amir and the merchants. As the administrators of the affairs of Kuwait, the Al Sabah also administered its oil revenues, which propelled the ruler into a position of absolute political preponderance, while in the context of the new oil and rentier economy, the merchant class became redundant as a source of national income. From then on, modern trade would take place within a framework set by legislation issued by the state—that is to say, in large measure by the Al Sabah. Demographically, the population of

which is traditionally one of liberal opposition to the regime. In Kuwait, political opposition to the Al Sabah is identified with the rich and not with the poor; the historical event that best illustrates this opposition is the merchant *majlis* movement to force the shaikh to consent to the creation of a legislative assembly in 1938. In this confrontation, the leading merchant families, all Sunni, and a few dissenting Sabahs were pitted against the ruling family supported by the majority of the Shi'i laborers (Crystal 1995).

2. Particularly the rise of the Wahabis as the most expansive military and ideological force in the peninsula.

Kuwait jumped from 200,000 in 1957 to 2.1 million in 1990, as many as 60–70 percent of whom were foreign migrant workers.[3] To understand society and state in Kuwait and the other Gulf countries, it is essential to understand that the presence of the migrant workers there is not merely an epiphenomenon of the economy but a major constitutive element of these societies (Longva 1997). In addition to being the whole of the productive forces in the region—cheap, docile, and easy prey to economic exploitation, and a market for the local trade—the migrants are the foil in relation to which the Gulf nationals perceive and define themselves. As nonnationals, the migrant workers are excluded from the social, economic, and legal privileges that Gulf citizenship entails and thus present a strong contrast that helps elicit national consciousness among the citizens. One could claim that nation building—or, more precisely, the awareness of national identity, of belonging to a modern nation-state—in the region owes much of its success to the overwhelming presence of the migrant workers.

In Kuwait from the very start, oil revenues were used to build a vast welfare state for the Kuwaiti people. Throughout the 1950s, houses, roads, schools, hospitals, and desalination plants were built. By the time the country became independent in 1961, a remarkable change in the quality of life of the inhabitants had already been achieved. In contrast to its neighbors, Kuwait also adopted a constitution in which basic rights and freedoms are guaranteed, with the important exception of political rights. It is clear that, from the beginning, the social rights of the Kuwaiti citizens were to take precedence over their political rights.

The Kuwaiti social rights are extensive. The most basic ones are entirely free education (from primary school to university studies, including studies abroad), entirely free health care (prior to summer 1999, when a small charge was introduced), and practically free housing. Until the late 1980s, all Kuwaiti adults were guaranteed a job in the public sector within one year of the application and a full retirement pension after twenty years for men and fifteen years for women of active work in the public sector. There are many other minor social benefits, such as the state contribution to the bride price for male citizens (KD 2,000 or approximately U.S.$8,000);[4] generous subsidies for water, electricity, and basic foodstuff; and the complex system through which the state helps its citizens to earn money in the private sec-

3. Until the Iraqi invasion in 1990, the majority were Palestinians (ca. 400,000). The remaining were made up of other Arab citizens and Asians (mostly from the subcontinent and the Philippines). After liberation, the Palestinians were expelled en masse and were replaced by Egyptians, Indians, and Filipinos.

4. On condition that it is their first marriage and that the brides are Kuwaiti citizens.

tor—by granting them legal rights over the non-Kuwaitis, by giving them business priorities and exclusive right to contracts, and so on (for more details, see Longva 1997). Except for compulsory military service for men,[5] practically no formal obligations are demanded from the citizens for the enjoyment of these rights, not even taxes (Kuwaitis do not pay income tax). The question is then not so much what civic responsibilities citizens have to assume in order to enjoy the comprehensive social rights, but rather what other rights they are expected to give up in exchange for these. The obvious answer is that most of the people have to give up the enjoyment of full political rights. Until 1996, this situation obtained on the basis of an uneven distribution of citizenship.

In his classic work on democracy based on the case of England, T. H. Marshall (1950) delineates the order in which rights were acquired: first came the civil rights in the eighteenth century, then political rights in the nineteenth century, and finally social rights in the twentieth century. Corresponding to this evolution, which seems to be generally valid for Western Europe, was the establishment of the law courts, Parliament, and the welfare state. In Kuwait, Marshall's order has been reversed. In this society, social rights were the first to be guaranteed when the modern state was formally established; they are undoubtedly extensive and solidly anchored. The situation of civil rights is somewhat more ambivalent.[6] As for political rights, it is only more recently that the prospect for all Kuwaiti citizens to aquire them seems reasonably good (see below).

Manipulating Citizenship in the Process of Nation Building

In Arabia, the notions of nationality and citizenship are recent. The nationality codes in the region date from the late 1940s, but their strict implementation did not start before the 1960s and in some cases (e.g., Bahrain and the United Arab Emirates) the 1970s. Initially, these codes followed a middle road between the two principles of jus sanguinis and jus soli, taking the former as the basic principle and the latter as an auxiliary principle. But as the Gulf countries turned into advanced welfare state societies and as the

---

5. It is relatively easy to avoid military service, and many Kuwaiti men, especially among the *hadhar*, shun it. There is a widespread consensus among Kuwaitis that army matters are of little concern to the urban people, who are more interested in commerce than in war.

6. The ambivalence is due to the fact that the *shari'a* legal precepts prevail in personal status law. Seen from a Western perspective, this system does not guarantee full justice because women do not enjoy equal rights with men.

volume of labor migration reached unprecedented proportions, their nationality laws underwent substantial changes.

In Kuwait, two decrees adopted in 1948 defined as *originally Kuwaiti (asil)* any "members of the ruling family, those permanently residing in Kuwait since 1899, children of Kuwaiti men and children of Arab or Muslim fathers also born in Kuwait" (Kuwait 1948, Order No. 3, 23–30). Naturalization was possible for people who had lived in Kuwait at least ten years, were employed, and spoke Arabic; it could also be granted "by special order for valuable services" (Kuwait 1948, Law No. 2, 35–49). In this original legislation, the jus soli principle was acknowledged because permanent residency and birth on Kuwaiti territory automatically gave access to Kuwaiti nationality. This is a noticeably modern innovation that sharply contrasted with the tradition in the region of classifying people according to the birthplace of their identifiable ancestors, not according to their own—which is the same as aligning nationality along the jus sanguinis principle.

Eleven years later, in the new Nationality Law of 1959, which is the one effective today, the category *originally Kuwaiti* was widened to include descendants of those established in Kuwait since 1920. At the same time, the category *children of Arab or Muslim fathers also born in Kuwait* was dropped. The jus sanguinis principle reasserted itself: only sons of Kuwaiti fathers could claim nationality. Naturalization was still possible for the others, but it became more limited. The law has been refined several times since 1959: in 1960, an amendment fixed the number of cases of naturalization of people originating from outside the Gulf to a mere fifty annually. Length of residence required before an application can be considered was extended to fifteen years for non-Arab applicants. In 1981, the National Assembly passed a bill restricting naturalization to Muslims only.

For the time being, citizenship in Kuwait primarily implies access to social rights. The political dimension of citizenship is somewhat underplayed as the exercise of one of the most basic political rights—namely, participation in parliamentary elections—has been granted to Kuwaiti citizens only sporadically since independence. Although Kuwait officially adopted a constitutional regime after independence in 1961, the National Assembly has been suspended twice (1976–81 and 1986–92). Besides, the suffrage was for many years the privilege of male citizens over twenty-one who belong to the so-called first category of citizens (originally Kuwaitis)—i.e., those whose forefathers were residents in Kuwait since at least 1920. The suffrage was thus denied to the majority of Kuwaiti nationals—all the women and the naturalized Kuwaiti males and their sons. Limitation of the male citizens' political rights was lifted after 1996, and for the first time all male

Kuwaitis could participate in the elections in June 1999. Women, however, are still disenfranchised at the time of this writing (September 1999). But an *amiri* decree issued in May 1999 in the absence of parliament should make it possible for them to vote and run in the next elections, on condition it is approved by the majority of the deputies.

From the perspective of identity and loyalty, the Kuwait case has several interesting aspects.

The year 1920 is not an arbitrary date. The story behind it is very much part of the story of Kuwaiti nation building. Until independence in 1961, the term *Kuwaitis* was used to refer exclusively to the inhabitants of the town of Kuwait. Beyond it, the bedouin nomads were known by the names of their tribes or their tribal subdivisions. Thus, independently of modern labor migration and long before the advent of oil, Kuwaiti society, as most societies in the Arabian peninsula, consisted of two sharply contrasted communities, the sedentary town dwellers *(hadhar)* and the nomads *(badu)*. The *hadhar* always earned their living from trade, mostly sea trade, whereas the *badu* lived from the products of sheep and camel. One major distinction between the nomads and the sedentary people was the *hadhar*'s attachment to the town of Kuwait. To the *badu*, the town had its pragmatic utility as a marketplace, but it was the desert that was vested with a more expressive and symbolic significance. To the *hadhar*, on the other hand, the town of Kuwait was not only an important source of livelihood but also the very locus where communal life arose and unfolded. The town also provided its inhabitants with a much needed physical security in a permanently hostile environment. Mutual identification among the town dwellers therefore derived importantly from the need to protect themselves against common dangers. One such danger—the memory of which is inscribed in the Kuwaiti history books and deeply engraved in their collective consciousness— occurred in 1920, when Ibn Saud unleashed his Ikhwan troops against Kuwait (Abu-Hakima 1982). For two months, the entire population of Kuwait worked round the clock to build a wall around their town. The Ikhwan never reached Kuwait but the wall and the collective efforts that went into its erection remained the symbol of Kuwaiti unity against external threats. The Battle of Jahra in 1920 created a special bond between the town dwellers who had taken part in it and invested them with legitimacy of membership in the Kuwaiti community. This event, it is often said in Kuwait, saw the birth of an explicit Kuwaiti "national" awareness by creating a nucleus of citizenry encompassing those who had taken part in the events and their descendents. These people qualify today as full-fledged first-category Kuwaitis, whose loyalty to Kuwait has never been questioned.

The others, who came onto the scene after 1920 and were granted nationality along the years, have never enjoyed the same degree of legitimacy.

Over and beyond this general suspicion of new citizens—which is by no means an exclusively Kuwaiti or Gulf phenomenon[7]—the urban Kuwaitis bear a special resentment against the new citizens of *badu* origin. When, after independence in 1961, the nomadic tribes came to settle down in Kuwait as citizens of the new nation-state, the *hadhar*[8] regarded them as trespassers, a reaction that is hardly surprising considering the traditional antagonism between settlers and nomads. But it takes more than tradition to account for the persistent and even growing suspicion that characterizes the urban Kuwaitis' attitude: from the mid-1960s to 1980, the government offered to naturalize thousands of nomads and to grant them housing facilities as well as other social benefits partly in order to build up a popular base of political support against the increasingly vocal liberal opposition led by the merchant class. Between 1963 and 1975, the electoral power of the *badu* more than doubled (Crystal 1995), and their proportion in the Kuwaiti population (excluding the migrant workers) was estimated to be 60 percent in the late 1990s. In contrast to a society that upon its independence in 1961 was made up of a clear majority of city dwellers with a long tradition in sea trade, the Kuwait of today is a predominantly *badu* society where conservative tribal values are rapidly gaining ground, socially and politically (Longva forthcoming). As this transformation took place, the ruling family consolidated its position: until the 1990s, the *badu* had consistently and loyally voted in support of the Al Sabah, thus defeating the merchants'

7. Examples of such suspicion can be found practically anywhere. One illustration is the collective internment of U.S. citizens of Japanese origin in the United States during World War II out of fear that they might side with their previous homeland against their present one.

8. The terms *badu* and *hadhar* are still used today, even though all Kuwaitis are now settled and, as inhabitants of this city-state, they are all "urban." It is interesting to note, however, that the urban people do not refer to themselves as *hadhar* but simply as "Kuwaitis" or as "the people from within the wall"—meaning the wall that used to surround the town. It is the *badu* who call them *hadhar*. Likewise, it is mainly the *hadhar* who speak of the "others" as *badu*. But badu is more common as it is also used in national politics to refer to the elected representatives or the political groupings from the "rural" or outlying constituencies with an exclusively tribal population. The press would speak for example of "a pragmatic alliance between islamist and *badu* (tribal) deputies." In contemporary political language, *hadar* and *badu* refer to two types of electorate rather than two actual ways of life. Although traditionally the *hadhar* have distinguished themselves from the *badu* by their education, their greater familiarity with the outside world, and a typically more sophisticated lifestyle, the *badu* are swiftly catching up. Today, to the untrained eye of the outsider, the difference between the educated *badu* and their "urban" compatriots may not always be easy to tell. Increasingly, the family names and not the lifestyle are becoming the best indications of people's social backgrounds.

demands for a modernization of politics. According to urban Kuwaitis, this unflinching political support is the supreme indication that the *badu* do not care for the interests of Kuwait, the land, and the community. All they care for, it is claimed, are the interests of their tribes and "the hand that feeds them"—namely, the ruling family.

Beside the urban folk and the tribal folk, there is a third native (i.e., nonmigrant) component in Kuwaiti society: the stateless or *bidoun,* from the Arabic phrase *bidoun jinsiyya,* which literally means "without nationality." The *bidouns,* who are not to be confused with the bedouins, consist mainly of unregistered former nomads whose pasture grounds centered around the area where Kuwait and Saudi Arabia meet. In the 1960s, modernity, in the form of national borders and oil exploitations, forced them to give up their traditional way of life. It seems that they did not register with the Kuwaiti authorities because they held on as long as they could to their nomadic migrations and because, initially, the young state of Kuwait went out of its way to permit and facilitate this tradition by leaving its borders open to their comings and goings. It was around these unregistered nomads that today's *bidoun* population grew. The Kuwaiti government was quick to realize that the presence of a stateless population could be an advantage. Throughout the Gulf, the small size of the native population combines with the privileged economic status of the citizens to make the question of recruitment for the army and the police a constant headache for the governments. Whereas the rest of the Gulf states employ mercenaries from Pakistan, Jordan, Syria, and Yemen to serve in their armed forces, the Kuwaitis have steadily relied on their *bidouns.* The advantages are clear: no one knows the local terrain as well or is as well adapted to it as the *bidouns.* Besides, they are, for all practical purposes, similar to the Kuwaitis themselves and are tied to the region in a way foreign mercenaries could never be. The problem of loyalty, it was thought, would be minimal with them. By rewarding them with free housing, health care, and educational facilities, the Kuwaiti state was offering the *bidouns* attractive incentives to enroll, and by depriving them of nationality and its socioeconomic trappings, it ensured that they would go on enrolling. Besides, the *bidouns* could always hope to be rewarded with naturalization in exchange for performing well in their duties. This system worked more or less satisfactorily for both parties until the outbreak of the Iran-Iraq war. From 1980 onward, however, less desirable elements joined the ranks of the stateless. These new *bidouns* were refugees, draft dodgers, infiltrators overwhelmingly from Iraq, and, increasingly, Arab migrant workers as well, either illegal aliens or absconders (Longva 1997). Toward the end of the 1980s, the Kuwaitis realized that they might have created for themselves an inextricable problem, but by then it was too late. The *bidoun* population had grown so large—to approximately two hundred thousand—and so shadowy that the authorities had difficulties in gaining control over it. On the eve of the Iraqi invasion, the threat to Kuwait's internal security deriving from the presence of the stateless was one of the country's major concerns. Although many of the bona fide *bidoun*s remained loyal to Kuwait during the Iraqi occupation, after liberation the Kuwaitis took it for granted that all the *bidoun*s had sympathized with Iraq. Sweeping measures were taken to expel them from the country and solve the problem once and for all.

Sectarianism, Tribalism, and the Question of Loyalty

Everywhere in the oil-producing states of the Gulf, the power elite is Sunni, whereas the population has a high proportion of Shi'a.[9] The Gulf is the center of *imami* Shi'ism, with the largest Shi'i sect and the one to which the Iranian population and regime subscribe. Among the sources of tension in the region is the reluctant coexistence of conservative Sunni communities, including Wahabi Saudi Arabia, and what they consider heresy par excellence, Shi'ism. Shi'ism's cradle and its holiest shrines are located in southern Iraq, and its most influential *ulamas* are based in the cities Najaf and Karbala (Iraq), Qom, and Mashhad (Iran). Since the creation of the Safavid Empire in the sixteenth century, Iran has been looked upon as the champion of Shi'ism, which, until then, had been a more or less persecuted minority sect throughout the Islamic world; and since Khomeini's revolution, Iran has sometimes been described as "the Vatican of the Shi'a." Although many Shi'a are ethnic Arabs, there is in the Gulf a persistent and widespread stereotype according to which *Shi'i* is the equivalent of *Persian (ajami)*, and *Sunni* is the equivalent of *Arab*. As ethnic Persians, the Shi'a are seen as outsiders by those for whom Kuwait is an integral part of the Arab nation. The political ideology of Arab nationalism or *qawmiyya* may be on the wane everywhere in the Middle East nowadays, but pan-Arabism is still a powerful and central source of identification that can mobilize the masses throughout the Arab world, as has been seen repeatedly in the series of confrontation between Iraq and the United States in the years since the invasion of Kuwait.

9. Altogether the Shi'a represent 75 percent of the total population of Iran, Iraq, and the six members of the Gulf Cooperation Council (Bahrain, Kuwait, Oman, Qatar, Saudi Arabia, and the United Arab Emirates). In Saudi Arabia, where they only make up 4 percent of the population, the Shi'a are all natives of the Eastern Province, where the whole of the Saudi oil reserves lie.

The various levels of identification between Iran and Shi'ism introduce an ethnic dimension to the sectarian conflicts that have been exacerbated since Khomeini came to power and that are proportional to the perceived or real military and ideological threats Iran poses to its Arab neighbors. Everywhere in the Arab Gulf states, the Shi'is suffer from a problem of ascribed disloyalty because of their faith and because of their real or putative connections with Iran. The most extreme cases of ascribed disloyalty are Saudi Arabia and Bahrain. In comparison, the Shi'is in Kuwait fare relatively well; however, their supreme loyalty has also always been questioned, most acutely during the period between 1979 until the Iraqi invasion.

Most sources put the percentage of the Shi'is in Kuwait at around 30. The majority are ethnic Persians who have settled in Kuwait in the past hundred years; with few exceptions, they used to work as sailors, pearl divers, and laborers before 1961. Many were until recently second-category citizens. Even those with first-category nationality have never enjoyed the same legitimacy as the Sunni Kuwaitis. During the Iran-Iraq war, as Kuwait resolutely supported Iraq, Shi'ite employees in the public sector and the army were discriminated against and removed from sensitive posts; many, who were Kuwaiti citizens, were even deported (Crystal 1995). It was widely assumed that their supreme loyalty went to the Islamic Republic, an assumption that was not always entirely ungrounded. A series of bomb attacks in the 1980s, including a near successful attempt on the amir's life, and three plane hijackings carried out by militants of the underground Da'wa, the oldest Shi'ite extremist movement in the Middle East with headquarters in Tehran, nurtured the Kuwaitis' worst suspicions. The fact that they were a marginalized minority made it necessary for the Shi'is to organize themselves in a tight network. Ironically, it was this very organization that allowed them to prove their loyalty to Kuwait in 1990: when the Iraqis invaded the country, it was the Shi'is who had the infrastructure needed to start a resistance movement against the occupiers. The Sunnis, meanwhile, were caught unawares and were much slower to organize themselves. Today, many Kuwaitis acknowledge that a great deal of the resistance was carried out by the Shi'is. Most of the people arrested, tortured, and executed during the occupation bore Shi'ite names. The Iraqi invasion was a turning point in the civic situation of the Shi'is. Practically all the Shi'is with whom I spoke during my fieldwork between 1994 and 1997, including those who did not fight actively against the Iraqis, told me that the war made them realize how deep their attachment to Kuwait was, and the experience led them to distance themselves somewhat from Iran, which they had until then viewed as the most critical source of their identity. The most common reason given for this change in attitude was that "the Iraqis treated us all as Kuwaitis" and did not differentiate between Shi'is and Sunnis. It was as if, through the eyes of the common enemy, the Kuwaitis had discovered a common national identity that transended their other identities and of which they had not been clearly aware previously. Not only that, but some Shi'is sought refuge in Iran during the war and discovered, to their dismay, that the Iranians looked on them as Kuwaitis and therefore as Arabs, not as one of them. Many also discovered that they were ill at ease in the Islamic Republic and that the Iranian sociopolitical reality did not quite correspond to what they had expected. The following statement by a Shi'ite informant adequately sums up a view shared by many: "Now I know who I am: first a Kuwaiti, then a Shi'i, then a person of Persian origin." In the case of the Kuwaiti Shi'is, it seems that national identity has indeed prevailed over sectarian and ethnic identities—all the more so as the state and most of the Sunnis seem for the first time to have acknowledged the Shi'is' loyalty to the nation. This acknowledgement has been expressed through the removal of all official discriminatory measures against them in the public sector.[10]

Although the Iraqi invasion seems to have helped the Shi'is realize and assert more confidently their civic belonging to Kuwait, the effect has been the opposite for the tribal Kuwaitis. Not only were they absent from the resistance movement, but there was also a tribally organized exodus toward Saudi Arabia at an early stage of the occupation. Those who remained in Kuwait and fought against the invaders in Kuwait, whether Sunni or Shi'i, were mainly people with urban roots. This fact deepened the historical cleavage between *hadhar* and *badu* after liberation and added fuel to the urban Kuwaitis' claim that the tribes only want to milk the Kuwaiti welfare state and have no loyalty whatsoever toward Kuwait itself.[11] To this accusation, the tribal apologists have replied that there are perfectly logical explanations for the exodus: the bulk of the Kuwaiti army was recruited from among *bidoun*s and tribal Kuwaitis, but not from among the *hadhar*. Unlike the *hadhar*, the *badu* lived in the so-called rural areas north of Kuwait city,

10. The Shi'is have always participated in parliamentary politics on the same footing as the Sunnis. The 1996 elections brought five Shi'ite deputies to the National Assembly.

11. In fact, there was and still is a lively debate going on about who did participate in the resistance movement. Many of the *hadhar* who criticize the *badu* for their lack of civic spirit were themselves in Cairo, Amman, Dubai, London, or the United States, far away from where the action took place. It may be more correct to say that those who put up with or fought against the Iraqi occupation were those who by chance found themselves in Kuwait at the time of the invasion. And experience shows that people who spend the hottest summer months in the country are, as a rule, those who cannot afford to travel to milder climates—that is to say, the lower middle class, both *hadhar* and *badu* (and migrant workers).

in the direction of the border between Kuwait and Iraq. These were the areas that the Iraqi troops crossed on their way to the capital and that fell under their occupation in the first place. Incapable of resisting the powerful Iraqi army, the Kuwaiti soldiers knew that they would not fare well in the hands of the occupiers; they had therefore no other alternatives but to flee with their families across the border to Saudi Arabia, where most of them had tribal relatives. Between the *hadhar*'s accusation of disloyalty and the *badu*'s logistical explanations for their exodus, there seems to have been a third reason for the latter's behavior, one that is related to the way tribal people conceptualize citizenship.

Two Ways of Conceptualizing Citizenship

Several decades of modernization and nation building under prosperous conditions have created an impression that the transplantation of the Western notion of citizenship onto Arabian soil has gone smoothly. Under peaceful conditions, a Kuwaiti citizen's pledge of attachment to Kuwait sounds very much like any Norwegian citizen's pledge of attachment to Norway. In both cases, we hear a modern discourse of citizenship and nation-state. What the war situation in Kuwait has reminded us, however, is that there are different ways of conceptualizing the relationship between an individual and those who govern him or her, and that modern citizenship is only one of those ways.

The tribes in Kuwait understand nationality and citizenship in the sense of *taba'iyya,* which can be translated as the "following" of or "allegiance" to a leader, in this case Kuwait's ruling family. The root verb of *taba'iyya* means, among other things, "to walk behind someone, to be subordinate to, to be under someone's command." The concept is clearly built on an idea of hierarchy and vertical allegiance. Urban Kuwaitis, on the other hand, understand citizenship as *jinsiyya,* from the root verb *jns,* meaning "to make alike, to assimilate, to naturalize." A derivative noun of *jns* is *jins,* which translates as "species, class, category, race," and, recently, "nation." There is here an idea of similarity and horizontal community; whether one can assume, by extension, an idea of equality is a matter of interpretation—a claim that can also be made about the term *citizenship.*[12] What is clear is that

12. Complete equality for all citizens before the law is a normative aspect of citizenship that derives from a political decision and not a characteristic integral to the very idea of membership in a city or a state—to wit, the late access in Europe and the United States of women and minorities, all of them technically members of the state, to the suffrage and other civic rights as compared with (white) men.

jinsiyya, unlike *taba'iyya,* does not posit a priori an idea of hierarchy or supreme authority. In this sense, it is much closer to the Western concept of citizenship. Although *jinsiyya* has no connection whatsoever with the city, the urban Kuwaitis relate this notion with a territorialized community that is Kuwait—previously the town, today the nation-state—rather than with a particular leadership. Thus, being Kuwaiti in the sense of *jinsiyya* implies an indissoluble bond between the citizen and the state of Kuwait; it is a condition that requires the existence of a national community, a national territory, and a state. Being Kuwaiti in the sense of *taba'iyya,* on the other hand, means that one's allegiance goes to a leader whom one follows and not to a territorialized sovereign state. In other words, whether Kuwait is ruled by the Al Sabah or another family or whether the regime changes from being an emirate to being a republic does not affect the feelings the citizens by *jinsiyya* have for their country; it does affect their views of and relations to the regime in place, but the object of their supreme loyalty—the territorialized imagined community—remains the same. But a change of the ruling family would make a critical difference to the citizens by *taba'iyya* because it would entail a change in the very object of their loyalty. They would be faced with the question of whether to follow the deposed leader in exile or to shift their loyalty to the new leader: in other words, exit or allegiance. Following this logic, some *badu* Kuwaitis had answered the accusations of their *hadhar* counterparts after the war by saying that, from their perspective, it would have been treason to stay behind in Kuwait under Iraqi occupation and not follow the amir into exile. Pursuing this logic further, one could indeed turn the question around and ask whether those who remained in Kuwait under Iraqi rule were to be looked upon as Kuwaiti citizens at all.[13]

Of the two, the *jinsiyya* model seems closer to the Western conceptualization of citizenship. The community to which the individual is attached through citizenship ties and for which "the state" serves as a metaphor is an urban, therefore territorialized, community. Furthermore, this urban space is perceived as the common achievement of the collectivity and not something a bountiful leader has bestowed upon his followers. In other words, the

---

13. Citizenship in Saudi Arabia is the prime illustration of this *taba'iyya* conception of citizenship. Here, the citizen's unmediated relationship to the land or an independent "imagined community" is not even thinkable because the country itself is appropriated by the ruling family whose name it bears. Formally, a Saudi citizen is Saudi by virtue of following the House of Sa'ud (literally, *taba'iyya*), not by virtue of any relationship to the land of Arabia—in which case he or she would have been identified as an Arabian instead of as a Saudi. Furthermore, this state of affairs raises the interesting question of whether the country could go on being called Saudi Arabia should the al-Sa'ud dynasty be removed from power. The obvious answer is no.

relationship between the imagined community and the land of Kuwait is perceived as a direct one, unmediated through a personalized leadership: the citizens have a legitimate claim to the land of Kuwait, for they have built it up over the years and have defended it. Regarding the citizens' relation to those in power, the *jinsiyya* model is heavily biased toward what we could call "entitlement citizenship"; that is, the community is conceived of as a community of watchful citizens, jealously guarding their rights in relation to the power holders, including the right to have a say in public life and the right to hold the leaders accountable. As to civic responsibilities, they are less clearly articulated in the daily discourse. One thing is clear, however: responsibilities are owed to the community, not to the leadership.

Part of this conceptualization arises, of course, from the organization of social life in an urban setting, where the division of tasks inevitably emphasizes the part played by professional competence in the allocation of roles and statuses at the expense of blood ties, which are central in the tribal system. But it also arises from the specific founding myth of the "pact" between the ruling family and the Kuwaiti people, in which the Al Sabah, being chosen by the people to administrate the town, do not have greater claim to this town than the rest of the Kuwaitis. Although the pact was agreed upon between the Al Sabah and the Sunni merchant community only, not the whole population, the oral transmission of the myth over the years has resulted in its being embraced by most of the urban population, including the Shi'is and the descendants of humble laborers. This has greatly contributed to strengthening the idea of "entitlement citizenship" among the *hadhar.*

Citizenship and the Welfare State

This pure *jinsiyya* conceptualization is, meanwhile, modified in practice by the peculiar character of Kuwaiti society as a uniquely paternalistic form of welfare, do-gooder state, one in which the citizens are not the producers of their own welfare goods and services, merely the beneficiaries.[14] Of particular significance is also the fact that in exchange for the enjoyment of exten-

14. This is the result of the Kuwaiti economy being a rentier economy, which according to Beblawi's definition (1990) is one in which (1) only a small fraction of the society is involved in the process of wealth generation, while the remainder is engaged in the distribution and utilization of this wealth, and (2) the state is an allocative state—i.e. it plays a central role in distributing this wealth to the population. It may also be added that the Kuwaiti citizens make up less than 20 percent of the labor force.

sive social rights, no obligations are required from the citizens, either in the form of taxes or in the form of military service. While privileging the citizens in many ways, this one-way relationship also disempowers them and puts them in a crippling dependency situation vis-à-vis the power holders. It also most effectively undermines the legitimacy of the notion of political entitlement that is intrinsic in the *jinsiyya* conceptualization of citizenship. In the context of the Gulf, what this type of welfare state does in practice is weaken the *jinsiyya* model in favor of the *taba'iyya* model.

In their majority, the *badu* do not identify themselves with the founding myth of the pact simply because, at the time it was agreed upon, most of them were not part of the Kuwaiti population. The notion of entitlement is by no means absent from the *taba'iyya* conceptualization of citizenship, but what the citizens are entitled to here are rights to material welfare and protection, traditionally rare values in desert life, rather than participation in decision making and political accountability. Thus, *taba'iyya* is a notion particularly suited to and compatible with the present Kuwaiti situation characterized by a rentier economy, a one-way welfare state, a liberal but not genuinely democratic regime, and heavy reliance on migrant labor. Whereas the *jinsiyya* model stresses the rights aspect of citizenship while remaining vague about the responsibilities, the *taba'iyya* model is clear about both rights and responsibilities: the citizen is entitled to social rights and is willing, in exchange, to give his political allegiance to the source of these rights—namely, the "state" represented by the Al Sabah.

Citizenship and Islam

In the Middle East today, Israel is the only state that explicitly links citizenship and creed. Among the Muslim countries, only Iran carries the designation *Islamic* in its official name, but it does not overtly claim that Iranian citizenship is predicated on membership in the Muslim community the way that Israel is said to be created by and for the Jews. That we do not find among the Muslim states as overt a linkage between citizenship and creed as in Israel does not mean, however, that this linkage does not exist. It is in fact quite real, cognitively—in people's minds—as well as legally—in the legal texts and, not least, in practice. This is, for example, clearly the case for Saudi Arabia, but as we have seen from the texts of the Kuwaiti nationality laws, being a Muslim is not a matter of indifference in Kuwait, especially when it comes to naturalization. In fact, the present legislation explicitly excludes non-Muslims from being considered for naturalization. Under normal circumstances, the correlation between citizenship and creed is hardly ever discussed as it is most unusual for non-Muslims to apply for naturalization in a Middle Eastern country.[15] I suggest that the citizenship-creed correlation is one of those deep-lying assumptions that make the conceptualization of citizenship in the Gulf, and probably throughout the Middle East, differ from the one we find in most Western societies. As mentioned, the assumption surfaces in the explicit discourse in cases of naturalization but also in cases of apostasy, which indicates that the linkage is more complex in the Gulf than in the case of Israel, where it is simply stated that one must be Jewish in order to be an Israeli citizen. In most Muslim countries, being Muslim is not a formal requirement for being a citizen, but because the personal status law is regulated by the *shari'a,* there is an implicit presupposition that, in order to be included as a full-fledged citizen in possession of all the rights guaranteed by the law, one has to be Muslim. Apostasy—i.e., conversion from Islam—therefore has immediate and extensive consequences for the legal status of the apostate: he or she loses his or her juridical capacity—the rights to remain married, to fulfill parental functions, to inherit, or to enter into any contractual relationship. It goes without saying that the principle of citizenship is seriously impaired by the devastating implications of apostasy, which have been equated by experts with "social and legal death" (Gibb and Kramers 1974, 414). Since the advent of the modern state, the question of whether the apostate should be deprived of his or her citizenship has been raised explicitly in various Arab countries (Peters and De Vries 1976–77). In Kuwait, this happened as recently as in 1996 in connection with the conversion to Christianity of Husain Ali Qambar, a Kuwaiti Shi'i (Longva 1996). On this occasion, the Islamists who have called for stripping the apostate of his Kuwaiti citizenship explicitly made the linkage between creed and citizenship.

It seems that for many Kuwaitis, membership in the state of Kuwait goes through membership in the supranational Muslim community, the *umma,* just as membership in the state of Israel goes through membership in the Jewish community. Although there is acceptance of Kuwaiti-born citizens who belong to another religion, the 1981 law restricting naturalization to Muslims only (and passed without noticeable opposition) clearly shows that the notion of citizenship, whether defined as *jinsiyya* or *taba'iyya,* is implicitly but nonetheless inherently conceptualized by most Kuwaitis not in terms of universal and abstract rights and duties but in the deeply cultural and particularistic terms of identity and loyalty.

---

15. The only exceptions are non-Muslim foreign women married to citizens of the Muslim countries. In most cases, these women would have converted to Islam upon marriage.

Conclusion

Born in Europe in conjunction with the nation-state, citizenship has for many years been treated by social scientists merely as a pragmatic mechanism to regulate the relations between citizens and state, so its symbolic significance has not been the object of much analytical scrutiny. But we have recently come to the view that although this institution is an effective mechanism for ordering societies, the kind of order it achieves need not always be the one we expect. History, tradition, and, above all, the circumstances under which the state is created and its legitimacy is maintained—all contribute to the way citizenship is conceptualized and put into practice. The interest of the oil-exporting states of the Arab Gulf in this regard lies primarily in that studying them forces us to examine familiar categories in a new light and to approach the topic of citizenship from an analytical perspective that takes into consideration the historical and sociocultural specificity of the region.

PART TWO

APPLICATIONS

Citizenship in Palestinian and Israeli Contexts

9

The Palestinians

From Hyphenated to Integrated Citizenship

ANIS F. KASSIM

WHEN THE IRAQI REGIME ordered its armed forces to invade the State of Kuwait in August 1990, the Palestinian community there was the second target of the occupation authority, which ordered the transfer of thousands of Palestinian employees, who constituted the backbone of the Kuwaiti civil service, to various districts in Iraq proper.[1] When the Kuwaiti government-in-exile was reinstated in liberated Kuwait, the Palestinian community, or the remnants thereof, was the first target of the Kuwaiti government. It accused the Palestinians of collaboration with the Iraqi occupation authority and launched a cleansing operation against the Palestinians in Kuwait.[2]

When the Palestine Liberation Organization (PLO) entered into the Declaration of Principles and subsequently the Oslo Agreements, Colonel Muammar Qadhafi, targeting the Palestinians working in Libya, ordered them to "go home" and threw them at the rim of the desert or on boats to carry them to Lebanon.[3] His declared objective was to "embarrass" the newly created Palestinian National Authority (PNA) and allegedly to prove that the premises of the Oslo Agreements were false. He also urged other

---

1. This account is based on my visit to Kuwait one month after the invasion. That experience is recorded in Kassim 1990.

2. Middle East Watch, *Nowhere to Go: The Tragedy of the Remaining Palestinian Families in Kuwait*, reproduced in *6th Palestine Yearbook of International Law* 87 (1990–91, 87). See also "Arbitrary Justice in Kuwait," *Guardian Weekly*, 26 May 1991; Lesch 1991, 34.

3. See a special report on this tragedy in *9th Palestine Yearbook of International Law* (1996–97).

Arab countries to expel Palestinians from their midst and drive them "home" (UNRWA 1995).[4]

In reaction to the Libyan cleansing operation, Lebanon declared that it would not accept the expelled Palestinians from Libya because Lebanon is "not a dumping yard of human remnants" (*Al-Hayat,* 12 September 1995), as one Lebanese official put it. The Lebanese government immediately issued new regulations requiring a Palestinian holding a Lebanese travel document to apply not only for a permit to return to Lebanon, but even for one to leave Lebanon.

As if so much agony were not sufficient to satisfy those regimes, two years earlier, in 1988, the Jordanian government suddenly discovered that the West Bank was not part of the kingdom and that West Bankers were not Jordanian citizens. More than a million people found themselves stateless virtually overnight. Not only did West Bankers turn out to be stateless, but unfortunate Palestinians who happened to be outside the West Bank when the severance of the ties with the East Bank took place were continuously threatened by the Ministry of Interior with being stripped of their citizenship. The ministry discovered that thousands of Jordanian citizens of Palestinian origin had been able to "forge" papers to acquire Jordanian citizenship. When so proven, and it turned out to be easy to prove, such "criminals" who had forged official papers were "awarded" "travel documents" for "humanitarian reasons."[5]

Considering the state of seige under which the Palestinians have been living in the autonomous areas, any movement of a Palestinian between the Gaza Strip and the West Bank has become more ludicrous. A student from Gaza who attends Birzeit University cannot, for example, travel directly from Gaza to Ramallah. Instead, he has to go from Gaza to Cairo, from Cairo to Amman, and then cross Allenby Bridge into the West Bank.

When Israel came into existence, it commenced the endless agony for the Palestinians, both those who remained under the new Jewish state and those who were expelled. If the creation of a Jewish state was intended to "normalize" the status of Jews, it also ironically resulted in "abnormalizing" the status of the Palestinians.[6]

The above examples demonstrate certain facts and raise certain issues, the most relevant of which to my purpose here are: to be a Palestinian means not to have a formal citizenship, with the resulting hardships that make the Palestinian life in various communities continuously dangerous; the legal

---

4. Also UNRWA Press Release, HQ/8/95, 29 September 1995. *Al-Hayat,* (Arabic daily—London) 19 September 1995.

5. See the text accompanying notes 21–29.

6. See the text accompanying notes 26–31.

status of a Palestinian in the Middle East is always in doubt and left to the political exigencies of each host country; and the absence of an internationally recognized State of Palestine will make this agony last indefinitely. This chapter therefore focuses on the legal definition of a Palestinian and traces that definition from its inception to the end of the twentieth century, the legal safeguards accorded to Palestinians, if any, and their legal status in the diaspora. Finally, it addresses the issue of who a Palestinian is under the new PNA and the recent attempts to integrate the citizenship status of the Palestinian.

The Early Legal Definition of a Palestinian

One of the most enigmatic sociolegal phenomena in contemporary studies is the definition of a Palestinian. At present, in the absence of the State of Palestine, if the label *Palestinian* were to be devised by an authoritative enactment or formal legislation, hardly any person would qualify for such an identification. Yet the Palestinian is pushed, shoved, oppressed, and deprived of elementary rights because he is a so-called Palestinian. Obviously, and as a result of the disintegration of the Palestinian community in 1948, others define who a Palestinian is, and the treatment of Palestinians is based on that other definition.

The legal definition of a Palestinian, as regulated by formal citizenship law, was developed historically in three stages: the British Mandate era, the Israeli phase, and the post-Oslo period.

Palestinian Citizenship: The Mandatory Phase

According to the Treaty of Lausanne, which came into force on 6 August 1924, it was determined, that those Ottoman nationals who were "habitually residents" of Palestine "will become *ipso facto*" nationals of that state (Hurewitz 1956, 119). The Mandate for Palestine provided in Article 7 that the mandatory power "shall be responsible for enacting a nationality law." That provision further directed the mandatory power "to facilitate the acquisition of Palestinian citizenship by Jews who take up their permanent residence in Palestine." However, Article 15 dictated that "No discrimination of any kind shall be made between the inhabitants of Palestine on the ground of race, religion or language. No person shall be excluded from Palestine on the sole ground of his religious belief" (Hurewitz 1956, 106).[7]

---

7. However, see the discriminatory nationality law that Israel has enacted and applied to Palestinians, in the section on "The Israeli-Palestinians," below, and in the text accompanying notes 27–36.

On 24 July 1925, the first Palestine Citizenship Order was enacted by the mandatory power (Drayton 1934, 2640). In its first article, that enactment defined a Palestinian as a "Turkish subject habitually resident in the territory of Palestine." This law followed the policy directions codified in the mandate in facilitating the acquisition of Palestinian citizenship by Jewish settlers who were transplanted to establish the "Jewish home." This legislation was the first official enactment that provided a legal definition of the Palestinian. It set out the territorial criteria for citizenship, and it was seemingly an nondiscriminatory legislation, which provided for granting citizenship to an applicant, irrespective of his race, religion, or language. This order remained in full force and effect until 14 May 1948, when the second phase began.

Palestinian Citizenship: The Hyphenated Phase

On 14 May 1948, the People's Council, representatives of the Jewish Community of Palestine and the Zionist Movement, unilaterally declared the establishment of Israel as "the Jewish state." The creation of a Jewish state resulted in multifaceted problems for those who once enjoyed equal Palestinian citizenship—more accurately, the non-Jewish Palestinians. On or about that date, the non-Jewish Palestinian polity was disintegrated, and Palestinian citizenship was disintegrated accordingly. Henceforth, those Palestinians had no citizenship but could be categorized under four groupings: (1) Palestinians who remained in Israel; (2) Palestinians who became refugees; (3) Palestinians who became citizens of Jordan; and (4) Palestinians who remained in or relocated in the Gaza Strip. In this phase, Palestinians became hyphenated citizens; they are now Israeli-Palestinians; Jordanian-Palestinians, United Nations Relief and Works Agency–Palestinians, and Gaza-Palestinians.

The Israeli Palestinians

The term *Palestinian,* as used here, is meant to include all persons who enjoyed Palestinian citizenship from 1925 until 14 May 1948. On this latter date, segregation began between Jewish Palestinians and non-Jewish Palestinians. When the term *Palestinian* is used hereinafter, it means the non-Jewish Palestinians.

During the period falling between 14 May 1948 and 14 July 1952, which is the time when the first Israeli Nationality Law came into force, Palestinians were considered "stateless." An overwhelming number of Israeli courts held during that interim period that the Palestinian citizenship was terminated on the same day Israel came into existence. In *Oseri* v. *Oseri,* the

Tel Aviv District Court held that the former Palestinian citizenship was now "devoid of substance," "not satisfactory and is inappropriate to the situation following the establishment of Israel" (*International Law Report* 1950, 111). In conclusion, the court held that plaintiff and defendant, both Palestinian citizens, were "stateless" during the period between the establishment of the state of Israel and the coming into force of Israel's Nationality Law. In *Hussein v. Governor of Acre Prison,* Israel's Supreme Court upheld the same principle (*International Law Report* 1950, 112).

The situation for the Palestinians did not much improve after the coming into force of Israel's Nationality Law in 1952. In fact, what the law did was to "legally" denationalize the Palestinians (Article 18[a]; text in *Laws of the State of Israel* [hereafter *LSI*] 1951/52, vol. 6, p. 50). The new legislation granted every "Jew" who immigrated to Israel, or, following the 1971 amendment, even expressed the desire to immigrate to Israel, "immediate" Israeli citizenship without taking any formal steps, but it determined, with retroactive effect, that the Palestinian Citizenship Orders "are repealed with effect from the day of the establishment of the State" (ibid.). The law then required those non-Jewish Palestinians to go through the process of "naturalization" to obtain Israeli citizenship.

Article 3 of the Nationality Law set out the conditions a Palestinian had to satisfy before he could obtain Israeli citizenship. The first paragraph of Article 3, subsection 3(a), stipulates that a Palestinian had to have been registered in the Inhabitants Registration in 1949, have been an inhabitant of Israel on 14 July 1952, and have been in Israel or in an area that later on became an Israeli territory between 14 May 1948 and 14 July 1952 or have entered Israel legally during that period. These conditions were in practice very difficult to fulfill. More significantly, they were cumulative conditions. As Professor Don Peretz (1958) recorded, most Palestinians at that time "had no proof of Palestinian citizenship," and those who had identity cards were forced to surrender them to the Israeli army during, or immediately after, the war. In addition, Peretz noted, many Palestinians were excluded from the Registration of Inhabitants because often there was a "deliberate attempt not to register many [Palestinian] villages" (123).

As a result of these legal hurdles, very few Palestinians were able to obtain Israeli citizenship. Those who failed to satisfy the above conditions, and they constituted the majority, remained in Israel as stateless persons. But that was not the end of this amorphous phase. The second paragraph of Article 3 of the Nationality Law, subsection 3(b), was sweetly drafted, but for a pernicious intent and purpose. It reads: "A person born after the establishment of the State who is an inhabitant of Israel on the day of the coming into force of this Law, and whose father or mother becomes an Israel national under subsection (a), shall become an Israel national with effect from the day of his birth" (51). This paragraph deals with the nationality of the minority of children born at the time to those Palestinians who were able to satisfy the difficult conditions of subsection (a) referred to above. The exact outcome of the application of these two paragraphs was that for the majority of the approximately 170,000 Palestinians who found themselves inside Israel when the 1949 armistice agreements were signed between Israel and the neighbouring Arab states, the remnants of the mass of the Palestinian people expelled from the territories that came under Israeli control, if a child is born to a Palestinian father or mother who was not a citizen of Israel, he or she will inevitably be stateless. Over the years, a situation developed in Israel whereby *stateless Palestinians were breeding stateless children.*

In an apparent attempt to soften that pinprick policy, an amendment to the Nationality Law was introduced in 1968 (*22 LSI* 1968, 241). The new conditions by which the amendment intended to relax the law proved to be a farce. According to the 1968 amendment, the applicant had to first apply within three years from reaching the age of eighteen years and had to prove that he had been an Israeli resident for five consecutive years immediately prior to his application. Once these two conditions were satisfied, the minister of interior would grant citizenship to the applicant unless he "has been convicted of an offence against the security of the State or has been sentenced to imprisonment for five years or more for another offence." Just prior to the time when that amendment was enacted, the Palestinians inside Israel were living under the Emergency Defence Regulations 1945, which virtually labeled every activity as a "security issue." It is needless to dwell on the pretext of "security" in the Israeli parlance because it has been used to a ludicrous degree, manner, and character. Consequently, very few stateless Palestinians were able to benefit from this amendment.

In 1980, another amendment was introduced and could be considered a turning point in the ordeal of Israeli-Palestinians (*34 LSI* 1980, 254). Although it does not do away with the discrimination between the conditions of acquiring citizenship for Jews and non-Jews nor alleviate the racist restrictions set out in Articles 3(a) and (b), the new amendment helped most Israeli Palestinians to obtain Israeli citizenship in that it waived the condition laid down in the said Article 3(a) and (b) of the law that the person was in Israel from the date of the establishment of the State of Israel in 1948 until the Nationality Law came into force in 1952.

The Jordanian Palestinians

That part of Palestine not occupied by the Israeli forces as a result of the 1948–49 war is now called the West Bank. This parcel of territory was soon united with the Hashemite Kingdom of Jordan. On 24 April 1950, both houses of the Jordanian Parliament, composed of equal representatives from both the East and West banks of the Jordan, adopted Resolution 1, which formally united the two sides of the river. The first paragraph of that resolution ensured "equality in rights and obligations" among all compatriots.[8]

The legal definition of Palestinians who remained in the West Bank would pass through three stages. While the West Bank was still under the "military administration" of the Hashemite Kingdom of Jordan, the Jordanian Council of Ministers issued on 13 December 1949 a Law Additional to the Citizenship Law of 1928. Article 2 of this law provided that "All those who at the time when this Law goes into effect habitually reside in Transjordan or in the Western part [of the Jordan] which is being administered by [the Kingdom], and who were holders of Palestinian citizenship, shall be deemed as Jordanians enjoying all rights of Jordanians and bearing all the attendant obligations."[9] Because this law was enacted before the West Bank was united with the East Bank, it in effect imposed Jordanian citizenship on Palestinians, and those Palestinians were defined, accordingly, as Jordanian Palestinians.

The second stage began when a new Citizenship Law was enacted in 1954, which, it appeared, was intended to regulate the irregular imposition of Jordanian nationality on Palestinians in 1949. The new law granted Jordanian citizenship to Palestinians living in the West Bank as well as to those Palestinians who crossed the river during the 1948–49 war and took refuge in the East Bank. Although Article 3(1) of that law confirmed the definition of Jordanians under the Citizenship Law of 1928, Article 3(2) granted Jordanian citizenship to "every person, other than a Jew, who was a holder of a Palestinian citizenship before 15.5.1948 and who normally resided in the Hashemite Kingdom of Jordan during the period between 20.12.1949 and 16.2.1954."[10] Ever since, all Palestinians in Jordan have been defined as Jordanians, entertaining full individual political, civil, economic, and religious rights.

The third stage commenced with the severance of Jordan's relationship with the West Bank. On the eve of 31 July 1988, King Hussein of Jordan delivered a televised speech in which he declared the severance of all administrative and legal ties with the West Bank.[11] In the royal speech, the king however asserted that:

---

8. Text of Resolution 1 in *Compilation of Jordan's Laws and Regulations* (in Arabic, 1961, 4).

9. This law went into effect when it was published in the *Official Gazette*, no. 1004 (20 December 1949).

10. Law No. 6 (1954).

11. Text excerpted in *4th Palestine Yearbook of International Law* (1987–88), 297.

it has to be understood in all clarity, and without any ambiguity or equivoca-
tion, that our measures regarding the West Bank concern only the occupied
Palestinian land and its people. *They naturally do not relate in any way to the
Jordanian citizens of Palestinian origin in the Hashemite Kingdom of Jordan.
They all have the full rights of citizenship and all its obligations,* the same as any
other citizen irrespective of his origin. (emphasis added)

In spite of that unequivocal royal directive, the successive Jordanian governments and officials set in motion a series of orders and regulations that have
had direct and negative bearing on Palestinians in the West Bank. The government decreed that all those who were living in the West Bank on 31 July
1988 were now "Palestinians."[12] Another negative consequence emerging
from the government's new approach was the revival, this time in a hard
and direct form, of the hyphenated citizenship of Jordanian Palestinians.[13]

The UNRWA Palestinians

On 8 December 1949, the United Nations General Assembly adopted its
famous Resolution 302(iv), which, inter alia, established the United Nations
Relief and Works Agency for Palestine Refugees in the Near East
(UNRWA). The major aim of the newly created world agency was to render
direct relief and work programs to the Palestinian refugees. This resolution
came about a year after the General Assembly had adopted its Resolution
194(III) of 11 December 1948, in which it was resolved that "the refugees
wishing to return to their homes and live at peace with their neighbors
should be permitted to do so . . . and that compensation should be paid for
the property of those choosing not to return."

According to UNRWA, a Palestinian refugee was defined as a person *(a)*
who lost his home and livelihood as a result of the 1948–49 hostilities, and
(b) who is in need (Tomeh 1968, Van Dusen 1972, Peretz 1993).[14] This

12. The government's instructions were released on 20 August 1988, but were never published in the *Official Gazette.* Text on file with the writer.

13. Mr. Adnan Abu Odeh, a Jordanian Palestinian, who once served as the head of the
Intelligence Service, minister of information, and minister of the royal court, was recently inter-
viewed in *Al-Dustour* (a Jordanian Arabic daily). He elaborated on his paradoxical situation as
being accepted neither by Palestinians nor by Jordanians. At present, Mr. Abu Odeh says he
prefers to be identified as "a Jordanian of Palestinian origin," whereas in the past he felt he was
"a Jordanian only." See *Al-Dustour,* 3, 5, 6, and 7 November 1996.

14. See also the excellent doctoral dissertation by Takkenberg, "The Status of Palestinian
Refugees in International Law" (1998). Dr. Takkenberg has traced the definition of a Palestinian refugees from its origins to the present time. He was able to site seven definitions.

restrictive definition excluded Palestinians who *(a)* did not leave their homes but lost their livelihood; *(b)* were displaced but found a substitute source of living in other countries; *(c)* were displaced and made refugees within Israel proper; and *(d)* were subsequently displaced from the Demilitarized Zones that were created by virtue of the Armistice Agreements of 1949. Subsequent Israeli wars created new refugees and made some people refugees for the second or third time (Zureik 1994).

Palestinian refugees were basically concentrated in five countries in addition to the West Bank. Jordan was the major recipient of Palestinian refugees, followed by Syria, Lebanon, Iraq, and to a far less extent Egypt. Other Arab countries, such as the Arab Gulf states and North African Arab states did subsequently receive Palestinian workers, but neither were such countries recipient states, nor were the Palestinians there as refugees.

The League of Arab States resolved that member states should accord the Palestinians living in their midst all rights accorded to their respective nationals, except for the right to citizenship. The rationale behind this exception was to keep alive the Palestinian identity and safeguard it against assimilation. All host countries, except for Jordan, issued Palestinian refugees with traveling documents. With time, these documents became straight jackets in some of the host countries, constricting virtually all rights purportedly granted to Palestinian refugees.

The Gaza Palestinians

Contrary to the public notions that the Gaza Strip was annexed by Egypt, Gaza in a strictly legal sense was the only parcel of the territory of Palestine that remained Palestinian. It was placed under the administration of Egypt, but it was never incorporated into the Egyptian jurisdiction. During the period between 1948 and 1967, the Egyptian administration retained most of the basic legislation that was inherited from the Ottoman and the mandatory periods, including the Palestinian Citizenship Order of 1925. All judgments issued by Gaza courts were rendered in the name of the "Palestinian people" (Kassim 1984).

The Gaza Palestinians were issued with Egyptian travel documents that enabled them to move outside the Gaza Strip and outside of Egypt. With time, this privilege was curtailed, as is shown below.

The Legal Status of Palestinians

This section addresses the legal status of all Palestinians, whether hyphenated or UNRWA Palestinians—namely, the refugees in the recipient countries.

The Hyphenated Palestinians

The Israeli Palestinians. Ever since the introduction of the 1980 amendment to Israel's Nationality Law, the citizenship status of the Israeli Palestinians is less harsh. Israeli Palestinians are now strictly legal citizens of the state of Israel, but they are not equal to the Jewish Israelis. Put differently and according to the Orwellian doctrine, the citizens of the State of Israel are all equal, but some are more equal than others. Jewish Israelis are more equal than Israeli Palestinians. This segregation is codified in Israeli laws and evidenced in Israeli official practices (Kretzmer 1990).

A Polish Jew, for example, who immigrates to Israel will be "immediately" granted Israeli citizenship. The new immigrant, or an *oleh* as the law calls him, is not required to take any action. He is not even required to apply for citizenship or to declare that he intends to reside in Israel or to take an oath of allegiance. In the eyes of the law, he is "returning home."[15] The presumption, therefore, is that a person "returning home" is not required to take any step or pursue any procedures except "to return." The law, emphasizing this premise, requires a Jew coming to Israel to take action if he does not want to be clothed with Israeli citizenship. The principle of "return" and the procedures attached thereto are codified in the Law of Return and the Nationality Law.[16]

It consequently follows from this dichotomy between an Israeli by return (Jewish) and an Israeli by residence, birth, and naturalization (Palestinian) that a whole set of preferential treatment is accorded each class of Israeli citizens. Some 20 percent of Israeli Palestinians, though legally a citizen of the state, are classified as "absentees" for the purposes of confiscating their lands, according to the Absentees' Property Law of 1950 (*4 LSI* 1950, 68). For any political party in Israel to have the right to run for the Israeli elections, the party's political program must first adopt the Zionist doctrine that the "State of Israel [is] the state of the Jewish people," according to the 1985 amendment of the Basic Law: the Knesset (*39 LSI* 1984–85, 216).[17] As Usama Halabi points out in his analysis of Supreme Court Justice Dov Levin's minority opinion in Elections Appeal No. 2/88 (Halabi 1991, 147), it was the view of Justice Levin that the objectives of the Progressive List for Peace, which was running in Knesset elections, contradicted that amendment because it called for complete equality of rights, and that anyone who

---

15. The ensuing text is based on Kassim (1972).

16. The Law of Return is, legally, an immigration law. However, the "right of return" as enunciated in that law has been incorporated in the Nationality Law.

17. See also Halabi (1991).

calls for equality between the Arab citizen and the Jewish citizen cannot run for the Knesset elections, as that objective is contradictory with the State of Israel being a Jewish state established to grant Jews more privileges and preferential treatment because they are Jews.[18]

An Israeli scholar has succinctly described the status of Israeli Palestinians as follows:

> The Palestinian citizens of Israel . . . have "passport citizenship" rights . . . but they are denied equal "democratic citizenship." . . . While enjoying equal access to the courts of law and to private property (civil rights), as well as to the ballot and to government (political rights), they are denied equal rights to social security, education and welfare (social rights), and to the land and water resources of the State (economic rights). (Davis 1995, 28)

The Jordanian Palestinians. When the Jordanian Citizenship Law of 1954 was enacted, Palestinians who became Jordanians enjoyed full individual political, civil, economic, and religious rights. Jordanian Palestinians, according to the Election Law of 1960, used to have one-half of the Parliament's seats.[19] They enjoyed equal opportunities in civil service, government portfolios, army, police force, schools, citizenship, business, and virtually all other sectors and fields of activity. Ownership to property, whether chattel or real, was also secured and safeguarded without discrimination.[20]

When Jordan unilaterally severed administrative and legal ties with the West Bank in 1988, the legal status of the Jordanian Palestinians was harshly undermined. On 31 July 1988, the Jordanian government stripped more than a million Palestinians living in the West Bank of their Jordanian citizenship. The government—without any authority under municipal law, let alone international law—made those Palestinians stateless. In an attempt to veil its nefarious intentions, it insisted that those who habitually reside in the West Bank are considered of "Palestinian citizenship."[21]

It should be highlighted that the Citizenship Law of Jordan dealt with the loss of Jordanian nationality in a highly restrictive and narrow manner. Article 18(1) provides that if a person was enlisted in the military service of a foreign country without advance permission from the Council of Ministers and refused to leave that military service when the government ordered him

---

18. For excerpts of this judgment, see 25 Israel Law. Rev. 219 (1991).

19. Law No. 24 (1960).

20. However, Mr. Abu Odeh has revealed that discrimination was actually practiced against Jordanian-Palestinians. See his interviews referred to in note 13.

21. See note 13.

to do so, his citizenship would be forfeited. A Jordanian may also lose his citizenship by a decree issued by the Council of Ministers and with the endorsement of the king if he joins the civil service of a foreign country and declines an order of the government for him to resign that service, if he serves in an enemy country, or if he commits or attempts to commit an action that jeopardizes the state's security and safety.

Article 19 deals with the loss of citizenship by a naturalized Jordanian. Once again, the loss of citizenship in this instance is subject to a decree by the Council of Ministers and the endorsement of the king. This article lists two events whereby a naturalized citizen may lose his citizenship: (1) if he attempts to commit or actually commits an action that endangers the state's security or safety; and (2) if he forges documents in his application for citizenship and based on such documents he was naturalized.

In practice, the reported cases involving the loss of citizenship by Jordanians, original or naturalized, are very rare. This remarkable history yields a very strong indication that because of the highly restrictive procedures and the significantly narrow situations that can cause a loss of citizenship, the Jordanian legislature has pursued a wise policy that is consistent with human rights requirements and international law imperatives.[22]

The government argument that residents of the West Bank are "Palestinian citizens" is groundless. The Jordanian executive or its legislative branch can legally designate who a "Jordanian citizen" is, but it certainly lacks authority under both municipal and international law to designate the citizenship status of persons who are not Jordanian citizens. The government argument is obviously intended to justify the stripping of more than one million Jordanian Palestinians of their citizenship in violation of both the domestic Citizenship Law and the international practice that dictates the obligation of sovereign states to reduce cases of statelessness.[23]

The Jordanian High Court of Justice adopted the government's arguments without scrutiny.[24] The Court ruled in a series of judgments that the severance of the legal and administrative ties with the West Bank is an "act of state" that falls outside its jurisdiction.[25] Adopting the government desig-

---

22. See the instructions issued by the Council of Ministers on 22 August 1988. These instructions were never published in the *Official Gazette* (in Arabic, on file with the writer).

23. For example, see Convention on the Reduction of Statelessness, which was adopted on 30 August 1961 and went into force on 13 December 1975.

24. See Jordanian High Court of Justice (HCJ), case no. 164/90, translated into English and published in *6th Palestine Yearbook of International Law* 68 (1990–91). This judgment incorporates all legal issues that were subsequently dealt with by the High Court of Justice.

25. In Law No. 11 (1989), constituting the Jordanian High Court of Justice, Article 9(b) provides that the court will not have jurisdiction over issues pertaining to "act of state." The law does not define or list examples of what constitutes an "act of state."

nation, it ruled that those who were living in the West Bank on 31 July 1988 were "Palestinian citizens." If any such Palestinian comes to Jordan, he is an "alien" and can be deported upon the expiry of his permit—so the High Court held. The Court did not address Articles 18 and 19 of the Citizenship Law and failed to apply them to the sudden loss of citizenship by more than one million Jordanian Palestinians. Furthermore, and probably more significant, the Court did not observe the imperative provision of Article 93(ii) of the Constitution, which reads: "A law shall come into force after its promulgation by the King and the lapse of thirty days from the date of its publication in the Official Gazette." Obviously, this constitutional imperative is important in that none of the governmental instructions dealing with the severance of ties with the West Bank were ever published in the official gazette. Neither was the royal speech of 31 July 1988.

The government, in an attempt to facilitate the movement of Palestinians who once were Jordanian citizens, decided to grant them a Jordanian passport valid for two years only, as opposed to a five-year passport that is normally issued to a Jordanian citizen. These new procedures, however, adversely affected the status of Palestinians in the West Bank. Traveling on a two-year passport was ipso facto evidence that the holder of the passport was a "Palestinian." Quite often, this fact precipitated denials of visas to other countries, of acceptance of the Jordanian Palestinian's children in Jordanian universities or civil service, and of entry in certain Arab countries, as well as the curtailment of job opportunities in the Gulf states, and so on.

Although this agony subsided in the period between 1988 and 1993, it again erupted after the Oslo Accords and especially after the arrival of the PNA to the autonomous areas. The issue became of such serious concern that many public figures became involved in the debate, including the Committee on Palestine and Occupied Arab Territories of the Jordanian Parliament.[26]

The Jordanian Ministry of Interior has further categorized Palestinians and Jordanian Palestinians into three groups: (1) those who were residents of the West Bank prior to 31 July 1988 are Palestinians; (2) those who were in Jordan (East Bank) are Jordanians; and (3) Palestinians who have yellow cards in their possession shall be treated as Jordanians living in the West Bank, and those who hold green cards are now deemed Palestinians. The

26. See the interview given by the chairman of the committee, Mr. Anwar al-Hadeed, to *Al-Sabeel* (a Jordanian weekly, in Arabic), 27 June 1995. See also the interview given by Mr. Hani al-Khasawna to *Al-Sabeel*, 6 June 1995. Mr. al-Khasawna was the minister of information when the West Bank was detached from Jordan in 1988. See also the interview by Mr. Taher al-Masri to *Al-Majd* (a Jordanian weekly, in Arabic) on 5 June 1995. Mr. Masri was the former prime minister of Jordan.

"Green Palestinian," according to the minister of interior, does not have the right to reside permanently in Jordan, establish a business, send his children to school, or participate in the elections either as a voter or as a candidate.[27]

This division was intensified in 1995 when the Ministry of Justice filed a case before the High Court of Justice against the Bar Association to order the annulment of the 1995 elections.[28] The grounds on which the minister based his case was that the Bar Association allowed lawyers who reside in the West Bank to participate in the elections of the Jordanian bar, and that was in violation of the decree that severed the relationship with the West Bank. The Ministry of Justice had not made such a move since 1988, the date of severance of ties between the West Bank and Jordan. Happily, the new government dropped the case before the High Court rendered its decision.[29]

The UNRWA Palestinians

UNRWA had been established two years before the 1951 Convention Relating to the Status of Refugees was adopted by the United Nations General Assembly (Takkenberg 1998). Paragraph D of Article 1 of the convention excluded from its scope of application the Palestinian refugees. It reads: "This Convention shall not apply to persons who are at present receiving from organs or agencies of the United Nations other than the United Nations High Commissioner for Refugees protection or assistance." In spite of that exclusion, I use some of the parameters defined in that convention as guidelines to explore how UNRWA Palestinians were treated in the recipient countries. In addition, certain resolutions passed by the League of Arab States are relevant, in particular the Casablanca Resolution of 1965, in which the Arab ministers of foreign affairs resolved to grant the Palestinians

27. See the interview with the minister of interior, Mr. Salama Hammad, in *Al-Dustour*, 23 October 1995, and in *Jordan Times*, 23 October 1995.

28. Jordanian HCJ case no. 108/95.

29. On 27 February 1996, the new minister of justice, Mr. Abdul Kareem al-Doughmi, instructed the deputy attorney general to drop the case. It should be noted that the High Court of Justice recently shifted its position in a few cases dealing with Jordanian Palestinians. In October 1997, the High Court held, inter alia, that the Jordanian government cannot deny a Jordanian his citizenship except in accordance with Articles 18 and 19 of the Citizenship Law and that the government cannot amend the law by regulations or instructions. Although the Court did not address directly the legality of the severance ties with the West Bank, that judgment is highly significant. See Jordanian HCJ judgment no. 212/97 (13 October 1997). It is early to determine if this new judgment will represent a new trend in the High Court rulings.

living in the host countries the right to work in, travel from and return to the country of their residence, obtain traveling documents, and receive entry visas to the Arab countries as any other national.

Palestinians in Lebanon. The status of the Palestinian refugees in Lebanon has been the most critical and perplexing ever. When Palestinian refugees first arrived in Lebanon in 1948, they were received by the president of the republic and his prime minister with warm and welcoming remarks (al-Natour 1993, 23).[30] Since the return of the refugees to their home country became a remote possibility, the treatment of the Palestinian refugees oscillated unpredictably (al-Natour 1993, 25 and passim).

In 1959, a decree was issued establishing the Palestinian Refugees Department, which was attached to the Lebanese Ministry of Interior.[31] It was charged with the responsibilities of dealing with Palestinian refugees affairs—namely, to make recommendations to the Public Security Department to issue travel documents, regulate personal status affairs (birth certificate, death certificates, marriages, and so on), help families reunite, locate the sites for establishing refugee camps, and regulate the residency rights or transfer from one refugee camp to another. Invariably, Palestinian refugees were issued travel documents that enabled them to travel abroad and to return to Lebanon. The residency right of the refugees in Lebanon had been confirmed by the ministerial Decree No. 319 of 1962,[32] which exempted the refugees from satisfying the requirements imposed on other foreigners who desired to reside in Lebanon. The Palestinian refugee was further allowed, like a Lebanese, to travel between Syria and Lebanon without having his travel document (Lebanon, Ministry of Interior, Decree No. 1 of 1970). He was also exempt from paying any fees whether for obtaining travel documents or for their renewal.

The right to work in Lebanon is regulated by the Labor Law of 1962. This law sets out the principle that a foreigner is allowed to work in Lebanon provided that *(a)* his country allows Lebanese to work in that country, and *(b)* he obtains in advance a work permit. As to the first condition, it was earlier codified in laws regulating the professional unions of pharmacists, engineers, medical doctors, and lawyers.[33] Hence, Palestinians, whether of similar professions or skilled or unskilled laborers, were not able

---

30. Mr. al-Natour himself was about one year old when his family from Acre left for Lebanon in 1948.

31. Decree No. 42 (31 March 1959).

32. This decree was issued as late as 2 August 1962. It was only intended to give exemption to Palestinian refugees from the law regulating the residency of foreigners in Lebanon.

33. Bar Association Law No. 8/70(1970); Medical Doctors Decree No. 1658 (1979); Pharmacists Law (1950); Engineers Law (1951).

to practice in Lebanon due to the lack of the principle of reciprocity. Several court judgments and official jurist opinions consistently upheld that principle.[34] No regard was given either to the fact that there was no state of Palestine to enact reciprocity rule or to the Arab League resolutions. Furthermore, it should be recalled that Article 7(2) of the Refugee Convention provides that "After a period of three years' residence, all refugees shall enjoy exemption from legislative reciprocity in the territory of the Contracting States." As to the second condition, the Lebanese authorities have issued a list of about sixty activities whereby work permits were not to be issued to foreign workers. The list excluded virtually all menial jobs. The immediate impact of that list was felt by the Palestinian community, and it is widely believed that they were the primary target of these regulations. One of the immediate results of this policy is that more than one-half of the Palestinian refugees do currently live below the poverty line.[35]

When Libya ordered the deportation of Palestinians in early September 1995, the Lebanese authorities were quick in taking all measures to prevent the return of those who were already on board a ship to Beirut. They were Palestinians holding Lebanese travel documents. The Lebanese authorities (as if desperately waiting for such a move) took swift measures not only with respect to those deportees, but also against all Palestinians who held Lebanese travel documents and resided in Lebanon at the time. The minister of interior issued Decree No. 478 that went into effect on 10 September 1995,[36] which provides that Palestinians who have been refugees in Lebanon since 1948 have to apply for an exit visa from Lebanon and an entry visa to return to Lebanon. Those Palestinians who happened to be outside Lebanon at the time have to apply for a return visa through the Lebanese diplomatic missions, which in turn have to obtain the prior approval of the Public Security Department. These measures are, in effect, a nullification of the residence and travel rights.

Palestinians in Egypt. Although the number of Palestinian refugees in Egypt has been relatively insignificant, the status of those Palestinians has been deteriorating rapidly since the 1970s. Prior to that, beginning with 1948, the Egyptian successive governments accorded the Palestinians a status equivalent to that of Egyptian nationals in many areas.

Palestinian professionals such as medical doctors, veterinarians, dentists,

34. See Lebanon, Opinion of the Legislation and Opinion of the Ministry of Justice, no. 0/117, dated March 26, 1966.

35. See the paper presented by Laila Zakharia in January 1996 to the Arab National Forum seminar on the Palestinians' situation in Lebanon (in Arabic).

36. Text in *Al-Nahar* (a Lebanese daily in Arabic), 23 September 1995.

pharmacists, and so on were exempt from any restrictions imposed on foreigners desiring to join any of these professions.[37] In 1963 the Palestinians,
like Egyptians but unlike foreigners, were allowed to own agricultural land.[38]
The Palestinians were also exempt from obtaining a work permit, which was
required of all non-Egyptian workers. The 1964 law regulating civil service
especially provided for certain exemptions in order to allow Palestinians to
work in government departments. On the other hand, in 1964 the government regulated the issuance of travel documents to Palestinian refugees and
ordered that the holder of such a travel document must obtain an exit visa,
an entry visa, or even a transit visa.[39]

Though as late at 1977 the Social Security Law was made to apply to all
Egyptians, citizens of Arab countries who accorded Egyptians similar treatment, and Palestinians without referring to reciprocity,[40] by the mid-1970s
the situation began to change rapidly. In 1976, and according to Law No.
81 of 1976, no foreigners were allowed to own real property in Egypt.[41] The
typical exemption accorded to the Palestinian refugees was missing. The
privilege that Palestinians had enjoyed of being able to work in the civil
service was canceled in 1978.[42] In 1985, a new law was enacted that repealed the exemption that allowed Palestinians to own agricultural lands.[43]
Whereas exit or entry visas used to be routinely granted to Palestinians, now
the process became a nightmare. The Salloum refugee camp, set up in the
fall of 1995 on the Egyptian-Libyan border, is evidence of this new Egyptian policy. Some of the present expellees in the camp are holders of Egyptian travel documents. Jordanian Palestinians who hold a two-year passport
are not allowed to enter Egypt without obtaining an entry visa in advance.
Palestinian students who fall under this category are also denied access to
Egyptian universities.

Palestinians in Syria. Syria has been consistent in its policy toward the
Palestinians who took refuge there in 1948. While Syria early on accorded
Palestinian refugees all rights of residence, travel, work, business, and own-
ership on an ad hoc basis, the status of Palestinian refugees was finally cod-

37. See Law No. 415 (1954) concerning medical practice; Law No. 416 (1954) concerning
veterinarians; Law No. 537 (1954) concerning dentists; and Law No. 127 (1955) concerning
pharmacists.

38. Law No. 15 (1963).

39. Decree No. 181 (1964).

40. Law No. 30 (1977).

41. Law No. 81 (1976).

42. Law No. 47 (1978).

43. Law No. 104 (1985). For an English translation of this law, see *2d Palestine Yearbook of
International Law* (1985), 153.

ified in Law No. 260 of 10 July 1956.[44] In its Article (1), the law provides that Palestinians residing in Syria at the date of its issuance shall be considered as Syrians in areas of employment, labor, trade, and national service provided that they keep their Palestinian citizenship. Based on this wide-scope law, Palestinians enjoy equal rights in employment, whether in the public or private sectors, and are entitled to social security benefits, labor benefits, residence, education, and travel. In matters of travel, the Syrian government issued Palestinian refugees with travel documents. Activities outside the scope of that law are also allowed and largely consistent with the spirit of the law.

Palestinians in Iraq. Palestinian refugees in Iraq do enjoy equal rights concerning residence, work, and ownership of residential areas. They have the right to join the civil service with virtually all the attached benefits.[45] However, under the circumstances prevailing in Iraq as a result of the economic sanctions and the brutal policies of the Iraqi regime, it is unfair to compare the present situation of Palestinian refugees with that of their counterparts in other Arab countries.

Palestinian Citizenship: The Integration Phase

The PNA Attempts to Define Who "the Palestinian" Is

The arrival of the PNA initially to the Gaza Strip and Jericho in mid-1994 and subsequently to the West Bank in late 1995 has created a new hard fact: the existence of a Palestinian public authority with internationally sanctioned powers and responsibilities. In spite of the limitations imposed on the PNA by the Oslo Accords[46] and subsequently by the de facto restrictions devised by the Israeli government,[47] there is a wide expectation that the newly established public authority is destined for statehood. One of the

---

44. *Parliamentary Record of Syria*, 10th sess. (7 July 1956), 191. See also the Uniform Civil Service Law of 1985, which provides in Article 7(2) that "Palestinian Arabs who fall within the purview of Law 260 for the year 1956 shall have the right to be appointed and retain their original Palestinian nationality." See *2d Palestine Yearbook of International Law* 151 (1985).

45. Decree No. 366 (1969). Travel documents for Palestinian refugees were regulated by Law No. 26 (1961). On 19 January 1981, Law No. 215 of 1980 was published in the *Official Gazette*, no. 2813. This law grants Palestinians enjoyment of real property rights. English text of this law was published in *2d Palestine Yearbook of International Law* 152 (1985).

46. See text of these accords in *7th Palestine Yearbook of International Law* 230 (1992–94) and *8th Palestine Yearbook of International Law* 353 (1994–95).

47. For example, see the Hebron Accord, signed on 15 January 1997, as dictated by the Israeli government.

most central tasks for the PNA is to define the manner in which and the procedures and modalities by which it will, first, liquidate the legacy that has plagued the hyphenated Palestinians as well as the UNRWA Palestinians, and second, reintegrate Palestinians into one citizenship body.

Admittedly, this task is neither simple nor easy. Like any other issue pertaining to the Palestine question, the problem is normally simple to define but too complex to handle. A Palestinian is a Palestinian because others have defined him as such, and that definition was largely motivated by national consideration, local interest, "transfer" purposes, and deprivation of jobs or seats in universities. These considerations should be present in the mind of the Palestinian legislature when it embarks on defining who the Palestinian is.

Since its arrival in Gaza and Jericho, the PNA has enacted several pieces of legislation that target Palestinians.[48] It would be illuminating to trace the policy thoughts of the PNA on who a Palestinian is. In the Election Law No. 15 of 1995,[49] the elector was defined as being "every Palestinian inhabitant of the Gaza Strip and the West Bank, including Jerusalem." Article 6 provides that every Palestinian "from the West Bank, including Jerusalem, and from the Gaza Strip . . . has the right to vote." Article 7 dictates that "For the purpose of this Law," a person shall be considered "Palestinian" if he/she " (a) was born in Palestine, as defined by the British Mandate, or could have the right to Palestinian citizenship according to the laws in force during that period; (b) was born in the Gaza Strip or in the West Bank, including Jerusalem; (c) irrespective of his place of birth, has one of his ancestors who meets the requirements in paragraph (a) above; (d) is the spouse of a Palestinian who meets the requirements mentioned above; and (e) has not acquired Israeli citizenship."

Furthermore, in mid-1995, the PNA circulated a draft Citizenship Law.[50] Article 2 of this law defines a Palestinian as any person who (1) was a holder of Palestinian citizenship (other than Jews) before 15 May 1948; (2) was born to a Palestinian father; (3) was born in Palestine to a Palestinian mother even if the citizenship of the father is not known; (4) was born in Palestine to unknown parents; and (5) was born outside of Palestine to a Palestinian mother and to a father whose nationality was not known—

---

48. See, e.g., Law No. 9 (1995 concerning press and publications, which requires the editor of a specialized publication or the manager of a publishing house to be a "Palestinian." Text of this law in *8th Palestine Yearbook of International Law* 127 (1994–95).

49. Law No. 15 (1995).

50. A copy of this draft is on file with the writer. The draft was circulated by the Council for Opinion and Legislation.

provided that this person opts for Palestinian citizenship within one year after reaching maturity, that he notifies the minister of interior of his intention to become a Palestinian citizen, that he becomes habitually resident of Palestine, and that the minister does not object to his application within one year from the time he receives the notice from the applicant.

Reading into these two major documents, one may ascertain that the concept of an integrated Palestinian citizenship is still not clear in the mind of the Palestinian policymakers. It is probably not unreasonable to add that the concept is blurred and traditionalist. Furthermore, the draft grants almost absolute authority to the executive branch of government.

The draft law is basically deficient in that it is conventional. It has not taken into consideration the very particular situation of the Palestinians in their diaspora. Although the draft draws on the Jordanian Citizenship Law of 1954, the latter was more advanced in that it had regulated the citizenship status of Palestinians who took refuge in the West Bank and in the East Bank of the Jordan. In fact, the PNA draft Citizenship Law was bashful in dealing with the status of the Palestinian refugees and their descendants, in contrast with its very clear wording when it deals with a far less important issue such as the status of those born to unknown parents. The draft law does not address the criteria in terms of which the UNRWA Palestinians would be normalized in a state of their own. How many UNRWA Palestinians, after almost five decades in exile, can prove that they were of Palestinian citizenship or that their fathers were citizens of Palestine? If the gist of the Palestine question is centered on the issue of Palestinian refugees, the draft law is surprisingly quiet about it.

The concept of citizenship as envisaged by the PNA draft follows the traditional pattern. It is well known to students of law that international law concerning citizenship recognizes two age-old methods of acquiring citizenship at birth: they are jus soli and jus sanguinis. According to the jus soli doctrine, a person is granted the citizenship of the state within whose territory he was born. The jus sanguinis doctrine provides that a person acquires, at his birth, the citizenship of one or both of his parents, regardless of the territory in which he is born.[51] Needless to add, there is also the method of naturalization that is applicable to persons of legal age.

These three principles are adopted in the Election Law and the draft Citizenship Law. However, none would be sufficient to liquidate the compounded legacy of hyphenated or UNRWA Palestinians. Consider the example of a Palestinian born to Palestinian parents in a refugee camp in

---

51. See Draft Conventions and Comments.

Lebanon, whose parents themselves were born outside Palestine: if one were to apply the jus soli, the conclusion is obvious; but the jus sanguinis would not be applicable because neither of the parents has a "citizenship status" to give it to his or her child. If the naturalization process is the only method left, the wishes of the executive branch decide the matter. According to the draft Citizenship Law, citizenship is not a "right" inherent to each and every Palestinian.

The draft law reflects the overriding character of the legislation enacted by the PNA. The executive branch enjoys a wide range of authorities at the expense of the legislative and judicial branches. While the draft refers in the body of the text to the minister of interior eleven times, to the Council of Ministers eleven times, and to the chairman of the PNA three times, it mentions the magistrate judge only once. That sole instance refers to when the naturalized person takes the oath of allegiance before the judge. The authorities granted to the executive branch are substantial and not merely formalistic in character.[52] Article 20 of the draft law, for example, provides that all decisions issued by the Council of Ministers with respect to granting or annulling citizenship are valid from the time they are published in the official gazette. According to Article 7, the council, in cases of naturalization, has the right to grant or not to grant Palestinian citizenship to the applicant. In both events, the draft law does not provide for a judicial review of the council's decisions. In the absence of judicial review and more definitive criteria, citizenship under the draft law has turned out, in effect, to be a privilege and not an inherent right.

Alternative Definition and Mechanism

As stated earlier, the international law has developed two methods for granting citizenship at birth—namely, the jus soli and the jus sanguinis. There is also the method of naturalization, which is the acquisition of nationality by adults. No legislature can avoid or ignore these conventional methods. In the Palestinian context, new methods should be innovated to liquidate the half-century legacy of dispersion and exile and ultimately to normalize the status of the Palestinian.

The definition of who a Palestinian is will remain the challenging issue to

---

52. See, e.g., Article 2(5) of the draft; Article 7 gives the Council of Ministers the right to grant or not to grant Palestinian citizenship; Article 8 gives the chairman of the PNA the right to grant citizenship to anyone "without being bound by any of the limitations provided for in the preceding provisions"; Article 15 grants the Council of Ministers the right to strip Palestinians of their citizenship in five instances.

be addressed by lawyers, policymakers, and lawmakers. Yet, one may venture to suggest the doctrine of return as one method to grant Palestinian citizenship to hyphenated and UNRWA Palestinians.

The Doctrine of Return

According to Resolution 194 of 1948, the UN General Assembly stipulated "that the refugees wishing to return to their homes and live at peace with their neighbours should be permitted to do so." This resolution has been repeated almost every year by the General Assembly, which converts it into customary international law, including, in particular, the right to return.[53] Those who are entitled to return pursuant to this resolution should be also entitled to acquire Palestinian citizenship. Because international law has accorded those Palestinians the right to return, a method to acquire citizenship based on this internationally sanctioned right would necessarily be permissible.

This suggestion may encounter several comments, but two of them seem the most relevant. The right to return, as enunciated by the General Assembly resolution, accords the Palestinian refugee the right to return to the Green Line area and not to the autonomous areas. Because Israel adamantly rejects the return of any Palestinian to the Green Line area, so the argument may go, granting such refugees Palestinian citizenship would therefore jeopardize their right to return to Israel. The doctrine of return as a method to acquire Palestinian citizenship does not compromise the right to return. The doctrine defines the Palestinian based on his right to return. There should be no confusion between the right to return and the acquisition of citizenship by return. A Palestinian refugee who acquired a Canadian or Australian citizenship did not forgo his right to return to his homeland.

The doctrine of return, furthermore, is not synonymous with the right of return as codified in Israel's Law of Return of 1950. The latter is, as described by an Israeli jurist, "the most Zionist law" in the State of Israel (Freudenheim 1967). It is therefore a legislation that codifies racial discrimination; it has granted a "Jew" the right to return simply because he is a Jew.

---

53. On the repetition of the UN resolutions on a certain issue and the effect thereof on customary law, see the dissenting opinion of Judge Tanaka in *Ethiopia* v. *South Africa; Liberia* v. *South Africa*. Second Phase (1966) ICJ 6, 291; Mallison and Mallison (1986, 143–48). On the right of return as a well-established right under international law, see *The Right of Return of the Palestinian People,* a study prepared for the Committee on the Exercise of the Inalienable Rights of the Palestinian People, ST/SG/SER.F/2 (New York 1978); Brownlie (1973, 673–77); Higgins (1963).

It is a law predicated on the biological accident, for he who is born to a Jewish mother and does not become a member of another religion is entitled to the right of return.[54] It is repugnant to the principles of the international law. The doctrine of return, as a method of acquiring Palestinian citizenship, is not based on any racial or religious preference. It would be accorded equally to Palestinians irrespective of religion, race, or color.

The Authority to Regulate Citizenship

The draft law grants the executive branch exclusively the right to grant, annul, or withdraw citizenship. The Palestinian legacy is too heavy for the executive branch to liquidate. It is certainly too sensitive a matter to be left solely to administrators to handle without a judicial review.

The constitution of a specialized agency, staffed with community experts who entertain credibility and impartiality is probably a more viable mechanism to regulate matters of citizenship. The proposed agency would have an independent status, work on the basis of well-defined legislation and pursue articulate procedures. Such an agency would mainly be charged with the definitive objective of redefining the Palestinian identity in order to reintegrate the Palestinian people in and outside of Palestine.

All decisions of this agency would be subject to judicial review by a specialized tribunal whose decisions would be final. The tribunal can have two tiers, a lower and a higher court in order to guarantee due process of law.

Undoubtedly, there are other proposals that would improve on the methodology of judicial review or on modalities to grant citizenship. The subject of Palestinian citizenship is so complex that lawmakers and policymakers should call for series of workshops to be able to develop the best methods and the most credible procedures to liquidate the hyphenated citizenship status and develop an integrated Palestinian citizenship.

Recommendations

Under conventional circumstances, one may argue that the major task of a state is to promote and safeguard the fundamental human values of its inhabitants. The right to citizenship is one of the basic values to which an individual is entitled. This right has been codified in international treaties and resolutions, and upheld by a wide spectrum of tribunals.

The situation in Palestine and that of Palestinians, the majority of whom

---

54. See the debate articulated by Israel's High Court of Justice in *Rufeisen* v. *Ministry of Interior* (1963); See also *Selected Judgments of the Supreme Court of Israel* (1971), 1.

are still in exile, is not conventional. There has never been an independent Palestinian authority that acted as a typical sovereign to define who a Palestinian is. This action has been reserved to outside sovereigns; citizenship granting and citizenship stripping have been exercises of foreign imposition. The Allied powers and, pursuant to their directions, the mandatory power determined in 1925 the citizenship status of Palestinians. Israel, in 1948, unilaterally stripped them of their citizenship. Jordan imposed on them its citizenship in 1949 and stripped them of their citizenship in 1988. The irony is that when the PNA assumed power, albeit of far less sovereign attributes, it ventured neither to advance innovative methods to normalize the status of the Palestinian nor to devise modalities to create an integrated status for Palestinians nor to consolidate the parameters for a peoplehood.

One of the venues that the PNA should explore and ultimately adopt is the right of return for all Palestinians, however defined. If, because of its universal adoption, confirmation, and reconfirmation, UN Resolution No. 194 has become part of customary international law, then the principle of return should be considered one of the methods for attaining Palestinian citizenship.

No state or public authority can adequately or effectively promote the basic values of its citizens without having institutions. In the Palestinian context, this requirement is paramount in many areas, especially in the area of citizenship. The authority of the executive branch, as envisaged in the draft Citizenship Law should be diminished. In addition, an impartial and independent body of jurists and learned personalities from various faculties should be constituted to set out criteria, procedures, and methods to put the principle of return in motion. This body may be established by the joint efforts of the legislative and executive council.

With clear policies intended to normalize the status of Palestinians, to establish citizenship as a right and not as a privilege, and to equip these policies with the proper institutions that enjoy authority, a new body politic, which is the basic ingredient of any state, will be in all likelihood part of making a democratic Palestinian state.

10

Democratization, Citizenship, Arab Unity, and Palestinian Autonomy

A Critical Reading of the New Middle East

URI DAVIS

BEFORE ATTENDING to the subject at hand, I wish to devote some time to consider whether and in what way the idea of citizenship, predicated on the twin principle of separation of religion and nationality from the state, could be validly challenged as culturally imperialist.

I submit that the fact that the idea of secular citizenship is Western in origin is itself of no consequence. Human cultural history is that of diffusion, integration, and reintegration of ideas, cultural implements, traditions, and innovations through trade and commerce, migration of population, and conquest. Cultures can be and have been destroyed. The history of imperialism is, among others, the history of massive destruction of indigenous cul-

The bulk of this paper was written before the May 1996 elections in Israel resulting in the defeat of Shimon Peres (Labor) and the election of Binyamin Netanyahu (Likkud) as prime minister, and it was completed after the May 1999 election defeat of Netanyahu by Ehud Barak (Labor).

This paper is based on work carried out in the framework of the UK Economic and Social Research Council (ESRC)–funded research program at the Department of Politics, University of Exeter, and the Centre for Middle Eastern and Islamic Studies (CMEIS), University of Durham (award ref. no. R00023446201), on citizenship and the state in the Middle East (1993–95) of which the author and Professor Tim Niblock were award holders. The substance of this paper is included in Uri Davis, *Citizenship and the State: A Comparative Study of Citizenship Legislation in Israel, Jordan, Palestine, Syria and Lebanon* (Reading: Ithaca, 1997).

tures and peoples by Western conquest. Yet, short of destruction, or in lieu of destruction, new ideas and values have forever been integrated and assimilated if they were conceived as beneficial or potentially beneficial to the indigenous population and rejected if perceived as harmful or destructive. Needless to say, the indigenous conception of an innovation as beneficial or destructive is itself historically constituted and changes in the course of time, often entailing profound cultural and political crisis and civil war. (Note, for example, the fraught history of Protestantism in medieval Europe and of Shi'a in medieval Middle East.)

It is my argument that the ideas of individual choice and democratic citizenship have become indigenous to the political debate of the Middle East today, though the terms of their introduction were colonial. They were not introduced to the Middle East on the basis of reciprocity. They were introduced as part of the cultural and political conquest of the region through the vehicle of Western imperialism. But so was Islam, in its own context. Reducing the history of an idea to its origin is bad history and bad logic.

The hub of the cultural and political conflict in the Middle East today could be phrased by one camp as whether the ideas of individual choice and democratic citizenship are beneficial to the peoples and the development of the cultural traditions of the region. Phrased by another camp, the relevant question is: To what extent are the cultural traditions of the region detrimental to the improvement of the human condition of the Middle East? The parties to the debate are not and ought not to be fictitiously conceptualized as a homogeneous indigenous traditional Middle East voice, on the one hand, and a unified, foreign cultural, hostile imperialist, outside power, on the other hand. I wish to point out that the debate is equally related to indigenous secular thinking and human rights organization in the region itself, to the achievement of political independence of the states of the Middle East, and to their affiliation as member states of the United Nations (UN). No country can be a member state in the UN and insulate itself from the universal norms of the UN organization, most specifically the Universal Declaration of Human Rights.

It is this aspect of the reality of contemporary international relations—together with the fact that the states of the Middle East are member states of the UN—that is as significant to the determination of the debate, if not more so, than the origins of any given idea. Since World War I, the world has been genuinely globalized, and no part of it can insulate itself from a dialogue with the rest of it in the manner that was (perhaps) possible before the Age of Imperialism. Simply put, the choice presented before the peoples of the Middle East today is the choice between democratic citizenship and a secular state (based on the twin principle of separation of religion and nationality from the state), on the one hand, and kin, tribal, or religious affiliation as the foundation for citizenship and state, on the other. The question is not debated between modern and nonmodern interlocutors. The fundamentalist political parties in the Middle East today are as modern and contemporary as the secularists. They use the same make of personal computers. And if the current regional Middle East peace process delivers, they will use the same Israeli-made Uzi submachine gun.

It is not only possible, it is also necessary to conceptually decouple in some fundamental ways the politics of imperialism from the assessment of the idea of democratic citizenship in order to consider the question whether the idea of democratic citizenship is a viable political proposition only on the basis of assuming continued Western imperial domination. Put differently, is it not the case that in order to defeat imperialist domination of the region, the Middle East must be restructured politically on the basis of democratic citizenship in the same way that in order for a colonial territory to win its political independence from the metropolitan power, it needs to equip its resistance with Western-produced arms?

Proponents of this position or similar positions are sometimes accused of cultural imperialism and insensivity to the indigenous traditions, notably the religious traditions, of the region. I deny the allegation. People like me are not enemies of religion, of tradition, of cultural pluralism. We are enemies of confessional and sectarian bigotry. We do not oppose and are not hostile to tradition. Our primary concern can be defined around one key focus: to promote a political system of governance that will constitutionally secure and make possible the continual expansion of individual and collective choices, including religious choices, within the normative parameters set out by the UN Declaration of Human Rights, UN covenants, and international law.

This is not a new concern. The imperative to choose between right and wrong and the continuing debate regarding what constitutes the good are as old as humankind. The choice of one religious tradition or another (Muslim, Christian, or Jewish) or one religious school or another (orthodox, reform, or liberal) or one secular ideology or another (liberalism, Marxism, existentialism) represents various sets of legitimate options, provided that the political system is not fundamentalist, where one tradition or one school or one secular ideology becomes the only choice.

The Western idea of democratic citizenship has been traditionally wedded in the West to the system of liberal political philosophy. As Bhikhu Parekh (1993) has brilliantly shown, the universal claims of liberalism and the statements that Western liberal philosophy pronounces regarding the individual in society and the desired economic, social, and political order are far from obvious. The destructive implications for the world of the liberal principle of individuation in society is recognized not only in the colonial periphery of the West, but at the heart of its metropolitan centers.

Different societies define and individuate people differently. They also define freedom, equality, rights, property, justice, loyalty, power, and authority differently. Yet it is striking that, for instance, "many a communitarian theorist has suggested restrictions on pornography, freedom of expression and immigration are not very different from those characteristic of traditional societies" (Parekh 1993, 169).

In this contribution to the debate, I suggest that we decouple the ideas of individual choice and democratic citizenship from their liberal ideological and culturally specific origin, in the same way that it is possible to decouple the idea of monotheism from its Jewish theological origin or the idea of the decimal numeral system from its Indian historical, economic, and cultural specificity transmitted to the West through the cultural heritage and the genius of Muslim civilization. Decoupling does not imply ignoring text and context or histories and ideas. It does mean, however, that in my view it is historical and conceptual nonsense to argue that the introduction of a new idea or artifact necessarily entails the uncritical introduction of the entire cultural and ideological baggage of its origin. There is no question that the introduction of the idea of democratic Western citizenship into the Middle East must entail some change. But it is not obvious that it must entail submission to cultural imperialism.

As already argued elsewhere (Davis 1996), whereas the claim of Western liberalism to universality can be readily rejected, the claim of the Universal Declaration of Human Rights cannot. Liberalism is an ideological narrative. It is not a legal requirement to membership in the UN. Accepting the norms of the declaration is. Citizenship is a key plank in the Universal Declaration of Human Rights, and because the world (with the odd exception) is now completely apportioned among member states of the UN, there is at least one important sense in which it is possible to say that the declaration is indeed universal in that it defines the normative prescriptions to which all the governments of member states of the UN (including Middle Eastern governments) of all ideological persuasions throughout the world have legally committed themselves. At the outset of this essay, I suggested that the Universal Declaration of Human Rights represents, in some important ways at least, a truly universal value system in that membership in the UN necessarily entails the introduction of the values of the declaration into each member country. It does not necessarily entail uniformity of application, interpretation, translation, and legislation of these values,[1] but it is equally true that the values of the declaration cannot be ignored anywhere in the world today. It is possible to decouple the declaration from its liberal Western origins, but it is not possible to ignore the established validity of the declaration in modern times as a universally applicable normative yardstick. The appeal of all dispossessed people throughout the world to the values of the declaration as the telos of their struggle and the rationalization of their moral claims is a recurrent living testimony of the case at hand.

It is my view that democratic citizenship (as a certificate of equal access to the civil, political, and social institutions and material resources of the state) and the separation of nationality from the state are necessary conditions for political democracy as a system of representative government. But democratic citizenship does not in and of itself entail the Western paradigm of multiparty parliamentary democracy, so it is possible to conceive of the institutionalization of equal access of the citizen to the civil, political, and social institutions and economic resources of the state in a political regime other than a multiparty political system (e.g., a one-party state).

Not so if the citizenship and the state are not decoupled and separated from nationality. As Nils Butenschon has convincingly argued, if citizenship is conceived of as a certificate of kin, tribal, or confessional affiliation, then apartheid, ethnocide, and genocide are almost inevitable outcomes (Butenschon 1993).

Democratization

I firmly believe that democratization efforts are critical for the future welfare of the Middle East, and I am joined in this belief by a huge number of men and women in and from the region. The debate on what are the appropriate paths toward democratization and which of the available political strategies are likely to be most effective is the substance of political life the world over. By committing myself to this work, I have been made part of that debate. The idea of democratic citizenship is fundamental to this debate in yet an additional way. It is, properly speaking, a necessary condition

---

1. The right to marriage as formulated in Article 16 of the declaration ("Marriage shall be entered into only with the free and full consent of the intending spouses") can be and is interpreted in different ways in different societies and in different culturally specific contexts as is the right to work as formulated in Article 23 ("Everyone has the right to work, to free choice of employment, to just and favourable conditions of work and to protection against unemployment").

for the debate to take place in the first place because only if everyone has the normative and practical equal access to the civil, social, political, and economic resources of the state can everyone participate in this debate on an equal footing and on the basis of reciprocity. In my lexicon, debate other than a debate on equal footing and reciprocity is not a debate at all.

The idea of democratic citizenship as a certificate of equal access to the resources of the state, decoupled from liberal ideology, is not insensitive to indigenous traditions. True, it is incompatible with political programs of fundamentalism and sectarianism and with all religious ideologies that resist the separation of religion from the state; it does promote affiliation to any society (traditional or civil) by choice; and it indeed denies the legitimacy of monopolizing the state by any one religious establishment or sectarian community. But it does not deny the legitimacy or the validity of Muslim, Jewish, or Christian traditional society.

In sum, the idea of democratic citizenship suggests that the welfare of all men and women in any territory of the Middle East (and throughout the world), regardless of national (kin, tribal, or confessional) affiliations and regardless of the existing political system of governance (democratically elected multiparty Parliament, democratic one-party state, or constitutional monarchy), will be hugely advanced if all the residents of the region have the right to equal access to the civil, political, and social institutions and resources of the state—namely, if the principle of democratic citizenship is upheld. The degree and the level to which any given political system upholds the principle of democratic citizenship (see, for instance, *jinsiyya* citizenship versus *muwatana* citizenship in Israel) provides a viable criterion to assess the degree and the level of democratization in that polity and the prospects for change, including change of the regime, through the democratic process.

The subject of this essay immediately impinges on the contemporary debate regarding democratization, secular politics, and civil society versus political Islam in the Middle East. As Rami Khouri (1995a) points out, in the context of this debate

The West often makes the mistake of seeing political Islam as a new danger, instead of seeing it for what it is: an expression of the failure of imported Western national structures and political concepts, and a sign of the Arab/Islamic quest for a more responsive, relevant political culture. Arab pluralistic democratization, to be successful, must emphatically respect and reflect indigenous Arab cultural norms (patriarchy, communalism, ethnicity, Islam, Arabism, etc.) but these norms do not appear to tend themselves to the sort of individualistic, almost libertarian, brands of democracy that dominate the West. (9)[2]

And further

> We have to discover how our cultural values and social traditions correspond to the key principles of Western democracy: pluralism, participation and accountability. I would suggest that these three principles are deeply entrenched in Arab/Islamic culture, but they are expressed in a different manner than in [the] Western political system. (Khouri 1995b, 9)

Rami Khouri and others are not seeking to dogmatically isolate the Arab and the Muslim worlds from the West. Rather, they are seeking a synthesis between Arab and Western political, social cultural traditions, "replacing confrontation and fear with a shared morality of human dignity as the common heritage of our civilization and the operative principles of our systems of national governance" (ibid).

If these and similar pronouncements are not intended to be legitimations for such Shari'a court sentences as cutting off the hand of the thief, then, I suggest, the best political and legal foundation for a shared morality and human dignity in a modern Middle East is the concept and the legal framework of democratic citizenship *(muwatana)* as outlined and developed in this essay (see chap. 8 for discussion of *muwatana*).

Identifying democratic citizenship as the desired legal foundation for a shared morality of human dignity for the entire region of the Middle East liberates the narrative from the false prevalent and contemporary Western assumption that the only valid universal paradigm for democracy is the Western paradigm of multiparty parliamentary democracy. Whether the political system is a constitutional dynastic monarchy like Jordan, a single-party state like Syria, or a multiparty state like Israel, the yardstick by which morality, human dignity, and equality of rights can be measured in the region is the universal yardstick of *muwatana*.

Arab Unity

One of the most vocal advocate (though not the only one) of the vision of the creation of a regional community of nations, with a common market

---

2. I am indebted to my colleague Tim Niblock for the reference.

and elected centralized bodies modeled on the European Community, is former prime minister of Israel Shimon Peres (Peres 1993, 63).

The cornerstone of the European Community structure is the political resolve to create a European Union (EU), where each individual citizen of any member state would enjoy the legal freedom of genuine choice of place of residence, place of work, and ownership of property, together with the full exercise of his or her democratic rights in the state of his or her residence (short of voting in elections for the state Parliament) regardless of his or her particular nationality or citizenship. Thus, for instance, in the UK, an Italian citizen has the right of residence, work, social security, and vote in all municipal, regional, and European bodies (but not yet the UK Parliament). The expansion of real individual legal choice was hugely advanced through the introduction of the Maastricht Treaty of 1992 of the legal concept of European citizenship:

Article 8
(1) . . . Every person holding a nationality of a Member State shall be a citizen of the Union.
(2) Citizens of the Union shall enjoy the rights conferred by this Treaty and shall be subject to the duties imposed thereby.
Article 8a
(1) Every citizen of the Union shall have the right to move and reside freely within the territory of the Member States, subject to the limitations and conditions laid down by this Treaty and by the measures adopted to give it effect.

If modeling the future of the Middle East on this vision were indeed Peres's vision, this change would be truly revolutionary. It would require the reform of many of the established regimes in the region. But it would also require, first and foremost, a radical reform of the State of Israel and the dismantlement of its Zionist legislation, notably its legislation on citizenship and the legislation limiting access to the economic resources of land and water to Jews only.

The question of citizenship immediately impinges on what I regard to be the most potent question in the Middle East today: the question of individual choice—specifically, individual choice of abode.

The beauty of a New Middle East modeled on the EU, with a single Middle East citizenship, would be that the same rights and opportunities and choices this would open up to the 1948 Palestinian refugee, including return to any locality inside Israel proper, would be available in all the states of the Middle East to every resident of the region: to the Lebanese, Iraqi, or Egyptian Jew who is a citizen of Israel; to the Egyptian Arab in Jordan; to the Yemeni Arab in Saudi Arabia and in Kuwait. All would have the same freedom of choice of place of residence, ownership of property, and work, with the full protection of their democratic rights wherever they reside, regardless of their particular nationality or citizenship. A new Middle East modeled on the EU would foster genuine cosmopolitanism throughout the region and offer new political, economic, and cultural opportunities to all the peoples in the area. Shimon Peres has yet to explain how his advocacy of the vision of modeling the Middle East on the EU squares with his uncompromising opposition to the return of the 1948 Palestine refugees and their descendants to localities of their choice inside Israel.

In opting for the EU model, I, together with many others, am opposed by the well-established legal order in the region. Two illustrations suffice to illuminate the case at hand.

Article 2 of the Constitution of the Hashemite Kingdom of Jordan, 1952 determines that Islam is the religion of the state, and Article 3 of the Jordanian Citizenship Law, 1954, defines a Jordanian citizen to be

> 1. Any person who had Jordanian citizenship or Jordanian passport under the stipulations of the Jordanian Citizenship Law of 1928 and its Amendments and the Jordanian Citizenship Law No 6 of 1954 and this Law;
>
> 2. Any person *who was not Jewish* and who had a Palestinian citizenship prior to 15 May 1948 and whose ordinary residence in the period of 20 December 1939 to 16 February 1954 was in the Hashemite Kingdom of Jordan. (emphasis added)

The State of Israel has no constitution, but the legal status of Jewish religion as the religion of the state is determined in Amendment No. 9, 1985, to the Basic Law: the Knesset, 1958, as follows:

> 7a A [parliamentary] List of Candidates shall not participate in the elections to the Knesset if its aims or actions, explicitly or implicitly, represent the following:
>
> (1) *Denial of the existence of the State of Israel as the state of the Jewish people;*
>
> (2) Denial of the democratic character of the state;
>
> (3) Incitement of racialism. (emphasis added)

Needless to say that (1) and (2) represent a contradiction in terms.

Regarding citizenship, Article 2 of the Israeli Nationality Law, 1952, determines that Israeli citizenship is obtained "by return":

2A Every *oleh* [Jewish immigrant] under the Law of Return 1950 shall become an Israel national.

See also the Law of Return, 1950, Article 1: "Every Jew has the right to come to this country as an *oleh*"—plural, *olim*, an immigration classification allocated uniquely to a Jew immigrating to Israel.

In this work, citizenship has been defined as a certificate regulating the relationship between the individual and the state where he or she is a citizen. But citizenship legislation also directly or by implication or both impinges on the status of any given individual in other states. The terms of naturalization and the possibility (or otherwise) of dual or multiple citizenship represent strategic instruments with which any given state can craft its relations with other states and determine the levels of its regional cooperation. Since World War II, the question of citizenship in the Middle East (as in Europe) is intimately linked to the debate on regional unity (federalism).

There is no question that multiple Arab-Arab citizenship and a form of Middle East passport union would fortify Middle Eastern unity (just as multiple European-European citizenship as a form of passport union does in Europe). Currently, the provisions of the League of Arab States (protocol of 5 April 1954) determines that an Arab citizen of a given member state of the League of Arab States is a foreigner in another member state: visas and work permits are required in most cases (Ahmad Sidqi Dajjani, interview with author, 11 August 1993).[3]

Why did the League of Arab States not follow the model of the EU, in terms of which citizens of all member states of the EU are entitled in each state to the same rights as the citizens of the said state (save the right to vote to the parliament other than the parliament of their citizenship)? The answer, at bottom, is that the governments of the member states of the League of Arab States do not wish, for various reasons, to implement this

---

3. Ahmad Sidqi Dajjani: "By defining themselves as Arab states all member states of the League of Arab States have constitutionally accepted the principle that citizenship of any one Arab state [*muwatana qutriyya*] and Arab citizenship in general [*muwatana arabiyya*] are one and the same. Judging by the Constitutions of all Arab states, constitutionally an Arab cannot be a foreigner in an Arab state. The legal reality, however, is that he/she can. Arab states have not articulated this constitutional principle in their laws. They did not legislate this principle. Still, it remains a valid question: if all member states of the League of Arab States are constitutionally Arab states, an Arab ought not to be a foreigner in any Arab state" (interview with author, Cairo, 11 August 1993).

Ahmad Sidqi Dajjani defined this situation as a "sickness." Instead of being a certificate of equal rights and equal access and a defense of individual human rights, citizenship became the modern vehicle of discrimination in the Middle East (ibid.).

model, probably because such a model must entail radical reduction in the ability of the governments concerned to control their peoples: control their movement, their travel, their access to the labor market, their access to new ideas and new associations.

For political regimes that regard citizenship as a certificate of loyalty of the individual to the regime—not a certificate of individual rights to equal access to the civil, political, social, and economic resources of the state— loss of control (democratization) is viewed with great apprehension. Oil politics are also central to the question. In the Gulf, citizenship in any member state of the Gulf Cooperation Council (GCC) indeed represents privileged access (though not equal access) to the superior social resources of the Gulf states that were made possible by oil wealth (free housing; free primary, secondary, and tertiary education; free medical care; etc.) This is one important reason why citizenship in all Gulf states is tightly controlled and why the mass of the skilled and unskilled labor force is recruited from outside the member states of the GCC on a Gastarbeiter basis. An EU model of citizenship for the Middle East would require that all citizens of member states of the League of Arab States who are resident in the Gulf be entitled to permanent residence and to the same access to the social resources of Gulf states as the citizens of the Gulf.

Such model citizenship would inevitably require a radical restructuring of the political economy of all Gulf states and a more equitable redistribution of oil wealth. None of the Gulf rulers hitherto has shown any willingness to contemplate such prospects, and all have a disreputable human rights record for their violence against any individual or political party advocating reform.

Palestinian Autonomy

The subject of this paper also immediately impinges on the current and pressing debate regarding the question of Palestinian autonomy. In democratic liberal states, autonomy is conventionally considered to be an option for self-determination (self-government) of a given communal or regional grouping, whose members are citizens of a state composed of a variety of such groupings. As Rudolph Bernhardt (1981) points out:

> The essential element of autonomy is the granting of certain rights to a specific part of the state population in view of its characteristics which differ from the majority of the population. (In democratic societies the majority hardly needs protection because it has the power to determine the law.) . . . As a rule, the minority enjoying autonomy has the same nationality as the majority of the population. (Otherwise the rights of aliens, diplomatic protection by other

states or problems of statelessness are involved). In the great majority of cases, the members of the autonomous groups have—outside the limits of the autonomy—the same rights as all other citizens. (26–27)

Examined under these standards, it is clearly misleading to refer to the Israel-PLO Declaration of Principles (DOP or Oslo I) and subsequent Cairo Agreement and Oslo II as accords for Palestinian "autonomy," "self-rule," or "self-government" as conventionally understood in international law. The Palestinian residents of the occupied West Bank and the Gaza Strip (the designated "autonomous areas") have anything but the same rights as all other citizens of Israel, whether inside the "autonomous areas" or inside "Israel proper." All international documents and UN resolutions relevant to the question of self-government are designated to protect the rights of the peoples concerned to freedom from colonial occupation either by way of integration with an independent state or by free association with such a state—either the former administering state or some other state (Sohn 1981, 9–10). Palestinian "autonomy" as negotiated in the accords named above is neither. For the transitional period 1994 to 1999, currently extended to the year 2000, these accords amount to little more than the normalization of continued Israeli occupation and settlement, on the one hand, and continued Palestinian statelessness, on the other, with the task of internal security (and violations of human rights) shared with the PLO.

The DOP and subsequent accords stipulated (at least during the transitional period now extended to 2000) "autonomy" ("self-rule") without citizenship for the Palestinians: not Jordanian citizenship and not Israeli citizenship. It is a caricature of autonomy. It is "autonomy" only in name, "autonomy" of a stateless population, a Bantustan autonomy, the "autonomy" of a "native homeland" under the sovereignty and in the shadow of an apartheid state. Under these terms, the independent Palestinian state will fare not much better in its human rights record than the "independent homelands" of apartheid South Africa.

It is a sad comment on international current affairs that the apartheid Bantustan order that was dismantled in the Republic of South Africa has been resurrected in Palestine, and that the leader some of us had hoped would grow to become the Palestinian Nelson Mandela has proven to be Palestine's Mangosuthu Buthelezi.

In 1987, I published *Israel: An Apartheid State,* with the concluding chapter entitled "The Alternative: The PLO" (74–119). In the intervening years, the PLO as an alternative to Zionist apartheid was defeated. The implications of the defeat are outlined in this study.

An overview of the current state of the Middle East today reveals an emerging new international legal framework. As the various pieces are placed inside the framework of the "Oslo process," the generative grammar of the current regional peace process seems to have been unveiled, producing an articulated new structure.

At center stage of the new structure stands the State of Israel as victor of half a century of war in the Middle East. If my reading of the grammar of the peace process is accurate, the linchpin of the "new order" in the Middle East will be the regional recognition of Israel as the successor of the British Mandate Government of Palestine and of Israeli sovereignty over the entire British Mandate territory of Palestine as defined by the League of Nations in 1922.

As the successor of the British Mandate Government of Palestine, Israel also inherited the responsibility for dealing with two additional players in the territories allocated to British influence by the League of Nations: the PLO as successor of the Higher Arab Committee, representing the Palestinian people and the Hashemite Kingdom of Jordan.

In return for Jordanian recognition of Israeli sovereignty over the entire territory of British Mandate Palestine as codified in the Israel-Jordan Treaty of Peace (October 1994), Jordan has been rewarded with a Vatican in Jerusalem.

In return for PLO recognition of Israeli sovereignty and PLO agreement to the Bantustanization of the West Bank and the Gaza Strip, Israel under Ehud Barak will agree to recognize a Palestinian equivalent of Andorra in Gaza and the West Bank, technically an independent state (with a representative in the UN)—but not a sovereign state (no army and no international border crossings). Correlatively, by 2000 the international community will have possibly declared the question of Palestine solved and the United Nations Relief and Works Agency (UNRWA) will be dismantled.

The political structure that I can see unfolding represents a complex arrangement. The arrangement is based on the distinction between *independence* (represented by international recognition as a member state of the United Nations Organization) and *sovereignty* (represented by the army patrolling internationally recognized borders). A state without an army patrolling its internationally recognized borders may declare itself to be sovereign, but it is not sovereign.

I submit that the political settlement currently unfolding accepts as point of departure the overarching sovereignty of the State of Israel over all British Mandate territory of Palestine, with Jerusalem as its internationally recognized capital boasting a new U.S. embassy; a Hashemite (possibly a Palestinian) "Vatican" administering the places of Muslim historical and religious significance in Jerusalem; the Pontifical Mission administration of the places of Christian historical and religious significance in Jerusalem (made possible by the establishment in 1994 of full diplomatic relations between the State of Israel and the Vatican); and a Palestinian Andorra-type ministate in Gaza and the West Bank. Like Andorra, the ministate of Palestine will be internationally recognized and represented in the United Nations, but ultimate sovereignty patrolling the international crossings as well as dominion over the territory of British Mandate Palestine will be vested in the State of Israel with the sanction of the Palestinian people as represented by a defeated PLO.

Andorra further provides an interesting paradigm for such powers as are anxious to formalize the surrender of the PLO in accepted international legal terms in that it offers a new framework for Israeli-Jordanian codominion and joint sovereignty over the remnants of British Mandate Palestine relegated to Palestinian self-government.

Andorra is a coprincipality whose political and legal institutions are based on the joint and indivisible sovereignty of its two coprinces (the bishop of Urgell, Spain, and the Count de Foix, whose duties are vested today with the president of the French Republic in a personal capacity). It does not mint its own currency and, needless to say, has no army. By the end of 1992, the constitutional process that began in 1990 was concluded, and following the referendum in March 1993, Andorra now has its first written constitution. In the same year, the Treaty of Good Neighborliness, Friendship, and Cooperation between the Kingdom of Spain, the French Republic, and the Principality of Andorra was signed. Article 1 reads that "[t]he Kingdom of Spain and the French Republic recognize the Principality of Andorra as a sovereign state."

Except that Andorra is not a sovereign state, at least not a sovereign state as defined in this work (with an army patrolling its internationally recognized borders), and there is no doubt in my mind that the international legal precedent of Andorra—recognizing a state as sovereign although it is not sovereign—is precisely the kind of veil needed for the government of Israel, the government of Jordan, and the defeated PLO to cover the reality of the Bantustanization of Palestine, its economy of underdevelopment, and its appalling human rights record in order to present it to the Palestinian people and to the international community as progress.

It took four decades of Palestinian resistance since 1948, culminating in the Palestinian Intifada (Uprising), to expose the Israeli cultivated lie regarding the mass expulsion of the Palestinian people from their homeland in 1948. It should not take as long to expose the reality of the calculated misrepresentation of the current regional peace process and its likely outcome. The State of Palestine, if and when it comes into existence as a result of the permanent status negotiations scheduled to have begun in May 1996 and end in May 1999, now sometime in 2000, may be packaged as a Middle East Andorra, but it will be soon exposed for what it is: a Palestinian Transkei of the apartheid State of Israel.

Conclusions and Recommendations

It is my belief that one fundamental reason why, after four decades of struggle for liberation, the PLO has been defeated and the attempts of the League of Arab States to reverse the results of the 1948–49 war have been frustrated is that they formulated their objectives and predicated their alternative vision for Palestine and the Middle East in terms that were not compatible with the basic values of the Universal Declaration of Human Rights. Continued attempts by human rights activists (including me) to effect appropriate changes and amendments in the political program of the PLO and the Palestinian national charter were not successful.

The current defeat of the Palestinian struggle and the PLO capitulation formalized in the series of the Oslo accords reveals pan-Arab nationalism at its weakest. Arab solidarity in general and solidarity with the Palestinian struggle in particular should have motivated Arab governments to offer Palestine refugees from 1948 and 1967 immediate asylum *plus* citizenship as a foundation for empowerment. How could anyone justify the pathetic provisions of the League of Arab States ordering the host Arab governments to deny citizenship to Palestine refugees and condemn them to half a century of statelessness in the name of solidarity with their cause? Statelessness is just about the worst legal status for any individual in a globe completely divided into independent states acting in concert (or otherwise) within the framework of the United Nations. Any citizenship is better than no citizenship. Dual or multiple citizenship is even better.

One could argue that the decision of the member states of the League of Arab States to deny Palestine refugees the option of naturalization in the neighboring host Arab countries was wrong at the human rights level, yet correct at the political level. Reality, it seems, has provided the answer to this argument. League of Arab States strategy and PLO srategy predicated on this argument for the past half-century have failed miserably and have been defeated. As the recommendations below suggest, I strongly believe that a new strategy is called for with a political program that is compatible with the values of the Universal Declaration of Human Rights.

Naturalization does not invalidate the legal claims of Palestine refugees to compensation or return or both under UN resolutions and international law. The correct response of the League of Arab States to the 1948 catastrophe and 1967 disaster should have been the offer of the citizenship of the host state accompanied by League of Arab States provisions for dual host state citizenship *plus* future Palestinian citizenship. This response was not to be, probably because the host Arab governments were not particularly anxious to provide for the empowerment of the Palestinian people, let alone their own people. It is also perhaps wrong to expect any government to be interested in the empowerment of its people unless compelled to do so by the people (see "Recommendations," below).

Citizenship is an advantage and a strength—never an obstacle. Instead of formulating its struggle in terms of the liberation of Palestine and dual Arab-Arab citizenship, the PLO accepted the stupid dichotomy of either naturalization or liberation.

Let me indicate at the outset that I fully and squarely support the naturalization of all refugees, including Palestine refugees, *not* as a political solution of one kind or another but as a basic human right, a precondition to a political solution. No political solution of any refugee situation is worth considering if it is formulated in terms that are incompatible with the right (and the most pressing basic need) of the refugee to citizenship. I am very much aware that this position can and ought to determine the kind of political solutions to be negotiated between the concerned parties, and I submit that adhering to this position will have far-reaching and beneficial political implications for the region as a whole.

The criterion for assessment of what political framework is more or less beneficial is whether the proposed framework is likely to improve or restrict the range of choice available to the individual. Examined in these terms, the question whether the unfolding new Middle East order is likely to be beneficial to the peoples of the region remains open.

The acceptability or otherwise of the emerging scenario for a "new Middle East" hinges on the kind of citizenship legislation that will underpin the process. It is by this standard that it will be possible to judge whether the "new Middle East order" represents a vision for a new Middle East patterned on the model of the European Union or a fiction of a "new Middle East" designated to veil the reality of Zionist apartheid now writ large over the entire Levant.

There is no doubt that the "new Middle East order" is beneficial to the governments and national authorities partaking in the process. They can see this as clearly as anyone else, and they meet and negotiate agreements on the basis of their common interests. But is the "new order" going to be beneficial to the peoples of the region, first and foremost to the Palestinian people?

In one important way it will. If my reading is correct, the process is likely to remove the condition of blatant statelessness from the region and thereby make possible an important and far-reaching empowerment of the people. But removing the blatant statelessness is one thing, and introducing equal citizenship is quite another. People who are unequal citizens are likely to fight for equal citizenship with the same determination, if not more, than stateless people are.

The state around which the "new Middle East" is being structured, the State of Israel, is typically an apartheid state, a state with two classes of citizenship, one for people recognized by the state as "Jews" and the other for "non-Jews," notably Palestinian Arabs. The most significant mobilizing element in the "new Middle East" equation will be the Palestinian citizens of Israel and their demand for equal citizenship, with all the law reforms that this needs to entail. The Jewish state will resist this demand. In the "new Middle East order," the constituency of the Palestinian citizens of Israel will emerge as the most important Palestinian constituency overall.

But the struggle of the Palestinian citizens of Israel directly impinges on all Palestinian constituencies, first and foremost the Palestine refugees. After all, some 20 percent of the Palestinians in Israel are "present absentees." Their struggle to recover their properties from the Israeli Custodian of Absentees Property will spearhead the struggle of all Palestine refugees, wherever they may be naturalized, to do the same. And as citizens of whatever state (any member state of the League of Arab States, the United States, any European state), they would have better leverage for their demands if they mobilized through regional and international bodies—not only for their claim for property, but of equal significance their claim to implement their right of return to localities of their choice inside Israel.

In a Middle East, where the war situation has ended and treaties of peace have been signed between Israel and its neighboring states, Israel may, under international law, deny an entry visa to a stateless person who does not have valid travel documents, if only as a tourist. It is unlikely to be able to deny, as a matter of policy, entry visas to persons with valid travel documents only because they are Palestine refugees, and with regional peace reigning, it will be unable to claim security reasons on a mass scale either.

Given the Israeli Zionist undaunted apartheid commitment to a guaranteed majority of citizens classified by the state as "Jews," what projection can we make on the basis of this study so far?

One such projection is the collapse of the PLO leadership after the departure of President/Chairman Yasser Arafat. A leadership and a leader that cannot recognize, admit, and take responsibility for defeat is a leadership that will be unable to recognize, admit, and take responsibility for victory. More critically, a leadership that misrepresents defeat as victory is guilty of cultivating a fundamental and debilitating lie. And predicating its existence and programs on such a lie blinds this leadership to important elements in the situation of defeat that can be salvaged to construct the elements of future victory.

One such element is the demand for dual and multiple democratic citizenship, the demand for a federal Middle East based on the European model.

The above analysis immediately impinges on the current and pressing debate regarding the question of Palestinian autonomy. As noted, in democratic liberal states, autonomy is conventionally considered to be an option for self-determination of given communal or regional groupings whose members are citizens of a state composed of a variety of such groupings and who wish to remain citizens of the same state after autonomy. The citizenship rights within the framework of the central state remain of crucial importance because they represent the rights of any individual (regardless of his or her affiliation to any particular grouping) to equal access to the civil, political, social, and material resources of the state. Autonomy is thus conceived of as an amplification and extension of the rock foundation of the democratic citizenship of the individual—improving, for instance, individual choice and equal access to his or her own cultural history (as well as the cultural history of other groupings in the state) and linguistic heritage (as well as the linguistic heritage of other groupings), control of educational and municipal resources, and so on. But all of this is possible only if underpinned by a system of rights represented in common and universal democratic citizenship.

The truth of our Middle East situation today is that the PLO and some of the governments of the Arab confrontation states have delivered to Zionist Israel what the African National Congress (ANC) and the governments of the African confrontation states have always refused apartheid South Africa: moral and legal legitimization of apartheid. The ANC insisted on linking the suspension of the armed struggle ("terrorism") and the commencement of the peace process to a firm and cast-iron guarantee by the government of South Africa to abolish the apartheid legislation of the land. The PLO did not act likewise. For reasons that are not rooted in the power-political advantage of the enemy, but (in my judgment) in serious flaws in its moral vision and political analysis, the PLO has committed itself to a negotiated peace process based on the renunciation of "the use of terrorism and other acts of violence" and the assumption of "responsibility over all PLO elements and personnel in order to assure compliance, prevent violations and discipline violators" *without linking* both commitments to a parallel commitment in writing by the State of Israel to dismantle its apartheid legislation.

As noted, unlike the ANC under the leadership of Nelson Mandela, the PLO under the leadership of Yasser Arafat did not link negotiations in the framework of the peace process to a program of reform inside apartheid Israel. It predicated its strategy on the erroneous political assumption that it is possible to achieve through a negotiated peace process a sovereign and independent State of Palestine alongside an apartheid State of Israel on the basis of the 1967 borders.

Another projection is that the fragmented interim solution outlined above is not likely to meet the long-term objectives of Zionist Jewish fundamentalism and apartheid commitment to a Jewish state with a *guaranteed* majority of "Jews." Resistance and opposition can and will augment this paramount ideological determination, and, in the new conditions of regional treaties of peace, such democratic opposition will be assisted by new factors. For instance, mass expulsion and mass dispossession are tried racist solutions in Palestine (Israel) as well as in the Gulf (Kuwait). But to be effective they seem to require the cover of war (1948 in Palestine and 1991 in the Gulf). A normalized Middle East—where financial, business, and security contracts of the order of multimillion and multibillion U.S. dollars are negotiated with the European Union, the United States, Israel, and the Gulf states, as well as between Israel and its neighboring Arab states—may discourage "media unfriendly" criminal solutions in the form of mass expulsion and dispossession.

It is the belief of many that the legal and political fragmentation of the Palestinian people through naturalization and Bantustanization leaves Israel the dominant state in the new Middle East order, with all its options open. But it does not.

More than fifty years after the establishment of the State of Israel, Zionism is no longer the only hegemoneous ideology directing the state. The Zionist success story and the progressive integration of Israel into the world economy has brought forth a parallel ideology, effectively competing and undermining the tenets of Zionism: privatization and economic liberalization. Privatization does not equal democratization, but in the Israeli context it is a precondition to democratization because when the state privatizes, the only assets it has available for privatization are Zionist assets. When these assets are privatized, they are made available through the market to everybody and anybody wealthy enough to compete for them, including non-Jews.

A conflict is emerging between the state and Zionist bodies such as the

Jewish National Fund and the Jewish Agency, and the cracks manufactured by the conflict represent opportunities for the struggle for democracy not only inside Israel but now in the region as a whole.

In the context of the regional peace process as it has already unfolded and the emerging diversion of interests between the state and the Zionist establishment, Israel seems to have accepted the naturalization of the 1948 Palestinians as *jinsiyya* citizens. Against the growing demand of the Palestinian citizens of Israel for equal *muwatana* rights and the progressive improvement of the Palestinian position inside the framework of a Zionist Jewish (apartheid) Israel, Zionist hegemony in Israel will change, and the struggle to improve the state of democracy in the region as a whole will begin. What was achievable for the ANC in South Africa is achievable in Israel—though not by the PLO.

Recommendations

The above analysis is directed to aid the intellectual, cultural, and political elites organized inside and outside the region who are committed to the defense of human rights and the democratization of the Middle East. A number of recommendations follow from the analysis, notably:

1. That the League of Arab States be renamed the Union of Middle Eastern and North African States (UMENAS). A necessary condition for membership in UMENAS would be confirming the Arabic language as the official language or one of the official languages. Sufficient conditions would entail submission to the provisions of UMENAS, inter alia, regarding citizenship.

2. That the League of Arab States protocol of 5 April 1954 regarding legislation on citizenship be nullified and replaced with a new protocol modeled on post-Maastricht European citizenship allows dual citizenship among members states of UMENAS.

3. That all member states of UMENAS change their citizenship legislation in accordance with the Universal Declaration of Human Rights and with UN conventions and covenants, and that these changes include the naturalization of Palestine refugees in the states of their ordinary residence, allowing for dual and multiple citizenship with the State of Palestine and the State of Israel.

4. That Palestine refugees organize in a representative NGO separate from the PLO and from the projected Palestinian state; that this NGO seek recognition by the United Nations as Observer (organization having received a standing invitation to participate in the sessions and the work of the

General Assembly as observer and maintaining permanent offices at head-quarters) to pursue the claims of Palestine refugees for material compensation or return or both and to mobilize for the reactivation by the UN of the Palestine Compensation Committee to determine the criteria for and effect the payment of compensations for Palestinian refugee properties.

5. That the United Nations exercise its leverage on Israel (including sanctions) with the view to nullify the annexation of Jerusalem to Israel and return sovereignty over the separate corpus of Jerusalem to the United Nations. The religious sites in Jerusalem as a city of significance to the three monotheistic religions will be decoupled from the question of sovereignty over the city and be governed by a tripartite council representing on equal footing Judaism, Christianity, and Islam. The United Nations will purchase from the government of Israel its government offices in Jerusalem to cover the Israeli cost of building a new government city.

6. That, with the advent of peace in the Middle East, all NGO activities be coordinated on Middle Eastern as well as Mediterranean levels, and an all–Middle East NGO lobby, led by Palestine refugee NGOs, be established under UN auspices to mobilize for the implementation of the above recommendations and for the adoption by the UN of an international convention on the suppression and punishment of Zionism as a form of racism and racial discrimination.

7. That the intellectual elite of the region work to reconstitute the Middle East in terms of the recommendations above with the view to model a new Middle East on the example of the European Union, leading to a democratic federal union.

11

Palestinian Political Culture, Civil Society, and the Conception of Citizenship

MANUEL HASSASSIAN

PALESTINIAN CULTURAL EXPRESSION has organically interwoven itself within the political development and reality of the historic struggle with Israel. Ironically, the failures of the national struggle have imbued Palestinian nationalism with a culture of resistance and a momentum of sociopolitical transformation. Since its early days of armed struggle, resistance has represented itself in popular demands for the protection of human and civil rights as well as the in popular need for democracy as an intrinsic element of self-determination. This representation has come hand in hand with developments in the shattered socioeconomic infrastructure of the Occupied Territories and with dramatic changes in the educational system.

Undoubtedly, the Intifada was instrumental in inducing the Palestinians toward institution building, thus expanding the democratization process among the grass roots of the Palestinian community through the growing number of trade unions, professional associations, as well as women and youth organizations and movements. A great number of Palestinians regarded their active participation in these organizations as effective methods of defying Israeli occupation and establishing democratic institutions. Consequently, alongside the ideas of national solidarity and struggle against occupation, the concept of democracy became a major ethos among Palestinians. It came to be perceived as the basis of Palestinian solidarity, popular mobilization, and steadfastness (*sumud*). Popular involvement in

Intifada activism incited a momentum of democratic awareness that took place along with other substructural changes, the expansion of education, and the growing political awareness among the lower strata of Palestinians, urban and rural alike.

Many of these transformations seem to be the result of lessons hard learned by the Palestinians, lessons that emphasize and continue to echo a forewarning that unless democratic practices are implemented at every level of daily life—in homes, schools, offices, organizations, and factories—the new State of Palestine would emerge as a replica of the surrounding authoritarian Arab regimes. One must recall that, in many senses, the twentieth century was marked by nothing short of tragedy for the Palestinians. They are the victims: the victims of a colonial settler movement, the victims of surrounding Arab government self-interest, the victims of the collective simplicity of their peasant roots in a world that imposed its will, modernity, and racism on them (Ghilan 1988). The road to collective redemption for the Palestinians has been a long one, marked only recently with the signs of a capacity to compete with the pen rather than the sword. Many Palestinian intellectuals (including proponents of the Islamic block) have led the way in popularizing political pluralism and freedom as essential elements and precursors to a multiparty system in the future Palestinian polity.

Today's Occupied Territories show strong signs of embarking on the process of state formation in an attempt to preserve the embryonic civil society that emerged during the last decades of the Israeli occupation (Rubenberg 1983b). This process can be seen as a consequence of a larger process of social transformation in Palestinian society highly noted during the Intifada period in which the patriarchal structure of Palestinian society was directly challenged. This challenge to the traditional authority of the Palestinian family by the youth and to a certain degree by women was made direct by claims "for a higher authority consecrated by political commitments to their political groups and therefore to the national cause" (Tamari 1991, 60). Although these changes have clearly made their mark on Palestinian society, the post-Intifada period has witnessed a regression of sorts, with Palestinian society returning to the familiarity and conservatism of traditional Palestinian life. This regression seems to have direct correlation to the health of the peace process and the national struggle as a whole, but one must forever be conscious that the possibility of returning to that which the population finds most familiar (be it religion, family, or tradition) always exists if more progressive forms of governance fail.

This chapter examines the status of democratic consciousness in the Palestinian context as a part of the contemporary Arab world, through a particular emphasis on the role that citizenship plays in this development.

Citizenship, Civil Society, and Democracy
in the Arab World

The question of Palestinian citizenship and gravitation to democratic elements must first be placed against a Middle Eastern backdrop. Here, the definition of *citizenship*, within the theoretical framework of contemporary Arab discourse and Middle Eastern politics, digresses from the widespread, Western-derived interpretation of the term. Unlike the Middle East, the West sees the evolution of citizenship as "an expression of aspirations towards individual liberty and democracy" (Muslih and Norton 1991, 5). Thus, the Western intellectual sees the need to specify the rights, roles, and obligations of the individual in society as essential, whereas the Middle Eastern definition is still ambiguous and presently maturing. The subsequent question to this line of argument is: Why hasn't the Arab world felt the overwhelming urge to detail the rights of its citizens?

Nazih Ayubi (1995) contends that the answer lies in the theories proposed by Arab thinkers such as Louis 'Awad and Kamal al-Haj: that the state and the individual in the Western world are intrinsically connected. Western brands of democracy are based on the idea that the state is a tool in the hands of the people and inherently should operate to satisfy their needs. Al-Haj goes even further in this interpretation, saying that according to Western ideas, the state alone can preserve the components of nationalism and enable the individual to experience freedom.

Applying these principles on a Middle Eastern stage is not so easy. Regionally, the people of the Middle East have always expressed a patriarchal relationship with their rulers, largely the remnants of cultural patterns as seen in tribal or clan formations and paralleled in family (father and child) relationships. This patriarchal system has continued even with the emergence of the modern states in the region. But it would be too dangerous to perceive Middle Eastern political trends through such an unscientific and perhaps orientalist lens. This is to say that the dynamic of unquestioned patriarchy and its governmental version is a difficult influence to measure. The autocracy of Middle Eastern leaders and the fear it has instilled among the masses make it difficult to collect reliable data as to whether loyalty to a given ruler is wrought from fear or from genuine support for the practices of the regime. The present makeup of contemporary Arab regimes dissuades any reliable data collection for the near future because questionnaires and even electoral results must always be considered with dubious credibility (al-Nasser 1989).

Clearly, elements of Western democracy have influenced the balance of power between state and people in the Middle East, however. This is most evident in the rise of Arab nationalism in the late nineteenth century and its subsequent evolution in the twentieth century—an evolution that has to a credible degree eroded monarchical infallibility and authority. Yet this erosion is not complete in that it seems impeded by the more deeply seated traditions of patriarchal respect still very much alive today. What seems to be left is a condition of neopatriarchy in which the relationship between the government and the people is neither fully patriarchal nor fully modern (Sharabi 1988, Tibi 1984).

Highlighting this transition are Arab intellectuals who are concerned about the suppression of individual expression and participation. Here, the distinction between the Western and Middle Eastern ideas of expression and participation needs to be pointed out. Class and individual in the Middle East are often seen as one, a reflection of socialist interpretations that equate the needs of the class as the only effective representative of the individual— i.e., the needs of the masses (Issawi 1956). The evolution of Arab nationalism during the latter part of the nineteenth century is attributed with emphasizing these needs within the sphere of the social class. This development was evidenced most prominently by the creation of the Wafd Party in Egypt, the Socialist Nationalist Party in Syria, and the Al-'Ahali Party in Iraq, and by the call for participatory elections on a mass level as expressed in the ideas of progressive radical thinkers such as Michel Aflaq, Khaled Bigdash, and Salameh Musa. The effect of this dynamic was an awareness and movement toward the presence of party representation and the use of elections among the masses.

Though the infusion of class, group, and party awareness of citizenship rights has been realized despite its failed implementation in the region, the "human dimension" of citizenship still seems to be lacking. Ironically, it is precisely the human dimension to citizenship from which one would expect group consciousness to emerge: how to define and defend the rights of the individual under the law within the context of a governing body. Although virtually no specific basic human rights are enumerated in Arab discourse, the growing influence of civil society highlights the move toward distinctly defining the rights of the individual. Here, the growing presence of interest groups or nongovernmental organizations (NGOs) seems to portend a dynamic in which people seek to buffer their relationship with the state and individual through the unity of a collective cause. It is, of course, hoped that such groups will be able to gather enough popular support that the government will choose to listen to their appeal rather than confront it. Interest groups set up precedents to curb or at least control the level of human rights violations. As Ayubi (1995) has said, "a pact of sorts appeared . . . and although the level of violations remained significant, it may be developing into a more distinct consociational formula" (37).

Interest-group existence is itself evidence of organized discontent and is combined with collective initiatives to change the system and how the masses are forced to act within it. In response, Arab governments have tended to give greater political and legal status to the judiciary. This could be conceived as a way for them to contend with direct appeals for democratic process and representation without making real constitutional changes that they would be responsible for implementing. Hence, the judiciary seems to have become a limited platform to contest diverse ideas and to appeal for safeguards to human rights in conjunction with popular demands for democratization. Morocco, Egypt, Tunisia, and Jordan are examples of countries that are witnessing the expansion and increased autonomy of their judicial systems as an outlet for popular democratic appeals (Tibi 1984).

Yet, at the same time, when all these positive movements seem to be taking place, there seems to be an equal movement of Arab governments in the opposite direction. The example of the Egyptian high constitutional court declaring in 1990 the elections law unconstitutional and calling for dissolving the parliament is indicative. A dissolving of elections in Algeria is perhaps the most extreme case and has led to the onset of a bloody civil war between the Islamic factions and the government, a war that to date has taken at least eighty thousand lives. Clearly, the Algerian case exhibits some interesting traits. Democratic reform in Algeria was construed by the Algerian government as democracy with limits: no Islamic party would gain a parliamentary majority. It is precisely examples like these that exhibit the limits to democratic momentum. Democracy in the Arab world seems to be at the stage where governors pay lip service to it as an ideal, initiating symbolic yet rather hollow reforms, while remaining steadfastly in positions of centralized power and decision making.

The inefficiency of the democratic movements in the Middle East can be traced to their conceptions of citizenship. The simple lack of a definition of *citizenship* is the major obstacle when trying to analyze those movements. Taken from the different liberal, socialist, and Marxist ideologies of Arab intellectuals, the most prevelant concept of citizenship seems to be an economic one. Whereas in the West citizenship has meant the right to freedom of expression and equity in the social and political arena, the Arab interpretation is limited to economic rights.

For these reasons, democracy in the Western sense does not exist in the Arab world. Most countries in the Middle East are run by autocratic or dictatorship regimes, with a powerful ruler flanked by a stalwart military (Muslih and Norton 1991). These dictatorships are kept in place through might and blood—i.e., a strong army and the practice of nepotism. The omnipresence of intelligence agents throughout Middle Eastern dictatorial regimes is evidence of the regimes' suspicion and fear that their power may be threatened by the people's discontent with the leaders' ways. Limited resistance, therefore, to the autocratic leaders of the region has more to do with "the republic of fear," as Kanan Makiya (1993) describes it, than with complicity and love of the rulers.

Though the above is generally true of the Arab states, the Palestinians seem to be an exception, perhaps a consequence of their precarious existence for the last fifty years. The Israeli occupation of the West Bank and Gaza during years of the Intifada saw Palestinians building various democratic civil institutions in fields such as welfare, health, and other social services in an attempt to make life more amicable (Rubenberg 1983b).

It is the growth of these institutions (still very much alive) that has given Palestinian society a more democratic posture than other Arab societies. Following the Israeli redeployment of forces as a result of the Israeli-Palestinian Interim Agreement, there were attempts to formalize these institutions into a governing authority. The Palestinian National Authority (PNA) became the quasi-governmental institution that had a president as well as a legislative council, but still seemed to lack a state. January 1996 witnessed the holding of free and open elections for the first time. Not only was Yasser Arafat elected president with more than 80 percent of the votes, but members of the legislative council were voted in as well (al-Khatib 1991). I return to the significance of democratic institutions and the PNA later on, yet only wish to convey here that the fundamental roots for a democratic government have been set in place. Whether this state will come to fruition is itself another question that remains to be answered.

Aside from the Palestinian model, however, it seems as though the rest of the Arab world is reluctant to adopt the Western concept of citizenship and institute democracy into their governments. Such concepts and the practices that go with them would undermine the autocratic leaders' authority and power, and would give governing ability to the people instead of the regime. Although many Arab countries have constitutions with democratically inspired rhetoric, the constitution merely serves as a symbolic element in the country's society, something that exists but is not adhered to (al-Nasser 1989). Democracy and citizenship would call for the end of such autocratic regimes and are therefore not compatible or accepted among the leadership. Furthermore, Arab societies lack the democratic institutions that exist in Palestinian society, which have served to raise awareness and protect the individual from blatant abuses of power. The "buffer" between government and grassroots Palestinian society, composed of civil society and its institutions, appears to be thicker in Palestinian society than in surrounding Arab regimes, where the individual is more exposed.

The Middle East appears to suffer from other societal factors that resist

Western practices of citizenship as well. In an effort to rejuvenate and revitalize their religion, Islamic fundamentalists reject all forms of Western "man-made" practices in their world. As a result, any concept of citizenship or democracy is not divine and therefore can play no part in the pure Islamic world. According to Islamic fundamentalists, Allah knows what is best for Muslims, making all laws stated in the Qu'ran and Shari'ah prescriptions for Muslims to live happy, free lives. Such an argument makes any call for a Westernized, free society virtually akin to blasphemy (Sid-Ahmed 1990).

If we bear all of the aforementioned ideas in mind, it seems unlikely that the Middle East will ever adopt a purely Western ideal of citizenship and democracy. Perhaps some countries will adopt a few elements of the Western ideology, such as elections and a legislative body. Yet for the most part, it seems as though for the near future a democratic Arab country is not possible. This situation is exacerbated by Western imperial and political practices in the region, both historically and presently, which have tended to incite Middle Eastern society to cling to precisely that which maintains their difference: traditional forms of Arab life. But it is these very traditions that, as has been mentioned, lack democratic roots and therefore impede the process of democratization.

Those countries that do adopt some practices, however, could set an example for the rest of the Arab world and a precedent for the years to follow. Perchance with the establishment of a democratic Palestinian state, other states will follow suit or at least be enlightened in some way. Through this enlightenment, much like the movement that originated in eighteenth-century France, neighboring Arab countries would come to see the benefits of that democratic order. For the meantime, however, solely an economic sense of equality (financial parity) does not appear to be appealing enough to bring about further democratic change. Only with a total change in the leadership and thinking—brought about through a change in education initiated both from the top and the bottom—will Western democracy and citizenship be accepted in Arab society. Furthermore, because it seems unlikely that any change of this sort will come about through the willful compliance of the ruling elite, a revolution may be the only way to alter the society. This does not bode well for the future of democracy or for the powerless within Arab society (Hijab 1989).

Despite these impediments, the term *civil society* has entered the discourse of the Arab world and has become a central concept in current debate over the direction of politics in the region. Evidence of such a process has materialized in the wake of the Cold War and the expansion of the global economy, in which societies are being transformed through political and economic liberalization (Sakamoto 1991). If liberalization has a home, it is in civil society, where clubs, syndicates, guilds, associations, unions, and political parties provide a buffer between the individual and the polity (Muslih and Norton 1991). Across the Arab world, people are adamantly requesting accountability from the political elite and a greater role in policymaking. There is no doubt that mounting pressure is put on governments in the Middle East to limit their authoritarian power as the regulators of civic organizations and to grant more freedom for discourse and organization.

The Middle East is in the process of witnessing the mushrooming of women's movements and charitable organizations (both secular and religious) in Kuwait, Algeria, Egypt, Jordan, and Yemen. These examples, to a certain degree, offer cautious optimism to the development of civil societies in the Arab world. Of course, if we believe that civil society is a precursor for democracy, the growth of civil societies in the Arab World should expedite the process of accountability and create a political ambiance for Arab governments to forge democratization in their political processes.

In all, it seems that the expanding role of the citizen through economic liberalization has created a mixed opportunity for societies to question their beliefs and values as related to state operation, priorities, and treatment of citizens. The overall effect, however, has been movement in two opposing directions: first, toward civic institutions that would undercut traditional kin-based, patriarchal, and matrilineal structures; or second, toward more traditional, familiar, and conservative values that are inherently less democratic in nature. These opposing movements have clearly polarized Arab society and left it in a state where little progress can be effected with the governments, which continue to run their autocracies through the strength of their militaries and through this very ambiguity in the ideologies of their populations.

Democratic Trends among Palestinians

In order for democracy to be entrenched in a society, it must be strengthened not only on the institutional level but also on the sociopolitical level.

The Palestinians are no exception to this rule. As actors in world politics, they have demonstrated considerable symbolic potency on the international stage, especially in the so-called third world. The fedayeen and the "children of the stones" conjure up strong images of a people who fight oppression and demand their right to freedom and self-determination. Yet their attempts have so far proved flawed as they have failed to establish an independent state, let alone one that could institutionally protect a democratic order. Furthermore, nationalism in principle bears no causal connection with democracy (Hassassian and Nammari 1992). Successful democracy must be institutionalized in a way that mediates the multiple and conflicting interests that emerge once statehood is declared. This process of transition is difficult as well as critical for developing societies because they lack experience in dealing with such conflicts, which often hampers their legitimacy and performance. It is further impeded by the diasporic nature of the Palestinian community. Achieving representative democracy when the Palestinian constituency is spread throughout the Arab world (indeed, the world), often living under harsh undemocratic systems, is close to impossible.

Understandably, this dilemma has raised a variegated assortment of Palestinian voices, each with his or her own political leanings. Pluralism in Palestinian politics has always been assessed in the context of the erosion evident in Arab politics reflected in fragmentation, repressive conditions, economic discrepancies, and lack of legitimacy and credibility (Abed and Kaufman).

An offshoot of Arab nationalism, Palestinian nationalism over the years developed a secular ideology committed to democracy. The process of democratization has been facilitated by the high level of education and literacy achieved by Palestinians, and by the existence of institutions and professional societies, especially embodied in the Palestine Liberation Organization (PLO). The PLO has portrayed itself as the institutional expression of Palestinian nationalism, a framework in which all Palestinian cultural, social, educational, political, and military activities have been integrated (Cobban 1984). By providing complex services to the Palestinians, it gained legitimacy and shouldered the burden of integrating the various attitudes and positions of Palestinian refugees, intellectuals, middle-class merchants, and commandos.

In recent years, the PLO has managed to emphasize certain democratic trends and pragmatism in its political program. The Intifada acted as a catalyst in changing the perceptions, attitudes, and even political strategies of Palestinians in the territories, most especially through the official declaration and espousal of the two-state solution in 1988 (Tamari 1991). This solution laid the groundwork for negotiations, political settlement, and accommodation, eventually implemented through the Oslo Accords.

Of course, there is quite a discrepancy between support for the rhetoric and support for the reality of democracy. Many Palestinian intellectuals genuinely support democracy, and they are followed by many of the people for the simple reason that it signifies dramatic change and the potential for prosperity. Whether the ruling elites support this cry remains to be seen (Moghrabi et al. 1991).

It is quite evident that the procedural definition of democracy is still inadequate among the Palestinians because one cannot presume the existence of the culture of accommodation that makes democracy operational. Nonetheless, Palestinians in the Occupied Territories have developed certain democratic behaviors on par with Western liberal democracy. These democratic trends have been embedded in the sociopolitical culture of a civic society that was initiated during the 1980s and 1990s by institution-building and grassroots organizations (Abed and Kaufman).

The Crafting of Democracy
and the Future of Palestine

The single strongest piece of evidence of a serious institutional demand for democracy comes from the Palestinian Declaration of Independence (November 1988). Its ideas can be traced back to the Democratic Front for the Liberation of Palestine (DFLP) under Naif Hawatmeh, who was the first to officially call for the creation of a secular democratic state. It addresses the question of the type of regime that the future, independent Palestinian state would have. The last paragraph in the declaration emphasizes that Palestinians will have full equality in rights and will be able to enjoy their national and cultural identity. Further, the Palestinian state will safeguard "their political and religious convictions and their human dignity by means of a Parliamentary democratic system of governance, itself based on freedom of expression and the freedom to form parties." Moreover, the declaration has made it clear in the area of authority and representation that

> the right of minorities will be duly respected by the majority, as minorities must abide by decisions of the majority. Governance will be based on principles of social justice, equality and non-discrimination in race, religion, color, sex under the aegis of a constitution which ensures the rule of law and the independent judiciary.

In principle, the language of the declaration reflects a philosophical commitment among Palestinians to the development of democratic institutions. Additional evidence of this democratic momentum includes the following:

Within the PLO, emphasis has been made on the importance of democratic procedures in relation to the decision-making process. A shift from consensus to majority politics is quite explicit.

Palestinians in the Occupied Territories have established a tradition of elections, and the 1972 and 1976 municipal elections are good examples, not to mention the current ongoing elections in the main professional associations, trade unions, labor unions, student movements, and women's organizations.

The high literacy rate among Palestinians has been instrumental in loosening the patriarchal traditional social structure. It is known that the development of education is a prerequisite for a democratic civil society (Abed and Kaufman).

For many years, the Palestinians have been engaged in heated debates among themselves concerning their future. Of course, the debates have led to a wider acceptance of the principles of negotiation and political compromise, two cornerstones of democratic development (Hourani 1980).

The concept of freedom is extremely important to the outlook of many Palestinian intellectuals and political elites in the Occupied Territories.

Emphasis has been placed on democracy as a means to encompass cultural diversity and variegated points of view among the interior and exterior Palestinians (Segal 1989).

Repression of Palestinian leaders of the Intifada has induced diffusion and decentralization of power to the grassroots organizations.

During the Intifada, Palestinians established new patterns of collective behavior and self-reliance—two characteristics of democratic behavior.

The role of women's organizations during the Intifada undermined the traditional perception of women in the Arab world and brought women closer to social and economic equality.

The Palestinian leadership represents to a certain degree a Western-educated leadership that may play a pivotal role in the crafting of the new regime of the Palestinian state (Abed and Kaufman). Furthermore, Palestinians cannot afford to build a nondemocratic state because they will be heavily dependent economically on Western donor countries.

The impact of Israeli occupation paradoxically prompted the Palestinians to become familiar with a political system that espouses the rule of law and democracy, the occupation notwithstanding. It has left a positive impact on the subculture and political culture of the Palestinians, who categorically reject a Palestinian authority that would be a replica of Arab authoritarian regimes.

The impact of the Intifada has been tremendous in institution building and in developing Palestinian infrastructure in the Occupied Territories (Tamari 1991).

The emergence of a middle class among Palestinians has been significant in the process of building a Palestinian civic society that would bolster a democratic Palestinian State.

Though the above reasons are encouraging signs of democracy, it must be clear that democracy as a whole still seems to be fighting a renewal of conservatism that prevents it from fully taking root. Furthermore, as a fledgling democracy, it:

> cannot pretend to start from the level of achievement at which the Western democracies have arrived. In fact, no democracy would ever have materialized if it had set for itself the advanced goals that a number of modernizing states currently claim to be pursuing. In a world-wide perspective, the problem is to minimize arbitrary and tyrannical rule and to maximize a pattern of civility rooted in respect and justice for each man . . . in short, to achieve a humane polity. Undue haste and overly ambitious goals are likely to lead to opposite results. (Sartori 1968, 120–22)

In many senses, the debate over whether the future Palestinian entity will be democratic or not is a moot one. As Hisham Sharabi has pointed out, "only a free and democratic Palestinian entity alongside Israel will guarantee a genuine and lasting peace. An autocratic regime, such as exists today in many Arab Countries, would not last but would inevitably lead to economic and political disintegration with unpredictable consequences" (1994).

Palestinian Civil Society in the Making:
Future Prospects

Ideally, civil society should both deal with government intervention and exhibit a dimension of tolerance within and among the institutions that it encompasses (Muslih and Norton 1991). The pertinence of civil society to the democratization process is solely based on the facts that (1) popular institutions lay the groundwork for grassroots training in the areas of plurality and democratic behavior, and (2) civil society can counterpoise the autocracy of the State.

The Palestinians' experimentation with the development of civil society involves a great deal more inclusivity when compared with that of rest of the Arab world. There is no doubt that the Palestinians have contrived to build institutions and organizations that are inclusive of an "array of political parties, municipal service organizations, cooperatives, educational institutions, student senates, women's organizations, health care associations, charitable organizations, labor unions, trade unions, business associations, child care facilities, religious group (including Welfare and social service organizations run by these groups), think tanks, professional unions and syndicates (e.g., lawyers' guilds and medical associations) and chambers of commerce" (Abed and Kaufman). Some estimates put the number of NGOs as high as twelve hundred for the Occupied Territories alone. Furthermore, NGOs have developed remarkable power given the difficult conditions under which they were wrought.

Consider, for instance, that NGOs came about under an oppressive Israeli occupation that saw little need or desire to in any way improve the well-being or livelihood of the people it dominated. Furthermore, the occupation forces were virulently opposed to NGOs, fearing that they would become warehouses of national allegiance. One tends to forget that the PLO was an outlawed institution in the Occupied Territories before the signing of the Declaration of Principles in 1993. Anyone vaguely associated with the PLO risked prison sentence or expulsion. This meant that NGOs developed a double face: an outer face that was apolitical and an inner face that witnessed the collection of people who followed one of the variegated political strains of the PLO. NGOs were in fact the principle way in which the PLO leadership in exile was able to maintain a presence in the territories and therefore could lay claim to representation of the Palestinian community at large.

These variegated organizations and groups have developed in the wake of the 1967 Israeli occupation of the West Bank (including Jerusalem) and the Gaza Strip and have been responsive in catering to the social needs of the Palestinians in the absence of any political or national authority. Of course, the services they rendered enabled the Palestinians to survive under Israeli military occupation. However, the work of these diverse formations will culminate in the building of an infrastructure of civil and political institutions—a prelude to an independent Palestinian state. Furthermore, the structure of Palestinian civil society has been enhanced by several significant attributes conducive to the process of democratization in the Palestinian autonomous areas.

One of the main attributes is the tolerance of divergent opinions, which has developed into a tradition among Palestinians, especially within the political infrastructure of the PLO. The concept of pluralism within the factions of the PLO evolved to become an intrinsic value within the Palestinian social system. It is no wonder that today the opposition forces within the Palestinian political spectrum is respected and tolerated by the mainstream. This is an essential element, indicating a level of "civility." Undoubtedly, the opposing groups would act as a check to the performance of the authority in a democratic environment. Furthermore, pluralist thinking is also embodied in a high number of women participating in political life.

Though such attributes are already present in Palestinian society, they still need to be bolstered and legitimized by the Palestinian National Authority. This is to say that Palestinian society has been severely distorted and affected by Israeli military occupation. It suffers from a weak economy largely dependent on Israel, high unemployment rates, poor education (especially the generation of the Intifada), and the adoption of the oppressor's logic to a certain degree. These seem to be the largest impediments to democracy, which only add fuel to the fires of conservatism.

Palestinian Democracy in the Post-Oslo Period

The post-Oslo period has witnessed the competition of various strains of Palestinian political culture. To begin with, the initial euphoria brought about by the eager hopes of a peaceful solution to the Palestinians' plight has quickly been dashed, most notably through the rise in ascendance of the Israeli right wing. In turn, Palestinians have been left with a desperate situation: the new political realities in which they find themselves are the direct opposite of their well-intentioned expectations in September 1993. Three particular strains of political momentum need to be noted, as it is through the crucible of their struggle that the fate of Palestinian democracy is likely to be decided.

The rise of conservatism in Islamic movements (Hamas and Islamic Jihad) is a phenomenon that can hardly be ignored. It is worth while noting that this rise only came about within the past ten years of Palestinian political life. Before the Intifada, political Islam scarcely had a face in Palestinian politics. Furthermore, support for such groups does not necessarily entail a renaissance of fundamentalism. Political scientists have noted the "balloon effect" of the popular support that Hamas receives. In a nutshell, the health of the peace process is inversely proportionate to the health and popular support of Hamas. What this means is that Palestinians need to see direct improvements and results on the political front (and indeed in their daily lives) if they are expected to support the PNA. Support of Hamas is a protest vote against both the ineffectualness of the PNA and the intransigence and oppression of the Israeli government. It is also a stern message that the Hamas demands need to be addressed.

Hamas also exhibits very interesting traits that are worth mentioning. To a greater depth than other Palestinian political organizations, Hamas has been able to create change in the daily lives of many of the poorest parts of Palestinian society. In this sense, it is very much a grassroots organization as well as a part of the complex matrix of NGOs previously mentioned. It cannot, however, be assumed to represent the values and traits of a civil society because its members preach a strain of political Islam that resists democratic procedure and appreciation of civil rights. Instead, we see an interesting dynamic: failure on the national front with the PNA and the Oslo process directly correlates to a victory of conservatism and nondemocratic standards. This tends to show that for society's poorest, democracy is an expendable notion that can be thrown out with the other failures of secular nationalism.

It is perhaps ironic that Hamas's inherently undemocratic nature does not prevent its members from claiming they are proponents of democracy in Palestine. As the most vocal political opposition to the PNA and the Oslo Accords, Hamas has done well to cultivate the growing resentment with the peace process, all at the PNA's expense. It therefore serves Hamas's interest to openly advocate a democratic form of governance and decision making because it would permit the voicing of popular opposition through the Islamic resistance movement. Instead, its voice is intentionally marginalized through *un*democratic means that include mass imprisonment and closure of its societal institutions. The irony of the situation draws into question two essential issues that the Palestinian national movement needs to address. First, given where Palestinian politics is at this moment, who maintains the moral right to speak on behalf of the people? Second, one must also question how democracy can ever be truly realized in a Palestinian state given that the two largest and most powerful elements in organized Palestinian political life, the PNA and Hamas, have ominous records of undemocratic practices, while at the same time claiming to be the first to demand a democratic state.

It is also important to resist the Western tendency to exaggerate Islamic fundamentalism. Support for Hamas, at its very highest, has never topped 30 percent of Palestinian society. This implies that there is a stalwart community in Palestinian society that will support the secular nationalist strain of politics that values democracy as a necessity in the future Palestinian state. This *must* be considered a victory for the forces of democracy as the majority of Palestinians have witnessed a number of reasons to give up any remaining faith in the peace process and perhaps even in the PNA itself.

The second strain of political momentum that seems to have emerged in the post-Oslo era is that of competing power between NGOs and the PNA. It must be remembered that for a long period of time NGOs were the only way in which Palestinians could attempt to improve their lives. They acted as a shadow government, providing the services that the occupation forces did not. With the arrival of the PNA to the Occupied Territories in 1994, a new dynamic emerged in which the NGOs were suddenly expected to step aside for the newcomers. Those associated with Fateh, the mainstream political party, often joined the PNA, but those associated with the opposition felt on the defensive, fighting to maintain a foothold in the political game. As time progressed, tensions emerged between the old grassroot-based NGOs and the "Tunisians," the Tunis-based PLO infrastructure under

Yasser Arafat's leadership. This tension had moments of conflict, most notably in the sphere of human rights. Leaders of renowned human rights organizations, Eyad Sarraj and Raji Sourani, were both imprisoned by the PNA for criticizing its record on human rights. Though they were later released, their imprisonment symbolically represented the clash of power between the old and new orders. Furthermore, this confrontation showed that democracy was going to be an issue that NGOs were not willing to compromise on, despite efforts to the contrary by the PNA.

This second issue is closely intertwined with the third issue that affects democracy: external pressure for safeguarding Israeli "security" together with the health of the peace process in general. It seems a never-ending demand on the PNA to eliminate by one means or another all organized opposition to the Oslo peace process. Beneath the guise of "terrorism," intense pressure has been placed on the PNA to imprison on a mass scale Hamas, Islamic Jihad, and even the Popular Front activists who oppose the current direction of Palestinian politics. The PNA has complied with these demands to a limited degree. In one sense, neutralization of the opposition makes Yasser Arafat's position easier: he can move forward in the talks while securing his power. Yet large-scale "snuffing out" of the opposition in the long run works against the power interests of the PNA, most notably when the peace process fails. Imprisoning opposition activists makes the PNA seem like the glove beneath which lies the hand of the Israeli occupying forces. This has shown itself most clearly in various instances where PNA police have turned over Hamas activists to the Israeli authorities. It has, understandably, made the PNA very unpopular in many circles of Palestinian society.

Here, the PNA has found itself in a catch twenty-two: if it refuses to comply with external pressure to crack down on the opposition, it fails to move anywhere at the peace tables and therefore fails to bring home any tangible results that would reinvigorate a dwindling faith in its ability to "redeem Palestine." Yet if Arafat does choose to make moves against the opposition, his domestic power base is weakened considerably, especially when the Israeli government endlessly demands compliance to its request without giving up one inch of territory or stopping the building of any settlements.

Conclusions

Amid the ruins of the peace process remains the fate and question of democracy. "Crack down on terrorism" many times simply translates to "abuse the human and civil rights of the population to service a personal interest and ingratiate a stronger enemy." Arafat treads a sensitive line, attempting to please the Israelis and U.S. "shepherd" on one front and his Palestinian constituency on the other. So far he has failed to please either sufficiently, seeming to be caught in a battle to maintain a grasp on his own legitimacy. It is unlikely that this situation can sustain itself for much longer.

Democracy in the Palestinian context has certainly exhibited strong evidence of a stable presence within civil society. Unfortunately, the role of civil society has been intentionally reduced with the arrival of the PNA. Although it is unlikely that democratic forces will ever go away, there is a great likelihood that they will be contained by the PNA because they could viably contest and confront it if they are able to mobilize the lower and middle classes. Though the pluralism of Palestinian politics is always guaranteed, whether such pluralism is embodied in a multiparty system remains to be seen. In many ways, it is the fate of the peace process that will determine the fate of the PNA, Yasser Arafat, Hamas, the opposition, civil society, and of course the question of the future Palestinian polity. In turn, the fate of Palestinian democracy seems to be held in the balance. As with many times in politics, there are many signs of encouragement, juxtaposed with an equal number of signs to be wary.

12

Citizenship and Its Discontents

Palestinians in Israel

REBECCA KOOK

CITIZENSHIP IS one of the fundamental concepts of modern politics. The term denotes both a community of membership as well as a legal status to which is attached a predefined set of rights and obligations. It is thus both an inclusionary political mechanism and an equalizing one. The membership it defines enjoys equality in respect to the rights that the status of citizenship bestows. In this sense, citizenship is a classic and pure public good: it is nonexclusionary and hence equal to all its members, and it is also joint in supply—i.e., one individual's partaking in the good does not in the least diminish its supply to all the others.

Citizenship first emerged during the eighteenth and nineteenth centuries as a political institution involved in combating class-based social inequalities. Increasingly, however, citizenship is becoming a vehicle for the struggles of different culturally defined minorities. Today, it is commonly perceived as the primary channel available to cultural and national minorities for increased inclusion in society—inclusion in the sense of distribution of rights, as well as in terms of belonging. The debate, both political and academic, centers around the question whether citizenship embodies the capacity to overcome social inequalities that either originate or simply manifest themselves culturally. Recognition of the potential limitations of citizenship has generated new and original ways of conceiving of the institution, such as differentiated or cultural citizenship. This new discourse has in effect ended the long-held monopoly of liberal thinking on citizenship and has raised the question, How "public" is this public good?

In Israel, citizenship is seen by many of the Palestinian minority within the state as embodying the capacity to overcome the social inequality and discrimination that pervades the society's main political, social, and economic venues. The recent establishment of the Palestinian National Authority and the negotiations between the leadership of Israel and of the Palestinians have brought this issue into strong relief. For some, these events have signaled the possibility that social equality will be attainable within the parameters of citizenship in Israel; for others, they have merely served to highlight its limitations. It is my argument in this chapter that because of the way in which citizenship is defined in Israel, its capacity to overcome social inequality is limited. The reason for this, I contend, is that ethnonational structures of inequality have been defined into the institution of citizenship, rendering it ineffective as a political and social equalizer. I demonstrate this by a close analysis of the two citizenship strategies adopted in Israel, illustrating the way in which they not merely fail to overcome inequality, but actually serve to perpetuate it.

The imagined community of citizenry is often (though not always) inextricably linked to that of the nation. Hence, on a more theoretical level, I suggest that the historically relatively new role assigned to citizenship (characteristic mainly of the twentieth century)—combating culturally embedded inequalities—reveals the limitations of the institution. I conclude therefore that minority groups seeking inclusion—be they religious, ethnic, or national—might be better off pursing nonstate vehicles of advancement.

The chapter is composed of four sections. In the first section, I discuss the development of citizenship in Israel. Next, I provide an overview of the literature on citizenship, focusing on the different strategies that have emerged to try and accommodate minority demands. In the third section, I illustrate how two of these strategies have been adopted in Israel. I conclude with both theoretical and operational suggestions.

The Parameters of Citizenship in Israel

Any analysis of citizenship must begin with two fundamental questions. The first: How is citizenship acquired or determined; or, who is, who can be, and who will never be a citizen? The second question concerns the so-called payoffs of citizenship: What does this status offer to its members; or, what rights are granted with citizenship, and are they granted equally? These two questions merely reflect the two primary functions of citizenship: membership determination and the means of distributing civil rights (Habermas 1994, 25).

Answering these questions in the context of Israel is not a simple task, as

Israeli citizenship is very much a hybrid institution, having developed hand in hand with the definition of Israel's national identity. Indeed, it is impossible to understand accurately the way in which citizenship operates without an understanding of the constitutive role the "nation" has played in determining Israeli citizenship.

Israel is very clearly a nation-state: it was self-consciously and by design established as a state for a specific nation, the Jewish nation. Indeed, few are the modern states that so clearly and self-evidently assign themselves this identity. In its constitutional arrangements, its parliamentary mechanisms, and its territorial assignations, Israel is most clearly a one-nation state. There are no consociational arrangements, for example, to negotiate political power between different national groups; there are no regions that enjoy an autonomous or semiautonomous status. Nonetheless, the citizenry of Israel is comprised of more then one nation, and in certain fundamental ways, this reality is acknowledged by the Israeli authorities: it maintains two official languages—Hebrew and Arabic; it supports parallel educational systems for its Jewish and Arab citizens; and, most tellingly (if not most simplistically), it distinguishes between nationalities in its public registration. (On Israeli ID cards, there is a designation for nationality: "Jewish," "Arab," "Druz," or countries of origin for non-Jews who are non-Arabs.)

Israel was conceived of, however, both ideologically and politically, as a *Jewish* state as well as a state designated *for* Jews. Both of these identities are reflected in the Citizenship Law of Israel and in the way it is carried out. As a state *for* the Jews, it was from the outset formally inclusionary only toward Jews. As a Jewish state, it was to establish a polity and a state culture that would promote a Jewish political and cultural identity. The maintenance of Israel as a Jewish state is manifested first and foremost in its identification between religion and nationality. Accordingly, the national identity of Israel's citizens *as well as* of Israel as a state is determined by religious identity. Thus, Israel's *national* identity is Jewish, in the same way as that of its Jewish citizens. Hence, Judaism, or some sort of Jewish ethos or heritage, is the basis not merely of the religious identity but of the political, national, and cultural identity in Israel as well.

At the same time, by defining itself as a democracy, Israel is committed to certain universalist criteria for the definition of its citizen body and its public sphere. Thus, citizenship is not shared exclusively by Jews, but by non-Jews as well. Indeed, Israel virtually *imposed* citizenship upon the then 150,000 Palestinians who remained within the territory of Israel in 1949— in the midst of its war of independence. In addition, the public sphere in Israel is not exclusively dominated by Jewish religious identity, and a secular culture thrives. The implementation of parallel educational systems, the recognition of Arabic as an official language, and the maintenance of distinct religious court systems are all testimony to Israel's presumption of cultural and normative pluralism and tolerance. However, a closer examination reveals a slightly different reality.

Thus, whereas de jure Israel is a nation-state par excellence, de facto it is a binational state. This dualism is clearly reflected in the types of citizenship strategies adopted by the state. In terms of political and civic rights, Israel maintains a liberal-based citizenship strategy, dispensing the same rights to all individuals regardless of group identity. For social rights, however, Israel has chosen a quasi-differentiated or collective-based citizenship strategy, dispensing rights toward groups on the basis of collective identity. Accordingly, the Palestinians, Israel's dominant national minority (constituting approximately 17 percent of the population), do not enjoy any particular civic or political rights not dispensed to all other citizens regardless of group identity. They qualify for no special treatment in terms of the right to political association or political participation: Israel maintains no affirmative action policies, nor does it allocate predetermined political positions to any group in particular. However, they do enjoy certain collective social rights. They enjoy the right to study and speak their national language, Arabic. Both primary and secondary school is conducted in Arabic, and citizens may choose to speak Arabic in any contact with public officials or public offices, including the Parliament. In addition, the Israeli state acknowledges the sovereignty of the Muslim, Christian, and other religious courts and law vis-à-vis the Arab population, much in the same way as it acknowledges the sovereignty of the Jewish religious courts and law vis-à-vis the Jewish population. Thus, the three primary spheres of social rights—language, education, and religion—are dispensed in Israel in accordance to one's collective national identity.

Despite the implementation of two strategies, aimed supposedly at establishing equality in the state, the Palestinian population is both marginalized within society and discriminated against. According to most socioeconomic indicators, the Palestinians in Israel fare way below their Jewish counterparts: this is true for income, education, employment, and political representation. The array of government services allotted to them is below the level of those allotted to centers of Jewish population. They live mainly in Palestinian towns such as Nazareth or in villages. There is no integrated settlement in the country, aside from the mixed cities of Haifa, Jerusalem, and Jaffa. But even there the Palestinian residents live separately from the Jews (Peled 1992, Bishara 1993).

Clearly, then, the tension between the universalist and particularist elements of the Israeli state render the distribution of rights unequal and biased in favor of the Jewish citizens of the state, and, ultimately, neither citizenship strategy—individual or collective—affords the Palestinians inclusion within Israeli society. When Tawfiq Tubi noted in 1952 that "Citizenship is given first of all to the population that was born in the country," he was reflecting an instinctual identification between belonging to the "country" and belonging to the "state" (quoted in Segev 1984, 56).

This identity was never instinctual in Israel. On the contrary, Israel was established through an inborn *distinction* between country, statehood, and citizenship. Indeed, the state did not evolve out of the struggles of the country and its inhabitants, but rather the state was imagined, its members created or "ingathered," and ultimately sovereignty was forcefully imposed against the wishes of most of the local inhabitants. All of this resulted in the fact that citizenship was conceived, from the outset, as a natural right (along with other such rights as liberty, life, possessions, etc.) not of members of the country, but only of the "ingathered" members of the state. To all others, citizenship was seen as conditional, and their civic rights were distributed at the discretion of the state (Pappe 1995, 621).

In Israel, we then find a good example of a case where citizenship does not necessarily serve as an inclusionary mechanism and where citizenship is actually incapable of seriously combating the structures of social inequality. Indeed, citizenship itself, its content and parameters, embody the structure of social inequality.

The Development of Citizenship

In Benedict Anderson's (1991) unassuming but pathbreaking book on nationalism, he provides a novel definition of the nation: the nation is an imagined community—imagined, he argues, as both sovereign and limited. It is imagined in the sense of a mental invention, yet not fabricated; it is a community in the sense that it inspires feelings of solidarity; it is limited insofar as the world is divided into many separate nations; and finally it is sovereign because it commands ultimate loyalty. In his attempt to explain how nationalism has come to dominate political reality, Anderson argues that nationalism is a historical outcome of various spontaneous historical processes that occurred toward the end of the eighteenth century, but which, having appeared, "became modular, capable of being transplanted, with varying degrees of self-consciousness, to a great variety of social terrains, to merge with a correspondingly wide variety of political and ideological constellations" (14). The establishment and then extension of citizenship status created an imaginary community similar both in its characteristics and in its historical significance to the imagined national community identified by Anderson. In fact, to a large extent, neither the imagined national community nor that of citizenship would have been *imaginable* without each other. Inherent in the notion of sovereignty that lies at the heart of Anderson's definition is the premise of equal participation, and equal participation is at the very least the sine qua non of citizenship (B. Anderson 1991). Citizenship, from its inception, aspired to create not merely a community of rights but a community of identity, membership in which would bestow both meaning and well-being. Thus, as most theorists of citizenship have noted, the development of citizenship and the development of the nation are inextricably linked. Any attempt to understand citizenship—both theoretically and empirically—must take its inherent relationship with the nation into account.

Historically, citizenship was established throughout the eighteenth and nineteenth centuries. It sought to create a community, coextensive with most residents of the state, who would have equal access to the benefits and goods available through residency in the state. Citizenship developed against the fundamental hierarchical worldview of the feudal and then absolutist eras, most notably against the notion of ascriptive rights and the religious primacy of the church. As a basic implement of the emerging bourgeois capitalist class, citizenship developed through a series of gradually inclusionary acts. It served simultaneously to strengthen the centralized rational state and, through the establishment of an equal public sphere, to allow for the expansion of a fundamentally unequal, market-driven civil society (Poggi 1990). The states that emerged from the kingdoms in France, England, Portugal, Spain, and Sweden were nation-states. The nation-state, in this original conception, allowed for rational administration, secured the fundamental rights necessary for free individual and collective action, and provided for a community of belonging that took the place of the previous local communities (Barbalet 1988). This community was a civic-national one.

It is unsurprising, therefore, that the study of citizenship has traditionally focused on two issues. The first concerns the parameters of the community defined by citizenship, and the second concerns the nature of the rights allocated by it. These two research concerns reflect the dual function of citizenship: to establish the existence of a limited community, distinguished from other such communities and capable of inspiring in its members a certain sense of solidarity and loyalty to the state; and to define the substance of the community—the nature of the rights allocated to the citizens and the different corresponding responsibilities expected of them.

What one scholar has called "traditional orthodoxy," represents the dominant way of thinking about citizenship which emerged after World War II, which marks the beginning of more systematic social science thinking about citizenship (Kymlicka and Norman 1994, 257–89). This orthodoxy, reflected most clearly in the writing of T. H. Marshall, is characterized by two main tenets.

1. "People can be full members and participants in the common life of society only if their basic needs are met" (Marshall 1965). These basic needs corresponded to different types of rights, which Marshall distinguished as civic, political, and social. He identified full citizenship only where all three categories were granted. As later critiques noted, Marshall's citizens were basically passive recipients of rights and not active participants in the promotion of the public good.

2. Citizenship was seen as both premised on and capable of establishing an integrated political community. It was posited "as a shared identity that would integrate previously excluded groups within . . . society and provide a source of national unity" (Kook 1995a, 5). All other identities, be they cultural or class based, were to be subsumed within this general civic identity. The political community was *the* community in more ways than one. It was paramount both in its expectations of allegiance and in its capacity to confer power through rights and access to resources. Unity and integration were perceived as both a premise of citizenship and an outcome of it (ibid.).

Both tenets share the assumptions that the main divisions that citizenship needs to combat are socioeconomic and that the best way to conduct this battle is through the equitable distribution of rights to individuals. A number of central transformations in the nature of politics, particularly but not exclusively in the West, have, however, altered both the academic and political agenda concerning citizenship. With the expansion of the welfare state and the decline of class-based politics, on the one hand, and the rise of immigration-related problems and sectarian politics, on the other, citizenship is less and less seen as a class-based vehicle for combating social inequality and increasingly as a vehicle for the advancement of cultural, racial, or religious minorities. This is obviously most clear—indeed, self-evident—in the case of excluded minorities, i.e., legal and illegal immigrants. For immigrants, citizenship is a highly valued good, attainment of which promises both entry into the targeted country as well as access to a variety of social and economic goods.

Citizenship as a vehicle for minority advancement is central in the struggles not only of *excluded* minorities, but also of those who are already at least partially included. Different minority groups, who share in the citizenship status, channel their demands for increased inclusion through the defining concepts and criteria of citizenship. As was the case for disenfranchised economic classes and for excluded immigrants, the struggle for equal citizenship for included minorities is aimed both at a more equitable distribution of rights and at increased inclusion in the community of membership. Thus, the battles of the economically disenfranchised classes to extend citizenship rights have been replaced by the struggles of discriminated minorities for increased and sometimes even overrepresentation and distribution of rights. Hence, the central question that emerges is whether citizenship has the capacity to overcome social inequalities that result in different forms of cultural or national disparity.

This political agenda has generated a new academic agenda, which roots itself in a critique of the previous intellectual orthodoxy. The fundamental critique of the liberal approach, articulated very much within this newly emerging political agenda, is that it fails to account for the existence of differences within society that perhaps cannot be accommodated into a general shared identity. The theorists who level this critique, generally referred to in the literature as cultural pluralists, argue that increasingly different types of groups feel excluded from society and from the institution of citizenship not because of their socio*economic* identity, but because of their socio*cultural* identity—or, rather, difference. Citizenship, they argue, should take account of these differences. A shared citizenship can only be a differentiated one. These studies have focused on the problems of different types of minorities: sexual, gender, ethnic, religious, and national. It is precisely what they have identified as the failure of liberal citizenship to extend its rights equally amongst discriminated and disenfranchised minorities that has brought them to devise alternative citizenship strategies (Kymlicka 1995, Phillips 1995, Young 1990).

The general category *differentiated citizenship* includes a variety of mechanisms. Of the different conceptions discussed, the most relevant to the case at hand involves the recognition of collective cultural rights *alongside* individual rights. This idea posits, simply, that separate and distinct cultural groups within the state deserve special rights as a group in addition to the array of rights they enjoy as individual citizens of the state. This is the idea behind the accommodation of small religious groups and their practices, affirmative action, and, of course, language and special educational rights (Kymlicka 1995, chap. 2). There are basically two rationales behind this concept. The first is that certain cultural or religious groups warrant these rights as a means of cultural or religious expression and that the "right" to culture should be acknowledged as basic a right as any other political or civic one.

Proponents of differentiated citizenship argue that the differences between groups, often embedded within a history of oppression and discrimination, render equality in the public sphere meaningless. As Marion Young (1990), a strong proponent of differentiated citizenship, argues:

In a society where some groups are privileged while others are oppressed, insisting that as citizens persons should leave behind their particular affiliations and experiences to adopt a general point of view serves only reinforce the privilege: for the perspective and interests of the privileged will tend to dominate this unified public, marginalizing or silencing those of other groups. (257)

The types of group rights that she promotes would entail, in practice, such measures as public funds for advocacy groups, guaranteed representation in political bodies, and veto rights over specific policies that affect the group directly—all measures aimed at reducing inequality based in group differences.

Kymlicka (1995) modifies this argument by distinguishing between three types of differentiated demands, which correspond to three categories of rights: for political representation, for cultural rights, and for differing degrees of self-government. The first two, he argues, are premised on the belief that the said group had either been historically disadvantaged or that the cultural practices of the group prevent it from being integrated into the norms of the dominant culture. Therefore, both categories of demands are fundamentally seen as measures that are aimed at enabling the members of the group to fully integrate into society either through the rectifying of former discriminatory practices through such measures as affirmative action, for example, or through the acknowledging of cultural practices, such as different dress codes, dietary needs, or religious practices, to allow the members to feel equal within the general community (chap. 4).

Kymlicka distinguishes these two types of differentiated demands from the third one—self-government. In this case, the demands are based on a sense of separate cultural and political identity and are fundamentally aimed at exclusion from society. They are premised on a different identity that is encompassing enough to maintain separate institutions—be they cultural, political, or economic. They are thus anti-integrationist in their essence. According to Kymlicka, only this latter category poses a threat to the stability of democratic regimes, because even when it does not aim at it, it often results in, the disintegration of the community.

What sense of identity does citizenship establish, and how does it stand in relation to other competing identities? To what extent is citizenship capable of inspiring the desire to participate in promoting the public good among its members and to engage in civic participation? These questions gain in significance when confronted with the constraints placed on citizenship in a multicultural context. The recent theories of differentiated citizenship highlight the fact that the reality of cultural or even national pluralism can perhaps be accommodated to the establishment of a shared citizenship community, but alternative mechanisms are necessary to achieve that goal. Two important constraints should be noted:

First, the promotion of collective cultural rights by the state entails not merely a commitment to integration and full equality, but also a commitment to allocate adequate resources to this endeavor. This is no simple task. Bilingual education, for example, needs schools, teachers, and many resources. Often, the groups demanding such resources are openly critical of the dominant national cultural norms and even at times hostile toward the state. In such cases, states might be unwilling or at the least reluctant to allocate significant funds to appease their demands. This situation may easily result in the allocation of the right without the necessary funding to back it up. The case of Israel illustrates the dangers in such a situation.

Second, the dispensation of any type of collective right should entail serious consideration of the impact this right might have on potential integration or disintegration of the society. This consideration is clearly highlighted in the cases of national minorities. Often, even "thin" demands for cultural rights or political representation are merely compromise requests veiling the ultimate desire for differing degrees of political autonomy. Because political autonomy clearly threatens the integration of the state, states will be suspicious of granting such rights to those minorities who possibly harbor such a desire.

Finally, given the inherent relationship between citizenship and the nation, and given the fact that in most cases the parameters of citizenship were developed in the context of the constitutive nation, citizenship is inherently incapable of extending equal treatment to members of a self-consciously differentiated nation; this inability is one of the central limitations of citizenship, which is more often than not national citizenship. Equal rights cannot be extended within the context of the civic community because that community was predefined in either explicit but more often implicit national terms. Therefore, in most cases, the efforts of national minorities to achieve equality through citizenship politics will remain frustrated, which is very well illustrated in the case of Israel and its Palestinian citizens, discussed in the following section.

The Limitations of Citizenship in Israel

The theoretical discussion above presented different citizenship strategies commonly aimed at promoting civic equality within culturally diverse societies. In Israel, two basic citizenship strategies are utilized. The first is rooted in the liberal approach, which posits that equality be attained through an individually based distribution of rights. This strategy governs the distribution of civic and political rights. The second is the collective or differentiated approach, which acknowledges that equality requires the distribution of certain rights differentially to different cultural or national groups. This is the strategy that governs certain social rights in Israel—namely, language, religion, and education. Clearly, the relevant group distinction that governs the distribution of such rights is that between Jews and Palestinians.[1]

The formative period during which Israel developed its citizenship policies toward the Palestinian populations was the first two decades of its existence. It was during this period that relevant civic legislation was passed: the Law of Return (1950), the Nationality Law (1952), Jewish National Fund Law (1953), the Israel Lands Administration Law (1960), and the Law and Government Ordinance of 1948, declaring official languages of the state. At the same time, this was the period of military rule over the Palestinian population (1948–66). Clearly overwhelmed by the reality of sovereignty, war, and the existence of a significant hostile national minority within their boundaries, Israel considered few other alternatives to this policy, which in effect isolated and controlled the Palestinian population to such an extent that they were virtually excluded from the realm of Israeli social, political, and economic life. Although some debate emerged within the Israeli political establishment later on as to the advantages of continuing this type of control, military rule was maintained virtually unopposed for the first decade of its implementation (Pappe 1995). The fundamental rationale underlying the military rule was the belief that the Palestinians would potentially serve as a fifth column within society, undermining its security and well-being at any given opportunity. For the Israelis, the national identity of the Palestinians was the dominant—to the point of exclusivity—characteristic of their identity.

Various documents, speeches, and formal policy guidelines show that the attitudes toward the Palestinians during this period are characterized by ignorance and imbued with stereotypic projections of "the Arab." One the one hand, he is to be feared—a potential fifth column, an enemy, a source of terror, and so on. (Interestingly, this portrait ran against clear evidence of passivity and lack of political involvement [Lustick 1980].) On the other hand, he is primitive, ignorant, the "other" who is characterized by exotic and Oriental characteristics—proud, traditional, and so on. This attitude

---

1. An additional cleavage also governs rights distribution in Israel, that between religious and secular Jews. Accordingly, there exists a separate religious educational system that is accorded to religious Jews as a collective right. This topic of research is interesting, but beyond the purview of this article.

was a typical modernization or colonial attitude. Often these perceptions colluded together: the proud, nationalist Palestinian merged with the obsequious, conniving one, resulting in such statements as that made by Golda Meir: "when I see an Israeli Arab pledging allegiance to the state three times a day I feel sick . . . and I feel the same way I do when I see an assimilating Jew" (quoted in Benziman and Mansour 1992, 19).

Thus, from the outset, the Jewish leadership and government of Israel would posit the Palestinians' reluctance or unwillingness to incorporate themselves as full citizens as the basis for Israel's unwillingness to accord them equal civic status. The inherent limitations of Israeli citizenship vis-à-vis the Palestinians were legitimized by such arguments as: "They are as yet unwilling"; "They suffer from a dual loyalty"; "they have not gone through a spiritual transformation toward authentic integration into the state" (Benziman and Mansour 1992, 20). The Israelis accused the Palestinian that it was his fault Israel did not grant him equal citizenship; after all, he was unwilling to behave like a loyal citizen. But at the same time they maintained the inherent belief (which was unconditional) that the Arab would never be able to fulfill authentic civic allegiance because by so doing he would betray himself.

Historical evidence shows that there was a debate, at the time, between the more liberal-minded policymakers and the security-oriented ones. The former argued for modification of the military rule and for the at least partial integration of the Palestinians within Israeli society (Pappe 1995, 634; Segev 1984, 56–83). Nonetheless, basic tenets enjoyed unanimous support. Primary among those tenets were, of course, the definition of Israel as Jewish state and the legitimacy of the government's right to expropriate land and property and to put it under the custodian guardianship of the state for Jewish settlements only. These two examples highlight the inherent difficulties in operationalizing a policy of equal citizenship in Israel.

Although certain amendments were made in key legislation, the incoherent and often ambivalent perception of the relationship between the state and its national minority has remained more or less intact. Consequently, what this discussion implies is that the fundamental limitations on citizenship imposed by the ethnonational definitions included within it are exacerbated and fortified by the sociopsychological and political attitudes toward the Palestinian population and its potential relationship with the Jewish majority. These two conditions—the Jewish definition of the state and the fundamental perception of and attitude toward this population— render citizenship inherently limited in its capacity to implement equality in society.

In this section, I demonstrate these limitations by analyzing four separate examples of rights. The first concerns the basic right to citizenship as exemplified in the Law of Return and the Citizenship Law. The second and third are basic civic and political rights—the right guiding property ownership and the right guiding political participation. Both are found within the liberal individualist approach to citizenship. The analysis illustrates that, despite the liberal premise, the advantages of Jews are inherent within the definition of these rights. The fourth right is a classic social right, concerning language, and is guided by the so-called collective approach. Also, close examination of the outcomes of this right uncovers the implicit advantages to Jews accrued from this type of distribution.

The Law of Return

The most prominent manifestation of Israel's Jewish state-identity is manifested in what is called the Law of Return. In terms of concrete implications concerning equality of rights within Israel, the Law of Return has minor ramifications. In a different sense, however, it is this law that is most fundamental in determining the discriminatory nature of rights distribution within Israel. It is this law that is the most explicit in stating the inherent connection between the State of Israel, as a legal entity, and the Jewish people of the world. It remains until today the primary symbol of Israel as a Jewish state.

The Law of Return was drafted in 1950, two years after the declaration of Jewish political independence. In its first version, it stated: "Every Jew has the right to come to this country as an *oleh* [Jewish immigrant]" (section 1). Section 4 describes the scope of the law as follows: "Every Jew who has immigrated into this country before the coming into force of this law, and every Jew who was born in this country, whether before or after the coming into force of this law, shall be deemed to be a person who has come to this country as an *oleh* under this law." Thus, in this law, the right of fundamental and natural membership is the natural right *not* of citizens of the state, but of Jews.

At the time the law was passed, its significance for the emerging state was very central because citizenship was already granted to non-Jews, the formal enemies of the Jewish community, in 1949. Hence, the different ways in which citizenship was attained and the differing legal reasoning adopted for each way caused some legal complications. Nowadays, however, these distinctions have been almost completely amended. Consequently, the distinction in the manner of acquiring citizenship is no longer as central. However, even presently, the ability to attain citizenship by return, which is equated with true membership in the nation, is possible only for Jews because this type of membership is equated with the act of "returning" to the homeland—an act possible only if one is Jewish.

To fully comprehend the ramifications of this type of membership one must consider an accompanying bill to the Law of Return—namely, the Nationality Law, passed in 1952. "The special feature of a people gathering from its dispersion in its historical homeland is expressed in this law by the provision which grants the absolute right of Israeli citizenship to an *oleh* under the law of return, that is to every Jew who comes to settle in Israel, and to every Jew who was born there" (*5710 Hatzaot Hok*, 194). This law is the basis of the nationality distinction in Israeli ID cards designating each citizen according to nationality: Jewish, Arab, Druz, and other. Hence, all Jewish citizens of Israel bear the nationality designation *Jewish;* most Arab citizens bear the designation *Arab;* and rather ironically and anach-ronistically, all non-Arab and non-Jewish citizens bear the nationality desig-nation of their previous nationality—e.g., Polish, German, or Swedish.

The lack of separation between religion and nationality, as it is manifested in the Law of Return and the Nationality Law is testimony to a larger issue. The essence of these laws corresponds to the ideological foundations of Israel's political existence as well as to the primary goals of the Israeli and related Zionist institutions: the establishment of a state dedicated to the "engathering of the exiles" and not necessarily the well-being of its citizen members. The Law of Return is then clearly considered the central legal pillar of the state and its related institutions. David Ben-Gurion, in present-ing the Law of Return and Nationality Law package, contended:

> The Law of Return and the Nationality Law which are before you are closely connected and have a common ideological basis, that derives from the histori-cal uniqueness of the state of Israel, a uniqueness that relates to the past and the future. . . . These two laws determine the special character and purpose of the State of Israel which carries the message of the redemption of Israel. (*6 Divrei Haknesset* 2035)

For the framers of these laws, the implications concerning the non-Jewish population were clear—if not consciously intended. The equation of the Jewish nationality with the core nationality of the state, and denying it any secular interpretation in no uncertain terms, excluded all non-Jewish indi-viduals—citizens and noncitizens—from actual or potential membership.

Property Rights

If one were to list two of the most fundamental tenets of Zionist ideol-ogy, which were later to become the pillars of Israeli political society, the first would undoubtedly be the Law of Return, and the second would most likely pertain to control of the land for Jewish settlement only. Indeed, throughout the prestate years, any activity that pertained to the land—whether it was cultivation or ownership—transcended in its significance the mere physical connection to the land and came to symbolize the psychological transformation that accorded to the Jew during the process of national liberation.

Since the declaration of Israel's independence in 1948, extensive land appropriations have been enacted. Up until today, the Israeli government is free to appropriate privately held land for government purposes under the British Defence (Emergency) Regulations, 1945, which have never been revoked.[2]

The various emergency regulations with which Israel appropriates land are used almost exclusively against Arab claims. This type of expropriation relies mainly on the "security" clause as its basis.[3] These regulations are nonetheless not formally discriminatory against non-Jews, in theory if not in practice. There is, however, another prominent legal instrument that guides the usage of state land and that is directly derivative from the definition of corporate national identity and, hence, discriminatory against non-Jews. This legal instrument is the charter of the Jewish National Fund.

The Jewish National Fund (JNF) was established in 1901 in order to purchase land in Palestine for the purpose of Jewish settlement. It was established as an official organ of the Zionist movement, and in 1907 registered as a company limited by guarantee in Britain. In the first decade of its operations in the Ottoman empire its land purchases were rather modest. But following World War I and the dismantling of that empire, which in Palestine was replaced by the British Mandate government guided by the

2. A number of legal statutes were used in order to expropriate Arab land. These include, primarily, the Absentees' Property Law of 1950 and the Land Acquisition (Validation of Acts and Compensation) Law of 1953. Also utilized were certain British Mandatory Laws, such as the Lands (Acquisition for Public Purposes) ordinance passed in 1943 as well as Defence (Emergency) Regulation 125. With the help of these laws, the State of Israel managed to recreate a reality in which, in addition to sovereignty over the land, they gained ownership as well. Indeed, today, fifty years following the war of independence, the state owns more than 90 percent of land in Israel. This fact, incidentally, implies that neither Arab nor Jewish citizens of the state own much of their own land; as explained below, even Jews are reduced, in most cases, to the status of lessees. See Jiryis (1976).

3. This clause indeed was the basis in the prominent case of Ikrit and Biram, which occurred in the midst of the war of independence. In the case of Ikrit and Biram, two Palestinian villages in Upper Galilee, the village lands were appropriated despite the fact that the villagers were friendly to the Jewish and later to Israeli authorities. The appropriation was ruled as illegal, and the Supreme Court ordered the lands returned to their Arab owners. This ruling has yet to be implemented, and the land has not been returned. See Ozacky-Lazar (1993).

Balfour Declaration, JNF operations took off, buying lands from private and communal Arab owners for the express purpose of Jewish settlement. However, in line with the collectivist sentiment of the Zionist movement at the time, the land purchased was not transferred to Jews in the form of private property, but rather it was to be "the perpetual property of the Jewish people" and was thus parceled out through a system of leasing.

In the first years of the state, in addition to the land that had been purchased by the Jewish National Fund prior to 1948 (approximately 936,000 dunams), the government transferred much of the land it had appropriated from the Palestinians both during and after the war to the Jewish National Fund. 101,942 dunams were transferred in 1949 (98.5 percent of which were rural—agricultural—lands); 1,271,734 dunams were transferred in October 1950 (again, most of which were agricultural lands). By the end of 1951, the Jewish National Fund had acquired more than three and a half million dunams of land (Granott 1936, Orni 1981).

In 1953, the Jewish National Fund Law was passed, which transferred title to these lands to an equivalent Israeli company called the Keren Kayemet Le'Israel. These lands were to be administered in the spirit of the charter of the Jewish National Fund, which clearly stated that all lands were held "for the purpose of settling Jews" (Orni 1981, 22). This statement has long been interpreted as meaning that no Keren Kayemet land would be leased out to non-Jews. By the late 1950s, along with the Keren Kayemet lands, the state owned more than 90 percent of the land of Israel.

In 1960, a law was passed whereby all Israel lands were to be administered by the Israel Lands Administration (ILA)—including, of course, the Jewish National Fund lands. Following the passage of this law, a formal covenant was signed between the government and the Jewish National Fund, establishing the terms under which the land was to be administered in the future. According to this covenant, "All state lands must be administered according to the principle that land is not sold, but is leased according to the land policy fixed by the Israel Lands Council. Jewish National Fund lands must also be administered in accordance with the memorandum and articles of association of the Jewish National Fund" (Orni 1981, 22). By the mid-1990s, approximately 19 percent of Israel lands, which are administered by the ILA, are Jewish National Fund lands and are administered "in accordance with the articles of association of the Jewish National Fund"—the implication being, of course, that these lands cannot be leased out to non-Jews. This has very severe ramifications for the Palestinian citizens.

To begin with, none of the Jewish National Fund lands can be leased to Palestinians. While this amounts to roughly 19 percent, it includes many of the best agricultural lands in Israel, which, were it not for the clauses of the covenant, could be leased to Palestinian farmers. Moreover, owners of private homes built on Jewish National Fund lands cannot sell their houses to non-Jewish buyers. Each transaction must be authorized by the ILA, and in the case of non-Jews the right to sell (or actually the right to transfer the lease) is denied. In addition, the majority of the remainder of land in Israel is owned by the state and administered by the ILA. The leasing of this land to Palestinians, although permissible, is intensely problematic. Aside from various technical reasons, many of the guidelines that regulate the leasing of public lands to individuals for both settlement and agricultural purposes are ideological. Given the ideological emphasis on Jewish settlement ("the redemption of the land" and so on), it is not surprising that since the establishment of the state, even though the Palestinian population has increased by almost fivefold, no new Palestinian agricultural settlements have been established, but many new Jewish settlements have been erected. In 1948–67, fifty new Jewish settlements were established within the so-called Green Line. In the aftermath of the "Land Day" demonstrations in 1976,[4] the government advisor on Arab affairs announced that no more additional Arab land would be appropriated by the state. This pronouncement, however, has not quelled the rumors or the leaked government plans for further Jewish settlement in Arab areas. A most recent plan was the "Seven Star" plan, which was proposed in 1991 in the wake of the massive wave of Jewish immigration from the former Soviet Union. This plan was to establish a network of new Jewish settlements that would ease the housing problem that arose in the wake of the immigration. However, the objective was twofold: alleviate the housing problem and "dilute" the dense Arab settlement in a region known as Wadi Ara. In a curious twist, recently, a young Palestinian couple managed to purchase a house, against the efforts of the members of one of the settlements, Katzir, which has set a significant precedent that may have an impact on the future of Jewish National Fund lands. Notwithstanding this incident, since the establishment of the state, Arab ownership of land has not increased, but rather, taking various episodic expropriations into account, has decreased.

4. Another prominent case is known as the case of "Area 9." In this case, the state attempted to appropriate roughly 100,000 dunams, also in the heavily Arab-populated region of Galilee. The attempt resulted in violent conflict between the army and the Palestinian residents; and six people were killed, and dozens were wounded. As a result of a public uproar, a compromise settlement was arrived at. The event, however, has been commemorated by Palestinians in Israel as "Land Day" and is observed yearly with mass demonstrations. See Kretzmer (1990, 60–66).

The Right to Political Association

Despite the exclusion of non-Jewish citizens from the Israeli national community, as exemplified in the Law of Return and in the right to land ownership, all Israeli governments have always prided themselves in granting one of the most fundamental and, for many, defining rights of democracy—the right to participate in elections, as voters and as potential candidates. Hence, the right to free, open, and periodic elections is a right that both Palestinians and Jews share in the State of Israel.

For the first seven rounds of elections (1949–69), most of the Arab votes were distributed among the Israeli Communist Party (Maki, later to become Rakach and later Hadash) and various Mapai and Mapam satellite lists. These satellite lists were formed by the said two main labor movement parties, Mapai and Mapam. Although headed by Arab candidates, they were for all intents and purposes extensions of the leading parties in terms of positions and coalition alignment. They are commonly described as satellite lists because of the patronage relationship between them and the Mapai and Mapam parties (Jiryis 1976, 162–63). The Israel Communist Party, however, was long considered the only party to truly represent Arab interests, despite the fact that some of its leaders were Jewish, until the appearance of the Progressive List for Peace (PLP) in 1984. In the elections to the Eleventh Knesset held that year, the PLP was established as a joint Arab-Jewish party perceived as a rival to the Communist Party in representing "real" Arab interests as well as in taking a relatively radical stand on the Palestinian issue.

The absence of local independent Arab lists may be perceived as somewhat of a conundrum in light of the growing level of politicization and the relatively high level of voter participation (both independently and in comparison with their Jewish counterparts). A survey of the development of the legislation pertaining to the right to free association will help explain the relative paucity of independent Palestinian lists. This review of the legal statutes concerning the right of political association and the rules regulating this activity reveals a structural discriminatory aspect that favors members of the Israeli corporate identity (i.e., of the Jewish nation) over nonmembers. Three cases mark the deterioration of the Arab's political rights.

The first attempt to organize politically by an independent Arab list was the case of al-Ard. The group, officially called Usrat al-Ard (Family of the Earth), was founded by two members of the Popular Front, a local group banned by Ben-Gurion at the end of 1959. It started out by publishing weekly reports for Palestinians that were highly critical of Israeli policies and that encouraged Palestinians to take their own issues in hand. They were identified as sympathetic to Arab nationalism and to the Nasserite movement. Their publications were confiscated, and all attempts at locally organizing lecture and study groups were met with severe objections from the Israeli authorities (Jiryis 1976, 187–90). Finally, in 1964, the two founders officially announced the establishment of the al-Ard Movement, hoping to be able to organize Arab nationalists into a list that would run for the next Knesset elections. The district commissioner refused to register their association on the grounds that it was unlawful in its aims. They appealed their case to the Supreme Court, which dismissed their petition. The basis for the ruling was that they intended, albeit implicitly, to persuade people of their platform through "subversive and hostile activity" and that it was in line with "Arab nationalistic propaganda . . . urging the destruction of Israel." Al-Ard was subsequently declared an unlawful association (Benziman and Mansour 1992, Zureik 1979).

The second case concerns the Socialist list, which was composed of many former al-Ard members and hoped to run for the elections to the Sixth Knesset in 1965. It was disqualified from running for elections by the chairman of the Central Elections Committee. The grounds for the refusal were that it was "an unlawful association because its promoters deny the integrity of the State of Israel and its very existence" (*Yardor* v. *Central Elections Committee* 1965).

The list appealed the refusal, and the Supreme Court, in what came to be known as the Yardor ruling, denied the appeal. The substance of the leading opinion, that of Chief Justice Agranat, is very significant. Essentially, he voiced the opinion that Israel was and is established not merely as a sovereign state but as a Jewish state in Eretz Yisrael and that "a list of candidates who reject the above fundamental principle, does not have the right, as a list, to participate in the elections for the house of representatives" (*Yardor* v. *Central Elections Committee* 1965, 387). The underlying rationale was that no regime could authorize the existence of a group or movement intent on undermining the existence and raison d'être of the regime. As such, the interpretation given to the opinion, that denying the Jewish existence and nature of the state was illegal, was but one way of understanding a more general statement. The conclusive opinion on this matter would occur twenty years later, with the Neiman case.

The Neiman case arose when the Central Elections Committee for the Eleventh Knesset decided to disqualify two lists—the Kahane Kach list and the PLP. The former disqualification was based on the racial arguments promoted by Rabbi Meir Kahane, and the rationale for the latter was that the list "believes in principles that endanger the . . . preservation of [Israel's] distinctiveness as a Jewish state." The decision of the committee was appealed by both lists. The PLP won its appeal, while the Kach list lost. In accepting the appeal, the judges implied that only lists dedicated to the *physical* destruction of the state would be deemed illegal. However, as a direct result of the Neiman case, the law governing political parties was altered in the form of Amendment No. 9 to the Basic Law: The Knesset (1985).

> A list of candidates shall not participate in the elections for the Knesset if its aims or actions, expressly or by implication, point to one of the following:
>   1. denial of the existence of the state of Israel as the state of the Jewish people.
>   2. denial of the democratic nature of the state.
>   3. incitement to racism. (Section 7a of Basic Law: the Knesset)

Undoubtedly, the implications of this amendment are more far-reaching then any previous court ruling or, for that matter, legal statute. In essence, this amendment granted legal status not merely to Israel's existence as a Jewish state, but placed a legal boundary on the limits to free association and free speech. For the first time, the Knesset put limits on political association that transcend the more acceptable "security" reasons—i.e., the need to safeguard Israel's democracy from those who want to destroy it. Thus, the amendment implies that *redefining* Israel as a state that belongs to its citizens is tantamount to attacking Israel's right to exist. Similarly, any list would be disqualified if it forwarded a binational arrangement to the Arab-Jewish relations within Israel. The majority opinion of the Supreme Court judges was that the definition of Israel as a state of the Jewish people was dependent on three characteristics: "a majority of Jews in the country; preference for Jews, over other groups, to return to their land; and a reciprocal relationship between the state and the Jews of the Diaspora (Kretzmer 1990, 30). Rejection of one of these characteristics automatically disqualifies a political association from running for election.

The Hadash list, the PLP list, and Darawshe's list, the Arab Democratic Party (founded in 1988), which are identified as the "Arab" lists, all incorporate this amendment in their platforms. They all call for the establishment of "two states for two nations," clearly implying that the State of Israel exists for the Jewish nation and calling for the establishment of a Palestinian state, alongside of Israel, which would exist for the Palestinian nation. Most recent developments mark a new direction, however. In the 1996 elections to the Fourteenth Parliament, a number of new lists were formed. The primary characteristic shared by many of them was the emphasis on the identity of the state. Demands ranged from recognition of the Palestinians as a national minority, and thus the need for varying degrees of cultural or even political autonomy, to demands for transforming Israel into a "state for all its citizens" rather than maintaining it as a Jewish state. The most direct and influential party in this context was the National Democratic Assembly headed by Dr. Azmi Bishara, a Palestinian intellectual and university professor at Bir Zeit University. This group ultimately merged with Hadash and gained a third of the Palestinian vote.[5] These concerns were reflected in many of the other groups that organized in this election campaign and definitely marked a new trend in the political discourse of Palestinians in Israel. The demands for cultural or political autonomy, as demands for the redefinition of Israeli citizenship, reflect the awareness and acknowledgment of the limitations of Israeli citizenship as it is defined today and thus mark a definite shift from the previous belief that civic equality is possible within the parameters of citizenship within the Jewish state (Ozacky-Lazar and Ghanem 1996).

In sum, the definition of the basic norms that underlie the State of Israel contradicts a fundamental tenet of democracy, which posits the sovereignty of the citizens of the state. The notion of a state as a mechanism that exists to further the interests of its citizens is redefined, *legally*, so as to read that the state exists to further the interests of the member nation. Non-Jewish citizens of Israel do not qualify for this membership, and hence the inference is that Israel is *not their state*.

Thus, as argued in this section, any reform of the Israeli legal *system* so as to make it more equitable would necessarily have to incorporate a reform of the legal *code*, which embodies within it certain laws that are testimony to the message of the declaration of independence—namely, defining Israel as a "Jewish state."

Language Rights

Designation of the official languages in Israel was actually inherited, and the status of those languages is contained in Article 82 of the Palestine Order-in-Council (1922), which designates three official languages—English, Arabic, and Hebrew. Although the article itself was never revoked, Section 15(b) of the Law and Government Ordinance (1948) repeals the status of English. Israel thus formally recognizes two official languages: Hebrew and Arabic (Kretzmer 1990, 165).

5. In the 1999 elections, the National Democratic Alliance headed by Dr. Azmi Bishara aligned with the Arab Movement for Change headed by Dr. Ahmad Tibi to form the Unified National Alliance. The alignment won two seats in the fifteenth parliament.

Nonetheless, it is widely acknowledged that for all intents and purposes, Hebrew is the primary official language of the state. The official status of Arabic by law demands that all laws and regulations must be translated into Arabic on request; that all correspondence with government offices may be conducted in Arabic; that letters may be addressed in Arabic; that Arabic may be used in the Parliament (Fisherman and Fishman 1975, 497–537). However, few of these regulations are enforced. Arabic is used on all official national symbols—including postal stamps, currency, and the plaques on some official monuments. The use of Arabic on street signs exists, but is inconsistent and can be found only in cities with a significant Arab population. Thus, for example, none of the street signs in Tel Aviv has the name written in Arabic (they are written in English and Hebrew), and even in Haifa, which is a binational city, one can find street signs in areas that are almost exclusively Jewish to be only in Hebrew. (The opposite is not to be found, however.)

Indeed, the sole area in which the official status of Arabic is enforced consistently is in education. Israel maintains three parallel public educational systems: the main one is designed for the secular Jewish population, the second for the Zionist religious Jewish population, and the third for the Palestinian citizens of the state. In the first two systems, the main language of instruction is Hebrew, and Arabic, when taught at all, is taught as a second or third language (following English and sometimes French). In the Palestinian educational system, Arabic is the main language of instruction, and Hebrew is taught as a second language. Thus, within both the primary and secondary schools of the majority of the Palestinian population in Israel, the language of instruction is Arabic: all subjects—including history, mathematics, geography, and the like—are taught in Arabic. In addition, Arabic language and literature as well as Hebrew language and literature are taught. Thus, for the first eighteen years of their lives, Palestinian citizens of Israel speak primarily Arabic: this is the language of instruction, the language of socializing, and the language at home. Although in recent years the number of hours allocated to the study of Hebrew has increased, and the grade in which instruction of Hebrew commences was changed from sixth to third, on the whole the proficiency of Palestinians in Hebrew is far lower than that of their Israeli-Jewish counterparts at the age of graduation from high school (al-Haj 1995, Benziman and Mansour 1992).

At the same time, although Arabic is the official language of school instruction, the mainstay of Israeli life—economic, political, and social—is conducted in Hebrew. This is true for both the public and private spheres. Affairs in all government offices—including all bureaucratic offices such as social security, welfare services, the Ministry of Education, and the like—are conducted in Hebrew. The language of instruction at the college and university level is Hebrew, and finally, economic life—businesses, industry, and the like—is dominated almost exclusively by Hebrew. In the economic sphere, one should add that although Arab-run business and industry are conducted in Arabic, they present a very small percentage of the country's economic structure because of the marginal socioeconomic status of this population (Shalev 1989b).

The implications are somewhat paradoxical. As Ben-Gurion himself stated, the maintenance of Arabic as a formal language and the implementation of this language as the formal language of instruction were granted as a right:

> we will not forbid [the Arabs] the use of their language in any way. . . . to be sure, this is not the way the issue is handled in most of the parliaments of the world, but we do not have to learn everything from others. There are a number of important things which we taught the world and we can be an example of a humane attitude toward the language of the minority. . . . the state must see to it that Hebrew be [not only] an official language, [but must provide the means for imparting the knowledge of Hebrew to immigrants and to all the residents of Israel] without depriving the Arab minority of the right to its own language.[6]

As Kymlicka (1995) and other theorists of collective rights argue—premised on the assumption of the centrality of the collective cultural and linguistic context to the fulfillment of the individual members' life plans—the significance of the culture and language to the identity of the members and to their ability to realize their full potential is fundamental. Given, however, the fact that Israeli society is dominated by Hebrew, then the right to language not merely does not help them advance their life plans, but actually inhibits their chances of success and attainment. The lack of proficiency in the main language of society serves to enforce the marginal status of the Palestinian citizens of Israel. This problem is reflected most clearly in their difficulties in the institutions of higher learning, where fluency in Hebrew is a necessary condition for success, and perhaps less directly but nonetheless as importantly in their ability to advance in other channels of life—business, social, and other.

An interesting aspect of this paradox is afforded by a close examination of

---

6. Representative speech of Ben-Gurion to the Parliament in 1952, in response to a suggestion made by then Herut member of parliament Raziel to make Hebrew the sole official language. Quoted in Fisherman and Fishman (1975, 505).

the psychometric exams instituted by the Israeli universities as a main entrance criterion. Recently, the supervisory committee of Arab education voiced a complaint that these exams serve to discriminate against the Arab students and bar their entry into the more selective faculties of law and medicine.[7] Indeed, although the sole language of instruction in the universities is Hebrew, the universities conduct psychometric exams in both Hebrew and Arabic. The supervisory committee, based on relative performance of Palestinian students compared with Jewish students on these exams and on testimonies by numerous Palestinian students, contend that the level of Arabic proficiency required by the Arabic exam is far higher than the level of Hebrew proficiency required by the Hebrew exam. In addition, the Arabic exam requires knowledge of three languages (Arabic, Hebrew, and English), whereas the Hebrew exam requires knowledge of only two. Furthermore, the language section in the Arabic exam is more extensive than that in the Hebrew exam, at the expense of the analytic sections.[8] The result is that choosing to take the exam in Arabic places students at an initial relative disadvantage.

To a large extent, Hechter's (1975) model of internal colonial domination, wherein economic peripheral status creates cultural peripheral status, ultimately resulting in a distinct national identity operates here in a slightly different causal interaction: economic and cultural peripheriality serve to complement each other, resulting in a distinct national-cultural and economic identity. Among other cultural markers that have developed as a result of this peripherialization and marginalization, one cannot help but note the distinct Arabic accent that most Palestinians have in Hebrew, which enables quick distinction between two ethnic groups that are otherwise indistinguishable from one another (as opposed to the distinction between blacks and whites or between indigenous and colonial populations).

Moreover, the content of the curricula approved (and designed) for both primary and secondary schools was clearly designed in such a way as to obliterate any cultural-national or even cultural-ethnic identity, which stands in stark contradiction to the contention that the designation of Arabic as an official language of education resulted from the respect of the Jewish leadership for the collective cultural-national identity of this population (al-Haj 1995, chap. 2). Indeed, it is quite curious that in the context of military rule

7. Only 5.8 percent of the national student body is Palestinian, 6 percent of the law students, 8 percent of the medicine students, 5 percent of social science students—despite the fact that they are close to 20 percent of the population. (*Statistical Abstract of Israel* 1995).

8. Based on interview with Ziad Assad, representative of the Druze students at Haifa University, 5 May 1995, and an article in *Ha'aretz*, 16 April 1995.

over this population, during which all activities—sports, education, politics—were closely regulated and controlled, the right to language was so keenly observed and granted.

Summary and Conclusions

It was the purpose of this chapter to demonstrate the limitations of citizenship in certain multicultural contexts. I argued that, in many cases, the role of the constitutive nation in the determination of citizenship renders citizenship incapable of combating inequalities that result from national differences within society. This theoretical notion was illustrated with the case of the Palestinians in Israel and the limited extent to which citizenship, as it is currently defined in Israel, is capable of eliminating the marginalized status they occupy within Israeli society.

The 1996 elections to the Israeli Parliament and the changes in the demands of some of the new Palestinian groups are clearly indicative of this point. Previous election campaigns were carried out under the general banner of fighting for equality within the parameters of citizenship and, indeed, reflected the belief among Palestinians that Israeli citizenship potentially embodied the capacity to implement equality. The platforms of many of the newly established parties and groups revealed a distinct departure from this mind-set: equality was now seen as attainable only through a redefinition of citizenship in Israel or through the formal recognition of the Palestinians as a national minority, with all that that entails.

However, as Kymlicka and other theorists of multicultural citizenship have demonstrated, demands for autonomy on behalf of national minorities invariably pose a threat to the stability and integrative function of political communities. They are also dependent on state resources for their full implementation. Granting such collective rights without adequate institutional and resource backing will result in perpetuating the inequality they supposedly set out to eliminate. Hence, from a theoretical perspective, such demands embody inherent limitations—indeed, the limitations of citizenship itself. The tentative conclusion would therefore be that demands of national minorities that reflect sincere dissatisfaction with the state will ultimately engender demands for the redefinition of citizenship. Only through a fundamental redefinition both of citizenship's membership and the measures it adopts for distributing rights will citizenship regain its original function as a social and political mechanism for equality.

13

The Contradictions of Palestinian Citizenship in Israel

Inclusion and Exclusion in the Israeli Welfare State

ZEEV ROSENHEK AND MICHAEL SHALEV

Some Problems with the "Arab Problem" in Jewish Scholarship

THE INVISIBILITY of Israel's Palestinian citizens in the viewfinder of Israeli sociology is a well-known feature of the discipline's past, now thankfully eclipsed by a decade-long wave of research. (For a fuller discussion, see Rosenhek 1998a). Traditionally guided by an implicit social map that defined the borders of "Israeli society" as synonymous with "Jewish society" (Kimmerling 1992), all but a handful of Jewish sociologists (notably Henry Rosenfeld and Sammy Smooha) treated the Arab minority as at most a footnote to the dominant Jewish text. Just as the Arab-Israeli conflict was seen largely as a matter for specialists on military and foreign-relations questions (Shafir 1996), so the study of the Arab citizenry of Israel was consigned mainly to the "orientalist" wing of the academy (Rabinowitz 1993). Insofar as sociologists or political scientists did become actively engaged, their principal interest was defined by the political concerns of the Jewish establishment: Why did so many Arabs reject the "Zionist parties" in favor of the communists? What was the import of the sense of kinship that Arab citizens came to display in their relations with the Palestinians in the Occupied Territories? Might either of these trends portend challenges to Jewish dominance of Israeli territory and the Israeli state? (See, for example, Rekhess 1989.)

After a flourish of quite substantial research activity—stimulated or complemented by the work of an increasing number of scholars who have emerged from the Palestinian minority itself (e.g., Zureik 1979, Haidar 1995, Sa'di 1992)—Jewish sociologists in Israel have fundamentally altered their approach. The Arab minority is being *endogenized;* that is, Palestinian citizens are increasingly seen as part and parcel of the society and a natural focus for research in diverse fields of inquiry. We rarely see anymore the defensiveness that to some extent underlay earlier reluctance to engage in the topic and that led those Jewish scholars who did approach it to wear the rose-colored glasses of modernization theory, bypassing issues of conflict and coercion, and presenting the Arabs' disadvantages as originating in their own backwardness. Although there are those who continue to take a benign view of the role of the state (as in two recent works by political scientists, Sandler 1995 and Landau 1993), the starting point for most Israeli researchers today is recognition of and curiosity about the economic and political disadvantages faced by the Arab population (see especially Lewin-Epstein and Semyonov 1993). Moreover, few have escaped the realization that both the ideological and institutional practices of the Israeli state have played a major part in the construction of the Arab-Jewish cleavage in Israel's stratification regime.

In this sense, Jewish scholars have, with a considerable time lag, achieved a certain convergence with the work of Arab scholars who insisted from the outset (e.g., Jiryis 1976) that Jewish-Arab inequality is deep, pervasive, and persistent, *and* that this deep divide is structurally rooted in the Zionist character of the state. In like fashion, a recent article by a Jewish scholar (Kook 1995a) argues that the exclusion of Israel's Palestinian citizens is inherent to the hegemonic (Zionist) ideology and its definition of Jewish corporate national identity. Or again, one may cite the conclusion of a new volume by a leading Palestinian researcher, who states, "The policy of discrimination derives primarily from the nature of Israel as a colonizing society and from its definition as a Jewish-Zionist state . . . anything good for the minority is seen as bad for the majority, and the reverse" (Haidar 1995, 180).[1]

There is, of course, a powerful kernel of truth to this realization. And yet, like *patriarchy* and the problem of women's subordination or *racism* and the issue of racial discrimination, in the context of majority-minority rela-

---

1. Ironically, despite this lip service to "Zionist functionalism," Haidar's book is actually a fine demonstration of the poverty of that approach.

tions in Israel, *Zionism* explains everything and nothing. The *definition of the state* is simply too general and static a category to be of much help in explicating complex and potentially dynamic realities. But there are other limitations as well.

Preoccupation with Zionism as a master explanation invites a functional analysis with all its well-known pitfalls: whatever happens can always be explained or rationalized and has no element of historical contingency; there is an expectation of and an interest in discovering continuity rather than change; and there is little analytical space for conflict and contradiction (that is, for politics).[2]

The emphasis on hegemonic ideology risks overlooking the material as well as political interests and the specific institutional practices that produce and reproduce this hegemony. It is more difficult still to entertain the notion (which has been central in the sociological literature on social closure generally and on ethnicity in particular) that ideologies of exclusivism may even originate in struggles for scarce economic and social resources (e.g., Bonacich 1972, Parkin 1974).

Zionism-centered explanations risk a kind of intellectual isolationism because by definition Israel is seen as a special case, and there is no obvious bridge to theories or comparisons that might pose new questions or offer new answers.[3]

The Potential Contributions
of a Citizenship-Based Approach

In our view, the best of the newer literature on the position of Israel's Palestinian citizens has taken one of two strategies for avoiding these analytical traps. One solution, inspired largely by Baruch Kimmerling's work (especially Kimmerling 1983), has been to treat Zionism's national exclusivism as a dependent as well as an independent variable. In this vein, building on the history and sociology of colonization and socioeconomic segmentation, Gershon Shafir (1989) has shown how Zionist nation-building and state-making practices and beliefs were formed out of the distinctive conditions— political, demographic, and economic—under which Jewish settlers con-

2. In the context of his critique of Lustick's early work, Rosenfeld (1983) has made similar arguments. Yet the alternative analysis suggested in the work of Carmi and Rosenfeld (1989 and 1992) is so voluntaristic and historically contingent that the realities of Zionist ideology and practice and of the Arab-Jewish conflict disappear altogether.

3. In some instances, of which Zureik's (1979) pathbreaking work is a good example, scholars proposing to adopt a cosmopolitan view of the Israeli case have ultimately fallen back on the argument that the Zionist character of the state is what explains Arab-Jewish inequality.

fronted the Arab inhabitants of late-Ottoman Palestine. Persistent and central characteristics of Israeli society—the political hegemony of the labor movement, the victory of militant Jewish separatism over Jewish-Arab integration and coexistence; the existence of gender, ethnic, and occupational inequalities *within* Jewish society—could only be explained, in this view, by the conflict (at bottom, material as much as "national") between Arabs and Jews.

From a similar starting point, Shalev's (1989b) study of persistence and change in the orientation of the Histadrut (the General Organization of Workers in Israel) to Arab labor argued that the labor organization's shifting mix of exclusionary and inclusionary policies could be linked to historical changes in the demographic balance, the threats or opportunities that the Arab minority posed to Jewish economic interests, and the substance of political exchange between the Histadrut and its partners in the Labor Party and the state. In other words, the historical conditions that gave rise to exclusionary practices were themselves subject to change, and so was the practical meaning of Zionism for Arab-Jewish inequality in Israel.

The political economy approach, with its focus on interests, profit seeking (or loss avoidance), and realpolitik, is not the only alternative to a reductionist interpretation based on Zionist hegemony. Some recent works offer new approaches to interpreting the politics of nationality in Israel that permit an understanding of contradictions, the possibility of change, and the structural divide between the Jewish and Arab sectors. The most radical contribution to date in this vein has been Ian Lustick's (1989) suggestion that by the mid-1980s Jewish politicians had unwittingly taken a political road to binationalism. Inspired not by ideological change but rather by considerations of gaining power in an increasingly competitive party system, even the Likud adopted a more inclusionary approach to the Arab electorate. Experience in the 1990s suggested that this is a perceptive but simplistic observation, the problem being in effect to incorporate the twin realities noted by Lustick—the repressive "control systems" discussed in his early work (Lustick 1980) and the potentially subversive logic of party competition on which he subsequently focused.

An important contribution by Yoav Peled (1992) has suggested that this dualism can be succinctly conceptualized in terms of two competing traditions in the theorization of citizenship. He demonstrates that what is interesting and distinctive about the Israeli case is the *coexistence* of a "liberal" floor of universal citizen's rights with Zionism's "ethnorepublican" tradition, which by definition renders only Jews (even those who are not Israeli citizens) eligible to contribute to the "common good." Peled illustrates how the resulting contradiction has been addressed and Arab-Israeli citizenship constituted by a series of judicial and political decisions on the legality of radical parties. This approach receives additional support and enrichment from Dan Rabinowitz's (1997) insightful microlevel account of Jewish-Arab relations in Upper Nazareth, a community created by the drive of the ethnorepublic to offset the country's most concentrated pocket of Arab demographic strength. Rabinowitz shows that even in this notoriously charged setting, there are Jews who genuinely espouse a liberalism that *coexists* with their nationalism, and the results are often paradoxical.

The recognition that citizenship in Israel is multilayered and potentially contradictory raises a variety of interesting research questions. Some of these questions have to do with the potential role of the Palestinian minority as an active force in Israeli politics. It is clear that for the most part Arab political leaders follow a strategy of using the rights and discourse of the liberal layer of citizenship to conduct political struggles that are not only instrumental but also implicitly or explicitly about identity and status. Might such struggles—particularly if they connect with the emergence of liberal political space in the Jewish sector—serve to undermine the ethnorepublican layer of citizenship, contributing to the kind of undramatic revolution foreseen by Lustick? Other questions arising out of the duality of citizenship concern the possibility of feedbacks from policy initiatives in the realm of liberal politics to ethnorepublican realities. *When the state, whatever its motivation (most probably grounded in Jewish politics), chooses to enrich the universal content of Israeli citizenship, is it held back by the ethnorepublican impulse to deny the new rights to its Arab citizens? What are the mechanisms that permit the state to make or prevent it from making ethnorepublican distinctions between rights of different citizens without repudiating the liberal floor of citizenship?*

The Welfare State as a Research Site

These are the questions that we seek to address in this chapter. We do so by studying the evolution of some salient features of Israel's welfare state over a period of significant economic and political change between the 1950s and the 1970s. The welfare state is a particularly fruitful site for investigating the dialectics of Palestinian citizenship in Israel. Unlike many of the cultural dimensions of citizenship, social policy presents the researcher with a palpable, formal mechanism that "operationalizes" citizenship and is one of the most important domains in which it is constituted.

In Israel, the welfare state has been a mechanism of special significance because of the relatively resource-rich and interventionist character of the state and the high level of economic dislocation suffered in different ways by large segments of both the Jewish and the Arab populations. Defined in broad terms (that include education, housing and employment policies, as well as income maintenance), the Israeli welfare state has been a crucial determinant of the life chances of its citizens.

Despite the rich potential of the welfare state as a site for investigating issues of Jewish and Arab citizenship in Israel, it remains the case that the Arabs have continued to be largely invisible in the study of social policy in Israel far more than in the study of distributional processes in the market arena. Or if visible, they have been the subject of essentially descriptive surveys with limited analytical ambitions.[4] Yet the literature on welfare states has long been fertile ground for theoretical disputation and innovation in macrosociology, and a growing body of this literature draws on theories of citizenship to understand the origins and consequences of inclusionary and exclusionary state policies. Some of the contemporary literature on welfare states—notably the work of Korpi (e.g, 1989) and Esping-Andersen (e.g., 1990)—has creatively melded insights from a citizenship perspective with a political economy approach. This analytical strategy, in light of our previous comments, seems to us to be particularly apt for the study of Arab-Jewish relations in Israel.

Turning now to the general literature on welfare states, one cannot help but be struck by the way that, unconsciously paralleling the classic distinction in political philosophy on which Peled drew, the literature on citizenship and social policy exhibits a number of interesting dualisms: between *universal* and *selective* policies, and between viewing the social rights of citizenship as either an equalizing or a stratifying force in modern societies. On the latter issue, the inevitable starting point is T. H. Marshall's classic *Citizenship and Social Class* (1950)—written, it must be remembered, in the first optimistic flush of the new postwar world when Keynesianism and socialist reformism were politically ascendant.

Marshall presented the welfare state as a liberating, inherently egalitarian counterpoint to the inequality of the market (Marshall 1950, Bulmer and Rees 1996). In contrast, much recent work has portrayed the welfare state as both reflecting and conferring *differentially graded citizenship* on the purely ascriptive grounds of race, gender, or nationality. Thus, recent studies of black and female disadvantage in the U.S. welfare state have demonstrated how exclusionary mechanisms (some implicit, others explicit; some

---

4. Until recently, the work of Abraham Doron, the doyen of social policy researchers in Israel, largely passed over the Arab population (see, however, Doron and Kramer 1991). Haidar (1991) and Cnaan (1985) have documented but offered only preliminary analysis of the discriminatory character of social policy vis-à-vis the Arab minority.

administrative, others economic, and still others cultural) have linked different types and conditionalities of social rights to different populations (e.g., Quadagno 1994, Mink 1995). Paralleling these concerns, research into the disadvantages faced by immigrants in Western Europe has demonstrated how "states create multiple forms of [citizenship] status by matching types of international migrants to types of . . . social rights" (Faist 1995, 221).

In the social policy literature, the same antimony has been associated with the choice between two different kinds of measures, *universal* and *selective* (Doron 1995). Universal benefits afford automatic entitlements as a matter of right, and they are typically administered by an independent, service-oriented bureaucracy committed to the mission of delivering benefits to those entitled to them. In contrast, selective benefits are targeted to specific exigencies and are available only to those with demonstrated need (e.g., meeting an income test or being approved by a professional forum). Frequently, the onus is on the needy person to actively seek out the benefit and present convincing evidence of eligibility. Clearly, universal benefits more obviously have the character of social rights of citizenship, whereas selective benefits often function as a residual system providing minimal economic security to groups on the margins of both the market economy and universal social programs.

One of the well-known criticisms of selective policies is that they tend to stigmatize the recipients, whereas universal policies more effectively reach the target population and carry no connotation of charity or discipline. Less well understood is the fact that because of their targeted nature, selective benefits may perform important political functions: as a means of creating dependency and offering rewards for citizen loyalty to political parties or their affiliated institutions, and as a way of denying benefits to "undesirables" and channeling them only to the "deserving." This is precisely what developed in Israel, yet in the course of time the welfare state experienced reforms (for reasons to be explained later) that transformed the selective basis of many benefits into universal citizens' rights. In the process, a real potential emerged for extending benefits to the Palestinian minority, injecting them into the liberal layer of citizenship.

This provides an ideal context for asking the questions raised earlier. *What was the role (if any) of nationality-blind political action by Arabs in bringing about these reforms? And how (if at all) did the ethnorepublican face of the politics of citizenship enter and perhaps frustrate the reform process?* We address these questions by referring to two policy areas where a potential emerged in the 1970s for benefits to become social rights of citizenship: child allowances (representing the income maintenance sphere of the welfare state) and housing (indicative of those social programs—health and education are other examples—that enhance consumption capacities by providing goods or services rather than income). At the end of the 1960s and the beginning of the 1970s, Israel's fragmented child allowance programs were formalized and centralized as part of their transformation into an ambitious antipoverty measure. At about the same time, housing policy shifted from an emphasis on planning and subsidizing home construction to offering mortgage assistance to newlyweds and needy families. In both of these cases, reforms carried with them a clear potential to generalize to the Arab population, ending their exclusion by transforming selective benefits into nationality-blind citizens' rights. In both cases, this potential was at least partially frustrated. Going into the archives and gleaning whatever can be mined from existing research has made it possible to largely reconstruct the processes by which the Arab minority's partial exclusion from the welfare state came to be challenged and then reinstated (Rosenhek 1995). Before turning to this fascinating story, however, we must at least schematically address the issue of how the Palestinian population came to be partially excluded in the first place.

The Origins of Palestinian Exclusion

The welfare state is one of the core institutions of Israeli society that, as one of us has previously argued in relation to the labor movement (Shalev 1992), is outwardly similar to its counterparts in the West yet has developed along a very different historical trajectory, linked to the pattern of Jewish colonization and the evolution of the Arab-Jewish conflict in the prestate period.[5] Both the political and the socioeconomic foundations of Arab exclusion were laid by the practices of nation and state building that emerged under the specific conditions of Jewish colonization of Palestine. Three constraints were especially important in the context: the Jews' demographic weakness in relation to the "native" population; their lack of sovereignty and the power resources that go with it; and the disadvantages that they faced in trying to gain control of land and access to employment through the market. The vanguard of the settlers (the propertyless "workers") and officials of the Zionist movement sought in response to these constraints to insulate Jews from Arabs and create islands of political and infrastructural autonomy. Consequently, exclusion of Arabs (or, in a few exceptional cases that prove the rule, dual organization) was the central operating principle of Zionist politics and economics. This exclusion dynamic was reinforced by

5. For a fuller elaboration of the arguments made here, see Shalev (1989a) and Rosenhek (1998b).

the development of animosity and violent conflict between Jews and Arabs, but it did not originate there.

In the Jewish community of mandatory Palestine, the *welfare state* (i.e., *decommodified* payments or services by public organizations that provide means of existence independent of the market [Esping-Andersen 1987]) developed in order to facilitate Jewish settlement in general and Jewish exclusiveness in particular. The key instruments of social policy were control over job allocation (labor exchanges and some actual job creation) and consumption subsidies (mainly by provision of goods or services, including housing). In cases of exceptional personal distress or acute economic crisis, income maintenance might also be offered but was never guaranteed as a matter of right. Access to these benefits depended on neither citizenship nor stratification. Instead, it was conditional on two criteria: *nationality* (being Jewish was a necessary requirement for all social protection; it was also a sufficient requirement for the residual antipoverty measures operated by philanthropic organizations and the "national institutions"); and *organizational affiliation* (either political or quasi-political affiliation, especially Histadrut membership, or for enterprise-based welfare schemes, employment in a particular workplace).

On the basis of this stylized account, it is easy to see the joint significance of "citizenship" and political economy for the welfare state of the Yishuv (prestate Jewish community). "Citizenship" (being Jewish) was essential for entry. But an individual's access to decommodifying social policy was also contingent on (1) his or her perceived contribution to the settlement process (special subsidies for new immigrants, kibbutzim, etc.); (2) class or market position (vulnerability to competition from Arab labor, variations in employee benefits between workplaces); and (3) political participation (especially Histadrut membership and allegiance to the parties that dominated the labor movement and Zionist politics alike).

To a significant extent, these principles persisted after sovereignty. Three different systems of welfare flourished during the first decade or so of Israel's existence. The first, benefiting mainly veterans, was a continuation of the "wage-earner's welfare" (Castles 1985) that had been spearheaded by the Histadrut in the earlier period and was now institutionalized and expanded with the help of the state. The second system was directed to new immigrants and was to a large extent financed and even administered by Zionist and Jewish philanthropic organizations. A third residual form of social protection was provided by the state in the form of highly selective and minimalist assistance. Evidently, the Palestinian citizens of the state could be eligible, if at all, only for this residual system. And, in fact, the Ministry of Social Assistance, responsible for the poor-relief system, was constructed in such a fashion that in accordance with their allegedly more modest needs, Arab recipients would be granted only substandard "rural" allowances (Doron and Kramer 1991).

The reasons for the Arabs' marginal position in Israel's fledgling welfare state are not hard to find. Indeed, their almost complete exclusion was *over-determined* by the conditions prevailing in the early 1950s—beginning with the fact that it was politically and fiscally convenient for the state and the dominant party vis-à-vis the *Jewish* population to let the welfare state languish and re-create essentially the prestate division of welfare that we have just discussed. But Jewish disinterest and Arab powerlessness also pointed in the direction of exclusion. So far as Jewish sentiments are concerned, a general atmosphere of Jewish prejudice as well as fear (however poorly grounded in reality) of Arab insurgency was multiplied in its effects by both objective and politically constructed conflicts of interest between Jews and Arabs (Beinin 1990). In addition, neither the state as such nor the chief political elites had any reason to regard Arab inclusion as a politically necessary or even desirable step. Although the Arabs who remained inside what became Israel were designated citizens, this offered them little more than the right to vote. State practices in relation to Arab citizens were segmented by the military government and the "Arab Department" system. The Palestinian minority was eminently controllable at minimal political cost. To the extent that the economic vulnerability was *not* ameliorated by decommodifying measures, Arab citizens would be that much more amenable to state control and political discipline because of their acute dependence on the goodwill of the authorities and on the authority of their traditional clan leaders.

In effect, the content of Arab citizenship after 1948 was hemmed in by the very same basic factors that shaped the prestate experience: the national conflict (the Arab minority as a "fifth column"); the drive to transfer Arab land and property to Jews; and the desire to shelter new immigrants from economic competition. No "legitimate" Jewish political body, with the partial exception of Mapam, raised demands to embrace liberal principles of citizenship that would override the forces supporting Arab exclusion. And under conditions of sponsored electoral mobilization and military government, the Palestinian citizens themselves faced a virtually nonexistent political opportunity structure.

Exclusionary Practices in the Child Allowances Scheme

Unlike other spheres of the Israeli welfare state, there were, as we have noted, no historical precedents from the prestate era for any kind of universal cash benefits or income guarantees. The reasons were simple. Lacking sovereign authority, the Jewish "national institutions" had no way of instituting a system of social insurance, and they preferred directing their limited funds to creating the infrastructure for Jewish colonization (including jobs) than wasting it on ephemeral investments in income maintenance. This opposition continued into the era of sovereignty, bolstered by the Treasury's budgetary concerns and the reluctance of the Histadrut and the Labor Party machine to sacrifice the political benefits of the system of "wage-earner welfare" they had developed in the prestate era and now (with the aid of state subsidies and guaranteed monopoly privileges) had honed to a very high level of effectiveness (Doron and Kramer 1991, Doron 1988).

Despite these obstacles, child allowances gradually became a key element of the welfare state. How can this be explained? We know that child allowances have generally been adopted only as part of the social security system of those Western nations with a large Catholic population and historically low birthrates (France being a good example). Given the character of child benefits as a potential inducement for raising the birthrate, one might assume that their prominence in the Israeli welfare state was the result of just such a demographic consideration and that, in consequence, the scheme would have been designed from the outset to apply solely to *Jewish* families. Instead, both the humble origins and to a large extent the further development of child allowances actually originated in the politics of intra-Jewish conflicts and in wage policy considerations.[6]

As part of the legacy of wage-earner welfare from the prestate era, the wage packet included what could be a quite substantial component based on the size of the (male) employee's family. One of the express purposes of the Large Families Allowances program instituted in 1959 was to relieve individual employers of this burden by turning the family supplement into a social benefit financed by all three social partners. But a second and more important motive was the desire to prevent impoverished Oriental immigrants employed at low pay in relief work from switching allegiance from the ruling Labor Party (Mapai) to the radical right or left (Herut or the Communist Party, respectively). In the colorful language of then minister of labor Mordechai Namir, "Nests of fascism and communism can be prevented very inexpensively through [social] insurance, when the workers contribute pennies [*prutot*] in order to identify with those on relief work." Characteristically, however, the Histadrut opposed the government's becoming involved in a social policy sphere in which it was already active (in this case, by means of wage policy). Even more important in this case—

6. For a fuller discussion, see Rosenhek (1995).

because the leaders of the labor organization recognized the political need for Mapai to fend off discontent among lower-class Orientals—was the fear that their core constituency, the veteran Ashkenazi wage earners, would have to bear the cost. As part of his attempt to assuage these fears, Minister Namir assured his colleagues that the number of recipients would be kept low, and "special arrangements will be made so that it doesn't include Arabs."[7] What really clinched the matter, however, was the first outbreak of political violence among slum dwellers (in Haifa's Wadi Salib quarter) in July 1959. Less than a month later the Knesset passed the necessary amendment to the National Insurance Law (adopted in 1953).

This first child allowance program was modestly proportioned, with benefits being paid only for the fourth and subsequent child and terminating when the child was fourteen. Nevertheless, the economic implications for Israel's Palestinian citizens might have been profound. Despite that fact, the minister of labor failed to make good on his promise of "special arrangements," and the law adhered in both theory and implication to the principle of universality. However, *implicit exclusionary practices* that limited the access of Palestinian families to the benefits *were embodied in its administration*. This pattern of exclusion was reflected in a significant gap between Jewish and Palestinian take-up rates that persisted until the mid-1970s.[8] As late as 1968, the take-up rate among Jewish families was 93 percent compared to 67 percent among Palestinian families.[9]

Without any apparent intentionality involved, the administrative routines under which the program operated limited the access of Palestinian families. (Let us be clear: had the blockages we are about to describe *not* operated, conscious steps *might* have been taken to prevent Arabs from receiving the benefits, but in practice the issue never arose.) Until July 1976, in order to receive the benefits, claims had to be personally presented at the National Insurance Institute (NII) office closest to one's residence (Sharon 1987, 203). In this period, the social and physical access of the Palestinian population to state institutions, including the NII, was notably limited. The number of NII branches in regions where the Palestinian population was concentrated, particularly in Palestinian towns, was very small, obliging would-be Arab claimants to travel to Jewish towns. Such travel was severely

7. This and the previous quotation are both from the Minutes of the Mapai Inner Secretariat, 31 October 1958; Labor Party Archives, 24/2.

8. Take-up rates refer to the proportion of families formally entitled to the allowances that actually receive them.

9. Based on figures in Keren-Yaar and Souery (1980) and National Insurance Institute (1975b); see also Shamai and Valdhorn (1972, 14).

hampered by lack of transportation and more especially by the restrictions on movement imposed on the Palestinian population by the Military Administration until 1966. In addition, the information supplied to Palestinians about their rights and about administrative procedures of the NII was worse than inadequate.[10] These factors produced differences in access and hence in take-up rates between Palestinians and Jews, generating a situation of partial exclusion even if specific and explicit political or administrative decisions were not involved in the process.

In 1965, two important reforms began the transformation of child allowances into a major instrument of income maintenance. The ceiling age for payment of the existing allowance was raised from fourteen to eighteen; in addition, a new scheme was introduced to cover the first three children (also up to age eighteen). However, the new program, Employees' Child Allowances, as its name reveals, was offered solely to wage earners. And harking back to one of the Histadrut's earlier concerns, the new allowance was paid as part of the wage, with employers being reimbursed by the NII. As a result of this absurd arrangement, the Histadrut was able to present the allowances to its constituency as an achievement in its struggle to improve wage levels (Doron 1969, 141). Even more important, insofar as the benefits were paid through the employer and were considered an integral part of salaries, they were taken into account in calculating employer and employee contributions to the Histadrut pension funds.[11] The labor organization successfully struggled for another decade against determined opposition to this arrangement by the NII.[12]

As in the original program for large families, discrimination against potential Arab recipients occurred via implicit exclusionary practices rather than through purposive measures deriving from the Israeli state's policy to-

10. All of these factors were cited by directors of NII branches complaining to the central office about the difficulties they faced in implementing social security programs vis-à-vis the Palestinians. See, for example, "Review of the Present Situation, and a Proposal for an Action Plan in the Arab Sector," memorandum submitted to the general director of the NII by his assistant for Arab affairs, 22 March 1955; letter of the Nazareth branch director to the general director of the NII, 17 June 1955; letter of the Zfat branch director to the general director of the NII, 15 February 1956 (NII Archives, 00–A-6/46).

11. This procedure was jointly agreed upon by the government and the Histadrut, despite the opposition of the employers (minutes of the meeting between NII representatives and a delegation from the Trade Union Department of the Histadrut, 26 August 1964 [NII Archives, 00–A-27/204]; "Reservations of Israel Manufacturers' Association to the Memorandum on the Employees' Children Allowances Program," 15 June 1964 [NII Archives, 00–A-27/204]).

12. Minutes of the Histadrut Central Executive Committee, 25 June 1972, 1 September 1974 (Labor Archives).

ward its Palestinian citizens. And once again, these practices significantly affected the chances of Palestinian families to receive the benefits. More precisely, because payment was effected by employers, take-up among Palestinians was primarily determined by their position in the Israeli labor market. A dualistic situation emerged that followed the well-established cleavage between sheltered employment in the public and Histadrut sector and in medium- and large-scale private firms, on the one hand, and workers employed by farmers, small building contractors, and small industrial and service employers, on the other. On several occasions, it was asserted that significant numbers of employers did not pay the allowances to their employees, even though they demanded and received the reimbursements from the NII (Doron 1969, 144; Roter 1973, 86).[13] Predictably, the employees who failed to receive the benefits were concentrated in disadvantaged social groups, particularly unskilled and temporary workers in the secondary sector of the labor market.[14]

Although direct evidence is lacking, it is reasonable to infer that one of the groups most harmed by this dualistic situation was the Palestinian employees. They were concentrated in the nonskilled and temporary occupations of the secondary labor market (Khalidi 1988, Lewin-Epstein and Semyonov 1993) and virtually banned from employment in the "bureaucratic labor market" (Farjoun 1983). Moreover, as small proprietors or unpaid family workers in agriculture, many Palestinians were altogether excluded from the program.

Exclusionary Practices in Housing Policy

After the establishment of the state, or more accurately after the end of the 1948–49 war, the building of public housing by the state became one of the central domains in which the Israeli welfare state was active (Roter and Shamai 1990, 171). In contrast to the income maintenance domain, institutional legacies and positive associations were inherited from the prestate period, and housing policy was consciously and deliberately formulated from the outset as an instrument for the fulfillment of Zionist national goals. The state's twin declared targets were "immigrant absorption" and "population

13. In a report of the NII in 1975, it was estimated that the allowances for between fifty thousand and one hundred thousand children were not paid to the employees (NII memorandum: "The Proposed Administrative Method for the Payment of Children's Allowances," 11 April 1975 [Labor Archives, IV-275–76]).

14. "Summary of the Histadrut Trade Union Department Meeting, 4 July 1967" (Labor Archives, IV-257–96); Minutes of the Fourth Council of the NII, Session No. 4, 17 July 1967 (Labor Archives, IV-257–96).

dispersion," and the two were conceived as intimately related. The settlement of the new immigrants in the periphery was intended to be the main instrument to attain the goal of population dispersion (Gonen 1979, 22; Tenne 1962, 445). The latter was of course a euphemism for strengthening the Jewish presence in those areas in which it was sparse in comparison to the Palestinian presence (Barkai 1981, 162; Gonen 1979, 22). Change in the demographic balance between Jews and Palestinians on the Jewish periphery was perceived as a way of both symbolically advertising the state's sovereignty and enhancing its effective control on the territory (Falah 1989, 248; Newman 1989, 220).[15] It is reasonable to assume in addition that, in the manner of and alongside other policies that kept newcomers out of the mainstream labor market, "population dispersion" was also desirable because it simply foreclosed potential competitive pressure by new immigrants on the wages and local services enjoyed by veterans (cf. Bernstein 1981).

The most dramatic illustration of the imbrication of the national conflict and housing policy was the government's decision—in pursuit of the strategic aims of ruling out the return of the 1948–49 refugees and of solving housing problems—to settle masses of newcomers in former Arab homes that were part of its enormous stock of "abandoned property" (Golan 1995). (Veterans also participated in this shareout, generally receiving the more valuable prizes.) In the related sphere of enlarging the housing stock by new construction, throughout the first two decades of sovereignty the state's preference was for interventions on the supply side of the housing market. State agencies and public organizations under its control were actively involved in planning, designing, financing, constructing, and distributing housing resources to defined population groups (Israel, Ministry of Finance and Ministy of Construction and Housing 1990b), and public housing represented a very significant proportion of the total housing units built during those years (Haber 1975).

Most of the state's expenditures on housing in this period were directed to the massive new immigrant population (Nissim 1969, 14; Roter and Shamai 1990, 179). The absolute dependence of the new immigrants on the state for access to housing and their lack of political power permitted state elites to freely employ the distribution of housing as an instrument for achieving political and geopolitical aims. Accordingly, most public construction for immigrants was carried out in peripheral areas in which the state was interested in strengthening the Jewish presence and the ruling party was

---

15. For evidence of these demographic intentions from publications of the Ministry of Housing and other state agencies, see "First report—The Inter-ministerial Committee for Population Dispersion," March 1964, and Haber (1975, 19–23; 1986, 5 and 14–5).

interested in establishing its dominance unhindered by political pluralism (Gonen 1979). In addition, more limited programs were directed to the veteran Jewish population (Drabkin-Darin 1957, Lavon 1974). Most of these projects were implemented in the more developed central region of the country, and the housing units were generally larger and of higher quality than those built for the new immigrants (Sleifer 1979, 11).

An important characteristic of housing policy in Israel in these years was the absence of formal and universalistic rules for the determination of entitlements in the housing domain. Even though at the declarative level the Israeli welfare state accepted the responsibility for the provision of at least basic housing resources to all citizens, this principle and any operative rules for its implementation were never formalized (Heymann 1981, 278). The absence of formal criteria and their nonimplementation in the few cases in which they were defined found expression in the decisions regarding both the execution of housing projects and the distribution of completed units among potential recipients (Israel, State Comptroller 1964, 366, and 1970, 585). This situation strengthened the political and bureaucratic apparatus in relation to the citizenry, enhancing the feasibility of using the distribution of housing assets as an instrument for co-optation and clientilistic political recruitment (Hasson 1981).

The absence of formal rules also facilitated the almost complete blockage of Palestinian access to the housing resources distributed by the state. Programs for new immigrants were obviously closed to them.[16] But Palestinian citizens were also excluded de facto from housing programs for the veteran population (Heymann 1981, 255).

Only in the late 1950s did the state begin to show some concern for the housing problems of the Palestinian population. This interest was motivated by the issue of Palestinian "internal refugees," a serious political problem for the Israeli state. The existence of a significant number of internal refugees was potentially damaging to Israel in the international arena, and there was also the domestic worry caused by the fear that the internal refugees would become a focus of political unrest. The state was interested in putting a definitive end to refugees' claims for the return of confiscated property. Consequently, any housing assistance provided to the refugees was conditional on their formally giving up their claims.[17]

16. The term *new immigrant* refers in Israel to a legal category applicable only to Jews immigrating on base of the Law of Return.

17. See, for example, letter of S. Cohen to Y. Cohen, both activists in the Arab Department of the Histadrut, 3 December 1961 (Labor Party Archives, the Arab Department—Economy, 2/H - 26/9).

Against this background, the government decided in 1958 to enlarge the direct involvement of the state in home construction for Palestinian citizens.[18] Following this decision, an official in the housing department of the Ministry of Labor was appointed as responsible for "minorities' housing affairs" (Israel, State Comptroller 1962, 203). Some public housing projects were executed in Palestinian towns and villages, but they were extremely limited in scope and grossly insufficient.

Three types of data concisely document the paucity of effort directed to addressing the acute housing problems of the Arab population.[19]

A publication of the Ministry of Housing reports the number of "housing solutions" that Palestinians received from state agencies between 1957 and 1970. Including loans for homeowner construction, this assistance reached only 7,500 families (Hirsh 1970, 102).

Between 1960 and 1973, only 3.4 percent of all public residential construction (in terms of built area) was carried out in Palestinian communities (Israel, Central Bureau of Statistics 1964, 48–49; 1966, 54–55; 1970, 40; 1972, 32; and 1974a, 31).

Between 1955 and 1977, only 0.6 percent of the government development budget for housing was allocated to projects for Palestinians (Israel various years). Furthermore, it was reported that sometimes actual spending was even lower than the sums allocated in the budget (Israel, State Comptroller 1962, 203–4).

In short, the access of Palestinian citizens to housing assets remained largely dependent on their ability to participate in the private housing market on the basis of personal or family resources or both.

From Implicit to Formal Exclusion

The next question on our agenda is, What happened to the Palestinians' partial exclusion from Israel's welfare state in the 1970s, a period of rising expenditure and in some cases also reorganization of policy along more universal lines? Before addressing that question, though, let us try to take stock of the story so far. Except for old-age allowances (which were already instituted in the 1950s, although on a very modest basis), child allowances were

18. In 1957, the ministerial committee for economic affairs decided to establish an interministerial committee to study the internal refugee problem and present proposals for its solution (Israel, State Comptroller 1962, 143). On the basis of its proposals, in February 1958, the government adopted a program for the economic rehabilitation of the refugees. Eighty percent of the program total budget was allocated for housing (Liskobscki 1960, 192).

19. For reports on the harsh housing conditions of the Palestinian population, see Abu-Keshek and Geraisi (1977), E. Cohen (1973), Kipnis (1978), and Peled (1986).

the first universal cash benefit offered by the Israeli welfare state. Although targeted to a specific need (the inadequate income of large families), the allowances were by law to be paid directly by the NII to all families with the appropriate number of young children. In fact, however, the intent of the program's political sponsors was to use child benefits as an antidote to political alienation among a specific Jewish constituency. Then came the inconvenient realization that the formal criteria adopted for this purpose would also benefit many Arab citizens, whose political allegiance could be obtained by other means and who were in no position to express their political alienation from the ruling party or the state.

Perhaps because of fear of the international repercussions (we can only speculate on the reasons), neither direct nor indirect attempts were made to bar Palestinians from receiving the benefit. Instead, the conditions under which the benefit was *administered* had the consequence of preventing a sizable minority of Arabs from actually receiving it. We know that the administrators were aware that not all of the entitlements were actually received. Hence, it may be fair to assume that their bosses (who apparently made no attempt to institute the needed reforms) were not unhappy with this state of affairs.

Precisely the same may be said for the additional child allowances program created in 1965, when once again the Palestinians' partial exclusion could be traced to the conditions of the program's administration. By now, however, clear institutional interests—having nothing to do with the Jewish desire not to "waste" money on Arabs—had come into play. The 1965 program was custom designed to assist the Histadrut, and the NII chafed under the program's circumvention of its authority. In respect to both programs, neither Labor Party politicians nor the leaders of the Histadrut had an interest in appealing the "nondecision" that no steps would be taken to ensure the delivery of benefits to those who failed to receive them (including but not only Palestinians). In contrast, the officials and supporters of the NII had precisely the opposite interest in the context of their ongoing struggle for autonomy and a recognized monopoly in the domain of income maintenance.

Housing, as we have seen, was a very different story. Here, there was an established prestate connection between Zionist settlement and immigrant-absorption aims and social policy that received added urgency and practicality in the conditions of the first two decades of sovereignty. The state had the means and its rulers had the political incentives to engage in massive direct interventions into the supply and distribution of housing. Entire neighborhoods and towns were created from the ground up to house Jewish newcomers, with the intention of fulfilling the state's territorial and political objectives. Only when the identical type of considerations—territorial and political—arose vis-à-vis the Arab population were any active steps taken to assist them. Given the selectivity and high level of discretion characterizing the operation of housing policy, the state's exclusion of the Arabs cannot be interpreted as merely a by-product of incidental circumstances (as appears to have been at least partly the case regarding child allowances). Instead, the state's revealed preference for discrimination along national lines was evidently housing policy's potential contribution to Jewish control of territory and Jewish political allegiance.

By the beginning of the 1970s, several important developments occurred that altered the parameters under which social policy was formulated in Israel. So far as the Palestinian minority was concerned, several key decisions (the formal integration of Arabs into the Histadrut, the creation of a state employment service, and later the dismantling of the military government) reflected the fact that Arabs were now welcome as insecure and low-paid jobholders in the Jewish sector's secondary labor market (Shalev 1989b). During the first half of the 1960s, as economic growth took off and unemployment fell, a "crisis of full employment" emerged that enhanced the job security of Jewish manual workers (predominantly Oriental immigrants) and eroded the authority of Histadrut and Labor Party bosses. The recession of 1966–67 temporarily (and harshly) interrupted both of these processes, but in the postwar boom, labor shortages (and for Jews, the expansion of the "bureaucratic sector") once again served to weaken the former dependency of low-status workers on the political machines (Grinberg 1993, Shalev 1984).

Despite the abolition of the military government, Palestinian citizens were still effectively under the state's control (Lustick 1980). But the Labor Party's influence among the Mizrachim (Oriental Jews) was becoming increasingly problematic. The electoral expression of Oriental and Arab discontent only came later, in the 1973 and 1977 elections. But already in 1970 the specter of the Wadi Salib riots more than a decade before came back to haunt the Ashkenazi establishment with the appearance of Israel's "Black Panther" movement (Cohen 1972, Etzioni-Halevy 1975a). The most pressing interest of the political elite was to restore its legitimacy and stem the threat that extraparliamentary protest posed to the very system by which it wielded power.

Under these circumstances, those bureaucrats and experts who could quickly come up with well-operational plans to ameliorate the material sources of discontent and restore the paternalistic authority of the ruling party found a very receptive audience among government leaders (Hofnung 1982; see also Etzioni-Halevy 1975b). The NII, which as we saw earlier had been seeking to extend its sphere of influence, was particularly well placed in this conjuncture. As a result, the social security system was extended at the expense of other players, such as the Ministry of Social Assistance and local government (Achdut and Carmi 1981, 65; Gross 1979, 101). In turn, the bolstering of the NII stimulated the process of universalization of the system. Contrary to the other organizations active in the field, which favored noninstitutionalized and selective programs based on means tests, the NII encouraged the enactment of statutory and universal welfare programs under its autonomous authority (Katz 1969). Its leaders and allies embraced universalism for both ideological and practical reasons—the latter being the institute's interest in increasing its financial independence from the Treasury and its political dependence on the government. In this connection, the loyalty of a large, efficiently served clientele was an additional desideratum.

This was the background to the expansion and institutionalization of the Israeli welfare state that characterized the 1970s (Doron and Kramer 1991). The import for the Palestinians was potentially enormous because—given their high level of need and record of prior exclusion—any tilt toward universality would have disproportionate effects: exceptionally beneficial for the recipients but unusually costly and visible to Jewish policymakers and possibly also to the Jewish public.

The Reform of Child Allowances

Urged on by the NII, the policy approach crystallized among political and bureaucratic elites was that an existent instrument, the child allowances scheme, could and should be used to provide additional means of consumption to the disadvantaged Jewish population. This goal would be achieved both by extending the scheme's coverage and by raising the level of the benefits.[20]

When the decision to turn child allowances into a meaningful component of large families' income was made, the issue of its distributional impact on Palestinians immediately arose. The state now had to confront the contradiction between its interest in a significant rise in the benefits level and the political and economic advantages of blocking the receipt of benefits by Palestinians. Because the reform to which policymakers were committed was

20. Between the beginning of the 1970s and the middle of the decade, child allowances, including veterans' benefits, doubled as a proportion of the average monthly wage. For large families (six or more children), the ratio of benefits to the average wage reached nearly 30 percent. (Rosenhek 1995, 167).

inextricably linked to the principle of universality, discussions inevitably focused on a variety of *formal* mechanisms to exclude Palestinian citizens from the expansion of the scheme. In order to adjudicate between various proposals, a special committee was appointed by the government in March 1970. Its task was to choose one of three alternatives: scaling benefit increases according to the official hierarchy of favored regions; using the Jewish Agency as a means to pay a supplement solely to Jews; or offering a supplementary benefit to families with at least one veteran of the armed forces.[21] The common objective of these alternatives was explicitly defined in an internal memorandum presented to the committee by the NII: ensuring that through the enlarged allowances a "basic level of welfare will be guaranteed in the case of Jewish families. For non-Jewish families a lower level of welfare will be secured."[22]

The committee chose increasing benefits to veterans' families as its preferred method for differentiating between the two national groups. Its reasoning was that adoption of a formally universal criterion—military service—would be the most politically acceptable solution in both the domestic and international arenas.[23] At the time, the almost absolute political marginality of Israel's Palestinian citizens and of the party that became their distinctive representative (Rakach, the New Communist list) defeated their efforts to challenge the legitimacy of this practice.

Accordingly, the partial exclusion of Palestinian families was formalized through the establishment in 1970 of Allowances for Veterans' Families. Eligible families were provided with additional cash benefits, at first for the fourth and then (after 1974) also the third child (Sharon 1987, 204). "Veterans' families" were defined in a very broad manner. The category included families with children having one or more parents, grandparents, or siblings with a record of service in any of the Israeli security forces (National Insurance Institute 1975a, 118). Obviously, this broad definition was aimed at incorporating the maximum number of Jewish families into the program, although inevitably some Arab families were also caught in the net.[24] More-

21. The committee was composed of representatives of the NII, the Treasury, the Ministry of Social Assistance, and the Ministry of Labor (Decision of the Ministerial Committee on National Insurance Law, 29 March 1970 [NII Archives, 00–A-84/599]).

22. "Children's Allowances for Families," memorandum presented to the "Special Committee" by the NII, 1 April 1970 (NII Archives, 00–A-84/599).

23. "Final Report of the Committee on Rise of Benefits for Families with Children," 12 April 1970 (NII Archives, 00–A-84/599).

24. For a number of years in the 1970s for which the calculation can be performed, approximately 8–9 percent of Arab families with four or more children received the veterans' allowances (Rosenhek 1995, 119).

over, additional steps were taken to include sections of the Jewish population—the ultraorthodox, new immigrants, and those exempted from military service for health or social reasons—who did not serve in the army.

Although the level of benefits was relatively low in the initial stages of the program, there was a constant increase in their real value. This process produced a growing differential between those families entitled to the special benefits and those that were not. Thus, in 1971, the gap for a family with four children was equivalent to only 2 percent of the average wage, but by 1977 it had reached 8 percent.[25] An important reason for this trend was that on several occasions during the 1970s increases in child allowances were used as a means of compensation for intended or unintended erosion of real wages, and the application of these increases favored veterans' allowances more than the standard benefits.[26]

At the same time, two other processes were working in the opposite direction to narrow the disadvantages of Arab families in the child allowances program. First, as a consequence of the unification of the two earlier systems of allowances and the adoption of automatic procedures for identifying and paying eligible families, the take-up rate for Arab families improved, rising from about three-quarters in 1970 to complete coverage by 1974 (Rosenhek 1995, 173). Second, when the real value of child allowances began to deteriorate in 1978 because of inadequate compensation for inflation and wage increases, the differential between standard and veterans' benefits was narrowed. As we discuss below, it was decided to phase out the differential altogether in the 1990s.

The Reform of Housing Policy

The early 1970s was also a period of significant change in the housing dimension of the Israeli welfare state. The magnitude of public housing built with direct state involvement declined, and the state began to direct its intervention toward the demand side of the housing market (Israel, Ministry of Finance and Ministry of Construction and Housing 1990b, 8). The earlier pattern in which the state produced and distributed housing resources to specific population groups outside the market arena was replaced by a policy in which the state implemented assistance programs to enhance citizens' chances to participate in the private housing market as consumers. A

25. Figures based on internal reports of the NII.

26. See, for example, "Final Report of the Commission for Examination of Compensation for the Rise in Prices as Consequence of Emergency Economic Policy," 9 November 1974 (Labor Archives, IV-275–183).

direct and important effect of this policy change was the growth and bolstering of the private construction sector (Israel, Ministry of Finance and Ministry of Construction and Housing 1990b, 6).

This change in policy was a response to economic and social trends that began to surface after the 1967 war. In view of the severe contraction suffered by the construction industry during the recession of 1966–67, the postwar revival of economic growth and immigration created a housing shortage (Lithwick 1980, 11). Housing prices increased at a much more rapid rate than the general price index (Hirsh and Paitelson 1972, 3–4), consequently lowering the chances of a significant part of the population— especially the second generation of Oriental Jews—to gain access to housing assets. This was an important part of the background to the political discontent of the Oriental poor expressed by the Black Panthers (Cohen 1972, 96; Hasson 1993). The rising cost and scarcity of housing also generated resentment among many middle-class newlyweds, and in 1971, a "young couples movement" formed to demand government action.

Policymakers proved responsive to the demands of both of these movements (Hofnung 1982, Etzioni-Halevy 1975b). Existing programs for housing based on the allocation of heavily subsidized mortgages and loans were expanded and new ones were established (Lerman 1976, 20; Ashuri 1988, 19). In tandem with informal measures to co-opt the most vocal activists by addressing their individual needs, it was decided to establish formal rules for the determination of entitlements to housing assistance in order to offer the promise of immediate and large-scale relief (Heymann 1981, 295). But just as in the case of child allowances, pressures to universalize and institutionalize housing policy invited the adoption of formal exclusionary practices that blocked or significantly reduced the access of Palestinian citizens.

The two main categories defined by the policymakers as targets for the new assistance programs were recently married couples and families living in substandard housing conditions. Mortgage and loan programs were established and were aimed at enhancing the prospects of these two groups to purchase housing in the private market. In addition, as a continuation of the policy of "population dispersal," special programs and benefits were designated for those acquiring housing in the periphery.

The first and most comprehensive program implemented was designed to offer mortgage assistance to young couples. *Eligibility* was universal, but assistance *rates* (both the principal and the conditions of repayment) were graded according to the socioeconomic situation of the beneficiaries (Lithwick 1980, 123). Two additional criteria were employed to entirely exclude Palestinian citizens from the entitled population. First, the benefits were provided only in situations where at least one spouse or a close relative (parent, grandparent, or sibling) had served in the army or other security service (Israel, Ministry of Housing 1976, 4). As in the case of the special child allowances for veterans, this requirement was defined by the Ministry of Housing in a very broad and flexible manner with a view to including as many Jewish households as possible (ibid. 18). Second, the program was implemented only in *specific* localities, and no Palestinian town or village was included in that list (ibid. 29). This procedure served to block access to those Palestinians (primarily Druzes and some bedouins) who are called upon to serve in the army, as well as others who serve in the police or the prison service. The efficacy of these practices is indicated by the fact that until 1977, among 16,394 mortgages granted by the program, only 34 were allocated to Palestinian couples (Lithwick 1980, 137).

In 1977, couples unable to claim veteran status were admitted to the program, but at a lower level of assistance. The mortgage to which most Palestinian couples were entitled was only 75 percent of the lowest mortgage provided to the veteran couples, and the conditions for its repayment were less favorable, embodying a lower level of subsidy (Israel, Ministry of Housing 1977b, 16 and 30–31). Furthermore, only one Palestinian community, Nazareth, was included in the list of towns in which the program was implemented (ibid., 37). Consequently, the take-up rate among Palestinian young couples continued to be extremely low (Barkai 1981, 165).

Palestinian citizens also fared poorly with respect to other housing assistance programs that operated in the 1970s. Needless to say, only Jews could benefit from the special mortgages and loans offered to new immigrants. Palestinians were also effectively shut out of selective assistance programs for families living in substandard housing (Sleifer 1979, 166; Israel, State Comptroller 1975, 617; Lithwick 1980, 161)—despite the fact that in 1975 Palestinian households constituted 48 percent of all households officially defined as overcrowded (Lithwick 1980, 81). Foreshadowing the Project Renewal model initiated in the late 1970s, only nonrural and non-Palestinian localities were selected for these programs (Israel, Ministry of Housing 1977a, 8, 27, 33). Moreover, even though the Palestinian population in the "mixed" cities such as Tel Aviv–Jaffa was formally entitled to participate, it was reported that in practice they were not provided with benefits.[27]

In the housing domain, then, the breakthrough to a nationality-blind

27. See Lithwick (1980, 158). Referring to the harsh housing conditions of the Palestinian population in Yaffo, Tel Aviv–Yaffo Deputy Mayor P. Onicobsky asserted in 1976 that the Arabs "cannot participate in the program '3 +' for the improvement of the housing conditions of families living in a density of three persons per room or more," adding, "In my opinion, this is really discrimination. They are city's citizens, as all the other citizens with rights and obligations, but this is the government policy" (*Ma'ariv*, 14 January 1976).

universality in social policy was either prevented outright or else rendered impotent. Instead, modest residual programs of a highly selective nature were adopted specifically for the Arab population. The mechanism employed was a dual administrative structure—one of the principal means by which the state had addressed the problem of controlling the Arab minority in the military government era. Thus, the "minorities department" of the Housing Ministry implemented a special loans program for that population. It was, however, notably limited regarding both the number of loans granted and their level (Abu-Keshek and Geraisi 1977, 3; Khamaisi 1990, 125). In 1971, for instance, the highest loan provided by the program amounted to fifteen thousand Israeli pounds, as against an *average* of twenty thousand provided by the young couples program (Israel, State Comptroller 1972, 581, and 1974, 48). The restricted scope of the program is further indicated by the fact that between 1970 and 1978 the mortgages granted by the minorities department of the Housing Ministry represented only 0.9 percent of the total sum allocated by the diverse housing programs implemented by the state (Haber 1975, 139; Israel, Central Bureau of Statistics 1973, 13, and 1974b, 11, and 1977, 22, and 1978, 22).

Conclusions

In the introduction to the empirical section of this chapter, we sketched two stylized portraits of the immediate postsovereignty years—one of the still-born Israeli welfare state, the other of the hypermarginality of the Palestinian minority in Israel's political economy. In view of the exceedingly bleak outlook that these two portraits suggested for the prospects of Palestinian entry into the sphere of public social provision, the development of exclusionary practices in welfare is hardly surprising. Indeed, if there is a surprise, it is that Arabs were not *completely* excluded.

In the case of child allowances, it is clear that the only partial exclusion of the Palestinians was a result of the degree to which the system operated universally as a right of (liberal) citizenship. The fact that the benefits had this universal character—and, indeed, the fact that there were benefits at all—was however not traceable to any political drive to enrich the social content of citizenship. Rather, it originated in considerations of intra-Jewish politics. The Arab population appeared to be invisible or irrelevant to policymakers, except when they realized that Jewish society might be required to bear the burden of finance should Arabs be incorporated into the system. The upshot was that Palestinian citizenship turned out to be relevant in a negative sense: denying Palestinians child allowances outright might have required steps that were irreconcilable with either the constitutional-legal fabric of the state or its all-important standing in the international community. It was in the fact that Palestinians could not be formally and explicitly discriminated against that their citizenship took on some meaning—not in the positive sense of their being "natural" candidates for entitlement to social rights.[28]

In any event, as we have stressed, a politics of social rights was not on Israel's welfare state agenda until the late 1960s. Instead, social provision was fragmented between multiple systems, and its overarching characteristics were the absence of formal definitions of entitlements and the deeply politicized character of the providing agencies (even those that were officially part of the state). When child allowances were instituted, Arabs were partially prevented from receiving them not by any active modification of the rules of entitlement, *but by the implicitly discriminatory effects of the normal operation of the political economy;* namely, the state failed to open local branches of the NII in Arab areas, and Arabs often failed to receive benefits paid out by employers because they existed on the margins of the economy.

Arab exclusion from the sphere of housing policy was quite a different matter because it was shot through from the outset with Zionist considerations. Two things are nonetheless noteworthy in this context from the perspective of the reservations we discussed at the outset of the chapter regarding what we called "Zionist functionalism." The first is precisely the contrast between the two policy domains. Neither Jewish inclusion in nor Arab exclusion from the child allowances programs were motivated by Zionist considerations, whereas this was most assuredly the case in housing policy. In other words, the variation and nuance here are worth accounting for. Second, even in housing it was not Zionism as a diffuse ideological commitment that determined the purposes and scope of housing policy. Rather, *substantive interests and practices deriving from Israel's character as a settler society*—namely, the state's drive to control Arab territory and minimize the implications of Arab demography—are what drove policy. And these interests and practices were closely intertwined with the political interest of the dominant party in basing its short- and long-term political strategy on a political economy of citizen dependency.

By the late 1960s, the Arab citizenry remained politically quiescent despite the passing of the phase of direct repression. Surveillance and direct

---

28. This conclusion is reminiscent of Peled's (1992) discussion of the banning of the racist Kach Party. He concluded that the state did not and could not regard Arabs as full members of the political community, but it was committed to defending their right not to be thrown out of their homes and their country.

dependency gave way to a measure of economic self-sufficiency and a politics of co-optation that at its most autonomous permitted local notables to engage in a degree of wheeling and dealing with the central authorities. (This is an important point: for their own political reasons, the partners of the state and the ruling party in the Arab sector themselves preferred particularistic gains to diffuse rights.) The initial story of child allowances was now replayed with still greater force: Jewish ethnic politics and the institutional interests of the NII led to a marked expansion of the system, this time along much more explicitly formal and universal lines. As predicted by both the theory of universal benefits and by the theory of liberal citizenship, Arabs were destined to become a part of this system. But along the way the very guardians of the principle of universality were called on to invent a legal mechanism for "capping" that universality by furnishing super (above standard) benefits for which only members of the ethnorepublic would be eligible. Not surprisingly—given the military's role as the principal institutional arena in which Israeli republican citizenship is constituted (Helman 1994)—criteria drawn from the military sphere were the preferred means of legitimizing this and other explicit exclusionary practices.

If there is a functionalist moral to this story, it is that preventing the decommodification of Palestinian citizens was functional. It kept them dependent on Jews (one of Lustick's control mechanisms). No less important, it kept them dependent on the *hamula* (clan) and on the traditional authority figures on which Jewish control relied. It was also "good for the economy" because Arabs proved to be cheap and flexible labor, and as such played an important role in the lowest echelons of the labor market, particularly prior to the entry of commuter labor from the Occupied Territories after 1967.

Yet nota bene: by the mid- to late 1970s, Palestinian citizens were as likely to receive child allowances as their Jewish counterparts, and the gap between standard and super benefits was narrowing. In the 1990s, as part of the price paid to the Arab parties in return for their support of the minority Labor government, the veteran's allowance was officially abolished. Even in the domain of housing, which as we saw remained almost impenetrable to Arabs and exclusively tied to Jewish territorial and political interests right through the reform era of the 1970s, some benefits began to be extended to the Arab population. Surely this is a testament not to the law of progress in human affairs generally or to the inevitable onward march of social citizenship in welfare state matters, but instead to the dialectics and conditionality of human history. As Haidar (1995) has shown, the new economic opportunities for Palestinian citizens that were unleashed by the occupation, along with other factors, made it possible for many to achieve a substantial degree of self-sufficiency and for some to accumulate quite substantial wealth.

Meanwhile, the control system that kept the Arabs in Israel quiescent for so long proved to be unsustainable over the long run because, among other reasons, the price of co-opting Arab leaders kept rising and Arabs "took full advantage of the opportunities provided by Israel's political system" (Haidar 1995, 40). The political cards were also reshuffled by shifts in party allegiances within the Jewish electorate, which rendered Jewish politicians more dependent on Arab votes or on the support of Arab parliamentarians; by the rise of a liberal conception of citizen rights in the Jewish middle class and intelligentsia; and by the growing effectiveness and autonomy of Arab politicians (based in no small part on their use of the discourse and practices of liberal citizenship). The Palestinians were still locked out of republican citizenship, but the difference was that they were no longer doomed to be only passive bystanders as Jewish politics caused them to be denied social rights or to receive these rights only to have them taken away. This process verifies the dynamic character of the position of Palestinian citizens in Israeli polity and social structure, even while the Israeli state still defines itself as Zionist.

14

Rights and Duties, Citizens and Soldiers

Conscientious Objection and the Redefinition of Citizenship in Israel

SARA HELMAN

THIS CHAPTER EXAMINES the development of selective conscientious objection to warfare and military service during Israel's war in Lebanon (1982–85). I contend that conscientious objection in Israel represents a radical attempt to redefine the obligations of citizenship and to institute a new right hitherto nonexistent in that society. My thesis is that the practice of conscientious objection embodies an alternative discourse on citizenship and on the subject of rights and obligations. The analysis of conscientious objection in Israel contributes to the current debate on citizenship by illuminating two analytically distinct yet connected issues within that debate: the first involves the social practices, discourses, and institutional arenas whereby citizenship is established and reproduced over time; the second issue touches on the conditions for the emergence of an alternative discourse of citizenship, which strives to redefine both the practices of citizenship and the subject of rights and obligations. Thus, conscientious objection is not conceived in this chapter in terms of a clash between the individual's

The research for this paper was generously supported by the Sheine Centre at the Department of Sociology, Hebrew University, and the United Institute for Peace. I would like to express my gratitude to Andre Levy, Baruch Kimmerling, Zeev Rosenhek, Jon Simons, and Niza Yanai for their comments on various versions of the manuscript and to Helene Hogri for her editorial assistance. My deep thanks to the interviewees, who devoted their time and energy and shared with me their thoughts and experiences. Without their cooperation, this paper would have remained an idea.

conscience and the law,[1] but as social practice that enables the individual to understand the institutions, practices, and discourses of citizenship, as well as the ways in which individuals and groups contest extant practices and institutions of citizenship.

This chapter is composed of three sections. In the first section, I analyze current debates on the theory of citizenship, while emphasizing how a comprehension of the organization of membership and participation in the political community may enhance our understanding of patterns of social action aimed at the redefinition of citizenship. The second section presents the methodology of the research, and in the third section, I analyze the conditions for the emergence of an alternative discourse on citizenship obligations embodied in selective conscientious objection and the main claims of this discourse.

Citizenship as a Contested Terrain

Citizenship is usually defined in legal terms or as a personal status—i.e., as a set of legal rights and obligations of individuals vis-à-vis the state. The extension of rights and obligations implies the inclusion of an individual or social category within the boundaries of the political community. Concomitantly, the act of inclusion defines who is considered "a competent member of society" and shapes "the flow of resources to persons and social groups" (Turner 1993a, 2). However, the very definition of citizenship as a personal status—even if the status symbolizes membership in a bounded community of citizens or in the nation-state as a "membership organization" (Brubaker 1992, 22)—connotes a preconstituted entity or individual to whom rights and obligations are naturally delegated or attached. Such a definition disregards the political, social, and symbolic practices of citizenship and the ways in which they constitute personhood.

A more appropriate definition of citizenship should take into account the

---

1. Conventional analyses of conscientious objection conceive of it in terms of a conflict between preconstituted individuals and the imperatives of the state (see Dworkin 1978 and Rawls 1971). These analyses adopt a minimalist version of what Turner (chap. 2) has conceptualized as the political definition of citizenship and disregard the broad sociopolitical context within which the phenomenon develops. Individuals are conceived of as bearers of moralities and identities that in specific situations, such as war, may collide with the imperatives of the state. However, conscientious objection in the twentieth century developed mostly after the extension of citizenship to different groups and strata, and not prior to it. (For a different analysis, taking into account state-society relations, see Gans 1992 and Walzer 1970.) Therefore, conscientious objection may reflect the coexistence within a single polity of different conceptions of citizenship (see Tilly 1995).

relations between social action, structural processes, and political-cultural discourses—all bounded by parameters of time and space (Somers 1993, van-Gunsteren 1978 and 1988). This definition taps the socially constructed, dynamic character of citizenship and enables us to uncover the cultural assumptions embodied in the social and symbolic practices that constitute the subject of rights and obligations. The former argument represents a shift in the analysis of citizenship from its emergence to its mode of institutionalization. This shift enables us to consider the mechanism through which citizenship is reproduced as well as the ways in which the practices, institutions, and discourses of citizenship are constitutive of different social categories—such as citizens and noncitizens (see, for example, Brubaker 1992, Soysal 1994) or different types of citizens (see Dietz 1992, Peled 1992, Silverman 1991 and 1992, Vogel 1994, Yeatman 1994)—as well as of different political identities.

Extant research on citizenship has tended to disregard, however, the ways in which citizenship in the sense of membership has been organized and the discourses, policies, and institutional arenas that establish and reproduce it over time (for exceptions, see Brubaker 1992, Silverman 1992, Somers 1993, Soysal 1994). Nor has much attention been paid to the social agents involved in this process or to relations between agents. Most of these analyses take models of membership (Soysal 1994) for granted and conceive of them as pressured from without or by groups that claim inclusion in the polity. Pressures on citizenship are conceived of as emerging from groups already incorporated into the market but not included in the political community (see, for example, Brubaker 1992, Silverman 1991 and 1992, Soysal 1994) or from groups that have been differentially included into citizenship.

It should not be assumed that models of membership reproduce themselves naturally; rather, these models should be conceived of as constantly reproduced and contested from within through state agents and through the routine activities of individuals and groups fully or partially included in the political community.

Little is known about the ongoing practice of citizenship—how the daily activities of individuals reproduce the institutions of citizenship and how the discourses legitimating particular forms of citizenship are embedded in daily practices, thereby reproducing the terms of participation in the political community and the relationship between the individual and the state. In this context, the mode of inclusion in that community and the arenas through which inclusion is concretized and symbolized are central in understanding patterns of participation, the constitution of political identity, and the terms of contestation over the institutions and practices of citizenship. Finally, as citizenship is closely related to the constitution of personhood and to the distribution of resources and entitlements, this dynamic defini-tion clarifies how institutions of citizenship may become arenas of contesta-tion for groups and individuals who reject their own political identity as it is constituted by extant practices, discourses, and institutions (Turner 1993a), for negotiations over citizenship are not only related to who gets what, but also to who is what (Brubaker 1992, 182; Yeatman 1994).

This chapter concentrates on a particular kind of contestation and nego-tiation by individuals constituted as "ultimate carriers" of civic value and worth—conscientious objectors during Israel's war in Lebanon (1982). While making no claims to universalize their kind of contestation to other kinds in Israel, it illuminates the main dynamics of the *hegemonic model of membership* and the ways in which this model frames challenges from within.

Citizenship in Israel: Zionism, the State, and War Management

Three main factors seem to have shaped the contours and dynamics of citizenship in Israel: the lack of struggle over the extension of citizenship, the Zionist character of Israel, and war and conflict management. With the establishment of the State of Israel, citizenship was granted from above, and the authority of the administrative apparatus was extended to all popula-tions within the boundaries of its sovereign territory. Nonetheless, the sep-aration into two political communities of Jews and Palestinians that had been constituted under British sovereignty (Kimmerling 1993b, Smith 1993) was transformed through differential practices of population man-agement under the umbrella of Israeli rule. Practices such as differential treatment by welfare agencies (Rosenhek 1995), differential access to occupational resources, and military and political surveillance of the Palestin-ian population (Lustick 1980) brought about the constitution of two com-munities of citizens within the framework of Israeli sovereignty: the Israeli Jews and the Palestinian citizens of Israel (or Israeli Arabs).

The constitution of these two communities of citizens reflects the Israeli hegemonic tradition of nationhood and national self-understanding. In Is-rael, nationhood has been constructed in ethnic-cultural terms rather than in relation to the administrative and territorial boundaries of the state (Bru-baker 1992, Habermas 1994). The Israeli state is committed to the fulfill-ment of the national aspirations of the Jewish people embodied in Zionist ideology, and this very commitment excludes non-Jews from being defined as full and competent members of society. Thus, although Palestinians are not denied access to citizenship, the institutions of citizenship and the practices of state agencies afford them differential access to the rights of citizenship.

Whereas the Zionist character of the Israeli state can explain how citizenship rights and obligations have been nationally framed, they cannot explain the type of citizenship developed in Israel or the institutions and practices that constitute the subject of rights and obligations, the standards of civic value, and consequently the flow of resources and rewards. Moreover, Zionism can explain who may be singled out as a potential candidate to be granted effective membership, but not how effective membership is instituted and reproduced.

In order to understand the form or type of citizenship developed in Israel, war and conflict management need to be taken into account. As the Zionist colonization and settlement of Palestine was characterized by a protracted state of conflict between Jews and Palestinians (Kimmerling 1993a, Shafir 1989), the management of conflict shaped the institutional makeup, infrastructural capacity, and legitimacy of the Jewish community there (Migdal 1989, Shafir 1989).

The Israeli state's monopoly over the societal means of violence and the consolidation of that monopoly through war and conflict management are not peculiar to this sociopolitical context; in fact, it is inherent in the logic of the modern state (Mann 1984 and 1987, Tilly 1985). War and conflict management in Israel, unlike other states, has not been limited to state making, however. Rather, it has become a permanent feature of the sociopolitical order, constitutive of the relations between the individual and the state, and between the state and society. Moreover, routine conflict management and its construction in terms of a struggle for survival have been central to the consolidation and enhancement of the power and autonomy of the Israeli state vis-à-vis various social groups (Ben-Eliezer 1995, Kimmerling 1993a and 1993b).

War and conflict management have been constitutive of the type of citizenship in Israel as well as of its practices and institutions. Full citizenship and effective membership have been constructed in republican terms—i.e., with an emphasis on the individual's contribution to the enhancement and fulfillment of collective goals (Habermas 1994, Oldfield 1990, Peled 1993, van-Gunsteren 1994). Fulfillment of these goals has been conceived of in terms of the preservation of Jewish sovereignty through participation in war and military service. Thus, civic virtue has been constructed in terms of and identified with military virtue. Institutions of war making and especially the military have been the main arenas of political, cultural, and social integration, and the signifiers of full and effective membership in society (Azarya and Kimmerling 1980, Horowitz 1982, Horowitz and Kimmerling 1974,

Kimmerling 1979). Moreover, war and the institutions of war making have been the main mechanisms for the construction of what Ben-Eliezer (1995, 280–308) has conceptualized as the *ethnic nation*. Therefore, participation in the furthering of collective goals has been one of the major criteria for the distribution of rights of citizenship (Haidar 1987, Kretzmer 1987, Rosenhek 1995).

This model of membership was not openly challenged until the late seventies. Although certain groups did question the relation between military service and citizenship a decade earlier, these groups were defined as marginal, especially in terms of their class and ethnic position, or as ultraorthodox sectors of society who were granted exemption from or postponement of military service. Thus, the conception of military service as the central arena for the fulfillment of obligations continued, on the whole, to be accepted. Few challenged the toll taken by the continuous state-of-war preparations, and even peace groups that questioned the war politics of the Israeli state were as yet unformed.

It was not until the late 1970s that the situation began to change. The occupation of the West Bank and Gaza Strip and the 1973 war (the Yom Kippur war) engendered divisions in Israel around issues of national security. The change in government in 1977 and the peace treaty with Egypt (1978) furthered the disagreement over issues of national security and promoted the crystallization of protest groups (left and right, doves and hawks). However, this process of open discussion and disagreement over the basic tenets of national security was not accompanied by a significant change in patterns of political obligation as expressed in military service.

The war in Lebanon represented a qualitative change in patterns of both political protest and political obligation. It was interpreted by wide sectors as a political war, waged as a political instrument rather than in response to a threat to Israel's survival. From the very first week of intensive fighting, expressions of protest could be observed. These expressions contradicted two tacit but firmly established agreements in Israeli society. The first was the view that as long as there was active warfare, the home front would express its solidarity with the front line and abstain from assuming any critical stance or from undertaking any action that might undermine that solidarity. The protest against the war was unprecedented in Israel mainly because it took place during the period of active fighting itself (after the first week of the war). The protest movements questioned the legitimacy of the war and the authority of the state's elites to declare and wage war. The other tacit agreement that was broken concerned the assumed linkage between the needs of national security and the soldier's sacrifice. The protest against the war was led by groups that perceived themselves to be directly affected by it—male-citizen soldiers and their parents—and that questioned the very necessity of the sacrifice required by the war. As the legitimacy of the war was challenged, so too, was the right of the state to command its soldiers to kill and be killed under any circumstances.

The most salient change that took place during the war in Lebanon was the emergence of selective conscientious objection. For the first time in Israel, opposition to the war gave rise to an alternative social practice. The practice of selective conscientious objection embodied an open questioning of the main terms of political obligation in Israel. The refusal of individuals to participate in war embodied a challenge to the state's authority both to declare war and to command individuals to participate in it. This challenge was made by individuals who were constituted as the prime carriers of civic virtue.[2] The purpose of this chapter, then, is to analyze how the hegemonic model of citizenship was challenged from within and the ways in which an alternative discourse unfolded from the very essence of that dominant model.

The Hegemonic Discourse of Citizenship

Interviews with Conscientious Objectors and Their Interpretation

The hegemonic discourse of citizenship in Israel and the alternative discourse that evolved were gleaned from in-depth, semistructured interviews with sixty-six soldiers who conscientiously refused their tour of duty during Israel's war in Lebanon (see note 3). Each interview consisted of broad questions covering subjects such as the interviewee's military service, reserve service, war participation, the story of his conscientious objection, his understanding of citizenship, and his understanding of the war in Lebanon.

The interviews were analyzed by relying on the interpretative approach.

2. The entire population of conscientious objectors included 130 individuals who were court-martialed and imprisoned for periods ranging from twenty-one to thirty-five days. Conscientious objectors to the war in Lebanon can be characterized as belonging to the dominant group or elite in Israel. Most were of Ashkenazi origin (81.8 percent), residents of major cities (Tel Aviv, Haifa, Jerusalem), or kibbutz members (25 percent), and former members of youth movements. They comprised a highly educated group: 36 percent held a bachelor's degree, 23 percent had obtained master's degrees, and 7.5 percent held Ph.D.s (mainly in the natural and exact sciences); the rest were undergraduate students or high school graduates. Their military service was in combat units, sometimes in elite units. After their period of conscientious objection, most (86 percent) continued their yearly tour of duty in the reserves. Most of the interviewees belonged to the center-left continuum of Israeli politics; a minority belonged to the radical left.

This approach assumes that the contents of interviews are individual and subjective expressions of intersubjective reality. In other words, it conceives of "ontological narratives" as subjective interpretations of public and cultural narratives (see Somers 1994).

The theory and methodology of this research were inspired by recent attempts in the social sciences to understand human action that is bounded by structural restraints (see Giddens 1976 and 1984). The renewed emphasis on the interaction between agency and structure leads to the use of cultural and ontological narratives as a method of analysis, thus distinguishing this research from current analyses of citizenship that focus on legal discourses and organizational structures. The present research allows us to understand how people come to conceive of their identities as constituted by "a person's temporally and spatially variable place in culturally constructed stories comprised of (breakable) rules, (variable) practices, binding and (unbinding) institutions" (Somers 1994, 67). The theoretical and methodological approach underlying this study conceives of narratives as embedded in an array of social and political relations constitutive of the social world (Friedland and Alford 1991, Laclau 1980, Somers 1994).

I interpret the ways in which the main terms of the discourse on Israeli citizenship obligations are articulated and how they frame the personal narratives of individuals. Analysis and interpretation of the interviews with conscientious objectors elicited two different, yet connected narratives of citizenship. One narrative expressed what I term the *hegemonic discourse of citizenship obligations,* and the other expressed the *alternative discourse* embodied in the practice of conscientious objection.

Military Service as Contribution and Belonging

The arguments raised by the conscientious objectors are expressive of their deep understanding and tacit acceptance of the Israeli model of membership. From these statements, we can glean what that model of membership is: "institutionalised scripts and understandings of the relationship between individuals, the state and the polity as well as the organisational structures that maintain this relationship" (Soysal 1994, 36).

Izhar,[3] a history teacher and a reserve soldier in the artillery corps, portrayed citizenship and its contents in strictly legal terms. He mobilized his wide knowledge of history and philosophy to denote the institutional arenas in which the practices of citizenship are embedded. He defined citizenship

---

3. All names are fictitious. Translations from Hebrew are by the author. Izhar was the first reserve soldier to be jailed for refusing military duty in the war in Lebanon (in August 1982).

mainly in terms of obligations and the duty to obey the law, subjecting rights to the fulfillment of obligations:

> In my classes, I constantly emphasize that citizenship consists of military ser-
> vice, paying taxes, and obeying the law. Paying taxes and going to the army
> both mean obeying the law, [and] they are the stuff of citizenship. That is
> what makes you a citizen and makes you eligible to enjoy the defense and the
> fruits that [the state] equally distributes. This may sound mechanistic and un-
> emotional, but this is how it is and the way it should be. There is nothing
> emotional in citizenship; citizenship is a technical concept. The basic rule, the
> basic rule in this soccer game is that the referee gives the final verdict. You may
> argue, play games, and even make all kind of gestures, but in this case the
> referee can kick you out of the game with the red card, and you are out of
> the game. I mean, the law establishes the final verdict. Why? Because this is
> the agreement upon which we entered the game. It may be right or wrong,
> good or bad; the law has the final word. I can ask what the limits are, but,
> look, this is not a good question. Because if I ask what the limits are, what the
> red lines are, I constantly cast doubts, and I need to test the law according to
> my own criteria. Have I the right to do so? This business works on the as-
> sumption that the verdict of the law is the final verdict, so he [the referee]
> called it, and so it ought to be.

According to Izhar, the fulfillment of obligations is the prime criterion of civic value and an essential prerequisite for the smooth functioning of the political community. Therefore, who is a citizen and who is considered a "person" or a competent member of society are contingent on two interrelated processes: legal codes or laws that establish and interpret the obligations of the individual toward the state and wider sociocultural narratives that equate civic value with the fulfilment of obligations. The "agreement" to join the political community implies that the individual surrenders to the state the interpretation of his obligations toward that community.

Whereas Izhar discussed citizenship in general and emphasized what he termed its "technical" character, other interviewees examined their obligations in greater depth. With an emphasis on the ideology of contribution and belonging, they played down the compulsory nature of military service, transforming its conception as the paramount obligation into almost a matter of personal choice. Take the case of Yotam, a psychology student and an officer in the parachutist corps, who discussed his obligations toward the state in a rational and reflective manner:

> First of all, let's talk about the formal aspect: it is an obligation because if I
> don't go [to the army], I may end up in jail. Well, that's the way it goes in this

country. The second thing is . . . that I think that the army is necessary for the security of the country. I'm willing to participate, and I think it is my duty to participate. It is my duty as a member of society. I would say [it is] my duty not only as an Israeli, but as a member of any community. As a member of a community, I receive something, and I am ready to give something in return. I think it is very important to be in the army—the army is a locus of power in Israel. I don't conceive of my military service only as a formal duty, but as a duty as a member of a community in which I live and which I want to influence. I would like to further clarify, because it sounds a bit confused, that I conceive of it as a social duty, not only in terms of pure defense, but in terms of influence upon a central institution.

Although Yotam mentioned the compulsory aspect of his obligations first, he did not elaborate on it. In fact, he played down its centrality by emphasizing the importance of the army and of each individual's military service for the attainment of national security. Yotam understands the centrality of the army in Israel, and this very centrality brings him to perceive the fulfillment of his military duties in terms of his loyalty and contribution to society—or, in his own words, to the "community." Moreover, his very being and his recognition by others are bound up in his military service, for "the army is a locus of power in Israel." By casting the legal compulsory aspects of military service in terms of contribution and influence on the destiny of the community, Yotam adopted the position enunciated for him in hegemonic discourse: the pursuer of the common good—a common good embodied in the Israeli army as an arena that incarnates collective goals.

Chanoch, a reserve soldier in the aerial defense corps, also adopted a reflective stance toward his obligations to obey the law. This stance allowed him to rationally examine the main arguments on which his obligations are premised and to conclude that military service is justified as a civic obligation. The ground for justifying his obedience and the fulfilment of his duties is the argument that the nation is constantly at war:

The obligation is that there is a law requiring each man to do a tour of duty of thirty days a year in the reserves and three years of regular military service. . . . But I feel that [by my military service] I contribute to the [state], and it is also part of my belonging to this society. And I think that the state is in such a situation that compulsory military service is justified. I mean, at this time or in the short run . . . I can't see right now any alternative to it. Should I conceive of [the Security Service Law] as unnecessary, as draconian, or as mere craziness, I would have thought of it differently. But I think that the country is still, from its inception until today, and maybe . . . surely in years to come. . . . I mean, I think the law is justified because the country is always in a state of war.

The discourse that emerges from the interviews constructs military service as the paramount duty of the individual toward the state, a duty that is justified by a protracted state of war. As the war situation endows obligations and their fulfilment with existential and survival meanings, the compulsory aspect of military service is blurred. Indeed, service in the armed forces becomes the ultimate criteria of membership and participation in the socio-political community. War making and war participation thus constitute the boundaries of the Israeli-Jewish community, and the discourse on war shapes the interpretative, cognitive, and emotional orientations of groups and individuals in Israel. The extent to which this discourse constructs the reality of Israeli Jews is evident in what Arnon, a kibbutz member and a reserve soldier in the infantry corps, termed the "moral law":

> The "moral law" means that the army is beyond [partisan] debate. . . . It means that when you are summoned, you go [because] it is your country, and you must fight for it whatever the consequences. [It means] that in war and in distress we cooperate, we are together. And that we fight when there is no other choice . . . right? . . . that our army is strong enough to cope with this lack of choice. And that we [the army] are ready to accept you [as you are] and to cope with you because you are part of this system and because it is necessary for victory. And these codes are agreed upon even by the extreme right. . . . I haven't said anything deviant; it is agreed upon by [both] the extreme right and the extreme left.

The mobilizing potential of the "moral law" must be interpreted within the cultural universe textured around war and threats to sovereignty. Within this universe, the contribution of each individual to the common war effort is deemed vital. Moreover, the army is the main constituent of a brotherhood, a brotherhood that is far beyond differences in political outlook. By constructing the army and war waging as the embodiments of the common good, both are depoliticized.

Michael, an infantry reserve soldier and a student of engineering, stated it clearly: "In our country, the army is a popular army. We are the army. We don't have militias. When everybody joins the army, your particular political outlook fades away." Within this cultural construct, the army is freed from narrow partisan interests and presented as embodying the broadest interest of the national collectivity in its struggle for survival. Each individual must suspend his particular political judgment while participating in military activities. The perception of soldiering—in particular, combat soldiering—as the epitome of "good citizenship" strengthens this conception by transforming each individual into a carrier of the general will.

The surrender of the soldier's personal or partisan political outlook does not deny him the possibility of interpreting the common good. On the contrary, individuals are required within this discourse to be involved and take the initiative (e.g., to take over from one's commander when he is killed in the line of duty) in order to enhance the common good. This remains true even though the state and its agents claim monopoly over the definition of the army's goals and activities. In other words, participation and involvement are conditional on obedience to the state's demands and the terms in which these demands are formulated. Yet because the fulfillment of duties is articulated in a discourse that emphasizes participation and involvement (albeit within distinct boundaries), individuals are placed in a position that enables them to evaluate critically the deeds of the army and through them the practices of the state.

Under special circumstances, this discourse on citizenship's obligations, articulated in terms of obedience and involvement, can generate a process of critical evaluation that may bring about the emergence of practices embodying an alternative conception of citizenship. These practices may challenge both the hegemonic conception of citizenship obligations and the monopoly the state claims over their formulation. Conscientious objection is such a practice. It involves an alternative conception of obligations as well as a claim to the institution of new rights.

The Alternative Conception of Citizenship Obligations

Israel's war in Lebanon (1982–85) was perceived by wide sectors in Israel as a political war, waged as a political instrument, rather than a defensive war aimed at countering a threat to existence. This overstepping of boundaries led individuals to perceive the state's war practices as irrational. It is in this sense that the war undermined the ideological construction of reality. In other words, the practices of this war could not be contained within or normalized by hegemonic war discourse, and a crisis of legitimation and motivation ensued (Habermas 1975, Pusey 1987). The war in Lebanon thus called into question the very construction of the army and military service as detached from narrow political interests.

Conscientious objectors utilized the hegemonic discourse that conceived of the army, war, and military service as apolitical in order to challenge the practices of the Israeli state. For instance, Jonathan, a journalist and an infantry soldier, appropriated central themes of the hegemonic discourse in his criticism:

> They took the army and used it for unjust purposes. They misused the IDF [Israeli Defense Forces]. The IDF was not meant to engage in such a thing. They used the IDF, I don't know, to force upon Lebanon a new political

order . . . to expel the PLO [Palestine Liberation Organization] from the whole territory . . . to conquer Lebanon, so Israel can police the place . . . and they wanted us to go up there and to die for that. It's not up to me to do that. It is not the mission of the IDF. The army recruits me to defend the country. There [in Lebanon] I was not recruited for that purpose. . . . Being in Lebanon was not for the defense of the country. They distorted the principles, and therefore I was not willing to go.

The claim that "they distorted the rules" presupposes the existence of a system of principles that establishes conditions for war waging (only when there is a threat to existence), its purposes (only for defense), and its targets (other armies). This system of rules serves as boundary conditions because it establishes discursive conditions of action (Hindess 1987) as well as the situations in which social agents are ready to fulfill their obligations.

Aware of the narrow interest embodied in the state's war practices, the conscientious objectors experienced a deep sense of deception and, as a consequence, perceived a gross violation of the unwritten contract between the individual and the state. Eyal, a history teacher and a soldier in the communication corps, pointed to the distortion of his commitment and its diversion to the pursuit of "political goals." The sense of deception is accompanied by the blunt accusation that the state and its political elites endangered his life without justification:

Look, I was called up to fight in a war, in Lebanon . . . while I'm not convinced of its goals. I think that somebody misused the army. . . . I don't think it is the army's mission to do things like this. And this is beyond my feelings that my life was endangered for a futile cause. We invaded a sovereign state, and we tried to rearrange things there. I felt that my life was endangered for unjust causes; they violated my right to life, so I felt that it is justified to refuse.

Eyal accused the state of invalidating the collective character of national security. In other words, the gross exploitation of the army by the state's political elites negates the very construction of war as a collective effort and therefore the existential urgency to participate in it. Moreover, under such conditions, death in war—or risking one's life—is perceived as unjustified and even illegitimate.

By questioning the war in Lebanon, conscientious objectors brought under scrutiny specific principles in the hegemonic discourse, such as the construction of the army as instrumental and nonpartisan. Commanding officers, whose duty it was to sentence the conscientious objectors, tried to convince them to change their minds, mainly making use of arguments about the nonpartisan character of the army and referring to the place of the army in a democratic society. In one such encounter with a commanding officer, Arnon realized the falsity of this "moral law." The reconstruction of his dialogue with his commander allowed him to break through this cultural construction. He suddenly realized that the army had never been apolitical:

> I told my commander: you are telling me that the army is beyond political debate. OK, I want you to say [that this is not true] to the state, to the government that mobilizes the army, because you are under their responsibility, isn't that right? You claim that the army is apolitical, and we know today that these things are not true. What is an apolitical army, huh? Can Kahane appoint the chief of staff? Or would they let someone belonging to Hashomer Hatzair be chief of staff? All this talk about the army being political or apolitical is pure bullshit.[4]

Statements such as Arnon's reveal a thorough questioning of deep cultural categories. These categories, which shape the discursive and practical consciousness of most Israeli Jews, differentiate between the political and the consensual. The political is always identified with narrow interests, whereas the consensual crosscuts group or particularistic interests.

Unveiling the narrow political character of the state's practices in the area of national security and negating the security effort as a collective enterprise, this comprehensive questioning led to a legitimation and motivation crisis. During their first tour of duty,[5] the future conscientious objectors became aware of the deep abyss between their own conception of soldiering and the principles embodied in the war in Lebanon. This widening gap brought these individuals into sharp confrontation with themselves and with the state at the very time they were required to enact their ultimate political obligation—i.e., to participate in war. This confrontation was expressed in a highly articulated narrative by Izhar, the artillery corps soldier and history teacher previously quoted:

4. Meir Kahane was elected to the Israeli Parliament as the head of an extreme rightist and racist party. He openly favored the expulsion of Palestinians from all of (greater) Israel and the establishment of a state based on religious Jewish laws. Kahane's faction was perceived as antidemocratic and was eventually banned from participating in the elections. Hashomer Hatzair is the generalized name for a Zionist left-wing movement and comprises a kibbutz movement, a political party (Mapam), and a youth movement. It has usually been identified with the radical wing of left Zionism.

5. Most conscientious objectors participated in the first stages of the war in Lebanon, which stretched from June to August 1982. Conscientious objection as a social phenomena developed from September 1982 on, more specifically after the massacre at the Sabra and Shatilla camps in Beirut.

I was a genuine product of a pre-1967 education,[6] the conventional Israeli education. . . . You are expected and you expect yourself to contribute to the common framework, to society. . . . You are expected to participate in frameworks that embody the highest values you believe in . . . and therefore it was only natural to go into the army and be a combat soldier. . . . This point is extremely important because it led me to break the rules in 1982 [during the war in Lebanon]. Since 1973 [the 1973 war], but even before that, since 1969, I have been haunted by doubts: whether I can participate—because I'm a soldier—in the subjugation of another people. For a long time, I thought that were I the ruler or the sovereign, I would be happy to have soldiers like myself. I would like to have soldiers who would do anything to justify their opposing attitudes. And the justification comes from your participation in the army, from your unconditional participation in every task you are summoned to. . . . The justification comes from the very fact that you did not evade anything, that you gave your best. . . . And then it came, the moment when I said to myself, "I'm playing into their hands, with my inner doubts, my tearful and self-righteous moral dilemmas" . . . and then the moment came when the spell was broken.

Izhar used the cultural narrative of the Israeli Jewish citizen-soldier in order to describe the experience of its breakdown during the war in Lebanon. Under the conditions of that situation, the rules and practices constructing soldiery as the paramount expression of citizenship collapsed and prevented the citizen-soldiers from continuing to fill their roles. Moreover, the statements "I could not continue living with the gap" and "the spell was broken" are directed at himself. He could no longer assume that citizenship and soldiering were consistent types of subjectivity. Consistency breaks down as soon as war is no longer considered a collective effort.

When the spell is broken, individuals reexamine the narratives that frame their identities and conceive of the rules as breakable, as open to challenge and contestation. This reconstitution of identity is an effort to regain coherence by opposing and even subverting the discourse that constituted them as the "carriers of civic virtue" and as "competent members of society." That discourse, which requires the surrender of personal political viewpoints for the sake of national security, is perceived as invalidating opposition and dividing individuals into "two different persons."

Legitimation and motivation crises paved the way in the Lebanon war for

6. The interviewee refers here to the period stretching from the establishment of the State of Israel to the 1967 war. This period has been constructed in the collective memory of the Zionist left in Israel as "the golden period" of a just society striving for peace and equality. Moreover, pre-1967 is considered as the period of the just wars and as the epitome of national solidarity.

an open challenge to Israeli state practices and to its monopoly over the definition of the scope and content of the individual's obligations to the state. However, in order to ascertain the radical alternative embodied in conscientious objection as a practice that seeks to redefine obligations and institute new rights—to redefine hegemonic discourse rather than reinstate it—we should turn to its specific contents.

Challenging the State's Monopoly over the Definition of National Security

The alternative conception of citizenship obligations embodied in conscientious objection challenges the state's monopoly over the definition of national security and of what constitutes a threat to security. By appropriating the state's hitherto exclusive right to define the meanings of security, the conscientious objectors opened the door to challenging the state's demands of the individual in terms of military service.

During his interview, Amotz, a physician in a tank battalion, insisted on tearing down the sacred aura that surrounds war and military service in Israel: "It really bothers me that people revere military service and, even worse, the very perception of participation in war as sacred. I don't like sacred things; I don't like things that are beyond critique . . . and most people in Israel are uncritical." Amotz distances himself from others in Israel, incorporating a critical stance toward the awe and obedience inspired by the sanctification of the national security. He demystifies war and military service, rejecting unconditional and unreflective obedience to the state's demands. As such, Amotz seizes from the "experts" (i.e., the state agencies) the capacity to define the meanings of defense and national security. Tearing down the halo of holiness surrounding national security paves the way for everyone to define the meaning of security and the struggle for existence. This perspective is reinforced by Chanoch's arguments, which emphasize not only the "profaneness" of security, but also the simplicity of its definition:

> I can't say that only the government can define what it means to defend the country. . . . Anyone can do that; I do not think it is so hard or complicated. There are cases in which the meaning is problematic, where there can be more than one interpretation, and there are cases in which it is crystal clear what defense is and what it is not.

This challenge to the hegemonic discourse and this denial of the state's monopoly over the enunciation of its main terms converge into a demand to allow each individual the leeway to decide where, when, and under what circumstances he will fulfill his military duties. Alexander, a physicist and an officer in the artillery corps, fashioned a "political-philosophical credo" during his interview, which allowed him to examine critically the Security Service Law, the legal framework that establishes his military obligations. Though he accepted the law as a rational arrangement, he did not accept the state's monopoly over the uses of war and the army:

First of all, it must be understood that [the Security Service Law] is not like other laws. There is no other law in this country that commands me to kill another person and to endanger my life. If so, I must ask myself what the goal of the law is, and here I have a long philosophical argument. . . . To make a long story short, my conclusion is that the only way to justify such a law—which is an absurdity because why should I kill a stranger? He did not threaten me or my relatives. If he threatens me personally, I have the right of self-defense, and if he threatens my children, I can extend this right to them. But if he threatens Boozaglo in Kiryat Shmona or Rabinowitz in Hamadia,[7] I couldn't care less. Am I an idiot who would die for them? So the whole story is not to be taken for granted, and the only reason I can accept the law as reasonable and justified is because Boozaglo in Kiryat Shmona can't defend himself alone, nor can I defend myself in Tel Aviv. So the justifying grounds for the law, a law that commands me to go to the army, is only in terms of a mutual defense pact. That's the story. But the government is not a partner in this pact, and the pact is a pact between inhabitants of the country and not between citizens.

Q: What's the difference?

The difference is that if an Israeli citizen living in Los Angeles gets into trouble with the African American community, I'm not obliged to defend him. To be part of the pact, he must come back to Israel. And the same rule applies to the Jewish settler in the Occupied Territories. If he wants to be defended, he must come back to the Green Line borders [the sovereign territory of Israel, the pre-1967 borders]. Now the government is not a partner in this pact; it is only a trustee. And it can only execute the agreement because I can't mobilize the army. But if [the government] bluntly declares that it executes the agreement not for defense's sake, but for a war of choice like the war in Lebanon, this is the grossest aberration that could possibly be.

7. The choice of names and places is not random. Kiryat Shmona is a small town on the Lebanese border that has been the target of rockets; its inhabitants are Israeli Jews of Moroccan origin. Hamadia is a kibbutz bordering Jordan; like most kibbutzim, it is populated by Israeli Jews of Eastern European origin. Hamadia, the neighboring settlements and towns were bombed during the seventies.

By constructing the law in terms of "a pact of mutual defense between inhabitants," Alexander was able to redraw the boundaries of his commitment and establish to whom, where, and when he was committed. This pact challenges and even denies the state's monopoly over the societal means of violence and their usage. This is a claim to extend the practices of democracy and citizenship—such as the active and even autonomous participation of individuals and groups in the shaping of political society (Offe and Preuss 1990)—to the sphere of national security. This claim is highly problematic; because the sphere of national security is the paramount symbol of the state's power and autonomy, the state can ill afford to allow leeway for a plurality of interests and their critical debate.

This radical demand is directed not only at the state, but also at each individual member of the political community. According to this argument, each citizen-soldier is required to express and enact his right to a personal political outlook each and every time he is summoned to war or military service. This demand represents what may be termed the "enabling limits" of citizenship,[8] especially the enabling limits of obligations in Israel. The very terms in which the subject of rights and obligations has been constituted—an emphasis on active involvement and initiative tempered by obedience—allow individuals to subject the state's practices to critical scrutiny and judgment. Moreover, by virtue of their participation, individuals can demand deliberation, negotiation, and change in the scope and contents of their obligations (Giddens 1984, Offe 1985, Offe and Preuss 1990, Turner 1993a). Thus, conscientious objection represents citizenship as an ever-reformulated endeavor (Mouffe 1992a), granting it flexibility and vitality. This representation implies a continuous reformulation of the meaning of security, especially in light of diverging viewpoints and conceptions about this issue.

The alternative conception of citizenship obligations refuses to leave the formulation of national security affairs to "professionals." It conceives of public affairs—especially those belonging to national security—as closely connected to the fashioning of collective and individual fates. As such, the sphere of national security must be opened up to participation according to criteria that are autonomous and even different from the interests represented in the practices of the state and its elites. This claim paves the way for the constitution of hitherto unrealized civic space around national security. Once this space is created, the scene is set for a second group of demands.

8. For the concept of "enabling limits," see Simons 1994.

The Institution of a New Right of Citizenship

The creation of a new civic space around the sphere of national security wherein individuals can challenge the practices of the state empowers them and paves the way for a call to reduce the state's demands on the individual and to institute a new right—conscientious objection.[9] This right can be summarily stated in the following terms: "Because I have the right to establish what security is, the state cannot recruit me unconditionally for every military activity."

This statement can be inferred from the words of Mark, a psychologist and army paramedic who expressed his beliefs concerning the role of the army in a democracy, clearly differentiating between soldiering and citizenship:

> The army in a democratic state should be used only for the defense of life or the defense of freedom. As we live under a democratic regime and we hold differing ideas on issues, if we are drafted into the army and obligated to sacrifice our lives, this can be done only if the army wages consensual wars. Well, you know there is no war that is completely consensual, but I would say that the army can be involved only in missions for survival. If a person is paid for his military service, if the army is a mercenary one, you can send it anywhere. But if I am commanded to obey totally, [the state and the army] can command my obedience only in situations in which as a citizen I can't oppose them, meaning the defense of existence and the defense of freedom.

For Mark, citizenship means the ability to express his political viewpoint and to disagree with others over the definition of the common good. In strong contrast, soldiering implies obedience, and obedience implies an abdication—however temporary—of his rights as a citizen. Thus, he sees soldiering and citizenship as two completely opposed modes of being. Further, he is ready to sacrifice the rights of citizenship in only limited situations: situations in which the realization of citizenship is contingent upon soldiering,

9. Conscientious objection does not exist as a civil right for males in Israel. Only religious girls are granted exemption from military service on grounds of conscience. However, young Orthodox men are granted a postponement of their military duties until they finish their religious studies, and as they tend to continue these studies indefinitely, they are rarely drafted. For all intents and purposes, theirs is also a case of conscientious objection, though not considered as such. The Palestinian citizens of Israel are not called up for military service, though nowhere in the "Security Services Law" can allusions to their exemption be found. For an extensive analysis, see Hofnung (1991, 249–56).

where survival is threatened, and there is a real danger that freedom could be jeopardized.

Embodied in Mark's arguments (and those of other interviewees) is the claim that the state, through the army, can command the fulfillment of obligations only under the condition that the goals of military activities are widely consensual. This demand derives from the following belief: because agreement between members of society is minimal and because the Israeli army is a popular army, the state can command the obedience of citizen-soldiers only when a threat to collective and personal existence is clear and agreed on by all. This condition is aimed at lowering the scope of demands made of the individual and in fact implies an attempt to control the military practices of the state. As the state's agencies can no longer assume unconditional obedience in light of the plurality of viewpoints, it must turn to a "rational" usage of the societal means of violence.

The demand to narrow the scope of obligations is coupled with the demand to institute a new right—the right of refusal to serve on grounds of conscience—and its universal application (Hofnung 1991, 250–56). Amir, a paramedic and a kibbutz member, complained about the double standard the authorities apply in Israel. He used students in orthodox religious academies (yeshivas) as examples to illustrate what he termed the unfairness and even hypocrisy of the state's agents.

> I think that it was unwise and unfair [to sentence us and send us to jail], especially in light of how [the state's agents] act toward other groups . . . yeshiva students, for instance. I assume that if we had political support, I would not end up in jail. Conscience has nothing to do with it; it's only bargaining. . . . Anyway, it is clear to me that what I did, and what others did, damaged the fabric of Israeli society.

The claim raised by the conscientious objectors derives from their elite status as individuals who have been granted a high civic value and not from a position of marginality. Their self-image as carriers of the highest civic value leads them to the statement: "what I did damaged the fabric of Israeli society," for they believe that by conscientiously refusing to serve, they have weakened the arena in which social integration and solidarity are built. Yet high civic value and elite status are seen as a hindrance. Whereas religious parties received privileges for their members mainly because of their political strength, the conscientious objectors experienced a sense of political isolation. They were not backed by political parties or by the vast majority of the protest movements against the war in Lebanon. High civic value diminished their strength as individuals vis-à-vis the state. Their very constitution as

carriers of paramount civic virtue trapped them in a total contract that reduced their leeway for bargaining and negotiating their obligations toward
the state. At the same time, it was the conscientious objectors' high civic
value and their deep consciousness of it that led them to make the following
claim: "It is because I have always been in the front line that the state's
agencies (the army) must withdraw its demands in situations in which my
conscience forbids me to participate."

This alternative conception of obligations entails a sweeping demand to
universalize processes of bargaining and negotiation. It also involves a demand to change the social contract from a full and unconditional partnership to a partial one—a partnership that is ever open to renegotiation and
change. This means that the state's agencies should honor individual motives and interpretations that may enter into open conflict with its own declared and undeclared goals of military activities. According to this
conception, the state can appropriate the resources of social agents only
when there is consensus between groups and organizations in civil society
and the state over the state's war practices; otherwise, the tacit contract
between the individual and the state should be open to deliberation. In
essence, the alternative conception of obligations implies an open demand
for the state to change its practices in the area of national security.

The Dialectical Relationship between
Sociopolitical Control and Agency

The present analysis of conscientious objection not only illuminates how
the practices, institutions, and discourses of citizenship are constitutive of
the subject of rights and obligations, of patterns of political participation,
and of political identity, but also sheds light on the ways in which individuals and social groups question and challenge those very aspects of citizenship, advancing alternative modes of political participation and identity by
means of this challenge. In that sense, conscientious objection can be seen
as part of the dialectic between sociopolitical control and agency.

The constitution of personhood by the act of inclusion within the
boundaries of the political community is not a static and closed endeavor,
for it implies the constitution of agency (Turner 1986). Agency endows
individuals with the capacity to examine discourses, practices, and institutions critically, to regard them as arbitrary, and, as a consequence, to view
them as open to reinterpretation (Mumby and Stohl 1991, Somers 1994).
The agency that is inherent in citizenship is the source of social action and
change, enabling individuals to question models of membership and the
ways in which they have been constituted as subjects of citizenship.

In the case of Israel, hegemonic discourse not only constituted the Israeli-Jewish subject of rights and obligations, as well as patterns of political participation and identity, but also contained the seeds for the emergence of an alternative practice and interpretation of citizenship obligations. The alternative discourse appropriated the hegemonic discourse, interpreted it, and, through its interpretation, challenged the authority of the state to declare war and demand the unconditional participation of citizens in it. This reinterpretation should not be seen as an attempt to redress distortions of hegemonic discourse or to reinstate it in its purity, as Kimmerling (1993a) claims. The very act of appropriation introduces significant changes in central components of the hegemonic discourse, thereby transforming it into a new discourse that challenges both state practices and the hegemonic model itself.

This alternative discourse should be seen as more than an attempt to institute the (new) right of conscientious objection. By challenging the state's monopoly over the definition of national security, individuals appropriate the definition of what constitutes a threat to security and come to perceive their obligations toward the state as open to deliberation and contestation. By demanding a redefinition of their obligations vis-à-vis the state, individuals reinterpret their political identity and claim recognition of alternative forms of participation in the public sphere, forms that in themselves constitute an open challenge to the hegemonic model of membership. This challenge enables individuals to question the terms of their unwritten contract with the state and to conceive of its rules as breakable and its practices as variable (Somers 1993 and 1994). The analysis of conscientious objection in terms of the dialectic between sociopolitical control and agency allows, then, for the understanding of citizenship as a contested terrain, a contest conducted not only over what we get, but also over what we are.

15

Internal Security and Citizenship under the Palestinian National Authority

BEVERLEY MILTON-EDWARDS

WHEN SOCIETIES characterized by decades of deep division and conflict over territory engage in a process of peacemaking or transition from one form of rule to another, the vexed issue of state control over its citizens or of law-and-order function can dominate future political processes and emerging political structures of rule and regulation. The Declaration of Principles (DOP) signed between Israel and the Palestinians in 1993 set the agenda for a new stage in Palestinian state building, a vision of citizenship for the Palestinians of the West Bank and Gaza Strip and for the law-and-order function. This new era of Palestinian self-rule through a project of limited autonomy has allowed the establishment of institutions, ministries, and near-governmental authorities with a facility for limited legislation and symbolic aspects of statehood such as citizen rights and internal security function, which in theory should promote a policing service designed to uphold and protect Palestinian citizens of the autonomous zones.

The DOP and accompanying appendixes outlined a vision of an interim period before Israeli and Palestinian politicians embarked on the final status negotiations to determine real peace and settlement of issues such as the status of Jerusalem, the refugees, and the removal of illegally constructed Israeli settlements in the West Bank and Gaza Strip. As such, the character

An earlier version of this chapter was published in the *British Journal of Middle Eastern Studies,* May 1998. I wish to thank all the staff of the Jubilee Hospital, BCH, Belfast, without whom the completion of this chapter would not have been possible.

of the interim has been important in creating or failing to create an atmosphere of mutual trust and development between Palestinians and Israelis as well as significant political and economic freedoms and developments for the previously subjugated, stateless, and occupied Palestinian residents of the areas conquered by Israel in the war of 1967. Such an interim need only exhibit enough democratic elements to satisfy the architects of the DOP and those from the international community funding the experiment in self-rule. The interim would, however, represent a carefully crafted security agenda, propelled chiefly by Israeli rather than Palestinian concerns in this area—an agenda that sacrifices citizens rights and encourages strong hegemonic control and limited democratic rights, and is sympathetic, encouraged by electoral mandate, to a monopoly of political control by a few in the Palestinian executive. In addition, political plurality has been perceived as a security issue threatening not just the interim but the future of final status negotiations. Such security fears have been further emphasized by the election of Binyamin Netanyahu and a Likud-led government in June 1996 on the platform "Security First."

The "Security First" mantra was mandated by a narrow majority of the Israeli electorate at a time when the country was reeling from the double blow of former Prime Minister Rabin's assassination at the hands of Israeli Yigal Amir and the Hamas suicide bombings that had struck at the heart of Israeli society, resulting in the deaths of women, children, urban commuters, pensioners, and ordinary citizens going about their daily business. This climate of fear should not be underestimated when balanced against Palestinian demands for greater freedoms, Israeli troop redeployment, maintenance of dialogue, and autonomy under the rule of the Palestinian National Authority (PNA). In response to these political realities, both Israel and the PNA were compelled to reinforce one of the institutions designed to facilitate the state-building process and good governance during the interim period. This structure is the state security apparatus, including the police and internal security forces. This police force, according to Article 8 of the DOP, should strive to create an atmosphere of "public order and internal security" for Palestinians during the interim period. In practice, however, it has acted as an institutional signifier of a state prototype of coercion rather than democracy. The deliberate ambiguities of the DOP have encouraged or allowed the "Security First" agenda to be pursued with explicit provision for a "strong police force," which concurrently fails to make precise delineation of the internal security structure and the policing function. The blurring of boundaries in this respect has led to the establishment of an institution known as the Directorate of Police Force under which a variety of official and unofficial internal security agencies have proliferated. This deliberate lack of clarity has filtered through to Palestinian society, where many have queried the identity of their own police force. In addition, the fusion or balance of a rights culture, which grew during the Palestinian uprising, and the creation of a protostate system predicated on the demand for a coercive policing model grants extra powers to police, and blurs the boundaries of internal and national security functions has to be questioned.

Foundations for the Future: State Building the Palestinian Way

Under the Oslo-inspired agenda, the state-building effort undertaken by the PNA is heavily circumscribed by Israel and its security fears. Mechanisms of control over the self-rule experiment, including internal security arrangements, have been propelled as much if not more by Israeli as by Palestinian concerns. Thus, as we know, external or national security is still Israel's sole concern, and the internal security agenda is subject to significant and persistent Israeli influence. The state-building agenda is, for the present, largely at odds with the liberal-democratic vision that has been promoted by so many. These dynamics in turn have shaped the nature of policing in the interim.

Many Palestinians believed that the establishment of the autonomy project in the Occupied Palestinian Territories would herald a new epoch in state building, the foundations of which would pave the way for a smooth transition from subjugated rule to citizens of an open democratic nation-state based on the Palestinian right to self-determination. The state-building endeavor in the West Bank and Gaza Strip has a long history (Sayigh 1997) but was institutionalized in the 1970s with developments in the local political arena, such as PLO support for municipal elections in 1976 and the establishment of nationalist higher councils for health, education, and other issues. These structures of self-rule were further consolidated during the Palestinian uprising when the nationalist movement under the United National Leadership of the Uprising (UNLU) established a formidable nongovernmental sector of institutions as part of a strategy of disengagement from and civil disobedience to Israeli rule. Such moves were paralleled by the nascent Islamist movement that later exceeded the nationalist movement in particular areas of social and welfare provision in the Gaza Strip. Through these activities and institutions there grew within Palestinian society a culture of right awareness centered on strategies of community-based education, politicization, and public debate that reflected a strong democratic impulse balanced against conceptualization of a future Palestinian state that acknowl-edged the prerequisite of a strong conception of citizenship.

The difficulties associated with Palestinian attempts at state building, however, were and remain myriad. They are affected by the model that is generally aspired to—a Western-based model that is perceived as a com-pulsory form (Zubaida 1993, 251). Indeed, it was believed that the DOP would encourage Palestinians to build institutions of government and state that would reflect the Western-inspired Israeli and European norm. Yet, in reality, during the interim period, the DOP has encouraged the opposite—a state-building effort that focuses on a highly centralized form of bureaucracy and hegemonic control through a pernicious and coercive state apparatus. The influence of regional state models such as those in neighboring Egypt, Jordan, and Syria become far more appropriate in measuring the Palestinian experiment in self-rule.

The Palestinian example greatly differs in one degree from its Arab neigh-bors: the state-building effort is heavily circumscribed by Israeli control over Palestinian destiny, and therefore the vision of Palestinian statehood (or po-litical development) is shared as Israel's politicians have engaged in a variety of attempts to place mechanisms of control over the Palestinian experiment in self-rule. In addition, although state building (by any other name) has been permitted, Israel has still not fully come to terms with Palestinian rights to self-determination and ultimately to territorially based statehood.

A Journey from Israeli Militarism to Palestinian Militarism

Since the signing of the Oslo deal and the limited redeployment of Israeli troops in the West Bank and Gaza Strip, many writers and scholars have focused on how Palestinian society can move from political limitations im-posed by more than quarter of a century of Israeli military occupation (with the development of economic and administrative practices of control and restriction) to a more democratic, pluralistic, citizen-rights, and accountable system of governance and political life. A variety of suggestions have been made and supported through externally funded development and education programs. For example, the scheduling and conduct of Palestinian elections in January 1996 to the Palestinian Legislative Council and the post of presi-dent of the PNA were widely supported by external backers of the DOP who were keen to dispel undercurrents of disquiet in the Palestinian com-munity about the PNA's apparent lack of accountability. Nevertheless, a significant obstacle to this move toward democratization was the militarism of Palestinian society characteristic of both the past and the present. By this, I mean the current proclivity of the PNA toward military methods, the uniform culture promoted by Arafat himself, aggressive patriotism, and the reliance on the gun for public order and internal security. Another feature of this approach is, once again, the irresistible regional model in this respect. In the Middle East, this model has resulted in national security agendas predicated on stable hegemonic control at any price. In this context, policing and internal security in defense of citizens are often taken to their extremes, and citizens are viewed as a subversive threat to the state. Such military involvement in politics and large internal security structures have been a feature of the region since the 1950s.

The military is associated with the modernization process—independence from the colonial past and the establishment of one-party rule. Securocratic control of politics has characterized a geographically diverse number of states including Iraq, Libya, Egypt, Syria, and Algeria. National security issues have been employed by Arab and other Middle Eastern states as a doctrine to maintain stability and control internal opposition, but this doctrine calls for political liberalization or pluralism. Elizabeth Picard (1993) argues that the militarized authoritarian model that characterized internal security in many Middle Eastern regimes in the 1990s represents a significant obstacle to meaningful democratization, greater accountability, and pluralism in these societies (269–70). States remain governed by politicians in army uniforms, increasingly dependent on the national and internal security structure to maintain rule. The institutions of security thus remain strong and rigid in the face of even the most limited suggestions for reform or liberalization. The distance between the state and its citizens is maintained and promoted by the security structure.

National security remains a primary preoccupation of these states in the face of instability from within as well as without. In this respect, they reflect the same features that mark the Latin American militarized landscape, where, according to Ugarte (1990), the distinction between the sphere of national defense (force to defeat external enemies) and internal security (protecting the rights of citizens) is blurred and sometimes lost entirely. In the Middle East, this loss has resulted in national security agendas predicated on a stable hegemonic state at any price, even if it results in the abuse or negation of citizens' rights, wide-scale oppression, criminalization of dissent, and subjugation of significant groupings of internal opponents. In this context, policing or internal security in defense of citizens is taken to its Kafkaesque extreme, and citizens are viewed as a subversive threat to the state, justifying extreme measures including imprisonment without trial, torture, death in detention, the establishment of state security courts, and murder of citizens.

As Picard (1993) notes, in the 1990s, the "balance sheet of security versus individual rights has deteriorated," with human rights labeled a "disaster" (270). Regarding the rights of citizens with respect to their own police force that Picard further notes, "it is especially in relation to enforcement of security laws by the police that the authoritarian state has been strengthened in the Arab world" (ibid.). In such a context, it is difficult even for civilian-led governments to pursue democratization of the political system.

In the Palestinian example of the interim period, however, an opportunity could have been afforded through new approaches to the issues of policing and associated internal security functions. However, there has already been a failure to separate external-national defense functions from policing and internal security. The failure to permit the establishment of a Palestinian national army and the maintenance by Israel of the national security function were early indicators of the problems that might beset the new experiment. For a variety of reasons, then, the Palestinian case failed to offer a new agenda. Further problems apparent almost from the start included the failure to separate the external from the internal security function, the absence of a national army, the incorporation of former freedom fighters (Palestinian Liberation Army [PLA]) into crime-fighting service, and the aforementioned proclivity toward militarism as a culture. Thus, any hope for the establishment of a civilian policing model was strangled at birth. The DOP encouraged the blurred boundaries approach to national and internal security, leaving the Palestinians bereft of a truly blank canvas on which to create a policy (after wide consultation within the community), administered by the PNA, that would maintain an important dichotomy between security functions and thus promote a positive relationship between society and the state, through its citizens. The incorporation of the PLA into internal security structures, along with local paramilitary organizations and armed bands such as the Fatah Hawks, has also hampered the promotion of a democratic impulse and has strengthened the likelihood that a democratic deficit will be maintained. An authoritarian militocratic or securocratic state will hamper Palestinian aspirations for liberal democracy. Conversely, however, they may provide the very stability through coercion that today's Palestinian state builders need and that Israel requires as part of the maintenance of its own security agenda.

In addition, Yasser Arafat's willingness to promote and incorporate the uniform culture through the proliferation of security forces, maintenance of military-style parades, funeral parades, and military commemoration days, as well as his own personal disinclination to shed army fatigues and uniform for the suited garb of politicians and civilian leaders, all point to the maintenance of militarism over liberalization. A project that embraces this path to internal and national security in the interim period, no matter how convincing the arguments for stability, will make it extremely difficult, if not impossible, for a truly civilian policing culture to emerge once stability or statehood has been achieved. The Palestinians need only witness the political developments in neighboring Jordan or Egypt, where the liberalization process has been adopted. In both cases, the continued militarism of the internal security function has hampered developments and resulted in the repression of opposition through states of emergency, imprisonment without trial, torture, and the establishment of military-security courts. The policing project implemented in the West Bank and Gaza Strip as part of the DOP offers little indication at present that the Palestinians will establish a civilian policing structure that would act on behalf of citizens rather than the state and will be supported by an independent judiciary, and whose personnel will be drawn from the population at large rather than from the ranks of former military and paramilitary organizations. The development of the Palestinian Police Force (PPF), to date, has proved a far cry from other attempts at policing a transition or interim, such as in Namibia, South Africa, or El Salvador. In these cases, although the long-term outcomes have not always been promising, initial designs did focus on a civilianized policing model, breaking away from a militarized, colonial, authoritarian security function. Even from the start, however, the Palestinian transition has been based on a militarized experiment in self-rule, where democracy and pluralism would be stifled.

Law Enforcement under Occupation

In the past seventy-five years, the Palestinians of the West Bank and Gaza Strip have witnessed five different police forces, from the 1920s with the establishment of the Palestinian Gendarmerie, followed by the Palestine Police under the British Mandate, to the 1950s, when both the Jordanian and Egyptian governments deployed their police forces and recruited Palestinian officers, to the post-1967 period, when Israel, along with its national army, the Israeli Defense Forces (IDF), deployed their police force in the West Bank, Gaza Strip, and Arab East Jerusalem. Under all these administrations, control of the policing function remained in the hands of outsiders. Although Palestinian officers were recruited and served in the ranks of all five forces, they never populated the highest echelons of the service. More importantly, the police forces were upholders of the law and government of Britain, Jordan, Egypt, and Israel, never the Palestinian state.

Policing the West Bank and Gaza Strip under the Israeli occupation became a marginalized feature of the blurred national and internal security boundaries. From 1967, when the then largely unprofessional Israel police force opened stations and deployed its policemen in West Bank and Gaza towns and cities, the police were by and large viewed as another institution in the Israeli occupation. Palestinians were recruited to the Israeli police force to serve in the Occupied Palestinian Territories, but the Israeli police culture dominated the force and dogged its role. Regarded as a "poor relation" to the IDF, the police were largely engaged in duties such as traffic incidents and petty crime, and the so-called real business of internal security was placed in the hands of the IDF. Until the late 1980s, the Israeli police force lacked credibility even with its own citizens, who regarded them as unprofessional. The model of policing adopted in the West Bank and Gaza Strip represented a classic authoritarian approach identified with the policing function in other deeply divided societies (Brewer 1991, 179–91). In this model, a dominant state is pitted against the interests of a subordinate community. Policing is associated with keeping the peace and with preventing, at all costs, communal violence and the breakdown of public order. Palestinian residents without citizenship were subjected to a plethora of laws and orders that competed in the suppression and criminalization of their activities. The state was interested only in stability through security and the pacification of the Palestinian population. Through its security structures, including the police, Israel has pursued this policy for more than twenty years.

The policing function, like so many other functions associated with internal and national security, was radically altered by the outbreak of the Palestinian uprising in December 1987. As part of a campaign of civil disobedience and the creation of alternative structures and institutions of self-rule, Palestinians who had become used to managing internal antisocial or petty criminal activity themselves were encouraged to jettison any dependence whatsoever on the Israel Police Force (IPF). Twenty years of Israeli occupation had already promoted the growth of alternative means of community-based law enforcement through the maintenance of strong family, clan, religious, or faction ties. The leadership of the uprising then called on the community to appropriate the policing function for themselves. In the spring of 1988, there were calls for mass resignations from serving Palestinian policemen and for the formation of popular committees and strike forces *(quwa dariba)* to ensure the maintenance of internal security and a semblance of law and order. Following the mass resignations, the Palestinians attacked Israeli police stations throughout the West Bank and Gaza Strip, and boycotted the police themselves. The police responded by scaling down their activities and even closing some police stations. Israeli police officers no longer patrolled the streets of Palestinian cities towns and villages alone;

rather, they accompanied the IDF and acted as an ancillary presence in collecting taxes or forcing shopkeepers to open their stores and break strike commands.

Following the mass police resignations in March–April 1988, the nationalist leadership pledged to ensure the formation of local committees to prevent a collapse of public order or the proliferation of petty crime. This initiative proved hugely popular and successful with the community for the first year of the uprising. Local people's courts were established, and at these courts complaints were dealt with by "popular judges" with their judgments based on *shari'a* law. In addition to the local committees and courts, traditional or notable figures from the community were identified as arbitrators of inter-Palestinian disputes. The Israeli authorities responded by criminalizing popular committees and declaring them illegal. Following a mass arrest campaign orchestrated throughout 1988, the popular committee system was severely weakened by the beginning of 1989. As noted in reports from human rights organizations, these committees *(lijan al-aslah),* had, however, presented the Palestinians with an opportunity to report crimes, disorder, and public grievances over issues such as "clan feuds, land disputes, financial questions and questions related to suspected collaborators" (B'tselem 1994, 31) The *lijan* were forced underground, but still managed to operate in severely reduced circumstances and perpetual threat of arrest and imprisonment. In addition, the *lijan* remained faction led and would reflect the prevailing political agenda of their organization rather than the community as a whole. Some disputes were thus considered the province of one faction, say the Popular Front for the Liberation of Palestine (PFLP), over another, such as the Fatah.

An unfortunate consequence of Israeli measures during this period was the subsequent rise in policing by the armed gangs associated with the various factions of the PLO and the Islamic movement. These groups—including the Fatah Hawks, the Black Panthers, and the PFLP's Red Eagles—initially enjoyed widespread community support. They actively pursued suspected collaborators and brought them down, often through execution. The leaders of these groups were largely young men *(shebab)* who reveled in their newfound status. They became subject to all sorts of myths designed to reinforce Palestinian notions of emancipation from Israeli authority. The increasing autonomy of the armed strike forces—not just from Israel, but from the Palestinian political leadership—became a worrying aspect of policing and the internal security function by the early 1990s. The nationalist leadership were unable to reign in the armed wings who were criticized, mostly by an external audience, for their suspected human rights abuses and increasing independence of action from the political committees. By 1991–

92, the specter of the type of internecine violence that had crippled and ultimately brought about the collapse of the first Palestinian uprising in 1936–39 stalked the Palestinian community. The internal security situation had deteriorated rapidly, so much so that, as Usher (1995c) remarks, the uprising had turned "into the property of rival bands of armed strike forces[,] . . . a domestic affair . . . drift[ing] to internecine struggle" (5).

The democratization of Palestinian society, which had been heralded by the uprising, was soured by the developments within the realm of policing and internal security. The pluralist civic culture that had been rights based and rights aware was soon dogged by the increasingly authoritarian and unprofessional ethics of the strike forces who were increasingly engaged in open conflict with one another for political dominance of the community. The strike forces became the provenance of individual men and explicitly associated with settling personal and political vendettas rather than with protecting the community from its own criminal elements as well as from the external threat of the IDF and associated security forces. They ultimately were not very good at policing, preferring a paramilitary function to a policing service to the community. They also possessed poor if any investigative skills, and some ignored human rights issues, particularly when dealing with individuals they considered collaborators. The developments of the early 1990s did not augur well for the future. Nevertheless, there is little doubt that the deterioration of internal security was something that the PLO wanted to avoid at all costs and may yet have been another factor that encouraged them to the negotiating table in Oslo.

The Peace Process: Policing to a New Beat

It is important to note that policing has been an important feature of the interim and has huge implications for the final status negotiations and any future political settlement. Palestinian policing is a dynamic phenomenon, and many changes have been discernible in the late 1990s. The new police force is entirely Palestinian in nature and completely independent of the IPF. It has also been established to provide express support for the Oslo formula. In addition, unlike other institutions of autonomy associated with the experiment in self-rule, the PPF has no ministry or directorate; decision making remains the provenance of the PNA president and his appointees, which has allowed the PPF to exceed its powers, its official remit, numbers of officers, all on the orders or with the express agreement of the president. As such the PPF currently stands as the most powerful institution within the PNA. The police force, most of whose officers are not actually engaged in ordinary policing duties, is for the most part an army and an internal security apparatus, with as few as one in fifteen wearing the blue uniform of the civil police. Nevertheless, all branches and units of the PPF have so-called normal policing powers, such as arrest. There are now, according to unofficial estimates, some forty thousand members of the PPF; the official remit provided for a maximum of twenty thousand officers. This implies a ratio of nearly 1 officer for every 110 people, compared to the international norm of 1 to 350. In practice, this means an agent of internal security or police stands on almost every street and at every roadblock in the densely populated centers of Palestinian community granted autonomy under the Oslo arrangements. Whether proto–Palestinian citizens find this proliferation of forces reassuring or intimidating has been the matter of fierce debate. The community has been literally swamped with police forces. Many of the police fulfill quasi-military functions in the absence of the national army and of a national security policy. Others remain dedicated to the proliferation of the internal security function and fall under the widely interpreted preventative security rubric. There is little or no distinction between the police and a military function, and the provision of a professional law enforcement agency is a largely unfulfilled wish among many sectors of the Palestinian community. The four official structures of the PPF are augmented by the unofficial proliferation of other "policing branches," including Preventative Security, headed by the now infamous Colonel Jibril Rajub and Mohammad Dahlan. More worrying is the level of policing expertise within the PPF as a whole. As the author of a confidential donor report written in 1996 remarked, "In general one can say that the lack of knowledge of policing is about 99 percent among members of the PPF."[1] In addition, those twelve thousand serving officers of the civil police are not "beat police"; rather, they fulfill guarding or station duties. This is an issue that the civil police themselves recognize, but they hope it reflects the interim rather than final status of the force. As Colonel Mohammad Shabawi, the Civil Police Training coordinator in Gaza, declared, "The civil police, like the police anywhere else in the first rather than the third world should be a police service not a police force. . . . But under the transition we cannot be a police service, we must be a force, we have experienced an armed opposition" (interview with author, 1997).

The PNA, headed by Yasser Arafat, has taken steps that guarantee rather than threaten the development of a militarized police force in the interim era. The responsibilities for national security and the civilian police are not defined; there is no clear division of responsibility. Military and paramilitary personnel from the PLA and other associated paramilitary groups have been

1. The report is still classified. It is in the author's possession, and the quote is from page 5.

allowed to join and head the new force, with ineffective provision for re-training or human rights issues. The transfer of thousands of PLA soldiers into the new policing structure was articulated in the Cairo Accords, with the promise of seven thousand PLA men (so long as they held a Jordanian or Egyptian passport) along with their spouses and children. Former com-manders of the PLA, including Colonel Nasser Yusuf (who is at least the only officer with police experience) and Major General Abd al-Razzaq Ma-jaideh, were appointed to head the new police force. Indeed, the provisions made in the Cairo Accords give the appearance of the almost wholesale import of the PLA into the new policing structure of the West Bank and Gaza Strip. This has had serious implications for the ethos of the policing service since the arrival of the PLA forces in the Gaza Strip in the spring of 1994. The force that arrived in Gaza was poorly equipped and ill-prepared for the job—"not a police force at all, but an army; a small lightly-armed and ramshackle army, but an army all the same," wrote one British journalist (Brown 1994, 23–27). Although there was provision for training, it re-mained underresourced and a low priority on the new policing agenda. The former officers of the PLA and the new recruits from within the West Bank and Gaza Strip, including the former members of the Fatah Hawks, were given a military approach to training and provision of policing. Today, the military ethos is still present at an everyday level in the civil police force; senior officers still talk of recruits as "soldiers," not police officers. Although senior officers also aspire to a civil police function—as one officer remarked, "it is our greatest project to build our state and this police service as a civilian institution"—they are hampered by a variety of factors (Lt. Col. Mohammad Samud, interview with author, 1997).

The DOP made provision for the funding of activities such as narcotics or traffic policing through appropriate disbursements received from and ap-proved by the donor community. It was believed that the donor community, in particular with support from the Scandinavian states, would guide the policing model to a more appropriate civilian function. Certainly, there has been no lack of willingness to provide police trainers with courses and tech-nical assistance in these areas, and the United Nations–sponsored office to coordinate the policing provision was optimistic in its ability to promote a full-scale range of professional assistance. In practice, however, international assistance has been unable to fulfill many of the plans it had to assist the full development of a professional democratic Palestinian police service. The do-nor community, like the Palestinian community, has had to reconcile itself to the clash of agendas with the need for the swift implementation of a strong, coercive police model, which has overridden the promotion of a long-term civilian-democratic policing service that would uphold the law on behalf of the state and the community. Disbursements have often been held up. The first year of deployment witnessed a Palestinian police without adequate housing, uniforms, and equipment. The payment of salaries was often held up, and the police were forced to rely on the local community for food and shelter. This was hardly the most auspicious start to a new police force with a professional approach. In addition, the problems reflected the universal issues that beset the transformation of any policing structure and more specifically what Stanley (1996) refers to as "the general absence of international police assistance programs" to support the reform of police, particularly in formerly deeply divided societies (44).

From Freedom Fighters to Crime Fighters: The Recruitment and Training Culture

The recruitment and training process involved in the establishment of the PPF has had an important impact on the organization's culture of policing. The recruitment and training agenda had the potential to shape an open police culture with a broad and positive emphasis on the respect for human rights and the state-building effort currently under way in Palestinian society. Whereas other cases, such as the South African experience, have highlighted the need for training programs that give police and civilian trainers a mixture of course cultures (police academies plus university degrees, community involvement, and practical courses), this need has been only partially reflected in the Palestinian example. In addition, the Palestinian case has often represented a very poorly coordinated training program developed on an ad hoc basis as need and funding have arisen. There is a distinct lack of "active partnership" in the training culture of the PPF; links between the police and the community sector, including human rights organizations, have been poor and ill-fated. Nevertheless, there has been progress in the recruitment and training culture of the PPF.

The need for the rapid deployment of a new Palestinian police force to coincide with the redeployment of Israeli troops away from Palestinian centers of population has already been emphasized. The text of the Oslo Accords signed in September 1993 and the Cairo Agreement signed in May 1994 allowed only a few months for the Palestinians (in coordination with the Israelis and the donor community) to establish and deploy a new police force in the Gaza Strip and Jericho area. The most striking example of this lack of preparedness took place on 11 May 1994, when 140 Palestinian police arrived in the town of Deir al-Balah in the Gaza Strip. The police didn't really know what they would be doing; they were greeted by the community as returning heroes, yet the majority of these men had not been in Gaza for more than twenty-seven years, and some had never lived there at all. It was, in essence, a homecoming of exiles rather than the deployment of a new police force. Delays in the implementation of the agreements coincided with the deployment of large numbers of police with no functions to fulfill. In the Gaza Strip, by the autumn of 1994, Palestinian police were posted on main arterial roads every few hundred yards, and the approach to the Erez border with Israel was literally littered with makeshift Palestinian police checkpoints posted by oil drums. The Israelis, who relinquished their police stations and other installations, left before the arrival of their Palestinian replacements; there was no official "hand-over" period in which to deal with coordination, briefings, and professional matters. It was only through the Joint Security Committee (JSC) that practical provision was made for the introduction of arms, equipment, and foreign assistance, as well as the management of the joint patrols of common boundaries that would take place between Palestinian and Israeli forces. This situation was a striking contrast to the arrangements made in South Africa, where, according to Justice Albie Sachs (1996), "joint activities were extremely important, particularly in the area of internal security where common agendas were discovered, everyone was made to feel an owner of the process of peace and there was a truly joint-functioning of the process" (author's notes from a meeting in Belfast in 1996).

The civil police opened police stations in the Gaza Strip and in Jericho in the old Israeli police installations. A training facility, known as the Academy, was partially initiated in Jericho; this facility consisted of old and worn tents (with no electricity or running water) for new recruits and four or five breeze block classrooms with no windows, air-conditioning, or desks, although one or two classrooms did have a blackboard and overhead fan. By the spring of 1997, the civil police academy in Jericho, which ran basic training (forty-five days) and management training, was operating on a budget of $3,000 a month; recruits received no living allowance for the first months; and the entire academy did not possess even one photocopier. In Gaza, the situation marginally improved with the completion of the first breeze block classrooms and washrooms, but accommodation and kitchens are still housed in old army tents, many of which are protected with plastic sheeting. There was no facility specifically equipped for this function, and police recruits were drilled and marched around the dusty streets of Gaza and Jericho by elderly PLA commanders. Costs were and remain a continual source of grievance and preoccupation. Nevertheless, it was hoped that the estimated $6 million needed for a purpose-built training facility in Gaza (which would train all PPF personnel, not just the civil police) would be raised by Germany, Denmark, Holland, Sweden, and Norway by the end of 1998.

The recruitment process was poorly organized and led to an immediate politicization rather than professionalization of the civil police force. Self-recruitment took place through the PLA and Fatah Hawks; service in these forces almost guaranteed entry into the new force. The only obstacle preventing this immediate flow of personnel was that the Cairo Accords gave Israel the power to veto any proposed candidate. An emphasis was put on prior military or paramilitary experience and on military-type physical training, fitness, and agility rather than on the intellectual abilities of police recruits. The ready association between the PNA, the Oslo Accords, and Yasser Arafat's Fatah organization, and the tensions between the PNA and the rejectionist camp also led to a partisan approach to police recruitment. Although recruits sympathetic to Hamas, for example, did join the force, the PPF was largely associated in people's minds with the Oslo process. Rejection of one often implied rejection of the other, and the legitimacy issue, as I explain in later sections, became particularly important. Inside the West Bank and Gaza Strip, advertisements for recruits to the police service were placed with the local press. Selection criteria were less than rigorous, and the result was an ad hoc recruitment policy that, as one commentator working in the human rights sector remarked, attracted a motley collection of "ex-prisoners, deportees, the poorly educated, convicted murders and former heroes of the Intifada" (anonymous, interview with author, 1995). Those recruits in the civil police who are educated and keen to adopt a professional approach to training and police practice are a distinct and increasingly frustrated minority.

Training the PPF is an essential element in shaping the context of police-community relations. The belief that training plays an essential part in the career of every police officer, from the highest to the lowest ranks, is generally regarded as a good thing. Training has a particular importance given the new policing context and the quality of the recruits that have been selected for the force. Given the military-activist profile, the need to retrain as well as provide a professional ethos to new recruits is vital to the force. As the UN coordinator in 1995 charged with the policing agenda remarked, "Our task is difficult, at present most of the officers of the PPF were formerly in the PLA. The task of training them therefore is to encourage the move from a military approach to policing to a civil approach" (P. Blekelia, interview with author, 1995). The ethos associated with the training and retraining of the PPF, as determined by the UN coordination officer, has been to get officers to accept a civilianized policing and law enforcement function. There has been a desire to move from an emphasis on war, military preparedness, and guerrilla tactics to a training based on community, impartiality, and a peacetime police. This move has been regarded as very important in shaping the training agenda while at the same time acknowledging the difficulties associated with transforming a military structure like the PLA and Fatah Hawks into a police force as part of a state-building exercise. Police advisor Thøger Berg Nielsen, who acted as coordinator in 1997, was slightly more circumspect, recognizing the context in which the police in general operate:

> They know that they are here to serve the community but there is no community policing model. There is no model, there is one chief of the police and I'm not sure whether the time is ripe yet for a real structure. . . . But what can you do but prepare police officers for the future, we're placing the tools in their hands. This at least is guaranteed but I cannot say that the future will allow them to put this approach into action. (interview with author, 1997)

Training has taken and is taking place at two levels. The first level concentrates on the provision of training and basic instruction to all recruits to the force. The second level, where the most resources have been committed, is taking place within the higher echelons of the force with the hope that a professionally trained officer corps will become the trainers of the lower ranks. Even at this stage, however, it is the trainers who are being trained or retrained, but the adoption of a training strategy and the resources to help implement it are still some way off. Training also has two emphases. The first places importance on physical training, knowledge of weapons, policing riots, public order duties, quasi-military functions such as marching, and guerrillalike maneuvers. The second focuses on police procedures, human rights training, forensic science, crime scenes, detection, the chain of command, and police management issues. At the highest level, officers receive training both locally and abroad in riot control, human rights, traffic police, rescue operations, and management. An effort has also been made to highlight the limitations involved in training; as the UN coordinator noted, "We are not able to train everyone" (Nielsen, interview with author, 1997). And even in this limited approach to training the trainers have been hampered by a further difference in training in the Gaza Strip and in the West Bank. The training agenda is also beset by other issues, such as rivalry between the branches of the PPF; some civil police have, for example, questioned the efficacy of traffic training for all nine branches of the PPF. In addition, the training program is affected by levels of bilateral assistance that is not coordinated through the UN coordinator's office. These additional factors have played their part in hindering the emergence of an organic approach to training, which is further exacerbated by the sheer logistical difficulties associated with the geographical separation and Israel's formal control of movements between the two areas. Thus, police personnel may not move freely to offer courses or participate in training in both areas, even high-ranking officers are often refused permission either to leave the West Bank or to enter Gaza. Training has been important, but a Hobbesian state of nature is assumed, and nurture is not promoted. Training priorities assume the worst case scenario—emergency police, riot control, the breakdown of public order, the use of arms against a civilian population, as well as an armed internal opposition in the form of the Islamists. The priorities in setting the training agenda are directed by the possibility of a state of chaos, not by a sense of stability. Under these circumstances, it is difficult to see how a community policing culture can be promoted and permeate the ranks of the PPF.

A Police State Without a State

The deployment of the PPF since 1994 has met with mixed fortunes characterized by a shortfall between expectation and reality within the organization and outside it. The hopes and optimism shared by everyone in the Palestinian community have been shattered and reshaped by the practical relationship that has grown up between the people and its police force in this interim period. The challenge of forging a police service established on the firm foundations of democracy has been hampered by the remit outlined in the Oslo and Cairo Accords, the widespread difficulties associated with the interim period, the dynamic of the politics of the interim period itself, and the inability or unwillingness on the part of the political leadership to relinquish power while they are establishing hegemonic control in the West Bank and Gaza Strip. Finally, the oblique lines of function between the civil police and other internal security agencies are predominant not only in the minds of the Palestinian public but also among some recruits to the force.

The remit on policing was initially warmly welcomed by the Palestinian population. The Palestinians regarded the deployment of their own police force as an important symbol of statehood without a state. The arming of this force was also a significant feature in the absence of a national army. In the first months of the deployment of the police, a honeymoon period was experienced. Although there were major logistical difficulties, such as the lack of training and equipment and the late payment of salaries, the presence of Palestinian police in the towns and refugee camps of the Gaza Strip and in Jericho was generally perceived as a good thing and an important step in the state-building process. Even members of the Palestinian opposition, and more specifically the Islamicists, initially agreed that although they themselves would not relinquish their arms, they did believe that the establishment of a Palestinian police force was a good thing. By the winter of 1994, however, the remit on policing had altered, the honeymoon period was officially over, and both the police and the Palestinian community faced up to the unpalatable fact that the remit on policing included coercive measures against the Palestinian community, largely at Israel's insistence.

The Islamists in particular believed they were being singled out in a campaign organized by Yasser Arafat and orchestrated by the security forces, including the civil police, to eliminate their presence. Throughout the summer of 1994, Gaza police chief Colonel Nasser Yusuf had made repeated calls on Hamas and Islamic Jihad to disarm in accordance with the conditions of the Oslo and Cairo Accords. The Islamicists vehemently refused, citing the call as an unpatriotic Israeli-led demand and likening the Palestinian security structure and its relationship with Israel to the South Lebanon Army led by General Anton Lahad (Milton-Edwards 1996b, 199–225). Hamas organized a campaign opposing the call to disarm, and the police in turn arrested and imprisoned Islamists in the Gaza Strip. By August 1994, Palestinian police were ordered to arrest Palestinians suspected of supporting or sympathizing with the Islamic movement and other rejectionist elements. Between August and November 1994, more than four hundred Palestinians were arrested. The tension culminated in a bloody clash between police and protesters leaving mosques in Gaza after Friday prayer on 18 November 1994. Black Friday, as it became known, resulted in Palestinian police firing on crowds of Palestinian demonstrators and a death toll of thirteen (Milton-Edwards 1996a, 176–77).

The Black Friday debacle attracted widespread censure of the police and the PNA, and served as an important watershed in the burgeoning policing remit. The failure of the police to maintain public order, the deaths as a result of police gunfire against their own people, and the determination of the PNA through its security forces to defeat Palestinian opposition served to alter the policing remit in the Gaza Strip and presented important indicators of the nature of police rule to come in the West Bank. Any hopes that the policing remit might herald an era of peace, democracy, and stability were shattered on Black Friday, and for the first time ever in the West Bank and Gaza Strip, the prospect of civil war between Palestinians looked like a distinct possibility. In the aftermath of Black Friday, widespread attempts at reconciliation, mediation, and negotiation took place between the Islamists, the PNA, and the police with Palestinian Arabs from Israel acting as neutral mediators. In addition, it was announced that the Arab-Israeli figures would investigate the Black Friday incident, but this announcement only served to highlight the failure of internal provision for independent investigation within the ranks of the police service. In addition, three years later there appeared to have been little long-term assessment within the civil police of the impact of this incident and its import in terms of police-community relations.

Beginning in November 1994, the civil police and other branches of the

PPF were increasingly ordered by the executive to devote their resources and energies to the quashing of Palestinian opposition. In February 1995, Yasser Arafat announced the establishment of the PNA's own State Security Court. The establishment of the court was widely condemned but was perceived within the security sector as an important facility in its campaign against the Palestinian opposition. The policing remit was boosted by the further increased deployment and proliferation of the security services and police. For example, following autonomy in the West Bank towns of Ramallah, Bethlehem, Tulkarem, Nablus, Qalqilya, and Jenin in the autumn of 1995, it was estimated that in the town of Jenin, some forty thousand Palestinian residents were to come under the authority of one thousand police and intelligence officers. The campaigns of mass arrest, imprisonment, and trial continued, and allegations of torture surfaced throughout 1995. The policing remit was perceived, particularly by a vocal Islamic opposition, to be directed away from the protection of Palestinians toward the persecution of the Palestinian opposition. A worrying trend emerged of a police and internal security apparatus that represented the state coercion of many segments, not just the Oslo rejectionists. It was not always acknowledged that much of this activity was Israeli inspired and part of the security agenda of the interim period, nor was Arafat's own position in this security equation.

Hostility and tension within the Palestinian community against the internal security forces resurfaced and reached new heights in the spring of 1996 following the heinous suicide-bombing campaign against Israel orchestrated by Hamas and Islamic Jihad. Succumbing to intense Israeli pressure and threats, Yasser Arafat ordered a mass arrest campaign against the Islamicists. By April 1996, the PNA announced that some nine hundred Palestinians had been arrested in the wake of the suicide bombings. The police were ordered to raid colleges, universities, and welfare and social institutions. Students, teachers, academics, doctors, lawyers, and human rights workers were detained and interrogated. Among the political elite, a perception began to emerge that the security situation under Palestinian control was becoming more repressive than under Israeli control. The aspirations of pluralism, multiplicity of opinion, and opposition were quashed under the increasingly authoritarian and invasive security structure established under the PNA. Events of the following year, 1997, further highlighted the growing gap between police and community as Israel used the security issue as a means of delaying resumption of peace talks and final status negotiations. The pressures on the police to initiate further campaigns of arrest, detention, and unlawful interrogation led to an increase in the number of deaths in police detention and a further decline in public confidence in the ability of the police to provide a service of law and order on an equal basis. This situation is likely to remain unchanged for as long as Israel insists that the peace talks will go no further until the PNA eradicates the threat of terror from Israel's doorstep.

Dealing in Dollars

In the absence of an International Police Assistance Program, the experiment in policing in the Gaza Strip and the West Bank has been supported by the donor community assisting the Palestinian autonomy project under the Oslo and Cairo Accords. Annex 1 of the Cairo Accords stipulated that finance would be jointly administered with Israel's approval. As previously mentioned, the disbursement of funds has not always been as smooth as hoped, but it has been eventually forthcoming, and the police and security services are in receipt of funds from the donor community. Indeed, it is questionable whether the service would survive in its current guise if it were dependent on funding raised locally through revenues from taxation. Can the international community, however, help determine and shape the Palestinian state-building effort through the donation of funds, assistance, and equipment? The donor community has aided this policing project with a commitment of pledges, funds, equipment, technical assistance, and other support. In 1994 alone, the PPF enjoyed disbursement from the donor states to the tune of U.S.$40.9 million, according to sources quoted in the *Journal of Palestine Studies* (1995, 142). Britain, for example, pledged £4.25 million in bilateral assistance to policing for 1994 to 1995 and 1996 to 1997. This amount compares to the £9 million in aid that Britain contributed to the United Nations Relief and Works Agency (UNRWA), which is charged with providing services and support to all the registered Palestinian refugees in the West Bank and Gaza Strip. Thus, there is no doubt that the donor community has provided important financial assistance in this area; however, funding directed to other sources has been affected as aid budgets only stretch so far and priorities are juggled.

Another difficulty associated with donor assistance and the policing issue is the problem of coherence raised in the absence of an international police assistance program. Although important efforts to help coordinate the disbursement of funds have been made through the UN Police Coordination Office, there is no coherent policing model visible in donor assistance. Thus, in practice, particularly in the area of technical assistance, Palestinian police are being taught techniques and policing practices that vary from one country to another. Management skills, for example, are learned in England, forensic investigation in the United States, and public order policing in

Holland, Denmark, and Sweden. In each of these countries, unique and different approaches to policing are in evidence. Hence, the civil police and other branches ultimately represent the "best or worst" practice of a variety of policing systems. For example, the efficacy of public order training from officers involved in the policing of Britain's contentious miners' strike has been raised in certain circles. Noticeably absent from this scenario is an attempt by the international community to provide or encourage training for police in other societies that have recently undergone similar changes in policing. The exchange of Palestinian and Namibian or South African police officers might prove more instructive than police visits to training colleges in the home counties of Britain. Yet, the UN Coordination Office has made no effort to date to incorporate such ideas into its training agenda for any branch of the PPF.

The issue of accountability in the disbursement of donor funding is also problematic. Rather, the accountability agenda itself could be questioned. For example, neither the donor community nor Israel has taken steps to stop the unofficial proliferation of security agencies under Arafat's control. Although complaints and protests have been aired, funding has not been linked to evidence of the establishment of a publicly accountable police force and security apparatus. The proliferation of arms has positively been encouraged, whereas issues of disarmament have remained largely unaddressed. Clearly, the donor community believes that the promise of funds is enough to support the Palestinian state-building effort; international tutelage does not seem to extend to ensuring certain ethical policing practices as well. This assessment of a greater or improved role for the donor community may in the short term prove simplistic and idealistic, but in the long term, the sponsorship of particular experiments in self-rule or autonomy, no matter where on the globe they are located, will adversely affect the nature of funding relations and assistance.

Learning Rights, Losing Rights

In 1995 and 1996, two of the most significant figures in the advocacy of Palestinian human rights under Israeli occupation, Raji Sourani and Dr. Eyad Sarraj, were arrested, detained, questioned, and imprisoned. Shortly before his arrest, Sarraj had been quoted as criticizing the security service and the PNA. He had declared, "There is an overwhelming sense of fear. The regime is corrupt, dictatorial, oppressive. . . . There are so many arbitrary arrests now, without charge, without reason. The [PN] Authority has nine security organizations, each with its own detention center. And people are systematically tortured" (*Middle East Realities* 1996). In 1996, the Pal-

estinian authorities announced that books authored by the Palestinian academic Edward Said, which called into question the Oslo Accords and criticized them, were banned from sale in shops and other retail outlets in the
Gaza Strip and West Bank. Police officers were ordered into shops to seize
books and newspapers critical of the policies of the PNA. In January 1996,
the international organization Human Rights Watch issued a report that
criticized the PNA for its violation of human rights, including "physical
abuse of detainees, newspaper closures, closed-door trials of opposition suspects, . . . acts of violence and intimidation against Palestinians by the over-
staffed security agencies, . . . the newly created state security courts, . . . [the
death of] two Palestinians . . . under suspicious circumstances during and
after interrogation by the Palestinian security services" (Human Rights
Watch 1996).

The abuse of human rights that has taken place under the authority of
the PNA and its security services has evoked widespread condemnation and
the identification of failures and problems in a number of areas. The first
significant issue at the heart of the human rights–policing equation is the
lack of clarity of law in this context. At present, there still is no clearly
functioning system of "domestic legal safeguards and political accountability
capable of providing the necessary level of protection for human rights"
(Bindman and Bowring 1994, 44). The police themselves are presented
with a plethora of laws and orders to enforce. In addition, which branch of
the police service is responsible for such abuses is made less than clear in the
media. The civil police, for example, claim that they have not been associated with any death in detention, yet they are commonly perceived as responsible for such acts.

This issue is complicated further by the legal dichotomy between the
Gaza Strip, which continues to function under an Egyptian-British mandate
legal system, and the West Bank, which continues to function under the
Jordanian legal system. In addition, Yasser Arafat, in direct contravention of
the Oslo and Cairo Accords, has declared all preexisting Israeli laws and
military orders null and void. The Basic Draft Law, which might have gone
some way in defining rights and delineating the context of law enforcement,
remains in draft format and is still undergoing consultation and revision.
The judicial system is confusing and hampered by the establishment of the
secretive security courts. Prisons are not subject to rigorous and effective
independent inspection: allegations of torture and death in detention have
already surfaced; the location of holding facilities, detention centers, and
prisons for each branch of the force is not known; and accountability in the
face of such allegations is glaringly absent. In addition, the PNA is not
solely responsible for the protection of human rights in the West Bank and

Gaza Strip. Israel, as an occupying power, still remains responsible for guaranteeing and protecting the right of those Palestinians who remain under occupation (Mar'i 1996, 37). Israel, nevertheless, appears to have absented itself completely from its responsibilities in the interim period and has only acted to urge Palestinian security officials to arrest suspects on its behalf.

In this context, the police have failed to enforce law because law is confused, human rights are abused, and the police remain relatively unaccountable for their actions. The police have regularly arrested hundreds of Palestinians without first possessing search or arrest warrants and have subsequently detained people over long periods without charge. It should be noted, however, that some police and security agents accused of torture have been tried in military courts and subsequently sentenced. The human rights issue is further complicated by the presence of a large number of police officers in the security services who themselves were victims of human rights abuses under the Israeli authorities or in other Arab states and who are now engaging in the same acts of violation. Those involved in the highest ranks of the police service are concerned to be seen to promote and protect human rights. A human rights officer is currently being trained in Geneva and will then be posted in the office of Gaza police chief Colonel Yusuf. Training in human rights issues has also been raised in the context of all police training, with the former UN coordinator Per Blekelia remarking, "It's important that we promote the idea of personal responsibility. The difficulty lies in the legacy of human rights abuse that so many officers have experienced themselves. Therefore we have a responsibility to help officers rehabilitate themselves and not act as occupiers to their own people" (interview with author, 1995). These sentiments are shared by officers serving in the highest ranks of the police force, including Colonel Yusuf, who has played an important role in supporting the promotion of human rights training. Courses have been organized by Palestinian human rights groups with assistance from Dutch and Swedish funders, but these courses have been of limited success given the small number of people who have enrolled in them. To date, there is very little evidence that a culture of human rights awareness and notions of public accountablity permeate the myriad ranks of the security structure in either the West Bank or the Gaza Strip.

The human rights record of the PPF was tarnished from the outset, and little has been done or achieved to secure public confidence in this area. There should be no doubt that this tarnished reputation has significant implications for the long-term nature of police-society relations. Human rights training should be a central feature of police training and the policing ethos in the West Bank and Gaza Strip, yet in practice human rights are sacrificed to maintain authoritarian control and stability in a period of building a state and new forms of political rule. Once again, good practice at an international level is ignored in favor of bad policy at a local level; there is no "integration of human rights into firearms training; the screening out of recruits with anti-rights disposition; application of international legal principles to practical everyday policing situations or support directed at police managers so that human rights perspectives are supported at a policy, managerial and supervision level and not merely amongst recruits" (Committee on Administration of Justice 1997, 3). This absence of a rights-based culture affects not just the realm of the political but everyday policing issues such as domestic violence or violence toward children. As a result, police officers and trainers lack a clear vision of their role as protectors—many expressing reservations, for example, about involving themselves in incidents of public violence against children, yet happy to detain (without appropriate warrants) suspected political activists. Thus, it is certainly clear that in the absence of a Draft Law, the branches of the PPF are left without a clear indication of what their responsibilities and duties to the Palestinian people are. In this context, the role of the PPF is perceived as increasingly in opposition to the people rather than in support of citizens. The threat from outside is largely unchecked, while the threat from within is promoted as the largest threat to the community and its future.

Setting a Stamp on Citizenship

The concept of citizenship is so inextricably bound up with statehood, democracy, and the nation-state that any discussion of policing and internal security arrangements in the post-Oslo era must address it. Yet, to date, the relationship between Palestinian citizens-to-be and their police force is relatively neglected and may be explored only through the predominant system of political rule that is emerging in the West Bank and Gaza Strip. Another important factor to bear in mind is the extent to which Palestinians, who officially remain stateless, experience contact with protostate institutions that serve to regulate their lives, raise revenue, police them, and determine welfare and education policy. In many respects, the type of citizenship that Palestinians might aspire to remains unexplored, or a certain type of citizenship is assumed. And this type of citizenship once again reflects regional rather than other norms. It may be assumed, therefore, that Palestinian citizenship may bestow more rights on some than others; for example, a gendered notion of citizenship has already been proffered during the interim period. Citizenship is likely to be patriarchal in nature and reflect the cultural and religious norms of Islam. Although there may be some attempt to secularize Palestinian citizenship, it will not be wholly successful. In this context, citizenship is also more likely to reflect a communal rather than individual dimension and is unlikely to serve, as Leca (1992) suggests, as a "weapon, or power for the weaker in the community" (21). An unequal sense of citizenship is highly likely to emerge "entropy-resistant," as Gellner (1983b, 64) refers to them, second-class citizens in a modern political state.

To date, then, the benefits of statehood that the Palestinians enjoy are minimal, but the demands of so-called citizenship (even in the absence of a state) are great. Indeed, it might be more appropriate to refer to Palestinian residents of the autonomous areas of the West Bank and Gaza Strip as subjects of the PNA. After all, Palestinians are currently under the rule of the PNA and the State of Israel; they remain under obligation—subordinate, dependent, subservient, exposed, and prone. One might argue that the people remain subjugated even under the authority of the PNA. Such an assessment alters the police-society relationship and could account for the lack of plurality and democracy as well as of other associated features in the internal security structure. One is thus led to question the current concept of citizenship being promoted in Palestinian society. Is *citizenship,* for example, yet another term that serves as nothing more than an empty signifier during an interim period of societal crisis (Laclau 1996, 36–46)? Can a meaningful notion of emerging citizenship—whether it be active-passive, public-private, or universal-particular—be identified during the interim state-building project? If it can, can it be identified as reflecting a certain state of affairs, or as Turner (1983a) remarks, "the embodiment of a wide range of modernizing processes in law, culture, society and politics" (12)?

These questions can be answered, at least in part, by assessing the nature of Palestinian society in the West Bank and Gaza Strip. Modernization is largely in evidence; despite the economic penalties accrued through Israel's occupation, the Palestinian economy has emerged as modernized. Civil society flourished, particularly during the Intifada, when some internal existing divisions were overcome by the larger national objective of overthrowing the occupation. In addition, one might add that Palestinian society is relatively secularized despite attempts by Islamists to imprint their agenda. Certainly within the political realm, the post-Oslo era has been characterized by secular-nationalist ascendancy and subjugation of political Islam as a dominant or challenging force. However, secularization is limited and has not always been formally incorporated into all aspects of Palestinian society in the West Bank and Gaza Strip. Rather, the tensions between secularist-modernizing forces and Islamist-modernizing forces have not been resolved or reconciled. Ultimately, this factor inhibits the development of any form of citizenship in the interim and allows coercive state force in pursuit of hegemony or unfettered power. After all, citizenship should contribute to the binding of a people together, yet any form of social solidarity is currently threatened by an internal security structure in pursuit of stable political rule.

In theory, citizenship should bestow certain rights to the stateless residents of the West Bank and Gaza Strip, which is precisely why Palestinians aspire to citizenship of an independent state. In the interim, however, when the Palestinians have neither the political nor the military authority that define a state, the PNA still demands the loyalty of the people—demands that are associated with the demands made by a state of its citizens. While Palestinians remain bereft of the privilege of citizenship, they are circumscribed in their ability to "exert control over government and make it aware of their demands" (Deegan 1993, 10), and the political rights associated with the demands for citizenship are once again diminished in the face of the state-building experiment, which involves the drive toward a strong state, a strong police force, and stability at any cost. The loyalty of the citizens-to-be is largely taken for granted, with the notion that any kind of Palestinian political rule is better than no Palestinian political rule.

Although many provisions about citizenship have been raised in the context of the Draft Law nothing has been finalized to date. The PNA has decided to put the Draft Law aside because issues of citizenship—its impact on Israel (i.e., recognition of citizenship would imply recognition of a Palestinian state) and the difficulty in defining who exactly would be entitled to Palestinian citizenship (who is a Palestinian)—have far-reaching political implications for the future. In the absence of a Draft Law, however, the police and security structure is left without a clear indication of their responsibilities and duties to the Palestinian population, which seriously hampers the policing remit in the interim period, leaving the force and its many branches free to improvise working practice. It also leaves the commanders of such forces increasingly dependent on the personalized executive authority of Yasser Arafat for policy, planning, and implementation, and removes the service one step further from the public domain. Even debate about the role of the police force and its relationship with the community has largely been absent, censored from the press and missing from other forums of public debate. Those who do raise the issue run the risk of arrest and detention without trial. The arrests of journalists, human rights workers, academics, and other professionals who have spoken out on this issue have set a disturbing precedence. The security service, then, remains largely immune from public opinion and occupies itself with the opinion of the PNA executive instead.

To reiterate, then, the role of the internal security structure and civil police is perceived largely in opposition to the people rather than in support of them. The threat to security from outside—from Israeli settlers, soldiers, or other elements—goes largely unchecked and is inhibited by the terms of the Oslo Accords, while the threat from within is promoted as the largest threat to the citizens-to-be. The security forces are granted powers that in a normal plural democratic society would be unthinkable. Opposition would not be regarded as a threat to the state but rather a reflection of a healthy democratic system of government. The main function of policing would not be euphemistically called "internal security," "preventative security," and "intelligence gathering," but rather a police service, publicly accountable and based on a model of community policing. Policing would take place in the context of clearly defined and enshrined notions of citizenship. Palestinians themselves still have to learn how to become citizens, let alone good citizens; after all, for more than two decades a culture of defiance in the face of state authority has dominated. Palestinians have to relearn their obligations to authority and teach the authority its obligations to them. To date, little ground has been covered in this respect, and large-scale programs of community education, of the type currently evident in Lebanon, are not present.

Principles for Better Policing

The objective of this chapter was to examine police-society relations in the Occupied Palestinian Territories in the interim period as a test of democracy and citizen rights.

Through analyzing the nature of the nascent security structure, the emphasis on coercion by executive authority, and the prevailing political climate, I show how there is small prospect at present for the emergence of a fully fledged liberal-democratic system of governance in any future political settlement between Israel and the Palestinians. There is a prevalent opinion in the discipline of politics that the prospects for state building and democracy can be enriched by a civilizing process. Conversely, the militarism of society is to be avoided at all costs. In Middle Eastern countries, where the military has assumed a dominant role, democracy has failed to flourish, and authoritarianism has prevailed. A policy of state building that thus embraces a civilized, accountable, and open internal security and policing structure will thus promote strong democratic relations between state and citizen.

Many of the features of the Palestinian experiment seem, at present, conducive to failure as a test of democracy. There has been no attempt to construct a new security structure in which old models and patterns of policing are abandoned for new ones. Instead, the same patterns of militarized authoritarianism have been repeated. Personnel from existing paramilitary structures have been incorporated into the new structure, and the logic behind such a decision is explicable and acceptable. What is not, however, has been the difficulty and lack of attention paid to the urgency of transforming former guerrillas and soldiers into police officers, particularly in the civil police. The PNA or, more specifically, those in charge of policy at the Directorate of Police Force have been unwilling or unable to introduce the necessary legislation to support an accountable police service rather than an unaccountable police force. The public debate about policing has been almost nonexistent, and those individuals who have offered constructive criticism have been imprisoned rather than recognized for playing their parts in active citizenship issues. The policing provision of the Oslo and Cairo Accords, therefore, made insufficient provision for the encouragement of an open democratic society in the interim, with a plural political base, protection of individuals' rights, and supporting institutions that would allow for a policing service for all. The resources devoted to the policing project have been predominantly channeled into salaries for a large force, basic uniforms, and provision of housing, arms, equipment, and riot-control training. The failure of the donor community to encourage accountability as a condition of disbursement of funds is also disappointing and further reflects the need for an international policing commission. In addition, at present, the nature of donor funding of the PPF has encouraged a financial dependency on outsiders that again has hindered the development of accountability to the public through the raising of police revenues by means of the taxation of the Palestinian community that the police force purports to serve. The police and internal security forces seem to be perceived as President Yasser Arafat's private army.

A number of lessons about policing from both the regional and international context could be learned for reforms that might steer the Palestinian policing project back on course. Many of these potential changes center on the principles of both legal and democratic accountability that should prevail in the interim period and form a major platform for any future political entity agreed on in the final status negotiations, should they ever take place. It is important to recognize that incremental reform is not enough to resolve tensions over the policing of societies formerly characterized by deep political, ethnic, and religious conflicts. The resolution of policing problems is dependent on political settlements of a wider nature and in particular on the rights culture or philosophy adopted as part of this broader settlement of conflict between Palestinians and Israelis. Subsequent policing arrangements must satisfy the majority if not the whole community, with the role of civic oversight bodies enshrined in legislation. Thus, any new policing service should be located under a liberal-democratic framework with appropriate legal and constitutional guarantees as well as mechanisms for accountability. Respect for human rights must remain an essential feature of a Palestinian police service, and police-community relations must be established through a variety of forums and take account of the diversity of opinion expressed by all in society.

The actual reformability of the PPF remains problematic and highly dependent on the nature of any final political settlement. What is certain is that the policing project is part of a peace process and state building in which high-ranking police officers feel they are hostages of Arafat and the mood of the Israeli government. The policing remit of the DOP, I would argue, has made insufficient provision for a policing model that encourages law enforcement and the provision of service as a long-term goal. The resources that have been devoted to the policing project illustrate my point. From the earliest days, the PPF and more specifically the civil police have been armed; hundreds of thousands of dollars have now been spent on issuing all forty thousand officers with arms of one sort or another. In particular, the use of Kalashnikov automatics within the civil police is not encouraging and is contradictory to the idea of a civil police force that presents itself as a policing service for the entire community. Indeed, although the issue of disarmament of police forces in other deeply divided societies has been the subject of fierce and contentious debate, the worrying trend in the Palestinian example has largely gone unchallenged. Money that has been spent on Kalashnikovs, pistols, bamboo beating sticks, batons, and so on could more usefully be diverted to address the pressing and urgent need for training. If, for example, the average cost of one Kalashnikov is five hundred dollars, the cost of just six of these would cover the entire budget for one month's training at the civil police "academy" in the West Bank. This facility in Jericho is obligated to provide forty-five days basic training to new recruits, officer training, plus six weeks "rehabilitation" training for currently serving officers. New recruits are housed in tents, and the officer cadets enjoy the luxury of concrete barns. The entire academy is served by classrooms without air-conditioning, windows, or chairs for everyone; there is not one single photocopier on site; and recruits do not receive a living allowance. Although everyone involved in the policing project recognizes the need for a police academy, echoing the 1994 words of Terje Rød-Larsen (in an interview with the author), "A Palestinian police academy should be a goal," to date, and despite early promises, the academy has still not been built, and the police service struggles to train its officers.

Indeed, within the PPF there is little evidence of any plans or future strategy thinking among the higher ranks. This reflects, in part, the political uncertainties of the situation in which the PPF finds itself, but in addition it highlights a surprising lack of management, particularly given the military culture that prevails. The desire to create a professional policing service is often rhetoric in the higher ranks; young officers in the lower ranks who share the same aspiration are ultimately frustrated, and some are already considering leaving the force. The PPF thus remains an ad hoc organization, with the civilian police the only branch able to articulate any future vision.

There is no sense within the community of ownership of the policing project that the chairman of the board enjoys a monopoly from within and that Israel directs from the outside. Policing is not even achieved in its most basic forms. To repeat an earlier point, the civil police, for example, behaves more like a soldier force based in a garrison and called out to deal with the breakdown of law and order; there is no beat police, patrols of officers in local neighborhoods. The civil police are restricted by lack of training and resources, poor management, power struggles, and poor initiative in their stations and guarding duties. There is no culture of accountability, no pocketbooks, no attempt to offer a policing service (despite the community policing agenda behind the provision of most donor training). This situation is in many respects one step away from a siege mentality pervading the forces of law and order that in an ideal world really should serve the Palestinian community of the West Bank and Gaza Strip and not regard it as the fifth column of the conflict with Israel.

16

Palestinian National Authority Toward a Permanent Status

The Contours of State Building "from Above"

CHRISTOPHER H. PARKER

ALTHOUGH MUCH HAS BEEN MADE of the authoritarian tendencies that have emerged within the Palestinian National Authority (PNA) and of the failure of Palestinian civil society to sustain a constructive engagement in defining the civic sphere of autonomy, few observers have suggested how each trend reflects the register of power embedded within PNA institutions. *Autonomy*—or *self-rule*—as defined by existing agreements between the Palestine Liberation Organization (PLO) and Israel refers to a limited but simultaneously rather specific power mandate. The scope and configuration of this power has a defining impact on activities within the civic sphere of the autonomy.

This chapter explores the contours of the emerging civic sphere of Palestinian autonomy as it is being shaped "from above." The central questions addressed include: What are the sources of and delimitations upon PNA power? How, in the classical sense of elite-based political mobilizations, is the PNA elite trying to reshape the interests of Palestinian society to more closely correspond with its own? To what extent do these sources and delimitations decisively inform the PNA's tactical use of power? And how are the subjects of PNA administrative coercion identifying their rights and ob-

This chapter draws considerably on ideas and evidence presented in my book *Palestine between Resignation and Revolt: Socio-political Development and the Predicaments of Peace* (London and New York: I. B. Tauris, 1998), especially chapter 5.

ligations within the new order? Embodied in the answers to these questions is a model and critique of the emerging civic sphere of Palestinian autonomy. After an introduction to the context of PNA powers as externally mandated and framed through international agreements, a conceptual and comparative framework is advanced. Incidents and episodes from the actual exercise of PNA rule are then discussed to show how the exercise of political consolidation from above is being rationalized and executed, and to show what impact it has in the Palestinian street.

Ultimately, it is argued that the limited powers of the PNA ratify the disempowerment of the Palestinian street; that is, inasmuch as the PNA lacks powers crucial to the regulation of Palestinian socioeconomic life, it is irrational to expect organization and affiliation on the Palestinian street to reflect attempts to engage the PNA constructively in a civil discourse about the use of power. The neopatrimonial and securitarian process of political consolidation informed by the powers currently wielded by the PNA will likely perpetuate and reproduce existing conditions of social mistrust, anomie, economic and social dependency, and the irrelevance of political institutions to addressing structural contradictions and tensions in the political economy of the Palestinian areas. The danger in this process is that as Palestinians prove unable to confront and address directly the politically imposed structural conditions of their current predicament, they will be increasingly alienated from their political institutions. Exclusion leads to rejection, and rejection can lead to violence. The Oslo framework and the context it provides for an attempt at consolidating political order from above are neither likely to promote sustainable political order in the emerging Palestinian polity nor firmly establish a basis for peace in the region.

PNA Power: Backgrounds, Contexts, and Sources

Although authoritarianism is often considered the product of absolute power, it is ironically the PNA's weakness in sectors other than security—a weakness that promotes inter alia the personalization of power and an emphasis on the ritual rather than on the sociological substance of politics—that encourages reactionary and authoritarian stances toward Palestinian society in the Occupied Territories. In short, powerlessness corrupts. It is suggested here that the neopatrimonial and securitarian tendencies of the PNA are in large part products of the agreements on interim Palestinian self-rule and of the structural environment in which they are being implemented (two variables that are themselves closely linked). Certainly, both bode ill for the prospects of a viable political order within the autonomy and thus for a lasting peace grounded in the trajectory of Oslo.

Determination by External Interests

Currently, the greatest portion of PNA power is circumscribed not by accountability to the society in which it operates, but rather by the demands and constraints placed on it by external actors and international agreements. Israeli historian Ilan Pappé has noted that the Oslo Accord "embodies the immense imbalance of power between the two sides: Israel can do what it wants, Arafat cannot even say what he wants" (Usher 1995a, 22). According to Ghassan al-Khatib, the peace process represents "a sort of dictation rather than negotiations. It starts with Israeli proposals and ends with agreements that are extremely similar to the initial Israeli proposals. Israel makes use of the weakness of the PLO [as well as] the lack of democratic decision-making process within the PLO" (Lindholm Schulz 1996, 24; al-Khatib 1998). Shimon Peres himself noted during the discussions on the transition to greater Palestinian autonomy that "in some ways we are negotiating with ourselves" (Murphy 1995, 36).

This imbalance of power within the context of the peace process means that the PNA must hold itself accountable to external demands that often seem to contradict the hopes associated with self-rule on the Palestinian street. Israeli authorities have taken a decidedly hostile stance toward the prospect of a Palestinian civil society capable of asserting itself in defining the boundaries of peace. Azmi Bishara bluntly argues that Oslo "inaugurates a process which sustains Israel's historic position of no withdrawal from and no annexation of the Occupied Territories; [but the process also] addresses the problem [of the unacceptable status quo ante that had emerged with the Intifada] by bringing in the PLO to solve it on Israel's behalf. This is the essence of autonomy" (Usher 1995b, 44). Usher goes further, arguing that the PNA's "obsessive ethos of 'national security' and 'national interest' . . . , once [its] political and ideological content is unpacked, turn[s] out to be no more than the practical implementation of Israel's territorial and security ambitions in the occupied territories" (Usher 1996, 33).

The major donors (particularly the United States) seem to have decided—their stated commitment to promoting a "culture of democracy" notwithstanding—that the peace process demands an authoritarian PNA to "deliver" the peace. Even formal participation in local political fora has been deemed a threat to peace. According to one source, Dennis Ross (the senior U.S. "peace envoy") has ordered that USAID not promote activities that might strengthen municipal and local administrations and thereby encourage bases of power and mobilization that might "diminish the power of Mr. Arafat and the PNA to carry out the tasks of the day" (Roy 1996, 74).

Former Israeli prime minister Binyamin Netanyahu has argued that Palestinian autonomy as currently constituted would not be allowed to lead to "a state in the classic sense, but [would represent] a completely new sort of political unit" (*Der Speigel*, 21 September 1996). The Israeli daily *Ha'aretz* has reported that Netanyahu openly likens the future of this unit to the U.S. protectorate of Puerto Rico (*Muslim World News*, 9 November 1996; *IMRA Review*, 8 November 1996). Netanyahu's groping to justify continued Israeli control over land and resources with an apparently benign reference suggests continued Israeli imposed conditionality on the future scope of obligations, rights, and sovereignty between authority and subjects in the spaces of what has been optimistically described as Palestinian "self-rule." As of January 1997, internal Israeli debates concerning the aim of eventual "final status negotiations" remained centered around whether Palestinians will have "a limited state" or "expanded autonomy." This debate is reflected in a document produced by Knesset members Yossi Beilin (Labor) and Michael Eitan (Likud), which was intended to draft a common document toward future negotiations (a.k.a., the Eitan-Beilin platform).

The Palestinian side is dependent on international arbitration if its polity is to transcend the limits suggested by the internal Israeli debate. The resulting predicament has been mocked in the Islamist press: "Arafat will resort to 'Arbitration' should his peace goal prove far from reality. Arafat has said: 'Arbitration. We have the United Nations, we have the Hague, we have the Security Council, we have the Europeans. We'll go to arbitration" (*Al-Quds*, ca. August 1996). The results of the Washington Summit in early October 1996 (as well as "summits" since) and the effective exclusion of Europe from anything but the paying of PNA bills highlight the weakness of Arafat's position in this regard.

Coercion and Administration: PNA Powers as Delimited by Current Agreements

Current agreements limit the PNA's ability to inject its power and will into society in meaningful ways. The present contours of Palestinian power are regulated through agreements with Israel, with whom the PNA shares the responsibilities of government by joint committee. The rights and obligations associated with citizenship remain bounded by accountability to the superior economic and coercive potential of the Israeli state, and in no way does any "inevitable" trajectory of the peace process ensure change.

The low degree of PNA governing potential represents a situation legitimized by the Oslo Agreement. The powerlessness of Palestinian politicians to articulate and execute positive policy, on the one hand, and the pressures of state building and social competition on underdeveloped and underempowered institutions, on the other hand, contradict the expectations and promise of self-rule. As Sara Roy (1995) has trenchantly noted, "with regard to autonomous decision making, the difference between the past and the present regimes is that there are now more Palestinians in positions of no authority" (78).

In spite of these debilitating shortcomings, however, the PNA does possess resources in certain sectors that allow it to exert influence over Palestinian society in the Occupied Territories. Pappé has noted that "Arafat in Gaza and Jericho has established a mechanism over which he has control. It is a limited control, but he has the powers of patronage, of salaries, of prestige, the rudiments, if you like, of a bureaucratic mini-state. This may bear little resemblance to the aspirations of the Palestinian people, but it is a form of power . . . [albeit] a wholly unstable form of power" (Usher 1995a, 22).

The argument that instability is inherent in circumstances where the demands of external patrons might contradict those of internal constituencies seems especially pertinent given the intentional vagueness and ambiguity as to the end result of the negotiations over power. The PNA has thus far managed to cover this contradiction by channeling its control over resource mobilization into vertically isolated clientist networks within which the ability to procure basic needs becomes conditional on political compliance. In essence, the regime nurtures vertical clientist networks—networks that essentially redistribute donor resources—designed to replace other potential poles of social self-organization. The problem with this approach is that although it secures the PNA a hold on the street, it does so by effectively neutralizing the street and thus undermining a source of power in the negotiations with Israel. Stability of a sort is procured through demobilization of society.

Furthermore, there are definite limitations on PNA administrative functions. The PNA is responsible for enforcing regulations, but it has only limited powers to amend existing regulation. Most crucial regulations are fixed or pegged according to Israeli standards. Joint committees are responsible for drawing up and ultimately approving regulations in vital areas. The PNA must consult Israel on issues such as where to build strategic infrastructure—e.g., the eventual Gaza port complex. And the PNA must even inform Israel of road repairs being made within the autonomous areas (Gaza-Jericho Agreement, Annex II, Article 2 B, 25). Article 2, paragraph 26, sets out regulations for what the Palestinians may put on postage stamps (postal services are still dependent on the Israeli postal system, a situation that has on occasion caused problems as Israeli postal workers refused to handle mail with PNA stamps). Erez Agreement Annex IV shows how the administrative functions give the right to issue the licenses regulating the tourist trade. However, the PNA lacks the powers that would be needed to promote a comprehensive tourist industry; it may regulate the provision of peripheral services, but not control the fundamental elements of infrastructure. Annex V of the same agreement notes that property taxes are still the domain of the Israeli government. According to the Gaza-Jericho Agreement Annex II, Article 2, paragraph B28b, custodial absentee land rights do not fall to the PNA. Finally, the PNA has no real foreign policy mandate (Interim Agreement Article 9; Gaza-Jericho agreement Article 6, paragraph 2a). These are merely a few examples illustrating the inability of the PNA to administer the autonomy in ways accountable to the interests of Gazans.

A second mechanism of PNA power is the securement of the autonomy. Although the powers associated with administration and redistribution are implicit features of existing arrangements, the agreements make clear an emphasis on "security" functions as the cornerstone of Palestinian authority. Article 8 of the original Gaza-Jericho First Agreement calls for a strong police force. The Interim Agreement signed in Washington on 28 September 1995 reaffirms this requirement in several places, including Articles 12 and 14, but it must not necessarily be seen as a phenomenon underpinning an emerging Palestinian state. Some observers have argued that the PNA's "legitimate use of force" constitutes a foundation of the PNA's emerging "stateness." However, the distinction between "legitimate use of force" and the classical Weberian definition—"monopoly on the use of coercive force"—is crucial here. It must be remembered that the PNA coercive functions are first and foremost legitimized by and held accountable to the peace process, and therefore do not represent legitimacy in ways denoting popular accountability.

At present, the failure to contain abuses of administrative privilege and coercive force within the self-rule areas suggests a lack of real institutional accountability within the autonomy—the failure of the Oslo process to promote constructive institutionalization at the core of much of the anomie in the autonomy today. This vagueness manifests itself in the apparent arbitrariness of self-rule's coercive face—a security apparatus characterized by structural amorphousness, factional proliferation, factional conflict, and a lack of terms of reference (Usher 1996, 24). It is thus difficult for Palestinians to distinguish between the unaccountable situation of occupation and the supposedly more accountable condition of autonomy. The imbalance of power has occasionally pressed the Palestinian security forces into tasks that made them appear more answerable to external interests than to the security of the society in which they operate.

Information on the various factions of the Palestinian security forces are sketchy. Observers put the number of factions at anywhere from ten to seventeen, a trend that allows Arafat to manipulate and suppress competing bases of power. At the same time, however, competition between the factions has sometimes resulted in violence, a phenomenon that does little to encourage morale and feelings of security on the Palestinian street. The primary factions include the General Intelligence Service, Military Intelligence, the Preventative Security Service, the Presidential Guard/Force 17, the Special Security Force; the National Security Forces, the Palestinian Police, and smaller forces such as the Naval Police, the Military Police, the University Police, the Women's Police, and the Disciplinary Police. Usher (1996) sees the security forces engaged in three tasks: (1) police functions; (2) finishing the business of seeking out and punishing collaborators; and (3) the surveillance of Palestinian opposition to Oslo (26). They have been undermined in the first task by a lack of training, a lack of standardization in operative procedure, the placing of organizational interests ahead of the unbiased enforcement of the law, and the entrenched antiauthoritarian attitudes among Gazans.

In theory, the agreements limit the number of security personnel within the autonomy to nine thousand under the Gaza-Jericho Agreement of 1994 and twelve thousand under the Interim Agreement of 1995. However, limits on the numbers of personnel are not observed by the PNA, Israel, or the various international sponsors. Usher (1996) reports that the police force of thirty thousand for the interim period in the West Bank and Gaza is a figure "not questioned by either PNA or Israeli officials. But this too is likely to be fluid. In June 1995, the head of Civil Police in Gaza City, Ghazi Jabali, said that the PNA would eventually require a police force of around 40,000 for the autonomy" (22–23). Israeli authorities have often played on apparent contradictions created by the agreement's limitation on the number of security personnel and the demands of securitization to accuse the PNA of violations of the autonomy accords (thus somehow legitimating Israeli violations). An Israeli critic of the Netanyahu government has pointed to the disingenuousness of his government's stance: "Increasing the number of Palestinian policemen? Israel is the one demanding day and night that the Palestinians step up their efforts to fight terrorism. And just who is supposed to do that?" (Levy 1998). In reality, the growth in this sector promotes security more by providing jobs in an atmosphere of acute economic hardship than by monitoring and disciplining the Palestinian population.

The numbers of police and their powers may seem frighteningly unlimited from the perspective of Gaza's inhabitants,[1] but the agreements ensure the accountability of the police to the interests and powers behind the peace process more than to the Palestinian street. Annex I, Article 9, of the Gaza-Jericho Agreement outlines the parameters of policing power down to the types of guns and ammunition allowed for the PNA security forces and to the top speeds and tonnage of the few boats allowed to the PNA coastal police. Furthermore, the PNA's strong policing and internal security mandate does not include jurisdiction over offenses committed in the settlements or in the military installation areas, nor may it arbitrate in offenses committed by Israelis in the self-rule areas. PNA powers are to be used only in arbitrating between and quelling unrest among Palestinians. In situations where Israelis are involved, the Israeli Defense Forces (IDF) have jurisdiction (Gaza-Jericho Agreement, Annex III, Article 1, paragraphs 2a and 2b; Article 3, paragraphs 2 and 3; Interim Agreement, Chapter 2, Article 8, paragraph 2b2). The high degree of integration between PNA and Israeli security forces undermines the perception of the accountability of Palestinian police to the population (Gaza-Jericho Agreement, Annex III, Article 1, paragraphs 5–9; Usher 1996, 21–22). Furthermore, "nothing shall affect the continued authority of the military government and its Civil Administration to exercise their powers and responsibilities with regard to security and public order, as well as with regard to other spheres not transferred" (Agreement on Transfer of Powers and Responsibilities, Article 6, paragraph 5.) This statement gives Israel broad scope for interference in Palestinian affairs. More information regarding actual applications and manifestations of the law is given in the next section.

This lack of effective PNA power clearly poses a predicament for Arafat: in order to increase his authority in the Palestinian social space, he must first prove that he can provide stability; in order to produce stability and consensus around his rule, he first needs the authority and scope of political power to produce and enforce political and economic outcomes acceptable to the Palestinian population; in order to acquire the scope of power that might allow for the presentation of positive incentives for social mobilization, he must first demonstrate his ability to neutralize and repress that society. Although it is tempting to attribute the failures of the PNA to fea-

1. It should be noted that support for policing exists in part because it provides much needed income for families, and in an environment where the rule of law is not consolidated but rather personalized, it becomes an imperative not to alienate any contacts one might have in the security apparatus.

tures of corruption and incompetence that undermine the efficiency of regimes elsewhere in the developing world (especially considering the combination of cronyism and a new *wabenzi*-ism[2] in the PNA), one must at least
consider how the externally enforced dynamic of emerging autonomy is denying the PNA the tools with which broad societal legitimation might be
pursued. More than just explanatory devices, they represent phenomena that
must themselves be explained.

The limitations of institutional power also indicate limitations on the
constituency of those institutions. In terms of citizenship, power might be
usefully analyzed with regard to how it organizes social forces to serve institutional ends or the ways in which people—people as the object and subject
of power because self-rule seems to imply some sort of twisting inward of
power relations—in turn shape its exercise. The failure of authority and a
constituency to reach a stable basis of power relations may be viewed as the
inability of power to strike a balance between services and coercion, between rights and obligations, within that community. Today, the limitations
of the PNA are the limitations of the Palestinians in Gaza. At the same time,
the powers of the PNA seem to be the powers only of the PNA and not
powers of the Palestinian inhabitants of the Occupied Territories.

In accepting the symbolic elements of autonomy (e.g., the public display
of the Palestinian flag, the Palestine postage stamp, and a telephone calling
code separate from that of Israel) and assuming that these elements would
inevitably lead to more substantive authorities, perhaps even a state, the
PLO elites seem to have assumed that their historical status would bear
legitimacy within Gaza throughout a new phase in the nationalist movement. But in this assumption they may have erred. Current limited PNA
powers might promote day-to-day stability by making Palestinian society
economically dependent on it. This arrangement could be inherently precarious, though, as the PNA is itself dependent on external funding and is
unable to promote the creation of an economic base capable of internally
sustaining self-rule institutions. Given the instability inherent in any transitional order and the limitations on the PNA's ability to shape consensus
(that is, to produce constructive initiatives that mobilize society from
above), it seems likely that any future stability in the Occupied Territories
may be based on dependence and repression.

---

2. *Wabenzi* refers to an indigenous class that has acquired wealth through their attachments
to the post-colonial state in Africa, i.e., through corruption. The name derives from the supposed preference within this group for Mercedes Benz automobiles (a symbol of conspicuous
consumption). Africans use the word pejoratively.

Meanings, Power, and the Civic Sphere:
The Degree of Government and Social
(De)Mobilization from Above

National Mobilization, State Building, and Power

Both the national movement and the state-building project refer to specific contexts for social mobilization and suggest different scopes of power, constituency, and possibility. These, in turn, shape a political dynamic that informs and orients individuals toward the ideas and institutions most likely to articulate and satisfy their interests. A national liberation movement is by its nature loose and inevitably presents an abstract ideal for government that clearly contrasts with existing inhibitions on rights and expression. The nationalist movement articulates general responses and mobilizes society in the face of perceived shared threats or challenges to a community that has become somehow socially, politically, economically, and psychologically "self-aware." State building, however, requires the establishment of an order with social structures deep and dependable enough to mitigate internal social conflicts. The state must be capable of asserting coercive force within the bounds of totemic (symbolic, psychological, and perceived historical) legitimacy. It does so by using power to enforce and reinforce institutions.

Ultimately, the sovereign political unit is recognizable through the exercise of power within identifiable social and geographic boundaries. Political power results from a variety of forces: inter alia, coercive technology, social mobilization, and the ability to regulate state-based economic privileges and incentives. All contribute to the way in which a particular regime conceives of and uses power. The political unit becomes functional as such when power is situated within institutions capable of both instrumentality and will. As things currently stand in the Palestinian situation, the elements of power that bind a society to its political institutions by uniting private and public interests and by creating an environment of security are lacking. Together, the ability of the PNA to repress its own subjects and its inability to protect Palestinians from continued settler violence or prevent intrusions of the IDF into PNA-controlled areas highlight this skewed balance of power in practice.[3]

State building represents a complex set of more or less recognizable po-

---

3. Certainly other states are in fact constrained by the interests of more powerful neighbors or global economic trends, but in no other case are the political authorities de jure subject to restrictions such as those imposed on the PNA. This greatly inhibits Palestinian society's and the PNA's ability to adapt to and plan for changing contingencies.

litical and socioeconomic processes. In the broadest civic sense, it might be said to represent processes of inclusion and consensus within institutions—institutions that have both the power to enforce rights and obligations, and to address and adapt to new demands and contingencies. In short, the power to instigate and reflect social change. In the context of Palestinian autonomy, however, there is no certainty about where the process of autonomous institution building is leading, in spite of the fact that the transition to a final status of Palestinian autonomy perhaps represents one of the most outlined, controlled, and observed of such processes in history. Some of this uncertainty has to do with imbalances of power between Israel and the PNA. It also has to do with the powerlessness of Palestinian society in relation to the PNA. PNA coercive potential raises a specter that hangs above its ineffectualness in other domains.

The Civic Sphere: Conflict, Consensus, and Consolidation

A theoretical exploration of the notion of the civic sphere is beyond the scope of this chapter, but a brief discussion of the concept is offered to provide context. Broadly speaking, I mean by the *civic sphere* the institutionalized field of power relations informing (consciously or implicitly) people's everyday choices and decisions. It constitutes a forum of interaction between historical extrapolations (subjective ideological interpretation) and actual institutions that gives meaning and predictability to understandings of rights and obligations both vis-à-vis agents of state power and among other people within a polity. It represents the totality of acts that reaffirm the political order and signifies the context within which meanings are attributed to those acts. The civic sphere is realized and observed through the conflicts, alliances, and accommodations between people and expressions of authority that are more or less institutionalized, as well as through the socioeconomic and political configurations that emerge as viable and orderly (at least in part through their contact with state regulations and interventions) even if they are not stable in any strict sense. It ultimately signifies the nature of power acting on and within state-society relations—whether that power is a function of the state, a pole of economic influence within society, the power embodied in a social mobilization, or the threat and use of violence.

In a somewhat idealized model of positive conflict in the civic sphere, people—informed by socioeconomic conflicts (opportunities and obstacles) and by developmental pressures—engage the political powers of the state in ways that resolve or work toward the resolution of structural tensions and disparities. Inasmuch as the state succeeds at mediating in these conflicts and in mitigating the negative impacts of socioeconomic change, thereby consolidating a consensus regarding the role of its institutions in performing these functions, the political order is legitimized. The involvement of both state and society in these conflicts is crucial in the incremental but constant relegitimation of political order. In this simplified conceptualization, the state is an omnipresent reference point, but it does not attempt to monopolize socioeconomic activity; it channels conflict rather than suppresses it. The state provides a focal point for energies aimed at navigating through socioeconomic constraints and possibilities. It is at various times a source of compensation for hardship resulting from unfavorable politicoeconomic circumstances and a mechanism for directly challenging and seeking to destroy both interior and exterior structural obstacles.

This description has been brought up as a starting point for comparison. PNA power is being used in a very different way to construct and manage the pseudoautonomous civic sphere of Palestinian self-rule. In a polity where consensus over the institutions that regulate and channel social conflict is weak or challenged, or where ruling authorities find themselves unable to mediate effectively or regulate with regard to structurally grounded socioeconomic phenomena that might lead to social conflict or that render suspect the legitimacy of the regime, conflict might be manufactured by regime elites using the resources they do have in order to pursue a specific strategy of political consolidation. In other words, in initiating a framework for conflict around resources and privileges associated with the limited powers it possesses, the regime sets itself up as the only viable agent of mediation, thereby enhancing (though not consolidating in institutions) its position as the primary politicoeconomic reference point for society.

It is such a top-down approach that characterizes the attempt to consolidate the civic sphere in Palestine today. In this framework, external patronage sustains both the factionalized social appendages of PNA institutions that define the contours of social conflict and the security forces that discipline those boundaries. The model deflects energies that might attempt to resolve structurally and politicoeconomically grounded predicaments and contradictions. The PNA is unable to address these issues and the governments of Israel and the United States find it not in their interests that such issues are resolved with the participation of the Palestinian street. PNA institutions are likely to develop accordingly and therefore to incorporate other mechanisms for ensuring its social relevance. This framework, intentionally or otherwise, is reinforced by the agreements.

Elites: Power and Legitimation

A conceptualization of state building from above in the Palestinian context requires a power-oriented notion of elites. As emphasized above, a precise notion of the tools (powers) "state"-based elites have at their disposal to confirm their elite status in society and of how this process of confirmation shapes other activities, incentives, and affiliations in the civic sphere is crucial in understanding the relationship between social activity, structural contexts, and political institutionalization. Shikaki (1996a) notes that throughout the early stages of the peace process, the PNA seemed to have held to the view that "the requirements of democracy may contradict those of national reconstruction, and that in the early stages of state building it is more important to assert the state's right to monopolize power and eliminate competitors for the people's loyalty" (9). The personalization of and reliance on central authority—or, at the very least, the reduction of authority to one faction (or one man)—precludes the consolidation of state institutions; Fatah is monopolizing power and thus far not transferring those powers into statelike institutions, at least not after the liberal model (Usher 1996, 31).

The PNA's effort to monopolize Palestinian civil society in the Occupied Territories from above has its roots in the attempt of the PLO to unite under its political umbrella the dispersed and vulnerable sectors of diaspora Palestinian civil society—sectors often struggling for survival in a variety of legal (or antinomian) conditions. Lacking the legal authority to insinuate itself into Palestinian society through formal regulation or positive policy initiatives, the PLO formula for national unity emphasized both a strong patron-client attachment by otherwise unintegrated communities to the central nationalist leadership and the mobilization of militant cadres to enforce politically correct stances vis-à-vis the PLO leadership and its political vision. PLO elites used the Intifada and the peace process that emerged from Israel's inability to deal with the uprising to reassert their primacy in Palestinian political life at a time when the core leadership was sidelined in Tunis and the nationalist structures in core Palestinian constituencies were disintegrating or unused. The Oslo Accords offered concrete mechanisms for the reinsinuation of the PLO into a core Palestinian constituency and brought with it the promise of donor patronage that allowed the PLO to restructure its bureaucracy and factional structure toward the task of ruling Palestinians in the Occupied Territories.

The current attempt by PNA elites to monopolize sociopolitical activity includes "laws" aimed at limiting, inter alia, press freedoms and freedom of association (Palestinian Center for Human Rights 1995a and 1995b). In particular, the 1995 Palestinian Draft Law Concerning Charitable Institutions (Draft Law) has aroused concern in the community of nongovernmental organizations (NGOs). During the Israeli occupation, NGOs arose to perform important social services and served as a focal point for criticism of the occupation regime. Inasmuch as they had a constituency and a source of economic viability not tied to the regime, they also represented a base of power and influence in society. The Draft Law put forward by the PNA represents an attempt to undermine the independence and freedom of operation of these organizations by making them legally accountable to and financially dependent on the PNA. By early 1997, with no apparent sense of irony, the PNA had established a Higher Council for Nongovernmental Organizations.

Whereas the figure of Yasser Arafat imbues the PNA with historical and revolutionary elite legitimacy, most other elites within the upper echelons of the PNA—the majority being "returnees"—owe their status more to their proximity to Arafat and their access to PNA resources than to any expertise or mass-based constituency. In the current climate of acute Palestinian unemployment, the Palestinian street has become in large measure directly or indirectly dependent on the PNA's distribution of resources (including jobs). The incentives structure of the PNA and the lack of a legal or structural environment that encourages the pursuit of civil alternatives have led to a demobilization of popular activity in the civic sphere. Usher (1996) notes that "The emergence of an increasingly authoritarian PNA has contributed to a process of depoliticization of Palestinian society in which many of its most able members have 'collectively withdrawn,' reverting to individualistic or clan-based (rather than political) solutions for their needs and aspirations" (32). Dependence deprives Palestinians of the resources needed to undermine or shape through challenge the contours of state building from above.

Constituency, Mobilization, and Institutionalization

Hinting that some of the weaknesses in the agreement might be attributed to a rush by PLO leaders to reassert the preeminence of the organization's institutions in Palestinian society at a time when it was threatened with relegation to the margins of Palestinian life, Hanan Ashrawi (1995) has pointed out that "it's not who makes the agreement but what's in it. . . . after you have signed, what power do you have?" (261). Samuel Huntington (1968) has argued that it is not the kind of government but rather the degree of government that determines whether a society is prone to violence and fragmentation or not: "The differences between democracy and dictatorship are less than the differences between those countries whose politics embodies consensus, community, legitimacy, organization, effectiveness, stability, and those countries whose politics is deficient in these qualities" (1). Huntington goes on to ask his central question and suggest an answer: "What was responsible for this violence and instability [in the developing world]? The primary thesis of this [Huntington's] book is that it was in large part the product of rapid social change and the rapid mobilization of new groups into politics coupled with the slow development of political institutions" (ibid.).

The current constitutive transition in the Palestinian autonomy undoubtedly represents a "rapid social change" that in turn encourages new patterns of social mobilization. The question is, however, whether the PNA possesses the kind of power needed to legitimize and make effective the channeling of social, political, and economic activity into the institutions of autonomy. The restrictions imposed by the agreement currently seem to impede the development of effective institutions. New institutions have sprung up overnight, but they lack institutionalization. They are shallow, weak, and have more symbolic than real power. Arafat is mobilizing society using some of the privileges of autonomy, but without incorporating social mobilization broadly within the institutions themselves.

In line with the above, we might argue that legitimacy is built through the exercise of governing and not only in the mobilization of symbols and the awareness of shared social experiences. The ability of ruling state ideologies to penetrate society and the willingness (or constructed need) of society to coalesce around governing institutions ultimately determine whether or not society and ruling elites can accommodate each other and identify the ruling order as legitimate. In short, Huntington identifies institutionalization as a precondition to social order, development, and the ability of society and ruling authorities to condition each other in the identification of legitimate symbolic and physical manifestations of power. Power that lends its weight to institutions inspires confidence in and enhances reference to those institutions.

The neopatrimonial strategy of state consolidation exemplified by the PNA tends to undermine the features that Huntington identifies as conducive to stability: it personalizes power relations and moves effective decision making beyond the reach of open and transparent institutions. As Brynen (1995) notes, neopatrimony is "generally corrosive of political institutionalization, since [it] suggest[s] the primacy of connections rather than the formal structures of law, constitutionalism and bureaucratic procedure" (25). Jameel Jum'a Salameh (1997), former deputy attorney general of Gaza, has forthrightly characterized the situation with regard to the autonomy: "we hear new expressions, 'you must have political support,' 'vitamin P—political influence,' 'you must look to someone important to speak on your behalf' and so on. [Elsewhere one's] rights are what is written in the laws. [Under Palestinian autonomy, one's] rights are none unless you have influence and power" (26). The coercive element involves more than just the threat or use of physical force in the streets; it might also mean the arbitrary denial of an established right, procedure, or privilege.

The limited "degree of government" currently accorded to the PNA inhibits the formation of enabling social and political institutions, and certainly affects the tactics used by ruling elites to consolidate and legitimate their authority. Rather than seeking legitimacy through the actions of governing—i.e., formulating and executing policy in the broad interests of society—the PNA, without effective control of the tools by which states usually attempt to control and manipulate the political economies of the social and territorial space in which they rule, has been forced into legitimacy building by (1) manipulative sloganeering that raises public expectations; (2) coercion (police functions being the one area where it almost enjoys an absolute power of state); and (3) co-opting strategically located elites with the limited patronage available—i.e., a factionally based divide-and-rule tactic that aims at breaking up possible broadly integrated opposition movements within Palestinian society. Ironically, it does not seem that self-rule has had the impact of strengthening and focusing the activity of civil society toward the construction of socially legitimate and productive institutions of political economy. Under the terms of the agreement, the PNA has very few of the powers usually invoked to co-opt the population to a state-building project. In fact, it lacks even most of the powers over resources and territory that most postcolonial elites in Africa and elsewhere had.

By Huntington's standards, therefore, the PNA's condition is conducive to neither development nor the types of predictable and efficacious institutions that promote a high degree of legitimacy. Although it would certainly be wrong to assume that democracy is not a priority for the Palestinian people, the East Asian examples indeed show that legitimacy can be built on aspirations other than the need to express choice over the names and faces of those who sit within ruling bodies. For example, in China today the dramatically successful free-market experiments have not been accompanied by political liberalization, and the upwardly mobile bourgeoisie do not seem to be demanding it as long as the regime allows them to get on with business. As a Palestinian academic noted when I asked for his thoughts about the likelihood of timely municipal elections, "who needs elections if you have services?" (interview, West Bank, 9 April 1998). To the dismay of modern artists and democratic theorists alike, people are generally more concerned with results than with process. This perhaps says something about the ability of the government to use coercion and incentives based on institutions that extend broadly and deeply into society to ensure the success of its social mobilizations from above to produce meaningful stability. However, the lack of democracy becomes more apparent to a population whose leadership seems unwilling or unable to ensure their more material needs and that stifles the resulting expressions of frustration.

Significance of the Distinction between Authority and Administration

Tamari's (1995) definition of authority as a phenomenon encompassing "issues of legitimacy and control" is useful here. Even more interesting is his implication that national identity is subject to a meaningful relationship with authority. Discussing a crisis of national identity as it is reflected in self-rule institutions, he notes that "This crisis is reflected in the symbolic national icons, on the one hand, and in the regulation of the relationship between civil society and the formative institutions of power—what can be called the institutionalization of authority—on the other" (10). PNA powers amount essentially to an administrative mandate; in other words, the PNA administers the peace accords during the interim period and does not in fact engage in a dynamic process of legitimating authority by shaping response to shared structural and ideological challenges. The important thing to note is that *administration* refers to the carrying out of preexisting arrangements, whereas *authority* denotes a positive, creative relationship between agents and subjects of power.

Jurisdiction and Law: Establishing the Boundaries and Content of Power

The imbalance between the protective and the coercive functions of the security apparatus represents another problematic feature of the autonomy. Many point to the role of the law in taking the first steps toward creating a comprehensible base for self-rule. However, the legal context of the transition and the behavior of the PNA suggest that its role might be complicating matters as much as clarifying them in the short term. The Israeli occupation was less a rule of law than a rule by whatever law was convenient. The PNA, with the implicit consent (and the steady insistence) of Israel and the United States, has done away with even this pretense of legalism.

First, the PNA has only limited scope to distance the legal context of self-rule from that of occupation. Article 18 of the Israeli-Palestinian Interim Agreement on the West Bank and the Gaza Strip states that

4.a. Legislation, including legislation which amends or abrogates existing laws or military orders, which exceeds the jurisdiction of the council or which is otherwise inconsistent with the provisions of DoP [Declaration of Principles], this agreement, or of any other agreement that may be reached between the two sides during the interim period, shall have no effect and shall be void ab initio.

    b. The Ra'ees of the Executive Authority of the Council shall not promulgate legislation adopted by the council if such legislation falls under the provisions of this Paragraph.

    5. All legislation shall be communicated to the Israeli side of the legal committee.

    6. Without derogating from the provisions of paragraph 4 above, the Israeli side of the Legal Committee may refer for the attention of the Committee any legislation regarding which Israeli considers the provisions of paragraph 4 apply, in order to discuss issues arising from such legislation. The legal committee will consider the legislation referred to it at the earliest opportunity.

This is basically the same as in the Agreement on Transfer of Powers and Responsibilities (29 August 1994), where PNA legislative authority is limited to promulgating secondary legislation "regarding powers and responsibilities transferred to it." Article 7, paragraphs 2–5, of the same agreement lists Israeli veto rights more specifically. A close reading shows that most of the powers to legislate cover the form of Palestinian administration but do not threaten its content, which follows the pattern of the occupation's civil administration functions. Israel's military sovereignty throughout the West Bank and Gaza Strip and its veto rights are maintained (Agreement on Gaza and Jericho Area, Annex I, Article 7, paragraphs 6 and 9). Those laws that the PNA does have the power to amend or replace are outlined in appendices to the agreement and include only a fraction of the laws and orders that were used to regulate the occupation.

Second, although the territorial integrity of the West Bank and Gaza Strip during the interim period is repeatedly reconfirmed throughout the text of the agreements (see, for example, Interim Agreement, Article 11, paragraph 1, and Article 17, paragraph 1), paragraphs subsequent to such reassurances usually reveal the actual patchwork of degrees and domains of jurisdiction. Article 17 of the Israeli-Palestinian Interim Agreement on the West Bank and the Gaza Strip notes the following exceptions to Palestinian jurisdiction: "a. issues that will be negotiated in the permanent status negotiations: Jerusalem, settlements, specified military locations, Palestinian refugees, borders, foreign relations and Israelis; and b. powers and responsibilities not transferred to the council."

The consistency of authority within given social and territorial spaces is also a factor that encourages individuals within a given community to identify common interests. In the Occupied Territories today, however, one might refer to the Palestinians as one nation divided under law. Questions of jurisdiction and legal precedent mean that Palestinians in different areas of the Occupied Territories experience the rule of the PNA through an inconsistent legal structure with uncertainty as who has the authority to arbitrate in many areas. This inconsistency is not as much a problem within Gaza, but it certainly does mean that Gazans will be experiencing self-rule through the lens of a different legal regime than inhabitants of the West Bank, just as the experience of occupation in Gaza was in many respects qualitatively different. The situation might not be conducive to creating the perception of equality in relation to institutions. The fact that people in different areas are experiencing the transition in different ways may be a factor undermining the future perception of the impartiality and independent character of self-rule institutions.

Third, current confusion and instability is exacerbated by the various poles of legal authority existing in the Occupied Territories, both in terms of personalities and in the hodgepodge of legal codes that prevail in the Palestinian areas. During occupation, the Israelis variously employed British, Jordanian, Egyptian, Israeli, and military legal precedent as it suited them, and under the terms of the agreements, these laws are the reference for the autonomy.[4] Many of these laws are draconian and designed to circumvent basic individual rights: "In 1945, the Mandate authorities issued a series of regulations called the emergency laws which were a compilation in one body of all the regulations and laws to deal with the special situation. . . . there was provision for all kinds of collective punishments—house demolitions, curfews and so on as well as detention and exile for those individuals suspected of engaging in anti-British activities. . . . these laws fell into disuse (under Egyptian administration) only to be resurrected by the Israelis when they occupied the West Bank and Gaza Strip in 1967" (Cossali and Robson 1986, 65).

More than one thousand military orders were issued by the Israeli military government in the Gaza Strip since 1967. Only seventy of these orders, which have the weight of law, are abrogated by the agreement (Roy 1995, 22). Arafat has contributed to the confusion by his declaration, in direct contravention of the agreements, that all military and occupation laws are null and void. The contingencies of the situation have of course not allowed him to act meaningfully on this, and inasmuch as he has, it has been by ignoring the primacy of the rule of law in general. He has, though, not hesitated to invoke preexisting laws when they increase his executive author-

---

4. For a brief but interesting overview of how these laws could be manipulated, see Cossali and Robson (1986, 75).

ity vis-à-vis the rights of Palestinians and the other institutions established within the autonomy. The role of law in the attempted "mobilization from above" has thus far been neither protective of subject rights nor institutionally constructive.

On top of this, "Palestinian leaders from outside have brought with them a criminal code applicable in Lebanon." Usama Halabi expands on these difficulties: "the head judge in Gaza issued a statement that courts in Gaza should make decisions based on Jordanian law, but Jordanian law does not apply in Gaza. How will the substance of legal matters be discussed and decided when there is not even a basic understanding about what laws apply[?] . . . It is a mess and no one has the authority to take any decisions to clarify matters" (Harlow 1995, 33).

Finally, with regard to powers and jurisdiction, not only are there problems with the nature and consistency of the laws themselves, but also with regard to who is to administer them. In most municipal zones in the West Bank (constituting about 3 percent of the West Bank territory) and in about 56 percent of the Gaza Strip, it is the PNA alone. In other areas, there is joint PNA and Israeli jurisdiction. And in other areas, only Israel is responsible for enforcement of the confusing legal situation. After the suicide bombings inside Israel in early March 1996, the IDF made arrests inside the autonomous areas in the West Bank, further obfuscating the character and boundaries of effective jurisdiction (as have school closings by the Israelis in spite of the fact that this function was explicitly turned over to PNA administration). The clarity of legal jurisdiction is further complicated by the lack of clear distinctions between the branches of Palestinian self-"government" and the vagueness of many job descriptions within the PNA (Harlow 1995, 34). There are many different courts, and the lack of effective powers means that there are institutions without immediate meaningful tasks.

In spite of all this apparent confusion, Palestinian legal and human rights advocates insist that the existing body of law is sufficient to ensure Palestinian rights. The problem is taking a case through the courts in a way that establishes legal precedent as to what laws and procedures apply. Thus far, the PNA has shown a tendency to cut a deal with the defendant(s) before a legal decision is reached that would undermine its future executive authority.[5] A publication of the Palestinian Human Rights Monitoring Group (Au-

---

5. These comments are based on interviews in April 1998 with Raji Sourani and Hamdi Y. Shaggura at the Palestinian Center for Rights and Law, and with Charles Lerchner at the Palestinian Human Rights Monitoring Group. See also the *Palestinian Human Rights Monitor*, no. 3 (August 1997), 2: "the existing legal framework is nothing less than an operating judicial system, capable of dealing with almost any *legal* task" (emphasis in original).

gust 1997) notes that "The Palestinian legal system, like other legal systems in the Middle East, is built up on layers placed by successive rulers. At first glance, it appears as though the various layers are in competition, creating confusion in the legal system. In fact, each new regime has usually adopted existing law in its entirety, and then proceeded to make alterations and changes as needed. At any given moment, the legal profession is aware of which laws are in use by the courts and which are not" (3).

The same report notes that competition between the PNA executive and the judiciary "presents the most severe challenge to the rule of law in Palestine." "The existence of this conflict is entirely the responsibility of the executive authority and the security forces, who are guilty of undermining the rule of law in Palestine, and thus pushing Palestinian society backward and into a state of anarchy and rule by decree" (ibid., 2). It should be added that this competition is borne of tensions resulting from the PNA struggle to implement the accords in line with the demands of its negotiating "partners" and from the Palestinian street's attempt to invoke the judicial system to imbue self-rule with an atmosphere of security and concrete, meaningful rights. A contradiction has developed between the two in the actual implementation of the Oslo Accords.

In years past, the lack of faith in and the inefficiency of the military courts set up by the Israelis encouraged people to use the traditional system of *mukhtars* (who were appointed by the military authorities) to arbitrate disputes (Cossali and Robson 1986, 71). During the Intifada and the general breakdown of the structures of military authority, Hamas (the Islamic Resistance Movement) played an increasingly important role in resolving disputes on the local level, with even Christians resorting to and respecting their arbitration (Ron Wilkinson, UNRWA information officer, interview with author, September 1995). The trends noted above have chipped away at faith in public institutions and have increased the tendency to resort to local and traditional modes of social mediation, perhaps strengthening the foundation for the PNA's factional control. Beyond the potential contradictions suggested by the imposition of diaspora national institutions on the inhabitants of the Occupied Territories, such a confusing situation of authority makes it difficult to see how the PNA is going to cement a stable and meaningful relationship between society and the provisional regime over the short term.

There are also cases that illustrate a dangerous trend toward the personalization and politicization of the justice system, as well as the limited ability of civil society to contain abuses of authority within the framework of current national institutions.[6] Arafat has openly declared that he refused to be a

---

6. On 11 May 1998, LAW issued the following press release; similar statements were sent

"puppet of the courts" (Beyer 1996, 25), a statement that reveals either ignorance or a lack of concern for due process in the content of self-rule. He has insisted on being consulted personally before the court makes any decision, particularly in regard to his freedom to decide the content and course of "internal security" (ibid.).

Usher (1996), for example, describes how Arafat in February 1995

> personally authorized the setting up of "special state security courts." These are independent of any civilian judiciary system, allow secret evidence, brook no appeal procedures, and are "judged" by PLO military personnel appointed by the PA. Verdicts are the prerogative of Arafat, who according to the PA's attorney general has sole power to "confirm, ease or stiffen" any sentence passed by the "courts." (32)

The legal precedent for these security courts is found in the mandate emergency laws, which were also invoked during Israeli occupation (Shikaki 1996b, 10). Palestinian lawyers generally refuse to appear before the court on behalf of clients so as not to in any way legitimize it (Hass 1997). Although these security courts have been widely condemned by Palestinians and international observers, international donors have not protested, and the results seem in line with Israeli expectations and perceptions of their interests.

In July 1996, a seventh victim died in PNA custody, apparently as a result of torture. The incident provoked a riot in the victim's hometown of Nablus. When unrest spread to Tulkarm, PNA forces responded to the demonstrations with violence, shooting and killing one demonstrator (Beyer 1996, 26). Immediately, PNA radio "switched to 'emergency broadcasting' and began featuring martial music and the rabble-rousing hits of the popular Arab singer Fayrouz to highlight 'our people's triumph over all vile conspiracies.'" The radio report went on to claim that Hamas militants had been responsible for the indiscriminate shooting and that an investigation was underway (Amayreh 1996, 8). Although an initial statement on the

---

out by other Palestinian NGOs: "LAW expresses its alarm over the recent resignation of Palestinian Attorney General Fayyez Abu Rahme, appointed to his office nine months ago. Mr. Rahme resigned his position because of continuous intervention by the Minister of Justice Freih Abu Meddein and the commanders of the security services. A precarious situation has developed in which the judiciary has been seriously undermined, its decisions disregarded, and the Attorney General's position eroded. LAW views with alarm the resignation of the Attorney General and its consequences for the future of the judiciary in Palestine. LAW demands an immediate halt to the interference in the work of the judiciary by the Executive branch, and calls for an investigation into the conditions that led to Mr. Rahme's resignation."

events referred to "suspicious attempts to distort the National Authority's image," the PNA admitted later that the victim was killed by police fire. By December 1997, the number of suspicious deaths of individuals in Palestinian custody had risen to sixteen.

Rabin had been clear in predicting such tendencies in 1993, noting that such a trend would be in Israel's interests: "'The Palestinians will be better at it than we were,' he said in September 1993, 'because they will allow no appeals to the Supreme Court and will prevent the Israeli Association of Civil Rights access to the area. They will rule by their own methods, freeing, and this is important, the Israeli army soldiers from doing what they will do" (Usher 1996, 28).

Palestinian unease is today palpable. Conducting interviews in Gaza in April 1998, I came across several people who openly referred to the "difficulty in expressing one's self on 'such issues' in the current circumstances" and others who after initial circumspection went on to describe methods of PNA intimidation that had been used against them. For example, one professor at a Gaza University noted with frustration that Palestinian security forces had been loitering in the street in front of his home for two full nights preceding the interview, making sleep all but impossible as he expected to be arrested at any time. Another Palestinian observer noted ironically that most of the security personnel in core services received their "human rights education" in Israeli prisons or through participation in the factional violence of Lebanon through the 1980s (Ibrahim Shehada, Gaza Center for Rights and Law, interview with author, September 1995). Beyond the routine use of torture in PNA detention centers and the deaths in detention, worrying trends include security force members using their positions to settle personal disputes or vendettas and to pressure business men to accept security force officers as "business partners."

In June 1996, Dr. Eyad Sarraj (1996), human rights activist and commissioner general of the Palestine Independent Commission for Citizens' Rights at the time, was arrested several times without charge and severely beaten while in detention. Sarraj has openly criticized the PNA, decrying the "corrupt, dictatorial, oppressive" nature of the regime and the arbitrary arrests of Palestinians, and referred to "an overwhelming sense of fear" among Palestinians. Political outspokenness was openly stated as the reason for his arrest. Following a national and international outcry against his arrest, police suddenly found illicit drugs on his premises and thereby charged him with possession and sale. Dr. Sarraj stated, however, that not once during his interrogation was he asked about drugs or drug dealing, but rather about a letter that he had sent to Arafat outlining criticisms and critical remarks he had made in an interview with the *New York Times*. The judge in the Palestinian Magisterial Court of Gaza dismissed the charges against Dr. Sarraj, who was released fifteen days later in the middle of the night before a scheduled hearing in front of a security court.

In another case in August 1996, the Palestinian High Court responded to the petition submitted on behalf of ten Birzeit students detained without charge or trial starting in March 1996 by ordering their immediate release. The High Court ruled that there was no legal basis to justify continuing the students' detention, especially given that no charges had been brought against them.[7] However, the next day Attorney General Khaled al-Qidra stated that the students would not be released before he had conferred with President Arafat. Commenting on the case, the Palestinian Society for the Protection of Human Rights (LAW) noted that "The Attorney General has interfered with the functioning of the court and violated Palestinian Laws, which require that the High Court's decision be immediately acted upon. . . . An independent judiciary is guaranteed by Palestinian law. According to the relevant Jordanian legal system, article 97 guarantees government respect and execution of the High Court's decisions. Article 101/1 ensures that no authority influence the free and fair functioning of the courts. The refusal to release immediately the students represents a violation of the law and provides a dangerous precedent against the free functioning of the Palestinian legal system" (LAW press releases, 18 and 20 August 1996).

By late August 1996, Arafat had pressured the judges involved in both the case against the students and the case against Eyad Sarraj to resign. These "excesses" and abuses by the plethora of different Palestinian security agencies have undermined public faith in the ability of the PNA to administer and enforce justice humanely and impartially. Violations include: prisoners being kept for periods in excess of their sentences; bad and violent treatment; detention without trail or hearing; the taking of hostages to pressure another wanted family member to turn him- or herself in; arrests due to Israeli pressure; food shortages in the prisons; and prisoners being forced to pay for necessary medicines while in detention (LAW, 26 March 1996). Hilal (1995) also notes the trend to rationalize repressive practices under the heading of "national interest," adding that, "all this is taking place be-

---

7. The statement of the court was as follows: "We find that the detention of the plaintiffs in Ramallah prisons since March 1996 and until now has happened without any legal reason and took place in the absence of procedures and in contravention of the rule of law, which gives us the power to accept this case and to find the arrest of the plaintiffs illegal. Release them immediately" (case no. 96/25). Source: Birzeit Human Rights Record No. 17 (April–September 1996).

fore any legal safeguards of basic human and democratic rights have been formulated and approved in a Palestinian constitution" (17).

Palestinians themselves are wary of this trend. According to an exit poll conducted by the Center for Palestine Research and Statistics: "When asked whether they supported unrestricted freedom of the press and human rights versus national interests as defined by the Palestinian authority, about two-thirds selected unrestricted freedom of the press and human rights. This clearly indicates that voters are not giving the president an unquestioning carte blanch" (Shikaki 1996a, 22).

Palestinian voters also expressed concern at the trend toward personalization of power: "the responses to one of the questions on the exit poll provide an important qualifier for Arafat's mandate: 40 percent of the voters polled on the election day said they wanted Arafat to have less power than the council; another 40 percent said they wanted the council and Arafat to have equal power, and only 20 percent thought that Arafat should have more power than the council" (Shikaki 1996a, 21). Hanf and Sabella (1996) conclude that Palestinians have to a significant degree "internalized the language of human rights and the rule of law in their struggle to bring down an efficient army of occupation" (169). In a survey conducted by these two political scientists, four-fifths of the respondents agreed with the statement: "the time of family/hamula politics is over. Leaders should be chosen on their own qualifications and merits" (ibid., 67). This survey also demonstrates Palestinian skepticism toward the unaccountable use of power in general, the consequences of which they were made too well aware of under occupation.

By way of summary, it can be said that the PNA lacks effective jurisdiction in several crucial domains. According to Raja Shehadeh (1994), "in three key areas, the arrangements imposed on the Palestinians by the Israelis [during occupation] were either preserved or augmented" (22): legal jurisdiction, jurisdiction over water, and jurisdiction over land. The PLO seems to have bungled the water rights issue by giving jurisdiction to the Israeli Mekoroth water company and agreeing in effect to keep water use distribution at the same levels (Gaza-Jericho Agreement, Annex II, Article 2b, paragraph 31). In the area of legal (civil) jurisdiction, Shehadeh argues that the agreement gives Israeli courts wider authority in disputes and offenses involving Israeli citizens than the pre-Intifada occupation jurisdiction did. The jurisdiction of Palestinian courts has been undermined at the current stage of the negotiations. Current zoning schemes allow settlers the freedom of movement in areas populated by Palestinians, but they are in no case accountable to Palestinian jurisdiction. The security of individual Palestinians is thereby threatened as settlers have continued leeway to harass and attack

Palestinians and vandalize their property. By putting the issue of Palestinian rights in Jerusalem under negotiation, the PLO has threatened to undermine a right that belonged to the Palestinians by international law. Shehadeh (1994) makes the argument that the PLO has failed to pay attention to and recognize the short- and long-term significance of the legal components of the changing relationship with Israel and the transition period itself. The impact of clear and understood law on the healthy functioning of Palestinian civil society and on long-term economic and social development has also been ignored. "The leadership must understand that, significant though the political transformations inaugurated by the PLO certainly are, the law also has a vital role: first, as a tool for achieving better success in future negotiations, and second, as a tool for peaceful and effective social transformation and economic and political development" (Shehadeh 1994, 24).

Electoral Legitimacy? Process versus Power in the Content of Ritual Elections

On 21 January 1996, the PNA's lack of substantive powers was obscured by the conduct of elections. Andoni (1996a) argues that: "While elections generally indicate a democratic process, in the Palestinian case, a democratic right has been permitted in order to legitimize a political process that could well lead to the perpetuation of Israeli control" (5). Shikaki (1996b) is somewhat more generous, but also notes the deviation from the standard meanings of elections: "For the PLO, since the old Palestinian consensus was gone, the elections were needed to give Arafat a mandate and to give legitimacy to a new political order. Therefore the democratic agenda is absent, and elections should not be seen necessarily as the start of a transition to democracy but in their role of nation building and peacemaking" (17).

The intended framework and scope of the elections is stated within the Interim Agreement: "These elections constitute a significant interim preparatory step toward the legitimate rights of the Palestinian people and their just requirements and will provide a democratic basis for the establishment of Palestinian institutions" (Article 2, paragraph 2). In fact, many Gazans who spoke enthusiastically of having taken this "significant interim preparatory step" became very cynical when asked what they expected the politicians to accomplish in the way of improving the basic conditions of life in Gaza. Elections that lead nowhere may only delegitimize the idea of election. Haidar Abd al-Shafi, a strong critic of undemocratic tendencies in the Fatah leadership and a prominent independent representative of left nationalist politics, did not spend a single shekel on his campaign for the Palestinian Legislative Assembly. His only campaign statement (according to word on the street) was that he would not make any promises because, if elected, he would not have the power to keep them. He was far and away the leading vote getter in Gaza. Elections restored a sense of pride, but hopes for substantive and qualitative change remained dim.

Before the elections, Shikaki (1996b) had noted that "while the peace process had dealt the final blow to the old consensus, it provided the basis for a new source of legitimacy: the popular will and the elections through which that will could manifest itself" (9). Elections, however, have seemingly failed to mold this new consensus. The subordination of the elections to the peace process in practice rendered them invalid as an arena for ideological contestation. The result is that national elections have in no way represented a foundation for popular rule or a safeguard in the Palestinian street against the insinuation of external interests and abuses of power.

In spite of reports from international election observers hailing free and fair elections, several Gazans told me that Palestinian police threatened them with harassment and denial of vital permits for travel and work if they failed to vote. Reinforcing this anecdotal evidence, a poll conducted in February 1996 found that slightly more than 20 percent of Gazans reported harassment at the polling stations and 48.1 percent of respondents either knew of vote buying or had heard of it (Jerusalem and Media Communications Center 1997, poll no. 13). There is also further evidence that the PNA used what powers it does have to ensure a desirable outcome to elections from their perspective. Arafat used his control over resources and privileges, as well as control over the timing of the elections and campaigning, to make sure that preferred candidates stood the best possible chance of election. Earlier, when many local (often young) candidates won a place on the Fatah list in the organization's internal caucus, Arafat declared the result null and void, placing his own preferred candidates on the "official" list. These candidates included many prominent returnees and representatives from strategically placed families (Andoni 1996a, 8–12). All in all, only 41.5 percent of respondents to the above-mentioned (February 1996) poll felt that elections were "free and fair." In spite of these attempts to manipulate the outcome, it is interesting to note that "some of the largest margins of victory went to prominent nationalist independents such as Haydar 'Abd al-Shafi, 'Abd al-Jawad Salih, and Hanan Ashrawi. . . . Another point of significance is the fact that eighteen or nineteen of the Fatah people who won as independents—the so-called 'Fatah rebels'—are very critical of Arafat and sometimes also of the peace process and therefore cannot be counted on to tow the party line" (Shikaki 1996a, 21). The Palestinian Legislative Council, in spite of its effective powerlessness, has used its platform to criticize corruption and human rights abuses under the PNA. However, Beyer (1996) reports that when a group of Palestinian councilors were asked "what percentage of their resolutions were implemented by the PNA, they broke out laughing. The answer was zero" (25). It seems that the council's main task was to give the Interim Agreement the veneer of popular legitimacy.

Election results may reflect attempts to connect oneself to the benefits associated with the PNA apparatus more than anything else. Although Shikaki offers evidence that cautions against the use of clan as a factor explaining voting preferences,[8] Andoni (1996) points out that the ability to access basic needs is still a primary factor of political allegiance rather than a good taken as a given: "One possible explanation for [the success of traditional returnee leadership in elections in spite of open resentment on the street] could be that the officials returning with Arafat relied heavily, perhaps even more than most Fatah candidates, on the PNA's structures, including security, in their campaigns. In some areas, they were called the 'authority's candidates,' a description denoting some resentment but also implying connections and the ability to deliver services" (15).

The process of appointing the municipal council of Beit Jala, a town in the West Bank, illustrates that clan affiliation continues to play a very important role in people's understanding of their interests within the political process. Muna Hamzeh-Muhaisen (1996) reports that "the municipal council, finally appointed in February 1998, is made up of ten Christians and three Muslims representing the various clans and social and political powers in the town" (4). Fuad Rizk adds that "each clan gathered and elected its own representative" (cited in Hamez-Muhaisen 1996, 4). When there is no context for voters to make rational long-term decisions about proposed policies, and elected politicians lack real legislative and regulatory function, one can expect that voters are making decisions based on immediate connections, concerns, and opportunities.

In democratic states, elections contest power. The essential thing is that every time we go to the polls we are not simply reaffirming our identity or acknowledging a lack of alternative to the status quo. Rather, we attempt to influence how power affects our personal and collective interests. If the elections were intended to serve as a referendum on a peace process, as was so often claimed in the press, then why not hold a referendum on that question instead of holding elections? In fact, the election results in Gaza—especially inasmuch as they demonstrated localized and factionalized outcomes—can be interpreted as people trying to position themselves as well as

8. "Based on our exit poll, we concluded that the most important primary selection criterion for the selection process was political affiliation, followed by the character of the candidate himself. . . . only thirdly did family or clan considerations figure" (Shikaki 1996a, 22).

possible in a new order that is grudgingly accepted as a fait accompli. The economic situation for many Palestinians at the time of the elections was such that any pondering of "to be or not to be" regarding the peace process as a whole was subordinate to trying to get someone in office who might remember them when it came time to distribute the crumbs of autonomy.

Nor have states historically been born by elections, but through the consolidation of power. From an elitist perspective, the boundaries of rule have been determined by the ability of elites to use power and influence to shape the interests of society in ways that conform to their own interests. Elections might be a tool used in such an endeavor. Given that democracy requires already clear boundaries, elections do not create or delimit states, but existing states can use elections to solve problems and revitalize legitimacy. Elections in the Occupied Territories have given the Palestinians the rituals and obligations of self-rule with few of its associated rights and privileges. The context of the elections of January 1996 allowed the Palestinians to go to the polls, but the politicians they elected do not have the necessary powers to deal directly with problems facing society. Furthermore, elections are a means and not an end. They work well when broadly defined goals of the society have been identified and when the basic consensual arrangement between state and society has been institutionalized, but they are less useful if the fundamental premise on which they are held is still deeply challenged within society. In the case of Palestinian autonomy, elections may only serve to dramatize the powerlessness of Palestinian political elites to manipulate autonomy toward the best interests of the Palestinian populations in the West Bank and Gaza Strip.

In other parts of the world, continuing unrest after "free and fair" elections shows that legitimacy is not merely the superficial and ritual observance of democratic practice. In cases such as Bosnia, elections must be backed up by the presence of international force. If a power vacuum exists, chaos and violence might break out as groups find advantage in challenging the results with violence—hence, perhaps the concern with coercive force as the cornerstone of PNA rule.

Elections also imply that voters have a rational basis for evaluating the correlation between proposed policies and their consequences. In its struggle to consolidate its position from above, the PNA has also been hard-pressed to control information on the street. Indeed, the PNA's attempts to control the street by closing independent newspapers and intimidating journalists constitutes a worrying trend. In the run up to elections, opponents were denied airtime, and journalists publishing reports critical of the PNA or the peace process were by various means denied access to their media of communication. Throughout the interim period, journalists have been arrested and beaten. Newspapers have been closed down or ransacked after publishing reports that failed to place the PNA in a positive light and even for failing to put the PNA in a positive enough light. Khalid Amayreh (1996) reports a tendency of the new leadership and their agents to "view all 'non-conformist elements' within the Palestinian society as impeding the 'national plan' and 'aborting the Palestinian new-born.'" Amayreh continues:

> many of the newcomers . . . view the slightest gesture of dissatisfaction with Arafat and his regime as a potential threat to their newly earned and previously undreamt of achievements. At a recent seminar in Beit Sahor on "Press Freedom under the Palestinian Authority," a high ranking military official said that Palestinians should concentrate on "bread winning" not "western-style freedoms" as their top priority. When confronted with "man does not live by bread alone," the official simply said "this is Palestine, not Sweden." This anti-democratic outlook, coupled with a scandalous lack of accountability and absence of discipline, [often with acquiescence from] the highest political echelons, [may have] tragic consequences.

In both democracies and dictatorships, leaders and societies communicate with and manipulate each other by adapting each other's terms to serve their own ends, but however vague and transcendental that dialogue may at times seem, it is a dialogue that has almost certainly responded to the survival needs of each.

The future of democracy in Palestine is in no small way connected to the devolution of meaningful powers in ways that make them accountable and contestable within Palestinian society. Elections that do not lead to change may only exacerbate frustration and highlight the emptiness of the exercise in the current environment. Democratization in its most vital sense refers to a context for social mobilization and not only to ideals of tolerance, individualism, and compromise. The framers of the agreement have called for democracy but have separated it from popular empowerment. Inasmuch as national elections represented any popular will, they were manipulated in service of social mobilization orchestrated from above. Effective democracy would demand that Palestinians be allowed to mobilize to influence issues over which the PNA or the Palestinian Legislative Council have no authority. People become citizens not by electing a *ra'ees* (president/chairman). They become citizens when they discover and appropriate the power to throw out a *ra'ees*. In short, real democracy in Palestine would amount to allowing the Palestinian street to contest the form and content of continued Israeli control over life in the Occupied Territories.

Conclusion

A pun commonly heard in the streets of Gaza after the signing of the Oslo Accords transformed the PLO slogan "revolution until victory" into the ironically more appropriate "chaos until victory." The Intifada had shown the Palestinians themselves and the world that the inhabitants of the Occupied Territories would not remain passive or submissive in the face of an increasingly unaccountable and economically disenfranchising military rule. The Palestinian street proved capable of initiating change. However, similar to the trajectory of events during the 1936–39 Palestinian uprising, by the time an occupying power was driven to the point of making concessions, Palestinians were too exhausted and fragmented to take advantage of any new opportunities. Although change was initiated from below, it remained for others to determine the nature and the boundaries of that change.

The current project of Palestinian autonomy, along with the trajectory of state building it implies, is a political undertaking with contours overwhelmingly determined from above. This view is suggested by the Israeli and U.S. roles in shaping the nature of PNA power and their demands on the PNA, and by a PNA leadership that often seems to envision the peace process primarily as a vehicle for pursuing the interests of nationalist elites. It is furthermore in the nature of the powers devolved on Palestinians by Oslo that they are unaccountable to the Palestinian street and unamenable to meeting the challenge of overcoming structural de-development in the West Bank and Gaza Strip. The agreements in the wake of Oslo must be seen as mechanisms to protect a diplomatic goal from the demands of the Palestinian public and not as viable mechanisms for the construction of a functional and independent Palestinian public life.

These factors have led to a dramatic corrosion of PNA legitimacy over the four years since Oslo was signed. The potential for instability inherent in this loss of legitimacy has been compensated for with a mixture of neopatrimonial payoffs and repression. This current nexus of limited power and external interest seems likely to condition and entrench neopatrimonial and securitarian tendencies in the emerging Palestinian polity. The inability of the PNA to promote new bases of social and political power (or legitimacy) by initiating processes of, for example, economic development or constitutional reform or both encourages it to pursue a neopatrimonial strategy of political consolidation premised on an ability to use its limited resourses— resources in most cases derived from external sources—to manipulate socioeconomic dependency, fragmentation, and conflict toward the ends of regime consolidation.

Palestinian society has few alternatives but to orient itself toward this system in order to meet immediate needs, which has the effect of consolidating an extrainstitutional pattern of PNA-society relations. This situation channels social energies away from developmental goals and leaves PNA institutions unaccountable to demands, however stifled they now are, for structural change. As the new order proves unable to address conditions of de-development, the ability of Palestinian society and economy to adapt or innovate in the face of structural challenges will remain limited, and political legitimacy will be attached to the redistribution of aid rather than to economic development or dynamic responses to structural constraints. These factors are already having profound consequences for political institutionalization and civic development in the self-rule areas.

One consequence of the vicious, deterministic circle encompassing the powerlessness of the PNA and the paralysis of Palestinian society is the failure of the PNA to represent and reflect a meaningful balance of individual and national rights and obligations in political institutions, patterns of social affiliation, and participation in everyday life. Indeed, the case of Palestinian autonomy suggests that the "strength" of civil society cannot be considered independent of broader politicoeconomic contingencies or without an understanding of the power embedded in the defining institutions of a polity (i.e., those institution that give the polity a sense of stateness). The power of one is dependent on and interacts with the power of the other, and powerlessness begets powerlessness. It cannot at present be said that Palestinian autonomy is encouraging the creation of a space from within which citizenship might be expressed and meaningfully understood.

Future stability in the Palestinian space and thus in the Palestinian-Israeli space generally will likely require the continuation of a high degree of external input in the form of material payoffs and "security"-oriented interventions. Yet the model is inherently unstable. It is in the margins of the neopatrimonial structures—in the spaces where patronage doesn't reach or is unable to compensate for the loss of ideological goals and dignity (or to use the power of governing to articulate and legitimate new hopes and structures of action)—that the inability of the current dynamic to produce a lasting peace is most apparent. Increasingly, individuals may turn to violence to assert their demands when all other channels of communication between society and power seem to have failed. However, feelings on the street that struggle is futile (the loss of hope has led and will lead to isolated acts of violence, but not to sustained activism) and the dependence on the PNA in daily coping strategies mitigate against concerted social action, violent or otherwise. One wonders whether or not this was the plan from the beginning.

In any case, the ultimate limitation of PNA power has been summed up by a senior Israeli military officer: "The Israeli army is prepared to move back into the PNA territories anytime it wants."[9]

---

9. Muslim World News, "Israeli army ready to return to PA territories: officer," November 27, 1966, posted at *MSA News,* http://www.mynet.net/~msanews. The Israeli daily *Ha'aretz* is cited by MNW as the source for this report.

Works Cited
Index

Works Cited

Books and Articles

Abdallah, S. 1986. *Lebanese Citizenship: A Comparison to the Arab Syrian and French Citizenship* (in Arabic). Beirut: Maktabat Matabi' al-Shuf al-Haditha, Darayya.

Abed, Shukri, and Kaufman, Edy. "The Relevancy of Democracy to the Resolution of the Israeli-Palestinian Conflict." Unpublished paper.

Abu-Hakima, Ahmad Mustafa. 1982. *The Modern History of Kuwait 1750–1965.* London: Luzac.

Abu-Keshek, Bakar, and Sammy Geraisi. 1977. *Housing Hardship in the Arab Sector: The Problem and Its Solution* (in Hebrew). Nazareth: Public Council for Social Welfare.

Achdut, Lea, and Menachem Carmi. 1981. *Twenty-Five Years of the National Insurance Institute* (in Hebrew). Jerusalem: National Insurance Institute.

Afkhami, Mahnaz, ed. 1995. *Faith and Freedom: Women's Human Rights in the Muslim World.* Syracuse: Syracuse Univ. Press.

Ahmed, Leila. 1992. *Women and Gender in Islam.* New Haven: Yale Univ. Press.

Alawiyya, H. 1984. *Lebanese Citizenship and Ways of Regaining It* (in Arabic). Beirut: n.p.

Alloula, Malek. 1986. *The Colonial Harem.* Translated by Myrna Godzich and Wlad Godzich. Minneapolis: Univ. of Minnesota Press.

Almond, Gabriel A. 1989. "The Intellectual History of the Civic Culture Concept." In *The Civic Culture Revisited,* edited by Gabriel A. Almond and Sydney Verba. Newbury Park: Sage.

Amayreh, Khalid. 1996. "Arafat Besieged by Domestic Trouble." *Palestine Times,* no. 63: 8.

Anderson, Benedict. 1991. *Imagined Communities: Reflections on the Origin and Spread of Nationalism.* London: Verso.

Anderson, Lisa. 1991. "Tribe and State: Libyan Anomalies." In *Tribes and State Formation in the Middle East,* edited by Philip S. Khoury and Joseph Kostiner. London: I. B. Tauris.

Andoni, Lamis. 1996a. "The Elections: Democracy or One Party Rule." *Journal of Palestine Studies* 25, no. 3: 5–16.

———. 1996b. "Jordan: Behind the Recent Disturbances." *Middle East International,* no. 536 (25 Oct.):17–18.

Andrews, Geoff, ed. 1991. *Citizenship.* London: Lawrence and Wishart.

"Arbitrary Justice in Kuwait." 1991. *Guardian Weekly,* 26 May.

Arendt, Hannah. 1967. *On Revolution*. New York: Viking Compass.

Aristotle. 1981. *Politics*. Translated by Hippocrates G. Apostle and Lloyd P. Gerson. Grinell, Iowa: Peripatetic.

———. 1985. *Nicomachean Ethics*. Translated by Terence Irwin. Indianapolis: Hackett.

Ashrawi, Hanan. 1995. *This Side of Peace*. New York: Simon and Schuster.

Ashuri, Amnon. 1988. "Assistance Programs for Housing" (in Hebrew). In *Israel Builds*, edited by I. Charlap. Jerusalem: Ministry of Construction and Housing.

el-Asmar, Fouzi, Uri Davis, and Naim Khader. 1978. *Towards a Socialist Republic of Palestine*. London and Kefar Shemaryahu: Ithaca Press and Miftah (Key) Publishers.

Ayubi, Nazih. 1995. *Overstating the Arab State: Politics and Society in the Middle East*. London: I. B. Tauris.

Azarya, Victor, and Baruch Kimmerling. 1980. "New Immigrants in the Israeli Armed Forces." *Armed Forces and Society* 6: 455–82.

Barbalet, J. M. 1988. *Citizenship*. Minneapolis: Univ. of Minnesota Press.

Barkai, Zeev. 1981. "On Housing Policy and the Problems in Its Implementation" (in Hebrew). *Bitahon Soziali*, no. 2 (Mar.): 162–69.

Batchelor, Carol. 1995a. "Stateless Persons: Some Gaps in International Protection." *International Journal of Refugee Law* (Oxford) 7, no. 2.

———. 1995b. "UNHCR and Issues Related to Nationality." *Refugee Survey Quarterly* 14, no. 2.

Beblawi, Hazem. 1990. "The Rentier State in the Arab World." In *The Arab State*, edited by Luciani Giacomo. London: Routledge.

Beiner, Ronald, ed. 1995. *Theorizing Citizenship*. Albany: State Univ. of New York Press.

Beinin, Joel. 1990. *Was the Red Flag Flying There? Marxist Politics and the Arab-Israeli Conflict in Egypt and Israel, 1948–1965*. Berkeley: Univ. of California Press.

Bell, Daniel. 1960. *The End of Ideology*. New York: Free Press.

Bellah, Robert N., et al. 1985. *Habits of the Heart*. New York: Harper and Row.

Bendix, Reinhard. 1977. *Nation-Building and Citizenship*, Berkeley: Univ. of California Press; orig. pub. 1964.

Ben-Eliezer, Uri. 1995. *The Emergence of Israeli Militarism 1939–1956* (in Hebrew). Tel Aviv: Dvir.

Benn, Stanley I. 1955. "The Uses of 'Sovereignty.'" *Political Studies* 3, no. 2:109–22.

Benn, Tony, and Andrew Hood. 1993. *Common Sense: A New Constitution for Britain*. London: Hutchison.

Benziman, Uzi, and Atallah Mansour. 1992. *Subtenants* (in Hebrew) Jerusalem: Keter.

Berhardt, Rudolph. 1981. "Federalism and Autonomy." In *Models of Autonomy*, edited by Yoram Dinstein. New Brunswick, N.J.: Transaction Books.

Berlin, Isaiah. 1969. *Four Essays on Liberty*. Oxford: Oxford Univ. Press.

Berman, Nathaniel. 1993. "'But the Alternative Is Despair': European Nationalism and the Modernist Renewal of International Law." *Harvard Law Review* 106: 1793.

Bernstein, Deborah. 1981. "Immigrant Transit Camps: The Formation of Dependent Relations in Israeli Society." *Ethnic and Racial Studies* 1: 26–43.

Beyer, Lisa. 1996. "Peace in Flames." *Time International* 148, no. 15 (7 Oct.): 23–27.

Bindman, Geoffrey, and Bernard Bowring. 1994. *Human Rights in a Period of Transition*. London: Law Society.

Bishara, Azmi. 1993. "The Palestinian Minority" (in Hebrew). In *Israeli Society: Critical Perspectives*, edited by Uri Ram. Tel Aviv: Breirot.

Bobbio, Norberto. 1987. *The Future of Democracy*. Minneapolis: Univ. of Minneapolis Press.

———. 1989. *Democracy and Dictatorship: The Nature and Limits of State Power*. Cambridge: Polity Press.

Bonacich, Edna. 1972. "A Theory of Ethnic Antagonism: The Split Labor Market." *American Sociological Review* 37: 547–59.

Boswell, John. 1990. *The Kindness of Strangers: The Abandonment of Children in Western Europe from Late Antiquity to the Renaissance*. New York: Vintage.

Brewer, John. 1991. "Policing Divided Societies: Theorizing a Type of Policing." *Policing and Society* 1: 179–91.

Bromley, Simon. 1994. *Rethinking Middle East Politics*. Austin: Univ. of Texas Press.

Brooks, Geraldine. 1994. *Nine Parts of Desire: The Hidden World of Islamic Women*. New York: Anchor.

Brown, Norman O. 1985. *Life Against Death: The Psychonanalytic Meaning of History*. 2d ed. Middletown, Conn.: Wesleyan Univ. Press.

Brownlie, Ian. 1973. *Principles of Public International Law*. Oxford: Oxford Univ. Press.

———. 1990. *Principles of Public International Law*. 4th ed. Oxford: Clarendon.

———, ed. 1992. *Basic Documents on Human Rights*, 3d ed. Oxford: Clarendon.

Brubaker, Rogers. 1992. *Citizenship and Nationhood in France and Germany*. Cambridge, Mass.: Harvard Univ. Press.

———. 1994. *Citizenship and Nationhood in France and Germany*. Cambridge, Mass.: Harvard Univ. Press.

———. 1996. *Nationalism Reframed: Nationhood and the National Question in the New Europe*. Cambridge: Cambridge Univ. Press.

Brynen, Rex. 1995. "The Neopatrimonial Dimension of Palestinian Politics." *Journal of Palestine Studies* 25, no. 1: 23–36.

B'tselem. 1994. *Collaborators in the Occupied Territories: Human Rights Abuses and Violations*. Jerusalem: B'tselem.

Bulmer, Martin, and Anthony M. Rees, eds. 1996. *Citizenship Today: The Contemporary Relevance of T. H. Marshall*. London: Univ. College London Press.

Busch, Diane Mitsch, and Stephen P. Mumme. 1994. "Gender and the Mexican Revolution: The Intersection of Family, State, and Church." In *Women and Revolution in Africa, Asia, and the New World*, edited by Mary Ann Tétreault. Columbia: Univ. of South Carolina Press.

Butenschon, Nils. 1985. "The Consociational Democracy Formula." *Scandinavian Political Studies* 8, nos. 1–2.

————. 1993. "The Politics of Ethnocracies: Principles and Dilemmas of Ethnic Domination." Working Paper 01/93. Oslo: Department of Political Science, Univ. of Oslo.

Canovan, Margaret. 1996, *Nationhood and Political Theory.* Cheltenham: Edward Elgar.

Carmi, Shulamit, and Henry Rosenfeld. 1989. "The Emergence of Militaristic Nationalism in Israel." *International Journal of Politics, Culture, and Society* 3: 5–49.

————. 1992. "Israel's Political Economy and the Widening Gap between Its Two National Groups." *Asian and African Studies* 26: 15–61.

Castles, Francis. 1985. *The Working Class and Welfare: Reflections on the Political Development of the Welfare State in Australia and New Zealand, 1890–1980.* Wellington: Allen and Unwin.

Chan, Johannes M. M. 1991. "The Right to a Nationality as a Human Right: The Current Trend towards Recognition." *Human Rights Law Journal* 12, nos. 1–2: 1–14.

Chomsky, Noam. 1969. *American Power and the New Mandarines.* Harmondsworth, Eng.: Pelican.

Clarke, Paul Barry. 1996. *Deep Citizenship.* London: Pluto.

Cnaan, Ram. 1985. "Racial Differences in Social Service Delivery: Jews and Non-Jews in Israel." *Social Development Issues* 9: 56–74.

Cobban, Helena. 1984. *The Palestine Liberation Organization: People, Power, and Politics.* London: Cambridge Univ. Press.

Cohen, Erik. 1972. "The Black Panthers and Israeli Society." *The Jewish Journal of Sociology* 14: 93–109.

————. 1973. *Integration vs. Separation in the Planning of a Mixed Jewish-Arab City in Israel.* Jerusalem: Levy Eshkol Institute for Economic, Social, and Political Research.

Cohen, Joshua, and Joel Rogers, eds. 1995. *Associations and Democracy.* London and New York: Verso.

Cohen, Saul B. 1973. *Geography and Politics in a World Divided.* 2d ed. Oxford: Oxford Univ. Press.

Combs-Schilling, M. E. 1989. *Sacred Performances: Islam, Sexuality, and Sacrifice.* New York: Columbia Univ. Press.

Connolly, W. E. 1995. *The Ethos of Pluralisation.* Minneapolis: Univ. of Minnesota Press.

Connor, Walter. 1994. *Ethnonationalism: The Quest for Understanding.* Princeton: Princeton Univ. Press.

Cossali, Paul, and Clive Robson. 1986. *Stateless in Gaza.* London: Zed.

Crossette, Barbara. 1996. "Muslim Women's Movement Is Gaining Strength." *New York Times,* 12 May.

Crystal, Jill. 1995. *Oil and Politics in the Gulf: Rulers and Merchants in Kuwait and Qatar.* Cambridge Univ. Press.

Dagher, C. 1993. "The Secrecy of Numbers and the Misery of Registries" (in Arabic). *Al-Safir,* 23 Mar.

Davis, Uri. 1990. *Israel: An Apartheid State*. London: Zed, orig. pub. 1987.

———. 1995."*Jinsiyya* versus *Muwatana*: The Question of Citizenship and the State in the Middle East—The Case of Israel, Jordan, and Palestine." *Arab Studies Quarterly* 17, nos. 1–2 (winter–spring): 19–50.

———. 1996. "The State, the Nation, and the People Examined in the Context of Conceptions of Citizenship in the Middle East." Guest Lecture, Staff Lunchtime Seminar, Department of Political Science, Univ. of Oslo, 21 Nov.

———. 1997. *Citizenship and the State: A Comparative Study of Citizenship Legislation in Israel, Jordan, Palestine, Syria, and Lebanon*. Reading: Ithaca.

Deegan, Heather. 1993. *The Middle East and Problems of Democracy*. Buckingham: Open Univ. Press.

Diamond, Stanley. 1974. "The Rule of Law versus the Order of Custom." In *In Search of the Primitive: A Critique of Civilization*. New Brunswick, N.J.: Transaction.

Dietz, Mary. 1992. "Context Is All: Feminism and Theories of Citizenship." In *Dimensions of Radical Democracy*, edited by Chantal Mouffe. London: Verso.

Donner, Ruth. 1994. *The Regulation of Nationality in International Law*. 2d ed. New York: Transnational.

Doron, Abraham. 1969. "The Development of Children Supplements in Israel, 1948–1967" (in Hebrew). *Keshet* 43: 132–47.

———. 1988. "The Histadrut, Social Policy, and Equality." *Jerusalem Quarterly* 47: 131–44.

———. 1995. *In Defense of Universalism: The Challenges Facing Social Policy in Israel* (in Hebrew). Jerusalem: Magnes.

Doron, Abraham, and Ralph Kramer. 1991. *The Welfare State in Israel: The Evolution of Social Security Policy and Practice*. Boulder, Colo.: Westview.

Doyle, Michael W. 1986. *Empires*. Ithaca: Cornell Univ. Press.

Drabkin-Darin, Haim. 1957. *Housing in Israel: Economic and Sociological Aspects* (in Hebrew). Tel-Aviv: Gadish.

"Draft Conventions and Comments." Prepared by the Research Institute in International Law of Harvard Law School. 1929. In *23rd American Journal of International Law* 1, spec. supp., 11.

Drayton, Robert H., ed. 1934. *The Laws of Palestine*. Rev. Ed. 3 vols. London: Waterlow.

Drysdale, Alasdair, and Graham Blake. 1985. *The Middle East and North Africa: A Political Geography*. New York and Oxford: Oxford Univ. Press.

Durkheim, Emile. 1992. *Professional Ethics and Civic Morals*. London: Routledge.

Dworkin, Richard. 1978. *Taking Rights Seriously*. Cambridge, Mass.: Harvard Univ. Press.

Ehteshami, Anoushiravan, and Emma Murphy. 1996. "Transformation of the Corporatist State in the Middle East." *Third World Quarterly* 17, no. 4: 753–72.

Eide, Asbjørn. 1998. "The Historical Significance of the Universal Declaration of Human Rights." *International Social Science Journal* (Blackwell/UNESCO), no. 158 (Dec.): 477–97.

Elshtain, Jean Bethke. 1991. "Sovereignty, Identity, Sacrifice." *Millennium* 20, no. 3: 395–406.

Esping-Andersen, Gosta. 1987. "Citizenship and Socialism: De-commodification and Solidarity in the Welfare State." In *Stagnation and Renewal in Social Policy*, edited by M. Rein, G. Esping-Andersen, and L. Rainwater. London: M. E. Sharpe.

———. 1990. *The Three Worlds of Welfare Capitalism*. Cambridge: Polity.

Esposito, John. L. 1982. *Women in Muslim Family Law*. Syracuse: Syracuse Univ. Press.

Etzioni-Halevy, Eva. 1975a. "Patterns of Conflict Generation and Conflict 'Absorption': The Case of Israeli Labor and Ethnic Politics." *Journal of Conflict Resolution* 19: 286–309.

———. 1975b. "Protest Politics in the Israeli Democracy." *Political Science Quarterly* 90: 497–520.

Faist, Thomas. 1995. "Ethnicization and Racialization of Welfare-State Politics in Germany and the USA." *Ethnic and Racial Studies* 18: 219–50.

Falah, Ghazi. 1989. "Israeli 'Judaization' Policy in Galilee and Its Impact on Local Arab Urbanization." *Political Geography Quarterly* 8: 229–53.

Fanon, Frantz. 1967. *A Dying Colonialism*. New York: Grove.

Farhi, Farideh. 1994. "Sexuality and the Politics of Revolution in Iran." In *Women and Revolution in Africa, Asia, and the New World*, edited by Mary Ann Tétreault. Columbia: Univ. of South Carolina Press.

Farjoun, Emmanuel. 1983. "Class Divisions in Israeli Society." *Khamsin* (London) 10: 29–39.

Farsoun, Samih, and Christina Zacharia. 1995. "Class, Economic Change, and Political Liberalization in the Arab World." In *Political Liberalization and Democratization in the Arab World*, edited by Rex Brynen, Bahgat Korany, and Paul Noble. Boulder, Colo.: Lynne Rienner.

Ferguson, Adam. (1773) 1995. *An Essay on the History of Civil Society*. Cambridge: Cambridge University Press.

Finley, Moses. 1963. *The Ancient Greeks: An Introduction to Their Life and Thought*. New York: Viking.

———. 1983. *Politics in the Ancient World*. Cambridge: Cambridge Univ. Press.

Fisherman, Haya, and Joshua A. Fishman. 1975. "The Official Languages of Israel: Their Status in Law and Police Attitudes and Knowledge Concerning Them." In *Multilingual Political Systems: Problems and Solutions*, edited by Jean-Guy Savard and Richard Vigneault. Quebec: Les Presses de L'Universite Laval.

Fransman, Laurie. 1989. *Fransman's British Nationality Law*. London: Fourmat.

Fraser, Nancy, and Gordon, Linda. 1994. "Civil Citizenship Against Social Citizenship? On the Ideology of Contract-Versus-Charity." In *The Condition of Citizenship*, edited by Bart van Steenbergen. London: Sage.

Freud, Sigmund. 1930. *Civilization and Its Discontents*. Translated by J. Riviere. London: Hogarth.

———. 1958. *Totem and Taboo*. Translated by James Strachey. Vol. 13, *The Standard Edition of the Complete Psychological Works of Sigmund Freud*, edited by James Strachey, Anna Freud, Alix Strachey, and Alan Tyson. London: Hogarth and the Institute of Psycho-Analysis.

Freudenheim, Yehousha. 1967. *Government of Israel*. New York: Oceana.

Friedland, Roger, and Robert R. Alford. 1991. "Bringing Society Back In: Symbols, Practices, and Institutional Contradictions." In *The New Institutionalism in Organizational Analysis*, edited by Walter W. Powell and Paul J. DiMaggio. Chicago: Univ. of Chicago Press.

Fukuyama, Francis. 1992. *The End of History and the Last Man*. Harmondsworth, Eng.: Penguin.

Gans, Chaim. 1992. *Philosophical Anarchism and Political Disobedience*. Cambridge: Cambridge Univ. Press.

Garlan, Yvon. 1988. *Slavery in Ancient Greece*. Rev. and expanded ed. Translated by Janet Lloyd. Ithaca: Cornell Univ. Press.

Geertz, Clifford. 1994. "Primordial Loyalties and Standing Entities: Anthropological Reflections on the Politics of Identity." Collegium Budapest, Institute for Advanced Study. Public Lecture no. 7 (Apr.).

Gellner, Ernest. 1983a. *Muslim Society*. Cambridge: Cambridge Univ. Press.

———. 1983b. *Nations and Nationalism*. Oxford: Blackwell.

———. 1994a. *Conditions of Liberty: Civil Society and Its Rivals*. London: Hamish Hamilton.

———. 1994b. *Encounters with Nationalism*. Oxford: Oxford Univ. Press.

Ghilan, Maxim. 1988. "The Palestinians: What Has Changed in the PLO." *Israel and Palestine* 146 (Nov.): 2–6.

Gibb, H. A. R., and J. H. Kramers. 1974. *Shorter Encyclopedia of Islam*. Leiden: E. J. Brill.

Giddens, Anthony. 1976. *The New Rules of Sociological Method*. London: Hutchinson.

———. 1984. *The Constitution of Society*. Berkeley: Univ. of California Press.

———. 1991. *Modernity and Self-Identity: Self and Society in the Late Modern Age*. Stanford, Calif.: Stanford Univ. Press.

Gloppen, Siri. 1997. *South Africa: The Battle over the Constitution*. Brookfield, Vt.: Ashgate.

Golan, Arnon. 1995. "The New Settlement Map of the Area Abandoned by Arab Population, Within the Territory of the State of Israel, during Israel's War of Independence and After (1948–1950)" (in Hebrew). Ph.D. thesis, Department of Geography, Hebrew Univ. of Jerusalem, Jerusalem.

Gonen, Amiram. 1979. "The Geography of Public Housing in Israeli Cities" (in Hebrew). *Bitahon Soziali*, nos. 18–19 (Dec.): 22–36.

Granott, A. 1936. *The Land Issue in Palestine*. Jerusalem: Keren Kayemet Le'Israel.

Greenfeld, Liah. 1992. *Nationalism: Five Roads to Modernity*. Cambridge, Mass.: Harvard Univ. Press.

Gresh, Alain. 1982. "The Banner of the Democratic State in the Palestinian Revolution, 1968–1971" (in Arabic). *Shu'un Filastiniyya*, nos. 122–23 (Feb.): 142–67.

Grinberg, Lev. 1993. *The Histadrut above All* (in Hebrew). Jerusalem: Nevo.

Gross, Ephraim. 1979. "The Development of the Transfer Payments System in Israel" (in Hebrew). *'Iyunim B'kalkalah*, 100–112.

Guy, Donna J. 1992. "'White Slavery,' Citizenship, and Nationality in Argentina." In *Nationalities and Sexualities,* edited by Andrew Parker et al. New York: Routledge.

Haber, Aliza. 1975. *Population and Construction in Israel* (in Hebrew). Jerusalem: Ministry of Construction and Housing.

———. 1986. *Expected Changes in the Population Distribution and Jewish and Non-Jewish Relationships until 2000, on the Basis of Growth Population Trends and Existent Housing Data* (in Hebrew). Jerusalem: Ministry of Construction and Housing.

Habermas, Jurgen. 1975. *Legitimation Crisis.* Boston: Beacon.

———. 1994. "Citizenship and National Identity." In *The Condition of Citizenship,* edited by Bart van Steenbergen. London: Sage.

Haggard, Stephan, and Robert Kaufman. 1992. "Economic Adjustment and the Prospects for Democracy." In *The Politics of Economic Adjustment,* edited by Stephan Haggard and Robert Kaufman. Princeton: Princeton Univ. Press.

Haidar, Aziz. 1987. "Social Welfare Services for Israel's Arab Population." Tel Aviv: International Center for Peace in the Middle East.

———. 1991. *Social Welfare Services for Israel's Arab Population.* Boulder, Colo.: Westview.

———. 1995. *On the Margins: The Arab Population in the Israeli Economy.* London: Hurst.

al-Haj, Majid. 1995. *Education, Empowerment, and Control.* Albany: State Univ. of New York Press.

Halabi, Usama. 1991. "Arab Citizens' Rights and Their Status in Israel" (in Arabic). *Majallat Al-Dirasat Al-Filastiniyya* 5 (winter): 127–48.

Halliday, Fred. 1994. "International Society as a Homogeneity." In *Rethinking International Relations.* London: Macmillan.

Halpern, Manfred. 1963. *The Politics of Social Change in the Middle East and North Africa.* Princeton: Princeton Univ. Press.

Hamid, Rashid. 1975. "What Is the PLO?" *Journal of Palestine Studies* 4, no. 4 (summer): 90–109.

Hamzeh-Muhaisen, Muna. 1998. "To Elect or Not to Elect: The Quagmire of Municipal Councils" *Palestine Report* 4, no. 42 (24 Apr.): 4.

Hanf, Theodor, and Bernard Sabella. 1996. *A Date with Democracy: Palestinians on Society and Politics, an Empirical Survey.* Freiburg: Arnold Bergstaesser Institute.

Harik, Ilya. 1990. "The Origin of the Arab State System." In *The Arab State,* edited by Giacomo Luciani. London: Routledge.

Harlow, Barbara. 1995. "There Is Not Even a Basic Understanding about What Laws Apply Here: Interview with Usama Halabi." *Middle East Report* 25, nos. 3–4: 33–34.

Hartshorne, Richard. 1950. "The Functional Approach in Political Geography." *Annals: Association of American Geographers* 40: 95–130.

Hass, Amira. 1997. "Arafat Critic Released." *Ha'aretz,* 28 Nov.

Hassassian, Manuel, 1990. *Palestine: Factionalism in the Palestinian National Movement (1919–1939)*. Jerusalem: Palestinian Academic Society for the Study of International Affairs.

Hassassian, Manuel, and Tahir Nammari. 1992. "An Independent Perspective of the Palestinian National Movement in the Occupied Territories." Unpublished paper delivered for the national Palestinians representative forces in Jerusalem, Jan.

Hasson, Shlomo. 1981. "Social and Spatial Conflicts: The Settlement Process in Israel during the 1950s and the 1960s" *L'Espace Geographique* 3: 169–79.

———. 1993. *Urban Social Movements In Jerusalem: The Protest of the Second Generation*. Albany, N.Y.: State Univ. of New York Press in cooperation with the Jerusalem Institute for Israel Studies.

Hechter, Michael. 1975. *Internal Colonialism: The Celtic Fringe in British National Development*. London: Routledge and Kegan Paul.

Held, David, ed. 1989. *Political Theory and the Modern State*. Cambridge: Polity.

Helman, Sara. 1994. "Conscientious Objection to Military Service as an Attempt to Redefine the Contents of Citizenship" (in Hebrew). Ph.D. thesis, Department of Sociology and Anthropology, Hebrew Univ. of Jerusalem, Jerusalem.

Heymann, Uriel. 1981. "Public Housing as a Welfare Service in Israel, 1948–1973." Ph.D. thesis, the F. Heller Graduate School for Advanced Studies in Social Welfare, Brandeis Univ.

Higgins, Rosalyn. 1963. *The Development of International Law through the Practical Origins of the United Nations*. London: Oxford Univ. Press.

Hijab, Nadia. 1989. "Strategy of the Powerless." *Middle East International*, no. 350 (12 May): 17–18.

Hilal, Jamil M. 1995. "The PLO: Crisis in Legitimacy" *Race and Class* 37, no. 2: 1–18.

Hindess, Barry. 1987. "Rationality and the Characterization of Modern Society." In *Max Weber, Rationality and Modernity*, edited by Scott Lash and Sam Whimster. London: Allen and Unwin.

Hinnebusch, Raymond. 1983. "Party Activists in Syria and Egypt." *International Political Science Review* 4, no. 1: 84–93.

———. 1985. *Egyptian Politics under Sadat: The Post-Populist Development of an Authoritarian-Modernizing State*. Cambridge: Cambridge Univ. Press.

———. 1990. "Government and Politics." In *Egypt: A Country Study*, edited by Helen Chapin Metz. Washington, D.C.: Library of Congress.

———. 1993a. "Class, State, and the Reversal of Egypt's Agrarian Reform." *Middle East Report* (Sept.–Oct.): 20–23.

———. 1993b. "The Politics of Economic Reform in Egypt." *Third World Quarterly* 14, no. 1: 159–71.

———. 1993c. "Syria." In *Economic and Political Liberalization in the Middle East*, edited by Tim Niblock and Emma Murphy. London: British Academic.

———. 1996. "State and Islamism in Syria." In *Islamic Fundamentalism*, edited by Abdul Salam Sidahmed and Anoushiravan Ehteshami. Boulder, Colo.: Westview.

Hirsh, Hila. 1970. "Attitudes to Homes among Tenants of Minorities Housing Schemes Initiated by the Ministry of Housing." In *Israel Builds,* edited by Y. Golani and A. Schwarze. Jerusalem: Ministry of Housing.

Hirsh, Hila, and Aran Paitelson. 1972. *An Outline for Assistance Housing Policy for Young Couples* (in Hebrew). Jerusalem: Ministry of Housing.

Hirst, Paul Q., ed. 1989. *The Pluralist Theory of the State.* London and New York: Routledge.

Hobbes, Thomas. 1968. *Leviathan.* Edited by C. B. Macpherson. Hammondsworth, Eng.: Penguin.

Hobsbawm, Eric J. 1990. *Nations and Nationalism Since 1780: Programme, Myth, Reality.* Cambridge: Canto.

Hodgson, Marshall G. S. 1974. *The Venture of Islam: Conscience and History in a World Civilization.* Chicago and London: Univ. of Chicago Press.

———. 1993. *Rethinking World History.* Cambridge: Cambridge Univ. Press.

Hofnung, Menahem. 1982. "Social Protest and the Public Budgeting Process: The Effect of the 'Black Panthers' Demonstrations on Allocations to Social and Welfare Needs" (in Hebrew). Master's thesis, Department of Political Science, Hebrew Univ. of Jerusalem, Jerusalem.

———. 1991. *Israel: Security Needs vs. the Rule of Law* (in Hebrew). Jerusalem: Nevo.

Hollander, Anne. 1994. *Sex and Suits.* New York: A. A. Knopf.

Horowitz, Dan. 1982. "The Israeli Defense Forces: A Civilianized Army in a Partial Militarized Society." In *Soldiers, Peasants, and Bureaucrats,* edited by R. Kolkowitz and A. Korbonski. London: George, Allen and Unwin.

Horowitz, Dan, and Baruch Kimmerling. 1974. "Some Social Implications of Military Service and the Reserves System in Israel." *European Journal of Sociology* 15: 262–76.

Hourani, Faysal. 1980. "The Palestine Liberation Organization and the Attitude Towards the Settlement" (in Arabic). *Shu'un Filastiniyya,* no. 99 (Feb.): 23–66.

Hudson, Michael C. 1977. *Arab Politics: The Search for Legitimacy.* New Haven and London: Yale Univ. Press.

Human Rights Watch World Report. 1996. *Israeli-Occupied West Bank and Gaza Strip.* New York: HRW.

Hunt, Lynn. 1992. *The Family Romance of the French Revolution.* Berkeley: Univ. of California Press.

Huntington, Samuel. 1968. *Political Order in Changing Societies.* New Haven: Yale Univ. Press.

———. 1994. "The Clash of Civilizations?" In *Foreign Affairs Agenda 1994: Critical Issues in Foreign Policy.* New York: Council on Foreign Relations.

Hurewitz, J. C. 1956. *Diplomacy in the Near and Middle East: A Documentary Record 1914–1956.* New York: Praeger.

Ibrahim, Saad Eddin. 1992. *The New Arab Social Order: A Study of the Social Impact of Oil Wealth.* Boulder, Colo.: Westview.

Issawi, Charles. 1956. "Economic and Social Foundations of Democracy in the Middle East." *International Affairs* 32 (Jan.): 28–45.

Jackson, Robert H. 1990. *Quasi-States: Sovereignty, International Relations, and the Third World.* Cambridge: Cambridge Univ. Press.

James, Alan. 1986. *Sovereign Statehood: The Basis of International Society.* Vol. 2, *Key Concepts in International Relations.* London: Allen and Unwin.

James, C. L. R. 1986. *Every Cook Can Govern and What Is Happening Every Day: 1985 Conversations.* Edited by Jan Hillegas. Jackson, Miss.: New Mississippi.

James, Paul. 1996. *Nation Formation: Towards a Theory of Abstract Community.* London: Sage.

Jiryis, Sabri. 1976. *The Arabs in Israel.* New York: Monthly Review.

Jorgensen, Connie. 1994. "Women, Revolution, and Israel." In *Women and Revolution in Africa, Asia, and the New World,* edited by Mary Ann Tétreault. Columbia: Univ. of South Carolina Press.

Kamali, Mohammad Hashim. 1995. *The Modern Revolutions of Iran: Clergy, Bazaris, and State in the Modernization Process.* Uppsala, Swed.: Uppsala Univ.

Kandiyoti, Deniz. 1992. "Women, Islam, and the State." In *Comparing Muslim Societies: Knowledge and the State in a World Civilization,* edited by Juan R. I. Cole. Ann Arbor: Univ. of Michigan Press.

Karam, J. 1993. *Lebanese Citizenship Between the Law and Reality* (in Arabic). Beirut: Matba'it Joseph al-Hajj.

Kassim, Anis F. 1972. *The Law of Return and the Nationality Law of the State of Israel: A Study of International and Municipal Law* (in Arabic). Palestine Monographs no. 89. Beirut: PLO Research Center.

———. 1984. "Legal Systems and Developments in Palestine." In *1st Palestine Yearbook of International Law.* Nicosia, Cyprus: al-Shaybani Society of International Law.

———. 1990. "The Gulf Crisis: The Palestinians between the Hammer and the Anvil" (in Arabic). *Majallat al-Disarat Al-Filastiniyya* 4: 3–8.

Katz, Israel. 1969. "The Large Families Problem" (in Hebrew). In *Conference in the Paul Barwald School of Social Work, The Hebrew University of Jerusalem.* Jerusalem: Paul Barwald School of Social Work.

Kellas, James G. 1991. *The Politics of Nationalism and Ethnicity.* London: Macmillan.

Kennedy, David. 1996. "International Law and the Nineteenth Century: History of an Illusion." *Nordic Journal of International Law* 65: 385–420.

Keren-Yaar, Hanna, and Miriam Souery. 1980. *Families with Children in Israel, 1968–1978,* survey no. 23 (in Hebrew). Jerusalem: National Insurance Institute.

Kerr, Malcolm. 1971. *The Arab Cold War: Gamal Abd al-Nasir and His Rivals, 1958–1970.* London: Cambridge Univ. Press.

al-Khafaji, Isam. 1995. "War as a Vehicle for the Rise and Demise of a State-Controlled Society: The Case of Ba'thist Iraq." *Amsterdam Middle East Papers No. 4.* Amsterdam: Research Center for International Political Economy and Foreign Policy Analysis.

Khalidi, Raja. 1988. *The Arab Economy in Israel.* London: Croom Helm.

Khalidi, Rashid. 1985. "The Palestinian Dilemma: The PLO after Lebanon." *Journal of Palestine Studies* 15, no. 1 (autumn): 88–103.

Khamaisi, Rassem. 1990. *Planning and Housing among the Arabs in Israel* (in Hebrew). Tel-Aviv: International Center for Peace in the Middle East.

al-Khatib, Ghassan. May 1991. "Let Our Democracy Truly Live Up to Our Aspirations" (in Arabic). *Sawt al-Watan,* no. 21.

———. 1998. "Let's Just Split the Difference." *Palestine Report* 4, no. 2 (24 Apr.).

al-Khayyat, Sana. 1990. *Honour and Shame: Women in Modern Iraq.* London: Saqi.

Khouri, Rami. 1995a. "Arab Democratization, Political Islam, and the United States." *Mideast Mirror,* 1 June, 9.

———. 1995b. "Wither Political Islam." *Mideast Mirror,* 7 June, 19.

Khoury, Philip S., and Joseph Kostiner, eds. 1991. *Tribes and State Formation in the Middle East.* London and New York: I. B. Tauris.

Kienle, Eberhard, ed. 1994. *Contemporary Syria: Liberalization Between Cold War and Cold Peace.* London: British Academic and Univ. of London.

Kimmerling, Baruch. 1979. "Determination of Boundaries and Frameworks of Conscription: Two Dimensions of Civil-Military Relations." *Studies in Comparative International Development* 14: 22–41.

———. 1983. *Zionism and Territory: The Socio-Territorial Dimensions of Zionist Politics.* Berkeley: Institute for International Studies, Univ. of California.

———. 1992. "Sociology, Ideology, and Nation-Building: The Palestinians and Their Meaning in Israeli Sociology." *American Sociological Review* 57: 446–60.

———. 1993a. "Militarism in Israeli Society" (in Hebrew). *Theory and Criticism: An Israeli Forum* 4: 123–40.

———. 1993b. "State Building, State Autonomy, and the Identity of Society: The Case of the Israeli State." *Journal of Historical Sociology* 6: 396–428.

King, Preston. 1987. "Sovereignity." In *Blackwell Encyclopedia of Political Thought,* edited by David Miller. Oxford: Basil Blackwell.

Kipnis, Baruch. 1978. *Assistance for Housing in the Arab Sector* (in Hebrew). Haifa: Haifa Univ.

Kook, Rebecca. 1995a. "Dilemmas of Ethnic Minorities in Democracies: The Effect of Peace on the Palestinians in Israel." *Politics and Society* 23: 309–36.

———. 1995b. "Towards the Rehabilitation of Nation Building and the Reconstruction of Nations." Paper presented at the annual meeting of the American Political Science Association, Sept., Chicago.

Korany, Bahgat, Rex Brynen, and Paul Noble, eds. 1993. *The Many Faces of National Security in the Arab World.* Basingstoke, Eng.: Macmillan.

Korpi, Walter. 1989. "Power, Politics, and State Autonomy in the Development of Social Citizenship: Social Rights During Sickness in Eighteen OECD Countries Since 1930." *American Sociological Review* 54: 309–28.

Kramer, Gudrun. 1994. "The Integration of the Integrationists: A Comparative Study of Egypt, Jordan, and Tunisia." In *Democracy Without Democrats: The*

Renewal of Politics in the Muslim World, edited by Ghassan Salamé. London: I. B. Tauris.

Kretzmer, David. 1987. *The Legal Status of the Arabs in Israel.* Tel Aviv: International Center for Peace in the Middle East.

———. 1990. *The Legal Status of the Arabs in Israel.* Boulder, Colo.: Westview.

"Kuwaitis Rival Saddam's Torturers in Brutality." 1991. *The Independent,* 19 Apr.

Kymlicka, Will. 1995. *Multicultural Citizenship.* Oxford: Clarendon.

Kymlicka, Will, and Wayne Norman. 1994. "Return of the Citizen: A Survey of Recent Work on Citizenship Theory." *Ethics* 104 (Jan.): 257–89.

Laclau, Ernesto. 1980. "Nonpopulist Rupture and Discourse." *Screen Education* 34: 87–93.

———. 1996. *Emancipation(s).* London: Verso.

Landau, Jacob. 1993. *The Arab Minority in Israel, 1967–1991: Political Aspects.* Oxford: Clarendon.

Lavon, Zelig. 1974. *Shelter* (in Hebrew). Tel-Aviv: Am Oved.

Lazreg, Marnia. 1994. *The Eloquence of Silence: Algerian Women in Question.* London: Routledge.

Leca, Jean. 1992. "Questions on Citizenship." In *Dimensions of Radical Democracy,* edited by Chantal Mouffe. London: Verso.

Leibowitz, Yeshaayahu. 1992. *Judaism, Human Values, and the Jewish State.* Cambridge, Mass.: Harvard Univ. Press.

Lemsine, Aïcha. 1993. *The Chrysalis.* Translated by Dorothy S. Blair. London: Quartet.

Lerman, Robert. 1976. "A Critical Overview of Israeli Housing Policy." Jerusalem: Brookdale Institute.

Lerner, Daniel. 1958. *The Passing of Traditional Society.* Glencoe: Free Press.

Lesch, Ann M. 1991. "Kuwait Diary: A Scarred Society." *Middle East Report* 21, no. 5 (Sept.–Oct.): 34–37.

Levy, Gideon. 1998. "The Nature of Naveh's Document" *Ha'aretz,* 18 Jan.

Lewin-Epstein, Noah, and Moshe Semyonov. 1993. *The Arab Minority in Israel's Economy.* Boulder, Colo.: Westview.

Lewis, Bernard. 1993. "Islam and Liberal Democracy." *Atlantic Monthly* (Feb.): 89–98.

Lijphart, Arend. 1969. "Consociational Democracy." *World Politics* 21 (Jan.): 207–25.

———. 1977. *Democracy in Plural Societies: A Comparative Exploration.* New Haven: Yale Univ. Press.

———. 1985. *Power-Sharing in South Africa.* Berkeley: Institute of Interational Studies, Univ. of California.

Lindholm Schulz, Helena. 1996. "Palestinian Identities and Self-Government: The Problematic Transition." Paper presented at the Conference on Citizenship and the State in the Middle East, Oslo, Norway.

Liskobscki, Aharon. 1960. "The 'Present Absentees' in Israel" (in Hebrew). *Ha-Mizrah HeHadash* 10: 186–92.

Lithwick, Irwin. 1980. "Macro and Micro Housing Programs in Israel." D-47–80. Jerusalem: Brookdale Institute.

Locke, John. 1963. *Two Treatises of Government*. Cambridge and New York: Cambridge Univ. Press.

Lohéac, L. 1978. *Daud Ammoun et la Création de L'État Libanais*. Paris: Klincksieck.

Longrigg, S. H. 1958. *Syria and Lebanon under French Mandate*. Lebanon: Oxford Univ. Press.

Longva, Anh Nga. 1996. "Apostasy and the Limits of Constitutionalism." *Midtøsten Forum* (Oslo) 1–2: 30–36.

———. 1997. *Walls Built on Sand: Migration, Exclusion, and Society in Kuwait*. Boulder, Colo.: Westview.

———. Forthcoming. *Democracy between Islam and Tribalism*.

Luciani, Giacomo. 1990. *The Arab State*. London: Routledge.

Lustick, Ian. 1980. *Arabs in the Jewish State: Israel's Control of a National Minority*. Austin: Univ. of Texas Press.

———. 1989. "The Political Road to Binationalism: Arabs in Jewish Politics." In *The Emergence of a Binational Israel: The Second Republic in the Making*, edited by I. Peleg and O. Seliktar. Boulder, Colo.: Westview.

Mabro, Judy, ed. 1991. *Veiled Half-Truths: Western Travellers' Perceptions of Middle Eastern Women*. London: I. B. Tauris.

MacFarlane, S. Niel. 1995. *Superpower Rivalry and Third World Radicalism: The Idea of National Liberation*. Baltimore: Johns Hopkins Univ. Press.

Makiya, Kanan. 1993. *Cruelty and Silence: War, Tyranny, Uprising, and the Arab World*. New York: W. W. Norton.

Makram-Ebeid, Mona. 1989. "Political Opposition in Egypt: Democratic Myth or Reality." *Middle East Journal* 43, no. 3: 423–36.

Mallison, W. Thomas, and Sally V. Mallison. 1986. *The Palestine Problem in International Law and World Order*. Harlow, Eng.: Longman.

Mann, Michael. 1984. "Capitalism and Militarism." In *War, State, and Society*, edited by Martin Shaw. New York: St. Martin's.

———. 1986. *The Sources of Social Power: A History of Power from the Beginning to AD 1760*. Cambridge: Cambridge Univ. Press.

———. 1987. "War and Social Theory: Into Battles with Classes, Nations, and States." In *The Sociology of War and Peace*, edited by Martin Shaw and Colin Creighton. London: Macmillan.

———. 1993. *The Sources of Social Power: The Rise of Classes and Nation-States 1760–1914*. Vol. 2. Cambridge: Cambridge Univ. Press.

Mannheim, Karl. 1992. *Essays on the Sociology of Culture*. London: Routledge and Kegan Paul.

Manning, C. A. W. 1962. *The Nature of International Society*. London: Bell; reprint, Macmillan, 1975.

Mansfield, Peter. 1973. *The Ottoman Empire and Its Successors*. London and Basingstoke: Macmillan.

Manzo, Kathryn A. 1996. *Creating Boundaries: The Politics of Race and Nation*. Boulder, Colo.: Lynne Rienner.

Marenin, Otis, ed. 1996. *Policing Change, Changing Police*. New York: Garland.

Mar'i, Mustafa. 1996. *Guarantees for the Respect of Human Rights in Palestine: Present Problems and Future Prospects.* L.L.M diss., Queen's Univ. of Belfast.

Marr, David G. 1981. *Vietnamese Tradition on Trial, 1920–1945.* Berkeley: Univ. of California Press.

Marshall, T. H. 1950. *Citizenship and Social Class and Other Essays.* Cambridge: Cambridge Univ. Press.

————. 1965. *Class Citizenship and Social Development.* New York: Anchor.

————. 1981. *The Right to Welfare and Other Essays.* London: Heinemann Educational Books.

Marshall, T. H., and T. Bottomore, eds. 1992. *Citizenship and Social Class.* London: Pluto.

Marx, Karl, and Friedrich Engels. 1972. *On Colonialism.* New York: International.

Massad, Joseph. 1995. "Conceiving the Masculine: Gender and Palestinian Nationalism." *Middle East Journal* 49, no. 3 (summer): 467–83.

Mayer, Ann Elizabeth. 1995a. "Reform of Personal Status Laws in North Africa: A Problem of Islamic or Mediterranean Laws?" *Middle East Journal* 49, no. 3 (summer): 432–46.

————. 1995b. "Rhetorical Strategies and Official Policies on Women's Rights: The Merits and Drawbacks of the New World Hypocrisy." In *Faith and Freedom: Women's Human Rights in the Muslim World,* edited by Mahnaz Afkhami. Syracuse: Syracuse Univ. Press.

McDowall, David. 1983. *Lebanon: A Conflict of Minorities.* London: Minority Rights Group.

————. 1966. *Lebanon: A Conflict of Minorities.* Rev. Ed. The Minority Rights Group, Report no. 2. London: Minority Rights Group.

McLuhan, Marshall. 1964. *Understanding Media: The Extensions of Man.* London: Routledge and Kegan Paul.

Mernissi, Fatima. 1987. *The Veil and the Male Elite: A Feminist Interpretation of Women's Rights in Islam.* Translated by Mary Jo Lakeland. Reading, Mass.: Addison Wesley.

————. 1992. *Islam and Democracy: Fear of the Modern World.* Translated by Mary Jo Lakeland. Reading, Mass.: Addison Wesley.

————. 1995. "Arab Women's Rights and the Muslim State in the Twenty-First Century: Reflections on Islam as Religion and State." In *Faith and Freedom: Women's Human Rights in the Muslim World,* edited Mahnaz Afkhami. Syracuse: Syracuse Univ. Press.

Migdal, Joel. 1988. *Strong Societies and Weak States: State-Society Relations and State Capabilities in the Third World.* Princeton: Princeton Univ. Press.

————. 1989. "The Crystallization of the State and the Struggles Over Rulemaking: Israel in a Comparative Perspective." In *The Israeli State and Society: Boundaries and Frontiers,* edited by Baruch Kimmerling. Albany: State Univ. of New York Press.

Mill, John Stuart. 1929. *On the Subjection of Women.* New York: E. P. Dutton.

Miller, Aaron David. 1983. *The PLO and the Politics of Survival.* Washington Papers

Series, vol. 11, no. 99. Washington, D.C.: Praeger Special Studies/Praeger Scientific. Published with the Center for Strategic and International Studies, Georgetown Univ.

Milton-Edwards, Beverley. 1996a. *Islamic Politics in Palestine*. London: I. B. Tauris.

———. 1996b. "Political Islam in an Environment of Peace?" *Third World Quarterly* 17, no. 2: 199–225.

Mink, Gwendolyn. 1995. *The Wages of Motherhood: Inequality in the Welfare State, 1917–1942*. Ithaca N.Y.: Cornell Univ. Press.

Mirhosseini, Akram. 1995. "After the Revolution: The Violation of Women's Human Rights in Iran." In *Women's Rights, Human Rights*, edited by Julie Peters and Andrea Wolper. New York: Routledge.

Moghissi, Haideh. 1994. *Populism and Feminism in Iran: Women's Struggle in a Male-Defined Revolutionary Movement*. New York: St. Martin's.

Moghrabi, Fouad, Elia Zureik, Manuel Hassassian, and Aziz Haidar. 1991. "Palestinians on the Peace Process." *Journal of Palestine Studies* 21, no. 1 (autumn): 36–53.

Moore, Barrington. 1966. *Dictatorship and Democracy: Lord and Peasant in the Making of the Modern World*. Boston: Beacon.

Mosca, Gaetano. 1935. *The Ruling Class*. New York: McGraw-Hill.

Mosse, George L. 1985. *Nationalism and Sexuality: Respectability and Abnormal Sexuality in Modern Europe*. New York: Howard Fertig.

Mouffe, Chantal. 1992a. "Democratic Citizenship and the Political Community." In *Dimensions of Radical Democracy, Pluralism, Citizenship, Community*, edited by Chantal Mouffe. London: Verso.

———, ed. 1992b. *Dimensions of Radical Democracy, Pluralism, Citizenship, Community*. London: Verso.

Moynihan, Daniel Patrick. 1993. *Pandaemonium: Ethnicity in International Politics*. New York: Oxford Univ. Press.

al-Mughni, Haya. 1993. *Women in Kuwait: The Politics of Gender*. London: Saqi.

———. Forthcoming. "Women's Associations and the Autonomy of Civil Society in Kuwait." In *Feminist Approaches to Social Movements, Community, and Power*, vol. 1, *Conscious Acts*, edited by Mary Ann Tétreault and Robin L. Teske. Columbia: Univ. of South Carolina Press.

Mumby, Dennis K., and Cynthia Stohl. 1991. "Power and Discourse in Organization Studies: Absence and the Dialectic of Control." *Discourse and Society* 23: 313–32.

Murphy, Emma. 1995. "Stacking the Deck: The Economics of the Israeli-PLO Accords" *Middle East Report* 25, nos. 3–4: 35–39.

Muslih, Muhammad. 1988. *The Origins of Palestinian Nationalism*. Institute for Palestine Studies Series. New York: Columbia Univ. Press.

Muslih, Muhammad, and Norton R. August. 1991. "The Need for Arab Democracy." *Foreign Policy*, no. 83 (summer): 3–19.

Mussalam, Sami. 1987. "The Infrastructure and the Institutional Structure of the Palestine Liberation Organization" (in Arabic). *Shu'un filastiniyya*, nos. 166–67: 16–59.

Muzaffar, C. 1993. *Human Rights and the New World Order.* Penang: Just World Trust.

Nakhleh, Emile A. 1979. *The West Bank and Gaza: Towards the Making of a Palestinian State.* Washington, D.C.: American Enterprise Institute for Public Policy Research.

al-Naqeeb, Khaldoun Hasan. 1990. *Society and State in the Gulf and Arab Peninsula: A Different Perspective.* Translated by L. M. Kenny. London: Routledge.

al-Nasser, Khalid. 1989. *The Crisis of Democracy in the Arab World* (Azmat al-demoqratiyyeh fi al-alem al-arabi). Beirut: Center of the Arab Unity Studies.

al-Natour, 1993. *The Situation of the Palestinian People in Lebanon* (in Arabic).

Newman, David. 1989. "Civilian and Military Presence as Strategies of Territorial Control: The Arab-Israel Conflict." *Political Geography Quarterly* 8: 215–27.

Nissim, Baruch. 1969. *Housing in Israel.* Jerusalem: Ye'utz u-Mehkar, Economic and Social Research Consultants.

Nussbaum, Arthur. 1954. *A Concise History of the Law of Nations.* New York: Macmillan.

O'Donnell, Guillermo. 1973. *Modernization and Bureaucratic Authoritarianism: Studies in South American Politics.* Berkeley: Univ. of California Institute of International Studies.

O'Donnell, Guillermo, and Phillippe Schmitter. 1986. *Transitions from Authoritarian Rule: Tentative Conclusions about Uncertain Democracies.* Baltimore: Johns Hopkins Univ. Press.

Offe, Claus. 1985. "New Social Movements: Challenging the Boundaries of Institutional Politics." *Social Research* 52: 817–68.

Offe, Claus, and Ulrich K. Preuss. 1990. *Democratic Institutions and Moral Resources.* Bremen: Centre for Policy Research.

Okin, Susan Moller. 1979. *Women in Western Political Thought.* Princeton: Princeton Univ. Press.

———. 1989. *Justice, Gender, and the Family.* New York: Basic.

Oldfield, A. 1990. *Citizenship and Community: Civic Republicanism and the Modern World.* London: Routledge.

Orni, E. 1981. *Land in Israel: History, Policy, Administration, Development.* Jerusalem: Jewish National Fund.

Orr, Okiva. 1981. "Socialism and the Nation-State." In *Debate on Palestine,* edited by Fouzi el-Asmar, Uri Davis, and Naim Khader. London and Kefar Shemaryahu: Ithaca Press and Miftah (Key) Publishers.

Ortner, Sherry B. 1974. "Is Female to Male as Nature Is to Culture?" In *Woman, Culture, and Society,* edited by Michelle Zimbalist Rosaldo and Louise Lamphere. Stanford: Stanford Univ. Press.

Owen, Roger. 1992. *State, Power, and Politics in the Making of the Modern Middle East.* London and New York: Routledge.

———. 1994. "Socio-economic Change and Political Mobilization: The Case of Egypt." In *Democracy Without Democrats: The Renewal of Politics in the Muslim World,* edited by Ghassan Salamé. London: I. B. Tauris.

Ozacky-Lazar, Sara. 1993. *Ikrit and Biram: Surveys on the Arabs in Israel.* No. 10 (in Hebrew). Givat Haviva: Institute for Arab Studies.

Ozacky-Lazar, Sara, and As'ad Ghanem. 1996. *The Arab Vote for the 14th Knesset, May 29, 1996.* No. 19. Givat Haviva: Institute for Arab Studies.

Palestinian Center for Human Rights. 1995a. *Critique of the Press Law 1995 Issued by the Palestinian Authority.* Gaza City: Palestinian Center for Human Rights.

———. 1995b. *Critique of the Second Palestinian Draft Law Concerning Charitable Societies, Social Bodies, and Private Institutions of 1995.* Gaza City: Palestinian Center for Human Rights.

Palestinian Human Rights Monitoring Group (PHRMG). 1997. "The State of Human Rights in Palestine II: The Judicial System." *Palestinian Human Rights Monitor,* no. 3 (Aug.).

Pappe, Ilan. 1995. "An Uneasy Coexistence: Arabs and Jews in the First Decade of Statehood." In *Israel: The First Decade of Independence,* edited by S. Ilan Troen and Noah Lucas. Albany: State Univ. of New York Press.

Parekh, Bhiku. 1993. "The Cultural Specificity of Liberal Democracy." In *Prospects for Democracy,* edited by David Held. Cambridge: Polity.

Park, Kyung Ae. 1994. "Women and Revolution in China: The Sources of Constraints on Women's Emancipation." In *Women and Revolution in Africa, Asia, and the New World,* edited by Mary Ann Tétreault. Columbia: Univ. of South Carolina Press.

Parkin, Frank. 1974. "Strategies of Social Closure in Class Formation." In *The Social Analysis of Social Structure,* edited by F. Parkin. London: Tavistock.

———. 1979. *Marxism and Class Theory: A Bourgeois Critique.* London: Tavistock.

Pateman, Carole. 1988. "The Fraternal Social Contract." In *Civil Society and the State,* edited by John Keane. London: Verso.

Patterson, Cynthia B. 1991. "Marriage and the Married Woman in Athenian Law." In *Women's History and Ancient History,* edited by Sarah B. Pomeroy. Chapel Hill: Univ. of North Carolina Press.

Peled, Nahum. 1986. *Population and Housing in the Arab Sector in Israel* (in Hebrew). Jerusalem: Ministry of Construction and Housing.

Peled, Yoav. 1992. "Ethnic Democracy and the Legal Construction of Citizenship: Arab Citizens of the Jewish State." *American Political Science Review* 86, no. 2: 432–42.

———. 1993. "Strangers in the Utopia: The Civic Status of Israel's Palestinian Citizens" (in Hebrew). *Teoriyah u-Biqoret* 3: 21–38.

Peled, Yoav, and Gershom Shafir. 1996. "The Roots of Peacemaking: The Dynamics of Citizenship in Israel, 1948–93." *International Journal of Middle East Studies* 28, no. 3 (Aug.): 391–413.

Peres, Shimon. 1993. *The New Middle East.* Shaftesbury: Element.

Peretz, Don. 1958, *Israel and the Palestine Arabs.* Washington, D.C.: Middle East Institute.

———. 1993. *Palestinians, Refugees, and the Middle East Peace Process.* Washington, D.C.: United States Institute of Peace Press.

Perthes, Volker. 1992. "Problems with Peace: Post-war Politics and Parliamentary Elections in Lebanon." *Orient* 33, no. 3 (Sept.): 409–32.

———. 1994. "The Private Sector, Economic Liberalization, and the Prospects of Democratization: The Case of Syria and Some Other Arab Countries." In *Democracy Without Democrats: The Renewal of Politics in the Muslim World*, edited by Ghassan Salamé. London: I. B. Tauris.

Peters, Julie, and Andrea Wolper, eds. 1995. *Women's Rights, Human Rights: International Feminist Perspectives*. London: Routledge.

Peters, R., and G. J. J. De Vries. 1976–77. "Apostasy in Islam." *Die Welt des Islams* 17, nos. 1–4: 1–25.

Peterson, V. Spike. 1994. "Gendered Nationalism." *Peace Review* 6, no. 1: 77–83.

Phares, W. 1995. *Lebanese Christian Nationalism: The Rise and Fall of an Ethnic Resistance*. London: Lynne Rienner.

Phillips, Anne. 1995. *Political Presence*. Oxford: Clarendon.

Picard, Elisabeth. 1993. "State and Society in the Arab World: Towards a New Role for the Security Services?" In *The Many Faces of National Security in the Arab World*, edited by Bahgat Korany, Rex Brynen, and Paul Noble. Basingstoke, Eng.: Macmillan.

Poggi, Gianfranco. 1990. *The State: Its Nature, Development, and Prospects*. Stanford: Stanford Univ. Press.

Pomeroy, Sarah. 1975. *Goddesses, Whores, Wives, and Slaves: Women in Classical Antiquity*. New York: Schocken.

Pool, David. 1993. "The Links between Economic and Political Liberalization." In *Economic and Political Liberalization in the Middle East*, edited by Tim Niblock and Emma Murphy. London: British Academic.

Pusey, Michael. 1987. *Jurgen Habermas*. Chichester and London: Tavistock.

Quadagno, Jill. 1994. *The Color of Welfare*. New York: Oxford Univ. Press.

Quandt, William, Fuad Jaber, and Ann Mosley Lesch. 1973. *The Politics of Palestinian Nationalism*. Berkley: Univ. of California Press.

Rabinowitz, Dan. 1993. "Oriental Nostalgia: How the Palestinians Became the 'Israeli Arabs'" (in Hebrew). *Teoriyah u-Biqoret*, 141–51.

———. 1997. *Overlooking Nazareth: The Ethnography of Exclusion in Galilee*. Cambridge: Cambridge Univ. Press.

Ranchod-Nilsson, Sita. 1994. "'This, Too, Is a Way of Fighting': Rural Women's Participation in Zimbabwe's Liberation War." In *Women and Revolution in Africa, Asia, and the New World*, edited by Mary Ann Tétreault. Columbia: Univ. of South Carolina Press.

Rawls, John. 1971. *A Theory of Justice*. Oxford: Oxford Univ. Press.

Rekhess, Elie. 1989. "Israeli Arabs and the Arabs of the West Bank and Gaza: Political Affinity and National Solidarity." *Asian and African Studies* 23: 119–54.

Richards, Alan. 1995. "Economic Pressures for Accountable Governance in the Middle East and North Africa." In *Civil Society in the Middle East*, edited by Augustus Richard Norton. Leiden: E. J. Brill.

Richards, Alan, and John Waterbury. 1990. *A Political Economy of the Middle East: State, Class, and Economic Development*. Boulder, Colo.: Westview.

Roche, Maurice. 1992. *Rethinking Citizenship: Welfare, Ideology, and Change in Modern Society.* Cambridge: Polity.

Rokkan, Stein. 1975. "Dimensions of State Formation and Nation-Building: A Possible Paradigm for Research on Variations Within Europe." In *The Formations of National States in Western Europe,* edited by Charles Tilly. Princeton: Princeton Univ. Press.

Rorty, Richard. 1993. "Human Rights, Rationality, and Sentimentality." In *On Human Rights: The Oxford Amnesty Lectures,* edited by Stephen Shute and Susan Hurley. New York: Basic.

Rose, Phyllis. 1983. *Parallel Lives: Five Victorian Marriages.* New York: Knopf.

Rosenberg, Justin. 1990. "A Non-Realist Theory of Sovereignty? Giddens' *The Nation-State and Violence.*" *Millenium* 19, no. 2: 249–59.

Rosenfeld, Henry. 1983. "History, Political Action, and Change as 'Aberrations,' and Zionism as an Irremediable 'Contradiction.'" *Israel Social Science Research* 1: 69–76.

Rosenhek, Zeev. 1995. "The Origins and Development of a Dualistic Welfare State: The Arab Population in the Israeli Welfare State" (in Hebrew). Ph.D. thesis, Department of Sociology and Anthropology, Hebrew Univ., Jerusalem.

———. 1998a. "New Developments in the Sociology of Palestinian Citizens of Israel: An Analytical Review." *Ethnic and Racial Studies* 21: 558–78.

———. 1998b. "Policy Paradigms and the Dynamics of the Welfare State: The Israeli Welfare State and the Zionist Colonial Project". *International Journal of Sociology and Social Policy* 18, nos. 2–4: 157–202.

Roter, Raphael. 1973. "The Reform of Children Allowances in Israel" (in Hebrew). *Bitachon Soziali* 4–5: 70–91.

Roter, Raphael, and Nira Shamai. 1990. "Housing Policy." In *Economic and Social Policy in Israel: The First Generation,* edited by M. Sanbar. Lanham: Univ. Press of America.

Rousseau, Jean-Jaques. 1968. *The Social Contract.* Hammondsworth, Eng.: Penguin.

Roy, Olivier. 1994a. *The Failure of Political Islam.* London: I. B. Tauris.

———. 1994b. "Patronage and Solidarity Groups: Survival or Reformation." In *Democracy Without Democrats: The Renewal of Politics in the Muslim World,* edited by Ghassan Salamé. London: I. B. Tauris.

Roy, Sara. 1995. *The Gaza Strip: The Political Economy of De-development.* Washington, D.C.: Institute of Palestine Studies.

———. 1996. "U.S. Aid to the West Bank and Gaza Strip: The Politics of Peace." *Middle East Policy* 4, no. 4: 50–76.

"Royal Lineage, The." 1959. *Burke's Genealogical and Heraldic History of the Peerage, Baronetage and Knightage.* 102d ed. London: Burke's Peerage.

Rubenberg, Cheryl. 1983a. *The PLO: Its Institutional Infrastructure.* Cambridge, Mass: Institute of Arab Studies.

———. 1983b. "The Civilian Infrastructure of the Palestinian Liberation Organization: An Analysis of the PLO in Lebanon Until June 1982." *Journal of Palestine Studies* 12, no. 3 (spring): 54–78.

Rubin, Gayle. 1975. "The Traffic in Women: Notes on a Political Economy of Sex." In *Towards an Anthropology of Women*, edited by Rayna Reiter. New York: Monthly Review.

Ruggie, John Gerard. 1986. "Continuity and Transformation in the World Polity: Toward a Neorealist Synthesis." In *Neorealism and Its Critics*, edited by Robert O. Keohane. New York: Columbia Univ. Press.

Sa'di, Ahmad. 1992. "Between State Ideology and Minority National Identity: Palestinians in Israel and in Israeli Social Science." *Review of Middle East Studies* 5: 110–30.

Sadri, Ahmad. 1992. *Max Weber's Sociology of Intellectuals*. New York: Oxford Univ. Press.

Said, Edward. 1989. "From the Intifada to Independance." *Middle East Report* (May–June): 12–16.

———. 1991. "Reflections on Twenty Years of Palestinian History." *Journal of Palestine Studies* 20, no. 4: 5–22.

Sakamato, Yashikazou. 1991. "Introduction: The Global Context of Democratization." *Alternatives* 16.

Salam, N. A. 1994. "Between Repatriation and Resettlement: Palestinian Refugees in Lebanon." *Journal of Palestine Studies* 24, no. 1 (autumn): 18–27.

Salamé, Ghassan. 1994a. "Small Is Pluralistic: Democracy As an Instrument of Civil Peace." In *Democracy Without Democrats? The Renewal of Politics in the Muslim World*, edited by Ghassan Salamé. London: I. B. Tauris.

———, ed. 1994b. *Democracy Without Democrats? The Renewal of Politics in the Muslim World*. London: I. B. Tauris.

Salameh, Jameel Jum'a. 1997. "What If Bar-On Was a Palestinian." *Palestinian Human Rights Monitor*, no. 3 (Aug.): 26.

Salibi, K. 1988. *A House of Many Mansions*. Berkeley: Univ. of California Press.

Sandler, Shmuel. 1995. "Israeli Arabs and the Jewish State: The Activation of a Community in Suspended Animation." *Middle Eastern Studies* 31: 932–52.

Sarraj, Eyad. 1996. "Arafat's Bastard Regime." *Middle East Realities*, 20 May.

Sartori, Giovanni. 1968. "Democracy." In *International Encyclopedia of the Social Sciences*, edited by David L. Sills, vol. 4. New York: Macmillan.

Saxonhouse, Arlene W. 1992. *Fear of Diversity: The Birth of Political Science in Ancient Greek Thought*. Chicago and London: Univ. of Chicago Press.

Sayigh, Rosemary. 1994. *Too Many Enemies: The Palestinian Experience in Lebanon*. London and New Jersey: Zed Books.

Sayigh, Yezid. 1997. *Armed Struggle and the Search for a State*. Oxford: Clarendon.

Schram, Gunnar, and Ineta Ziemele. 1999. "Article 15." In *The Universal Declaration of Human Rights: A Common Standard of Achievement*, edited by Gudmundur Alfredsson and Asbjørn Eide. The Hague: Kluwer.

Seddon, David. 1994. "Austerity Protests in Response to Economic Liberalization in the Middle East." In *Economic and Political Liberalization in the Middle East*, edited by Tim Niblock and Emma Murphy. London: British Academic.

Segal, Jerome M. 1989. *Creating the Palestinian State: A Strategy for Peace.* Chicago: Lawrence Hills.

Segev, Tom. 1984. *1949: The First Israelis.* Jerusalem: Domino.

Seligman, Adam. 1992. *The Idea of Civil Society.* New York: Free Press.

Shaaban, Bouthaina. 1988. *Both Right and Left Handed: Arab Women Talk about Their Lives.* London: Women's Press.

Shafir, Gershon. 1989. *Land, Labor, and the Origins of the Israeli-Palestinian Conflict.* Cambridge: Cambridge Univ. Press.

————. 1996. "Israeli Decolonization and Critical Sociology." *Journal of Palestine Studies* 25: 23–35.

Shalev, Michael. 1984. "The Mid-Sixties Recession: A Political-Economic Analysis of Unemployment in Israel" (in Hebrew). *Mahbarot Le Mehqar u-le-Biquoret* 9: 3–54.

————. 1989a. "Israel's Domestic Policy Regime: Zionism, Dualism, and the Rise of Capital." In *The Comparative History of Public Policy,* edited by F. G. Castles. Cambridge: Polity.

————. 1989b. "Jewish Organized Labor and the Palestinians: A Study in State/Society Relations in Israel." In *The Israeli State and Society: Boundaries and Frontiers,* edited by B. Kimmerling. Albany: State Univ. of New York Press.

————. 1992. *Labour and the Political Economy in Israel.* Oxford: Oxford Univ. Press.

Shamai, Nira, and Hanna Valdhorn. 1972. *Families with Children in Israel, 1969–1970* (in Hebrew). Survey no. 7. Jerusalem: National Insurance Institute.

Sharabi, Hisham. 1966. *Nationalism and Revolution in the Arab World.* Princeton: Van Nostrand.

————. 1988. *Neopatriarchy: A Theory of Distorted Change in Arab Society.* New York: Oxford Univ. Press.

————. 1994. "Only a Democratic Palestine Can Survive," *Washington Post,* 12 July, op-ed page.

Sharon, Esther. 1987. "The Children's Allowances System in Israel: 1959–1987" (in Hebrew). *Riv'on le-Kalkalah* 33: 202–16.

Sharoni, Simona. 1995. *Gender and the Israeli-Palestinian Conflict: The Politics of Women's Resistance.* Syracuse: Syracuse Univ. Press.

Shehadeh, Raja. 1994. "Questions of Jurisdiction: A Legal Analysis of the Gaza-Jericho Agreement." *Journal of Palestine Studies* 23, no. 4: 18–25.

Shikaki, Khalil. 1996a. "The Palestinian Elections: An Assessment" *Journal of Palestine Studies* 25, no. 3: 17–22.

————. 1996b. "The Peace Process, National Reconstruction, and the Transition to Democracy in Palestine." *Journal of Palestine Studies* 25, no. 2: 5–20.

Sid-Ahmed, Mohammad. 1990. "Initiatives for Deepening Democracy in the Middle East." *Alternatives* 15.

Silverman, Maxim. 1991. "Citizenship and the Nation State in France." *Ethnic and Racial Studies* 14: 333–49.

————. 1992. *Deconstructiong the Nation: Immigration, Racism, and Citizenship in Modern France.* London: Routledge.

Simons, Jon. 1994. *Foucault and the Political.* London: Routledge.

Sleifer, Yosef. 1979. "Urban Housing During the State Years" (in Hebrew). *Bitachon Soziali,* 5–21.

Sluglett, Peter, and Marion Farouk-Sluglett, eds. 1993. *Guide to the Middle East: The Arab World and Its Neighbours.* London: Times, Harper Collins.

Smith, Anthony D. 1991. *National Identity.* London: Penguin.

Smith, Barbara. 1993. *The Roots of Separatism in Palestine.* Syracuse, N.Y.: Syracuse Univ. Press.

Sohn, Louis. 1981. "Models of Autonomy Within the United Nations Framework." In *Models of Autonomy,* edited by Yoram Dinstein. New Brunswick, N.J.: Transaction.

Somers, Margaret R. 1993. "Citizenship and the Place of the Public Sphere: Law, Community, and Political Culture in the Transition to Democracy." *American Sociological Review* 58: 587–620.

———. 1994. "Reclaiming the Epistemological 'Other': Narrative and the Social Constitution of Identity." In *Social Theory and Politics of Identity,* edited by Craig Calhoun. Oxford: Basil Blackwell.

Soysal, Yasemin Nuhoglu. 1994. *Limits of Citizenship.* Chicago: Univ. of Chicago Press.

Springborg, Patricia. 1986. "Politics, Primordialism, and Orientalism: Marx, Aristotle, and the Myth of Gemeinschaft". *American Political Science Review* 80, no. 1: 185–211.

Springborg, Robert. 1975. "Patterns of Association in the Egyptian Political Elite." In *Political Elites in the Middle East,* edited by George Lenczowski. Washington, D.C.: American Enterprise Institute.

Stanley, Walter. 1996. "International Tutelage and Domestic Political Will: Building a New Civilian Police force in El Salvador." In *Policing Change, Changing Police,* edited by Otis Marenin. New York: Garland.

Steinberg, Matti. 1989. "The Pragmatic Stream of Thought within the PLO: According to Khalid al-Hasan." *Jerusalem Journal of International Relation* 11, no. 1: 37–57.

Stenberg, Leif. 1996. *The Islamization of Science: Four Muslim Positions Developing an Islamic Modernity.* Vol. 6. Lund: Lund Studies in the History of Religions.

Strauss, Leo. 1950. *Natural Right and History.* Chicago: Univ. of Chicago Press.

Takkenberg, Lex. 1998. *The Status of Palestinian Refugees in International Law.* Oxford: Clarendon Press.

Tamari, Salim. 1991. "The Palestinian Movement in Transition: Historical Reversals and the Uprising." *Journal of Palestine Studies* 20, no. 2: 57–70.

———. 1995. "Fading Flags: The Crisis of Palestinian Legitimacy." *Middle East Report* (194/195) 25, nos. 3–4: 10–12.

Tekiner, Roselle. 1994. "The Nonexistence of Israeli Nationality." *Contention* 4, no. 1 (fall): 29–46.

Tenne, David. 1962. "Housing in Israel's Development" (in Hebrew). In *The Economy of Israel: Theory and Practice,* edited by I. Ronen. Tel-Aviv: Dvir.

Tétreault, Mary Ann. 1991. "Autonomy, Necessity, and the Small State: Ruling

Kuwait in the Twentieth Century." *International Organization* 45, no. 4 (autumn): 565–91.

———. 1994a. "Women and Revolution in Vietnam." In *Women and Revolution in Africa, Asia, and the New World,* edited by Mary Ann Tétreault. Columbia: Univ. of South Carolina Press.

———. 1994b. "Women and Revolution: What Have We Learned?" In *Women and Revolution in Africa, Asia, and the New World,* edited by Mary Ann Tétreault. Columbia: Univ. of South Carolina Press.

———, ed. 1994c. *Women and Revolution in Africa, Asia, and the New World.* Columbia: Univ. of South Carolina Press.

———. 1995. *The Kuwait Petroleum Corporation and the Economics of the New World Order.* Westport, Conn.: Quorum.

———. 1997a. "Accountability or Justice? Rape as a War Crime." In *Feminist Frontiers IV,* edited by Laurel Richardson, Verta Taylor, and Nancy Whittier. New York: McGraw-Hill.

———. 1997b. "Justice for All: Wartime Rape and Women's Human Rights." *Global Governance* 3: 197–212.

———. Forthcoming. *Stories of Democracy: Politics and Society in Contemporary Kuwait.*

Tétreault, Mary Ann, and Haya al-Mughni. 1995. "Gender, Citizenship, and Nationalism in Kuwait." *British Journal of Middle Eastern Studies* 22, nos. 1–2: 64–80.

Tibi, Bassam. 1984. "Political Freedom in Arab Societies." *Arab Studies Quarterly* 6, no. 3: 222–27.

Tillion, Germaine. 1983. *The Republic of Cousins: Women's Repression in Mediterranean Societies.* London: Al Faqui Books.

Tilly, Charles. 1985. "War Making and State Making as Organized Crime." In *Bringing the State Back In,* edited by Peter Evans, Dietrich Rueschemeyer, and Theda Skocpol. Cambridge: Cambridge Univ. Press.

———. 1995. "The Emergence of Citizenship in France and Elsewhere." *International Review of Social History* 40: 223–36.

Tocqueville, Alexis de. 1955. *The Old Regime and the French Revolution.* Translated by Stuart Gilbert. Garden City: Doubleday Anchor.

Tomeh, George J. 1968. "Legal Status of Arab Refugees." *Law and Contemporary Problems in International Law* 33, no. 1.

Tönnies, Ferdinand. 1957. *Community and Society.* Translated and edited by Charles P. Loomis. East Lansing: Michigan State Univ. Press.

"Total Disbursements from Total Pledges 1994–95." 1996. *Journal of Palestine Studies* 25, no. 3: 141.

Turner, Bryan S. 1978. *Marx and the End of Orientalism.* London: Allen and Unwin.

———. 1986. *Citizenship and Capitalism: The Debate over Reformism.* London: Allen and Unwin.

———. 1990. "Outline of a Theory of Citizenship." *Sociology* 24, no. 2: 189–217.

———. 1993a. "Contemporary Problems in the Theory of Citizenship." In *Citizenship and Social Theory,* edited by Bryan S. Turner. London and Newbury Park: Sage.

———. 1993b. "Outline of a Theory of Human Rights." *Sociology* 27, no. 3: 489–512.

Turner, Bryan S., and Peter Hamilton P., eds. 1994. *Citizenship: Critical Concepts.* 2 vols. London: Routledge.

Ugarte, Jose. 1990. "Police Reform in Latin America." In *Policing Change, Changing Police,* edited by Otis Marenin. New York: Garland.

Usher, Graham. 1995a. "An Israeli Peace: Interview with Ilan Pappé." *Race and Class* 37, no. 2: 19–26.

———. 1995b. "Bantustanization or Bi-nationalism: an interview with Azmi Bashara." *Race and Class* 37, no. 2: 43–50.

———. 1995c. *Palestine in Crisis.* London: Pluto.

———. 1996. "The Politics of Internal Security: The PA's New Intelligence Services." *Journal of Palestine Studies* 25, no. 2: 21–34.

Van Dusen, Michael. 1972. "Jerusalem, the Occupied Territories, and the Refugees." In *Major Middle Eastern Problems in International Law,* edited by Majid Khadduri, Washington, D.C.: American Enterprise Institute for Public Research, 37–63.

van-Gunsteren, Herman. 1978. "Notes on a Theory of Citizenship." In *Democracy, Consensus, and Social Contract,* edited by Pierre Birnbaum, Jack Lively, and Geraint Parry. London: Sage.

———. 1988. "Admission to Citizenship." *Ethos* 98: 731–41.

———. 1994. "Four Conceptions of Citizenship." In *The Condition of Citizenship,* edited by Bart van Steenbergen. London: Sage.

van Steenbergen, Bart, ed. 1994. *The Condition of Citizenship.* London: Sage.

Verdi, Guiseppe. 1861. *La forza del destino.* Librettist, Francesco Maria Piave.

Vogel, Ursula. 1994. "Marriage and the Boundaries of Citizenship." In *The Condition of Citizenship,* edited by Bart van Steenbergen. London: Sage.

Waltz, Kenneth N. 1959. *Man, the State, and War: A Theoretical Analysis.* New York: Columbia Univ. Press.

Walzer, Michael. 1970. *Obligations: Essays on Disobedience, War, and Citizenship.* Cambridge, Mass.: Harvard Univ. Press.

———. 1994. *Spheres of Justice: A Defence of Pluralism and Equality.* Oxford and Cambridge: Blackwell; orig. pub. 1983.

Weber, Cynthia. 1995. *Simulating Sovereignty: Intervention, the State, and Symbolic Exchange.* Cambridge: Cambridge Univ. Press.

Weber, Max. 1968. *Economy and Society.* Berkeley: Univ. of California Press.

———. 1978. *Economy and Society.* Edited by Guenther Roth and Claus Wittich. Berkeley: Univ. of California Press.

———. 1981. *The City.* New York: Free Press.

Weis, Paul. 1979. *Nationality and Statelessness in International Law.* Alphen aan den Rijn: Sijthoff and Noordhoff.

Wolf, Eric R. 1982. *Europe and the People Without History.* Berkeley: Univ. of California Press.

Yeatman, Anna. 1994. "Beyond Natural Right: The Conditions for Universal Citizenship." In *Postmodern Revisionings of the Political,* edited by Anna Yeatman. New York and London: Routledge.

Young, Marion. 1989. "Polity and Group Difference: A Critique of the Ideal of Universal Citizenship" *Ethics* 99: 250–74.

———. 1990. *Justice and the Politics of Difference.* Princeton: Princeton Univ. Press.

Yuval-Davis, Nira, and Floya Anthias. 1989. *Woman-Nation-State.* London: Macmillan.

Zamir, Meir. 1978. "Emile Eddé and the Territorial Integrity of Lebanon." *Middle Eastern Studies* 14, no. 2 (May): 232–35.

———. 1982. "Smaller and Greater Lebanon: The Squaring of a Circle." *The Jerusalem Quarterly,* no. 23 (spring): 34–53.

———. 1985. *The Formation of Modern Lebanon.* London: Croom Helm.

Ziemele, Ineta. 1998. "State Continuity and Nationality in the Baltic States and the Russian Federation: International and Constitutional Issues." Ph.D. thesis. Cambridge Univ.

Zubaida, Sami. 1992. "Islam, the State, and Democracy: Contrasting Conceptions of Society in Egypt." *Middle East Report* 22, no. 6: 2–10.

———. 1993. *Islam, the People, and the State.* London: I. B. Tauris.

Zureik, Elia. 1979. *Palestinians in Israel: A Study in Internal Colonialism.* London: Routledge and Kegan Paul.

———. 1994. "Palestinian Refugees and Peace." *Journal of Palestine Studies* 24, no. 1: 5–17.

Documents

International and Regional

1869. *Ottoman Citizenship Law.*

1924. *Treaty of Peace,* Lausanne.

1945. The League of Arab States. *Pact of the League of Arab States.*

1949. *Geneva Conventions.*

1950. Council of Europe. *The European Convention for the Protection of Human Rights and Fundamental Rights.*

1954. The League of Arab States. *Agreement of 5 April 1954 on Provisions Regarding Citizenship among Member States of the League of Arab States.*

1955. International Court of Justice. *Reports on Judgements, Advisory Opinions and Orders.*

1965. The League of Arab States. *The Casablanca Resolution.*

1966. International Court of Justice. *Ethiopia v. South Africa; Liberia v. South Africa.*

1978. *The Inter-American Convention on Human Rights.*

1979. *The Camp David Accords.*

1992. The European Union. *Treaty on European Union,* Maastricht.

1993. *Declaration of Principles on Interim Self-Government Authority.* 13 Sept.

1994. *The Gaza-Jericho Autonomy Agreement* (Cairo Agreement). 4 May.

1994. *Agreement on Preparatory Transfer of Powers and Responsibilities signed between the PLO and Israel* (Early Empowerment Agreement/Erez Agreement). 29 Aug.

1994. *Treaty of Peace between the State of Israel and the Hashemite Kingdom of Jordan.* 26 Oct.

1995. Israeli-Palestinian Interim Agreement on the West Bank and the Gaza Strip. 28 Sept.

1997. *Protocol Concerning the Redeployment in Hebron.* 17 Jan.

1997. *The Council of Europe. The European Convention on Nationality.*

United Nations Documents

1945. United Nations Charter.

1947. General Assembly Resolution 181.

1948. Universal Declaration of Human Rights.

1948. General Assembly Resolution 194.

1949. General Assembly Resolution 302.

1951. Convention Relating to the Status of Refugees.

1958. The Convention on the Nationality of Married Women.

1960. Declaration on Granting Independence to Colonial Countries and Peoples.

1961. Convention on the Reduction of Statelessness.

1966. The International Covenant on Civil and Political Rights.

1966. The International Covenant on Economic, Social and Cultural Rights.

1966. International Convention on Elimination of All Forms of Racial Discrimination.

1973. International Convention on the Suppression and Punishment of the Crime of Apartheid.

1978. The Right of Return of the Palestinian People (Committee on the Exercise of the Inalienable Rights of the Palestinian People, ST/SG/SER.F/2).

1979. The Convention on the Elimination of All Forms of Discrimination Against Women.

1989. The Convention on the Rights of the Child.

1994. World Population Prospects: The 1994 Revision.

1997. The United Nations High Commission for Refugees (UNCHR), Regional Bureau for Europe. *Citizenship and the Prevention of Statelessness Linked to the Disintegration of the Socialist Federal Republic of Yugoslavia.* European Series 3, no. 1. June.

Country Legislation and Other Official Documents

Egypt. 1954. Law No 415.

———. 1954. Law No 416.

———. 1954. Law No 537.

————. 1955. Law No 127.

————. 1963. Law No 15.

————. 1964. Law No 181.

————. 1964. Decree No. 181. *Official Gazette*, no. 94.

————. 1969. Decree No. 366.

————. 1976. Law No 81.

————. 1977. Law No 30.

————. 1978. Law No 47.

————. 1980. Law No 215.

————. 1985. Law No 104.

France. 1789. Declaration of the Rights of Man and the Citizen.

Germany. 1935. German Reich Citizenship Law (one of the so-called Nuremberg laws).

Iran. 1975. Family Protection Law.

Iraq. 1961. Law No 26.

————. 1969. Decree No 366.

————. 1980. Decree No 215.

————. 1990. Resolution 111 of the Revolutionary Command Council.

Israel. 1943. Lands (Acquisition for Public Purpose) Ordinance.

————. 1948. Law and Government Ordinance.

————. 1949–50. 4 Laws of the State of Israel.

————. 1950. Law of Return.

————. 1950. Absentees Properties Law.

————. 1952. Nationality Law.

————. 1952. 6 Laws of the State of Israel.

————. 1953. Jewish National Fund Law.

————. 1953. Land Acquisition (Validation of Acts and Compensation) Law.

————. 1953. National Insurance Law.

————. 1958. Basic Law: The Knesset.

————. 1960. Basic Law: Israel Lands.

————. 1960. Israel Lands Law.

————. 1960. Israel Lands Administration Law.

————. 1962. Judgments of the Supreme Court, Case No 72/62.

————. 1963. The Supreme Court. *Rufeisen v. Ministry of Interior.*

————. 1965. Judgments of the Supreme Court, Case No 1/65.

————. 1968. 22 Laws of the State of Israel.

————. 1971. Selected Judgements of the Supreme Court of Israel.

————. 1973–74. National Insurance Institute. *Statistical Yearbook, 1973–74.*

————. 1975. National Insurance Institute. *Rights and Duties in the National Insurance Institute* (in Hebrew).

————. 1980. Nationality Law [Amendment No 4].

————. 1980. 34 Laws of the State of Israel.

————. 1984. Judgments of the Supreme Court, Case No 2&3/84.

————. 1985. Basic Law: The Knesset [Amendment No 9].

———. 1995. Statistical Abstract of Israel. Central Bureau of Statistics.

———. Various years. *Budget Proposal* (in Hebrew). Jerusalem: Government of Israel.

———. Central Bureau of Statistics. 1964. *Construction in Israel, 1960–1963* (in Hebrew). Jerusalem: Central Bureau of Statistics.

———. Central Bureau of Statistics. 1966. *Construction in Israel, 1962–1965* (in Hebrew). Jerusalem: Central Bureau of Statistics.

———. Central Bureau of Statistics. 1970. *Construction in Israel, 1966–1968* (in Hebrew). Jerusalem: Central Bureau of Statistics.

———. Central Bureau of Statistics. 1972. *Construction in Israel, 1969–1971* (in Hebrew). Jerusalem: Central Bureau of Statistics.

———. Central Bureau of Statistics. 1973. *Monthly Prices Statistics* (in Hebrew). Vol. 24. Jerusalem: Central Bureau of Statistics.

———. Central Bureau of Statistics. 1974a. *Construction in Israel, 1971–1973* (in Hebrew). Jerusalem: Central Bureau of Statistics.

———. Central Bureau of Statistics. 1974b. *Monthly Prices Statistics* (in Hebrew). Vol. 25. Jerusalem: Central Bureau of Statistics.

———. Central Bureau of Statistics. 1977. *Monthly Prices Statistics* (in Hebrew). Vol. 28. Jerusalem: Central Bureau of Statistics.

———. Central Bureau of Statistics. 1978. *Monthly Prices Statistics* (in Hebrew). Vol. 29. Jerusalem: Central Bureau of Statistics.

———. Ministry of Finance and Ministry of Construction and Housing. 1990a. *Financing Housing Construction.* Jerusalem: Ministry of Finance and Ministry of Construction and Housing.

———. Ministry of Finance and Ministry of Construction and Housing. 1990b. *Government Housing Programs.* Jerusalem: Ministry of Finance and Ministry of Construction and Housing.

———. Ministry of Housing. 1976. *Assistance Programs—Young Couples, 1976* (in Hebrew). Jerusalem: Ministry of Housing.

———. Ministry of Housing. 1977a. *Assistance Programs—Housing Conditions Improvement* (in Hebrew). Neighborhoods Rehabilitation, 3 + . Jerusalem: Ministry of Housing.

———. Ministry of Housing. 1977b. *Assistance Programs—Young Couples, 1977* (in Hebrew). Jerusalem: Ministry of Housing.

———. State Comptroller. 1962. *Year Report No. 12, 1961* (in Hebrew). Jerusalem: State Comptroller.

———. State Comptroller. 1964. *Year Report No. 14, 1963* (in Hebrew). Jerusalem: State Comptroller.

———. State Comptroller. 1970. *Year Report No. 20, 1969* (in Hebrew). Jerusalem: State Comptroller.

———. State Comptroller. 1972. *Year Report No. 22, 1971* (in Hebrew). Jerusalem: State Comptroller.

———. State Comptroller. 1974. *Year Report No. 24, 1973* (in Hebrew). Jerusalem: State Comptroller.

———. State Comptroller. 1975. *Year Report No. 25, 1974* (in Hebrew). Jerusalem: State Comptroller.

Transjordan. 1928. Nationality Law.

Jordan. 1949. Law Additional to the Nationality Law of 1928.

———. 1952. Constitution of the Hashemite Kingdom of Jordan.

———. 1954. Citizenship Law No 6.

———. 1960. Elections Law No 24.

———. 1961. Compilation of Jordan's Laws and Regulations (in Arabic).

———. 1989. Law No 11.

———. 1990. High Court of Justice, Case No 164/90.

———. 1995. High Court of Justice, Case No 108/95.

———. 1997. High Court of Justice, Case No 212/97.

Kuwait. 1948. Order No 3.

———. 1948. Law No 2.

———. 1959. Nationality Law.

———. 1985. Amendment of the Electoral Law.

Lebanon (The French Mandate). 1921. Resolution 763.

———. 1922. Newcome-Paulet Agreement (French & British Mandate Power).

———. (The French High Commisioner). 1922. Regulation 1307.

———. (The French High Commisioner). 1923. Resolution 2825.

———. 1925. Resolution 15.

———. 1932. Decree No 8837.

———. 1944. Decree No 1822.

———. 1949. Decree No 398.

———. 1950. Pharmacists Law.

———. 1951. Engineers Law.

———. 1959. Decree No 42.

———. 1962. Decree No 319.

———. 1962. Labour Law.

———. 1967. Law No 67/68.

———. 1970. Decree No 1.

———. 1970. Bar Association Law No 8/70.

———. 1979. Medical Doctors Decree No 1658.

———. 1985. Ministry of Information. *Da' irat ma' arif ash-sharq.*

———. 1994. Citizenship Decree.

———. 1995. Decree No 478.

Morocco. 1923. Nationality Decree.

Palestine (The British Mandate). 1925. Order in Council.

———. Palestine Citizenship Order.

———. (The British Mandate). 1945. Defence (Emergency) Regulations.

———. (Palestine Liberation Organization). 1988. Declaration of Independence.

———. (Palestine National Authority). 1995. Law No 9.

———. (Palestine National Authority). 1995. Elections Law No 15.

———. 1985. 2d Palestine Yearbook of International Law.

————. 1987–88. 4th Palestine Yearbook of International Law.

————. 1990–91. 6th Palestine Yearbook of International Law.

————. 1992–94. 7th Palestine Yearbook of International Law.

————. 1994–95. 8th Palestine Yearbook of International Law.

————. 1997. 9th Palestine Yearbook of International Law.

Syria. 1956. Law No 260.

————. 1956. Parlimentary Record of Syria, 10th sess. 7 July.

Tunisia. 1923. Nationality Decree.

Other Documents

Committee on the Administration of Justice. 1997. *Human Rights on Duty, Principles for Better Policing, International Lessons for Northern Ireland.* Belfast: CAJ.

International Bank for Reconstruction and Development. 1995. *Aid to Palestine: Total Disbursements from Total Pledges, 1994–95,* Washington, D. C.

International Law Report. 1950.

Jerusalem Media and Communications Center. 1993–96. *Public Opinion Polls on Palestinian Attitudes Toward Politics.* Nos 1–18. East Jerusalem: JMCC.

World Bank. 1994–95. *World Population Projections 1994–95.* Baltimore and London: John Hopkins Univ. Press.

Newspapers and Other Media

Al-'Amal (Lebanese Daily)

Al-Anwar (Lebanese Daily)

BBC Summary of World Broadcasts

Ad-Diar (Lebanese Daily)

Al-Dustour

Foreign Radio Broadcast Service (FBIS)

Ha'aretz (Israeli Daily)

Al-Hayat (Arabic Daily, London)

The Jerusalem Post (Israeli Daily in English

Jordan Times (Jordanian Daily in English)

Kull Shay' (Lebanese Weekly)

Ma'ariv (Israeli Daily)

Al-Majd

An-Nahar (Lebanese Daily)

Al-Quds (Palestinian Daily, Jerusalem)

Return Magazine (London)

Al-Sabeel

Al-Safir (Lebanese Daily)

Der Spiegel (German Daily)

UNRWA Press Release HQ/7/95 (13 Sept. 1995)

UNRWA Press Release HQ/8/95 (28 Sept. 1995)

Internet Sources

Middle East Realities. <http://www.MiddleEast.org (Email: MER@MiddleEast. org; subscriptions: LISTSERVER@MiddleEast.org)

MSA News. <http://www.mynet.net/~msanews (Subscriptions to *MSA News:* <listserver@lists.acs.ohio-state.edu>) The information cited as from the following organizations was posted at or received via *MSA News:*

Al-quds interfax: <alquds@palestine-net.com>; Independent Media Review and Analysis, Aaron Lerner: <imra@netvision.net.il>; Land and Water Establishment (LAW), Palestinian Society for the Protection of Human Rights and the Environment: <lawe@netvision.net.il >; Muslim World News (MWN), Friday Journal News Service): bayan@ghgcorp.com

Middle East Realities. 1996. "Arafat's Bastard Regime: Police Reservations Taking Root." Middleast@aol.com.

Palestine Times. <http://www.ptimes.com>

Interviews

Anonymous. 1995. Interview with Beverley Milton-Edwards.

Anonymous Palestinian academic. 1998. Interview with Christopher H. Parker, Apr., West Bank.

Assad, Ziad. 1995. Representative of the Druze students at Haifa Univ. Interview with Rebecca Kook, 5 May.

Blekelia, Per. 1995. Interview with Beverley Milton-Edwards.

Djanni, Ahmad Sidqi. 1993. Interview with Uri Davis, 11 Aug., Cairo.

Hammad, Salameh. 1995. Interview with Rania Maktabi.

Ifram, Habib. 1996. Interview with Rania Maktabi, Feb.

Lerchner, Charles. 1988. Interview with Christopher H. Parker, Apr.

Mirhij, Bishara. 1996. Interview with Rania Maktabi, 5 Feb.

Nielsen, Thøger. 1997. Interview with Beverley Milton-Edwards.

Ni'man, Isam. 1996. Interview with Rania Maktabi, 10 Feb.

Quteish, Hussein. 1996. Interview with Rania Maktabi, 9 Feb.

Rød-Larsen, Terje. 1997. Interview with Beverley Milton-Edwards.

Samud, Mohammad (Lt. Col.). 1997. Interview with Beverley Milton-Edwards.

Shabawi, Mohammad (Col.). 1997. Interview with Beverley Milton-Edwards.

Shehada, Ibrahim. 1995. Interview with Christopher H. Parker, Sept.

Sourani, Rani, and Hamdi Y. Shaggura. 1988. Interview with Christopher H. Parker, Apr.

Wilkinson, Ron. 1995. Interview with Christopher H. Parker, Sept.

Index

Contemporary Issues in the Middle East

This well-established series continues to focus primarily on developments that have current impact and significance throughout the entire region, from North Africa to the borders of Central Asia. Other titles in the series include:

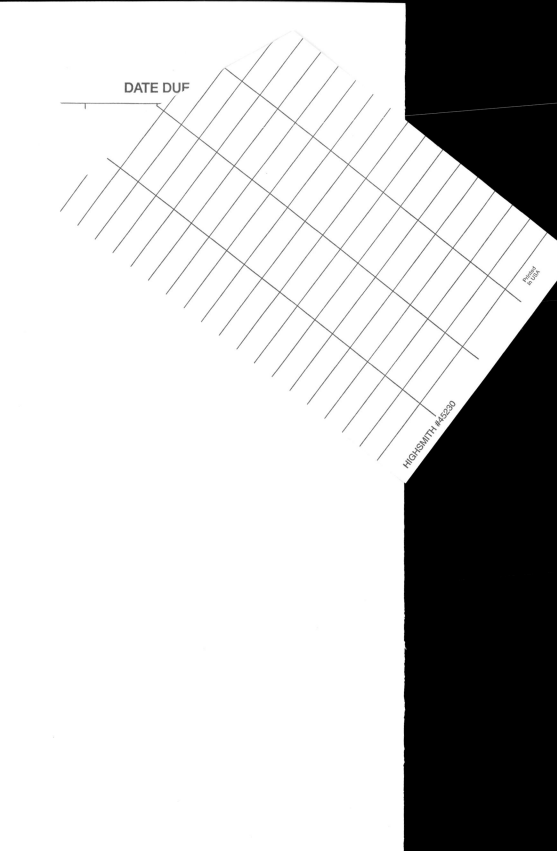

DATE DUE

HIGHSMITH #45230

Printed in USA

Citizenship and the State in the Middle East introduces a pioneering approach to politics in the Middle East by analyzing key factors in the constitution of political communities and collective identities in terms of citizenship.

As a response to processes of globalization, regional integration and ethnic conflicts, the study of citizenship has regained new interest among social scientists and legal experts. This approach focuses on the relationship between the state and the people—as individuals and collectivities, citizens and non-citizens—both those living within or outside its borders. Citizenship defines the terms of rights and obligations in a society, regulates political participation and access to public goods and properties. Together, with its companion volume, *Gender and Citizenship in the Middle East,* this book represents the first systematic critical attempt to interpret the complex nature of Middle East politics from a citizenship perspective.

In addition, the book provides both theoretical contributions and case studies, and includes a significant section on Israel and Palestine.

◆   ◆   ◆

Nils A. Butenschon is associate professor of international politics and relations and director of the Norwegian Institute of Human Rights, the University of Oslo. **Uri Davis** is chair, AL-BIET: Association for Defence of Human Rights in Israel. **Manuel Hassassian** is professor of international politics and executive vice president of Bethlehem University.

Front cover: Detail of wall mosaic in the mosque of Ahmed el-Bordeyny (17th century), from *Arabic Art in Color,* edited by Prisse D'Avennes.

Contemporary Issues in the Middle East

SU
Syracuse University Press
Syracuse, New York 13244-5160

ISBN 0-8156-2829-3

90000

9 780815 628293